The **LEGAL ADVISOR**
for **LIBRARIANS,**
EDUCATORS, &
INFORMATION
PROFESSIONALS

THE LIBR
LEGAL COMP

Licensing
Information
Resources
and
Services

TOMAS A. LIPINSKI

Neal-Schuman

An imprint of the American Library Association

Chicago   2013

The Legal Advisor for Librarians, Educators, & Information Professionals

No. 1—*The Complete Copyright Liability Handbook for Librarians and Educators*, by Tomas A. Lipinski

No. 2—*Professional Liability Issues for Librarians and Information Professionals*, by Paul D. Healey

No. 3—*The Digital Librarian's Legal Handbook*, by John N. Gathegi

No. 4—*The Librarian's Legal Companion for Licensing Information Resources and Services*, by Tomas A. Lipinski

© 2013 by the American Library Association. Any claim of copyright is subject to applicable limitations and exceptions, such as rights of fair use and library copying pursuant to Sections 107 and 108 of the U.S. Copyright Act. No copyright is claimed for content in the public domain, such as works of the U.S. government.

Printed in the United States of America

17 16 15 14 13   5 4 3 2 1

Extensive effort has gone into ensuring the reliability of the information in this book; however, the publisher makes no warranty, express or implied, with respect to the material contained herein.

NOTE TO THE READER
"This publication is designed to provide accurate and authoritative information in regard to the subject matter covered. It is sold with the understanding that the publisher is not engaged in rendering legal, accounting, or other professional service. If legal advice or other expert assistance is required, the services of a competent professional person should be sought." *From a Declaration of Principles adopted jointly by a Committee of the American Bar Association and a Committee of Publishers*

ISBNs: 978-1-55570-610-4 (paper); 978-1-55570-919-8 (PDF).

Library of Congress Cataloging-in-Publication Data
Lipinski, Tomas A., 1958–
    The librarian's legal companion for licensing information resources and services / Tomas A. Lipinski.
        p. cm. — (The legal advisor for librarians, educators, & information professionals; no. 4)
    Includes bibliographical references and index.
    ISBN 978-1-55570-610-4 (alk. paper)
    1. Copyright licenses—United States. 2. Librarians—United States—Handbooks, manuals, etc. I. Title.

KF3002.L57 2013
346.7304'82—dc23

                                                                    2012018173

Cover design by Rosemary Holderby/Cole Design and Production
Text design in New Baskerville and Franklin Gothic Condensed by UB Communications

♾ This paper meets the requirements of ANSI/NISO Z39.48-1992 (Permanence of Paper).

▶ Dedication

To Eileen, my wife, the muse of my life!

► Contents

► PART I
BEFORE YOU READ THE LICENSE:
ESSENTIAL BACKGROUND CONCEPTS

▶ PART II
THE RANGE AND NATURE OF
INFORMATION RESOURCE LICENSES
THAT LIBRARIES ENCOUNTER

▶ PART III
A LICENSING REFERENCE TOOLKIT
FOR EVERYDAY USE

► Series Editor's Foreword

This book is the fourth in a series on a range of legal topics in libraries, from licensing to liability, from privacy to an array of protected speech issues, and more. The series is titled The Legal Advisor for Librarians, Educators, & Information Professionals. While the number of legal titles published in the library and information science (LIS) area is proliferating, numerous areas have yet to be addressed. This results in an imbalance of represented topics. In addition, the existing titles are somewhat discordant in style. Others lack the level of legal scholarship that is desired by the series editor and publisher, as well as series authors. This series serves to ratchet the discussion of legal issues in LIS up a notch or two, toward a more in-depth and intense level or paradigm of inquiry.

Practitioners in the library or information center in both the private and public sectors, including those serving schools, archives, manuscript and special collections, and, to a lesser extent, museum collections as well, should find this monograph and others in the series useful. This book, like others in the series can be viewed as a "why," "what," and "how" book: *Why* do we engage in a certain course of conduct or response? *What* is the law governing that conduct or response? *How* does it affect me? And *how* do we comply with it and use the law where we can to our advantage?

This series presents a range of legal topics of interest to a wide variety of information organizations in both the private and public sectors: libraries, schools, archives, special collections, and, to a lesser extent, museum collections. Each monograph in the series follows a similar pattern: presentation of the law and its application through discussion of the law and examples specific to library (in its varied iterations), archive, or educational circumstances; case studies (in question-and-answer or another format) and bullet-point summaries concluding each substantive chapter; the final part of the book includes compliance or practice tools such as checklists, audits, model policy, or other sample language, such as signage or notices where appropriate.

The goal of the series is to provide practical, readable information drawn from sound legal analysis on a variety of specific legal topics. Each title is based on sound legal scholarship written by leading experts in the field and offers practitioners a useful tool for compliance. One way this will be accomplished is for each title to contain at least two resource chapters, one including some sort of Q&A or audit that can be used as both a professional teaching tool and as a compliance and risk management device. The other resource chapter would contain a model policy or series of policies that would implement the legal principles of the subject matter. Where appropriate, a third resource chapter might contain sample language of use in contracts or licenses, signs or notices, or other appropriate contexts.

As a result, this monograph accomplishes two additional goals: it serves as a tool for creating a compliant environment within your library and its broader institutional context and, as a result, can help create a "law-aware" environment within your organization—and thus it also functions as a risk-management device. Because licensing is a two-way street between licensor and licensee-library, a bit of advocacy is involved here, too.

The series editor has used an array of contacts in the legal-library information community to solicit submissions and interest from prospective authors. Interested authors can contact either the series editor or the publisher, and new author suggestions and recommendations are welcomed as well. Future topics in the series include free speech in public library content and spaces, gifts, privacy, and confidentiality. The series editor and publisher are committed to including only the highest quality titles in this series from contributors who have strong research foundations as well as experience in both law and libraries or related information settings. We hope you enjoy and, moreover, find useful our efforts. We look forward to your feedback as well as your ideas for new additions to the series.

Tomas A. Lipinski, JD, LLM, PhD
Professor, School of Library and Information Science
Indiana University–Purdue University, Indianapolis

▶ Preface

Well, now that you have decided to actually read this book, or at least browse this preface, several comments about the purpose of this book, including some suggestions on how to use it—depending upon your interest and level of expertise on legal issues, in specific licensing (or contract) law and, where relevant, copyright and other laws—are in order.

Maybe you are one of those persons who bought the book weeks or months ago but is just now getting around to reading it, or maybe you are one of the those users who religiously reads from cover to cover every page of a new book. Then again, perhaps you have used or consulted this book before but never bothered to read the preface. It may be possible that this book or a part of it is assigned to you as a required text in a course you are taking or is recommended in conjunction with a seminar you are attending and you are seeking a fast and painless way to get a sense of what the book is about, its content, and its value without having to read it. If so, well then, this preface is for you.

PURPOSE

My reason for writing *The Librarian's Legal Companion for Licensing Information Resources and Services* is simple: to allow you to read and understand the law surrounding the contracting of information content and, to a lesser extent, information services in library and related settings.

Contract law serves as the legal foundation for interpreting licenses. In addition, understanding copyright law often helps one understand the practical impact of licenses. The scope of this book is the former, emphasizing contract law. Many, many books have been published on understanding copyright law; significantly fewer center on licensing. However, reference is made to those places where there is an intersection of license and copyright, offering brief explanation on the latter and indicating where additional information can be obtained. The book begins with several chapters on basic contract law and where at times this can be applied in library settings. More advanced concepts in contract and licensing law are presented—concepts impacting licensing today and in the future. Purchasing or licensing information content and services is essentially the law of contract. Though these transactions may raise additional issues such as advertising, fair trade, and related consumer law issues, the focus of this book is on the factors you can control rather than the regulatory issues often raised by these legal concepts. In other words, you may have an opportunity to play an active role in determining or at least contributing to the terms by which an acquisition is made. Where the transaction does not offer such opportunity, a so-called "take it or leave it" offer, you will at least be able to evaluate whether you can live with those terms, whether it is better to take it or leave it. Later, more practical chapters build upon these foundations.

By learning a bit of the law of licensing you also learn some contract law and vice versa. While a fair amount of law is discussed—more than in other books on licensing—this book provides the necessary foundation for those readers seeking advanced knowledge into the "why" behind many license provisions. How much of the book is consumed dictates whether the treatment is intermediate or advanced, at least as far as librarian use is concerned. (Chapter 14 can be consulted for a introductory look at an alphabetical listing and discussion of licensing terms, but even this treatment is far more robust than that found on websites or other articles and monographs.) More and more librarians are being asked to step up to the licensing counter when placing their order for library content (databases, e-books, etc.) and services (software, devices such as e-book readers, etc.). As contract law (including the law of licensing) is state based, this book cannot address the laws of each of the fifty states, even if limited to contract concepts alone. Librarians need to understand the legal aspects regarding acquisition by purchase or license of information in the library and to use that understanding to their advantage. The laws surrounding gifts and donations will be discussed in another title in this series, I hope.

Second, not all library schools prepare students to delve into such issues in any great detail. At best, course work in copyright and license is elective, or given mention or short treatment in other courses. As a result, information professionals continue to enter practice without adequate, significant, or advanced and practical exposure to these issues. This book will help you overcome that deficiency or further increase your professional competence. I hope it also serves to empower you as well by providing a thorough discussion of the context, law, and application of that law to your information acquisition practices.

While use of the terms *library* and *librarian* is made throughout the text, the principles here would of course be of assistance to archivists (in archives) and curators (in special and perhaps museum collections), as well as those in educational settings. The book does not, however, cover purchase and license of works of art, cultural artifacts, and the like.

A BRIEF COMMENT ON THE LAW

As mentioned, purchasing books or licensing information content, such as access to a proprietary database, or information services, such as library automation software or a system with its various modules (serials management, public access catalog, etc.), is essentially based on the law of contract. While there are sources of countrywide guidance on contract principles well-known to the law librarian readership, they tend to be less commonly known to other librarians—for example, the Restatements of Contracts (which has a first and second edition) with its series of "statements" followed by "comments" and "illustrations" for each of the hundreds of so-called black-letter rules or restatements, and the Uniform Commercial Code (UCC).

The Restatements are not laws per se but an attempt to restate in general terms what the law is across the jurisdictions and the courts that rule or make law in a particular area. Restatements exist on a variety of topics, from "agency" to "unfair competition." The second edition "constitutes a thorough revision and updating of the original 1932 Restatement. It embodies additions inspired by the Uniform Commercial Code and improves the black-letter formulations by altering the order or scope of topics to enhance clarity or reduce redundancy." Consulting the second edition (referred to in later discussions simply as "the Restatements" or "Restatement" when reference is made a specific statement), a reader can get an approximation of the law in a particular area across the states—a sort of legal snapshot, if you will. The Restatements offer a series of concise statements (known as black-letter law) regarding the aspects of the Restatement topic, followed by official comment and illustrations for each such statement, all built upon existing case law. The second edition contains hundreds of these statements and accompanying comments and illustrations.

As the name implies, the UCC is a standardized codification of contract law. Uniform laws are proposed by the National Conference of Commissioners of Uniform State Laws (NCCUSL). Such uniform laws are proposed (and, it is hoped, adopted by the state legislatures) in an attempt to create standardization across the states in a given area of law. There are many, many uniform laws, from the Adult Guardianship and Protective Proceedings Jurisdiction Act to the Unsworn Foreign Declarations Act.

In the case of contract law and the UCC, all states have adopted in some form or another the text of the uniform code. In the original proposed version by NCUSL, the statutory text is followed by an "official comment" accompanying each UCC provision. The comments provide a sort of readers guide and help in interpreting each provision.[1] Contract law remains state law, codified by individual state legislatures and interpreted by the courts, either by the state's own courts or by the federal courts of the jurisdiction applying it in diversity[2] cases. This state-based contract law is often a combination of code, that is, the statutes enacted by state legislatures (which are often from the UCC, except in licensing cases, as most courts conclude the UCC does not apply to information and software licenses) and court, or the decisions of the courts interpreting the code and advancing the development of the common law, including consideration of sources that comment upon that law (often the Restatements), or both. Even federal courts dealing with contract issues under diversity jurisdiction principles use the law of the state in which the dispute is being adjudicated.

As a result, the law can vary from state to state. For example, the Restatement may reflect the majority or trend but alert the reader to the minority position as well, or merely restate a general concept that not all state appellate courts have had opportunity to consider. "Restatements are secondary sources that seek to 'restate' the legal rules that constitute the common law in a particular area... Restatements are one of the most highly regarded types of secondary authority and have exerted considerable influence on the judicial process. Many courts have adopted Restatement sections verbatim as the law of their jurisdiction."

However, while all states have adopted the UCC, the precise language of its provisions may vary from state to state. Of course, the interpretation of similar language may vary from court to court as well. This occurs because each state's respective case law (and, to an extent, each federal district court's case law) operates merely as persuasive precedent, though it may be influential. So the decision of one state's court may not matter much in another state, but this is not to say that books such as this one are of no value. Rather, this legal reality should alert you to the practical limitation of trying, without involving a multivolume treatise, to have a single place be the first and last place you look. (Indeed, I hope this book will be one of your first resources on the topic, but it should not be the last you consult in resolving an issue concerning contract or licensing law.) So, rather than lengthen the book even further, discussion of the Restatements and the UCC is placed in the beginning contract-based chapters to provide a sense of the overall status of the law.

The goal is to bring to you, the reader, in one volume an exposition of the basic, intermediate, and advanced contract law principles—and this will in part depend upon the point from which you are beginning, both in terms of your knowledge and which parts of the book you decide to read—involved in the license of information content and services most likely applicable in the library setting. As a result, the case examples used throughout the book are expository, intending to explain or describe the application of a particular concept (such as the idea of unconscionability, for example) or to represent the extant or emerging case law in the area (such as the application of the doctrine of copyright misuse in the context of licensing). If you are searching for a final answer, it may or may not exist; the matter might not yet have been addressed by a legislature or reported by a court, but the place to uncover that answer will require eventual consultation with the applicable governing local law. This governing law would be the law of your state, that is, its code and its case law (made up of the decisions by the state and federal courts that have applied the law). However, this book will surely get you started in that direction, informing you of the basic issues and possibilities. The book also attempts to apply the content in a practice-oriented chapter that lists and comments upon the various terms typical in a license agreement, as well as providing several chapters that review different agreements, offer an inventory of questions useful in license review, and suggest a basis for library-friendly clauses. The latter content—a reference toolkit of sorts—can get you up and running quickly, but often the discussion in those chapters refers to the basic concepts covered in earlier chapters, which could then be consulted for additional explanation.

One other point about copyright law should be made at this early point: it will be reinforced throughout this book as well. While you do not need an understanding of copyright law to understand the legal issues involving a particular license clause (or before you read and use this book), you will be challenged to both appreciate the significance of that clause and assess (or alter) its practical impact in your library. Having some understanding of copyright can assist you in meeting that challenge. This is because a license clause may give you more rights than you might otherwise be entitled when using content protected under the copyright law, such as right to digital first sale; conversely, a license might take away or limit a right, such as fair use. This understanding is an obvious prerequisite to figuring out whether a particular license agreement or a particular clause is palatable to your information tastes. This initial understanding leads to the ability to determine the overall costs and benefits of a particular agreement your library is being asked by the licensor to enter; for example, you may be granted the convenience of online access but asked to forgo some fair-use rights in return. Based on the examples and trends in current license agreements reviewed in conjunction with the preparation of this book, the author will alert you to those circumstances where the copyright-license interface is significant or troublesome (at least to the author), as well those circumstances where other legal rights might be implicated, such as patron privacy or librarian free-speech rights to make public comment on the product, for example.

ORGANIZATION AND USE

You can use *The Librarian's Legal Companion for Licensing Information Resources and Services* in a number of ways. You can read it cover to cover (the advanced approach), but another way is to scan the table of contents, which is detailed and gives a list of the subtopics within each chapter so you can jump from issue to issue if you like. Another way to do this would be to begin with Chapter 14, "A Basic Licensing Glossary, A–Z," that lists and discusses a variety of license terms and either work backward or forward as needed (the intermediate approach). Or you might just want to look up a specific term or two (Chapters 14 and 17) or review one of the actual license agreements analyzed in Chapter 15. To be sure, licensing is not for the faint of heart; if you think copyright law is challenging, licensing law is even more complex, but any unease you feel likely stems from your unfamiliarity with subject. The more you get used to it, the more comfortable and knowledgeable you will become in moving within its contours. So do not cower from these issues. Read this book, and remember that help is only a page or two away.

Synopsis of Parts and Chapters

Part I, "Before You Read the License: Essential Background Concepts," discusses basic and at times essential concepts in contract law upon which the law of licensing is based, as a license is a form of agreement or contract. Many of these concepts have direct connection to topics discussed later.

> Chapter 1, "The Information Acquisition Landscape Today," reviews the ascent of licensing and sets the stage and perspective of the book, contrasting essential differences between acquisition by sale (governed by copyright) and acquisition by license.
>
> Chapter 2, "Basic Contract Law Concepts," shows that historically contracts are based upon the understandings of the parties regarding the nature of their relationship. This chapter reviews some simple fundamentals and sets the stage for later topics, such as website permissions and access, or determining whether a scenario is governed by contract.
>
> Chapter 3, "Contract Formation and Enforceability," completes the discussion of basic contract concepts, again laying the groundwork for later interpretation of license terms, such as *material breach*. It gives a good overview on how to begin thinking in terms of contract/license law.
>
> Chapter 4, "Broader Legal and Policy Issues in Licensing," discusses a handful of concepts that courts use to question the value of a contract in a broader societal context. Contracts and licenses do have limitations, and recent doctrines have emerged to address overzealous licensors.

Part II, "The Range and Nature of Information Resource Licenses Libraries Encounter," covers the day-to-day basics of licenses that libraries and other organizations encounter.

> Chapter 5, "Electronic Signatures in Global and National Commerce Act and the Uniform Electronic Transactions Act," reviews the basic laws that paved the way for online contracts.
>
> Chapter 6, "Negotiated and Nonnegotiated Licenses," discusses the two general forms of licenses encountered daily. Knowing the difference is important, and each has advantages and disadvantages.
>
> Chapter 7, "Shrink-Wrap, Click-Wrap, and Browse-Wrap Licenses," covers another layer of difference by detailing the several contractual forms where assent or agreement is performed by some action, such as tearing the wrapping, clicking an icon, and so forth. Courts focus on basic issues of notice of

terms, assent to those terms, and so on, most based on basic concepts drawn from Part I.

Chapter 8, "End User License Agreements (Websites)," involves website transactions often for access alone and without any payment or exchange. The chapter discusses the legal status of website permission and use restrictions.

Chapter 9, "General Public Licenses, Open Source Agreements, and Creative Commons Agreements," covers agreements viewed by some as an alternative to copyright. It is important to know that Creative Commons licenses and other agreements are based on the concepts of license formation and enforceability.

Chapter 10, "Basic Music and Media Licenses," discusses musical works and sound recordings that librarians, teachers, and students often use in the course of a workday. This chapter reviews the basics of licensing such uses and when the copyright law allows such use without permission (remember that a license is a form of permission).

Chapter 11, "The Uniform Computer Information Transactions Act," reviews the controversial law of contract designed specifically for information products and services.

Chapter 12, "The Developing Law of Implied Licenses," is a picture of today. There may be some circumstances where a license, though not formally entered into, is nonetheless determined by courts to grant permission (the essence of a license) to make use of content posted on a website or in other circumstances. This determination is again based upon the application of basic contract principles.

Chapter 13, "The Future Look of Licenses," presents a few thoughts on potential future issues regarding licensing.

Part III, "A Licensing Reference Toolkit for Everyday Use," contains resources to use in evaluating license terms and provisions and maximizing those terms and provisions to the library's advantage.

Chapter 14, "A Basic Licensing Glossary," contains dozens of license terms, often with some mention of the legal status of such terms, examples from actual agreements, comments on the effect the term can have, unintended consequences, suggestions for alternative approaches, pluses and minuses, and so on.

Chapter 15, "Four Common Library Licenses Deconstructed," may be the most-consulted chapter in the book. It provides clause-by-clause/provision-by-provision review of the practical and legal aspects of licensing in four different agreements and in the context of and in relation to the provisions of the same agreement.

Chapter 16, "Twenty Sample Key Clauses to Look For in Content Licenses," is also designed for quick reference. It reviews the major licensing provisions with suggestions that are library friendly.

Finally, Chapter 17, "Look Before You License: 126 Questions and Answers for Evaluating Licenses," provides questions to ask about a license. It can also be used as a review of license issues in general. The questions are grouped with commentary regarding the major issues.

PERSPECTIVES AND ATTITUDES

It was in conjunction with a presentation I was making at InfoToday a decade ago that Neal-Schuman Publishers editor Charles Harmon asked me to consider writing a book on licensing. The presentation was in essence a reflection on recent developments in licensing law, rather than a how-to session. However, its conclusion established the perspective for this book: licenses will not go away, so why not use licenses to our advantage? Or stated perhaps a bit more figuratively, we need to stop looking at licensing as a dirty word, embrace the challenge licensing poses without fear, and where possible adopt its circumstances to our advantage.

I suppose the premise and purpose, then, of *The Librarian's Legal Companion for Licensing Information Resources and Services* is to show that licensing can and should be a positive experience, if we in the library prepare for it, combat it at times, and, dare I say, exploit it as well.

Consider one simple observation in support of this idea. I lecture frequently on the topic of copyright (and licensing) law in libraries and schools to library consortia and systems, school districts, colleges and universities, and the like, and at a variety of library conferences and professional meetings. While I can say much about what we know to be true of our rights as copyright users and facilitators of use to others (our patrons), when we make content and services protected by copyright available to our patrons there remains a great deal that is unsettled within the copyright law. Why not settle it, remove the copyright guesswork, and let a license govern your use of content in the library? The additional up-front cost of the license (negotiation, drafting, etc.), for example, can be more than recaptured in the savings resulting from the legal certainty of subsequent uses being compliant under the license instead of working under copyright principles alone. Although some of these savings may be negated by the actual cost of the license fee, remember that in a copyright regime you would need to pay the acquisitions cost of the item anyway. Certainty reduces risk, and this benefit alone may be worth the price of the license. The license agreement can define those uses. Of course, the license giveth and the license can taketh away, so understanding what the licensor might be asking you to surrender is paramount.

Does this mean that publishers and licensors (two more dirty words?) are out to get us? Of course not. They merely have an agenda of their own: to stay in business, which likely entails the maximization of profits and minimizations of costs, which translates into a desire for the best terms for their products that the market will carry. And we are the market. A license, then, is merely a tool to achieve an end. When that tool is not of assistance, we seek another tool, but we need to know how to use the tools we have. As the adage states, we need the right tool for the job.

I hope *The Librarian's Legal Companion for Licensing Information Resources and Services* will provide you with an understanding of licensing, the law behind it, the various associated terms and their meanings, and, to a lesser extent, how an understanding of copyright can increase the instruments at your disposal, allowing you to select from an array of tools to solve distinct problems.

ENDNOTES

1. "The Uniform Commercial Code (UCC), a comprehensive code addressing most aspects of commercial law, is generally viewed as one of the most important developments in American law. The UCC text and draft revisions are written by experts in commercial law and submitted as drafts for approval to the National Conference of Commissioners on Uniform State Laws (now referred to as the Uniform Law Commissioners), in collaboration with the American Law Institute. . . . The UCC is a model code, so it does not have legal effect in a jurisdiction *unless* UCC provisions are enacted by the individual legislatures as statutes. Currently, the UCC (in whole or in part) has been enacted, with some local variation, in all 50 states, the District of Columbia, and the Virgin Islands." Uniform Commercial Code, available at http://www.law.duke.edu/lib/researchguides/ucc.

2. BLACK'S LAW DICTIONARY 502 (9th ed.) (Bryan A. Garner ed., St. Paul, MN: West Publishing, 2009) defines diversity jurisdiction as "[a] federal court's exercise of authority over a case involving parties who are citizens of different states and an amount in controversy greater than a statutory minimum [$75,000.00]" (no pagination in Westlaw).

► Acknowledgments

Thanks to the great folks at West Librarian Relations—through their support, Westlaw and other research tools are made available to like-minded researchers in the LIS field.

► PART I

BEFORE YOU READ THE LICENSE: ESSENTIAL BACKGROUND CONCEPTS

► 1

THE INFORMATION ACQUISITION LANDSCAPE TODAY

Read this chapter to gain an understanding of these licensing issues:
- ► Differences between contracts and licenses and their relationship to copyright law
- ► Basic issues in contract law and the application of that law to licenses
- ► Assessing permissions granted or taken away in a license to ensure that the agreement matches the rights under copyright
- ► Application of the first-sale doctrine in license agreements
- ► Possible impacts from recent litigation on the libraries' use of traditional library content

In the preface, the concept of licensing law was presented in contrast to copyright law. It is often difficult to understand the full impact of a license or a particular provision in a license without some understanding of copyright. This is especially true of licenses or provisions that relate to use rights and restrictions governing material that is protected by copyright law. This book does not attempt to present both understandings. Its focus is upon the former and not the latter. Where relevant, the book presents the essential difference between a particular right or restriction under a license versus the result that would occur under the copyright law (i.e., the legal concepts that would operate if the copyright law had applied), instead of the license or particular license provision. In addition, this chapter attempts to overview the foundation for this dichotomy from a definitional as well as a larger, big-picture perspective.

BASIC CONCEPTS: CONTRACT, LICENSE, AND COPYRIGHT

A license is a type of contract:

> A contract has been defined as an agreement upon a sufficient consideration to do, or refrain from doing, a particular lawful thing. Similarly, a "contract" has been defined as an agreement, obligation, or legal tie by which a party binds itself, or becomes bound,

expressly or impliedly, to pay a sum of money or to perform or omit to do some certain act or thing. Also, a "contract" has been defined as a private, voluntary allocation by which two or more parties distribute specific entitlements and obligations.[1]

The provisions of the contract are determined by the parties (or at least by one party in the case of a so-called mass-market or consumer contract, such as for a rental car, cell phone application, etc., but this is getting ahead of ourselves, as contract basics are covered in the next two chapters and the various license types are covered in more detail in Part II). An important feature to note here is that a contract is a sort of private ordering of events, circumstances, responsibilities, obligations, and so forth. In other words, the "rules" under which the parties must operate are determined by the parties (or, at least in the situation of a nonnegotiable license, the terms are set by one party, and the other party nonetheless agrees). Of course, legislatures can impact this ordering through codified contract law, the basic rules under which any such private ordering proceeds. For example, a legislature might make voidable contracts entered into by minors (and courts can establish such basic rules as well), but upon this foundation the parties are free to build their own set of rights and responsibilities and other circumstances under the contract; this is true of licenses as well. In this way, legislatures draw the general contours of the contract, but within those contours the parties have the freedom to choose the particular legal shape of their agreement. So, too, courts interpret and apply the "ordering" that the contract through its provisions established, again in light of any existing statutory law and previous interpretations made by the court.

So what is a license? A license is a type of contract that does not generally result in the transfer of ownership rights in physical objects. Unlike a contract for a purchase of a new set of encyclopedias, a license is in a sense ephemeral: "The word license means permission, or authority; and a license to do any particular thing is a permission or authority to do that thing; and if granted by a person having power to grant it, transfers to the grantee the right to do whatever it purports to authorize."[2] For libraries and similar institutions, these permissions relate to services (e.g., a license for a library automation system) or information access (e.g., a database license) or devices (e.g., an e-book reader). So a license is an agreement between at least two parties wherein one party grants permission to the other to engage in some course of conduct. In the previously noted examples, this would be permission to load and use the automation software to process library acquisitions, holdings, and circulations; the right to have authorized users access and use the online database; and the right for a library to lend (circulate) the e-readers to its patrons (although, without getting ahead of ourselves, a legal argument can be made that the software on devices such as cell phones, readers, tablets, etc., is actually a sale; this exception is covered in detail in Chapter 4). The permission granted by one party may be dependent upon the other party undertaking additional obligations besides paying a fee. Likewise, there may be obligations upon the party granting the permission, known as the licensor. As long as the basic agreement contours established by a legislature or court are adhered to, the parties are free to craft or order their series of rights, responsibilities, obligations, future conduct, and so forth, as the parties see fit.

PRIVATE ORDERING OF CONTRACTS VERSUS PUBLIC ORDERING OF COPYRIGHT

In the absence of a license, the law most likely to apply to the sort of content libraries come into contact with-that is, the law that would govern the use rights, restrictions, obligations, and so on, for such areas as automation or device software or "information" such as books—is copyright law.[3] The private ordering of a contract-license is in contrast to copyright law, where the basic rules are established by the U.S. Congress through the codified copyright law and as applied by the courts.

This landscape is in contrast to contract-license, representing then a sort of public ordering. It is public in two senses. First, the laws are made with opportunity for public input through our system of elected representatives and legislative processes. Second, since copyright law is federal law, this law applies to all citizens, owners or providers, and users or consumers alike. For example, when the use of a book is subject to copyright law, then fair use of that book under the copyright law can be made by all users; it need not be negotiated or obtained from each publisher but applies to all members of society. Of course, courts may interpret fair use slightly differently depending upon the jurisdiction of the user, as discussed in the next example. This private-public dichotomy was explained by Judge Easterbrook in *ProCD v. Zeidenberg*, a decision of the 7th Circuit:

> Copyright law forbids duplication, public performance, and so on, unless the person wishing to copy or perform the work gets permission; silence means a ban on copying. A copyright is a right against the world. Contracts, by contrast, generally affect only their parties; strangers may do as they please, so contracts do not create "exclusive rights." Someone who found a copy of SelectPhone (trademark) on the street would not be affected by the shrinkwrap license—though the federal copyright laws of their own force would limit the finder's ability to copy or transmit the application program.[4]

In contrast, the rights, responsibilities, conditions, limitations, obligations, and so forth, governing the use of works protected by copyright is public law in the sense that the rights and responsibilities are determined by the copyright statutes and regulations (and the interpretation the courts give to the statutes and regulations), and not by the individual copyright owner and user.[5] There are numerous points of public input, both direct and indirect, in addition to traditional legislative processes and inputs. The copyright statutes are enacted by legislators (elected officials). In the copyright arena, the U.S. Copyright Office reporting and rule-making processes often include opportunity for public comment through hearings,[6] roundtables,[7] public comment, and so on.[8] Finally, the federal judiciary is at least nominated by an elected official (the president) and confirmed by elected officials (members of the Senate). To some extent, as licensing and private ordering increases, the significance of copyright is lessened or made less relevant; or, in a more critical phrasing, it could be said that copyright law is threatened through some situations of licensing.[9]

There are several reasons why understanding basic issues in contract law and the application of that law to licenses is important in library and archive-related information settings, and educational environments as well—the latter environments being those in which libraries or archives can reside. This understanding is enhanced by an understanding of basic copyright law. However, other legal concepts, such as privacy and free speech, can also be implicated by license provisions, but because much, if not all, of what is licensed—be it content (e.g., a database)[10] or a service (e.g., a computer program)[11]—is protected by copyright, the copyright law is most relevant here.[12] Remember, a license is a form of permission; the range of use (the scope of the permission) that can be made of licensed content is determined by the provisions of the license. In contrast, content protected by copyright that is purchased (not licensed) by the library (e.g., a book or set of encyclopedias) is governed by copyright law.

COPYRIGHT LAW AND UNDERSTANDING LICENSES

First, without an understanding of basic copyright law, the librarian may not be aware of his or her use rights[13] under the copyright law or the conditions or obligations[14] placed upon him or her to secure those use rights—rights that under the law allow the library and its staff to use and make available to patrons content acquired through purchase to the maximum extent possible under the copyright law. If, for example, a library desires to circulate a computer program that it has purchased (as opposed to licensed), what rights or restrictions, if any, are imposed on the library to make use of the program in this way?[15] Understanding what is possible under copyright law can assist in assessing and ensuring that the rights under a license are at least as great as those under the copyright law (and the licensor may propose terms that offer rights far less than those under the copyright law), but it is impossible to undertake that assessment without some knowledge of copyright law. The author is not suggesting you run out and buy a copyright book to have on hand as you use this book (unless your knowledge of copyright law is very limited) but asks instead that you be aware of the alternative world of rights and restrictions that a license may present. Further, this book will alert you to those specific license provisions that purport to "take away" these copyright use rights.

"Use," under the copyright law, refers to those acts that implicate, or in the colloquial "step on," one or more of the exclusive rights of the copyright owner. These uses are *reproduction* (photocopying or scanning a book), *public distribution* (circulating a VHS cassette or DVD), *public display* (think transmission or display of multiple images of the same item in the same place but not "display" as in holding up a map or poster and showing it to an audience during a book talk), and *public performance* (playing the VHS cassette or DVD during a library programming) of content protected by copyright, and also perhaps the *preparation of derivative works* (scripting a young adult novel into a play), and even the *public performance through the digital transmission of a sound recording* (streaming a music CD through an online reserve or course content delivery system such as Moodle or Desire2Learn).[16] These are the sort of uses librarians and patrons often make of content found in the library and related educational settings. However, these are the exclusive rights of the copyright owner. As a result, the often complex interplay of copyright rights and restrictions (and obligations) already mentioned apply. A license can change all of that, realigning both rights and restrictions (or from the library and patron perspective, the uses the copyright law otherwise might allow) from the public ordering of the copyright law to the private ordering of the license.

With a knowledge of the basic copyright concepts, the librarian can assess what permissions might be missing in a license and work toward getting language into the agreement that matches the rights under copyright as well as press for additional rights; in situations where the negotiation of terms is not possible, this understanding of copyright versus license can help the librarian to determine whether the license, taken as it is, is worth its cost.

Take, for example, the same computer program mentioned previously and make library acquisition of it subject to a license agreement that includes a prohibition on further distributions. Without some understanding of section 109, the provision of the copyright law that allows for circulation (public distributions) of protected (by copyright) material, including a special provision for circulation of computer programs, you may not realize that you have contracted away your so-called first-sale rights, restoring to the copyright owner his or her right to control distributions after the first sale or transaction of a copy of the work (i.e., the software program the library acquired). Without an understanding of basic copyright law, it is often difficult to appreciate the significance of a particular clause in a license agreement and to assess whether the library might lose more that it gains by entering into the license; for example, the cost (in terms of price, conditions, obligations, and limitations) may not be worth the benefit of increased access (in terms of content, format, etc.). Even worse, the cost of licensing content is increasing, in actual and associated costs.[17]

With a license agreement, the use of the content (or service) is governed by the terms of the license agreement and the law that applies to interpreting that language is essentially the law of contract. License agreements in various forms, even shrink-wrap, web-wrap, and new iterations (all of which are discussed in subsequent chapters), can be enforceable. This legal position reflects the deference by the courts to an underlying policy of American society and its focus upon commerce: the freedom to contract is honored by the court, even when that contract might not be in the consumer's best interest because its terms are in some way less than fair. The agreement can alter what would be the result in the absence of the agreement—what would exist under the copyright law (or other law, for that matter, such as privacy).[18] This can have enormous implications for the library and its patrons. It may be a better or a worse result in terms of use rights, restrictions, obligations, and so on. A license, like any contract, can give you rights that you might not otherwise have, or the license can take away rights that you would otherwise have:[19]

> What rights are acquired or withheld depends on what the contract says. This point only is implicit in Article 2 [of the Uniform Commercial Code] for goods such as books; UCITA [Uniform Computer Information Transactions Act, discussed in Chapter 11] makes it explicit for the information economy where, unlike in the case of a book, the contract (license) is the product.[20]

The hope is that you come to realize this potential or possibility and use this book to become familiar with such contractual implications. Without understanding the underlying legal concepts, you cannot fully appreciate what it is you might be giving up and, likewise, what you might be gaining through the license agreement. This book focuses on the former in detail but also covers the latter, where relevant, at least in as much detail as to explain its significance within the licensing context and offer additional sources where more information may be found.

Other rights may be implicated as well. Does the copyright law impose any limitations on the librarian who desires to write a review of the same software program the library purchased? The answer is no.[21] However, if the computer program is instead acquired by the library through a license agreement, then the terms of the license agreement will govern the use of the software program. License agreements may contain language that restricts the ability to undertake and disseminate such reviews or to undertake related product or benchmark testing.[22] While this is not a book on copyright law (or free speech or privacy law, for that matter), the author endeavors where appropriate to point out to the reader where copyright and contract converge from opposite ends of a continuum and where other rights, such as privacy and free speech of librarians and patrons alike, may be implicated by license terms and conditions and likewise intersect at the license agreement.

Another reason why understanding licensing is important in libraries and other information-rich environments is obvious: From both supplier and consumer perspectives, and for many sorts of works, the digital format is becoming the dominant if not also the preferred method of delivery and consumption.[23] Nothing prevents a content provider from licensing content that was traditionally purchased, for example, as an analog item (and by logic, a physical item) such as a book or cassette, or even digital-physical items such as a music CD.[24] (There is some discussion among commentators on whether the doctrine of copyright preemption[25] limits or should limit the reach of license terms,[26] but more on this in Chapter 4.)

It could be argued that content providers already consider the use of contractual terms to limit the use of analog-physical items or digital-physical items that are purchased for library and patron use.[27] Consider a VHS cassette (analog-physical) or DVD (digital-physical) that contains one of these warning screens: "By continuing to view this work you agree to limit the use of the work to home-use or personal use only, and make no public or commercial use of the work whatsoever"[28] or "Your viewing of this motion picture obligates you to send us an additional $25.00." Is either an enforceable contract? If so, what is the impact on section 110(1) or 110(2) of the copyright law that allows qualifying public performances to be made of protected content in educational settings? Contract can indeed override copyright, so does this mean you may not play or stream a portion of the VHS cassette or DVD of *To Kill a Mockingbird* (the 1962 movie adaptation starring Gregory Peck) during a class session on American literature? It depends on whether a valid contract with this language ("By continuing… /Your viewing…") was formed between the copyright owner (e.g., Walt Disney Studios or another movie studio, producer, authorized distributor, or rights holder) and the home viewer (e.g., the patron who checked out the VHS cassette or DVD from the public library). Chapters 2 and 3 address these questions with discussions of the basic rules of contract law, especially contract formation.

Some digital-physical items are subject to license agreement already, such as a CD-ROM that comes shrink-wrapped (terms and agreement printed inside the box or container) or click-wrapped (terms and conditions viewable upon installation or use). Books could be next![29] Whether this is a good idea—whether the expansion of licensing regimes into all areas of content acquisition in the library or elsewhere in society is good information policy—is not the primary focus of this book (though such considerations are unavoidable when discussing the topic in any detail); rather, the focus here is to understand the legal possibility of such a result.[30] An obvious result here is that the license also determines what use rights our patrons possess. With a book that is purchased, librarians can rest assured that their patrons will have fair-use rights in that book, for example. This is not so with a license agreement governing the same book read through a database or on an e-reader. The use rights in the content are determined by the provisions of the license agreement, which often govern use of e-book content. The point is that while content providers are experimenting with digital and online formats as well as migrating more content to these formats, patrons are likewise expecting the wider range and convenience of access that such formats provide. Why does licensing matter here? Licensing matters because the content (e.g., iTunes music downloads) as well as the delivery devices (e.g., an e-book reader) that libraries are now using are governed by license.[31]

UNDERSTANDING THE LICENSE-CONTRACT DICHOTOMY AND THE FIRST-SALE DOCTRINE

As alluded to earlier, a license agreement could alter the application of the first-sale doctrine that allows one in possession of a lawfully acquired copy of a protected work to make further public distribution of the copy of that work. The first-sale doctrine is of paramount importance to libraries and in essence limits the public distribution right of the copyright to "first sale" or first transaction of the copy alone, not to every subsequent public distribution that might occur: publisher through a bookstore sells book (the first sale) to customer; customer donates book to library; library uses book for a time and then sells book through its "friends" group; library patron buys book and gives it to a friend to read. All subsequent transfers beyond the first sale are in theory public distributions, but does each implicate the exclusive right of the copyright owner, the first-sale right? No, because the first-sale doctrine as codified in section 109 of copyright law limits the right of public distribution to the first sale—the first transaction point alone. The practical effect is that while the author gets a percentage of the sale by the publisher/book-store in the form of royalties, the author is not entitled to subsequent earnings on any subsequent public distributions, such as donations or further sales. This right applies to content that is purchased but not to content that is licensed. As discussed in Chapter 4 (see When Is a License Not a License?), recent courts have struggled with determining whether an acquisition of software can be in fact a purchase even if the agreement that accompanies it claims the use of the computer program is subject to a license.

The first-sale doctrine applies to items the library purchases for its collection and allows to circulate (use in public distribution). "For example, a library may lend an authorized copy of a book that it lawfully owns without violating the copyright laws."[32] As long as the copy of the item the library owns is a lawfully made copy, the doctrine applies and the distribution right of the copyright owner is limited. The concept is codified in section 109,[33] but there are exceptions, such as for computer programs[34]—and exceptions to the exceptions for libraries if a warning notice is used![35] Here we've scratched the surface of the often complex sequence of rights, responsibilities, conditions, limitations, obligations, and so forth, at play within the copyright law. However, a license can change all of that. A license can make your "information life" simpler or more complex. A license agreement can indicate that the e-book you download cannot be further distributed to the public in any way and is for the personal use of the immediate licensee alone. Likewise, a license agreement can include language to the effect that use of the downloaded music file or e-book is limited to "personal, noncommercial uses" and that "no further distribution" may be made of the acquired content. Content subject to these terms in a school or public library could not be used in the classroom or circulated to patrons as these would be public distributions of the work.

Some courts have concluded—and not all courts have addressed this question—that the terms of the license would override the provisions of the copyright law, such as the first-sale doctrine, because the license transaction is not a sale transaction. The licensee never acquires any lawfully made copy of the work to which the first-sale doctrine can apply.[36] However, the license binds only the parties to the agreement; the license cannot bind or restrict third parties, such a school student or library patron.[37] This is one reason many licensors desire to have the library monitor at some level what use students or patrons make of the licensed content or promise that its patrons will comply with the use rights and restrictions established by the license. The broader policy impact is that a license can alter the balance that the copyright law strives to achieve in section 109[38] or other provisions of the copyright law, such as section 107 (fair use) or 108 (library and archive reproduction and distribution), if the librarian allows the license to do so, that is. A license can override other use rights that the "limitations on exclusive rights" granted by sections 107 through 122 of the copyright law allow. Courts have observed that a license can override section 117,[39] the provision that allows the making of a "copy or adaptation of that computer program" in certain circumstances, such as for backup or maintenance.[40] Fair use may also be in similar jeopardy, making users subject to the terms of a license agreement.[41] However, this may not be applied to nonnegotiated, so-called mass-market licenses (more will be said of this later). Even Raymond Nimmer admits that in a mass-market license a clause that overrides fair-use rights, such as the right to reverse-engineer, "may very well preclude enforcement of a contract clause ... but that issue has never been settled."[42] It is important to remember that the realignment of copyright uses, rights, restrictions, obligations, and so forth, offered by a license agreement can improve or exacerbate the situation either by offering a greater array of uses than would otherwise be available under the copyright law alone or by limiting use rights the librarian or patron would otherwise have had under the copyright law; and in either instance, the agreement may make it worse by imposing additional responsibilities, conditions, limitations, obligations, and so on, than would otherwise exist under the copyright law. Of course, a license can do a little of both. Sorting out which clauses in a license agreement are likely to do the former and which are likely to do the latter is a major objective of later chapters, including Chapters 5 and 6.

THE POTENTIAL IMPACT OF RECENT LITIGATION

Courts are beginning to wrestle with these issues as well, as they may impact the uses libraries have made of traditional library content, such as books. In a case involving watches, but with implications for any work manufactured overseas— that there could be no first-sale or public distribution rights if, say, the book were manufactured overseas—courts have interpreted the first-sale doctrine in a narrow way. One appellate court concluded that the "general rule that § 109(a) refers 'only to copies legally made . . . in the United States," *id.* [*BMG Music v. Perez*, 952 F.2d 318, 319 (9th Cir. 1991)], is not clearly irreconcilable with *Quality King* [*Quality King Distributors, Inc. v. L'anza Research International, Inc.* 523 U.S. 135 (1998)] and, therefore, remains binding precedent. Under this rule, the first sale doctrine is unavailable as a defense to the claims under §§ 106(3) [the copyright holder's right of public distribution] and 602(a) [[43]] because there is no genuine dispute that Omega manufactured the watches bearing the Omega Globe Design in Switzerland."[44] If this holding applies to library items such as books, CDs, DVDs, and so on, then a library would violate the copy owner's right to make a public distribution of works manufactured overseas and imported without the permission of the copyright holder. If this applies to libraries and their books (and other items), a library would be prohibited from circulating the item[45] per the previous discussion. This decision was appealed to the U.S. Supreme Court, but the Court affirmed the decision without opinion.[46]

In a follow-up to *Omega S. A. v. Costco Wholesale Corp.*, the 2nd Circuit appellate court answered the question left undecided by the U.S. Supreme Court: "The Supreme Court recently seemed poised to transform this dicta into holding when it granted a writ of certiorari to review the Ninth Circuit's decision in *Omega S. A. v. Costco Wholesale Corp.* . . . After hearing oral argument, an equally divided Supreme Court (with Justice Kagan recused) was obliged to affirm the judgment rendered by the Ninth Circuit. Without further guidance from the Supreme Court, we now consider the extent to which the protections set forth in § 109(a) may apply to items manufactured abroad. In doing so, we rely on the text of § 109(a), the structure of the Copyright Act, and the Supreme Court's opinion in Quality King."[47] In *John Wiley & Sons, Inc. v. Kirtsaeng* the 2nd Circuit likewise considered the application of the first-sale doctrine to books manufactured overseas: "The principal question presented in this appeal is whether the first sale doctrine, 17 U.S.C. § 109(a), applies to copies of copyrighted works produced outside of the United States but imported and resold in the United States."[48]

Under section 602 of the copyright law, importation of copies of a work without the authority of the copyright owner is infringement, violating the owner's right of public distribution. The question in *John Wiley & Sons, Inc. v. Kirtsaeng*, as with the *Costco Wholesale Corp. v. Omega S. A.* litigation, was whether the first-sale doctrine applies to such copies, operating, as do all of the user rights granted in sections 107 through 122 of the copyright law, as an affirmative defense to a claim of infringement. If the first-sale doctrine applies to such works, then the public distribution of such works is not infringing and, therefore, any public distribution of those works does not violate the owner's right under section 106(3); and if the right to make public distributions is allowed, then such acts, including importation, are also not infringing:

> Finally, because conduct covered by § 109(a) does not violate § 106(3), and because absent a violation of § 106(3) there cannot be infringement under § 602(a), conduct covered by § 109(a) does not violate § 602(a). In short, infringement does not occur under § 106(3) or § 602(a) where "the owner of a particular copy...lawfully made under this title" imports and sells that copy without the authority of the copyright owner.[49]

Section 602(a)(3)(C) contains an exception:

> [I]mportation by or for an organization operated for scholarly, educational, or religious purposes and not for private gain, with respect to no more than one copy of an audiovisual work solely for its archival purposes, and no more than five copies or phonorecords of any other work for its library lending or archival purposes, unless the importation of such copies or phonorecords is part of an activity consisting of systematic reproduction or distribution, engaged in by such organization in violation of the provisions of section 108(g)(2).[50]

However, this exception suggests that acquisitions of foreign-made works could not be done in order to serve as a source of "systematic reproduction or distribution" but would allow for the occasional interlibrary loan or reproducing service for patrons under section 108(g)(2), which provides:

> The rights of reproduction and distribution under this section extend to the isolated and unrelated reproduction or distribution of a single copy or phonorecord of the same material on separate occasions, but do not extend to cases where the library or archives, or its employee—engages in the systematic reproduction or distribution of single or multiple copies or phonorecords of material described in subsection (d): Provided, That nothing in this clause prevents a library or archives from participating in interlibrary arrangements that do not have, as their purpose or effect, that the library or archives receiving such copies or phonorecords for distribution does so in such aggregate quantities as to substitute for a subscription to or purchase of such work.[51]

Subsection (d) authorizes the reproduction and distribution "of no more than one article or other contribution to a copyrighted collection or periodical issue, or to a copy or phonorecord of a small part of any other copyrighted work,"[52] either for a patron of a qualifying library or archive or the patron at another qualifying library or archive. That works so acquired might on occasion be the subject of such requests for reproduction and distribution would appear acceptable.[53] The legislative history of the provision does little other than to repeat the exception:

> The bill specifies that the third exception does not apply if the importation "is part of an activity consisting of systematic reproduction or distribution, engaged in by such organization in violation of the provisions of section 108(g)(2)." If none of the three exemptions applies, any unauthorized importer of copies or phonorecords acquired abroad could be sued for damages and enjoined from making any use of them, even before any public distribution in this country has taken place.[54]

The 2nd Circuit observed the possible interpretations of the phrase "lawfully made under this title": "But while a textual reading of § 109(a) does not compel the result favored by Wiley, it does not foreclose it either. The relevant text is simply unclear. '[L]awfully made under this title' could plausibly be interpreted to mean any number of things, including: (1) 'manufactured in the United States,' (2) 'any work made that is subject to protection under this title,' or (3) 'lawfully made under this title had this title been applicable.'"[55] Nevertheless the appellate court decided that "we conclude that the District Court correctly decided that Kirtsaeng could not avail himself of the first sale doctrine codified by § 109(a) since all the books in question were manufactured outside of the United States. In sum, we hold that the phrase 'lawfully made under this Title' in § 109(a) refers specifically and exclusively to copies that are made in territories in which the Copyright Act is law, and not to foreign-manufactured works."[56]

If such items are not "lawfully made under this title," then libraries would be infringing if such items are circulated and, arguably, when also made available for public access in such libraries short of being actually circulated. However, all is not lost, as explained by Jonathan Band: "a combination of defenses, including section 602(a)(3)(C) of the Copyright Act, the Ninth Circuit's *Drug Emporium* [*Parfums Givenchy, Inc., v. Drug Emporium, Inc.*, 38 F.3d 47 (9th Cir. 1991)] exception, implied license, and fair use, allow libraries throughout the country to continue their existing purchasing and circulation practices with a fair degree of confidence that they will not infringe copyright by doing so."[57] Band also opines that for libraries in the 2nd Circuit the decision in *John Wiley & Sons, Inc. v. Kirtsaeng*

> is actually worse than the Ninth Circuit's decision in *Costco* in a manner significant to libraries. The Ninth Circuit realized that its interpretation had a negative policy impact...So, the Ninth Circuit created an exception to its interpretation, and ruled that the FSD [First-Sale Doctrine] still applied to a foreign manufactured copy if it was imported with the authority of the U.S. copyright owner. Thus, if a library buys a foreign printed book from an authorized dealer in the U.S., the FSD applies to that book and the library can lend it...Unfortunately, the Second Circuit rejected this exception as not having a foundation in the language of the FSD. Accordingly, a library in the

Second Circuit that wants to lend foreign manufactured copies must rely on fair use or the ambiguous exception in 17 USC 602(a)(3)(C) that allows a library to import 5 copies (except audiovisual works) for lending purposes, but doesn't specifically allow the library to actually lend those copies.[58]

For now, this narrow interpretation of the first-sale doctrine is the law only in those circuits where the question has been litigated, the 9th and 2nd Circuits. Other circuits may follow. However, the Supreme Court granted certiorari in April 2012. If oral arguments occur in the fall, a decision may be forthcoming in 2013. It is hoped the Court would interpret "lawfully made under this title" to make clear that foreign-sourced or -manufactured materials fall within the phrasing and first-sale rights would apply to owners of lawfully made copies. This decision might also impact other provisions where the same appears, such as section 110 (classroom use). Depending on the decision rendered by the Court, Congress, if pressured, may seek to craft a legislative solution, allowing distribution of such works so acquired to be lawful.[59] For example, Congress could limit such exception to works in the current holdings of a library and let the market decide future acquisitions; or it could limit the application to another of the possible interpretations considered but rejected by the 2nd Circuit—that the work must be made (manufactured) in a country where the work also is subject to copyright protection.[60]

A BRIEF WORD REGARDING COURT DECISIONS

So far this chapter has mentioned and referenced different sorts of courts, such as the 9th Circuit, the 2nd Circuit, and the U.S. Supreme Court. A brief comment should be made on the sources of law discussed in this and succeeding chapters. There are legislative laws, codes, and statutes. In the contract-license area, such law is most often created by state legislatures, resulting in codified or statutory standards for creating and executing agreements between parties, establishing a sort of legal minimum and maximum, if you will (think contours), regarding what the parties can and cannot agree to in their agreement. In the contract arena, states have enacted slight variations on the Uniform Commercial Code (UCC), as discussed in the preface. Courts then interpret this law in given situations. In the area of modern copyright law, Congress enacts or amends the copyright law. Courts then interpret and apply this law. As is often the case with the licensing of software (automation or devices) or information (databases), the codified law does not always apply, so courts apply their own "rules," with the resulting court-made law referred to as the common law. (Most codifications of contract have origins in the common law.)

One more point about court interpretations. The parties to a contract-license, as well as those making fair use or other use of content governed by copyright law, exist in jurisdictions. The parties may be in the same or different jurisdictions. Here the concept of jurisdictions relates to which court or courts possess the authority to govern the parties. Which court decisions represent "the law" for a particular contract-license or use under the copyright law depends on which court or courts have jurisdiction.[61] The short version is that the rulings of the U.S. Supreme Court apply to all citizens across all jurisdictions. The Supreme Court rules on both contract-license issues as well as copyright issues. Likewise, decisions of state supreme courts govern the parties within that state. The trial courts of a state are often organized by circuit or district (other terms may be used), which can be organized into different appellate districts. All states have a supreme court, decisions of which can bind persons in the entire state. Likewise, the federal courts are organized into a similar three-tiered system, with the trial courts known as district courts. Some states have more than one federal district. In general, states are then organized into courts of appeal or circuit courts. Federal courts can apply contract-license law as well as copyright law. As copyright law is federal law, state courts do not have subject matter jurisdiction to decide copyright cases. From the individual's perspective, each court's decisions in the chain of command or hierarchy represent "the law." In other words, a person in Indianapolis is governed by the law of the federal district court of southern Indiana, the 7th Circuit Court of Appeals (as district courts in Indiana, Illinois, and Wisconsin are within the jurisdiction of this appellate court), and the U.S. Supreme Court (whose decisions have binding authority across the United States). The decisions that constitute "the law" for a given jurisdiction are known as mandatory authority. But what of the courts of other jurisdictions, federal or state? This book cites cases from federal and state courts all over the country. These decisions are known as persuasive authority. In the case of our sample person from Indianapolis, what impact does a decision from Arizona (state or federal court) or the 9th Circuit (the federal appellate court with jurisdiction over cases arising in Arizona) have? Such decisions are not the law but can be used to persuade a court in the Indianapolis jurisdiction that this other court was correct and its decision should also be followed in Indianapolis.[62] Suffice it to say that the cases cited and discussed in this book may represent either mandatory (what the law is here) or persuasive (what the law is elsewhere and could be here) authority for the reader, depending on where the case is from and where the reader resides. Moreover, the cases cited in this book are not exhaustive but are included to offer example illustrations—not to represent a comprehensive review of contract case law or, to a lesser extent, copyright law.

ENDNOTES

1. 17A AMERICAN JURISPRUDENCE 2D CONTRACTS § 1, footnotes omitted (Westlaw database, updated November 2011).
2. Federal Land Bank of Wichita v. Board of County Commissioners of Kiowa County, 368 U.S.146, 154, note 3 (1961), quoting Gibbons v. Ogden, 9 Wheaten 1, 22 U.S. 1 (1824).

3. "The right to copy; specifically, a property right in an original work of authorship (including literary, musical, dramatic, choreographic, pictorial, graphic, sculptural, and architectural works; motion pictures and other audiovisual works; and sound recordings) fixed in any tangible medium of expression, giving the holder the exclusive right to reproduce, adapt, distribute, perform, and display the work" per BLACK'S LAW DICTIONARY (9th ed.) (Bryan A. Garner ed., 2009) (no pagination in Westlaw). The subject matter or protected works is found in 17 U.S.C. § 102(a)(1)–(8): "Copyright protection subsists, in accordance with this title, in original works of authorship fixed in any tangible medium of expression, now known or later developed, from which they can be perceived, reproduced, or otherwise communicated, either directly or with the aid of a machine or device. Works of authorship include the following categories: (1) literary works; (2) musical works, including any accompanying words; (3) dramatic works, including any accompanying music; (4) pantomimes and choreographic works; (5) pictorial, graphic, and sculptural works; (6) motion pictures and other audiovisual works; (7) sound recordings; and (8) architectural works."

4. ProCD v. Zeidenberg, 86 F.3d 1447, 1454 (7th Cir. 1996). See also Universal Gym Equipment, Inc. v. ERWA Exercise Equipment Ltd., 827 F.2d 1542, 1550 (Fed. Cir. 1987): "Parties to a contract may limit their right to take action they previously had been free to take." See also Ryan J. Casamiquela, *Contractual Assent and Enforceability in Cyberspace*, 17 BERKELEY TECHNOLOGY LAW JOURNAL 475 (2002).

5. See Niva Elkin-Koren, *What Contracts Cannot Do: The Limits of Private Ordering in Facilitating a Creative Commons*, 74 FORDHAM LAW REVIEW 375, 407 (2005) (Symposium, Law and the Information Society, Panel 1: Intellectual Property and Public Values): "We often think of property and contracts as two distinct legal mechanisms that together constitute the market. There seems to be a division of labor between the two: Copyright law is responsible for allocating the initial entitlements, while contract law governs their transfer; copyright law creates rights against the world (*in rem*), whereas contract law applies only to the parties (*in personam*). Property rights differ from contract rights in that a property right 'runs with the asset,' namely, it can be enforced against subsequent transferees of the asset. Enforcing standard licenses against third parties blurs the distinction between property and contracts. It allows distributors, right holders, and possibly others to establish rights in rem through contracts. Typically, the law does not enforce contracts that run with the asset, and claims against third parties are normally denied" (footnote omitted).

6. See, for example, United States Copyright Office Field Hearings, Copyright Office Study On Distance Education, Library of Congress, Copyright Office, Docket No. 99-12A, Promotion of Distance Education Through Digital Technologies, Request for Comments and Notice of Public Hearing, available at 63 FEDERAL REGISTER 71,167 (December 23, 1998); UNITED STATES COPYRIGHT OFFICE, III. REPORT ON COPYRIGHT AND DIGITAL DISTANCE EDUCATION (1999), transcripts of hearings.

7. See, for example, United States Copyright Office Public Roundtables, United States Copyright Office and the Office of Strategic Initiatives, Library of Congress, Docket No.

06-10801, Section 108 Study Group: Copyright Exceptions for Libraries and Archives, available at 71 FEDERAL REGISTER 70434 (December 4, 2006), DePaul University College of Law, Lewis Building, Room 1001, 25 E. Jackson Boulevard, Chicago, Illinois, 60604, January 21, 2007, transcripts available at http://www.loc.gov/section108/roundtables .html; and United States Copyright Office Public Roundtables, United States Copyright Office and the Office of Strategic Initiatives, Library of Congress, Docket No. 06-10801, Section 108 Study Group: Copyright Exceptions for Libraries and Archives, 71 FEDERAL REGISTER 7999 (February 15, 2006), Rayburn House Office Building, Room 2237, Washington, DC, March 16, 2006, transcript available at http://www.loc.gov/section108/ docs/0316-topic1.pdf.

8. See recent cycle of § 1201(a)(1)(C) rule making: 71 FEDERAL REGISTER 68472 (November 27, 2006). Comments available at http://www.copyright.gov/1201/2006/comments/ index.html; reply comments available at http://www.copyright.gov/1201/2006/reply/. Status and documentation from the current section 1201 rule making can be found at http://www.copyright.gov/1201/.

9. Steven A. Heath, *Contracts, Copyright, and, Confusion: Revisiting the Enforceability of "Shrinkwrap" Licenses*, 5 CHICAGO-KENT JOURNAL OF INTELLECTUAL PROPERTY 12, 26 (2005): "[W]hile the case law discussed has provided valuable information to software producers seeking to uphold their licensing agreements, the ultimate effect is to reinforce the licensing norm within an ill-suited paradigm. The rise of licensing as 'private governance' has eroded the scope of the Copyright Act; the remedy for which can surely only be found through appropriate legislative action."

10. Of course, some licensed content may not be protected. A statistical database—for example, one made up of facts—can still be subject to copyright protection as a compilation. See 17 U.S.C. § 101 (2006), defining compilation as "work formed by the collection and assembling of preexisting materials or of data that are selected, coordinated, or arranged in such a way that the resulting work as a whole constitutes an original work of authorship." The way in which the noncopyrightable facts in the database are selected, coordinated, or arranged might be protected by a compilation copyright, but the underlying facts would not be protected.

11. A computer program is also protected by copyright: "It is not disputed that a computer program is a form of literary work, and thus is copyrightable," per Greenberg v. National Geographic Society, 533 F.3d 1244, 1262, at note 6 (11th Cir.), cert. denied 129 S.Ct. 727 (2008). A "computer program" is a set of statements or instructions to be used directly or indirectly in a computer in order to bring about a certain result per 17 U.S.C. § 101 (2006). See also Apple Computer, Inc. v. Franklin Computer Corp., 714 F.2d 1240, 1249 (3d Cir. 1983): "[A] computer program, whether in object code or source code, is a 'literary work' and is protected from unauthorized copying, whether from its object or source code version," cert. dismissed 464 U.S. 1033 (1984).

12. A good review of basic copyright principles is found in KENNETH D. CREWS, COPYRIGHT LAW FOR LIBRARIANS AND EDUCATORS: CREATIVE STRATEGIES AND PRACTICAL SOLUTIONS (3d ed.) (Chicago: American Library Association, 2012).

13. The headings of § 107 through § 122 of the copyright law (title 17 of the U.S. Code) all begin with the phrase "Limitations on Exclusive Rights" to indicate that these sections offer "uses" or, in a legal sense, privileges to make what would otherwise be an infringing use, in other words, a use that limits on one the exclusive rights of the copyright owner. These use rights then operate as a limitation on or an exception to the exclusive rights granted to copyright owners in § 106: to reproduce the work, to make derivative works, to distribute the work to the public, to make public performance or display, and to make public performance of a sound recording through a digital audio transmission, for example, to make a webcast of a music CD. The most well-known of these exceptions is found in § 107, Limitations on Exclusive Rights: Fair Use.

14. Again, § 108 through § 122 of the copyright law often impose conditions or obligations upon users as a prerequisite to the availability of the limitation on exclusive rights granted by a particular section. In addition, the use right granted may be limited to particular works or to certain types of users or circumstances, or apply to selected exclusive rights. For example, the requirement in § 108(d) for library and archive reproduction and distribution, the section of the copyright that allows interlibrary loan transactions, obligates display of a warning notice under § 108(d)(2), imposes a condition under § 108(d)(1) that the item reproduced and distributed "becomes the property of the user," and restricts through the limitation under § 108(i) that reproduction and distribution to patrons under § 108(d) cannot "not apply to a musical work, a pictorial, graphic or sculptural work, or a motion picture or other audiovisual work other than an audiovisual work dealing with news." 17 U.S.C. § 108 (2006).

15. See 17 U.S.C. § 109(b)(2)(A) (2006): "Nothing in this subsection shall apply to the lending of a computer program for nonprofit purposes by a nonprofit library, if each copy of a computer program which is lent by such library has affixed to the packaging containing the program a warning of copyright in accordance with requirements that the Register of Copyrights shall prescribe by regulation."

16. 17 U.S.C. § 106 (2006).

17. Elkin-Koren, *supra* note 5, at 375, 381: "The cost associated with licensing copyrighted materials has increased exponentially in recent years. This can be attributed to two developments: one substantive and the other procedural. The substantive element concerns the expanded scope of copyright protection, and the procedural one the removal of formal requirements. The expansion of copyright protection to cover more subject matters, extended duration, and additional rights reduced the volume of works that are freely available to build upon. Furthermore, in addition to the expansion of copyrights, the characteristics of the digital environment also make informational works less available" (footnotes omitted).

18. See, for example, ProCD Inc. v. Zeidenberg, 86 F.3d 1447, 1454 (7th Cir. 1996): "A copyright is a right against the world. Contracts, by contrast, generally affect only their parties; strangers may do as they please, so contracts do not create 'exclusive rights'"; and Universal Gym Equipment, Inc. v. ERWA Exercise Equipment Ltd., 827 F.2d 1542,

1550 (Fed. Cir. 1987): "Parties to a contract may limit their right to take action they previously had been free to take." See also Casamiquela, *supra* note 4.

19. "[L]ibraries need to be aware that licensing arrangements may restrict their legal rights and those of their users," per the Association of Research Libraries, *Reshaping Scholarly Communication: Principles for Licensing Electronic Resources* (July 15, 1997), http://www.arl.org/sc/marketplace/license/licprinciples.shtml.

20. Uniform Computer Information Transactions Act (UCITA) (2000), Prefatory Note.

21. See NXIVM Corp. v. Ross Institute, 364 F.3d 471, 482 (2d Cir. 2004): "It is plain that, as a general matter, criticisms of a seminar or organization cannot substitute for the seminar or organization itself or hijack its market. To be sure, some may read defendants' materials and decide not to attend plaintiffs' seminars . . . But that sort of harm, as the district court properly recognized, is not cognizable under the Copyright Act. If criticisms on defendants' websites kill the demand for plaintiffs' service, that is the price that, under the First Amendment, must be paid in the open marketplace for ideas," cert. denied 543 U.S. 1000 (2004).

22. See Genelle I. Belmas and Brian N. Larson, *Clicking Away Your Speech Rights: The Enforceability of Gagwrap Licenses*, 12 COMMUNICATIONS LAW AND POLICY 37, 38, at note 4 (2007), referencing the Oracle license as one such example of an agreement prohibiting dissemination of any benchmark test results without prior permission of Oracle.

23. For a snapshot of licensing practices across 70 major academic libraries, see Research and Markets Primary Research Group, THE SURVEY OF LIBRARY DATABASE LICENSING PRACTICES, 2011 EDITION (January 2011), http://www.researchandmarkets.com/product/d9b5d9b2/the_survey_of_library_database_licensing_prac.

24. See Ticketmaster Corp. v. Tickets.com, Inc., 2003 WL 21406289, at *2 (C.D. Cal. 2003): "The 'shrinkwrap' cases find the printed conditions plainly wrapped around the cassette or CD enforceable." See also Aundrea Gamble, *Google's Book Search Project: Searching for Fair Use or Infringement*, 9 TULANE JOURNAL OF TECHNOLOGY AND INTELLECTUAL PROPERTY 365, 383–384 (2007): "Even the 'public benefit' inherent in the [Google] Book Search program could lead to increased contracting for consumers, forcing publishers to include license agreements with every new book"; and Joseph P. Liu, *Owning Digital Copies: Copyright Law and the Incidents of Copy Ownership*, 42 WILLIAM AND MARY LAW REVIEW 1245 (2001): "Book publishers can shrink-wrap their books."

25. 17 U.S.C. § 301 (2006): "[A]ll legal or equitable rights that are equivalent to any of the exclusive rights within the general scope of copyright as specified by section 106 [the exclusive right of the copyright owner] in works of authorship that are fixed in a tangible medium of expression and come within the subject matter of copyright as specified by sections 102 and 103, whether created before or after that date and whether published or unpublished, are governed exclusively by this title."

26. Viva R. Moffat, *Super-Copyright: Contracts, Preemption, and the Structure of Copyright Policymaking*, 41 U.C. DAVIS LAW REVIEW 45, 71 (2007): "As a general matter, courts rarely hold that federal statutes preempt the operation of state contract law, and, more specifically,

contractual restrictions on baseline copyright principles have generally been upheld over preemption challenges. This approach has been misguided and the results skewed, however, because courts have failed to engage in the interpretive preemption task."

27. See Paul Deane, posting to LISNews (June 7, 2005), http://lisnews.org/node/14943: "This year I have been recieving [*sic*] reference books with a license on shrink wrap"; and G. M. Filisko, *Shrink-Wrap Contracts 'Booked': Publishers Stretch Software-Type Licensing to Ink-on-Paper Products*, ABA JOURNAL E-REPORT (July 29, 2005):"Librarian Paul Deane from Arlington Heights, Ill., says he's seen shrink-wrap agreements on at least five books in the past four months, one a directory of medical practitioners, the others reference books." See also Charles McManis, *The Privatization (or "Shrink-Wrapping") of American Copyright Law*, 87 CALIFORNIA LAW REVIEW 173, 173–174 and 176 (1999).

28. See, for example, Michael J. Madison, *Legal-Ware: Contract and Copyright in the Digital Age*, 67 FORDHAM LAW REVIEW 1025, 1068, at note 152 (1998): "Pre-recorded videotapes typically bear a notice that the film is 'licensed for home [or personal] use/exhibition only.'"

29. John A. Rothchild, *The Incredible Shrinking First-Sale Rule: Are Software Resale Limits Lawful*, 57 RUTGERS LAW REVIEW 1, 56–57 (2004): "This could be done by placing the license agreement on top of the book, covering the book in shrinkwrap, and placing a label on the outside stating that important terms are enclosed. The purchaser of the book acquires it subject to the terms of the license agreement. The agreement licenses the acquirer to read the book as many times as she likes, and to distribute it to members of her immediate family. (Just for fun, the agreement might prohibit her from reading the ending before slogging through the entire book, or require the publisher's written permission before publication of any review of the book" (footnote omitted). This result was hypothesized by the U.S. Supreme Court a hundred years ago! See Bobbs-Merrill Co. v. Straus, 210 U.S. 339, 349–350 (1908): "What does the statute mean in granting 'the sole right of vending the same?' Was it intended to create a right which would permit the holder of the copyright to fasten, by notice in a book or upon one of the articles mentioned within the statute, a restriction upon the subsequent alienation of the subject-matter of copyright after the owner had parted with the title to one who had acquired full dominion over it and had given a satisfactory price for it? It is not denied that one who has sold a copyrighted article, without restriction, has parted with all right to control the sale of it. The purchaser of a book, once sold by authority of the owner of the copyright, may sell it again, although he could not publish a new edition of it." The "license" at issue in the case included the following notice: "The price of this book at retail is $1 net. No dealer is licensed to sell it at a less price, and a sale at a less price will be treated as an infringement of the copyright." *Id.* at 341. See also L. J. KUTTEN, 2 COMPUTER SOFTWARE: PROTECTION LIABILITY LAW FORMS § 9:72 (database updated April 2012): "This author finds EULAs [End User License Agreements] disturbing from a public policy perspective . . . Further, if EULAs are valid, why must they be limited to software? Why wouldn't the following nonsoftware transactions also be valid contractual restrictions? . . . A book publisher put a shrink-wrap agreement on its back covers prohibiting the loaning of its books by a public library."

30. See Niva Elkin-Koren, *Copyright Policy and the Limits of Freedom of Contract*, 12 BERKELEY TECHNOLOGY LAW JOURNAL 93 (1997) (Symposium: Digital Content: New Product and New Business Model), http://www.law.berkeley.edu/journals/btlj/articles/vol12/Elkin-Koren/html/reader.html.

31. See IFLA's Committee on Copyright and other Legal Matters (CLM), *Licensing Principles* (2001), http://www.ifla.org/V/ebpb/copy.htm: "P3. Licenses (contracts) for information should not exclude or negatively impact for users of the information any statutory rights that may be granted by applicable copyright law."

32. Hotaling v. Church of Jesus Christ of Latter-Day Saints, 118 F.3d 199, 203 (4th Cir. 1999). "When a public library adds a work to its collection, lists the work in its index or catalog system, and makes the work available to the borrowing or browsing public, it has completed all the steps necessary for distribution to the public" (*id.* at 205).

33. 17 U.S.C. § 109(a) (2006): "Notwithstanding the provisions of section 106(3) [establishing the copyright owner's right of public distribution], the owner of a particular copy or phonorecord lawfully made under this title, or any person authorized by such owner, is entitled, without the authority of the copyright owner, to sell or otherwise dispose of the possession of that copy or phonorecord."

34. 17 U.S.C. § 109(b)(1)(A) (2006): "Notwithstanding the provisions of subsection (a), unless authorized by the owners of copyright in the sound recording or the owner of copyright in a computer program (including any tape, disk, or other medium embodying such program) . . . may, for the purposes of direct or indirect commercial advantage, dispose of, or authorize the disposal of, the possession of that . . . computer program (including any tape, disk, or other medium embodying such program) by rental, lease, or lending, or by any other act or practice in the nature of rental, lease, or lending."

35. 17 U.S.C. § 109(b)(2)(A): "Nothing in this subsection shall apply to the lending of a computer program for nonprofit purposes by a nonprofit library, if each copy of a computer program which is lent by such library has affixed to the packaging containing the program a warning of copyright in accordance with requirements that the Register of Copyrights shall prescribe by regulation."

36. See MGE UPS Systems, Inc. v. Fakouri Electrical Engineering, Inc., 422 F. Supp. 2d 724, 733 (2006): "[I]f MGE transferred ownership of copies of Muguet and Pacret, the first-sale doctrine would bar MGE from claiming copyright infringement; however, the first-sale doctrine would not apply if MGE simply licensed the software"; Novell, Inc. v. Unicom Sales, Inc., 2004 U.S. Dist. LEXIS 16861, at *30 (N.D. Cal. 2004): "Accordingly, the Court finds that the SLA is a license, rather than a sale, and the first sale doctrine has no application to defendants' distribution of SLA software they obtained from Joy"; Adobe Systems, Inc. v. Stargate Software, Inc., 216 F. Supp. 2d 1051,1054 (N.D. Cal. 2002): "The issue before the Court is whether Adobe, through its OCRA and EULA, transferred ownership of each particular copy of its software to its distributors D.C. Micro and Dallas Computers. Having transferred such ownership would bar Adobe from claiming copyright infringement by Stargate under the first sale doctrine. An issuance via license, however,

would not. Rather, the establishment of a license by Adobe would protect Adobe under the first sale doctrine"; and Microsoft Corp. v. Harmony Computer and Electronics, Inc., 846 F. Supp. 208, 213 (E.D.N.Y. 1994): "Entering a license agreement is not a 'sale' for purposes of the first sale doctrine. Moreover, the only chain of distribution that Microsoft authorizes is one in which all possessors of Microsoft Products have only a license to use, rather than actual ownership of the Products . . . Defendants' argument is unpersuasive. First, to the extent that defendants' argument invokes the first sale doctrine, it must fail for the reasons stated above" (references and footnote omitted); see also ProCD Inc. v. Zeidenberg, 86 F.3d 1447, 1450 (7th Cir. 1996): "Whether there are legal differences between 'contracts' and 'licenses' (which may matter under the copyright doctrine of first sale) is a subject For Another Day"; and Step-Saver Data Systems, Inc. v. Wyse Technology, 939 F.2d 91, 96 (3d 1991): "There Was No Need to characterize the transactions between Step-Saver and TSL as a license to avoid the first sale doctrine because both Step-Saver and TSL agree that Step-Saver had the right to resell the copies of the Multilink Advanced program." But see SoftMan Products Company, Inc. v. Adobe Systems, Inc., 171 F. Supp. 2d 1075 (C.D. Calif. 2001): "The Court finds that the circumstances surrounding the transaction strongly suggests that the transaction is in fact a sale rather than a license . . . [T]he purchaser commonly obtains a single copy of the software . . . for a single price . . . The license runs for an indefinite period . . . the ultimate consumer . . . pay[s] full value for the product, and accept[s] the risk that the product may be lost or damaged. This evidence suggests a transfer of a title in the good . . . Ownership of a copy should be determined based on the actual character, rather than the label of the transaction by which the user obtained possession . . . If a transaction involves a single payment giving the buyer an unlimited period in which it has a right to possession, the transaction is a sale" (*id.* at 1086). It would appear that most if not all mass-market software products are characterized by a single price for an indefinite period. However, the case appears to be an anomaly, relegated to the unique facts of unbundled software products, and not a general call for the proposition that a software license or any other license for that agreement cannot override first-sale rights.

37. SoftMan Products Inc. v. Adobe Systems, Inc., 171 F. Supp. 2d 1075 (C.D. Cal. 2001): "However, the existence of this notice on the box cannot bind SoftMan. Reading a notice on a box is not equivalent to the degree of assent that occurs when the software is loaded onto the computer and the consumer is asked to agree to the terms of the license" (id. at 1087). "In this case, Adobe seeks to control the resale of a lawfully acquired copy of its software . . . The Court finds that SoftMan has not assented to the EULA and therefore cannot be bound by its terms" (*id.* at 1089). Contra, Vernor v. Autodesk, Inc., 621 F.3d 1102, 1111 (9th Cir. 2010): "We hold today that a software user is a licensee rather than an owner of a copy where the copyright owner (1) specifies that the user is granted a license; (2) significantly restricts the user's ability to transfer the software; and (3) imposes notable use restrictions. Applying our holding to Autodesk's

SLA, we conclude that CTA was a licensee rather than an owner of copies of Release 14 and thus was not entitled to invoke the first sale doctrine or the essential step defense" (footnote omitted), petition for cert. filed, 79 USLW 3674 (May 18, 2011, No. 10-1421, 10A990), cert. denied 132 S.Ct. 105 (Oct. 3, 2011).

38. H. R. Rep. No. 101-735, at 8 (1990), reprinted in 1990 U.S.C.C.A.N. 6935, 6938: "The first sale doctrine represents an important balancing of interests. The doctrine prohibits copyright owners from controlling the terms and conditions of further distribution of lawfully made copies of a work once the initial authorized distribution of those copies has taken place. At the same time, the limitations on the doctrine preserve other, essential rights of copyright owners, including the right to authorize public performances. Congress has, in the past, resisted proposals to alter the balance achieved in section 109, requiring those seeking amendments to make a compelling case for change. Proposals to reform the first sale doctrine are neither easy nor without controversy. They occur in a shifting legal, technological and economic landscape. Frequently, calls to amend the first sale doctrine are made in response to a new technology developed for reproduction of copyrighted works."

39. See MAI Systems Corp. v. Peak Computer, Inc., 991 F.2d 511, 518, at note 5 (9th Cir. 1995): "Since MAI licensed its software, the Peak customers do not qualify as 'owners' of the software and are not eligible for protection under § 117." See also DSC Communications Corp. v. Pulse Communications, Inc., 170 F.3d 1354 (Fed. Cir. 1999): "Plainly, a party who purchases copies of software from the copyright owner can hold a license under a copyright while still being an 'owner of a copy of the copyrighted software for purposes of section 117. We therefore do not adopt the Ninth Circuit's characterization of all licensees as non-owners. Nonetheless, the MAI case is instructive, because the agreement between MAI and Peak, like the agreements at issue in this case, imposed more severe restrictions on Peak's rights with respect to the software than would be imposed on a party who owned copies of software subject only to the rights of the copyright holder under the Copyright Act. And for that reason, it was proper to hold that Peak was not an 'owner' of copies of the copyrighted software for purposes of section 117" (*id.* at 1360). Rather it depends on the terms of the license: "The question of ownership of the copies of the software, by contrast, was a matter that needed to be addressed in the contracts" (*id.* at 1361). "We conclude that the district court read the market rights clause too broadly... [W]e hold that it was improper for the court to conclude, as a matter of law, that the RBOCs were 'owners' under section 117 of the copies of DSC's software that were in their possession" (*id.* at 1362).

40. 17 U.S.C. § 117(a)(2) (2006): "[F]or archival purposes only and that all archival copies are destroyed in the event that continued possession of the computer program should cease to be rightful"; and 17 U.S.C. § 117(c) (2006): "[M]ake or authorize the making of a copy of a computer program if such copy is made solely by virtue of the activation of a machine that lawfully contains an authorized copy of the computer program, for purposes only of maintenance or repair of that machine."

41. Davidson & Associates, Inc. v. Internet Gateway, 334 F. Supp. 2d 1164, 1180 (E.D. Mo. 2004): "The defendants in this case waived their 'fair use' right to reverse engineer by agreeing to the licensing agreement. Parties may waive their statutory rights under law in a contract." See also Bowers v. Baystate Technologies, Inc., 320 F.3d 1317, 1335 (Fed. Cir. 2003): J. Dyk, concurring in part, dissenting in part; referring to the majority opinion: "By holding that shrinkwrap licenses that override the fair use defense are not preempted by the Copyright Act," cert. denied, 539 U.S. 928 (2003).

42. Raymond T. Nimmer, 2 Information Law § 11.149 (updated in Westlaw, November 2011); Marshall Leaffer, *The Uncertain Future of Fair Use in a Global Information Marketplace*, 62 Ohio State Law Journal 849, 855 (2001) (Symposium: The Impact of Technological Change on the Creation, Dissemination, and Protection of Intellectual Property): "Ultimately, Congress may be forced to decide whether copyright policy should allow copyright owners to circumvent by contract copyright law's balance of rights and limitations. The truth is that in American law the ambit of fair use has receded; its contours ever more uncertain. Determining what constitutes a fair use of a copyrighted work in a given situation is a hazardous undertaking. Providing guidance on fair use is the last thing that a practicing lawyer, even one versed in copyright, would prefer to do. Despite the uncertainty, the clear tendency as manifested in the case law is becoming apparent: in cases that really count, that is, anytime large group rights are involved, courts have progressively sided with information providers against the user's right to access" (footnote omitted).

43. 17 U.S.C. § 602(a) provides that the "[i]mportation into the United States, without the authority of the owner of copyright under this title, of copies or phonorecords of a work that have been acquired outside the United States is an infringement of the exclusive right to distribute copies or phonorecords under section 106."

44. Omega S. A. v. Costco Wholesale Corp., 541 F.3d 982, 990 (9th Cir. 2008); judgment affirmed by an equally divided court without opinion, Costco Wholesale Corp. v. Omega S. A., 131 S.Ct. 565 (2010).

45. Omega S. A. v. Costco Wholesale Corp., 541 F.3d 982, 986 (9th Cir. 2008): "The statute would not apply because Omega made copies of the Omega Globe Design in Switzerland and Costco sold the copies without Omega's authority in the United States"; judgment affirmed by an equally divided court without opinion, Costco Wholesale Corp. v. Omega S. A., 131 S.Ct. 565 (2010).

46. Costco Wholesale Corp. v. Omega S. A., 131 S.Ct. 565 (2010).

47. John Wiley & Sons, Inc. v. Kirtsaeng, 654 F.3d 210, 218 (2d Cir. 2011), petition for Writ of Certiorari granted, 2012 WL 1252751 (Apr. 16, 2012) (Docket No. 11-697).

48. *Id.* at 212.

49. Omega S. A. v. Costco Wholesale Corp., 541 F.3d 982, 985 (9th Cir. 2008), and observing that the Supreme Court "adopt[ed] this interpretation" in Quality King Distributors, Inc. v. L'anza Researc International, Inc., 523 U.S. 135, 144–145 (1998).

50. 17 U.S.C. § 602(a)(3)(C).

51. 17 U.S.C. § 108(g)(2).

52. 17 U.S.C. § 108(d).

53. For a more detailed discussion of "systematic" in § 108, TOMAS A. LIPINSKI, THE COMPLETE COPYRIGHT LIABILITY HANDBOOK FOR LIBRARIANS AND EDUCATORS (New York: Neal-Schuman, 2006).

54. H. Rpt. No. 94-1476, 94th Cong. 2d Sess. 125 (1976) reprinted in 5 U.S.C. CONGRESSIONAL AND ADMINISTRATIVE NEWS 5659, 5786 (1976).

55. John Wiley & Sons, Inc. v. Kirtsaeng, 654 F.3d 210, 220 (2d Cir. 2011), petition for Writ of Certiorari granted, 2012 WL 1252751 (Apr. 16, 2012) (Docket No. 11-697).

56. *Id.* at 222, footnotes omitted.

57. Jonathan Band, *The Impact of the Supreme Court's Decision in Costco v. Omega on Libraries*, 1 (2011), http://www.arl.org/bm~doc/lcacostco013111.pdf. This paper is a follow-up to a similarly focused paper on the 9th Circuit decision.

58. Jonathan Band, *Second Circuit Makes the First Sale Situation Worse for Libraries*, ARL POLICY NOTES (2011), http://policynotes.arl.org/post/9005206450/second-circuit-makes-the-first-sale-situation-worse-for.

59. See John Wiley & Sons, Inc. v. Kirtsaeng, 654 F.3d 210, 222 (2d Cir. 2011), petition for Writ of Certiorari granted, 2012 WL 1252751 (Apr. 16, 2012) (Docket No. 11-697): "If we have misunderstood Congressional purpose in enacting the first sale doctrine, or if our decision leads to policy consequences that were not foreseen by Congress or which Congress now finds unpalatable, Congress is of course able to correct our judgment."

60. This interpretation is offered by the dissent: "Unlike the majority, I conclude the first sale defense should apply to a copy of a work that enjoys United States copyright protection wherever manufactured. Accordingly, I respectfully dissent," per John Wiley & Sons, Inc. v. Kirtsaeng, 654 F.3d 210, 225 (2d Cir. 2011), petition for Writ of Certiorari granted, 2012 WL 1252751 (Apr. 16, 2012) (Docket No. 11-697), J. Murtha, dissenting.

61. Jurisdiction is a "geographic area within which political or judicial authority may be exercised," per BLACK'S LAW DICTIONARY 502 (9th ed.) (Bryan A. Garner ed., St. Paul, MN: West Publishing, 2009).

62. For on the various sorts of law and authority, see CHRISTINA L. KUNZ, DEBORAH A. SCHMEDEMANN, ANN BATESON, and MEHMET KONAR-STEENBERG, THE PROCESS OF LEGAL RESEARCH (New York: Aspen Publishers, 2008); AMY E. SLOAN, BASIC LEGAL RESEARCH: TOOLS AND STRATEGIES (New York: Aspen Publishers, 2009); MORRIS L. COHEN and KENT OLSEN, LEGAL RESEARCH IN A NUTSHELL (10th ed.) (St. Paul, MN: West Publishing, 2010).

▶ 2

BASIC CONTRACT LAW CONCEPTS

Read this chapter to gain an understanding of how contract law concepts might be applied these situations:
- ▶ A purchase agreement including both goods and services
- ▶ Advertisements, unsolicited merchandise, and instructor review copies
- ▶ Acceptance and rejection of offers
- ▶ Counteroffers, conditional acceptance, and requests for additional terms
- ▶ Revocation by the offeror and repudiation by the offeree
- ▶ Interpretation of contract clauses and the presence of parol evidence

Any first-year law student would know that for a contract to exist three elements must be present: an offer, an acceptance, and some form of consideration.[1] The offer and acceptance elements represent the mutual assent of the parties, the desire of each to enter into a contract expressed through the give-and-take of negotiation (or at least a communication of some sort) between the parties. Consideration is the glue, so to speak, and proves each party is serious, taking the form of payment, promises, or conduct. These concepts can help determine whether certain "contract" language is enforceable, for example: a click-to-agree button on a website the web development librarian visits; the similar "I agree to the terms" language that might appear on a website a library patron visits for a cell phone application ("app"); the "for home use only" warning notice that precedes the start of a DVD the literacy librarian is playing as part of an instructional session; the "not for resale or other use" warning that might accompany a complimentary review copy of the latest edition of a textbook.

APPLICABLE LAW

The goal of this chapter is to lay the legal foundation for examining issues in greater detail in subsequent chapters related to contract and licensing formation and application, as well as negation and the contract-licensing intersection. In other words, are the circumstances of the transaction indicative of a license or a sale? As indicated earlier, the law of licensing is contract law. As a result, this chapter is generally applicable to sales of tangible things like books, library tables and chairs, and so forth, with examples attempting to demonstrate how contract law concepts might be applied to such traditional acquisitions, and anticipates such application in licensing settings as well.

Because contract law is state-based law—even if the case is heard in federal court through diversity jurisdiction principles—the federal court will look to state law to interpret the contract and its circumstances. As indicated in the preface, this book cannot cover the variations of law in all 50 states but uses two significant sources and offers examples from across a variety of states to illustrate basic principles. Rather than reference specific state statutes, two general sources are used: the Restatement (Second) of Contracts and the Uniform Commercial Code (UCC). The Restatements (various topics include agency, property, law governing lawyers, torts, etc.), published by the American Law Institute,[2] represent an attempt by scholars to distill the common law across the United States into a series of rules or so-called black-letter expressions in order to restate what the law is or where the law appears to be heading.[3] Each of the hundreds and hundreds of statements (within a given restatement each is given a section number) is accompanied by a useful explanation ("comment"), an example ("illustration"), and a citation list. The source of the UCC (as well as numerous other "uniform" and "model" laws) is the National Conference of Commissioners on Uniform State Laws (NCCUSL).[4] The strategy behind the UCC and the other uniform or model laws is forward-looking. Rather than summarize, the goal of NCCUSL is exemplary, proposing legislation that can then be enacted by each jurisdiction. If the contract is for information or services, the UCC generally does not apply.

For example, in *Respect Inc. v. Committee on Status of Women*, the district court, in concluding that a dispute involving a book purchase agreement was in fact a contract for services and not tangible things, summarized the law regarding mixed instances of both oral and written instruments: "the cases governing such mixed contracts require this Court to determine whether the 'predominant purpose, or 'raison d'etre' of the contract was primarily the provision of goods or the rendition of services. If the contract is predominantly for goods, then the entire contract falls within the ambit of UCC Article 2. If it is primarily a contract for services, then the entire contract must be tested by common-law standards."[5] To eliminate such quandaries, some scholars saw a need either to update the UCC in such a way as to include information or services or to create (as eventually occurred) a separate law to govern "pure" information-based transactions. As a result, the Uniform Computer Information Transactions Act (UCITA) was born. UCITA has been adopted by only two state legislatures to date: Maryland and Virginia. In the future, further adoption is unlikely.[6] Such transactions are therefore governed by the common law and the Restatements for most parties. Chapter 5 discusses further recent "uniform" legislation, including the Uniform Electronic Transactions Act (UETA),[7] facilitating the adoption of existing contract principles in the online setting.

THE OFFER

An offer[8] requires intent and terms that are definite. Intent is determined from the conduct of the offeror (the person who makes the offer) in light of the surrounding circumstances and context. There might be clear intent to make an offer but a lack of definiteness upon which the other party could be expected to proceed upon that offer: "I would like to sell you this encyclopedia set, but I'm not sure if it's the new edition or not and, if it is new, what the price will be." Here, the intent is present (the publisher's rep wants to sell you a set of books!), but the will is lacking, in a sense, as there is no definiteness to the offer that would allow a reasonable offeree (you, the collections development librarian, the person receiving the offer) the ability to determine whether the offer should be accepted.

The offer must address the subject of the offer (not "Would you like to buy some books?" but "Would you like to the buy the 2012 edition of *The Worst Dictionary in the World* for your collection?"), the quantity ("Would you like to purchase a single copy of *The Worst Dictionary in the World* at the new low price of...?"), and the price ("I can offer the first copy of *The Worst Dictionary in the World* for $129.95 and discount subsequent copies by $30, so each additional copy would be $99.95").

In a sense, after the initial offer, the offeree has a bit of power, with the proverbial ball now being in his or her court once a clear and definite offer has been made, either to reject or accept—or to counteroffer, as discussed later in this chapter. The law demands some measure of specificity to ensure an efficient response; without it, the offeree is left to guess at whether the request to buy was just talk or a firm offer. These principles of offer and acceptance are at play in the world of licensing as well, including counteroffering, at least in those licenses which are able to be negotiated. We'll discuss this more later.

RECEIVING AN INVITATION TO BARGAIN VERSUS RECEIVING AN OFFER

In library acquisitions, as in other commerce, distinguishing between an "offer" and a mere "invitation" to enter into a bargain is paramount, as the latter is not an offer. In the area of licensing, either for a so-called negotiated license (e.g., most database subscriptions where it is possible to negotiate over the terms of the agreement) or for a nonnegotiated license (e.g., with a software program that is downloaded from a website), there is a contract to review indicating the terms, referencing a price, or providing other consideration.

An invitation to bargain (to begin the general process of offer-acceptance-consideration) is not an offer. This "invitation" might take the form of your book vendor contacting you with information and asking, for example, "The ninth edition of *The Best Reference Book in the World* is due for release soon. Would you be interested in ordering several copies?" as opposed to "I am returning your call inquiring about the new edition of *The Best Reference Book in the World* to let you know that it will be available next month. I can give you an additional 15 percent off and free shipping if you order a copy today, so the price would be $95.99 with your loyal customer discount." The latter is an offer; the former is not. An invitation often asks questions (or raises more questions than it answers), whereas an offer has enough information for the librarian-offeree to make a tactical decision on whether to accept it on behalf of the library. Of course, strategic issues may prevail. For example, the librarian may respond, "That's a great offer, but I have to check with the reference supervisor to see if there is need for the new edition" or "We've been waiting for the ninth edition to be available, but I have to determine whether there are funds left in this month's book budget to acquire it." As discussed in the next section, statements in catalogs, promotional brochures, and the like are considered invitations, not offers, by the courts.

THE RULE FOR ADVERTISEMENTS

Even though an advertisement might contain the requisite specificity as to product or item description, price, and so on, there are exceptions to the "offer" concept or rule for these and other propagations like brochures, flyers, circulars, catalogs, and so forth. The reason for this result is that advertisements are deemed inconclusive or indefinite as to who is being solicited and as to quantity and possibly other terms. This stands to reason, as such brochures, flyers, circulars, catalogs, and so on, are sent somewhat indiscriminately, extended to literally hundreds of potential customers. In the example of a newspaper advertisement, anyone who picks up and browses through the paper will come across the advertisement. This is too tenuous a scenario to constitute the mutual assent the law requires, as there is not the requisite meeting of the minds of both parties (the offeror and offeree) necessary for the certain and determinable flow of commerce. If such material constituted an offer, havoc would result. A typical complicating example is a scenario in which the inventory of the item expressed in the ad expires (the store runs out of it) before the customer possesses the opportunity to "accept" (goes to the store to buy it). Can the customer later demand under contract principles purchase at the sale price or claim damages for not having the item in the present stock, even if the item is no longer available?

Assuming there is no other violation of law—for example, a violation of fair trade law that prohibits so-called bait-and-switch advertising whereby the seller has no intent to make good on the advertisement but uses the ad merely as a ploy to attract shoppers into the store—the answer is generally no. We know this from our personal shopping experience, and that learned experience is built upon contract law principles.

> Merchandising systems, such as catalogues or advertising, are treated as solicitations for an offer, rather than offers themselves, at least where they are made to a broad audience. The significance is that the person seeking to acquire the product does not have the power to create an enforceable contract by merely accepting the offer (e.g., ordering the product). Rather, and in the case of an acquisitions librarian who reads the brochures, flyers, circulars, catalogs, etc. the library's order will be treated as an offer, leaving the vendor the discretion to accept or reject it, or to provide the product only under different terms ["That item is out of stock at the moment. We can have it shipped by the end of next month, but the new book discount of 25 percent listed in the information we sent will not apply"] that constitute a counter-offer. This [legal as well as practical result] protects vendors against contractual obligations where inventory has been exhausted or prices changed.[9]

The vendor or the stores (in the case of our personal shopping transactions) may nonetheless make good on the offer, but in the absence of an unfair trade practice this response is more likely an effort to garner the goodwill of the customer instead of a requirement to honor a contractual (read: legal) obligation with every person who claims to have read the advertisement. Also, sellers ought to have some discretion, within the limits of other laws, again, such as fair trade or discrimination, to choose the terms with which it extends an actual offer. Consider the car dealer that includes 100,000 sale inserts in the local Sunday paper regarding new cars "just arrived." After a mere ten customers purchase automobiles during the subsequent week, the dealer decides that any customers who buy through the end of the month will qualify for preferred or discounted pricing ("If we sell you this car at MSRP, would you buy the car today?"). The question the sales representative asks the prospective buyer is the offer; the initial newspaper sales insert is not.

Courts have concluded, however, that some advertisements might constitute an offer. A rare book dealer that places an ad in *Library Journal* with words to the effect that it will pay $250 for each first edition copy of *The Rarest Title Ever* sent to it by December 31, 2015, is an offer.[10] Likewise, early case law set forth the principle that an advertisement in the personals for reward of a lost item is also an offer—"LOST RING. Will pay $500 to finder of lost gold wedding ring, claddagh design. Inside engraved with letters TAL, outside engraved shamrocks and inset with emerald, lost at the Milwaukee Irish Fest School of Music building on or about September 9, 2012. Call 777-888-9999."—that, if accepted (i.e., a reader finds and returns the ring), must be honored.[11] How so? Such circumstances suggest that such an ad is an offer where overacceptance is unlikely—there can be only one person who could accept the offer: the person who finds and returns the ring. This is unlike the general indiscriminate weekend sale advertisement in the newspaper or the magazine advertisement that invites specific action without further communication (the rare book or reward solicitation).

Specificity rules the day here. Thus, if the advertisement or solicitation is directed at a particular person or institution, it may be an offer. Suppose the librarian receives an envelope addressed to him or her but under circumstances that lead the librarian to believe it is still a generic mail-merged letter. Inside the envelope is a brochure for a new reference series. The brochure appears to be a routine promotion flyer, sent out quarterly from the publisher, folded to fit and sent in a regular letter envelope. This is likely not an offer. The situation would be a different if the envelope instead contained a letter from the vendor, addressed to the collection development librarian by name, thanking him or her for the loyal business over the past few years, and also acknowledging the vendor's awareness of a new degree program starting next year at the librarian's institution. The letter is hand-signed by the account representative with whom the librarian has phoned, e-mailed, or otherwise communicated with in the past, offering the librarian a new reference set on a topic related to the new program at a special discount if ordered by the end of the month. If specific details are included as to title, price, and so on, the letter constitutes an offer.

UNSOLICITED MERCHANDISE AND THE LIBRARY COLLECTION

Questions often arise regarding receipt of merchandise the library did not order. What if the library receives an item such as a book or DVD that was not ordered? Is a contract formed if the processing clerk opens the package? If the library decides to keep the item and add it to the collection, does the library have pay for it? What if the item comes with a note that says "Promotional item, not for sale or further distribution," or words to that effect? Is the library prohibited from adding the book to its circulating collection (which would likely be a public distribution under the copyright law) or, if deciding it does not want the item, placing it on its "used books cart" for sale to patrons? (Again, this discussion poses these questions from a legal perspective, not an ethical or practical one. For example, what if the item was sent in error? Future relationships with vendors might be compromised if we do not allow amends for human error.) What if, inside the packaging, there is a cover letter introducing the item as a possible addition to the library's collection—"for your consideration"—but an invoice is also enclosed? The library never ordered the item or asked that it be sent for review, nor is the item part of any approval plan or similar mechanism. In fact, the library has never heard of this vendor-publisher before. The item is what is known as unsolicited merchandise. What is the library's legal obligation under these circumstances? Is the cover letter and invoice an offer? Does the library accept the offer by keeping the item beyond some reasonable time period, as stated in the accompanying letter (e.g., beyond 30 days after opening), or by placing the item on the used books cart on which it will be available for sale to library patrons for 25 cents? Is the library now obligated to pay for the item?

Recall that an advertisement in a catalog is an invitation, not an offer. Yet in the case of unsolicited merchandise, the item is obviously available. From the general principles of contract law discussed so far, it could be concluded that keeping the item, depending upon the circumstances, is tantamount to acceptance of the offer to purchase it. As a leading source on contract law explains:

> When an offeree takes or retains possession of chattels or other property which have been offered, the taking or retention may constitute an acceptance in the absence of other circumstances. As such, the offeree may come under a duty to return money or property in its possession belonging to the offeror, unless the offeree accepts an offer for its acquisition. The offeree's silence and failure to return the property in such a case may amount to an assent to purchase it.[12]

If the library chooses not to retain the item, must it pay the expense of returning the item? Is the dilemma either keep (and pay for) the item or pay the expense of returning the item? In short, no. Federal and state statutes foreclose the possibility of any contractual obligation arising out of such trolling practices by vendors and resolve the recipient's legal (but perhaps not its moral) dilemma in favor of the recipient.

Federal postal law treats the sending of unsolicited items through the mails as "an unfair method of competition and an unfair trade practice."[13] The law deems these items as "unordered merchandise."[14] It is also an unfair method of competition and an unfair trade practice if the item is accompanied by or the sender otherwise "mail[s] to any recipient of such merchandise a bill for such merchandise or any dunning communications."[15] Instead, items so received may be treated as a gift: "Any merchandise mailed in violation of subsection (a) of this section, or within the exceptions contained therein, may be treated as a gift by the recipient, who shall have the right to retain, use, discard, or dispose of it in any manner he sees fit without any obligation whatsoever to the sender."[16] In fact, the package must include a statement to that effect—that the item so received is indeed a gift.[17]

There is scant litigation under the federal statute. In *Marshall v. Little Professor Book Center, Inc.*,[18] the plaintiff sent ten copies of his magazine to 148 independent booksellers around the country along with the following statement:

> I am delighted to send you 10 copies of my new monthly magazine—PHOTO COMPE-
> TITION U.S.A. Our targeted customers are millions of amateur photographers all
> across this land. The cover date of this issue is August 92, therefore you have about 60
> days to sell it. THIS SHIPMENT IS ON A CONSIGNMENT BASIS. I am also sending it

to 1500 booksellers across the USA, Canada, England, Germany and Japan. The price of the magazine is $3.00. YOU CAN KEEP 50% OF THE SALE PRICE AND SEND ME THE OTHER 50%. In other words, if you sell it all, please send me your check for $15.[19]

After the defendant indicated that the magazines could be treated as a gift in its weekly newsletter, Marshall filed suit on numerous tort theories such as libel, interference with contract, and negligent misrepresentation, all of which were dismissed. However, the court made the following comment when discussing the libel claim: "The Postal Reorganization Act clearly states that the franchisees were not legally responsible for returning to Marshall either the magazines or half of the profits from the sale of the magazines. Rather, the franchisees could legally keep the magazines and consider them 'a gift.' The newsletter thus simply and accurately informed the franchisees about relevant law."[20] This may appear unfair to the merchant-sender-vendor, who has lost out on both the product and the payment. However, in the larger picture of the marketplace, the result is a good one. Otherwise, the sending of unsolicited merchandise would constitute a unilateral way for the merchant-sender-vendor to create a binding purchase or, in the *Marshall* case, a consignment agreement; worse, at the recipient's expense, it would force the financial obligation of returning the merchandise in lieu of acceptance and contract formation.

From a practical perspective, if the merchandise is from a source with which the library is in current communication or other transaction, or so desires to be in the future, a prudent response might be to make contact with and inform the sender of the unsolicited (and moreover unwanted) items that the library is in possession of and request that a postage-paid return mailer be sent at the expense of the vendor-sender (or other similar return arrangements), within a specified and reasonable time period, or the library will indeed treat the item as a gift and dispose of it as it sees fit.

Suppose a publisher or other vendor sends an unsolicited demo CD or DVD, sample book, or other item with this note: "Promotional use only. This item is the property of the publisher and is licensed to the intended recipient for personal or trial use only. Retention of this item beyond 30 days shall constitute an agreement to comply with the terms of the license. Public distribution of the item is prohibited by the license. Any reproduction is limited to 0.000000001 percent or an otherwise infinitesimal portion of the content. If a public distribution is made of the item, please remit $100.00 for each distribution. Each time the content is accessed (listened to, watched or viewed, read or browsed, etc.) please remit $1,000.00. Resale or transfer of possession is not allowed and may be punishable under federal and state laws." Is the library obligated to pay the amount requested if it keeps the unsolicited promotional material? Must the library abide by the use restrictions? Is this a valid license? Was a contract formed?

A recent 9th Circuit decision sheds light on the obvious answer (which is no) and is consistent with the concepts discussed so far. In *UMG Recordings, Inc. v. Augusto*,[21] the court described the underlying facts of a copyright infringement case that revealed a similar promotional scheme:

> The copies in issue comprise eight specially-produced compact discs, each embodying a copyrighted sound recording. UMG, the copyright owner, used the discs solely for marketing purposes, sending them unsolicited to individuals such as music critics and radio disc jockeys. Although Augusto was not one of those individuals, he managed to obtain the discs from various sources. He later sold them at auction, an act which UMG contends infringed its exclusive right to distribute the discs.[22]

Under the copyright law, those in possession of lawful copies, which is a prerequisite for so-called first-sale rights discussed in Chapter 1, have the right to make public distributions of the copies.[23] Here, the copies were not bootleg recordings but lawfully made copies. How Augusto acquired those copies is not relevant to the copyright law, so in theory he had a right to resell, give them away as gifts, or make other public distribution of the CDs under section 109, such as by sale. This is the right of every possessor of a lawfully made copy of an item protected by copyright except, according to the same provision, sound recordings and computer programs.[24] "UMG argues that the statements on the discs and the circumstances of their distribution granted only a license to each recipient, not a transfer of ownership (or 'sale') of the copy."[25] The promotional discs, similar to the language of other items received by the library in the previous examples, contained the following "terms": "This CD is the property of the record company and is licensed to the intended recipient for personal use only. Acceptance of this CD shall constitute an agreement to comply with the terms of the license. Resale or transfer of possession is not allowed and may be punishable under federal and state laws."[26] Some discs contained a simpler admonition: "For Promotional Use Only—Not for Sale."[27] In discussing the applicable law, the 9th Circuit cited the same postal statute regarding unsolicited merchandise sent through the mail as did the *Marshall v. Little Professor Book Center, Inc.* court.[28] Did the language the merchant used somehow create a contract, a license to use the items—the CDs—for promotional purposes alone?

If no license was created, then the ownership of the items belonged to the recipients and the rights of such possessory owners are determined under the copyright law, at least as far as making use of the item that might otherwise interfere with the copyright owner's exclusive rights (e.g., to make a public distribution). Such a possessory owner of a copy, in this instance Augusto, could resell, gift, or otherwise give away such items:

> The same question is presented here. Did UMG succeed in creating a license in recipients of its promotional CDs, or did it convey title despite the restrictive labeling on the CDs?

> We conclude that, under all the circumstances of the CDs' distribution, the recipients
> were entitled to use or dispose of them in any manner they saw fit, and UMG did not
> enter a license agreement for the CDs with the recipients. Accordingly, UMG trans-
> ferred title to the particular copies of its promotional CDs and cannot maintain an
> infringement action against Augusto for his subsequent sale of those copies.[29]

However, the merchandise was not actually sent to Augusto, so the Unordered
Merchandise Statute did not apply to him, but it did apply to those to whom the
promo discs were sent, who then had the right to treat them as gifts and in turn
dispose of the discs as they saw fit, including placing the CDs into the waiting
hands of Augusto, who in turn sold the discs.[30]

It is hoped this case demonstrates a logical result and avoids the havoc that any
alternative conclusion (contract formation, obligation to return at receiver's
expense, license for limited and enumerated uses, etc.) would wreak upon such
similarly situated recipients, including institutions such as schools or libraries.[31]

> Because we conclude that UMG's method of distribution transferred the ownership
> of the copies to the recipients, we have no need to parse the remaining provisions in
> UMG's purported licensing statement; UMG dispatched the CDs in a manner that
> permitted their receipt and retention by the recipients without the recipients accepting
> the terms of the promotional statements. UMG's transfer of unlimited possession in the
> circumstances present here effected a gift or sale within the meaning of the first sale
> doctrine [codified in section 109 as observed previously and discussed in Chapter 1 as
> well as Chapter 4 and elsewhere] . . . UMG's distribution of the promotional CDs under
> the circumstances effected a sale (transfer of title) of the CDs to the recipients. Further
> sale of those copies was therefore permissible without UMG's authorization.[32]

A similar message at the start of a DVD "for home use only" likely appears when a
teacher attempts to show some of the disc's content to illustrate a class topic. (The
right to show an audiovisual work in a classroom is found in section 110 of the
copyright law.[33]) In an obviously absurd example, what if another introductory
message likewise prompted the viewer at the commencement of the playing of
the DVD or at the start of a track on a CD that such viewing or listening is "for
personal or home use only . . . your use of this disc in any other context constitutes
an agreement to remit to us $100 billion or, if you prefer, a more reasonable
$29.95 at your earliest convenience." Is this language binding? Most persons
would answer no. This is correct, as logic would dictate that such results are not
possible, but this conclusion has its basis in contract law. Such statements do not
form binding contracts or licenses, nor do they in such unilateral fashion take
away rights under copyright, such as those enabling teachers and students to play
a DVD in the context of the classroom per section 110(1) or to play a CD in
public.[34]

In a dispute between Avon Products, Inc. and its sales representatives regarding the return and crediting of unsolicited and unsold products,[35] a California state court, after an exhaustive interpretive discussion, concluded that this same postal "unsolicited merchandise" statute did not apply to "the mailing of unordered merchandise as between parties to an ongoing contractual relationship involving the sale of the same merchandise."[36] While the statute is broad enough to reach beyond consumers, "instead using the word 'recipient'..., the legislative history of the statute as reported in case precedents, similar state statutes, and the FTC's [Federal Trade Commission] own orders enforcing section 3009 show that it is addressed to the mailing of unordered merchandise by the seller to the consumer of that merchandise, not to parties who have contracted with each other to promote the sale of the same merchandise to third persons."[37] Such a relationship would be more distant than, say, that between a library and one of its regular vendors-publishers but would be more akin to the relationship between a publisher and a new independent book retailer or consigner. The latter relationship is too close to have one party take refuge and treat such wares as unsolicited gifts.

Relying on an FTC consent order regarding another company that sent unsolicited lightbulbs to other businesses (i.e., its customers, who were nonetheless recipients),[38] the *Blackemore* court observed that the statute was intended to "forbid...the mailing of unordered merchandise by sellers to consumers, and was not intended to apply to independent jobbers or wholesalers or, as in this case, where a contractual relationship exists between the parties relating to the sale of the merchandise."[39] The *Blakemore* court acknowledged, as did the consent order, that a business or other entity can be a consumer under such circumstances.[40] Not only did the lightbulb company send its unsolicited wares, but it also pursued collection measures against those who did not pay, reported the deficiency to credit companies, and billed the recipients for any storage expenses incurred when delivery of the items was refused.[41]

So, can a library be a consumer? Can it be the requisite "recipient" under the statute and seek its protection—to, in other words, treat such merchandise as unsolicited gifts? Even though a library may have a past or ongoing relationship with a vendor, the library is nonetheless a customer for or a "consumer" of books, magazines, CDs, DVDs, and so on. There would need to be an agreement in place for receipt of unsolicited items, for example, an approval plan, for section 3009 not to apply ("contractual relationship exists between the parties relating to the sale of the merchandise"). If the library had no relationship whatsoever with the sender of the items, as in the previously discussed photography magazine case, the library should be able—as would any other recipient, such as the independent bookstore that was in receipt of the unsolicited magazines—to treat the receipt of the unsolicited item as a gift.

Many states have similar statutes indicating that those who receive unsolicited merchandise have no legal obligation to pay for such items and can treat the items as gifts.[42] Several states also provide that the recipient of unsolicited merchandise possesses a statutory right to bring legal action to enjoin the vendor from sending bills or otherwise making repeated attempts to collect payment through so-called dunning letters[43] and to obtain reasonable attorney fees and costs associated with bringing the action.[44]

The federal statute does not provide injunctive relief but nonetheless prohibits the sender of unsolicited merchandise from billing or otherwise attempting to obtain payment through aggressive and repeated communication.[45] Submission of invoices and other attempts to render payment (dunning letters) are prohibited by section 3009 as an unfair method of competition and an unfair trade practice. To this end, federal courts have concluded that enforcement rests with the Federal Trade Commission, without a private right of action on the part of the recipient. "In short, the text and structure of § 3009 strongly suggest that Congress did not intend to supplement FTC enforcement with a parallel system of private litigation but absentmindedly forgot to mention an intended private action."[46] While a previous 9th Circuit opinion suggested that a private right of action for declaratory relief is implied,[47] this decision predates more recent Supreme Court precedent governing the analysis of implicit congressional intent of private enforcement rights in federal statutes. As the *Wisniewski* court explained: "*Kipperman* is not persuasive authority for us because its analysis is inconsistent with the Supreme Court's subsequent decisions . . . which restructured the implied private right of action test to focus solely on legislative intent."[48]

The state statutes have likewise seldom been the focus of litigation. In dismissing a request for class-action certification over an unsolicited monthly cable guide,[49] a state court commented that while the Missouri statute would make charges for the unsolicited channel guide unenforceable, the plaintiffs' choice to pay their monthly cable bills that included a clearly identified additional fee for the guide operated as a bar—under the voluntary payment doctrine[50]—to later seeking the protection of the unsolicited merchandise statute:

> Thus, the statute makes negative option billing not legally enforceable. However, the voluntary payment doctrine applies to payments of money made on demands that are not legally enforceable . . . [The statute] does not prevent a consumer from waiving his or her statutory rights by paying for the merchandise. Finally, while negative option billing is an unfair practice, it does not rise to the level of fraud or duress as would bar the voluntary payment doctrine.[51]

Again, in contract law, one's actions and the reasonableness of reliance by others upon those actions are paramount.

Of course, another issue with such statutes is practical. Is it to the library's advantage to argue that an item was shipped in error, is unsolicited, and therefore can be treated as a gift? That might be the legal result, but consider this: If the item is from a vendor with which the library is familiar, having done business with the vendor in the past and wanting to do so again, or perhaps the library would like to establish such a relationship the future, asserting such a claim might not be in the best interest of any continued or future relationship. Everyone makes mistakes, and the library might at some point desire a similar consideration for its error, as might the vendor, with both parties desiring common sense to prevail.

For example, the author sent the following e-mail looking for more information about a title and inquiring if any customer discount was available: "Hi West Group / I have a West Group account but not sure if it [sic] active or not so I don't have my number / I am intersted [sic] in the Nimmer and Dodd, Modern Licensing Law, listed for $259, is there any customer discount you can offer (sounds affordable if under $200 with our shrinking state budgets) and can you send a table of contents so I can make a decision to puchase [sic] or not / thanks, tom." Here is the text of the e-mail reply received on the same day: "The CE Ops Academic Center has received your recent west.bookstore@thomson.com email order. It will now be handled through the standard order fulfillment process. If your order does not appear in your Order Status Report within 5 business days, please contact your designated CE Ops Academic Center Representative. Thank you, CE Ops Academic Center." So if the book arrives (it sounds like Thomson is going to send it), can the author treat it as unsolicited merchandise and keep it? Oddly, one of the few cases reported involved a dispute with West Publishing Company!

In *Wehringer v. West Publishing Co.*, a prior relationship existed as the "plaintiff... ordered, received and paid for an earlier edition"[52] of *Federal Rules of Civil Procedure* three years previous. Wehringer "notified the defendant that he was treating the new book as an unconditional gift."[53] However, the court observed that the "single billing by the defendant thereafter, established by the affidavits on the motion to dismiss, does not constitute the continued sending of bill statements required by the General Obligations Law to warrant its injunctive relief, whether or not the sending of such a book under the circumstances here would qualify as an unconditional gift."[54] The court left unanswered whether the actual sending qualified as unsolicited merchandise under the New York law and could be treated as a gift, but the decision at least stands for the proposition again that disputes can arise and can involve the so-called big names in the publishing industry as well. Fortunately, in my own e-mail exchange recounted earlier, calmer minds prevailed (or intervened), and the account rep from West e-mailed back with the information requested, including a 25 percent discount if the item was ordered by the end of the year (an offer!; see previous discussion), which the author accepted via e-mail (dispatch rule!; see following discussion).

APPLICATION OF CONTRACT CONCEPTS TO INSTRUCTOR "REVIEW COPIES"

What circumstances in a "review copy" scenario indicate the item is complimentary, that is, unordered or unsolicited? There is a meaningful difference between true review copies, where some agreement is in place regarding the book or other item under review (license, loan, or other transaction in the form of a bailment whereby possessory interest alone is transferred such that first-sale rights do not apply), and unordered or otherwise complimentary copies (no restrictions, possessory and ownership interest in the book or item transferred).

A so-called label license is ineffectual as a binding contract restriction:

> Even so, there are other situations beyond promotional CDs where this case [referring to *UMG Recordings, Inc. v. Augusto*] almost certainly provides a useful answer. For example, many casebook publishers send unsolicited review copies to law professors. Starting in the past year or two, publishers have put anti-First Sale label licenses onto the books (in some cases engraved onto the cover; in other cases, as a sticker slapped on the cover). As an example, West's label license reads "Professor Review Copy//Not for Resale." I'm pretty sure this opinion means that those label licenses stuck onto unordered review copies are ineffectual, making the review copies freely re-sellable. (I note that law professors have had extensive discussions about the non-legal considerations of reselling review copies).[55]

Under the *Augusto* decision, the use restrictions that accompany an unsolicited or unordered or complimentary or promotional book or other item would not be enforceable, as there is no contract—whether in the form of a license, loan, or other transaction—in the first place.

In the case of a review copy, it might depend on the circumstances of the "acquisition" of the review copy. If the book or other item is subject to a valid agreement, and the agreement takes the form of a license of sorts (e.g., the professor possesses the book or other item if and only if and subject to the condition that he or she restricts use to their own personal circumstances), then use beyond those personal circumstances (e.g., placing the book or other item on reserve—a public use) would be outside the scope of the license. Under typical terms or understanding, the instructor only owns the copy if he or she adopts the book or item as a requirement in a class. If the instructor does not and further desires to make public uses of the work (under section 106 of the copyright law: display, performance, or distribution), then he or she must purchase the item, in which case he or she would then become the owner of the copy.

Did the library or instructor communicate with the publisher regarding the review copy? For example, did the sales representative say something like, "Sure, we'll send a copy out for review on the condition that you buy the book, adopt it for a class in the upcoming school year, or return it within 45 days of delivery," to which the instructor replied, "Okay. I understand I either have to buy it, adopt it for a class, or return it." If so, then a verbal agreement was likely in place regarding the circumstances of how the instructor came into possession of the book, what he or she could do with the book (i.e., if the item is not purchased or adopted as required reading by the instructor, the item would have to be returned within a certain time period), and that the item was not an unsolicited or a complimentary copy. This agreement indicates that if the item is for review alone (the instructor examines the book and decides not to adopt it, so he or she must send it back), the transaction is in the form of a loan without transfer of ownership unless the item is adopted. If not adopted but the instructor decides to retain the item nonetheless, he or she must purchase the item. Only in the case of subsequent adoption or purchase does ownership of the item occur.

Review arrangements suggest that the instructor is merely a possessor or holder of the item and not an owner of a physical embodiment of the copyrighted work. Under the recent decision in *Vernor v. Autodesk, Inc.* and discussed in detail in Chapter 4, the "first sale doctrine does not apply to a person who possesses a copy of the copyrighted work without owning it, such as a licensee."[56] Under this reasoning, an instructor holding a review copy, if such agreement applied (if the restrictions were valid), could not forward the item to a student to use in a final project, to the library for its collection or to place on reserve, or to a book jobber who purchases used or otherwise unwanted textbooks.

Section 109 of the copyright law indicates that first-sale rights are not available in some situations, even if the copy is nonetheless lawfully made under this title: "The privileges prescribed by subsections (a) and (c) do not, unless authorized by the copyright owner, extend to any person who has acquired possession of the copy or phonorecord from the copyright owner, by rental, lease, loan, or otherwise, without acquiring ownership of it."[57] Moreover, such downstream transferees would likewise not have any first-sale rights—that is, the library, like the plaintiff in *Vernor v. Autodesk, Inc.* who acquired the software from the initial transferee of Autodesk, Inc. (a company that licensed the software from Autodesk, Inc.), is not an owner of the software but a licensee. A later decision of the same circuit summarized the application of the rule in *Vernor*: "In applying this test to Autodesk's SLA, which explicitly reserved Autodesk's title to Release 14 copies and imposed significant transfer and use restrictions, we held that Autodesk's customer from whom Vernor acquired the used copies was a licensee, not an owner of the copies. Thus, neither Autodesk's original customer nor Vernor could sell or resell copies of Release 14 under the first sale doctrine."[58] As a result, neither Vernor nor the initial recipient possessed first-sale rights in the software. By analogy, in the instance of a review copy where the request for review is made by the instructor with terms agreed upon at the time of the request for review, neither the instructor (like the initial customer of Autodesk, Inc.) nor the library (like Vernor), although possessing a copy of the item, owns that copy; rather the copy is, under section 109(d), on "loan" or in some other state of nonownership from the publisher. The instructor must either adopt the item as required for a class in an upcoming semester, return the item, or purchase it (in which case the loan would cease and the instructor would now own that copy of the item). Thus, a person in possession of a review item on loan would not have first-sale rights in the item. Subsequent transferees of the item would not have such rights either, with the result that the instructor could not circulate the item to students, put it on reading reserve, use it in a distance-education classroom, sell it at a book sale or to a used-textbook jobber, or donate it to the library.

Such arrangements (review and return unless adopted or purchased) may be more like a bailment[59] with the instructor the bailee.[60] "The elements of a bailment are delivery of personal property by one person to another to be used for specific purpose, acceptance of that delivery, and an express or implied contract that the purpose will be carried out and that the property will then be returned or dealt with as otherwise directed. Ordinarily a bailment is created by delivery and acceptance and consent or agreement of the parties, but it may also result from actions and conduct of people concerning the goods in question."[61] In the case of a requested copy for review, the specific purpose is, of course, review. Once the review is completed, the item is to be returned if not adopted. Up until this point, while possession of the copy obviously resides with the educator, ownership of that title has not been transferred. Rather, if the book is adopted, then the educator may keep the item; in other words, ownership of the item is then also transferred. If not adopted and the educator desires nonetheless to retain the item, it must then be purchased, in which case the ownership of the item also passes to the educator. At that point of ownership transfer, the educator is free to keep or dispose of the item as he or she sees fit. Bailments often occur in the world of libraries, for example, when patrons check out books.[62] While material circulated to library patrons may come into possession of the patron, ownership of the item remains with the library. The patron is not allowed to keep the item; such material must be returned to its rightful owner—the library—unless of course the patron loses the item or decides to keep it, but in those cases the items are not transferred freely, as patrons must pay for items loaned but not returned. Courts have characterized these transactions as part of a bailment.[63] Another form of bailment with which the reader might be familiar is a bailment for sale, for example, when you take your set of first editions to the book dealer and he or she attempts to sell them on your behalf in return for a percentage of the sale price. Another name for a bailment for sale is consignment.[64] Bailments are not contracts per se but implied contracts, a topic covered in Chapter 3. The remedy for a breach of bailment obligations is an action for conversion.[65] In a bailment case involving books that a publisher transferred to another company so that the books could be destroyed, the court characterized the "arrangement between Little, Brown and APR pursuant to which APR would pick up books from Little, Brown for purposes of recycling was not a contract for the sale of books, but rather a contract for services . . . that from the time APR picked up the books at Little, Brown until such time that the sale of the paper after destruction of the books was consummated, APR had possession of the books as a bailee."[66] Under these circumstances, the ownership of the books in question remained with the publisher and the bailee; the recycling company retained possession alone.[67] However, the recycling company did not destroy all of the books but instead sold or otherwise transferred the books to others. While the court did not discuss the first-sale doctrine, the court did indicate nonetheless that the right of the copyright owner to control public distributions of the books for which it still retained ownership indeed remained with the publisher:

> It is undisputed that copies of two novels, *Vineland* and *Masquerade*, were among the books consigned by Little, Brown to APR, and thereafter sold by APR to Advantage . . . I find that APR did not obtain title to or ownership interest in the books pursuant to its contract with Little, Brown. I further find that Little, Brown did not authorize, either expressly or impliedly, the sale of the four shipments of books by APR to Advantage. I conclude that in selling the four shipments of books to Advantage, APR infringed Little, Brown's rights under the Copyright Act, to wit, the exclusive right to distribute copies . . . of the copyrighted work to the public by sale or other transfer of ownership.[68]

Likewise, in the case of a requested review copy where the terms are made known, the transfer of the book or other item is for a particular purpose (adoption or return), and other purposes are not authorized under the copyright law. Of course, there is a difference between a book or other item that arrives without previous action and is marked "for review" and a book or other item that is requested by the instructor, for which the terms of "adopt, purchase, or return" are made known at the time of the request, and with some acknowledgment (e.g., a verbal "Yes, I understand" made to the customer representative on the phone) made by the requesting instructor. With the latter, it is reasonable to conclude that unless the book or item is adopted by the librarian or instructor, it is to be returned, and that only possession has been transferred at this point because the item is under review. Ownership of the book or item is not transferred and so, like the books in the *Little, Brown and Company, Inc. v. American Paper Recycling Corp.*, the transferee does not have the right to make further distributions of the items under the copyright law.

See Table 2.1 for an overview of first-sale rights in situations involving unordered merchandise and review copies.

▶ **TABLE 2.1** First-Sale Rights in Unordered Merchandise and Review Copies

Item Origin	Relevant Statutory or Case Law	Application of Law to the Facts	Immediate Impact on Librarian or Educator	Subsequent Impact on Library
Item obtained through purchase by librarian, educator, or library	Items purchased by librarian, educator, or library are governed by the copyright law: § 109 and § 110 are the most relevant, but fair use (§ 107) and other provisions apply as well. Further requirements may apply if public distribution is made of a computer program under section 109(b)(2)(A). See also TOMAS A. LIPINSKI, THE COMPLETE COPYRIGHT LIABILITY HANDBOOK FOR LIBRARIANS AND EDUCATORS 232–336 (2006). Other rights and restrictions under the copyright law apply as well.	§ 109 first-sale rights allow for further public distribution as long as the copy is "lawfully made under this title" (title 17 of the U.S. Code, i.e., the copyright law). Use of items manufactured in a foreign country may require further analysis (see discussion in Chapter 1 of the impact of the *Omega S.A. v. Costco Wholesale Corp.*, 541 F.3d 982, 986 (9th Cir. 2008), judgment affirmed by an equally divided court without opinion; *Costco Wholesale Corp. v. Omega S.A.*, 131 S.Ct. 565 (2010); and *John Wiley & Sons, Inc. v. Kirtsaeng*, 654 F.3d 210, 218 (2d Cir. 2011), petition for Writ of Certiorari granted, 2012 WL 1252751 (Apr. 16, 2012) (Docket No. 11-697), decisions.	First-sale rights allow the librarian to give it as a gift to a colleague or allow an educator to hand it out to a student to take home. Educator could also make a display or performance of the item in the classroom under § 110(1). If the item performed by the educator in the classroom is an audiovisual work such as a DVD, then a "lawfully made under this title" requirement also exists. See TOMAS A. LIPINSKI, COPYRIGHT LAW AND THE DISTANCE EDUCATION CLASSROOM 16–22 (2005). Additional rights and conditions apply if the item is used in a distance-education scenario under § 110(2). See TOMAS A. LIPINSKI, COPYRIGHT LAW AND THE DISTANCE EDUCATION CLASSROOM 35–108 (2005).	First-sale rights allow the library to circulate a copy "lawfully made under this title" of the item so acquired. Additional requirements apply if the library circulates computer programs.
Gift of item made to librarian, educator, or library	Same as for "Item obtained through purchase."	Same for "Item obtained through purchase."	Same for "Item obtained through purchase."	First-sale rights allow the library to circulate a "lawfully made under this title" copy of the item so received as a gift.

(continued)

▶ **TABLE 2.1** First-Sale Rights in Unordered Merchandise and Review Copies *(Continued)*

Item Origin	Relevant Statutory or Case Law	Application of Law to the Facts	Immediate Impact on Librarian or Educator	Subsequent Impact on Library
Complimentary item received by the librarian, educator, or library	Under 39 U.S.C. § 3009 and the case law applying it, such items can be treated as a gift unless subject to specific statutory exceptions: "(1) free samples clearly and conspicuously marked as such, and (2) merchandise mailed by a charitable organization soliciting contributions" per 39 U.S.C. § 3009(a). Under federal law such items are defined as "unordered merchandise": "merchandise mailed without the prior expressed request or consent of the recipient" per 39 U.S.C. § 3009(d). State law also suggests a similar result, see discussion and state statutes referenced chapter note 42.	As the item is a gift and, assuming the item is "lawfully made under this title," § 109 and § 110 (where this phrase is also found) would apply, as would any other section of the copyright law for that matter. Remember that other rights and restrictions under the copyright law apply as well. See "Item obtained through purchase."	Same for "Item obtained through purchase."	Same as for "Item obtained through purchase" and "Gift of item made."

(continued)

▶ **TABLE 2.1** First-Sale Rights in Unordered Merchandise and Review Copies *(Continued)*

Item Origin	Relevant Statutory or Case Law	Application of Law to the Facts	Immediate Impact on Librarian or Educator	Subsequent Impact on Library
Unsolicited (unordered) merchandise received by the librarian, educator, or library ("for your consideration" or invoice enclosed)	Same as for "Complimentary item received." In specific, under *Marshall v. Little Professor Book Center, Inc.*, 1992 WL 309627 (E.D. Pa. 1992) (unpublished), those in receipt of such items would not be obligated to either return the item or pay for it. (See *id.* at *3.) Under 39 U.S.C. § 3009(c), "mail[ing] to any recipient of such [unordered] merchandise a bill for such merchandise or any dunning communications" constitutes "an unfair method of competition and an unfair trade practice in violation," per § 3009(a), and is subject to enforcement action by the Federal Trade Commission.	Same as for "Complimentary item received."	Same as for "Complimentary item received."	Same as for "Complimentary item received."
Promotional item received by the librarian, educator, or library accompanied by label license (restrictions on public display, public performance, or public distribution)	Same as "Unsolicited merchandise received." In specific, under *UMG Recordings, Inc. v. Augusto*, 628 F.3d 1175 (9th Cir. 2011), language that restricts use to those that are "personal" or language that states the item is "promotional" and "not for sale" or that purports to create a license or "constitute an agreement to comply with the terms" as stated above is not legally binding (*id.* at 1177–1178).	Items so received are treated the same as if a gift. See "Unsolicited merchandise received."	As the item is a gift, the same first-sale rights apply: "We also hold that, because the CDs were unordered merchandise, the recipients were free to dispose of them as they saw fit under the Unordered Merchandise Statute," per *UMG Recordings, Inc. v. Augusto*, 628 F.3d 1175, 1180 (9th Cir. 2011).	The library possesses the same rights and restrictions regarding its use of the item as if it were a gift. See "Unsolicited merchandise received."

(continued)

▶ **TABLE 2.1**   **First-Sale Rights in Unordered Merchandise and Review Copies** *(Continued)*

Item Origin	Relevant Statutory or Case Law	Application of Law to the Facts	Immediate Impact on Librarian or Educator	Subsequent Impact on Library
Promotional item received by the librarian, educator, or library accompanied by label license (restrictions on public display, public performance, or public distribution) *(continued)*			("Accordingly, UMG transferred title to the particular copies of its promotional CDs and cannot maintain an infringement action against Augusto for his subsequent sale of those copies" (*id.* at 1180).) Section 110, fair use (section 107) or other rights as well as restrictions under the copyright law apply.	
Review copy received by educator, scenario I (circumstances where educator did not request item but conditions of use—adoption, purchase, or return—are indicated by enclosure accompanying review copy or stamped on item or its cover or jacket)	Under *UMG Recordings, Inc. v. Augusto*, 628 F.3d 1175 (9th Cir. 2011), the same result as "Promotional item received." Label licenses that read, for example, "Professor Review Copy/Not for Resale" "are ineffectual, making the review copies freely re-sellable," per Eric Goldman, Technology and Marketing Law Blog: *Top 5 Cyberlaw Developments of 2010, Plus a 2010 Year-in-Review*, Cyberspace Lawyer, March 2011. "[I]t it is very doubtful that the publisher has any legal right to restrict their resale, notwithstanding any statements to the contrary stamped on the books," per Richard F. Blake, *Overview of Educational*	Same as for "Promotional item received."	Same as for "Promotional item received."	Same as for "Item obtained through purchase."

(continued)

▶ **TABLE 2.1** First-Sale Rights in Unordered Merchandise and Review Copies *(Continued)*

Item Origin	Relevant Statutory or Case Law	Application of Law to the Facts	Immediate Impact on Librarian or Educator	Subsequent Impact on Library
Review copy received by educator, scenario I *(continued)*	*Textbook Publishing*, LEGAL AND BUSINESS ASPECTS OF BOOK PUBLISHING 425, 445 (Richard Dannay and E. Gabriel Perle eds., 1986) (PLI Course Handbook #222).			
Review copy received by educator, scenario II (circumstances where educator requested item and conditions of use—adopt or either return or purchase—were indicated at time of request by publisher, which the educator acknowledged, and were enclosed with review copy or stamped on item or its cover or jacket)	If a contract is formed, then the copyright law does not govern as above. Rather the terms under which the review copy was transferred by the publisher and obtained by the librarian or instructor govern. An argument can be made that such transfers do not result in the librarian or instructor obtaining ownership of the review copy but are mere possessors of the item—perhaps less than a license but more similar to a loan or other form of bailment. If so, then first-sale rights under 17 U.S.C § 109(d) do	The terms of the agreement indicate that the item is not given as a gift but possession is transferred for purposes of review alone. If the item is not adopted, it must be returned. In this case, the transfer appears more in the form of a loan or bailment than a license. If the item is adopted, then the publisher will indeed deem the transfer of possession as a gift and the librarian or instructor may keep possession of the item forever (with accompanying ownership rights in the item, which would then include first-sale rights). In the absence of either	If the librarian or instructor does not own the item under review but obtains mere possession of it, the First-Sale Right does not apply: "the privileges prescribed by subsection . . . (a) . . . do not, unless authorized by the copyright owner, extend to any person who has acquired possession of the copy or phonorecord from the copyright owner, by rental, lease, loan, or otherwise, without acquiring ownership of it" per 17 U.S.C. § 109(d). "The first sale doctrine does not apply to a person who	If the transaction is a license, loan, bailment, or other transfer of possession with ownership rights in the item, i.e., not a gift (or purchase for that matter), then neither the librarian or educator nor the library would possess any first-sale rights under the transaction, and the library could not make further public distributions of the item, such as by circulation, if prohibited by the agreement. "In applying this test to Autodesk's SLA, which explicitly reserved Autodesk's title to Release 14 copies and imposed significant transfer and use restrictions, we held that Autodesk's customer from whom Vernor acquired the used copies was a

(continued)

▶ **TABLE 2.1** First-Sale Rights in Unordered Merchandise and Review Copies *(Continued)*

Item Origin	Relevant Statutory or Case Law	Application of Law to the Facts	Immediate Impact on Librarian or Educator	Subsequent Impact on Library
Review copy received by educator, scenario II *(continued)*	not apply "unless authorized by the copyright owner, extend to any person who has acquired possession of the copy or phonorecord from the copyright owner, by rental, lease, loan, or otherwise, without acquiring ownership of it."	return or adoption, if the librarian or instructor desires to nonetheless retain the item, he or she must purchase the item, which would result in both possessory and ownership rights being transferred, and first-sale rights would again apply.	possesses a copy of the copyrighted work without owning it, such as a licensee," per *Vernor v. Autodesk, Inc.*, 621 F.3d 1102, 1107 (9th Cir. 2010), cert. denied 132 S.Ct. 105 (Oct. 3, 2011). See further discussion in Chapter 4.	licensee, not an owner of the copies. Thus, neither Autodesk's original customer nor Vernor could sell or resell copies of Release 14 under the first sale doctrine," per *Apple Inc. v. Paystar Corp.*, 658 F.3d 1150, 1156 (9th Cir. 2011, citing *Vernor v. Autodesk, Inc.*, 621 F.3d 1102 (9th Cir. 2010) at 1111–1112 and 1116), cert. denied 132 S.Ct. 105 (Oct. 3, 2011). This case implies that similar terms of a contract outlining the conditions upon which the review copy would be sent also preclude application of the First-Sale doctrine and preclude such transfers.

THE END OF THE POWER TO ACCEPT

Once an offer is made, the ball is in the offeree's court, as the saying goes. As a result, the person or entity in receipt of a true offer has power at that point: accept or reject the offer. The offeree, through the act of acceptance, possesses the power to bind the maker of the offer so that the offeror must keep his or her word and fulfill the terms of the offer. This power comes at a price, however, in that the offeree cannot leave the offeror waiting or expect that the offeror should be bound by the initial offer if the offeree shows unreasonable conduct. The offer will not be available forever, but while the offer stands the power to make the next move resides with the offeree.

The power to accept can be revoked for various reasons, one of which is lapse of time. Again, the idea of reasonableness comes into play here. Offers are not open forever; in fact, the offer may state a time period within which the acceptance must occur. Barring that, courts apply a reasonableness standard, with the reasonable time period beginning with receipt of the offer.[69] The reasonableness depends on the circumstances, however. The Restatement suggests that unless there is a clear statement to the contrary ("You can think about whether to take the job as director of the ABC Public Library, but get back to us by the end of the month"), for face-to-face or phone negotiations, when an offer is made, the offer is good for a period only as long as the duration of the conversation.[70] In spite of the reasonableness standard, the Restatement indicates that unless circumstances exist to the contrary, or if the offer states otherwise, "an offer sent by mail is reasonably accepted if an acceptance is mailed at any time before midnight on the day on which the offer is received."[71]

It should be obvious that the power to accept is also ended by a rejection of the offer—for example, when a librarian responds to an unsolicited call from a vendor, "Sorry, but I'm not interested in the new edition of *The Best Reference Compendium Ever Written*," then thinks better of the offer the next day and calls back to say, "I'll take it." In addition, the offeree can undertake more complicating conduct that ends the offer. This would include situations in which the initial offer is met with a counteroffer, acceptance is forwarded but with some additional term, or the vendor-offeror withdraws the offer outright (called revocation).

COUNTEROFFERS AND THE END OF THE POWER TO ACCEPT

Suppose the vendor leaves the following message on the librarian's voicemail: "Hi, Tom. This Eileen from ABC Books. I'm returning your call inquiring about the new edition of *The Best Reference Book in the World*. It will be available next month, and I can give you an additional 15 percent off and free shipping if you order by the end of the week. The price would be $95.99. If you order additional copies now, I can give you an extra 10 percent off, for a 25 percent savings, free shipping included." Is this message a solicitation (an invitation to receive an offer from the librarian) or an offer? This is an offer because there is definiteness as to subject, quantity, price, and so forth, as previously discussed.

Now suppose that the librarian is on vacation and does not return and make the acceptance call to the vendor until a week later. This delay in response time would likely be deemed a lapse, as discussed. However, what if the librarian calls the vendor back the next day and says, "I'm interested in ordering a copy of *The Best Reference Book in the World*, but I want the 25 percent discount on the first copy as well"? This request would be considered a counteroffer and not an acceptance, as the contract is not yet clear as to price (amount of the discount available). If the librarian instead says, "I'll take two copies of *The Best Reference Book in the World* only if I can have the first year's supplement for free as well." Rather than a counteroffer, this request might be better characterized as a conditional acceptance, as discussed later in this chapter. The difference is significant, as counteroffers end the offeree's power of acceptance.

There is an exception for so-called options, where consideration is made to keep the offer open for a set period. This is known as an option contract. If this occurs, then the option to accept must remain open and a counteroffer will not terminate the power to accept.

Acceptances that are accompanied by further inquiry or a mere request for different terms do not terminate the power to accept but can bind the offeror. The difference often depends again on reasonableness. In other words, would a reasonable person in the position of the person who made the offer believe that a counteroffer was made? If not, and the conversation fell short of negotiating (offers and counteroffers), with the result that better terms cannot be secured, the offeree-librarian is still committed to buying the book.

There is a difference between true counteroffers—acceptances that come with mere inquiry or a request for different terms and acceptances that come with additional questions: For example, the offeree might respond, "I'll take two copies of *The Best Reference Book in the World*, but I'm wondering: What would be your lowest price on the first year's supplement?" A counteroffer terminates the power of acceptance. Here, there is no additional condition and no counteroffer; rather, it is an acceptance with further inquiry.

Perhaps the discount schema in the previous example—first copy at 15 percent discount, additional copies at 25 percent discount—is typical; it is also typical for the librarian to ask for the larger discount across the board, with the sales representative having to check with the home office to see if that discount is possible. This scenario has played out numerous times between the vendor-offeror and the librarian-offeree. Suppose the librarian, regardless of the response to the acceptance with inquiry or request, has always taken the latest edition of the item irrespective of the amount of the discount the sales representative could secure. In light of these circumstances, a request such as "I'd like to order two copies of *The Best Reference Book in the World*, but can I get the 25 percent discount on the first copy?" is likely an acceptance with a request for different terms, not a conditional acceptance. The sales rep may reply, "Sorry, I can't get you 25 percent, but would you take 20 percent off the first copy?," and this may result in negotiation over the additional term.

The response "I'll take two copies of *The Best Reference Book in the World*, but can I have the first year's updates for free as well?" is also an acceptance with a further inquiry about free updates (different from a true conditional acceptance, as discussed later in this chapter). Here, even if the discount or free updates are not available, there was a clear indication of a desire to purchase two copies of *The Best Reference Book in the World*, one at the 15 or 20 percent discount and a second at the 25 percent discount offer, with the possibility of free supplements for the first year.

This should make sense because if mere inquiry or request for different terms would terminate the power of acceptance, commerce would quickly grind to a halt.

> SALES REP: Hi, Tom. I'm returning your call inquiring about the new edition of *The Best Reference Book in the World.* It will be available next month, and I can give you an additional 15 percent off and free shipping if you order by the end of the week. The price would be $95.99. If you order additional copies now, I can give you an extra 10 percent off, for a 25 percent savings, free shipping is included.

> LIBRARIAN: I'd like to order a copy of *The Best Reference Book in the World,* but can I get the 25 percent discount on the first copy too?

> SALES REP: I'm sorry, but the extra discount is no longer available.

> LIBRARIAN: Okay. I'd still like a copy.

> SALES REP: I'm sorry, but now I can only offer free shipping.

To keep the good and steady flow of commerce in place, the law views a contract formed with the necessity of ironing out the remaining terms later.

There may also be times when a response includes intent to accept the offer but is accompanied by a further condition. This is known as a conditional acceptance. For example, "I want to renew our subscription to your retrospective bar coding service, but only if I can have the first quarter-year's service at a 15 percent discount." While this statement expresses a clear intent to accept, it also conditions the acceptance on the inclusion of a discount. The difference may appear subtle, but this is not quite a counteroffer. A counteroffer could be worded, "I would consider taking another year's subscription to your retrospective bar coding service, but instead of the 5 percent discount you offered I want to receive a 15 percent discount over last year's price for the first three months of the year."

CONDITIONAL ACCEPTANCE AND THE END OF THE POWER TO ACCEPT

The general rule is that a conditional acceptance terminates the power of acceptance (as does the counteroffer), but of course it can constitute an offer by the librarian back to the sales rep, which then vests the sales rep/vendor with the power to accept.

> SALES REP: Okay. You can have the first three months with the 15 percent discount.

> LIBRARIAN: No, thanks. I changed my mind. I don't want your service anymore.

> SALES REP: Hey, wait a minute. That's not fair!

Grumbling acceptances are acceptance nonetheless ("Okay, I will take another year of retrospective bar coding, but I sure wish you could give us a better price!"), as long as they stop short of actual dissent, such as a rejection or a counteroffer.

However, the general rule of conditional acceptance as termination does not apply if the offer is for a sale of goods. This change reflects the impact of the UCC and the development of modern contract law. In the old days, the acceptance had to mirror the offer precisely. This was known as the so-called mirror image rule. This would mean that the parties would have to continue negotiations (or the offer would terminate), restating the terms back and forth until the parties were in perfect synchronization, often with formation of the entire contract in doubt throughout the process. Making a response with different terms meant the prior offer was terminated and the response of different terms was treated as a new offer. If a counter response was forthcoming that also contained different terms, then the first response was likewise terminated and this second response constituted a new offer. Whoever managed in their response to mirror the response immediate and prior to it would be deemed to accept that immediate and prior response. This became known as the "last shot" rule,[72] especially when merchants traded forms back and forth, for example, sales and purchase orders, order confirmations, and acknowledgments, each always with slightly different terms from those contained in the counter form that preceded it.[73] With so many opportunities to terminate an offer, it is a wonder that commerce ever progressed.

ADDITIONAL TERMS

What happens when the parties intend to form a contract and one party accepts the other's offer but desires to make additional terms part of the agreement (neither a counteroffer nor a conditional acceptance)? This might occur in close proximity to contract formation or weeks or even months after the moment the law would deem the contract was formed. In a sense, the UCC rule solves these quick-trigger terminations of offer, rapid-fire counteroffers, mirror images, and last-shot rules, and on the like. Under the UCC, a contract indeed exists where a new term or conditional acceptance is treated as a circumstance requiring additional bargaining: "A definite and reasonable expression of acceptance or a written confirmation which is sent within a reasonable time operates as an acceptance even though it states terms additional to or different from those offered or agreed upon, unless acceptance is expressly made conditional on assent to the additional or different terms."[74] Suppose the librarian says to the vendor, "We'll take the new furniture we discussed and you described in your offer of July 18 and at the price indicated in the same letter, but you must be able to guarantee delivery by September 1 or the deal is off." Here the library desires to accept the terms in the written offer referenced but with the additional condition of the delivery date stated. Is this sufficient under the UCC rule? Is it a true conditional acceptance, with a contract formed if and only if the delivery date conditions are agreed to by the vendor, "thus converting the response to a counteroffer which must be accepted by the original offeror"?[75] Yes. As stated by one court, "the offeree must explicitly communicate his or her unwillingness to proceed with the transaction unless the additional or different terms in its response are accepted by the offeror."[76] The UCC rule regarding additional terms allows commerce to proceed, with a contract formed and negotiation commencing regarding the additional terms. There is a slightly different rule when the transaction is between merchants, however, with those additional terms becoming part of the contract unless certain elements exist.[77]

Suppose a person reads an advertisement on a website or in the newspaper for a laptop. This is not an offer but a solicitation to receive an offer. The consumer calls to place an order, at which time the terms of the sale are reviewed (an offer is now made), and provides his or her credit card and mailing information. The company sends the computer in the mail or via a third-party shipper but includes in the box the terms of the agreement, a so-called "pay now,[78] terms later" contract. So when is the contract formed? Is this an acceptance with the result that a contract is formed but with additional terms inside the box, with the extant terms prior being the description of the product (the specs of the laptop) and the price and other information exchanged during placement of telephone order? Courts have held that a contract is formed after the terms arrive and the purchaser possesses a reasonable opportunity to inspect the computer and the accompanying terms—and, if not pleased, return the product.[79] However, a contract does not occur if the original offer prohibited different terms or the conditional acceptance required the additional terms to be part of the contract or else—that is, an "express condition," as the UCC rule reflects.

In the "pay now, terms later" scenario, there are no additional terms to construe, material or otherwise. However, when there is a contract and an exchange of additional terms ensues (a so-called battle of the forms), then UCC section 2-207(2) is triggered, with "additional terms [...] construed as proposals for addition to the contract."[80] If the transaction is between merchants, the additional terms become part of the contract unless the terms are material (in which case the terms require additional bargaining), the offer prohibits additional terms, or the material terms have been rejected already within a reasonable time. For example, in *Wachter Management Co. v. Dexter & Chaney, Inc.*, where a contract was formed by signing a proposal in the office of the software vendor, the court observed that "continuing with the contract after receiving a writing with additional or different terms is not sufficient to establish express consent to the additional or different terms."[81] As an agreement was established, there could be no battle of the forms, and the shrink-wrap language involved was treated as an additional term.

Determining what is a material term in a contract between merchants is not always easy.[82] "Although the phrase 'material' is subject to interpretation, it has been defined as 'affect[ing] the purpose of a contract in an important or vital way.'"[83] Many, many disputes have arisen between merchants and consumers and among merchants themselves over material terms, with the purchaser/licensee attempting to argue for contract formation at an early point in time, for example, when walking out of the store or when the order is placed over the phone, such that under the UCC additional and material terms rule of section 2-207 any subsequent terms would need to be bargained over in a consumer transaction as well as in a transaction between merchants (unless the circumstances qualify for one of the exceptions in section 2-207). Courts have not viewed these disputes as governed by the conditional acceptance rule but rather treated them as a sort of delayed acceptance until some later point in time:

> A vendor, as master of the offer, may invite acceptance by conduct, and may propose limitations on the kind of conduct that constitutes acceptance. A buyer may accept by performing the acts the vendor proposes to treat as acceptance. And that is what happened. ProCD proposed a contract that a buyer would accept by *using* the software after having an opportunity to read the license at leisure. This Zeidenberg did... Ours is not a case in which a consumer opens a package to find an insert saying "you owe us an extra $10,000" and the seller files suit to collect. Any buyer finding such a demand can prevent formation of the contract by returning the package, as can any consumer who concludes that the terms of the license make the software worth less than the purchase price.[84]

A number of courts have analyzed whether agreements where terms are not revealed until a later time (pay now, terms later transactions) are conditional acceptances or completed contracts with a request for additional terms. Courts disagree in the application of these pay now, terms later agreements to transactions involving software, so-called shrink-wrap licenses. For example, the court in *Arizona Retail Systems, Inc. v. Software Link, Inc.*, interpreting UCC section 2-207,

> reject[ed] TSL's argument that the...license agreement constituted a conditional acceptance. The court is very reluctant, in light of the purposes underlying section 2-207 and the circumstances of this case, to interpret section 2-207 in such a way that a package disclaimer constitutes a conditional acceptance even though the disclaimer arrives after the parties have entered into an agreement for the sale of goods. The court believes that it is much more consistent with the policies underlying section 2-207 to assume that package disclaimers, that arrive only after the parties have reached a general agreement under section 2-207, constitute proposals to modify the agreement.[85]

This decision is consistent with the UCC provision governing agreements between merchants. Likewise, so is the decision in *ProCD, Inc. v. Zeidenberg*, which involved a transaction between a merchant and a consumer.[86]

A recent dispute between RealNetworks, Inc. and the DVD Copy Control Association (DVD CCA) demonstrates the "terms later" concept. DVD CCA is the nonprofit entity that administers industrywide use of the CSS (Content Scramble System) technology that prevents copying of DVDs. RealNetworks, the same company that makes RealPlayer, entered into a nonnegotiable license agreement with DVD CCA in order to "build a product that implements CSS technology."[87] Various CSS specifications were then provided to RealNetworks by DVD CCA after the license was executed. "These specifications are never provided to prospective licenses prior to execution of the CSS License, and thus were not provided to Real prior to August 2007,"[88] the date RealNetworks, Inc. executed Version 1.2 of the CSS License Agreement. The dispute, for breach of contract, arose when RealNetworks distributed its RealDVD product that allowed users to save copies of DVDs played on personal computers. In order for RealDVD to accomplish this task, the product must circumvent the CSS protection technology, thus violating section 1201 of the copyright law. As a result, aggrieved parties "are permitted to bring both DMCA [Digital Millennium Copyright Act] claims for circumvention of CSS technology and breach of contract claims under the CSS License Agreement."[89] Returning to the breach of contract claim, RealNetworks argued that the specifications relating to the CSS copy control requirements were not binding because it received the specifications after the contract was executed. However, RealNetworks was aware that such additional specifications ("terms later") would be forthcoming.[90] "That the confidential technical specifications were not delivered until after selection of the appropriate membership category by Real and execution of the agreement does not mean they were not part of the contractual agreement between Real and DVD CCA"; as the court pointed out, RealNetworks had the opportunity to return or destroy the specifications after receipt: "This behavior indicates that Real understood it to be bound by the CSS General Specifications as well as the other technical specifications received after execution of the CSS License Agreement."[91] The general rule under the UCC sets contract formation at an earlier point in time, for example, when the computer is ordered over the Internet or via phone or the customer pays for the software at the local Best Buy, with additional terms construed as proposals for additions to the contract. If the contract so formed is one between merchants, then "such terms become part of the contract unless: (a) the offer expressly limits acceptance to the terms of the offer; (b) they materially alter it; or (c) notification of objection to them has already been given or is given within a reasonable time after notice of them is received."[92] If the customer is a merchant and the terms of the offer prohibited any additions or the customer fails to object, then additional terms become part of the contract unless the terms are material. This raises two immediate questions that later become important in license interpretation: Who is a merchant? What is a material term? The former is discussed in the next section, and the latter is discussed in the context of licenses that relate to "material" terms.

THE LIBRARY AS MERCHANT

The question of course is whether, in a transaction between a vendor and a library, the library is treated as a merchant or a consumer. The UCC defines a merchant as "a person that deals in goods of the kind or otherwise holds itself out by occupation as having knowledge or skill peculiar to the practices or goods involved in the transaction or to which the knowledge or skill may be attributed by the person's employment of an agent or broker or other intermediary that holds itself out by occupation as having the knowledge or skill."[93] The UCC defines the concept of "between merchants" to mean "any transaction with respect to which both parties are chargeable with the knowledge or skill of merchants."[94]

While the librarian certainly possesses "knowledge or skill peculiar to the practices or goods involved in the transaction," for example, books and periodicals, and how to assist patrons in use of those goods, the librarian is not necessarily involved in producing the products; in other words, the librarian is not a publisher. "Yet again, for what little it is worth we observe that the Hills misunderstand the setting of *ProCD*. A 'merchant' under the UCC 'means a person who deals in goods of the kind or otherwise by his occupation holds himself out as having knowledge or skill peculiar to the practices or goods involved in the transaction', § 2-104(1). Zeidenberg bought the product at a retail store, an uncommon place for merchants to acquire inventory."[95] However, the official comment to UCC section 2-104 states: "This Article assumes that transactions between professionals in a given field require special and clear rules which may not apply to a casual or inexperienced seller or buyer."[96] Librarians would like to think of themselves as professionals, at least in the broad commercial sector of information goods. In terms of the business of the licensor—the creation, maintenance, and offering of searchable databases—a library is all too familiar with this and, in fact, is a database vendor of sorts to its own patrons as a library creates, maintains, and makes its own database(s) available to its patrons (e.g., its online catalog). Further UCC comment indicates: "In this type of provision, banks or even universities, for example, well may be 'merchants.' But even these sections only apply to a merchant in his mercantile capacity; a lawyer or bank president buying fishing tackle for his own use is not a merchant."[97] If a university can be a merchant when transacting goods and services related to university functions, it would appear a library in a university, public library, school library, or special library in a corporation could also be said to be a merchant, possessing the specialized knowledge or skill peculiar to the practices of the information profession but perhaps not when it buys tables and chairs. However, as explained by one court:

> The issue is whether the University is a "merchant in goods of the kin" with respect to the dryer unit... Minnesota courts have labored, however, to find some principled basis for distinguishing consumer transactions from commercial transactions. In making this distinction, courts have had particular difficulty where, as here, both parties to the transaction are "merchants," as that term is defined in the UCC.[98]

A library, in addition to purchasing books, periodicals, and the like with frequency, might also be viewed in a similar light when it purchases study carrels and technology workstation furniture. The Minnesota

> court conclude[d] that the University was a merchant with respect to the purchase of the ["agricultural gas-fired blower"] dryer unit. The purchase of the dryer unit by the University was not an isolated transaction; the University had purchased six such units over the past thirty years. The University solicited bids for the purchase and thus possessed some bargaining power in the transaction. The University was a sophisticated purchaser and employed an agent who was an acknowledged national expert in dryer units.[99]

True, a library might not be a merchant when it purchases a microwave for its employee break room, but the library might be expected to know a bit about—or, in other words, be deemed a merchant for the purposes of purchasing furniture designed specifically for use in libraries—media stations, computer labs, and so on.

REVOCATION OF THE OFFER (BY THE OFFEROR)

The general rule is that revocations must be communicated to be effective. Exceptions are for offers made to the public at large, for example, the rare book solicitation or the reward for lost items in the classifieds examples discussed previously. Where a revocation is published in the same medium—for example, another ad in *Library Journal* indicating the book dealer who placed the original ad will no longer accept any more first editions—the revocation is deemed effective. Again, there are exceptions when the offer must be held open during the duration of the option because the offeree has given consideration in return for a promise from the offeror that the offer remains open for a stated time period.

A firm offer is an offer within which a time period for acceptance is indicated in the offer. Like any other offer it may be revoked, even prior to the final acceptance date occurring. However, if the offeree gives consideration for this definiteness, then the offer is irrevocable. This is then known as an option contract. Even nominal consideration can qualify.[100] This is the majority rule indicated in the Restatement: "An offer is binding as an option contract if it is in writing and signed by the offeror, recites a purported consideration for the making of the offer, and proposes an exchange on fair terms within a reasonable time."[101] A firm offer is also irrevocable if it is reasonable for the offeror to foresee that the offer would induce the offeree to rely on the offer, and the offeree so relies.

The practical realities of commerce can make revocation a bit tricky. For example, a vendor leaves the original offer as a voicemail message on the first day that the offer is available. When the librarian returns from vacation two weeks later, he picks up the phone and orders 11 copies based on the terms that were offered in the voicemail. However, a week after the initial offer via voicemail, the vendor had sent an e-mail message to the librarian indicating that "the discounts are no longer available." But the librarian has not yet read this e-mail, checking and clearing his voicemail first. Can the vendor be forced to honor the voicemail offer, or was the e-mail revocation effective?

The Restatement indicates that revocation is effective upon receipt, but acceptance is effective upon dispatch (the so-called mailbox rule, i.e., historically, when the response of acceptance was placed in the proverbial "the check is in the mail" scenario or other common, expected mode of delivery). "An offeree's power of acceptance is terminated when the offeree receives from the offeror a manifestation of an intention not to enter into the proposed contract."[102] So it is easier to change your mind about revoking (assuming the revocation is retrieved in time) your offer than about accepting the offer of another to you (because acceptances are effective upon dispatch, which is known as the dispatch rule).

In the previous example, does receipt of the revocation message in the inbox of the librarian's e-mail constitute receipt, or must it be read to be deemed received? The revocation is effective, as the Restatement again indicates: "[a] written revocation, rejection, or acceptance is received when the writing comes into the possession of the person addressed, or of some person authorized by him to receive it for him, or when it is deposited in some place which he has authorized as the place for this or similar communications to be deposited for him."[103] When is a "receipt" a receipt? It would appear that an e-mail message awaiting review in the inbox of the vacationing librarian would be "some place which he [or she] has authorized as the place for this or similar communication to be deposited." Likewise, a retraction of an offer for a reward is effective even if every person who first saw the ad in the Sunday paper did not read the next Sunday's edition in which the retraction was published. A minority of states, however, provide that revocation is effective upon dispatch.

ACCEPTANCE BY THE OFFEREE AND THE COMPLICATION OF CROSS-COMMUNICATIONS: REJECTION

In the historical development of contract law, a distinction was made between bilateral (a promise for a promise or a performance for a performance)[104] and unilateral contracts.[105] A bilateral contract can be accepted only by a promise to reciprocate in turn (A promises to let B use his riding mower and B promises in return to mow A's lawn for each use made of the mower).[106] "More succinctly put, unilateral and bilateral contracts differ in that the offeror of a unilateral contract seeks performance in exchange for a promise [A promises to give B $25 if in return B will mow A's lawn], while the offeror of a bilateral contract seeks a return promise."[107] There are many ways to accept an offer: a promise (where a promise equals acceptance), acknowledgment ("I promise to buy XYZ from you for the price you offered"), conduct that implies acceptance ("I will give you $100 for your collection of rare ABC books; if you would like to accept my offer, please leave the books in the night book drop of my store over the weekend"), conduct identified by the offeror to designate acceptance ("By going to the following webpage and submitting a search query you will have accepted our offer to purchase ABC"[108]), or at times even silence (in situations where the offeree solicited the offer and drafted its terms, the offer is worded in such a way that it is reasonable to deem it accepted unless rejected, and offeror relies on the silence as acceptance[109]).

The idea of silence might also be thought of as a lack of action or conduct—but not in the sense of asking, for example, "Will you buy this rare book for $100?" and the librarian says nothing, with the result that his or her silence is not deemed an acceptance. Rather it would be based on a statement by the offeror. Perhaps the rare book dealer says to the librarian, "If you ever deaccession any of those volumes in the ABC series from the 1920s we've talked about, send them to me. Unless I send them back within a week, I'll buy each volume you send for $100" (an offer). Eventually, the librarian sends out one such rare book to the dealer (an acceptance) and then after a month passes sends an invoice for the book to the dealer for $100. (The librarian can expect payment, as a contract was formed with the rare book dealer keeping the book for more than a week; it would not be an unsolicited offer of merchandise.) The rare book dealer does nothing (silence). In fact, because he keeps the book, this silence can be deemed an acceptance under the circumstances.

In the instances of a bilateral contract (promise for a promise or a performance for a performance), the return promise, or the acceptance, must be communicated to the offeror. Remember also the so-called mailbox rule states that acceptance is effective upon dispatch, in other words, when the response is put in the mail: "While a revocable offer to a bilateral contract may be revoked at any time prior to acceptance, that revocation, or rejection, is effective at the moment of receipt. On the other hand, acceptance is effective upon dispatch."[110] A unilateral contract (promise for an act) can be accepted only by performance where commencement of the performance protects the offeree from revocation: A says to B, "If you seal my driveway, I promise to pay you $100." B buys the tar and begins to paint A's driveway with it. Once tarring commences, A views how ugly it looks and says to B, "I changed my mind. I've decided to repave the driveway in concrete instead." A's attempt at revocation is not valid. In a bilateral contract, the acceptance is effective when the return promise is fulfilled or at least fulfillment is begun. Many courts hold that in an option contract (a promise to keep the offer open) acceptance takes place upon receipt; this makes sense, as the offer is being held open so that there is no need to protect the offeree against a cross-communication revocation.

The medium of communication must be reasonable, again under the circumstances. In the examples provided, if the sales rep routinely used both e-mail and voicemail to communicate with the librarian, it would appear that either mechanism would suffice. Assume that in response to the voicemail offer from the vendor the librarian sends off an acceptance through e-mail five days after the offer was left on voicemail. Two days later, the sales rep calls the librarian and informs him that the offer is no longer available (attempted revocation). This revocation is not effective because on day five the acceptance was effective upon its dispatch using a reasonable medium for its conveyance, and a contract was formed. "In fact, a fairly persuasive argument in favor of the acceptance-is-good-when-posted rule is that offerors can protect themselves from the uncertainty concerning when a contract has been made and offerees cannot. If an offeror fails to avail itself of that protection by prescribing a time of acceptance in the offer, then the law should favor the offeree."[111] The revocation (attempted on day seven) being effective upon receipt did not reach the offeree librarian until after a contract was formed on day five, when the acceptance was posted (per the mailbox rule). The mailbox rule prevents the offeror from reneging in this way. Of course, an easy way for the offeror to retain the control over the transaction is to make explicit that the acceptance of the offer is not valid until receipt by the offeror. Many contracts, including licenses, do this, defining when and how notices, including for example acceptance, nonrenewal, a change in license terms, and so forth, are deemed effective. Absent such precise and clear language, the acceptance would be effective upon dispatch to the e-mail inbox of the sales representative on day five.

Instead of the attempted revocation of the offer by the sales rep (effective upon receipt by the librarian, planned for day seven), suppose the librarian rejects the offer (effective upon receipt by the sales rep) on day four through the post and then thinks better of it and on day six e-mails to accept before the slower postal rejection is received by the sales rep. What is the result? Although the rejection was mailed before the acceptance was posted, it depends on which communication the sales rep receives first. If the rejection arrives first, the mailbox rule does not apply and there is no contract. This is a sound result. The reason is that from the offeror's perspective the sales rep concludes that the possibility of a successful transaction is over. However, where the acceptance arrives first, there is a contract. Why? Reasonable assumptions on the part of the offeror would lead the offeror to conclude that a contract is formed.[112] The law protects the reasonable conclusions drawn by the offeror. So if the rejection posted on day four really does take three days to arrive (receipt on day seven), the acceptance upon dispatch (mailbox rule) on day six supersedes and a contract is formed. However, if the rejection went by overnight mail and the acceptance e-mail was sent a day after that, there is no contract, as the rejection was received (and is effective upon receipt) before the acceptance was dispatched; the power of acceptance by the offeree ended upon receipt of the rejection by the offeror. Thus, the power of acceptance is a great thing (effective upon dispatch, not on receipt), but once surrendered it places the recalcitrant offeree at the mercy or good nature, as the case may be, of the offeror.

This is a different scenario from the one in which the acceptance is mailed first (a contract is formed) with a rejection phoned in later (a so-called repudiation, discussed later in this chapter), even if the sales rep receives or checks e-mail or voicemail messages before the postal mail arrives. Why does the acceptance rule trump all other efforts? Here the mailbox rule applies and a contract is formed even though the sales rep receives the rejection first. This prevents the offeree from speculating at the offeror's expense: "After mailing an acceptance of a revocable offer, the offeree is not permitted to speculate at the offeror's expense during the time required for the letter to arrive."[113] An example would be a price change. Offer is received on day one. Acceptance is given by post on day three. Librarian locates the same item at half the price on day four, at which time the acceptance has yet to arrive at the offeror's place of business. The librarian calls to reject the offer. The librarian is prevented from this sort of price shopping after committing to the acceptance. The moral is, do your homework first!

Of course, you might be thinking that much can go wrong even in the simplest of transactions. These examples are given for two reasons, neither of which is to scare or confuse readers. First, the examples demonstrate the concepts in familiar circumstances. Second, the reader will soon recognize that these sorts of disputes in reality often fail to materialize because the parties (sales representative and librarian) often can come to a reasonable reconciliation when the sale price is no longer available, the books do not arrive in time for the beginning of the semester, the cost of shipping rises, the librarian changes his mind, and so on—though these reconciliations themselves may constitute a series of negotiations, offers, or counteroffers.

These concepts can be at play in license agreements as well. Suppose the library receives a copy of the proposed license agreement from the vendor. The library crosses out all the "prohibited use" provisions and instead types in its place, "There are no prohibited uses. The authorized users may do whatever they wish with the licensed content," and sends it back with payment. Is this a contract? Of course it is not. Or in another not unheard-of scenario, is a handwritten note on a purchase order returned with payment from the library to the vendor stating that the purchased DVDs listed on the order all come with "public performance rights included" a contract? No, it is not. At best these are counteroffers; at worst, they are contracts with proposals for additional terms with which the licensor is likely not to agree! Suppose the library director signs the contract and sends it back with payment using the U.S. mail. Before the signed agreement is delivered to the vendor, the vendor calls to say the discount listed in the contract is too high; the discount per item has gone down. What is the result? The mailbox rules would indicate that acceptance was executed when mailed and a contract was formed, so the stated price discount must be honored by the vendor. Depending on circumstances, the mailbox rule for acceptance can favor the offeree-librarian/library.

REPUDIATION BY THE OFFEREE (AS OPPOSED TO REVOCATION OF THE OFFER BY THE OFFEROR)

Now suppose the librarian changes his mind and calls first thing the next morning to rescind or repudiate the acceptance he dropped in the mailbox the day before. This is different from sending both a rejection and an acceptance. Here the acceptance has been sent, but now the librarian would like to withdraw that acceptance. What is the result? The rules are much the same as when both rejection and acceptance are sent with the determination of effect turning on which communication is received first. Again, the predictable result regarding acceptance carries the day: a contract is formed when the acceptance arrives first and the subsequently arriving repudiation is not valid. If the repudiation arrives first (acceptance in the post, repudiation in overnight service), again the power of acceptance rules the day and the Restatement holds that a contract is formed: "The fact that the offeree has power to reclaim his acceptance from the post office or telegraph company does not prevent the acceptance from taking effect on dispatch. Nor, in the absence of additional circumstances, does the actual recapture of the acceptance deprive it of legal effect, though as a practical matter the offeror cannot assert his rights unless he learns of them."[114] The librarian cannot use the receipt/dispatch rules to his benefit. Suppose the librarian sent the acceptance on day three, but then, erroneously believing a better price could be had elsewhere, sends a repudiation by overnight service on day four, with it arriving on day five and the prior acceptance arriving on day six. However, if the offeror in good faith relies on the rejection and sells the remaining copies to another library, the librarian may be estopped from enforcing the contract the law might otherwise deem was formed according to the dispatch rule.[115]

CONSIDERATION

Assuming that it can be determined that a valid offer and acceptance are present, the third element for a valid contract is consideration. The requirement of consideration ensures that the parties are serious and not just testing each other or musing in regard to actions each might do. Suppose A says, "If I pay you $100, will you water my garden once a week this summer?" If A never pays B, B is not obligated to do anything, as there is no contract. A promise can be valid consideration (remember a promise for a promise and the concept of bilateral contracts). A bargained agreement is sufficient even if the promises are of unequal value. This disparity may impact defenses against contract formation, such as unconscionability, however (discussed in Chapter 4). Such disparity is an important issue in certain types of license agreements known as mass-market licenses where the consumer has no ability to bargain and the terms are rather one-sided, but more on that in Chapter 4. There are exceptions to the general "bargain as consideration" rule. Examples include nominal consideration ($1 for a used bookmobile worth $100,000), the surrender of an enforceable legal claim based on a reasonable good faith belief in its validity ("the plaintiff's alleged agreement to forbear from suing the defendants is insufficient consideration since the plaintiff cannot sustain a claim against the defendants for failure to pay on a usurious loan"[116]),[117] illusory promises[118] (e.g., a promise for a promise but where the offeror has the right to terminate at any time so there really is no promise[119]), or a promise to perform what one possesses a legal duty to perform anyway.[120] Significant exceptions exist for so-called donative promises (promises to make a gift) unless it is reasonable to expect that such promise would induce reliance and such reliance is made (promissory estoppel). The former is not enforceable; the latter is an enforceable promise.

Now, as a reader, you have the basics of modern contract law (offer-acceptance-consideration) along with a few nuances as well. Of course, there is far more detail, but at least this discussion forces you to begin thinking like the contract law does, which in later chapters is essential to understanding how licensing operates (or how it cannot operate) and the impact its operation can have in the library, archives, and related settings.

INTERPRETATION OF CONTRACTS AND THE CONCEPT OF PAROL EVIDENCE

Once the terms and conditions of the agreement are written down, or in an oral contract exchanged between the parties, the obvious question is how to determine what the terms mean. For example, a clause promising that a database systems vendor will provide "reasonable support" may mean during the workday and into the early evening, Monday through Saturday, to you, or perhaps 24/7 phone availability, but to the vendor it may mean 10 a.m. to 5 p.m., Monday through Thursday. This can be a big difference for a library on the West Coast or in Hawaii with a vendor based in New York City or Washington, DC. Moreover, in a license agreement, as in any contract, terms may have legal meaning, being defined by courts or statute to precise definition, such as a clause disclaiming an "implied warranty of merchantability,"[121] for example, or a provision requiring that the licensee execute a response under circumstances where "time is of the essence."[122] Generally, a trier of fact (the jury or the judge in a bench trial) applies a reasonable person test, which is an objective standard examining not whether the interpretation by the party raising the point is reasonable but whether a reasonable person in the place of the person with the knowledge of this person would conclude the same meaning. This can create obvious issues regarding interpretation. As a result, it is best to define as much as possible as well as possess awareness that legal terms of art may have meaning independent of what the standard dictionary meaning might suggest. In addition, performance of the current contract, past dealings, common practice if each party knew of it, and customary practice of the trade, if such practices exist, are all factors to consider in the interpretation of contract terms. For example, in *Random House, Inc. v. Rosetta Books, LLC,*[123] the appellate court observed that consideration by the district court of the standards and practices in the publishing industry in support of its refusal to enjoin the public distribution of books by the publisher in e-format was proper.

A major concept in the interpretation of written contracts is the parol evidence rule.[124] Often there may be other documentation, such as a prior contract, written note or other writing (like a brochure), or even recollections of verbal promises or recollections of conversations, that one party is claiming relates to how a term or condition should be interpreted.

> Numerous decisions state, in effect, that such evidence is excluded—not for any of the usual reasons requiring the exclusion of evidence, such as lack of probative value, materiality or relevancy, and not because of its untrustworthiness—but because, as a matter of substantive contract law, evidence regarding earlier words or conduct cannot be used to prove the parties' agreement where they have set forth their agreement in an unambiguous writing.[125]

For example, a clause in a vendor license indicating that the content is offered "as is" or that the content of the database is "subject to change without notice" may be at odds with what the librarian recalled the sales rep stating at last year's American Library Association midwinter convention, for example, that the title would remain in the database for at least three years. Suppose, then, that two months after the librarian enters into the license, the title is withdrawn from the database. Can the statements of the sales rep be used to interpret the content clause of the agreement so that the absence of the title is a breach of a promise to provide it for at least three years? The answer is no, as the agreement entered into by the vendor and the library stated the complete understanding of the parties, and the sales rep statement is not interpreted as an exception to the "as is" or "subject to change" clause. Courts will not rewrite the license to read "as is except for ABC title" or "subject to change except for XYZ title." This is an example of the parol evidence rule in operation.

The general rule is that parol evidence is not allowed to vary, add, or contradict a written contract. Parol evidence is not allowed when it is clear that a contract excludes such external evidence. This is often accomplished by a provision that states, in effect, "This agreement is all there is." In a technical sense, the clause indicates that any relevant information from other sources (e.g., prior version of the contract) has been rolled into the new agreement. This clause often includes a phrase to the effect that all prior agreements are superseded by the current version. As the intentions of both parties have been expressed in the present agreement, nothing else matters. This concept is known as integration.[126] Contracts often contain such merger or integration clauses, including database or other content license agreements. The majority rule holds that a merger clause is dispositive of integration while the newer minority rule is that it is just one factor to consider. The Restatement expresses this concept as complete or "completely integrated." As a result of the bringing together of the various parts into one new agreement, the clause is often known as an integration or merger clause.[127] Generally, evidence of a prior oral or contemporaneous agreement is not allowed.

There are exceptions to the rule, of course. Parol evidence may be allowed when it can show a lack of consideration, fraud, duress, or mistake.[128] All four scenarios serve as defenses in a sense to valid formation of a contract—in other words, situations where the contract will not be enforced. Parol evidence is also allowed if needed to demonstrate a condition precedent to the "legal" effectiveness of the contract (as opposed to a performance of a condition within the contract itself), to explain or interpret the contract (relating to the terms and conditions that are in fact in the agreement), or if the evidence relates to a modification of the contract (information that is relevant after integration occurred).

If separate consideration was rendered for the parol agreement, evidence of this other agreement can be allowed.[129] Parol evidence can also be allowed to address a naturally omitted term. In either case of separate consideration-agreement or naturally omitted term, the presumption is that neither is contradictory but instead complimentary to the agreement. Under the Restatement, if the term does not conflict with the agreement and the omission of the term appears natural ("such a term as in the circumstances might naturally be omitted from the writing"[130]), it will also be considered. "This situation is especially likely to arise when the writing is in a standardized form which does not lend itself to the insertion of additional terms."[131] The UCC has a liberal, "more parol-friendly,"[132] and "certainly would have been included" approach reflecting a similar theme of making under section 2-202.[133] An extension of this concept is a modern trend to entertain information that does not contradict the existing terms and conditions but which can be said to fill in gaps. "The determination whether a contract is integrated in the first instance can pose conceptual difficulty. The proof that a contract is not integrated may well depend on seemingly prohibited parol evidence. As with many of the issues associated with the application of the parol evidence rule, the question of integration and the admissibility of extrinsic evidence can, at least in theory, become maddeningly circular."[134] There are differences across the states and between state law and the interpretations offered by the UCC and its comments. Remember that parol evidence relates to contract interpretation, not to contract enforceability, the latter being a potential statute of frauds or other enforceability issues that are covered in the next chapter. For example, oral evidence cannot by definition cure a statute of frauds issue, but it can help interpret an ambiguous clause[135] in a license regarding vendor assistance and availability in a valid, enforceable license.

APPLICATION OF BASIC CONTRACT LAW PRINCIPLES: EXAMPLES FROM THE BOOK WORLD OF PUBLISHERS, LIBRARIES, AND EDUCATIONAL ENTITIES

So what does one make of the contract law and its application in the library setting? Does the potential for dispute appear remote and more the topic of law school professor hypotheticals—or in this instance, library school professors? I hope that the relationship between you, your library or its institution, and your vendors is open and peaceful. However, disputes do arise over sales, returns, and so forth, of library or school materials and can illustrate some of the concepts discussed in Chapter 2. Some of the cases included here are indeed old, and some involve library-related disputes such as book publishing or manuscript adoption deals gone sour, but, again, they can demonstrate that the law of contract applies equally to libraries, schools, and related entities and directly relates to the use of essential materials such as books and other associated media.

A recent case involved a contract dispute, among other issues, between a community college in Florida and Follett Corporation regarding the discounts offered in the purchase of new textbooks (at least 75 percent off the full sale price) and the returns of used textbooks (not less than 50 percent of the purchase price) to students in return for the exclusive rights to operate the campus bookstores. "The operation of these bookstores during the time period relevant to this case was governed by a single bookstore operating agreement ('Agreement') between DBCC [Daytona Beach Community College] and Follett."[136] Follett was rounding up return amounts and the college cried foul. Unfortunately, there was no specific language in the agreement dealing with the issue of the dollar round-up practice. Is this an issue of parol evidence or contract interpretation of an existing term? As explained by Follett executives in their depositions, "[A] common pricing procedure in the bookstore industry is to round up used textbook prices to the next higher chosen increment, i.e., $0.05, $0.10 or $0.25. Although there is no provision in the Agreement either permitting or prohibiting such rounding practices, it is common practice at the DBCC bookstores operated by Follett to round up the prices of used textbooks to the nearest $0.25 increment."[137] Lesson number one: if you are not sure, ask and get the clarification in writing, that is, in the contract. Otherwise, evidence of common practice in the industry will be used to assess the reasonableness of the interpretation of the contract. In this case, it was the students, not the college, suing over the discount practice. The plaintiffs were students, third parties to the contract. The facts demonstrate another principle of contract law: third parties such as students, library patrons, and so on, in general do not have the right to enforce the terms of a contract. As the court stated: "Florida recognizes a non-party's right to sue on a contract only where that party was an intended beneficiary of the contract; non-parties who receive merely an incidental or consequential benefit from a contract have no right to its enforcement."[138] The court concluded that the contract did not express such benefit.[139]

Disputes do, however, sometimes arise between the heavy hitters in the field and major state university systems. One such dispute involved Alabama State University and Baker & Taylor,[140] where the reported decision involved review of whether diversity jurisdiction was appropriate, with the vendor arguing that diversity jurisdiction (removal of the case to federal district court) was appropriate and the university arguing it was not.[141] Other disputes have involved, among others, agreements over book ownership between the founder and former dean of Delaware Law School (DLS) of Widener University and the university and its library,[142] reconsideration of a bookbinding contract bid for a public library,[143] delivery and payment of books to a free county library,[144] a handful of old cases between school districts or statewide school systems over textbook adoptions and other supply contracts,[145] and cases, some still older, involving sales of books to library corporations or societies.[146]

SUMMARY POINTS

▶ While both federal and state courts may hear cases involving contract disputes, including licensing contracts, the underlying law is essentially state law, often codified by adoption of the Uniform Commercial Code, though based on common principles. Consulting the law of the relevant jurisdiction is therefore crucial.

▶ Intent is an element of a valid offer. An offer cannot be made by accident. However, intent can be determined from conduct or the circumstances. In addition, the offer must be definite (in subject, quantity, and price) so that its recipient can make a decision to accept, reject, make a counteroffer, and so on.

▶ Invitations to bargain, for example, statements including questions, are not offers. Advertisements are generally not offers but invitations to make an offer (or submit an order), unless the advertisement is specific and relates to unique or singular items such as a reward for a lost item, a dealer seeking collectibles.

▶ Federal and state statutes both indicated that recipients of unsolicited merchandise are under no contractual obligation to pay for items so received and may treat the "solicitation" as a gift.

▶ If an educator requests a copy for review and the conditions of the review are made known (adopt, purchase, or return), then while the educator may have possession of the review copy he or she does not likely own that copy, with the result that the educator does not have first-sale rights in the copy of that book or other item, nor would a third party to whom the educator subsequently disposes of the book. Circumstances are important, as an unordered copy that turns up on the desk of educator with a note stating "for your review" is not a true review copy and can be treated as unsolicited merchandise.

▶ Offers can lapse. In other words, an offer must be accepted within a reasonable time, with reasonableness dependent upon the circumstances. A rejection closes the offer and ends the power to accept.

▶ A counteroffer is not an acceptance. A counteroffer terminates the power of acceptance.

▶ An acceptance can be accompanied by additional inquiry or terms, as distinct from a counteroffer or a conditional acceptance.

▶ As a general rule, a conditional acceptance operates as a termination of the power of the offeree to accept the offer, except where the offer is for a sale of goods.

▶ Under the UCC rule concerning contracts for goods, conditional acceptances with additional terms are not terminations but negotiable. Where the transaction is one between merchants, the terms become part of the contract, unless the offer states that additional terms are not allowed, the terms are material to the contract, or the offeree already rejected the terms.

▶ Under the interpretation of the UCC rule, a library (and certainly a university) can be considered a "merchant" of certain items, like library-dedicated furniture, for purposes of the conditional acceptance rule, with the terms becoming part of the contract unless the offer states that additional terms are not allowed, the terms are material to the contract, or the offeree already rejected the terms. However, it is also likely that terms relating to price and discount *are* material and would need to be negotiated.

▶ Revocation of the offer by the offeror is effective upon receipt, but acceptance by the offeree is effective upon dispatch (the mailbox rule).

▶ Acceptance is effective upon dispatch, not on receipt. Rejections are not good upon dispatch but upon receipt. If the rejection arrives first before an acceptance is made, no contract is formed. But where the rejection arrives first but was actually made after the offer was accepted (which is effective upon dispatch), the repudiation of the acceptance is not valid and a contract is deemed formed.

LEARNING EXAMPLES

▶ **Example 2.1**

Situation: A catalog or other advertisement arrives in the mail. A set of reference books is listed at a ridiculously low price and you suspect it is an error. Knowing that acceptance is good upon dispatch, you send off an e-mail immediately ordering two copies of the reference set. Is a contract formed? Can your e-mail bind the publisher?

Legal Analysis: Advertisements of this sort are not offers, which the librarian can then accept. Rather advertisements are invitations to bargain or to make an offer. For example, by calling or e-mailing the publisher and offering to order item #12345ABC listed on page 20 of the catalog at the ridiculously low price, the librarian is beginning the bargaining process. In a case of catalog error or misprint, the publisher will likely make a counteroffer for the reference set at the correct price.

▶ **Example 2.2**

Situation: Suppose the library receives a catalog or other advertisement perhaps via e-mail that offers an encyclopedia at a 25 percent discount for orders received before the end of the month, and states that this offer includes free online updates for one year. The ABC Library responds by sending a purchase order. After the item arrives at the library, the library sends the payment along with the accompanying invoice, and on the back of the invoice the acquisitions librarian types, "Can we also have free updates for an additional two years?" Is there a contract? If so, what are its terms?

Legal Analysis: The catalog information is not an offer but an invitation to enter into a later transaction. The purchase order submitted by the library is the offer, with the sending of the item and its invoice the acceptance. The payment is the consideration and a contract is formed. The inquiry for additional updates at no cost is not a counteroffer that terminates the power of acceptance; nor is it a conditional acceptance but an inquiry alone.

▶ **Example 2.3**

Situation: Suppose the same facts as in Example 2.2, but now the librarian types, "Acceptance is hereby conditional upon the agreement of the publisher to provide free updates for five years" on the return invoice. What is the result of the statement?

Legal Analysis: The conditional statement is an additional term. However, as the term is material, additional bargaining would have to occur before it could become part of the contract.

► Example 2.4

Situation: After several conversations regarding a retrospective fiche set, the publisher makes a final offer as to price that includes a set of cabinets to house the collection. The librarian tells the sales rep the she will get back to the publisher in a couple of days. The next day, the librarian sends an e-mail accepting the offer. The day after that, the librarian thinks better of it and calls the sales rep just as he is coming into the office in the morning, hoping to repudiate the acceptance before the rep checks his e-mail. Which is effective, the e-mail acceptance or the phone call repudiation?

Legal Analysis: The acceptance rule (valid upon dispatch) trumps the repudiation and a contract is formed. In reality, the sales representative may realize that it makes good customer relations to let the librarian renege in this fashion; it may also be the case that the publisher has a return policy.

► Example 2.5

Situation: Same initial facts as Example 2.4, except the librarian mails a letter of rejection, changes her mind, and two days later e-mails an acceptance. However the postal mail and other deliveries arrive before the e-mail is sent and so the rep sells the last copy in stock to someone else. Can the librarian insist the acceptance is valid and a contract be formed?

Legal Analysis: As the rejection was received first, the power to accept ended upon receipt of the rejection by the sales rep, and there is no contract upon the later phone call.

► Example 2.6

Situation: An educator receives the latest edition of a textbook. The item was unsolicited but includes a statement from the publisher: "For consideration, please accept this review copy. Please adopt or return to us, or keep it by paying the enclosed invoice." Is this statement enforceable?

Legal Analysis: Although this may be a "review copy," it is unordered merchandise and can under federal and most state law be treated as a gift. The instructor thus receives both a possessory as well as ownership interest in the review copy and may dispose of the book or other item so received as he or she sees fit.

► Example 2.7

Situation: The same note accompanies a copy of a book or other item received by the educator as in Example 2.6, except that the educator, hearing that a new edition of the current text was available, called the publisher beforehand to request a copy to review. The customer representative who took the phone call reiterated the terms under which items for review are sent out: for possible adoption, purchase, or return.

Legal Analysis: Under the circumstances the copy sent by the publisher to the educator is like a bailment (or the library loan of a collection item to patron). The recipient obtains possession of the item but not ownership over it. As library materials must be returned, so too must the review copy, unless, according to the terms of the bailment, the educator either adopts or purchases the book or other item. At purchase or adoption, ownership of the item would transfer to the educator. Without such ownership right, the educator does not have first-sale rights and under the relevant and analogous case law further public distribution, such as by sale to a used textbook jobber or by gift to the library, would infringe the copyright of the publisher or other copyright holder under section 106.

ENDNOTES

1. RAYMOND T. NIMMER, 2 INFORMATION LAW § 11.2 (updated in Westlaw, November 2011): "Creating an enforceable contract requires only an offer and acceptance and sufficient consideration to render that agreement enforceable. The consideration can come from a variety of sources, not just from property rights."
2. See ALI Overview (2012), http://www.ali.org/index.cfm?fuseaction=about.creation.
3. "Restatements are highly regarded distillations of common law. They are prepared by the American Law Institute (ALI), a prestigious organization comprising judges, professors, and lawyers. The ALI's aim is to distill the "black letter law" from cases to indicate trends in common law and occasionally to recommend what a rule of law should be. In essence, they restate existing common law into a series of principles or rules." Secondary Sources: ALRs, Encyclopedias, Law Reviews, Restatements, & Treatises (Intro to Restatements), found at http://libguides.law.harvard.edu/content.php?pid=103327&sid=1036651.
4. "The Uniform Law Commission (ULC, also known as the National Conference of Commissioners on Uniform State Laws), established in 1892, provides states with non-partisan, well-conceived and well-drafted legislation that brings clarity and stability to critical areas of state statutory law. ULC members must be lawyers, qualified to practice law. They are practicing lawyers, judges, legislators and legislative staff and law professors, who have been appointed by state governments as well as the District of Columbia, Puerto Rico and the U.S. Virgin Islands to research, draft and promote enactment of uniform state laws in areas of state law where uniformity is desirable and practical." About the ULC (About Us), found at http://www.nccusl.org/Narrative.aspx?title=About%20the%20ULC.
5. Respect Inc. v. Committee on Status of Women, 781 F. Supp. 1358, 1363–1364 (N.D. Ill. 1992) (citations omitted).

6. On August 11, 2003, the NCCUSL disbanded its UCITA standing committee, effectively ending active attempts to pass the model act on a state-by-state basis. See also http://nccusl.org/Act.aspx?title=Computer%20Information%20Transactions%20Act.

7. See Electronic Transactions Act, http://uniformlaws.org/Act.aspx?title=Electronic %20Transactions%20Act.

8. Many of the topics covered in this chapter are likely found in any basic text on contract law. A number of the topics discussed in this chapter are outlined in MELVIN ARON EISENBERG, GILBERT LAW SUMMARIES: CONTRACTS (14th ed.) (Chicago: Gilbert Law Summaries, 2002).

9. Nimmer, *supra* note 1, at § 12.35.

10. Restatement (Second) of Contracts § 26 (1981) (Preliminary Negotiations), Illustration 2: "A advertises that he will pay $5 for every copy of a certain book that may be sent to him. This is an offer, and A is bound to pay $5 for every copy sent while the offer is unrevoked."

11. See, for example, Pierson v. Morch, 37 Sickels 503, 1880 WL 12594 (N.Y. 1880): "The publication of an advertisement offering a reward for information respecting a loss, or the return of lost property, is a general offer, and the acceptance of it by any person who is able to give the information asked, or to return the property, creates a valid contract."

12. RICHARD A. LORD, 2 WILLISTON ON CONTRACTS § 6:55 (4th ed. 2008, database updated in Westlaw, May 2012), from a section titled Silence as Acceptance of Offered Terms—Acceptance by Taking or Retaining Property; Acts Inconsistent with Offeror's Ownership (footnote to relevant Restatement and UCC sections omitted).

13. 39 U.SC. § 3009(a) (2006). There are exceptions "for (1) free samples clearly and conspicuously marked as such, and (2) merchandise mailed by a charitable organization soliciting contributions." See also Validity, Construction, and Application of 39 U.S.C. § 3009, Making It an Unfair Trade Practice to Mail Unordered Merchandise, 39 A.L.R. Fed. 674 (originally published in 1978).

14. 39 U.SC. § 3009(d) (2006) defining "unordered merchandise" as "merchandise mailed without the prior expressed request or consent of the recipient."

15. 39 U.SC. § 3009(c) (2006).

16. 39 U.SC. § 3009(b) (2006).

17. *Id.*: "All such merchandise shall have attached to it a clear and conspicuous statement informing the recipient that he may treat the merchandise as a gift to him and has the right to retain, use, discard, or dispose of it in any manner he sees fit without any obligation whatsoever to the sender."

18. Marshall v. Little Professor Book Center, Inc., 1992 WL 309627 (E.D. Pa. 1992) (unpublished).

19. *Id.* at *1.

20. *Id.* at *3, citations to 39 U.SC. § 3009 and Kipperman v. Academy Life Insurance Co., 554 F.2d 377 (9th Cir. 1977) omitted.

21. UMG Recordings, Inc. v. Augusto, 628 F.3d 1175 (9th Cir. 2011).

22. *Id.* at 1177.

23. 17 U.S.C. § 109(a) (2006): "the owner of a particular copy or phonorecord lawfully made under this title, or any person authorized by such owner, is entitled, without the authority of the copyright owner, to sell or otherwise dispose of the possession of that copy or phonorecord."

24. 17 U.S.C. § 109(b) (2006): "unless authorized by the owners of copyright in the sound recording or the owner of copyright in a computer program (including any tape, disk, or other medium embodying such program), and in the case of a sound recording in the musical works embodied therein, neither the owner of a particular phonorecord nor any person in possession of a particular copy of a computer program (including any tape, disk, or other medium embodying such program), may, for the purposes of direct or indirect commercial advantage, dispose of, or authorize the disposal of, the possession of that phonorecord or computer program (including any tape, disk, or other medium embodying such program) by rental, lease, or lending, or by any other act or practice in the nature of rental, lease, or lending."

25. UMG Recordings, Inc. v. Augusto, 628 F3d 1175, 1177 (9th Cir. 2011).

26. *Id.* at 1177–1178.

27. *Id.* at 1178.

28. *Id.* at 1179: "In the alternative, Augusto argues that the original recipients were entitled to treat the CDs as gifts under the Unordered Merchandise Statute, enacted as part of the Postal Reorganization Act of 1970, and therefore had 'the right to retain, use, discard, or dispose of [them] in any manner [they saw] fit,' in this case, by selling those CDs to the thrift shops and second-hand stores where Augusto states he purchased them."

29. *Id.* at 1180.

30. *Id.* at 1180: "We also hold that, because the CDs were unordered merchandise, the recipients were free to dispose of them as they saw fit under the Unordered Merchandise Statute..."

31. *Id.* at 1182: "It is one thing to say, as the statement does, that 'acceptance' of the CD constitutes an agreement to a license and its restrictions, but it is quite another to maintain that 'acceptance' may be assumed when the recipient makes no response at all. This record reflects no responses... Because the record here is devoid of any indication that the recipients agreed to a license, there is no evidence to support a conclusion that licenses were established under the terms of the promotional statement. Accordingly, we conclude that UMG's transfer of possession to the recipients, without meaningful control or even knowledge of the status of the CDs after shipment, accomplished a transfer of title."

32. *Id.* at 1183.

33. See 17 U.S.C. § 110(1) (2006): "Notwithstanding the provisions of section 106, the following are not infringements of copyright: performance or display of a work by instructors or pupils in the course of face-to-face teaching activities of a nonprofit educational institution, in a classroom or similar place devoted to instruction, unless, in the case of

a *motion picture or other audiovisual work,* the performance, or the *display of individual images,* is given by means of a copy that was not lawfully made under this title, and that the *person responsible for the performance knew or had reason to believe was not lawfully made.*"

34. See 17 U.S.C. § 110(4) (2006): "performance of a nondramatic literary or musical work otherwise than in a transmission to the public, without any purpose of direct or indirect commercial advantage and without payment of any fee or other compensation for the performance to any of its performers, promoters, or organizers." There is no performance right in a sound recording unless by means of a "digital audio transmission," per 17 U.S.C. § 106(6) (2006). See also In re Cellco Partnership, 663 F. Supp. 2d 363, 375 (S.D.N.Y. 2009): "The playing of a ringtone by any Verizon customers in public is thus exempt under 17 U.S.C. § 110(4) and does not require them to obtain a public performance license."

35. Blakemore v. Superior Court, 27 Cal. Rptr. 3d 877, 881 (Cal. App. 2005): "The crux of their complaint is that Avon engages in a practice they characterize as 'channel stuffing,' in which Avon forces or 'stuffs' products onto its sales representatives— Avon's 'channels of distribution'—by deliberately shipping them products they did not order, or products far in excess of the quantities they ordered. When the sales representatives return the unordered products for credit, Avon refuses to grant the credit, in violation of its own return policy."

36. *Id.* at 888.

37. *Id.*

38. In re Commercial Lighting Products, Inc., 95 F.T.C. 750, *4 (1980): "For purposes of this order the following definitions shall be applicable: 'Person' shall mean a recipient of Products from the Respondent or the recipient of any telephonic, written or other type of communication from Respondent in connection with the advertising, offering for sale or sale of products, as defined. *Provided, however,* that Person shall not mean a natural person, business establishment or institution which does not purchase said Products for consumption (i.e., independent jobbers or wholesalers)."

39. Blakemore v. Superior Court, 27 Cal. Rptr. 3d 877, 890 (Cal. App. 2005).

40. *Id.* at note 16: "The small businesses are plainly the consumers of the products in question."

41. In re Commercial Lighting Products, Inc., 95 F.T.C. 750, *1 (1980): "Persons who do not pay for light bulbs or other products will have their alleged delinquent accounts referred to an attorney, debt collection company, credit bureau, or credit reporting agency. Respondent will adversely affect the credit rating or persons with alleged delinquent accounts. Failure to accept delivery of respondent's products will result in the persons being liable for storage charges or other charges assessed by common carriers attempting to deliver such products." The FTC concluded that such acts were and are deceptive trade practices.

42. Alabama (Ala. Code § 35-1-3: "Unless otherwise agreed, where unsolicited goods are delivered by mail or common carrier to a person, he has a right to refuse to accept

delivery of the goods and is not bound to return such goods to the sender. If such unsolicited goods are addressed to or intended for the recipient, they shall be deemed a gift to the recipient, who may use them or dispose of them in any manner without any obligation to the sender"); Alaska (Alaska Stat. § 45.45.105: "(a) A person may not offer merchandise for sale, in any manner, when the offer includes the voluntary and unsolicited sending of merchandise not actually ordered or requested by the recipient, either orally or in writing. (b) Unsolicited merchandise received shall be considered an unconditional gift to the recipient who may use or dispose of it in any manner the recipient sees fit without obligation to the sender"); Arizona (Ariz. Rev. Stat. § 44-1222(A): "If unsolicited goods are delivered by mail or common carrier to a person, such person may refuse to accept delivery of the goods and shall not be bound to return such goods to the sender. If such unsolicited goods are addressed to and intended for the recipient, they shall be deemed a gift to the recipient, who may use the goods or dispose of them in any manner without any obligation to the sender); Arkansas (A. C. A. § 4-86-103: "When unsolicited merchandise is delivered in this state to the person for whom it is intended, the person shall have a right to refuse to accept delivery of this merchandise, or may deem the merchandise to be a gift and use it or dispose of it in any manner he or she chooses without obligation to the sender"); California (Cal. Civ. Code § 1584.5: "No person, firm, partnership, association, or corporation, or agent or employee thereof, shall, in any manner, or by any means, offer for sale goods, wares, merchandise, or services, where the offer includes the voluntary and unsolicited sending or providing of goods, wares, merchandise, or services not actually ordered or requested by the recipient, either orally or in writing. The receipt of any goods, wares, merchandise, or services shall for all purposes be deemed an unconditional gift to the recipient who may use or dispose of the goods, wares, merchandise, or services in any manner he or she sees fit without any obligation on his or her part to the sender or provider"); Connecticut (Conn. Gen. Stat. § 42-126b(a): "No person, firm, partnership, association or corporation, or agent or employee thereof, shall, in any manner, or by any means, offer for sale goods, wares or merchandise, where the offer includes the voluntary and unsolicited sending of goods, wares or merchandise not actually ordered or requested by the recipient, either orally or in writing. The receipt of any such unsolicited goods, wares or merchandise shall for all purposes be deemed an unconditional gift to the recipient who may use or dispose of the same in any manner such recipient sees fit without any obligation on such recipient's part to the sender"); Delaware (Del. Code. Ann. Tit. 6, § 2505: "Where unsolicited merchandise is delivered to a person for whom it is intended such person has a right to refuse to accept delivery of this merchandise or such person may deem it to be a gift and use it or dispose of it in any manner without any obligation to the sender"); Florida (Fla. Stat. Ann. § 570.545: "When unsolicited goods are delivered to a person, the person may refuse delivery of the goods, or, if the goods are delivered, the person is not obligated to return the goods to the sender. If unsolicited goods are either addressed to or intended for the recipient, they shall be deemed a gift and the recipient may use or dispose of them in any manner without obligation to the sender"); Georgia (Ga. Code Ann., § 10-1-50: "No person, firm, partnership, association, or corporation, or agent or employee thereof, shall, in any manner or by any means, offer for sale goods, wares, or merchandise where the offer includes the voluntary and unsolicited sending of such goods, wares, or merchandise not actually ordered or requested by the recipient, either orally or in writing. The receipt of any such goods, wares, or merchandise shall for all purposes be deemed an unconditional gift to the recipient, who may use or dispose of such goods, wares, or merchandise, unless such goods, wares, or merchandise were delivered to recipient as a result of a bona fide mistake, in any manner he sees fit without any obligation on his part to the sender"); Hawaii (Haw. Rev. Stat. § 481B-1: "No person, firm, partnership, association, or corporation, or agent or employee thereof, shall, in any manner, or by any means, offer for sale goods, property, or merchandise, where the offer includes the voluntary and unsolicited sending of goods, property, or merchandise not actually ordered or requested by the recipient, either orally or in writing. The receipt of any such unsolicited goods, property, or merchandise shall for all purposes be deemed an unconditional gift to the recipient who may use or dispose of the same in any manner the recipient sees fit without any obligation on the recipient's part to the sender"); Idaho (I. C. § 28-2-329: "No person, firm, partnership, association or corporation, or agent or employee thereof, shall, in any manner, or by any means, offer for sale goods, wares, or merchandise, where the offer includes the voluntary and unsolicited sending of goods, wares, or merchandise not actually ordered or requested by the recipient, either orally or in writing. The receipt of any such unsolicited goods, wares, or merchandise shall for all purposes be deemed an unconditional gift to the recipient who may use or dispose of the same in any manner he sees fit without any obligation on his part to the sender"); Iowa (I. C. A. § 556A.1: "Unless otherwise agreed, where unsolicited goods are mailed to a person, that person has a right to accept delivery of such goods as a gift only, and is not bound to return such goods to the sender. If such unsolicited goods are either addressed to or intended for the recipient, the recipient may use them or dispose of them in any manner without any obligation to the sender, and in any action for goods sold and delivered, or in any action for the return of the goods, it shall be a complete defense that the goods were mailed voluntarily and that the defendant did not actually order or request such goods, either orally or in writing"); Kansas (K.S.A. 50-617: "(a) Whenever any supplier shall, in any manner, or by any means, deliver property or services not affirmatively ordered or requested by the recipient, the receipt of any such unordered property or services shall for all purposes be deemed an unconditional gift to the recipient who may use or dispose of the same in any manner the recipient sees fit without any obligation on the recipient's part to the supplier. Property or services are considered to be unordered unless the recipient specifically requested, in an affirmative manner, the receipt of the property or services according to the terms under which they are being offered"); Kentucky (Ky. Rev. Stat. Ann. § 365.710(1): "Where unsolicited goods are delivered to a person, he has a right to refuse to accept delivery of the goods and is not bound to return such goods to the sender. Such unsolicited goods shall be deemed a gift to the recipient, who may use them or dispose of them in any manner without any obligation"); Louisiana (LSA-R.S. 51:461: "A. No person, firm, partnership, association or corporation shall offer for sale in any manner any goods, wares or merchandise if the offer includes the voluntary and unsolicited sending of such goods, wares or merchandise not ordered or requested by the recipient, either orally or in writing. All such goods, wares or merchandise shall be deemed to be an unconditional gift to the recipient, and he may use or dispose of such goods, wares or merchandise in any manner he sees fit without any obligation to the sender"); Maine (Me. Rev. Stat. Ann. Tit. 33, § 1101: "Where unsolicited merchandise is delivered to a person for whom it is intended, such person has a right to refuse to accept delivery of this merchandise or he may deem it to be a gift and use it or dispose of it in any manner without any obligation to the sender"); Maryland (Md. Code Ann., Commercial Law § 14-1304(a): "(1) A person may not offer any merchandise for sale in any manner or by any means if the offer includes the voluntary and unsolicited sending of merchandise not actually ordered or requested by the recipient orally or in writing. (2) If a person receives any merchandise offered for sale in violation of this subsection, it is an unconditional gift to him for all purposes. He may use or dispose of the merchandise in any manner without any obligation on his part to the sender"); Massachusetts (Mass. Gen. Laws Ann. ch. 93, § 43: "Any person who receives unsolicited goods, wares or merchandise, offered for sale, but not actually ordered or requested by him orally or in writing, shall be entitled to consider such goods, wares or merchandise an unconditional gift, and he may use or dispose of the same as he sees fit without obligation on his part to the sender"); Michigan (Mich. Comp. Laws Ann. 445.131: "Sec. 1. No person, firm, partnership, association or corporation, or agent or employee thereof, in any manner, or by any means, shall offer for sale goods where the offer includes the voluntary and unsolicited sending of goods by mail or otherwise not actually ordered or requested by the recipient, either orally or in writing. The receipt of any such unsolicited goods shall be deemed for all purposes an unconditional gift to the recipient. The recipient may refuse to accept delivery of the goods, is not bound to return them to the sender, and may use or dispose of them in any manner he sees fit without any obligation on his part to the sender"); Mississippi (Miss. Code Ann. § 75-65-101: "No person, firm, partnership, association or corporation, or agent or employee thereof, shall in any manner or by any means offer for sale goods, wares or merchandise where the offer includes the voluntary and unsolicited sending of goods, wares or merchandise not actually ordered or requested by the recipient, either orally or in writing. The receipt of any such unsolicited goods, wares or merchandise shall for all purposes be deemed an unconditional gift to the recipient who may use or dispose of the same in any manner he sees fit without any obligation on his part to the sender"); Missouri (Mo.

Ann. Stat. § 407.200: "Where unsolicited merchandise is delivered to a person for whom it is intended, such person has a right to refuse to accept delivery of this merchandise or he may deem it to be a gift and use it or dispose of it in any manner without any obligation to the sender. Where unsolicited merchandise is delivered to a person for whom it is intended, such person has a right to refuse to accept delivery of this merchandise or he may deem it to be a gift and use it or dispose of it in any manner without any obligation to the sender"); Montana (Mont. Code Ann. § 70-3-104: "Unless otherwise agreed, where unsolicited goods are delivered to a person, he may refuse delivery of the goods, or if the goods are delivered, the person is not bound to return the goods to the sender. If unsolicited goods are either addressed to or intended for the recipient, they shall be deemed a gift, and the recipient may use or dispose of them in any manner without obligation to the sender"); Nebraska (Neb. Rev. Stat. § 69-2201: "Unless otherwise agreed, where unsolicited goods or merchandise are sent through the mail to a person, he has a right to refuse to accept delivery of the goods or merchandise and is not bound to return such goods or merchandise to the sender. If such unsolicited goods or merchandise are either addressed to or intended for the recipient, they shall be deemed a gift to the recipient who may use them or dispose of them in any manner without any obligations to the sender"); Nevada (Nev. Rev. Stat. § 597.950(1): "Any person who receives unsolicited goods, wares or merchandise offered for sale, but not actually ordered or requested by him orally or in writing, is entitled to consider those goods, wares or merchandise an unconditional gift, and he may use or dispose of them as he sees fit without obligation on his part to the sender"); New Jersey (N.J. Stat. Ann. § 46:30A-1: "No person, firm, partnership, association or corporation, or agent or employee thereof, shall, in any manner, or by any means, offer for sale goods, wares or merchandise, where the offer includes the voluntary and unsolicited sending of goods, wares or merchandise not actually ordered or requested by the recipient, either orally or in writing. The receipt of any such unsolicited goods, wares or merchandise shall for all purposes be deemed an unconditional gift to the recipient who may use or dispose of the same in any manner he sees fit without any obligation on his part to the sender and no civil action may be instituted for the recovery of the value of such goods, wares or merchandise or for their return"); New York (N.Y. General Obligations Law § 5-332(1): "No person, firm, partnership, association or corporation, or agent or employee thereof, shall, in any manner, or by any means, offer for sale goods, wares, or merchandise, where the offer includes the voluntary and unsolicited sending of such goods, wares, or merchandise not actually ordered or requested by the recipient, either orally or in writing. The receipt of any such goods, wares, or merchandise shall for all purposes be deemed an unconditional gift to the recipient who may use or dispose of such goods, wares, or merchandise in any manner he sees fit without any obligation on his part to the sender"); North Carolina (N.C. Gen. Stat. Ann. § 75-27: "Unless otherwise agreed, where unsolicited goods are delivered to a person, he has a right to refuse to accept delivery of the goods and is not bound to return such goods to the sender. If such unsolicited goods are addressed to and intended for the recipient, they shall be deemed a gift to the recipient, who may use them or dispose of them in any manner without any obligation to the sender"); Ohio (Ohio Rev. Code Ann. § 1333.60: "Where any merchandise is offered for sale by means of its voluntary delivery to an offeree who has neither ordered nor requested it, the delivery of such merchandise constitutes an unconditional gift to the recipient"); Oklahoma (15 Okl. Stat. Ann. Tit. 15, § 721: "No person, firm, partnership, association or corporation, or agent or employee thereof, shall, in any manner, or by any means, offer for sale in this state, goods, wares, or merchandise, where the offer includes the voluntary and unsolicited sending of such goods, wares, or merchandise not actually ordered or requested by the recipient, either orally or in writing. The receipt of any such goods, wares, or merchandise shall for all purposes be deemed an unconditional gift to the recipient who may use or dispose of such goods, wares, or merchandise in any manner he sees fit without any obligation on his part to the sender. Provided, however, that where solicited goods, wares, or merchandise are delivered to the wrong person by accident or by the mistake of the delivery or mail service, such delivery shall not constitute an offer subject to this act, and provided that the provisions of this act shall not apply to goods of equal or greater value and at no additional cost, substituted for goods ordered or solicited by the recipient"); Pennsylvania (73 Pa. Cons. Stat. Ann § 2001: "Unless otherwise agreed between the sender and the recipient of the goods prior to delivery, where unsolicited goods are delivered to a person, he has a right to refuse to accept delivery of the goods and is not bound to return such goods to the sender. If such unsolicited goods are sent by mail to and intended for the recipient, they shall be deemed a gift to the recipient, who may use them or dispose of them in any manner without any obligation to the sender"); Rhode Island (R. I. Gen. Laws § 6-13-10: "The receipt of unsolicited goods, wares, or merchandise through the mail or otherwise shall for all purposes be deemed an unconditional gift to the recipient who may use or dispose of the unsolicited goods, wares, or merchandise in any manner he or she sees fit without any obligation on his or her part to the sender." R. I. Gen. Laws § 6-33-1: "If unsolicited goods or merchandise of any kind are either addressed to or intended for the recipient, the goods or merchandise shall, unless otherwise agreed, be deemed a gift to the recipient who may use them or dispose of them in any manner without any obligation to the sender"); South Carolina (S. C. Code Ann. § 39-1-50: "Any unsolicited merchandise, except stolen merchandise, received through the mails, shall be deemed an absolute gift and the addressee-recipient may retain and use such merchandise without any liability for payment. The provisions of this section shall not apply to ordered merchandise deemed unsatisfactory by the addressee-recipient for any reason or to merchandise received by him by mistake or misdelivery"); South Dakota (S. D. Codified Laws § 37-24-2: "Unless otherwise agreed, if unordered merchandise is delivered in person or by mail or common carrier to a person, he has a right to refuse such merchandise and is not obligated to return such merchandise to the sender. Such unordered merchandise shall be deemed an unconditional gift to the recipient, who may use it in any manner without any obligation to the sender. This section does not apply if there is evidence of an obvious misdelivery, or the merchandise is offered in good faith in substitution for merchandise ordered"); Texas (Tex. Bus. & Com. Code Ann. § 35.45: "(a) Unless otherwise agreed, if unsolicited goods are delivered to a person, the person: (1) is entitled to refuse to accept delivery of the goods; and (2) is not required to return the goods to the sender. (b) If unsolicited goods are either addressed to or intended for the recipient, the goods are considered a gift to the recipient, who may use them or dispose of them in any manner without obligation to the sender." Tex. Bus. & Com. Code Ann. § 602.003: "(a) Unsolicited goods that are addressed to or intended for the recipient are considered a gift to the recipient. (b) The recipient may use or dispose of goods described by Subsection (a) in any manner without obligation to the sender"); Virginia (Va. Code Ann. § 11-2.2: "If any person, firm, partnership, association or corporation, or any agent or employee thereof, shall in any manner or by any means offer for sale goods, wares or merchandise when the offer includes the voluntary and unsolicited sending of any goods, wares or merchandise not actually ordered or requested by the recipient, either orally or in writing, then the sender of any such unsolicited goods, wares or merchandise shall for all purposes be deemed to have made an unconditional gift to the recipient thereof, who may use or dispose of such goods, wares or merchandise in any manner he deems proper without any obligation to return the same to the sender or to pay him therefor"); Washington (Wash. Rev. Code Ann. § 19.56.020: "If unsolicited goods or services are provided to a person, the person has a right to accept the goods or services as a gift only, and is not bound to return the goods or services. Goods or services are not considered to have been solicited unless the recipient specifically requested, in an affirmative manner, the receipt of the goods or services according to the terms under which they are being offered. Goods or services are not considered to have been requested if a person fails to respond to an invitation to purchase the goods or services and the goods or services are provided notwithstanding. If the unsolicited goods or services are either addressed to or intended for the recipient, the recipient may use them or dispose of them in any manner without any obligation to the provider, and in any action for goods or services sold and delivered, or in any action for the return of the goods, it is a complete defense that the goods or services were provided voluntarily and that the defendant did not affirmatively order or request the goods or services, either orally or in writing"); West Virginia (W. Va. Code Ann. § 47-11A-12a: "No person, firm, partnership, association or corporation, or agent or employee thereof, shall, in any manner, or by any means, offer for sale goods, wares or merchandise, where the offer includes the voluntary and unsolicited sending of goods, wares or merchandise not actually ordered or requested by the recipient, either orally or in writing. The receipt of any such unsolicited goods, wares or merchandise shall for all purposes be deemed an unconditional gift to the recipient who may use or dispose of the same in any manner he sees fit without any obligation on his part to the sender"); Wisconsin (Wis. Stat. § 241.28: "If unsolicited goods or merchandise of any kind are either addressed to or intended for the recipient, the goods or merchandise shall, unless otherwise agreed, be deemed a gift to the recipient who may use them or dispose of them in any manner without any obligation to the sender"); and Wyoming (Wyo. Stat. Ann. § 40-12-103: "Unless otherwise agreed, when unsolicited merchandise is delivered to a person, he has a right to refuse such merchandise and is not obligated to return such merchandise to the sender. Such unsolicited merchandise is deemed an unconditional gift to the recipient, who may use it in any manner without any obligation to the sender. This section does not apply if there is evidence that the merchandise has been misdelivered, or if the delivered merchandise is offered as a good faith substitution for merchandise previously solicited by the recipient").

43. *Dun* means "to demand payment from a delinquent debtor"; see BLACK'S LAW DICTIONARY 502 (9th ed.) (Bryan A. Garner ed., St. Paul, MN: West Publishing, 2009). "Debt-collection letters, therefore, are frequently referred to as 'dunning letters'" (Owens v. Hellmuth & Johnson, PLLC, 550 F. Supp. 2d 1060, 1063, at note 1 [D. Minn. 2008]).

44. California (Cal. Civ. Code § 1584.5: "If, after any receipt deemed to be an unconditional gift under this section, the sender or provider continues to send bill statements or requests for payment with respect to the gift, an action may be brought by the recipient to enjoin the conduct, in which action there may also be awarded reasonable attorney's fees and costs to the prevailing party"); Georgia (Ga. Code Ann., § 10-1-50: "If, after any such receipt deemed to be an unconditional gift under this Code section, the sender continues to send bill statements or requests for payment with respect thereto, an action may be brought by the recipient to enjoin such conduct, in which action there may also be awarded reasonable attorneys' fees and costs to the prevailing party"); Louisiana (LSA-R.S. 51:461: "B. If the sender of such goods, wares or merchandise continues to send bill statements or requests for payment therefor, the recipient may institute proceedings to enjoin such action. In addition, the sender may be liable for reasonable attorney fees and the costs of court"); Maryland (Md. Code Ann., Commercial Law § 14-1304(c): "After the receipt of any merchandise considered to be an unconditional gift under this section, if the sender continues to send any bill, statement of account, or request for payment with respect to the merchandise, the recipient may bring an action to enjoin the sender's conduct. In that action, the court may award reasonable attorney's fees and costs to the prevailing party"); New York (N. Y. General Obligations Law § 5-332(1): "If after any such receipt deemed to be an unconditional gift under this section, the sender continues to send bill statements or requests for payment with respect thereto, an action may be brought by the recipient to enjoin such conduct, in which action there may also be awarded reasonable attorney's fees and costs to the prevailing party"); and Oklahoma (15 Okl. Stat. Ann. Tit. 15, § 721: "If after any such receipt deemed to be an unconditional gift under this section, the sender continues to send bill statements or requests for payment with respect thereto,

an action may be brought by the recipient to enjoin such conduct, in which action there may also be awarded reasonable attorneys' fees and costs to the prevailing party").

45. 39 U.SC. § 3009(c): "No mailer of any merchandise mailed in violation of subsection (a) of this section, or within the exceptions contained therein, shall mail to any recipient of such merchandise a bill for such merchandise or any dunning communications."

46. Wisniewski v. Rodale Inc., 510 F.3d 294, 307 (3d Cir. 2007) (internal quotation and citation omitted), cert. denied, 129 S.Ct. 47 (2008).

47. Kipperman v. Academy Life Insurance Co., 554 F.2d 377, 380 (9th Cir. 1977): "However, subjecting it to national law is within the power of Congress and the limited private right we recognize will further the purposes Congress sought to serve by enacting the section." And ultimately concluding that, "such an unaccepted offer to insure is not merchandise in the meaning of 39 U.SC. § 3009 and therefore does not result in free insurance coverage for the recipients of Academy Life's solicitation" (*id.* at 381).

48. Wisniewski v. Rodale Inc., 510 F.3d 294, 308 (3d Cir. 2007) (reference to Supreme Court decisions omitted), cert. denied, 129 S.Ct. 47 (2008).

49. Hutch v. Charter Communications, Inc., 2008 WL 1721868, *1 (Mo. App. 2008) (unpublished). They alleged that they did not request Charter's "Paper Guide," also known as the "Channel Guide Magazine" (the Guide); that Charter did not inform plaintiffs that it would charge them for the Guide; that the cost of the Guide was not included as part of their monthly cable channels or services; that the Guide "has been appearing as a separate line item" on their monthly bills; and that Charter "charged plaintiffs $2.99 or $3.24 per month for the Guide."

50. "The voluntary payment doctrine is the name given to 'the universally recognized rule that money voluntarily paid under a claim of right to the payment, and with knowledge of the facts by the person making the payment cannot be recovered back on the ground that the claim was illegal, or that there was no liability to pay in the first instance.'" Hutch v. Charter Communications, Inc., 2008 WL 1721868, *4 (Mo. App. 2008) (unpublished), citing, American Motorists Ins. Co. v. Shrock, 447 S.W.2d 809, 811–812 (Mo. App. 1969), quoting 40 AMERICAN JURISPRUDENCE § 157 (Payment), at 820, 821.

51. Hutch v. Charter Communications, Inc., 2008 WL 1721868, *7 (Mo. App. 2008) (unpublished).

52. Wehringer v. West Publishing Co., 387 N.Y.S. 2d 806, 807 (1976).

53. *Id.*

54. *Id.*

55. Eric Goldman, *Top 5 Cyberlaw Developments of 2010, Plus a 2010 Year-in-Review,* CYBERSPACE LAWYER, March 2011. See also Richard F. Blake, *Overview of Educational Textbook Publishing,* in LEGAL AND BUSINESS ASPECTS OF BOOK PUBLISHING 425 (1986) (Practising Law Institute Patents, Copyrights, Trademarks, and Literary Property Course Handbook Series, 222 PLI/Pat 425, PLI Order No. G4-3785): "Mailing review copies to thousands of professors . . . a large number of review copies end up on bookstore shelves . . . books

are purchased by the college bookstore directly from professors and placed on the shelf. It is becoming common, however, for middlemen to buy up review copies from a number of professors and resell them to bookstores in large quantities. This practice has prompted publishers to stamp or imprint the covers of examination copies with various legends, usually to the effect that the books are not for resale. Although this has made it more difficult to sell review copies as new books, it has not significantly reduced the number of copies being bought and resold. Since the books are sent out unsolicited, it is *very doubtful that the publisher has any legal right to restrict their resale, notwithstanding any statements to the contrary stamped on the books*" (*id.* at 445, emphasis added).

56. Vernor v. Autodesk, Inc., 621 F.3d 1102, 1107 (9th Cir. 2010), citing section 109 (d), cert. denied 132 S.Ct. 105 (Oct. 3, 2011): "The privileges prescribed by subsections (a) and (c) do not, unless authorized by the copyright owner, extend to any person who has acquired possession of the copy or phonorecord from the copyright owner, by rental, lease, loan, or otherwise, without acquiring ownership of it." See also Quality King Distributors, Inc. v. L'anza Research International, Inc., 523 U.S. 134, 146–147: "[B]ecause the protection afforded by § 109(a) is available only to the 'owner' of a lawfully made copy..., the first sale doctrine would not provide a defense to...any nonowner such as a bailee, a licensee, a consignee, or one whose possession of the copy was unlawful."

57. 17 U.S.C. § 109(d).

58. Apple Inc. v. Paystar Corp., 658 F.3d 1150, 1156 (9th Cir. 2011), citing Vernor v. Autodesk, Inc., 621 F.3d 1102 (9th Cir. 2010) at 1111–1112 and 1116, cert. denied 132 S.Ct. 105 (Oct. 3, 2011).

59. A *bailment* is a "delivery of personal property by one person (the *bailor*) to another (the *bailee*) who holds the property for a certain purpose, usually under an express or implied-in-fact contract. Unlike a sale or gift of personal property, a bailment involves a change in possession but not in title," from BLACK'S LAW DICTIONARY, *supra* note 43.

60. A *bailee*, then, is a "person who receives personal property from another, and has possession of but not title to the property," from BLACK'S LAW DICTIONARY, *supra* note 43.

61. RICHARD A. LORD, 1 WILLISTON ON CONTRACTS § 53:2 (4th ed. 2008, database updated in Westlaw, May 2012) (footnote omitted).

62. See Mezo v. Warren County Public Library, 2010 WL 323302, *2 (Ky. App. 2010): "Mezo further contends that his library card represents a contract between him and the library, stating that he would be responsible for lost or damaged items. The trial court [...] held that Mezo had entered into a bailment relationship with the library and that he was, therefore, liable for loss of the books. We agree. A bailment occurs when one person (the bailor) delivers possession of some personal property to another person (the bailee). The defining element of the transaction is the requirement that the property be returned to the bailor, or duly accounted for by the bailee, when the

purpose of the bailment is accomplished . . . It is not necessary for a contract to define a bailment; rather, a bailment is created by lawful possession by virtue of an entrustment and the duty to account for the thing as the property of another. A bailment can be for the benefit of the bailor or the bailee, or for the mutual benefit of both parties. When a bailment benefits only one party and no consideration is given, the bailment is gratuitous. The bailee who is the sole beneficiary of a bailment must exercise extraordinary care and will be liable for even a slight neglect . . . The case before us involves a gratuitous bailment. Mezo lawfully possessed the library's books and clearly understood that he had the duty to return them" (quotations and citation omitted).

63. See Smith v. C. I. R., 3 T.C. 696, 704–705 (1944): "The contract between petitioner and the public library is not shown. We may assume that the loan of the book was a bailment for the exclusive benefit of the bailee and that petitioner would be liable to the library for the payment of damages to the book arising from slight negligence on his part. By leaving the book unguarded in a public conveyance petitioner was guilty of negligence. The payment of $3.50 to the library was apparently in satisfaction of such damages. This payment was made to the owner of property by a gratuitous bailee for damages to the property caused by the bailee's negligence."

64. A bailment for sale is a "bailment in which the bailee agrees to sell the goods on behalf of the bailor; a consignment," from BLACK's LAW DICTIONARY, *supra* note 43.

65. "A bailee in possession of a chattel who disposes of it in a manner not authorized by the bailment is liable to his bailor for conversion," per 198 Metropolitan Vacuum Cleaner Co. v. Douglas-Guardian Warehouse Corp., 208 F. Supp. 195, 198 (D.C.N.Y. 1962).

66. Little, Brown and Company, Inc. v. American Paper Recycling Corp., 824 F. Supp. 11, 16 (D. Mass. 1993).

67. *Id.* at 17: "In the present case, Little, Brown as the bailor of the books retained ownership of and title to the books; APR, as the bailee, had the right to possession."

68. *Id.*, citing § 106 where the exclusive rights of copyright owners are listed.

69. Restatement (Second) of Contracts § 41 (1981) (Lapse of time): "(1) An offeree's power of acceptance is terminated at the time specified in the offer, or, if no time is specified, at the end of a reasonable time. (2) What is a reasonable time is a question of fact, depending on all the circumstances existing when the offer and attempted acceptance are made."

70. Restatement (Second) of Contracts § 41 (1981) (Lapse of time) Comment d (Direct negotiations): "Where the parties bargain face to face or over the telephone, the time for acceptance does not ordinarily extend beyond the end of the conversation unless a contrary intention is indicated. A contrary intention may be indicated either by express words or by the circumstances."

71. Restatement (Second) of Contracts § 41(3) (1981) (Lapse of time).

72. Brewster of Lynchburg, Inc. v. Dial Corp., 33 F.3d 355, 362 (4th Cir. 1994): "This code section [UCC § 2-207] displaces the common law's 'last shot rule' which recognized

that, when the parties exchanged conflicting forms but nonetheless performed their obligations, the contract encompassed the terms contained in the last writing submitted immediately prior to performance."

73. UCC § 2-207 (Additional Terms in Acceptance or Confirmation), Official Comment 1: "A frequent example of the second situation is the exchange of printed purchase order and acceptance (sometimes called 'acknowledgment') forms. Because the forms are oriented to the thinking of the respective drafting parties, the terms contained in them often do not correspond."

74. UCC § 2-207(1) (Additional Terms in Acceptance or Confirmation).

75. Lee R. Russ, Annotation, What constitutes acceptance "expressly made conditional" converting it to rejection and counteroffer under UCC § 2-207(1), 22 A.L.R.4th 939, § 1[a] (originally published in 1983, updated in Westlaw): "In deciding whether or not a response to an offer, which response contains additional or different terms, is made expressly conditional upon assent to the new or different terms, and thus converting the response to a counteroffer, most courts have held that, to convert the acceptance to a counteroffer the conditional nature of the acceptance must be clearly expressed in a manner sufficient to notify the offeror that the offeree is unwilling to proceed with the transaction unless the additional or different terms are included in the contract... The focus of inquiry is on the explicit rather than the implicit intent of the parties." 67 AM. JUR. 2d *Sales* § 164 (database updated May 2011) (view that acceptance must explicitly notify offeror of conditional nature to be "expressly conditional") (footnotes omitted).

76. Daitom, Inc. v. Pennwalt Corp., 741 F.2d 1569, 1577 (10th Cir. 1984).

77. UCC § 2-207(2) (Additional Terms in Acceptance or Confirmation): "The additional terms are to be construed as proposals for addition to the contract. Between merchants such terms become part of the contract unless: "(a) the offer expressly limits acceptance to the terms of the offer; (b) they materially alter it; or (c) notification of objection to them has already been given or is given within a reasonable time after notice of them is received."

78. This form of contract is also known as a rolling contract. See MICHAEL L. RUSTAD, INTERNET LAW IN A NUTSHELL 115 (St. Paul, MN: West Publishing, 2009): "This is an example of a 'rolling contract' where the consumer pays for the product and receives the terms in the packaging of the product when the shipper sends in at a later point."

79. Hill v. Gateway 2000, Inc., 105 F.3d 1147, 1150 (7th Cir. 1997), referring to ProCD, Inc. v. Zeidenberg, 86 F.3d 1447, 1454 (7th Cir. 1996): "The question in *ProCD* was not whether terms were added to a contract after its formation, but how and when the contract was formed—in particular, whether a vendor may propose that a contract of sale be formed, not in the store (or over the phone) with the payment of money or a general 'send me the product,' but after the customer has had a chance to inspect both the item and the terms. *ProCD* answers 'yes,' for merchants and consumers alike."

80. UCC § 2-207(2) (Additional Terms in Acceptance or Confirmation).

81. Wachter Management Co. v. Dexter & Chaney, Inc., 144 P.3d 747, 752 (Kan. 2006).

82. For a review of the case law by jurisdiction and by type of term, see generally, William H. Danne Jr., Annotation, What Are Additional Terms Materially Altering Contract Within Meaning of UCC § 2-207(2)(b), 72 A.L.R.3d 479 (first published 1976, updated weekly in Westlaw).

83. H. WARD CLASSEN, A PRACTICAL GUIDE TO SOFTWARE LICENSING FOR LICENSEES AND LICENSORS 65 (3d ed.) (Chicago: American Bar Association, 2008), quoting K&K Management, Inc. v. Lee, 557 A.2d (Md. 2989) and WILLISTON ON CONTRACTS § 866.

84. ProCD, Inc. v. Zeidenberg, 86 F.3d 1447, 1452 (7th Cir. 1996), emphasis original.

85. Arizona Retail Systems, Inc. v. Software Link, Inc., 831 F. Supp. 759, 765–766 (D. Ariz. 1993), footnote omitted.

86. Compare ProCD v. Zeidenberg, 86 F.3d 1447, 1452 (7th Cir. 1996): "As their titles suggest, these are not consumer transactions. Step-Saver [Step-Saver Data Systems, Inc. v. Wyse Technology, 939 F.2d 91, 102-03 (3d Cir. 1991)] is a battle-of-the-forms case, in which the parties exchange incompatible forms and a court must decide which prevails... Our case has only one form; UCC2-207 is irrelevant." Footnote omitted, and referring to Arizona Retail Systems, Inc. v. Software Link, Inc., as well as Step-Saver Data Systems, Inc. v. Wyse Technology, 939 F.2d 91 (3d Cir. 1991); and Vault Corp. v. Quaid Software Ltd., 847 F.2d 255, 268–70 (5th Cir. 1988).

87. Real Networks, Inc. v. DVD Copy Control Association, Inc., 641 F. Supp. 2d 913, 921 (N.D. Cal. 2009).

88. *Id.* at 922.

89. *Id.* at 934.

90. *Id.* at 946: "Moreover, the record is clear that Real had knowledge that it would receive the technical specification in the order that it did-after membership selection and execution of the CSS License Agreement."

91. *Id.*

92. UCC § 2-207(2) (Additional Terms in Acceptance or Confirmation).

93. UCC § 2-104(1) (Definitions: "Merchant"; "Between Merchants"; "Financing Agency").

94. UCC § 2-104(3) (Definitions: "Merchant"; "Between Merchants"; "Financing Agency").

95. Hill v. Gateway 2000, Inc., 105 F.3d 1147, 1150 (7th Cir. 1997), referring to ProCD, Inc. v. Zeidenberg, 86 F.3d 1447 (7th Cir. 1996).

96. UCC § 2-104 (Definitions: "Merchant"; "Between Merchants"; "Financing Agency"), Official Comment 1.

97. UCC § 2-104 (Definitions: "Merchant"; "Between Merchants"; "Financing Agency"), Official Comment 2.

98. Board of Regents of University of Minnesota v. Chief Industries, Inc., 907 F. Supp. 1298, 1300 (D.Minn. 1995), affirmed 106 F.3d 1409, 1412 (8th Cir. 1997): "The University had purchased a number of such units over the prior thirty years, and had the advantage of a centralized purchasing department that solicited bids for the purchase. Before purchasing the unit, the Southwest station's superintendent (who had been responsible for other such purchases) consulted a prominent expert in grain drying, who provided

advice on such specifications for the unit as fan size and BTU requirements... To be sure, not all large, sophisticated purchasers are necessarily merchants in goods of the kind they buy, just as an informed and careful individual consumer does not become a 'merchant.' But based on the particular and undisputed facts of this case, we agree with the district court that the University possessed specialized knowledge with respect to the grain drying unit." Both district and circuit courts discussed Lloyd F. Smith Co. v. Den-Tal-EZ, Inc., 491 N.W.2d 11, 17 (Minn. 1992), concluding that the plaintiff-dentist was not a "merchant in goods of the kind" and that the purchase of the dentist chair was not a "commercial transaction."

99. Board of Regents of University of Minnesota v. Chief Industries, Inc., 907 F. Supp. 1298, 1302 (D.Minn. 1995).

100. Restatement (Second) of Contracts § 87(1)(a), Comments and Illustrations b (1981) (Option Contract): "Offers made in consideration of one dollar paid or promised are often irrevocable under Subsection (1)(a). The irrevocability of an offer may be worth much or little to the offeree, and the courts do not ordinarily inquire into the adequacy of the consideration bargained for. See § 79. Hence a comparatively small payment may furnish consideration for the irrevocability of an offer proposing a transaction involving much larger sums. But gross disproportion between the payment and the value of the option commonly indicates that the payment was not in fact bargained for but was a mere formality or pretense."

101. Restatement (Second) of Contracts § 87(1)(a) (1981) (Option Contract).

102. Restatement (Second) of Contracts § 42 (Revocation by Communication from Offeror Received by Offeree). See also comment c: "Once the offeree has exercised his power to create a contract by accepting the offer, a purported revocation is ineffective as such."

103. Restatement (Second) of Contracts § 68 (What Constitutes Receipt of Revocation, Rejection, or Acceptance).

104. BLACK'S LAW DICTIONARY, *supra* note 43, defines a bilateral contract as a "contract in which each party promises a performance, so that each party is an obligor on that party's own promise and an obligee on the other's promise; a contract in which the parties obligate themselves reciprocally, so that the obligation of one party is correlative to the obligation of the other." An example would be where A says to B "if you promise to pay me a $100, I promise to walk across the Brooklyn Bridge backwards." Once B pays A $100, A is obligated to perform the bizarre walk. "Typical examples of bilateral contracts are contracts of sale, the buyer promising to pay the price and the seller promising to deliver the goods. A typical example of a unilateral contract is a promise of a reward for the finding of lost property followed by the actual finding of the property." P. S. ATIYAH, AN INTRODUCTION TO THE LAW OF CONTRACT 32 (3d ed.) (Oxford: Clarendon Press, 1981).

105. A unilateral contract is one "in which only one party makes a promise or undertakes a performance; a contract in which no promisor receives a promise as consideration for the promise given," per BLACK'S LAW DICTIONARY, *supra* note 43. "If A says to B, 'If you

walk across the Brooklyn Bridge I will pay you $100,' A has made a promise but has not asked B for a return promise. A has asked B to perform, not a commitment to perform. A has thus made an offer looking to a unilateral contract. B cannot accept this offer by promising to walk the bridge. B must accept, if at all, by performing the act. Because no return promise is requested, at no point is B bound to perform. If B does perform, a contract involving two parties is created, but the contract is classified as unilateral because only one party is ever under an obligation." JOHN D. CALAMARI and JOSEPH M. PERILLO, THE LAW OF CONTRACTS § 2-10(a), at 64– 65 (4th ed. 1998).

106. Another example would a litigation settlement where "the debtor's promise to release joint tortfeasors in a personal injury settlement agreement in exchange for a lump-sum payment and periodic payments was a classic example of a bilateral contract in which consideration was given in the form of a promise for a promise or a promise to forbear from taking some action." In re Hayes, 168 B.R. 717, 725 (Bkrtcy. D. Kan., 1994).

107. Owen v. MBPXL Corp., 173 F. Supp. 2d 905, 915 (N.D. Iowa, 2001). See also B&D Appraisals v. Gaudette Machinery Movers, Inc., 733 F. Supp. 505, 507–508 (D.R.I., 1990) (citations omitted): "Bilateral and unilateral contracts create distinguishable rights, duties, and obligations. A bilateral contract involves mutual promises which simultaneously obligate the parties. A unilateral contract arises when a party makes a promise in exchange for another's act or performance ... Since the act or performance sought constitutes the bargained for detriment (consideration), a return promise has no effect on the bargain. Only the fulfillment of the performance will create a contract and establish the rights and duties of the parties ... In a unilateral contract, no mutuality of obligation exists—only the promisor becomes bound when the promisee executes the bargained for act."

108. See, for example, Register.com v. Verio, 126 F. Supp. 2d 238, 248 (S.D.N.Y. 2000): "Nor can Verio argue that it has not assented to Register.com's terms of use. Register.com's terms of use are clearly posted on its website. The conclusion of the terms paragraph states 'by submitting this query, you agree to abide by these terms.' (Ex. 27 to Pl.'s Sept. 8, 2000 Motion) ... However, in light of this sentence at the end of Register.com's terms of use, there can be no question that by proceeding to submit a WHOIS query, Verio manifested its assent to be bound by Register.com's terms of use, and a contract was formed and subsequently breached."

109. See, for example, Hill v. Gateway 2000, Inc., 105 F.3d 1147, 1148 (7th Cir. 1996), cert. denied 522 U.S. 808 (1997): "A customer picks up the phone, orders a computer, and gives a credit card number. Presently a box arrives, containing the computer and a list of terms, said to govern unless the customer returns the computer within 30 days. Are these terms effective as the parties' contract, or is the contract term-free because the order-taker did not read any terms over the phone and elicit the customer's assent?" The answer: "Like Zeidenberg, the Hills took the third option. By keeping the computer beyond 30 days, the Hills accepted Gateway's offer, including the arbitration clause" (id. at 1150).

110. Buchbinder Tunick & Co. v. Manhattan Nat. Life Ins. Co., 219 A.D.2d 463,466, 631 N.Y.S.2d 148, 151 (N.Y.A.D. 1 Dept. 1995) (citations to Calamari and Perillo omitted).

111. ROBERT A. HILLMAN, PRINCIPLES OF CONTRACT LAW 61 (St. Paul, MN: West Publishing, 2004).

112. Restatement (Second) of Contracts § 40 (Time When Rejection or Counter-Offer Terminates the Power of Acceptance): Comment b: "Since a rejection or counter-offer is not effective until received, it may until that time be superseded by an acceptance."

113. Restatement (Second) of Contracts § 63 (Time When Acceptance Takes Effect), Comment c.

114. *Id.*

115. *Id.*: "A purported revocation of acceptance may, however, affect the rights of the parties. It may amount to an offer to rescind the contract or to a repudiation of it, or it may bar the offeree by estoppel from enforcing it."

116. Venables v. Sagona, 925 N.Y.S.2d 578 (N.Y.A.D. 2 Dept., 2011) (slip opinion).

117. Restatement (Second) of Contracts § 74 (1981) (Settlement of Claims): "Forbearance to assert or the surrender of a claim or defense which proves to be invalid is not consideration unless (a) the claim or defense is in fact doubtful because of uncertainty as to the facts or the law, or (b) the forbearing or surrendering party believes that the claim or defense may be fairly determined to be valid."

118. BLACK'S LAW DICTIONARY, *supra* note 43, defines an illusory promise as one "that appears on its face to be so insubstantial as to impose no obligation on the promisor; an expression cloaked in promissory terms but actually containing no commitment by the promisor. An illusory promise typically, by its terms, makes performance optional with the promisor. For example, if a guarantor promises to make good on the principal debtor's obligation 'as long as I think it's in my commercial interest,' the promisor is not really bound."

119. This is often known as the mutuality rule (a good promise for a good promise) and it applies only to bilateral contracts (promise for a promise) and not to unilateral contracts (a promise for performance), for obvious reasons, as such contract requires a promise to be given in return so that promise must be one of substance. See, for example, Chados v. West Publishing Co., Inc., 292 F.3d 992, 997 (9th Cir. 2002), where the court concluded that a term that allowed the publisher to reject the manuscript if not suitable in "form and content" was not illusory: "It is correct that the agreement at issue imposes numerous obligations on the author but gives the publisher 'the right in its discretion to terminate' the publishing relationship after receiving the manuscript and determining that it is unacceptable. However, we conclude that the contract is not illusory because West's duty to exercise its discretion is limited by its duty of good faith and fair dealing."

120. See US Ecology, Inc. v. State of California, 111 Cal.Rptr.2d 689, 702 (Cal. App. 4 Dist., 2001): "Ecology made a single promise in the MOU that it would maintain the promised schedule set forth in its license-designee application and, if it did not, it

would be subject to forfeiture of its performance bond. However, Ecology was already bound to perform these obligations on this same schedule or forfeit its performance bonds. The MOU language was identical to the governing regulations," citing and referring to 17 California Code of Regulations § 30483.). See also Scott v. Savers Property and Casualty Ins. Co., 663 N.W.2d 715, 726 (Wis., 2003), footnote omitted: "The general rule is that the performance of a legal duty, or the promise to perform a legal duty, is not sufficient consideration to create a contract. Here, Johnson's and the District's performance was induced not by the plaintiffs but by the laws of the state. The plaintiffs had a right to have Johnson perform his job, but no contract was created between the plaintiffs and the District or Johnson."

121. BLACK'S LAW DICTIONARY, *supra* note 43, indicates that an implied warranty of merchantability is "[a] warranty that the property is fit for the ordinary purposes for which it is used." "The *implied warranty of merchantability* attaches when the seller is a merchant with respect to the goods involved in the exchange. Accordingly, the product must meet certain standards; it must pass without objection in the trade under the contract description and it must be fit for the ordinary purposes for which such goods are used. The concepts of marketability, operability, and repairability have emerged as varying criteria for merchantable goods," 1 JULIAN B. MCDONNELL and ELIZABETH J. COLEMAN, COMMERCIAL AND CONSUMER WARRANTIES 1.02 [1], at 1–7 (1991) (emphasis in original).

122. BLACK'S LAW DICTIONARY, *supra* note 43, states that "time is of the essence" in "a contractual requirement [is] so important that if the requirement is not met, the promisor will be held to have breached the contract and a rescission by the promisee will be justified." RICHARD A. LORD, 15 WILLISTON ON CONTRACTS § 46:2 (4th ed. 2008), footnotes omitted, states: "When it is said that time is of the essence, the proper meaning of the phrase is that the performance by one party at or within the time specified in the contract is essential in order to enable that party to require performance from the other party. It does not simply mean that delay will give rise to a right of action against that party, although the breach of any promise in a contract, including one dealing with the time of performance, will have that effect. Nor does the phrase merely mean that performance on time is a material matter, but rather, that it is so material that exact compliance with the terms of the contract in this respect is essential to the right to require counterperformance."

123. Random House, Inc. v. Rosetta Books, LLC, 283 F.3d 490, 492 (2d Cir. 2002): "the reasonable expectations of the contracting parties 'cognizant of the customs, practices, usages and terminology as generally understood in the . . . trade or business' at the time of contracting," quoting Random House, Inc. v. Rosetta Books, LLC, 150 F. Supp. 2d 613, 618 (S.D.N.Y. 2001), citing Sayers v. Rochester Telephone Corp. Supplemental Management Pension Plan, 7 F.3d 1091, 1095 (2d Cir. 1993).

124. See RICHARD A. LORD, 1 WILLISTON ON CONTRACTS § 3:4 (4th ed. 2008), footnote omitted: "[T]he parol evidence rule, which plays such an important role in determining the

existence and meaning of contracts, is based on the assumption that where a written memorial of the transaction is made, its terms, and not the subjective intent of the parties, will govern." See also RICHARD A. LORD, 11 WILLISTON ON CONTRACTS § 33:2 (4th ed. 2008), footnotes omitted: "Despite its name, the parol evidence rule is not a rule of evidence and even though it is generally discussed in connection with the interpretation of writings, it is not a rule of interpretation or construction, but is a rule of substantive law. Although not itself a rule of interpretation, the parol evidence rule identifies what is the proper subject matter of interpretation."

125. RICHARD A. LORD, 11 WILLISTON ON CONTRACTS § 33:3 (4th ed. 2008), footnotes omitted.

126. Restatement (Second) of Contracts § 210(1) (1981) (Completely and Partially Integrated Agreements): "A completely integrated agreement is an integrated agreement adopted by the parties as a complete and exclusive statement of the terms of the agreement."

127. Restatement (Second) of Contracts § 216 (1981) (Consistent Additional Terms), comment e, written term excluding oral terms ("merger" clause): "Written agreements often contain clauses stating that there are no representations, promises or agreements between the parties except those found in the writing."

128. See, for example, UCC § 2-202 (2004) (Final Expression in a Record: Parol or Extrinsic Evidence) (Official Comment 4).

129. Restatement (Second) of Contracts § 216 (1981) (Consistent Additional Terms), comment c, separate consideration and illustration 3: "A and B in an integrated writing promise to sell and buy a specific automobile. As part of the transaction they orally agree that B may keep the automobile in A's garage for one year, paying $15 a month. The oral agreement is not within the scope of the integration and is not superseded."

130. Restatement (Second) of Contracts § 216(2)(b) (1981) (Consistent Additional Terms).

131. Restatement (Second) of Contracts § 216 (1981) (Consistent Additional Terms), comment d, terms omitted naturally.

132. Ralph James Mooney, *A Friendly Letter to the Oregon Supreme Court: Let's Try Again on the Parol Evidence...*, 84 OREGON LAW REVIEW 369, 385, n. 55 (2005).

133. UCC § 2-202 (2004) (Final Expression in a Record: Parol or Extrinsic Evidence) (Official Comment 3): "Whether a writing is final, and whether a final writing is also complete, are issues for the court. This section rejects any assumption that because a record has been worked out which is final on some matters, it is to be taken as including all the matters agreed upon. If the additional terms are those that, if agreed upon, would certainly have been included in the document in the view of the court, then evidence of their alleged making must be kept from the trier of fact. This section is not intended to suggest what should be the evidentiary strength of a merger clause as evidence of the mutual intent that the record be final and complete. That determination depends upon the particular circumstances of each case."

134. RICHARD A. LORD, 11 WILLISTON ON CONTRACTS § 33:16 (4th ed. 2008).

135. RAYMOND T. NIMMER, 2 INFORMATION LAW § 11.46 (database updated in Westlaw, November 2011): "When extrinsic evidence is admissible to determine the intent of the parties

under parol evidence concepts differs among the states and depending on what contract law governs. In many states, under common law, use of extrinsic evidence to explain the terms of a contract requires a determination that the written contract terms are ambiguous...The case law on this issue under common law varies widely." Footnotes omitted.

136. Rebman v. Follett Higher Educ. Group, Inc., 575 F. Supp. 2d 1272, 1274 (M.D. Fla. 2008).

137. *Id.* at 1275, citations to depositions omitted.

138. *Id.* at 1276, citation omitted.

139. *Id.* at 1277; "Mr. Shapiro identified two other reasons that the stores offer to buy back used books from students—savings on freight charges and aid in Internet competition—both of which directly benefit Follett and DBCC, not the bookstores' customers. Consequently, Mr. Shapiro's testimony is not the type of clear expression of intent required to confer third-party-beneficiary status upon Brandner and Rebman" (*id.* at 1278).

140. Alabama State University v. Baker & Taylor, Inc., 998 F. Supp. 1313 (M.D. Ala. 1998).

141. *Id.* at 1315, citations omitted: "A district court has original jurisdiction over all cases between citizens of different states and where the amount in controversy exceeds $75,000, exclusive of interest and costs. When federal subject matter jurisdiction is predicated on diversity of citizenship, all plaintiffs must be diverse from all defendants."

142. Avins v. Moll, 610 F. Supp. 308, 320–321 (D.C. Pa. 1984): "Plaintiff's sixth and seventh causes of action refer to promises allegedly made by various defendants in this action regarding books given by plaintiff to the DLS library, and duties performed by Avins in establishing the DLS library. Plaintiff claims the books belonged to him, not to DLS, and that he actually lent them to DLS. Avins alleges that he was entitled to certain 'books' and 'shelving' and that promises of his entitlement were made 'in consideration of plaintiff's agreement to retire as Dean, and to continue his acquisition of books for the library...and otherwise to help sort and arrange the library during the academic year 1974-75...Defendants argue that these claims are barred by the applicable statutes of limitations, and I agree."

143. Glick v. Trustees of Free Public Library of City of Newark, 67 A.2d 463, 464 (N.J. 1949): "The defendant Trustees of the Free Public Library of the City of Newark appeal from the judgment of the Appellate Division of the Superior Court setting aside, on certiorari, a resolution adopted by the Trustees on March 24, 1948, whereby a contract for the binding and rebinding of the Library's books during the year 1948 was awarded to defendant Wm. H. Rademaekers & Son Co., on a bid of $23,811.25. The respondents submitted a bid of $23,112.95. No reason was assigned for the rejection of the lower bid; want of responsibility is not alleged."

144. S. H. Roemer Co. v. Board of Chosen Freeholders, 220 A.2d 211 (N.J. 1966); "Plaintiff is a wholesale bookseller, limiting its operation to the State of New Jersey...For the past 17 years plaintiff has been supplying books to the Free County Library of the County of Camden. There has never been any public advertisement for bids by the library, the Library Commissioners or the county...The county admits that all of the

books were delivered by plaintiff, were accepted and used by the library and that they were fairly priced...The county's refusal to pay is based upon the fact that it did not advertise for bids as required...it was prohibited by law from entering into a valid agreement with plaintiff...Thus the county contends that plaintiff may not recover from it" (*id.* at 212). "It is quite understandable that where the practice of purchasing books by the county library has been of many years standing, county officers and employees might sincerely believe the long established practice to be the correct one...Plaintiff should therefore be entitled to be paid by the county on its claim of Quantum meruit" (*id.* at 216).

145. See, for example, Pendry v. Edgar, 129 P. 936, 936 (Kan. 1912): "This is an action in mandamus to compel the defendant school board to install a primary reading chart in the district school, and to pay the plaintiff $12 therefor"; Ginn & Co. v. School Book Board of Berkeley County, 59 S.E. 177, 177 (W.Va. 1907): "Ginn & Co. had a contract with the school board of Berkeley county for furnishing certain books for use in the free schools of that county, dated February 24, 1902, and expiring July 1, 1907... before the expiration of the contract the school board met to select books to be used for the five years succeeding the expiration of the contract . . . Ginn & Co. offered to renew their said contract for the succeeding five years; but the school board refused to renew the contract, and Ginn & Co. ask of this court a mandamus to compel the school board to do so"; Silver, Burdett & Co. v. Indiana State Bd. of Education, 72 N.E. 829, 830 (Ind. App. 1904): "Appellant brought a suit in equity to enjoin the State Board of School Commissioners, and the individual members thereof, from entering into a contract with D. C. Heath & Co., a book publishing corporation, to furnish certain text-books for the use of the public schools of the state"; Attorney General v. Board of Ed. of City of Detroit, 95 N.W. 746, 748 (Mi. 1903): "If the complainant, D. C. Heath & Co., has any standing in the court, it is because it has made a valid contract with the defendant for five years, either for its entire series of arithmetics, or for the Grammar School Arithmetic. It seeks an enforcement of this contract in equity. If it has a valid contract, its remedy at law is complete, in the appropriate action for breach of contract"; and Roland v. Reading School District, 28 A. 995, 995 (Pa. 894): "The books enumerated in the contract were provided and paid for. An additional number of books of the same kinds set out in the contract was ordered and furnished, and the plaintiff's account therefor is $1,625.36, for the recovery of which this suit is brought. The defense made is that these books were to be furnished at cost, and that their cost was but $1,226.67; and evidence was given for the purpose of showing the offer of the plaintiff to furnish them at cost in case the contract was awarded to him, and its acceptance and the award of the contract by the school board. Witnesses were then called to show that, when the plaintiff and the president of the school board met to execute the contract, the plaintiff insisted upon adding the sentence beginning with the words 'with the addition of six per centum on the cost price.' The words were finally incorporated into the contract without any previous authority from the school board."

146. See, for example, Fifth Ave. Library Sco. v. Gates, 127 N.W. 714, 715 (Mich. 1910): "As it was subsequently admitted and held to make a prima facie case, there is no occasion to discuss this question further. The court held that under this contract it was necessary that the books be delivered to the defendant in Dexter, and that delivering the same to an express company directed to defendant at Dexter did not constitute a delivery to defendant at Dexter. There was no error in this. The intention, as shown by the contract, was that the defendant was to have the books delivered to him at Dexter, before becoming liable for their price. The order should receive no other construction. Hence the receipt of the books by the local agent of the express company was not sufficient"; Appleton v. Norwalk Library Corp., 22 A. 681, 681 (Conn. 1885): "This case depends upon the construction to be given to a certain contract...The books were delivered, and the defendant paid a number of installments according to the contract; but finally it ceased payment, and tendered the books to the plaintiffs, informing them that it should make no further payments under the contract. The plaintiffs refused to receive the books...This contract is an absolute one. The plaintiffs agreed to sell the books to the defendant for the sum of $90, to be paid in installments at certain specified times...There is no conditional agreement here...It is said that the plaintiffs had the right, at their option, to retake the property at any time if the defendant fail to pay any installment for a period of 30 days after it became due...But this is not their only remedy. The contract expressly further provides that, in case of such breach, all the remaining unpaid installments shall immediately become due and payable. If they become due and payable in consequence of non-payment, of course a suit could be maintained for their recovery. The plaintiffs base their suit upon this right given them in the contract, and we think it can be sustained."

▶ 3

CONTRACT FORMATION
AND ENFORCEABILITY

Read this chapter to gain an understanding of how these concepts affect contract enforceability:

- ▶ Indefiniteness—when a contract does not explicitly state the terms of the agreement
- ▶ Mistakes—when a contract includes either mutual or unilateral errors
- ▶ Misrepresentation, nondisclosure, duress, and undue influence—when external pressure renders the contract unfair for one of the parties
- ▶ Oral contracts—when they can be used and when written contracts are required
- ▶ Lack of capacity—when the person entering into the contract lacks the mental capacity to do so
- ▶ Impossibility—when a person can no longer fulfill the terms of a contract due to "acts of God" or acts of third parties
- ▶ Performance and breach of contract—when a person is perceived to have not met the terms of the agreement, and the application of remedies and damages in such situations

There may be circumstances where the responsible person failed to review and understand the terms, and the deal nonetheless struck with the responsible person signing the agreement, thus binding the library. Now the library is, for lack of a more expressive word, stuck with the terms of the agreement. Can anything be done to get out of the contract, short of asking for reconsideration of the terms (a request for additional terms or a superseding agreement altogether) or forcing a breach of those terms, which may result in the licensor exercising a right to end the agreement—though likely not without some cost to the licensee, such as loss of the licensing fee, which is often paid a year in advance? Several doctrines may, given the right circumstances, be used to "destroy" or, in legal parlance, void the contract—or at least void specific provisions of the contract. To be sure, these scenarios will not be present in every setting. More likely it is the rare case when one of the issues in contract formation or enforceability would apply. Many of the concepts are now perhaps more historical anomaly—seldom asserted by a litigant and even less often found present by courts—often rectified by advances in drafting between the parties. However, discussion is included for two reasons. The first is for the sake of completeness. Second, and more important, there have been developments in case law in recent years (and in contract trends as well) that relate to licensing, so having a basic understanding here lays the legal foundation for discussion of these concepts in the following chapters. Cases discussed in this chapter are drawn from library, school, and book trade to demonstrate that over time these concepts do impact the world of libraries, schools, and their books.

INDEFINITENESS

This concept may be obvious, but if the contract does not state the essentials, subject matter, price, and so forth, then there can be no agreement. Here, terms are so incomplete or indefinite that it appears the agreement was still in the stages of negotiation or formation. This is not the same as an agreement where details still need to be worked out.[1] In terms of incompleteness, this can be a result of the party's conduct (e.g., negotiations had not ended), or it can be upon determination by the court, which might conclude the terms are so indefinite that the contract cannot be formed.

The UCC rules reflect a more liberal position regarding indefiniteness, including a number of gap-filler provisions, default rules of sorts, supplying missing terms so that the contract can survive a legal challenge: price (section 2-305(1)), place of delivery (section 2-308), time for shipment of delivery (section 2-309), time for payment (section 2-310), and duration[2] (section 2-309). This reflects the modern trend of courts striving to honor terms and conditions if there is evidence that the parties intended a contract to be formed. Where the parties fail to include a material term, the court may, and often does, insert one.[3] But where the parties leave its determination for a later time in a so-called agreement to agree, the traditional rule is not to enforce the agreement. If the term is a minor one, the general rule is to insert it and enforce the agreement. In other situations, the lack of more than one material term in spite of the existence of gap-filler provisions might suggest that the intent to form an agreement was not manifested by the parties.[4] Oversight is one thing, but the existence of too many holes suggests some other purpose than to form a contract.

Solving an indefiniteness problem might raise other problems, such as the statute of frauds, discussed in this section, and vice versa. In brief, the statute of frauds requires that certain contracts be in writing to be valid; one exception is a contract for services of less than a year in duration.[5] In a dispute involving a mixed contract of goods and services, that is, for books as well as the program and consultation that went with the books, the court concluded that the oral agreement lacked essential terms. The court commented upon the interplay between the concept of indefiniteness and the exception to the writing requirement of the statute of frauds:

> Indeed, the final nail in Respect's coffin on this issue is driven by the recollection that the contract *must* be labeled as one for Mast's services if it is to survive the Statute of Frauds requirement that it be capable of performance in less than a year. Respect cannot have it that way for one purpose, then shift the contract's dominant purpose to the sale of goods (which would fail the Statute of Frauds test) when it suits Respect's other goal of avoiding invalidity because of uncertainty. For Respect it comes down to a choice (to shift metaphors from land to sea) between Scylla and Charybdis rather than any possibility of steering between those perils—either way, its contractual ship sinks. In light of the required determination that the parties' contract was predominantly one for services, common law principles apply. Under those principles the contract is so permeated with undefined essential terms that this Court cannot enforce it.[6]

Similarly, in *Academy Chicago Publishers v. Cheever*, the court found that numerous crucial items absent from the agreement between the widow of a famous author and a publisher regarding a collective edition of the author's short stories suggested the meeting of the minds never occurred:

> Trial testimony reveals that a major source of controversy between the parties is the length and content of the proposed book. The agreement sheds no light on the minimum or maximum number of stories or pages necessary for publication of the collection, nor is there any implicit language from which we can glean the intentions of the parties with respect to this essential contract term. The publishing agreement is similarly silent with respect to who will decide which stories will be included in the collection. Other omissions, ambiguities, unresolved essential terms and illusory terms are: No date certain for delivery of the manuscript. No definition of the criteria which would render the manuscript satisfactory to the publisher either as to form or content. No date certain as to when publication will occur. No certainty as to style or manner in which the book will be published nor is there any indication as to the price at which such book will be sold, or the length of time publication shall continue, all of which terms are left to the sole discretion of the publisher.[7]

While courts may insert missing material terms where some implication of the term can be found, this case demonstrates that when many significant terms are missing, courts are reluctant to concoct those terms.

MISTAKE

It is possible to sort the mistakes that can occur in contract formation into two groups: mutual mistakes[8] and unilateral mistakes.[9] A mutual mistake occurs when both parties err as to a basic assumption of fact on which the contract was made, and the error has a "material effect on the agreed exchange of performances, [in which case] the contract is voidable by the adversely affected party unless he bears the risk of the mistake."[10] The adversely affected party must evidence harm:

> It is not enough for him to prove that he would not have made the contract had it not been for the mistake. He must show that the resulting imbalance in the agreed exchange is so severe that he cannot fairly be required to carry it out. Ordinarily he will be able to do this by showing that the exchange is not only less desirable to him but is also more advantageous to the other party.[11]

In contrast, a "unilateral mistake occurs where one party to a written contract is negligently mistaken as to the subject matter of a contract in such a way as to justify the other party's reliance upon the stated assent to the written terms; such a mistake is unilateral and the contract is enforceable."[12] Courts are reluctant to void a contract where the error is not shared among the parties, that is, when the error is not a mutual mistake.

> As a matter of traditional policy, each party must protect its own position. This principle has been sometimes adjusted in modern case law to hold that a unilateral mistake may allow avoidance of the contract if enforcement against the party making the mistake would be oppressive while rescission of the contract would impose no substantial hardship on the other party (a "no harm, no foul" premise) . . . The other side of this principle, however, places responsibility on the person making the unilateral mistake if the mistake caused reliance by the recipient.[13]

Exceptions exist to the "buyer-beware" attitude of the unilateral mistake rule. To void a contract based upon a unilateral mistake, the elements of a mutual mistake (assumption, materiality, and risk) must first be satisfied,[14] and, in addition, there must be present either "(a) the effect of the mistake is such that enforcement of the contract would be unconscionable, or (b) the other party had reason to know of the mistake or his fault caused the mistake."[15] This may result in harsh assessments, but a party is generally responsible for its own errors, incorrect assumptions, and so forth.[16] "The sender of a mistaken message, whether electronic or not, ordinarily has responsibility for its mistake if the recipient relied on the message without any reason to suspect that it was a mistake."[17] Instances of unilateral mistake often occur in construction or government contractor and other bidding scenarios, as can be imagined. For example, in *Information International Associates, Inc. v. U.S.,* after a dispute arose over the failure to include the salary for a library assistant position at Malmstrom Air Force Base, the court "determined that Plaintiff has demonstrated by clear and convincing evidence that Plaintiff would have bid an additional $174,882.00, but for the mistake. Accordingly, the court has determined that there is no genuine issue of material fact between the parties and the five requisite elements of a unilateral mistake have been established by clear and convincing evidence."[18] Numerous cases involve school districts. Where the error is not so egregious, courts are reluctant to reform the contract. In *Lassiter Const. Co. v. School Bd. for Palm Beach County*, a 4 percent error regarding a contractor bid was deemed insufficient to revise the contract.[19] The lesson of these cases is to read and understand any agreement, including any license the library is considering, as a unilateral mistake is often allowed to let stand, usually to the disadvantage of the erring party: "Moreover, there is no evidence that appellant behaved or acted in any way to mislead or take advantage of respondent. In fact, an employee of appellant made further inquiry into respondent's bid and confirmed respondent's confidence in that bid. Respondent cannot now ask that the courts provide a remedy for respondent's unilateral mistake. Respondent won the informal bidding process, and it will find no refuge to escape from its contract with the school."[20] In cases where costs estimates are submitted, such as bid submissions, courts are not sympathetic to errors made by those who engage in such services for a living, such as contractors.

MISREPRESENTATION, NONDISCLOSURE, DURESS, AND UNDUE INFLUENCE

In some circumstances, a meeting of the minds, so to speak, cannot occur because of some external pressure, such as misrepresentation, nondisclosure, duress, or undue influence. These create an uneven playing field with respect to external factors surrounding contract formation and result in the inability for the two minds to, in essence, meet. These situations speak to the unfairness of the contract to one of the parties. Where the unfairness is internal to the contract, that is, found within the language of the contract, a second impediment to contract formation known as unconscionability (discussed in Chapter 4) may be found.

Misrepresentation

As with many of the claims against contract formation, misrepresentation is rooted in concepts of equity, with the option of voiding the contract then resting with the aggrieved party. This is a choice the aggrieved party must exercise, as the contract is not automatically voided. However, where a misrepresentation goes to what is sometimes called the "factum" or the "execution," rather than merely the "inducement,"[21] then the contract is void, as there was no manifestation of intent in the first instance, induced or otherwise.[22] "This distinction has important consequences. For example, the recipient of a misrepresentation may be held to have ratified the contract if it is voidable but not if it is 'void.'"[23] In other words, if the misrepresentation is based on execution or factum, the contract is void—there is no contract at all—but if the misrepresentation is due to inducement, then a contract does indeed exist but is deemed to be somehow tainted. Such contract is voidable at the option of the induced, now-harmed party.[24] Misrepresentations relating to an essential term without knowledge of the misrepresentation prevent contract formation[25] and result in a void contract.

Those contracts which involve fraud or material misrepresentation are voidable:[26]

> Three requirements must be met in addition to the requirement that there must have been a misrepresentation. First, the misrepresentation must have been either fraudulent or material. Second, the misrepresentation must have induced the recipient to make the contract. Third, the recipient must have been justified in relying on the misrepresentation.[27]

The misrepresentation must substantially impact the assent of the other party: "It is not necessary that this reliance have been the sole or even the predominant factor in influencing his conduct. It is not even necessary that he would not have acted as he did had he not relied on the assertion. It is enough that the manifestation substantially contributed to his decision to make the contract."[28] If a representation is made with some sense of dishonesty, it is a fraudulent misrepresentation. This implies that the misrepresentation must be made with intent to induce the other party to enter the contract with some knowledge of the problem.[29] According to Williston,

> contractual fraud in the sense in which it is pertinent here is defined by the courts with some regard for the difference between tort claims and contract disputes, to mean and include: misrepresentation known to be such, concealment, [and] nondisclosure where it is not privileged, by any person intending or expecting thereby to cause a mistake by another to exist or to continue, in order to induce the latter to enter into or refrain from entering into a transaction.[30]

Knowledge, belief, and lack of confidence in the veracity of the statement or the underlying facts must be present.[31] "If the mistake of one party is induced by the other with neither knowledge of the error nor willful indifference in regard to it there is misrepresentation but not fraud," although there can be constructive fraud, in other words, fraud without intent but where "reckless, negligent and in certain circumstances innocent misrepresentations" are present.[32] Likewise,

> an assertion need not be fraudulent to be a misrepresentation. Thus a statement intended to be truthful may be a misrepresentation because of ignorance or carelessness, as when the word "not" is inadvertently omitted or when inaccurate language is used. But a misrepresentation that is not fraudulent has no consequences under this Chapter unless it is material.[33]

This leads to a second type of misrepresentation, one that is not fraudulent or meant to deceive but made by accident—yet nonetheless so significant that a court would consider voiding the contract. A material misrepresentation is "[a] false statement that is likely to induce a reasonable person to assent or that the maker knows is likely to induce the recipient to assent."[34] In other words, it goes to a material fact.[35]

Nondisclosure

There may also be situations where the misrepresentation derives from nondisclosure or more aggressive concealment, rising to a level of misrepresentation: "Concealment necessarily involves an element of non-disclosure, but it is the act of preventing another from learning of a fact that is significant and this act is always equivalent to a misrepresentation. Non-disclosure without concealment is equivalent to a misrepresentation only in special situations"[36]; that is, it must be either fraudulent or material. "If a fact is intentionally withheld for the purpose of inducing action, this is equivalent to a fraudulent misrepresentation."[37] A nondisclosure may be innocent, with no intent to deceive, but nonetheless be material,[38] and thus it may also constitute a misrepresentation, making the contract voidable.

> It is settled that there is no general requirement of full disclosure of all relevant facts in every business relationship, and consequently agreed by the majority of jurisdictions that, at least in courts of law, it is not necessarily fraudulent for one party to a bargain consciously to take advantage of the ignorance or mistake of the other party by failing to disclose material facts...and there is no duty existing between the parties that compels disclosure of the facts.[39]

In some cases, there may be a duty to disclose, however. "The duty to disclose material facts may arise as a result of a fiduciary or confidential relationship between the parties, or from the particular circumstances of the case, and may be legal or equitable in nature."[40] The difference between fraud and mistake is that the latter must relate to a material term in order to provide remedy, whereas the former may require relief under any degree of term importance.[41]

> However, it is important to bear in mind that while some courts state as a general rule that nondisclosure of a material fact may constitute fraud sufficient to invalidate a contract generally without applying that broad statement to the facts under consideration, many courts have distinguished between simple silence and concealment or suppression, holding that the former is not without more fraudulent, while the latter may be a basis for a fraud claim even in the absence of a statutory or common law duty to the other party.[42]

This is the concept underlying nondisclosure as a contractual harm for which the law provides remedy and those results which offer no remedy other than a lesson hard-learned.

Duress

The concept of duress[43] involves some threat of action that leaves the other party cornered, in a sense, without recourse: "If a party's manifestation of assent is induced by an improper threat by the other party that leaves the victim no reasonable alternative, the contract is voidable by the victim."[44] Unlike the agreement described in a scene from *The Godfather* ("My father made him an offer he couldn't refuse"), it would be the odd case in a library or educational setting where the threat of physical force (the historical confines of duress) is used to induce someone to assent to a contract.[45] However, one may threaten through nonphysical measures, such as threat of litigation.[46] This scenario may sound familiar; for example, a vendor threatens to sue a university over its e-reserve, online course management practices, or streaming practices with respect to use of the content supplied by the vendor unless the university renews its current subscription at an increased rate. However, there is a difference between this scenario and one without reasonable alternative—the true circumstance of duress. In this case, for the university, arguing fair use in defense of the infringement claim is a reasonable alternative.[47]

Again, the distinction between a contract being void or voidable is apparent here: "Duress by threat results in a contract voidable by the victim. It differs in this important respect from duress by physical compulsion, which results in there being no contract at all."[48] There may be other scenarios of effective duress in the absence of physical harm, that is, where a contract is properly formed but one party refuses to deliver the goods unless the other party also agrees to purchase some other item[49] or to alter the price of the existing contract.[50] The illustrations to the Restatement suggest that if the other party is in dire straits, where loss of the good or service would cause "heavy financial loss," or is in urgent need of the good or service, there may be duress.[51] It is the result of the threat that is of paramount importance.

> In order to constitute duress, the improper threat must induce the making of the con-
> tract...A party's manifestation of assent is induced by duress if the duress substantially
> contributes to his decision to manifest his assent. The test is subjective and the question
> is, did the threat actually induce assent on the part of the person claiming to be the
> victim of duress. Threats that would suffice to induce assent by one person may not
> suffice to induce assent by another.[52]

A recent case involving an unsuccessful claim of duress involved students subject to their school district's rule requiring that all student assignments be submitted to Turnitin.com, a plagiarism detection website:

> Though Plaintiffs plead duress, there is no evidence that anyone was coerced in any
> fashion by Turnitin or iParadigms. Insofar as Plaintiffs' duress defense is asserted against
> Plaintiffs' respective schools, rather than Defendant iParadigms, there is no support for

the proposition that a contract can be invalidated on the basis of third party duress... If Plaintiffs' objection is that their schools' policies requiring students to use Turnitin are wrongful, Plaintiffs' proper redress is with the school systems... Thus, Plaintiffs' duress defense fails.[53]

The court also concluded that use of the student papers was fair use.

Undue Influence

Again, the concept underlying undue influence is that circumstances prevent the party from making an adequate assessment of the terms of the agreement and so a true meeting of the minds cannot be said to occur.

> If a party in whom another reposes confidence misuses that confidence to gain an advantage while the other has been made to feel that the party in question will not act against its welfare, the transaction is the result of undue influence... Undue influence is equivalent to that which constrains the will or destroys the free agency of the person and substitutes in its place the will of another.[54]

The Restatement focuses upon the domination in the agreement of one party over another: "Undue influence is unfair persuasion of a party who is under the domination of the person exercising the persuasion or who by virtue of the relation between them is justified in assuming that that person will not act in a manner inconsistent with his welfare."[55] A contract formed under undue influence is voidable by the victim of the undue influence.[56] The victim of the undue influence must be under the domination the other party. This can often occur based upon the relationship of the parties. "Relations that often fall within the rule include those of parent and child, husband and wife, clergyman and parishioner, and physician and patient."[57] The concept of undue influence can offer one party remedy where duress or misrepresentation is not present; as both of the latter require conduct undertaken by the offending party, undue influence can result from the surrounding circumstances alone.

> The degree of persuasion that is unfair depends on a variety of circumstances. The ultimate question is whether the result was produced by means that seriously impaired the free and competent exercise of judgment. Such factors as the unfairness of the resulting bargain, the unavailability of independent advice, and the susceptibility of the person persuaded are circumstances to be taken into account in determining whether there was unfair persuasion, but they are not in themselves controlling.[58]

The emphasis is not on the other party but on the victimized party, so to speak:

> Additional circumstances involved in any determination of undue influence include the age of the party imposed upon, any existing mental condition or physical infirmities the

victim suffers, and the adequacy of the consideration exchanged for the benefit received. However, where there has been no proof of fraud or undue influence, proof of weakness of mind which does not amount to imbecility is insufficient to warrant setting aside a contract. These are all elements which will be considered by the courts when making a determination as to the existence of undue influence.[59]

However, given the nature of the disposition of the aggrieved party required, it is unlikely the concept would arise in the library or related setting.

ORAL CONTRACTS AND THE STATUTE OF FRAUDS: WHEN CONTRACTS MUST BE IN WRITING

Oral contracts are just as enforceable as written contracts. However, the law developed over time to require that certain contracts should be in writing. The rationale was that such rules were necessary so that the terms would be set down on paper and this in turn would prevent fraud and perjury. The historical list of contracts for which a written form is required includes contracts for the sale of land and for the sale of goods over $500, contracts in consideration of marriage (such as a prenuptial agreement), service contracts where the performance dates are beyond one year, and surety situations (where one promises or secures another's debt, as in when a parent cosigns a car loan for an adult child). By reflecting on the list, you can likely see the need for and benefit to having these sorts of contracts in writing. Under modern commercial contract law, the UCC requires that indeed a "writing" is necessary (again, there are numerous exceptions) for "contracts for sale" of goods, but the amount is now set at $5,000.[60] Under the increased limit, most library purchases would likely not exceed the new limit. The point is that contracts which did not conform to the requirements of the statute of frauds were not necessarily void but that "[f]ailure to satisfy the requirements of this section does not render the contract void for all purposes, but merely prevents it from being judicially enforced in favor of a party to the contract."[61] Some exceptions are relevant to the library setting, for example, where the buyer accepts and receives all or part of the goods, and buyer makes a partial payment. Also recall that books are goods, so acquisition of such items is by sale, but a subscription to a database or an outsourced bar-coding project is in the nature of a contract for a service, not a good. As Nimmer and Dodd point out, most licenses are not sales and thus courts should not apply UCC law to these transactions.[62] (The recharacterization of licenses into sales and the implications of that recharacterization are covered in Chapter 4.)

In this way, asserting a statute of frauds issue can operate as a defense of sorts to contract enforcement. This raises an issue of contract formation, by arguing that the contract should have been in writing and therefore one is not bound by the oral terms that do exist.[63] As one court observed: "It is undisputed that the agreement, whatever its content, was oral. To be sure, some documents most likely exist that support the existence of the contract. But even if such documents do exist and are construed as part of the contract—and the contract is thus found to be partly written and partly oral—then the law governing oral contracts still applies."[64] Statute of frauds issues still occur, with several somewhat recent cases involving authors and their publishers. For example, in a dispute regarding a book purchase agreement, a district court observed that "[u]nder Illinois' version of the Statute of Frauds an oral contract is unenforceable unless by its terms it is capable of full performance within one year, as measured from the date of its making. By Mast's admission the pilot program was to run for more than one year: Mast says that Committee promised to buy books over a three-year period, the duration of the pilot study. Hence the contract is unenforceable."[65] Consider a scenario where an editor claims that an oral agreement with a publisher to name her a coauthor should be enforced. This was the issue in *Kwan v. Schlein*, where the requirement that service contracts beyond one year in duration be reduced to writing was an issue.[66] The concepts underlying the statute of frauds raised questions for the expansion of online contracting, prompting additional uniform codes to be promulgated.[67] "Often, the issue of whether the statute of frauds is satisfied will be vital in the online context to determine if a meeting of the minds occurred that created a binding agreement."[68] The Uniform Computer Information Transactions Act (UCITA) identifies this problem as well: "Similarly, the performance tendered and accepted must be sufficient to show that a contract exists and cannot consist of minor acts of ambiguous nature. Thus mere access to information at an Internet Web site does not satisfy the statute of frauds when there is no indication that a contract exists or that the access resulted in assent to contract terms."[69]

LACK OF CAPACITY

It may also be that the person entering into the contract does not have the capacity to enter a contract. This often relates to "legal" capacity due to age or some infirmity that makes consent—or makes the meeting of the minds—impossible. When this occurs, the law reasoned that it was not fair for a person so positioned to be bound by the terms of the contract, as the terms often disadvantage the weaker party, for example, children,[70] the senile, or the mentally disabled.[71] "Among them are congenital deficiencies in intelligence, the mental deterioration of old age, the effects of brain damage caused by accident or organic disease, and mental illnesses evidenced by such symptoms as delusions, hallucinations, delirium, confusion and depression."[72] The general rule is that such contracts are voidable, not void per se. As a result, a particular state law may indicate that a contract involving a minor is voidable rather than void. Of course, it is the minor or other person of incapacity who may void the contract with the thought that it was his or her diminished position that was taken advantage of, so to speak. In cases where the contract is to the disadvantage of the other party, the minor may not, in a sense, take advantage of the law and use the law to later void the contract.[73] While it is unlikely to arise in the context of library licensing, this question often arises in conversation or at the reference desk as an inquiry by a patron. Again, it is best to check state law for a statute dealing with the legal capacity of minors or other individuals and the relevant case law.

IMPOSSIBILITY

Another concept that again makes a contract voidable is impossibility. "Where, after a contract is made, a party's performance is made impracticable without his fault by the occurrence of an event the non-occurrence of which was a basic assumption on which the contract was made, his duty to render that performance is discharged, unless the language or the circumstances indicate the contrary."[74] Unlike incapacity, this concept does find its way into most contracts, including licenses. Three historical circumstances triggered the application of the doctrine: supervening death or incapacity of a person necessary for performance,[75] supervening destruction of a specific thing necessary for performance,[76] and supervening prohibition or prevention by law.[77] The modern Restatement rule indicates a more general concept: "Events that come within the rule stated in this Section are generally due either to 'acts of God' or to acts of third parties."[78] In modern practice, this clause is often a part of the contract as a force majeure clause, or act of God provision, whereby natural disasters, such as fire, flood, and so on, destroy the product or ability to supply the service; for example, a fire burns down the distribution center so that the books no longer exist or a flood fries the servers of the database vendor. "Although the rule stated in this Section is sometimes phrased in terms of 'impossibility,' it has long been recognized that it may operate to discharge a party's duty even though the event has not made performance absolutely impossible . . . Performance may be impracticable because extreme and unreasonable difficulty, expense, injury, or loss to one of the parties will be involved."[79] As with many of the concepts discussed in this chapter, the modern license anticipates these issues and includes language addressing the circumstance in the agreement. "However, 'impracticability' means more than 'impracticality.' A mere change in the degree of difficulty or expense due to such causes as increased wages, prices of raw materials, or costs of construction, unless well beyond the normal range, does not amount to impracticability since it is this sort of risk that a fixed-price contract is intended to cover. Furthermore, a party is expected to use reasonable efforts to surmount obstacles to performance, and a performance is impracticable only if it is so in spite of such efforts."[80] Frustration excuses performance when the underlying good or service is destroyed; that is, the purpose for which the contract was formed is affected due to changed circumstances, but the ability to perform is not affected.[81] "In modern legal parlance, frustration of purpose refers to a situation where an unforeseen event has occurred, which, in the context of the entire transaction, destroys the underlying reasons."[82] If the event is foreseeable, then frustration cannot result. Impossibility or impracticability arises where circumstances make it impossible or extremely difficult to perform but do not change the underlying purpose for the contract. Suppose, due to forest fires out west, a paper company cannot get the pulp it needs, which in turn makes the paper the publisher and printer need for the second edition of *The Library's Legal Answer Book* astronomically expensive. This circumstance is not frustration because the contract's purpose, to print and sell books, can still be fulfilled. It will just be far more expensive to do so until the fires recede and supply returns to normal cost and availability.[83]

PERFORMANCE, CONDITIONS, BREACH, AND REMEDIES (DAMAGES)

Once the agreement is in place, there is hope that each party will be satisfied with the bargain struck. However, it may come to be that one party does not believe the other is performing the contract as expected or to the satisfaction of this party. These sour scenarios raise questions of performance and breach. When does performance fall so short of the terms that one can consider the other party in breach, and what is the character of this breach? In other words, is it a material or minor breach and is there an opportunity to cure the breach? Of course, it is best to consider these issues before the contract is formed and to define the course of proper conduct and response in the agreement. The concepts of performance (and the standards by which such conditions are to be measured, such as reasonableness, or the extent to which the party "reasonably" performs or executes the condition of use) and breach are found in many content licenses and are discussed in later chapters.

The Good Faith Requirement

In general, each party to a contract has an obligation to perform that contract in good faith. This sounds like a logical and a reasonable thing to expect, but defining what constitutes good faith is a more difficult issue. UCC section 1-203 includes a simple statement commanding that parties execute a contract in good faith.[84] Section 1-201(20) of the UCC indicates that good faith is "honesty" in fact and standard practices of fair dealing.[85] "Although 'fair dealing' is a broad term that must be defined in context, it is clear that it is concerned with the fairness of conduct rather than the care with which an act is performed."[86] The Restatement, section 205, suggests that good faith is anything outside the bounds of bad faith:

> But the obligation goes further: bad faith may be overt or may consist of inaction, and fair dealing may require more than honesty. A complete catalogue of types of bad faith is impossible, but the following types are among those which have been recognized in judicial decisions: evasion of the spirit of the bargain, lack of diligence and slacking off, willful rendering of imperfect performance, abuse of a power to specify terms, and interference with or failure to cooperate in the other party's performance.[87]

Both the obligations of good faith and fair dealing are often imposed in contract dealings among parties: "Good faith contains a subjective component, but fair dealing imposes an objective one."[88]

Is the Breach Material or Minor?

Breach occurs when the promises made by the parties are broken (e.g., the content provider fails to make the content accessible for a minimum contract hours per month), exceed a limitation of the agreement (e.g., the licensee makes an infringing use in terms of the copyright law of the content of the licensed database), or undertake conduct that constitutes a repudiation or refusal to comply (e.g., a subscriber's nonpayment of the renewal fee). A license as a form of contract may in its simplest sense be characterized as a promise not to sue if certain conforming obligations or conduct is met (e.g., "If you don't let remote third-party users access the database, then you can use the content for in-house course packs that would otherwise, in at least some instances, exceed fair use"). The modern concept of contractual expectation views each party as undertaking mutual obligations that are enforceable under the contract. This may appear a fine point, but it is an important one—especially when assessing the validity of online contracts that govern websites. "The more complete view recognizes that reciprocal obligations exist in any contract, including a license, and that mutual promise or obligations arise in a relationship without there being explicit promissory language attached to each and every type of conduct...the licensor promises to not sue for acts within the scope of the license and the licensee promises to not go beyond the terms of the licensed conduct."[89] Viewing the license in a more limited way can lead some courts to conclude that a copyright preemption issue exists (discussed in Chapter 4), as the contract does nothing more than copyright law does already. The right to cure a breach is implicit in modern contract law if not otherwise defined by the terms of the agreement. Again, when applied to licensing, and as discussed in later chapters, the right to cure a breach is often included and provides a saving mechanism limiting the right of the nonbreaching party to terminate the contract.

While a breach gives rise to a right to claim damages by the aggrieved party, the breach may or may not excuse the aggrieved party from the continued obligation of performance. The critical factor is whether or not the breach was material, which often provides the aggrieved party the right to cancel the contract. If a minor breach is involved, then the obligation to perform—to continue with the contract—remains, though in some cases it may be suspended. If the breach was material, the obligation is excused. There is a relationship between substantial performance and breach, as a party that has substantially performed its part of the bargain cannot commit a material breach because the essence of the contract has been fulfilled. Likewise, a party in material breach cannot fulfill its obligation under the contract; that is, said party cannot substantially perform the contract. On the other hand, substantial performance with those elements which are the focus of the breach cures the breach. When a license addresses these issues, it is important to determine how the terms define and apply to these concepts: When is a breach material? What right of cure exists? When can termination due to breach occur? Contracts in which language that defines a material breach is absent can be problematic. The concept is related to good faith and so involves objective as well as subjective factors. The Restatement focuses upon the loss of a reasonably expected benefit, ability to compensate for the loss of the benefit, the likelihood of forfeiture if the breach is deemed material, the possibility for cure, and whether the breaching behavior nonetheless conformed to good faith and fair dealing.[90] The Restatement views the following circumstances important in determining whether a breach of the term is material: the extent to which the aggrieved party is deprived of a reasonably expected benefit and can be compensated adequately for that loss; the extent to which the breaching party will suffer loss, and the likelihood of cure by that party, including reasonable assurances to accomplish the cure; and an evaluation of the extent of good faith (subjective) and fair dealing (objective) of the party in breach.[91] Applying these factors suggests that the determination of material breach is a question of fact for the trier of fact (judge or jury), whereas the result of the breach, termination, operates as a matter of law.[92]

The concept behind materiality, or what sorts of breaches are material,[93] in essence asks what terms, conditions, promises, and obligations under the contract are so critical to it that, if unmet, unfulfilled, or broken, for example, one would say the heart of the bargain or its essential purpose or element is destroyed. As with all contract principles, determining material breach requires an interpretation of state law, but as the Restatement suggests, themes apply across jurisdictions.[94] Based on these standards, price would appear to be a material term in a library license, as might content or subject matter—what journal titles are offered by the vendor, for example, or how many hours per month the service must be available.

The Concept of Anticipatory Breach

What if the library sends a letter to the vendor stating, "We don't intend to monitor or report any violations of the terms of the license by our authorized users to you as is required under the terms of the agreement," or the vender conveys to the library, "We are sorry, but due to rising costs we will be deleting half the titles from our database for the duration of the current license term. This change will take place on the first of the month"? If a party repudiates the contract, must the other party wait until these events actually occur before any action can be taken against the party about to breach? It might depend on the other provisions of the agreement, but in the common law of contract, in the absence of language in the agreement addressing such circumstances, the aggrieved party can consider the breach as constructively present and material. This circumstance is often referred to as an anticipatory breach. It is anticipatory because the act of breach has not occurred yet, but other conduct has—for example, conduct that provides a clear indication of a desire not to fulfill an obligation under the contract. This evidence may be through words or deed, but the expression must be clear and it must be unconditional. A clear expression of one's doubt as to the party's ability to perform is not enough;[95] it must clearly indicate no intention of performing an obligation under the contract. Repudiation "generally gives rise to a claim for damages for total breach even though it is not accompanied or preceded by a breach by non-performance. Such repudiation is sometimes elliptically called an 'anticipatory breach,' meaning a breach by anticipatory repudiation, because it occurs before there is any breach by non-performance."[96] As a result, it is best to define what will be considered a material breach, whether anticipatory breach can occur, and what the remedy is for a particular breach.

Understanding Covenants (or Promises) and Conditions (Precedent and Subsequent)

Another issue to consider is whether a provision is an independent promise, also called a covenant (the failure to perform or otherwise fulfill the promise constitutes a breach, which can then be enforced), or a condition or some other obligation (the failure to meet a condition is not enforceable; i.e., the party cannot be forced to comply, but failure to meet the condition impacts the duty of the other party under the contract). Going back to our examples, the statement "I'll sell you the second edition at a 25 percent discount if it's still in print" is a condition. The condition (the book being in print) triggers the promise (to sell it at a 25 percent discount). A condition can likewise release a party from a duty to perform under the contract. Consider a clause such as the following in a library software license: "If the circulation module operates error free for a period of 30 days after initial installation or upgrade installation, the commitment to provide installation or upgrade service support is hereby fulfilled." A condition that upon occurrence gives rise to an obligation to perform a later act or obligation is known as a condition precedent (e.g., selling the book that's currently still in print), whereas a condition that upon occurrence releases a party from performance is known as a condition subsequent (e.g., discontinuing system support).[97] If the book is out of print, there is no right on the part of the other party to force the vendor to print more, as this is a condition. Whether the book is still in print or not is not an enforceable right or promise but a condition precedent to the selling of the book; if the book is in print, then a promise (covenant) exists upon the part of the vendor to sell the book at the agreed-upon discount. (Of course, this assumes that such communications and statements meet the other requirements for valid contract formation.)

In disputes over such scenarios, it should be obvious, or at least logical if one thinks about it, that the burden of proof shifts depending on whether the condition to be proved is precedent to some future act/obligation or is subsequent to an event/release of an obligation. The burden to prove a condition precedent is on the plaintiff (the one alleging that a triggering event occurred), who must demonstrate that the defendant now has the obligation to follow through on some conduct. The burden to prove a condition subsequent is on the defendant (the party claiming that the obligation under the contract was fulfilled), who must show that the initial obligation was satisfied and further conduct by the defendant party is no longer necessary.[98]

Express and Implied Conditions

Conditions can also be expressed as a provision in the contract or implied. "An express condition, typically, entails an explicit term that provides that one event is not required unless the other (the condition) previously occurs."[99] A useful example of an implied condition relates to notice. Suppose the condition is "When we deposit the grant funds, you may begin filling our order" or "When we receive the new storage cabinets and fiche readers, you may begin shipping the fiche." While the provision does not state, "Upon notification from us that the grant funds have been deposited into our account..." or "Upon receipt of notice provided upon the arrival of the fiche cabinets and readers...," it is implied that the obligation to begin filling the book order or fiche set does not arise until the vendor has been notified of the triggering event. (How would the vendor otherwise know of it?) Thus, there is an additional condition, albeit an implied (and somewhat obvious) one, that the vendor will be provided notice when the condition precedent has occurred and can then begin shipping the books or fiche. Implied conditions are inferred by law. Consider the following exposition by one court regarding these issues:

> The court, however, finds that the language of the contract is clearly a condition. Provision C9.21 does not create a specific right or duty under the contract [which if deemed a covenant or promise would give rise to an enforceable and compensable (damages for breach if material) right under the contract], but seeks to limit the time within which claims may be filed. The time limitation is clearly an event, not certain to occur, which must occur...before performance under a contract becomes due. Because the event (filing within the time limitation period) did not occur, plaintiff failed to meet the condition, and therefore acquired no right to enforce the promise. Plaintiffs, by failing to file within the time provided in the contract, have lost their right to receive refunds. The time limitation is not a covenant, as plaintiffs argue, because it does not create a right or duty in and of itself...the provision merely limits the contractor's right to recover the refunds.[100]

A covenant (or promise), on the other hand, is a commitment to perform or to refrain from performing some designated act. A database license might be structured along these lines: "If you refrain from the following uses [often introduced with the heading "Prohibited Uses"] and comply with the following undertakings [licensee's obligations such as reporting noncompliance with the terms of the license by authorized users], then we promise not to sue you and your authorized users for the following uses [often prefaced by the heading "Permitted Uses"]"— uses that in some instances might otherwise be infringing under the copyright law.

Covenants can be express or implied as well. As the labels suggest, an express covenant is one stated by the terms of the contract, whereas an implied covenant is inferred from the terms. An example of an implied covenant is good faith and fair dealing,[101] and that both parties enter into the agreement in good faith and apply the terms fairly as well.[102] This is important in a license agreement governing the use of copyrighted content, as the true nature of many provisions may be that the vendor promises (i.e., provides a covenant) not to sue for copyright infringement for engaging in what would otherwise be an infringing use of the content. For example, a clause might allow you to create course packs with articles from the licensed database if certain conditions listed in the agreement (express) are fulfilled—for example, that only authorized users have access to the course packs or that no commercial use is made of the course packs (the course packs cannot be sold to students). The condition precedent (the licensee's use of the content in designated ways) triggers a promise not to sue for copyright infringement.

Observing the Difference between Covenants and Conditions in Practice

To use the example of notice, suppose a license clause allows for termination upon the condition that 30 days' notice is first given. The licensee terminates, or ceases fulfilling, its other obligations under the agreement, but after giving only 20 days' notice. Can the vendor sue the library-licensee for damages? No, because this provision is not a covenant. It does mean, however, that the vendor has no obligation to release the licensee from the agreement, as the condition precedent (30 days' notice) was not met—in other words, the licensor need not terminate the agreement and can still, for example, expect payment for future availability of the database. Now suppose the licensee does not see it this way, believes the agreement is terminated effective the upcoming month, and so stops payment for further access to the database. What result? The fee obligation provision is likely a promise: if the vendor makes the database available, there is a promise by the licensee to pay for it. This would be an enforceable promise, likely giving rise to damages, too, as payment issues are material to most contracts; nonpayment constitutes material breach, and absent a cure right, the remedies indicated under the agreement would be available. (Worse, many licenses have a provision indicating that in response to a material breach by the licensee the licensor may suspend service and need not give a refund for any payments received.)

> The correctness of this position depends on whether the thirty day requirement in the contract is a "condition precedent" or a "covenant"... A condition precedent is a fact which must exist before a duty of immediate performance of a promise arises. A covenant, as distinguished from a condition precedent, is an agreement to act or refrain from acting in a certain way. A breach of a covenant which is a part of a legally enforceable contract gives rise to a cause of action for damages rather than affecting enforceability of the provisions of the agreement... Normally a term such as "if", "provided that", "on condition that", or some phrase of conditional language must be included that makes performance specifically conditional.[103]

Perhaps a little confusing is that a contractual provision can operate as both a condition and a convenant (or promise).[104] Concluding that the provision in question constituted a condition as well as a covenant, the *James Klein Ins., Inc. v. Select Office Solutions* court observed: "There was a condition (Klein's determining the copier was compatible with his other systems) coupled with a covenant (Select's promise not to deliver the copier or submit the lease to GECC until the condition was satisfied). The breach of the covenant entitled Klein to recover his damages."[105] In a license agreement governing the use of content protected by copyright, breach of a promise can give rise to an action for both contract (damages for breach of the promise) and copyright infringement.

Recent case law demonstrates that courts continue to observe the difference between conditions and promises (or covenants). In *PAJ, Inc. v. Hanover Insurance Co.*, the court observed:

> The distinction between condition and covenant is significant in this case. PAJ argues the contract's notice provision is a covenant [a promise]. Given that understanding,

PAJ's untimely notice would excuse Hanover's performance only if the untimely notice were a material breach, i.e., only if Hanover was prejudiced by the breach. Hanover, on the other hand, argues the notice provision is a condition to Hanover's performance. Thus, under Hanover's understanding, Hanover would have no obligation to perform unless PAJ gave timely notice, and prejudice to Hanover would be irrelevant.[106]

It is often difficult to determine whether a clause is a condition or a covenant, as one court observed:

Admittedly, it is frequently difficult to determine whether a particular stipulation in a contract constitutes a condition or a covenant. We adopt the reasoning that the difference relates largely to the remedy, and if the breach of the agreement pertains to the validity of the instrument or is a ground for forfeiture it is a condition, while if the remedy is an action at law for damages the agreement is a covenant.[107]

If a party's promise is subject to condition, there can be no breach until the condition has been fulfilled; that is, the promise was in a status where the now-triggered obligation could be broken and failure to perform the promise is now a breach. For example, a circulation module agreement contains a provision that once the module has been installed and runs error free for 30 days, the licensee-library has an obligation to pay for the module within 30 days. Suppose the module after 45 days is still not functioning properly. There is no obligation to pay for it, as the condition (error free for 30 days) has not yet been fulfilled by the licensor. Then suppose that finally the bugs are eliminated and the program runs error free for 30 days; now the condition precedent has been met and the library has an obligation (as it made a promise) to pay for the module. If it does not pay for the module within 30 days, the licensor may respond accordingly under the agreement, as the library in now in breach—and by the terms likely in material breach.

Breach of a promise by one party may or may not excuse the obligation of the other party to still perform under the contract, whereas the nonoccurrence or nonfulfillment of a condition generally excuses the other party of the duty to perform that which was subject to the condition, that is, the promise that the condition would have triggered. To reiterate, words such as *provided, if,* and *when* indicate that the following is intended to be a condition. Returning to a previous example, if the book is out of print, the party that wants to buy the book cannot force the other party to order another print run; it is a condition that is not enforceable. But once it is established that the book is in print, the promise to offer it for sale at a 25 percent discount must be upheld. Likewise, the library cannot force the vendor to get the circulation software to run properly; this is not an enforceable covenant but instead a condition. On the other hand, until the condition is met and the software runs error free for 30 days, the library has no obligation to pay for it. When in doubt, courts often construe provisions as promises. Sometimes the word *covenant* is used to describe that which is not deemed a condition. Failure to meet a condition creates an obligation to perform, but it does not create a right to force the other party that has failed the condition to perform; it merely releases the nonbreaching party from their return obligation.

Breach of a covenant (or promise) may give rise to damages if the breach is material. However, if the provision is a condition, there is no breach and no right to claim damages. But if the condition is not met, it releases the other party from its obligation because the triggering event requiring a return act has not occurred. This might mean a use by the library is now unauthorized and infringing, and the licensor can sue for copyright infringement. This is the harsh lesson of the cases discussed. Is the provision that the vendor provides costumer service to end users a promise, and, if so, is it material to the contract, such that failure to provide the service constitutes a breach for which a damage remedy is available? Or is the provision a condition precedent, which then triggers the licensee's obligation to pay the monthly license fee? It of course depends on how the provision is drafted. If the provision is a condition that the vendor has not met, the licensee cannot treat the failure as a breach; it is not an enforceable right under the contract. However, if it is a part of the mutual promises the parties exchanged, then it can be an enforceable provision and may be subject to damages as a breach. The question is whether the failure to fulfill this promise is material or not: Does it go to the heart of the bargain, so to speak? As a result of these issues, many agreements define what acts constitute a breach and what the remedy is for this breach.

If there is a condition precedent, then its execution is excused by prevention or hindrance, by waiver, by impossibility or impracticability, or by forfeiture. If not, and the condition is fulfilled such that an obligation to perform exists, then performance can be excused by some other mechanism, such as occurrence of a condition subsequent; actual performance; material breach; doctrines such as impossibility, impracticality, frustration, mutual rescission, release, or accord and satisfaction; or novation (replacement)[108] or modification of the agreement. Examples of prevention or hindrance include illegal conduct or termination of a business (bankruptcy). Parties may also waive a right of performance owed to them. Impossibility, impracticality, and forfeiture can excuse the fulfillment of a condition if fulfillment does not go to a material term or condition.

Conditions and Covenants in Licenses in the Case Law

As Nimmer explains, whether a term is a condition or a covenant can have significant implications for contracts involving use of content protected by copyright that is then licensed:

> If the nature of a licensee's violation consists of a failure to satisfy a condition to the license (as distinguished from a breach of a covenant), it follows that the rights dependent upon satisfaction of such condition have not been effectively licensed, and, therefore,

any use by the licensee is without authority from the licensor and may therefore, constitute an infringement of copyright. Thus, if a license to exhibit a motion picture film is subject to the condition that any such exhibition must occur at specified times and places, an exhibition by the licensee that does not satisfy such condition is without authority from the licensor and is therefore, a copyright infringement. By the same token, when a license is limited in scope, exploitation of the copyrighted work outside the specified limits constitutes infringement...Conduct that constitutes both a breach of covenant and the failure of a condition will permit an election of remedies based either upon breach of contract or copyright infringement.[109]

If the license, however, transfers all of the copyright owner's rights, the license is considered exclusive and there would be no rights left under the copyright law to enforce. Any violation of an agreement in this situation would give rise to rights under the contract law alone. In the copyright-licensing enforcement arena, the granting of a nonexclusive license in essence leaves the copyright owner without any copyright rights to enforce, and so if the conditions of that use are met, the copyright owner would be unable to pursue a remedy for violation of the license under copyright law but must proceed under the contract law alone.[110]

If the agreement is one for, say, access to a database of journal articles where the content is still protected by copyright and the rights of use given are nonexclusive,[111] then the vendor can claim a remedy in both contract and copyright law if the use is conduct that is also infringing and beyond the scope of the license. Suppose the license includes a provision that the licensee must cooperate to the fullest extent possible where excessive downloading of articles occurs. There is also a provision indicating that, in return for fulfillment of various conditions (like that pertaining to excessive downloading), the licensee may use the database to create course packs and e-reserves, as well as populate its online course management system and e-anthologies with the licensed content. Now suppose excessive downloading occurs and the vendor does not believe the library is doing its part to stop it, though it pays the vendor invoice on time. What is the result? The excessive downloading provision is likely a covenant (conduct the licensee promised to do) and a condition (if cooperation is not to the fullest extent possible, then the licensor does not have to fulfill its part of the bargain to allow use of articles for course packs, e-reserves, etc.). The promise (remember that covenants are promises) not to sue the library for such uses is no longer in effect now; so if the use of articles in course packs, e-reserves, and so forth, is infringing, the vendor can sue the library for copyright infringement. The vendor might also have other remedies under the agreement, such as suspension of service until the library starts cooperating in enforcement efforts.[112] "Since a nonexclusive license does not transfer ownership of the copyright from the licensor to the licensee, the licensor can still bring suit for copyright infringement if the licensee's use goes beyond the scope of the nonexclusive license."[113] These principles are demonstrated in several cases involving license agreements and the use of content protected by copyright.

Consider *Graham v. James*,[114] where the publisher alleged its obligation to pay royalties to the programmer and include a notice of authorship (not an exclusive right of the copyright owner under section 106 of the copyright law) on the software disks were covenants (promises), not conditions, of the contract. This case also involved the downstream commercial use of content that was derived from various kinds of open source content.[115] As discussed previously, the difference between a covenant and a condition is in the nature of the claim that the aggrieved party— in this case, the licensor—can make: "Graham claims that even if James owns the copyright in the C version [of the software], Graham was licensed to use the copyright under a licensing agreement, and that the district court therefore erred in finding that Graham was an infringer. According to Graham, James was entitled at most to recover for Graham's breach of the licensing agreement."[116] Failure to include attribution did constitute copyright infringement even in the absence of the license (permission to use the software): "Moreover, Graham's failure to credit James with the copyright on the C version did not itself amount to copyright infringement."[117] This result is sound, as attribution is not an exclusive right of the copyright owner under section 106. However, in cases where violation consists of a failure to satisfy a condition, then the rights that are dependent upon that condition (e.g., access to the database as long as use of the licensed content in course packs to students is made without any direct remuneration or that use of the licensed content to fill interlibrary loan requests be in print form alone) have not been licensed (as the conforming condition of use is not met) for use by the licensee beyond those terms and, without additional authority of the copyright owner, can constitute copyright infringement.

Assuming the conditions are met by the licensee—whereby the prohibited uses are avoided and the uses permitted are adhered to by the licensee—then use of the licensed content remains authorized under the license and the remedy of the licensor rests with the contract law alone; the conditions precedent of the licensee in the agreement are fulfilled, which triggers a promise on the part of the vendor-licensor not to sue the library-licensee for the authorized uses granted and articulated in the agreement.

> [C]ourts recognize a distinction between conduct that merely breaches the contract (or a covenant within the contract), and conduct that exceeds the license scope resulting also in a claim for infringement. The distinction rests on contract interpretation under state contract law principles... A breach of a mere covenant entitles the licensor to damages perhaps, but does not support an infringement claim so long as the licensee continues to perform within the license scope [i.e., uses the content in course-packs or for interlibrary loan according to the terms of the license but breaches some other

covenant]. On the other hand, breach of a scope provision [uses the licensed content to populate e-reserves when such use is prohibited by the license terms and where the use also exceeds fair use under the copyright law] entitles the licensor to both a contract remedy and an infringement claim, providing of course that there can be no double recovery.[118]

The breach of a promise is an enforceable right, for example, "I promise to pay you the subscription fee if you make the database available." If the condition is met (the database is made available) and payment is not forthcoming, the vendor can sue the library for breach of contract—but the remedy would not lie in copyright law as an infringement. However, where a condition exists to limit use of the database to authorized users alone (a condition precedent) and in return a number of uses are permitted, such as use of the licensed content in course packs and e-readers or anthologies, then failure to comply with the condition (the library allows unauthorized users access to the database) allows the vendor to sue under a copyright infringement theory when the licensed content is used to make course packs and e-readers. Such use would be infringing, as the vendor's promise not to sue no longer governs because this promise was conditional on an obligation of the licensee, which is now unmet.[119] (Of course, not all use of copyrighted content in course packs and e-readers is infringing, but some uses might be; this is one reason such uses are included in licenses—so the library need not worry if such uses might be infringing. For those uses which would otherwise be infringing in the absence of the license, the licensor retains the option to sue for copyright infringement if the promise not to sue is negated by some conduct of the licensee-library, such as failure of a condition.) This is why many scope (permitted and prohibited uses) provisions in license agreements are phrased at least as conditions: to preserve the right of vendors to sue licensees for copyright infringement as well as under contract theory.

In the *Graham v. James* case, instead of breaking a promise, the licensor argued that the condition was breached and thus ended the contract, making the uses complained of infringements as well as breaches of the contract: "James argues that the license was voided when Graham breached its conditions by nonpayment of royalties and removal of James's copyright notice. This argument turns—and fails—on the distinction in contract between a condition and a covenant."[120] The basis for the court's comment was once again rooted in fundamental differences under contract law between covenants and conditions: "the payment of royalties and the inclusion of a notice crediting James's authorship are to be considered covenants, not conditions."[121] If truly conditions, then the failure of Graham to fulfill the royalty and attribution provisions would release James from his obligation not to sue under the contract, as the condition precedent ("If you pay me, I won't sue you") would not be met. The court said such provisions were not conditions but instead covenants. This is the expected result, as fee provisions are typically presented as promises to pay a specified amount for access or use of the content. Citing New York state law, the court observed the rule that presumes clauses to be promises or covenants rather than conditions.[122] Likewise, in a recent case involving the publication of images, such obligation was characterized as a covenant, not a condition.[123] Similarly, a provision requiring the licensee to include technological controls to prevent users from disabling subtitling was a covenant, not a condition precedent.[124]

The 9th Circuit addressed a similar question in *Sun Microsystems, Inc. v. Microsoft Corp.*[125] regarding a dispute between the two computing giants over Java:

> The district court did not elaborate on why the case was a copyright infringement rather than a contract interpretation dispute...It contends that the disputed compatibility requirements of the license agreement are affirmative covenants rather than limitations on the scope of the license [conditions limiting the use of the licensed content], and that accordingly contractual rather than copyright remedies are appropriate if there has been any breach.[126]

Differing expectations laid the foundation for the eventual dispute: "Sun had created Java so that programmers could write a single program that would work on any operating system. Because Sun wanted Java to remain cross-platform compatible, the TLDA includes compatibility requirements."[127] Relations soured under the Technology License and Distribution Agreement (TLDA) when Sun came to believe Microsoft was "polluting" the program by using modified versions that were no longer compatible with Sun's Java systems. Sun moved to enjoin "Microsoft from using Sun's 'Java Compatible' logo on products that failed Sun's compatibility tests."[128] The court could not make that determination based on the evidence before it but indicated again that the crux of the ability to sue under copyright infringement claim revolved around whether conditions or covenants applied.[129] Again, it is state contract law that often determines the characterization of terms as conditions or covenants: "The principles illustrated by *Video Trip*[130] and *S.O.S.*[131] indicate that the disputed question in this case, whether the compatibility terms in the TLDA are license restrictions or separate covenants, is a preliminary contractual issue that must be resolved under California law favorably to Sun before Sun is entitled to the copyright presumption of irreparable harm."[132] Unfortunately, the 9th Circuit referred the matter back to the district court for this determination. The district court ultimately concluded: "The language and structure of the TLDA suggest that the compatibility obligations are separate covenants and not conditions of, or restrictions on, the license grants."[133] A court recently decided that it was possible also to bring a breach of contract suit and a claim for circumvention of access control technologies under the Digital Millennium Copyright Act (DMCA). Circumvention suits are separate from a claim based on copyright infringement but are nonetheless based on the protection of the underlying work whose access or control was circumvented vis-à-vis the copyright law:[134] "This court holds that the Studios are permitted to bring both DMCA claims for circumvention of CSS [Content Scrambling System] technology and breach of contract claims under the CSS License Agreement."[135] Actually, the DMCA claims were brought under anti-trafficking provisions, which prohibit distribution of products that allow technologies to circumvent control of access to and duplication of protected content, among other uses. RealNetworks, Inc. developed, marketed, and sold RealDVD, which included what it referred to as Vegas and Facet software. For example, "Real's Vegas software, in addition to permitting storage of DVD content on a hard drive, also allows for portability of the DVD content by allowing users to create and save personal copies of DVDs onto a laptop computer or portable hard drive."[136] The technology RealNetworks developed circumvented the CSS access control provision when a RealDVD user accessed a stored copy of a DVD: "The only time RealDVD accesses the CSS keys with authorization is the first time RealDVD reads a physical DVD that is inserted in the DVD drive. Thereafter, RealDVD circumvents CSS when it accesses the DVD content from its hard drive, after having performed the 'save' or 'play and save' function. Every time the RealDVD product, be it Vegas or Facet, accesses DVD content from its hard drive, it does so by circumventing CSS technology and violating the access-control provision of the DMCA."[137] RealNetworks was engaged in prohibited trafficking of such a circumvention device when it made the RealDVD product available to the consuming public. The RealDVD technology also circumvented copy-control technology. This is not a violation of the DMCA per se, but trafficking in technologies that allow others to do so is also a prohibition of the antitrafficking rules of the DMCA. "RealDVD circumvents the copy-control provision of the DMCA through RealDVD's utilization of the CSS authentication codes and algorithms for an unauthorized purpose, namely, to copy the content from a CSS-protected DVD to a hard drive."[138]

See Table 3.1 for examples of common covenants and conditions and the resulting effects of a breach or failure of these license provisions.

Remedies and Damages

Remedies for breach of contract, or for most legal harms, fall into to two broad categories: monetary and nonmonetary. Most folks think of dollars and cents, but in the contract area, nonmonetary remedies can be as powerful. For example, a nonmonetary outcome might require a specific performance—that is, a court may tell the reneging party that it must fulfill its end of the bargain and deliver the goods as planned or carry out the terms of the service agreement, and so forth. Nonmonetary damages, often called equitable remedies, include injunctive relief ("Stop doing that") or specific performance ("Start doing this"). Breach by the seller or vendor in a contract for goods where the buyer seeks delivery of goods is a

▶ **TABLE 3.1   Covenants and Conditions in Licenses**

Character of License Provision	Example	Effect of Breach or Failure	Definition from the Case Law
Covenant (promise)	"The Licensee promises to pay the annual subscription fee within thirty days of receipt of invoice." (There is likely an implied condition here in that the licensor must submit an invoice to the licensee, which then obligates the licensee to fulfill its promise to pay the annual subscription fee.)	Breach of a covenant allows the vendor-licensor to terminate the agreement under many licenses. See, e.g., *Graham v. James*, 144 F.3d 229, 237 (2d Cir. 1998): "A material breach of a covenant will allow the licensor to rescind the license and hold the licensee liable for infringement for uses of the work thereafter." See also *Madison River Management Co. v. Business Management Software Corp.*, 387 F. Supp. 2d 521, 534 (M.D.N.C. 2005), holding that a licensee's use of a copyrighted work in excess of that which was authorized under the license was a breach of a covenant under the terms of the license agreement between the parties, and therefore the copyright holder was entitled only to breach-of-contract damages and not copyright remedies: "Because the payment term is a covenant of the Agreement, Defendant's remedy does not lie in copyright infringement, but in breach of contract. Summary judgment will therefore be granted in favor of Madison on this claim."	"A copyright owner who grants a nonexclusive, limited license ordinarily waives the right to sue licensees for copyright infringement, and it may sue only for breach of contract. However, if the licensee acts outside the scope of the license, the licensor may sue for copyright infringement. Enforcing a copyright license raises issues that lie at the intersection of copyright and contract law. We refer to contractual terms that limit a license's scope as conditions, the breach of which constitute copyright infringement. We refer to all other license terms as 'covenants,' the breach of which is actionable only under contract law. We distinguish between conditions and covenants according to state contract law, to the extent consistent with federal copyright law and policy" (*MDY Industries, LLC v. Blizzard Entertainment, Inc.*, 629 F.3d 928, 939 (9th Cir. 2010), citations and quotations omitted). See also *Quest Software, Inc. v. DirecTV Operations, LLC*, 2011 WL 4500922, *4 (C.D. Cal., 2011): "Stated somewhat circularly, conditions are contractual terms that limit a license's scope . . . the breach of which constitutes copyright infringement. All other license terms are covenants which the Ninth Circuit has defined to mean a contractual promise, i.e., a manifestation or intention to act or refrain from acting in a particular way" (citations omitted).
Condition precedent	"If our warehouse receives the library's order by the 20th of	Not enforceable if unfulfilled, but without fruition of the act or event (warehouse did not receive the order in time), the obligation regarding future	"Normally a term such as 'if', 'provided that', 'on condition that', or some phrase of conditional language must be included that makes performance specifically conditional" (*Matter of*

(continued)

► **TABLE 3.1** Covenants and Conditions in Licenses *(Continued)*

Character of License Provision	Example	Effect of Breach or Failure	Definition from the Case Law
Condition precedent *(continued)*	December, we will process and ship the order before the end of the year."	conduct (process and ship before the end of the year) does not arise.	*5300 Memorial Investors, Ltd.*, 973 F.2d 1160, 1170 (5th Cir. 1992) (internal quotations and citations omitted). "The rationale for imposing the burden of proof on the one attacking the validity of the claim for failure to perform assessment work may also be explained in terms of *conditions precedent* and *subsequent*. Briefly, a *condition subsequent* is a provision or condition which cuts off an existing legal right, entitlement or benefit. Upon its occurrence, a *condition subsequent* operates to defeat or annul a right or benefit. On the other hand, a *condition precedent* requires certain performance or condition which must take place before a legal right can vest. The condition must occur or be performed before a right, entitlement or benefit comes into existence and becomes binding" (*Tosco Corp. v. Hodel*, 611 F. Supp. 1130, 1186 (D.C. Colo., 1985), italics in the original).
Condition subsequent	"Once the number of downloads exceeds 100 in a calendar year, the e-book will no longer be available."	Not enforceable if unfulfilled, but once requirement is satisfied (number of downloads by the licensee exceeds 100) the obligation to continue present conduct or circumstances ceases (the licensor need not continue to make the database available).	See "Condition Precedent." "A condition subsequent has been defined as a future event upon the happening of which the agreement or obligations of the parties would be no longer binding . . . The term 'condition subsequent' as normally used in contracts in contrast to 'condition precedent,' should mean an event which occurs subsequent to a duty of immediate performance, that is, a condition which divests a duty of immediate performance of a contract after it has once accrued and become absolute. True conditions subsequent are very rare in the law of contracts." RICHARD A. LORD, 13 WILLISTON ON

(continued)

▷ TABLE 3.1   Covenants and Conditions in Licenses *(Continued)*

Character of License Provision	Example	Effect of Breach or Failure	Definition from the Case Law
Condition subsequent *(continued)*			Contracts § 38.9 (4th ed. 2008, database updated in Westlaw, May 2012) (footnotes omitted).
			See also *Century 21 Al Burdack Realtors v. Zigler*, 628 S.W.2d 915, 916 (Mo. App. E.D. 1982) ("such a provision [financing contingency] is a condition subsequent to the existence of the contract, which, upon the non-occurrence of the stipulated event, may be raised to avoid the contract . . ."); and *Frankel v. Board of Dental Examiners*, 54 Cal.Rptr.2d 128, 137 (Cal. App. 3 Dist., 1996): "The potential lack of approval by the Board is simply a condition subsequent, i.e., a future event upon the happening of which Frankel's agreements and obligations no longer would be binding on him."
Covenant and condition	"If you monitor users for compliance with the terms of this agreement, we will let you and your patrons use the contents of our database to fill e-ILL [interlibrary loan] or create e-course packs."	Conduct that constitutes both a breach of covenant (users are not complying with the terms of the agreement) and the failure of a condition (library fails to monitor users to ensure compliance) will permit an election of remedies based either upon breach of contract or copyright infringement (without the covenant in place, some ILL and course pack creation may be infringing).	*Jacobson v. Katzer*, 2008 WL 3395772 (Fed. Cir. 2008): "The heart of the argument on appeal concerns whether the terms of the Artistic License are conditions of, or merely covenants to, the copyright license" (*id.* at *5). "Thus, if the terms of the Artistic License allegedly violated are both covenants and conditions, they may serve to limit the scope of the license and are governed by copyright law. If they are merely covenants, by contrast, they are governed by contract law" (*id.* at *5).

court action known as replevin.[139] Remedies, in addition to a reasonable period within which the breaching party has a right to cure, include nonmonetary alternatives (those relating to performance, e.g., cancellation, rescission, or termination) and monetary remedies (those related to recovery of damages). Rescission allows the party to act as if the contract never existed, whereas termination as a form of cancellation allows one to end continued obligations under the contract.

Damages—the bottom line in any assessment of costs and benefits—are a major factor in the assessment of legal risk associated with any scenario of contemplated action. In other words, is this breach of the agreement worth it in terms of the remedies the other party may obtain? Or from the library's perspective as the aggrieved party, is it worth suing the seller, vendor, or licensor in light of the remedy that could be obtained? Again, the discussion in this chapter relates to the default rules, so to speak, developed by the case law. However, the terms of the license may indicate (or limit) what remedies are available as well as the maximum amount recoverable—often capped at the amount of the annual subscription rate. Of course, no person or entity prefers litigation, and likely most disputes in the library environment might not come to legal blows, but it is a possibility. Moreover, such extreme response may be avoided if the other party can be persuaded that compromising or settling is in its best interest. Damages can play a role here as well, as leverage—again, from the perspective of library as harmed party—in that the seller, vendor, or licensor believes that an agreed-upon alternative holds far less risk than what might result from a court- or jury-awarded amount of damages or scope of remedies. As a result, it is important to understand the range and scope of possible damages and then to realize that provisions in many license agreements may operate to limit or eliminate certain sorts of damages or remedies, or they may foreclose litigation altogether in favor of arbitration.

Contractual monetary damages are generally concerned with several sorts of interests. The Restatement characterizes these interests as reliance, restitution, and expectation interests.[140] A reliance interest focuses upon reimbursement for losses caused by reliance on the terms of the contract being fulfilled, thus placing the nonbreaching party in as good a position as before the contract was made. A restoration (or restitution) interest is concerned with restoring to the nonbreaching party any benefit that the breaching party reaped or obtained as a result of the breach.[141] This is a concept known as unjust enrichment. Finally, an expectation interest focuses on assessing the value the party would have been entitled to had the contract materialized, restoring to the nonbreaching party the anticipated benefit of the bargain. Where a court finds an implied contract (discussed in Chapter 4), it can award monetary compensation for services performed (known as *quantum meruit*) or for the value of property received (known as *quantum valebant*).

In rare circumstances, punitive damages may be awarded, but contract law does not focus on punishment; rather, the concern is to make the nonbreaching party whole again. Also frowned upon in court are liquidated damages, where dollar amounts are assigned for particular breaches. Again, these amounts may have little to do with the actual harm suffered and they are therefore scrutinized by the courts: "Liquidated damages are a predetermined good-faith estimate of damages the Customer will incur as a result of the Licensor's breach or that the Licensor will incur as a result of the Customer's breach, which eliminates the necessity that the injured party proves its damages."[142]

Expectation damages fall into two categories: those which could be expected, often described in such terms as general damages or ordinary damages, and those which in the normal circumstances would be unexpected, often termed special damages. The latter are not typically available unless some knowledge of the peculiar circumstances that would cause such harm is held by the breaching party. "The distinction is intended to call attention to the difference between losses that could be seen as ordinary and predictable consequence of the breach, and losses that are not chargeable to the breaching party unless it had knowledge or notice of the risk of causing them because they flow from special requirements of the injured party."[143] Under article 2 of the UCC, where the buyer breaches the agreement, typically by not paying, the seller can obtain the contract price, the general or compensatory damages, and any incidental damages. Where the seller breaches, typically by some breach of warranty or other act or nonact subsequent to delivery, such as lack of service, the remedy for the buyer is to recover the value of the goods as if the warranty or follow-up service would have been provided. Incidental and consequential damages are also possible. In cases where the goods have not been retained or tendered and the buyer breaches, the seller can recover the contract price (adjusted for market price or resale) or lost profits; incidental damages are also possible. In cases where the seller is in breach, the buyer can recover a similar contract price adjusted for market price at the time of breach or cost of substitute goods or specific performance (often where the goods are unique and there is no substitute to offset), including incidental and consequential damages.

Understanding when remedy is available is important because a misconception or misidentification of material breach can mislead the initial nonbreaching party to breach:

> The most common case occurs where one party believes that a breach occurred and ceases making payments required by the contract because of that breach. In such cases, if a less than material breach or repudiation has occurred and there is no basis to suspend performance, the non-paying party risks placing itself into breach of the contract because of nonpayment. Its own breach may, indeed, override the other breach and lead to cancellation of the license.[144]

This is why the license may define material breach and eliminate the guesswork. It is typical in many licenses to limit the potential for liability for the licensor or for both parties to the price of the contract, or the amount of license fees paid under the agreement. Courts often enforce such limitations, which represent in essence a refund remedy.[145]

Liquidated damages are those indicated by agreement. In a contract with a seller, vendor, or licensor, it would be found in the terms and conditions of the agreement; in an agreement between a library and a patron, in a registration form, for example, it might be the fee established for each day a book or other item is late being returned.[146] The amount must be reasonable in the court's view and cannot represent in effect a penalty.[147] "In licensing, one common form of liquidated damage provision is to provide that the licensee must pay all remaining license or service fees for the remaining term of the license in the event of breach. Such provisions produce mixed results in court... clauses that purport to escalate and increase the amount of fees owing as a result of breach, often are treated as penalties that are unenforceable."[148] Regardless of how the agreement labels the clause granting liquidated damages as a remedy, it cannot operate as a penalty. "The licensee should be careful, however, to include a provision that provides that if the liquidated damages reach a certain level, the licensor shall be deemed to be in material breach and the licensee may terminate the contract."[149] The concept of contract remedies is compensatory, not punitive.[150] A clause in a database license agreement awarding $10,000 for each hour of service the system is down would likely be a penalty, especially if disproportionate to the cost of an annual subscription. Again, the goal of damages in contract law in general is to make the parties whole and to compensate them for loss based on the reasonable reliance on promises made. Liquidated damages are often sought when it is very difficult to ascertain at the time the contract is made what actually would result if there was a breach.

A final type of monetary damages is nominal damages, which are also known as token damages. In some cases, no actual loss is proved, but courts will award a token amount, such as one dollar.

SUMMARY POINTS

▶ Under common law, there may be numerous reasons why a meeting of the minds could be said not to have occurred regarding the essential elements of the transaction and a contract be deemed not to have been formed. This concept is articulated as indefiniteness.

▶ Courts are unlikely to reform a contract based on a unilateral mistake unless the effect of the mistake is such that enforcement of the contract would be unconscionable, the other party had reason to know of the mistake, or the other party's fault caused the mistake.

▶ Misrepresentations relating to an essential term without knowledge of the misrepresentation prevent contract formation in the first instance, while those which involve fraud or material misrepresentation are voidable by the reliance party.

▶ Duress results when a contract is formed in response to some threat of physical harm or monetary loss or necessity that leaves the party with no reasonable alternative course of action.

▶ In situations where one party exerts domination over the other party, often based upon the disparate positions of or relationship between the parties, undue influence can be used to void the contract.

▶ Many state statutes reflect the historical notion of when agreements should be committed to writing and when oral agreement suffices. This concept is embodied in the statute of frauds. The current UCC rule exempts from the writing requirement contracts for a sale of goods less than $5,000.

▶ A contract with a minor is generally voidable by the minor if to his or her disadvantage.

▶ Natural disasters, so-called acts of God, may render performance of contractual obligations impossible. Licenses often address this concept in what are known as force majeure clauses.

▶ A covenant (or promise) in a contract is an enforceable provision, and if a party breaches a promise, it may give rise to a remedy for damages, if the breach is material.

▶ Material breaches relate to those aspects going to the heart of the bargain. Prices or license fees are generally material. The loss of one title from a subscription database of hundreds is likely not material.

▶ A condition can be express (in the contract) or implied by the court. A condition does not give rise to a remedy for damages, nor is it enforceable. Rather, conditions operate as "triggers," obligating the party to some other act or course of conduct or releasing a party from further obligation.

▶ Conditions may be precedent, triggering an obligation to act, such as a duty to notify the licensee when substantial changes to the list of titles available in a database are made, or they may be subsequent, releasing a party from the duty to act, such as a provision indicating when installation service obligations have been fulfilled.

▶ Remedies may include award of monetary and nonmonetary benefits. The purpose of monetary damages in contracts is to make the aggrieved party whole. Damages come in many forms: reliance, expectation (general and special), restitution, punitive, liquidated, and nominal.

LEARNING EXAMPLES

▶ **Example 3.1**

Situation: A library purchases new tables and chairs for its main reading room. Delivery and setup of the furniture is scheduled to occur on the first of the next month. The vendor's factory has a fire, and the whole order goes up in smoke. The vendor then contracts with a competitor to fill the order according to the original specifications, but there is a labor strike at the plant where the replacements are to be made.

Legal Analysis: In the unlikely event that there is no written contract, a statute of frauds issue arises, with the result that the vendor may be able to assert this issue as a defense for contract enforcement by the library. Another issue raised by this situation is impossibility. While it is more likely for a writing to exist, in the absence of language addressing the current facts, the common law result, again, as a defense asserted by the vendor when the library attempts to enforce the vendor's end of the bargain (in this case, delivery of the promised furniture), would be one of impossibility due to an "act of God"—the factory fire. Many contracts address the circumstances under which a party may terminate the agreement and thereby be released from an obligation to perform the contract. It is typical to include fire but less likely that labor strikes or work stoppages are included, as such events are not acts of God but man-made.

► **Example 3.2**

Situation: A license agreement contains the following provisions: "The Vendor will supply a print copy of any article from the Content provided should the Licensee inform the Vendor of any article inaccessible for more than one day"; "The Vendor will supply an online help desk 24 hours a day for the duration of the agreement"; and "The Vendor promises to offer access to the Content for a period of one year."

Legal Analysis: The first clause is a condition. The latter two clauses are covenants or promises. The second clause is not a material clause, as online help in using the product is not the heart of the agreement. Damages may be a remedy depending on the other provisions of the agreement, such as those for downtime or routine maintenance, but the licensee would have no right to claim remedy for a breach. Access to the content, noted in the third clause, does go to heart of the agreement and so is material; depending on the duration of the loss of access, the vendor may be considered in breach. The first clause is a condition precedent. An obligation on the part of the vendor to supply a substitute print version of an article in the database (the content) is triggered only when the licensee informs the vendor of the article's unavailability online.

► **Example 3.3**

Situation: Suppose a librarian is drifting through the exhibit hall at the annual conference of the American Library Association. One database vendor indicates that by filling out and signing an interest card, the librarian will qualify her library for a free set of e-book readers and laptops—if the librarian agrees to participate in a follow-up call and sales pitch by a representative of the vendor in the next month or so. The librarian does this and places the interest card through the slot in a wood box labeled "Reader and Laptop Drawing." The vendor representative calls the following week to ask when the library would like its subscription to begin, indicating that the card the librarian filled out was actually a contract with the disclaimer "Terms available on our website" written in very small print on the reverse of the card.

Legal Analysis: This situation would likely not occur because vendors are not this unscrupulous, but it represents a misrepresentation in factum or execution, as there was no indication that the card the librarian signed was anything other than an interest card.

▶ **Example 3.4**

Situation: Suppose the same initial scenario as in Example 3.3, but the vendor tells the librarian the database is updated by weekly data dumps and its title list of magazines and newspapers will double in the next month. The librarian enters into the license based on these claims by the vendor. However, in actuality, the database is updated only once a year and the list of titles actually decreases over the course of the first quarter of the annual subscription.

Legal Analysis: Currency and content are likely material terms to the library and as such could be grounds for a claim of material misrepresentation or inducement, making the contract voidable by the party harmed if reliance on the assertions was reasonable by the librarian. Most license agreements address this issue by a clause that says the licensee agrees not to rely on any information provided by any promotional material or on assertions made by its representatives. Such clauses undermine any claims of reasonable or justifiable reliance, an element of a claim of inducement.

ENDNOTES

1. Cape Motor Lodge, Inc. v. City of Cape Girardeau, 706 S.W.2d 208, 215 (Mo.1986): Contract between a university and a municipality "not avoided for indefiniteness because the specific details are not fully established."
2. See also Restatement (Second) of Contracts § 33(3) (1981) (Certainty), comment d, uncertain time of performance: "Valid contracts are often made which do not specify the time for performance. Where the contract calls for a single performance such as the rendering of a service or the delivery of goods, the time for performance is a 'reasonable time.'"
3. Restatement (Second) of Contracts § 33(3) (1981) (Certainty), comment a, certainty of terms: "An offer which appears to be indefinite may be given precision by usage of trade or by course of dealing between the parties. Terms may be supplied by factual implication, and in recurring situations the law often supplies a term in the absence of agreement to the contrary."

4. Restatement (Second) of Contracts § 33(3) (1981) (Certainty): "The fact that one or more terms of a proposed bargain are left open or uncertain may show that a manifestation of intention is not intended to be understood as an offer or as an acceptance."

5. RICHARD A. LORD, 9 WILLISTON ON CONTRACTS § 24:3 (4th ed. 2008): "It is well settled that the oral contracts invalidated by the Statute [of Frauds] because they are not to be performed within a year include only those which *cannot* be performed within that period. A promise which is not likely to be performed within a year, and which in fact is not performed within a year, is not within the Statute if at the time the contract is made there is a possibility in law and in fact that full performance such as the parties intended may be completed before the expiration of a year" (emphasis in original, footnotes omitted).

6. Respect Inc. v. Committee on Status of Women, 781 F. Supp. 1358, 1365 (N.D. Ill. 1992), emphasis original.

7. Academy Chicago Publishers v. Cheever, 578 N.E.2d 981, 984 (Ill. 1991).

8. BLACK'S LAW DICTIONARY (9th ed.) (Bryan A. Garner ed., St. Paul, MN: West Publishing, 2009) indicates that a mutual mistake is a "mistake that is shared and relied on by both parties to a contract. A court will often revise or nullify a contract based on a mutual mistake about a material term. Also termed common mistake" (no pagination in Westlaw).

9. *Id.*: "A mistake by only one party to a contract. A unilateral mistake is generally not as likely to be a ground for voiding the contract as is a mutual mistake."

10. Restatement (Second) of Contracts § 152(1) (1981) (When Mistake of Both Parties Makes a Contract Voidable). "A mistake of both parties does not make the contract voidable unless it is one as to a basic assumption on which both parties made the contract" (*id.* at comment b, basic assumption).

11. Restatement (Second) of Contracts § 152(1) (1981) (When Mistake of Both Parties Makes a Contract Voidable), comment c, material effect on agreed exchange.

12. RICHARD A. LORD, 27 WILLISTON ON CONTRACTS § 70:104 (4th ed. 2008).

13. RAYMOND T. NIMMER, 2 INFORMATION LAW § 12.41 (database updated in Westlaw, November 2011).

14. Restatement (Second) of Contracts § 153 (1981) (When Mistake of One Party Makes a Contract Voidable), b. Similarity to rule where both are mistaken: "The mistake must be one as to a basic assumption on which the contract was made; it must have a material effect on the agreed exchange of performances; and the mistaken party must not bear the risk of the mistake."

15. Restatement (Second) of Contracts § 153 (1981) (When Mistake of One Party Makes a Contract Voidable).

16. *Id.* at comment a: "Courts frequently show lack of sympathy with claims that one party 'did not understand' a term, even if the legal consequences of the term are far from self-evident."

17. Nimmer, *supra* note 13.

18. Information Intern. Associates, Inc. v. U.S., 74 Fed. Cl. 192, 207 (2006). The five elements are "(1) a mistake in fact occurred prior to contract award; (2) the mistake was clear-cut, clerical or mathematical, or a misreading of the specifications and not a judgmental error; (3) prior to award the Government knew, or should have known, that a mistake had been made and, therefore, should have requested bid verification; (4) the Government did not request bid verification or its request for bid verification was inadequate; and (5) proof of the intended bid is established" (*id.* at 191).

19. Lassiter Const. Co. v. School Bd. for Palm Beach County, 395 So.2d 567, 569 (Fla. App. 1981): "Appellant has failed to demonstrate that the mistake was not due to Lassiter's own negligence. We further note from the record that the error is less than four per cent of the intended bid, and that without the increase of $100,000 appellant would still receive some profit." See also Mountain Home School Dist. No. 9 v. T.M.J. Builders, Inc., 313 Ark. 661, 858 S.W.2d 74, 78 (Ark. 1993): "Under requirement No. 1, the mistake was not of such magnitude as to render enforcement of the contract unconscionable. The proof shows that T.M.J. was doing about $5,000,000.00 in business annually at this time and that its net worth was more than $80,000.00. T.M.J.'s president testified that to perform the contract would have put the company out of business. However, the error involved the sum of $80,400.00, or 3.9% of the total bid." Observing the four requirements: "1. the mistake must be of so great a consequence that to enforce the contract as actually made would be unconscionable; 2. the matter as to which the mistake was made must relate to a material feature of the contract; 3. the mistake must have occurred notwithstanding the exercise of reasonable care by the party making the mistake; and 4. it must be able to get relief by way of rescission without serious prejudice to the other party, except for loss of his bargain," citing State ex rel. Arkansas State Highway Commission v. Ottinger, 334 S.W.2d 694 (1960). Accord, similar four elements, James T. Taylor & Son, Inc. v. Arlington Independent School District, 335 S.W.2d 371 (Tex. 1960): "They are (1) the mistake is of so great a consequence that to enforce the contract would be unconscionable; (2) the mistake relates to a material feature of the contract; (3) the mistake occurred despite the exercise of ordinary care; and (4) the parties can be placed in status quo in the equity sense."

20. A. A. Metcalf Moving & Storage Co., Inc. v. North St. Paul–Maplewood Oakdale Schools, 587 N.W.2d 311, 318 (Minn. App. 1998), quotation includes reference to note 3, the text of which follows: "We note that respondent's total charge for the move is $69,013, which is three and a half times the amount of its bid. This unexplained disparity by professional movers questions the good faith and claimed error of the bidder."

21. Dougherty v. Mieczkowski, 661 F. Supp. 267, 274 (D. Del., 1987): "Under the common law of contracts, there is a distinction between fraud in the inducement and fraud in the 'factum,' or execution. Fraud in the factum occurs when a party makes a misrepresentation that is regarded as going to the very character of the proposed contract itself, as when one party induces the other to sign a document by falsely stating that it has no legal effect. If the misrepresentation is of this type, then there is no contract at all, or

what is sometime anomalously described as a void, as opposed to voidable, contract. If the fraud relates to the inducement to enter the contract, then the agreement is 'voidable' at the option of the innocent party. The distinction is that if there is fraud in the inducement, the contract is enforceable against at least one party, while fraud in the factum means that at no time was there a contractual obligation between the parties." See also Iron Workers' Local No. 25 Pension Fund v. Nyeholt Steel, Inc., 976 F. Supp. 683, 689 (E.D. Mich., 1997): "In other words, fraud in the execution (a.k.a. 'fraud in factum') occurs when a misrepresentation is made which induces a party believe that he is not assenting to any contract or that he is assenting to a contract entirely different from the proposed contract"; and Downes v. Morgan Stanley Dean Witter, 2002 WL 31247980, *7 (Pa. Com. Pl., 2002): "Fraud in the inducement, on the other hand, occurs where the party proffering the evidence alleges he or she was fraudulently misled during the negotiations leading up to the agreement and would not have entered into the agreement otherwise yet the agreement is consistent on its face with those fraudulent misrepresentations."

22. Restatement (Second) of Contracts § 163 (1981) (When a Misrepresentation Prevents Formation of a Contract), comment a, rationale: "If, because of a misrepresentation as to the character or essential terms of a proposed contract, a party does not know or have reasonable opportunity to know of its character or essential terms, then he neither knows nor has reason to know that the other party may infer from his conduct that he assents to that contract. In such a case there is no effective manifestation of assent and no contract at all."

23. Restatement (Second) of Contracts § 163 (1981) (When a Misrepresentation Prevents Formation of a Contract), comment c, "Void" rather than voidable.

24. "Fraud in the inducement consists of inducing one by some fraudulent representation or pretense to execute the very contract to be executed. An agreement based on such an inducement is voidable. Fraud in the inducement has three requirements: first, the misrepresentation must have been either fraudulent or material; second, the misrepresentation must have induced the recipient to make the contract; third, the recipient must have been justified in relying on the misrepresentation. If each of these elements is met, the contract is voidable. Fraud in the execution, on the other hand, occurs if a misrepresentation as to the character or essential terms of a proposed contract induces conduct that appears to be a manifestation of assent by one who neither knows nor has a reasonable opportunity to know of the character or essential terms of the proposed contract. If the elements of the defense of fraud in the execution are met, the contract is not merely voidable, it is void *ab initio*." Colorado Plasterers' Pension Fund v. Plasterers' Unlimited, Inc., 655 F. Supp. 1184, 1186 (D. Colo. 1987), citations and quotations omitted.

25. Restatement (Second) of Contracts § 163 (1981) (When a Misrepresentation Prevents Formation of a Contract), comment a, Rationale: "If, because of a misrepresentation as to the character or essential terms of a proposed contract, a party does not know or have reasonable opportunity to know of its character or essential terms, then he

neither knows nor has reason to know that the other party may infer from his conduct that he assents to that contract. In such a case there is no effective manifestation of assent and no contract at all." See also Restatement (Second) of Contracts § 163 (1981) (When a Misrepresentation Prevents Formation of a Contract), comment c, "Void" rather than voidable: "It is sometimes loosely said that, where the rule stated in this Section applies, there is a 'void contract' as distinguished from a voidable one."

26. "A contract is voidable if a party's assent is induced by either a fraudulent or a material misrepresentation by the other party, and is an assertion on which the recipient is justified in relying." Carpenter v. Vreeman, 409 N.W.2d 258, 260–261 (Minn. App., 1987).

27. Restatement (Second) of Contracts § 164 (1981) (When a Misrepresentation Makes a Contract Voidable), comment a, Requirements.

28. Restatement (Second) of Contracts § 167 (1981) (When a Misrepresentation Is an Inducing Cause).

29. Restatement (Second) of Contracts § 162 (1981) (When a Misrepresentation Is Fraudulent or Material), comment a, meaning of "fraudulent": "In order that a misrepresentation be fraudulent within the meaning of this Section, it must not only be consciously false but must also be intended to mislead another."

30. RICHARD A. LORD, 26 WILLISTON ON CONTRACTS § 69:2 (4th ed. 2008), footnote omitted.

31. Restatement (Second) of Contracts § 162(1)(a)–(c) (1981) (When a Misrepresentation Is Fraudulent or Material): "A misrepresentation is fraudulent if the maker intends his assertion to induce a party to manifest his assent and the maker knows or believes that the assertion is not in accord with the facts, or does not have the confidence that he states or implies in the truth of the assertion, or knows that he does not have the basis that he states or implies for the assertion."

32. Lord, *supra* note 30.

33. Restatement (Second) of Contracts § 159 (1981) (Misrepresentation Defined), comment a, Nature of the assertion.

34. BLACK'S LAW DICTIONARY, *supra* note 8.

35. Restatement (Second) of Contracts § 162(2) (1981) (When a Misrepresentation Is Fraudulent or Material): "A misrepresentation is material if it would be likely to induce a reasonable person to manifest his assent, or if the maker knows that it would be likely to induce the recipient to do so."

36. Restatement (Second) of Contracts § 161 (1981) (When Non-Disclosure Is Equivalent to an Assertion), comment a, Concealment distinguished. See also Restatement (Second) of Contracts § 160 (1981) (When Action Is Equivalent to an Assertion) (Concealment), comment a, scope: "Concealment is an affirmative act intended or known to be likely to keep another from learning of a fact of which he would otherwise have learned. Such affirmative action is always equivalent to a misrepresentation."

37. Restatement (Second) of Contracts § 161 (1981) (When Non-Disclosure Is Equivalent to an Assertion), comment b, Fraudulent or material.

38. *Id.*: "But the failure to disclose the fact may be unintentional, as when one forgets to disclose a known fact, and it is then equivalent to an innocent misrepresentation. Furthermore, one is expected to disclose only such facts as he knows or has reason to know will influence the other in determining his course of action."

39. RICHARD A. LORD, 26 WILLISTON ON CONTRACTS § 69:16 (4th ed. 2008), footnotes omitted.

40. *Id.* at § 69:17.

41. "The importance of distinguishing whether the transaction can be called fraudulent as distinguished from one based on mistake without fraud, even where no other remedy than rescission is sought, lies in the fact that fraud as to any circumstances actually inducing a bargain may justify relief, although mistake must be as to a matter that formed a fundamental basis of the bargain" (*id.* at § 69:16, footnotes omitted).

42. *Id.* at § 69:17, footnotes omitted.

43. "Few areas of the law of contracts have undergone such radical changes in the nineteenth and twentieth centuries as has the law governing duress... Today the general rule is that any wrongful act or threat which overcomes the free will of a party constitutes duress. This simple statement of the law conceals a number of questions, particularly as to the meaning of 'free will' and 'wrongful.'" JOHN D. CALAMARI AND JOSEPH M. PERILLO, THE LAW OF CONTRACTS § 9-2, at 337 (3d ed. 1987).

44. Restatement (Second) of Contracts § 174(1) (1981) (When Duress by Threat Makes a Contract Voidable).

45. See Restatement (Second) of Contracts § 174 (1981) (When Duress by Physical Compulsion Prevents Formation of a Contract), comment a, rationale.

46. Restatement (Second) of Contracts § 174(1) (1981) (When Duress by Threat Makes a Contract Voidable), illustration 2: "A makes an improper threat to commence a civil action and to file a lis pendens [a request for the court to exercise "jurisdiction, power, or control acquired by a court over property while a legal action is pending." BLACK'S LAW DICTIONARY, *supra* note 8.] against a tract of land owned by B, unless B agrees to discharge a claim that B has against A. Because B is about to make a contract with C for the sale of the land and C refuses to make the contract if the levy is made, B agrees to discharge the claim. B has no reasonable alternative, A's threat is duress, and the contract is voidable by B."

47. Restatement (Second) of Contracts § 174(1) (1981) (When Duress by Threat Makes a Contract Voidable), illustration 1: "1. A makes an improper threat to commence civil proceedings against B unless B agrees to discharge a claim that B has against A. In order to avoid defending the threatened suit, B is induced to make the contract. Defense of the threatened suit is a reasonable alternative, the threat does not amount to duress, and the contract is not voidable by B."

48. Restatement (Second) of Contracts § 174 (1981) (When Duress by Threat Makes a Contract Voidable), comment d, Voidable.

49. Restatement (Second) of Contracts § 174 (1981) (When Duress by Threat Makes a Contract Voidable), illustration 3 (repair of necessary machine, amended contract

for additional repairs) and illustration 4 (vacate premises under lease, additional agreement to purchase furniture).

50. See Restatement (Second) of Contracts § 174 (1981) (When Duress by Threat Makes a Contract Voidable), illustrations 5 and 7.

51. Restatement (Second) of Contracts § 174 (1981) (When Duress by Threat Makes a Contract Voidable), illustrations 3 and 4 ("heavy financial loss"), illustrations 5 ("urgent need of the goods"), and illustration 7 ("urgent need of cash").

52. Restatement (Second) of Contracts § 174 (1981) (When Duress by Threat Makes a Contract Voidable), comment c, Subjective test of inducement.

53. A.V. v. iParadigms, Ltd., 544 F. Supp. 2d 47, 481 (E.D. Va. 2008), affirmed 562 F.3d 630 (4th Cir. 2009).

54. RICHARD A. LORD, 28 WILLISTON ON CONTRACTS § 71:50 (4th ed. 2008), footnote omitted.

55. Restatement (Second) of Contracts § 177(1) (1981) (When Undue Influence Makes a Contract Voidable).

56. Restatement (Second) of Contracts § 177(2) (1981) (When Undue Influence Makes a Contract Voidable): "If a party's manifestation of assent is induced by undue influence by the other party, the contract is voidable by the victim."

57. Restatement (Second) of Contracts § 177 (1981) (When Undue Influence Makes a Contract Voidable), comment a, required domination or relation. "The required relation may be found in situations other than those enumerated. However, the mere fact that a party is weak, infirm or aged does not of itself suffice, although it may be a factor in determining whether the required relation existed" (*id.*).

58. Restatement (Second) of Contracts § 177 (1981) (When Undue Influence Makes a Contract Voidable), comment b, unfair persuasion.

59. RICHARD A. LORD, 28 WILLISTON ON CONTRACTS § 71:50 (4th ed. 2008), footnotes omitted.

60. UCC § 2-201(1) (2004): "A contract for the sale of goods for the price of $ 5,000 or more is not enforceable by way of action or defense unless there is some record sufficient to indicate that a contract for sale has been made between the parties and signed by the party against which enforcement is sought or by the party's authorized agent or broker."

61. UCC § 2-201(1) (2004), Official Comment 5.

62. RAYMOND T. NIMMER AND JEFF C. DODD, MODERN LICENSING LAW § 3:47 (database updated in Westlaw, November 2011): "The court's reasoning [referring to Grappo v. Alitalia Linee Aeree Italiane, S.p.A., 56 F.3d 427 (2d Cir. 1995)] betrayed an implicit assumption, common among commercial lawyers, that if the Uniform Commercial Code does not apply, the parties will be case out into a dark wilderness. That attitude is a conceit of U.C.C. lawyers. It explains why many cases rush to the Uniform Commercial Code to resolve licensing disputes. The fact is that there is a world of law outside of the Uniform Commercial Code."

63. "Under state law, the statute of frauds is an affirmative defense requiring that specified classes of contracts be in writing to be enforceable. A contract for the sale of real estate

falls within the class of contracts that must be in writing to be enforceable." Petrello v. Prucka, 2011 WL 305444, *3 (S.D. Tex. 2011) (slip copy).

64. Respect Inc. v. Committee on Status of Women, 781 F. Supp. 1358, 1363 (N.D. Ill. 1992), footnote and citation omitted.

65. *Id.*, citations omitted.

66. Kwan v. Schlein, 441 F. Supp. 2d 491, 501–502 (S.D.N.Y. 2006): "However, for the same reason that Kwan's contract claim may not be time-barred, it is barred by the Statute of Frauds. In New York, a contract that 'by its terms is not to be performed within one year from the making thereof' is void if it is not in writing [Citing New York General Obligations Law § 5-701(a)(1)]. If Kwan is correct to contend that the contract requires continuous performance—i.e., that Schlein and BRB continue to label 'Find It Online' as coauthored by Kwan and continue to pay Kwan royalties—it falls within the ambit of the Statute of Frauds because it cannot be performed within a year. In this way, the statutes of limitation and frauds operate in tandem to bar Kwan's claim: the contract either required ongoing performance such that it is void because it is not in writing, or was susceptible to immediate performance and is therefore barred by the statute of limitations."

67. See Ronald J. Mann, *Just One Click: The Reality of Internet Retail Contracting*, 108 COLUMBIA LAW REVIEW 984, 989 (2008), footnotes omitted: "With respect to traditional contract doctrine, the shift to an online contracting environment poses a particular challenge. The statute of frauds traditionally requires a writing to form a binding agreement involving a substantial sale of goods. To deal with an online electronic contracting environment, the statute of frauds has been revised to permit online retailers the same ability to enter into binding arrangements with their customers that their bricks-and-mortar predecessors enjoyed. To that end, the central provisions of the Uniform Electronic Transactions Act (UETA) and of the Electronic Signatures in Global and National Commerce Act (ESIGN) also require parity of treatment for electronic records and paper documents."

68. JONATHAN D. ROBBINS, ADVISING E BUSINESSES, § 8-1.20 (database updated in Westlaw, November 2011) (Forming contracts online).

69. Uniform Computer Information Transactions Act, § 201 (1999), Official Comment 4. Exceptions to the Basic Rules, a. Partial Performance.

70. Restatement (Second) of Contracts § 14 (1981) (infants). The Restatement indicates that in the absence of a statute to the contrary "a natural person has the capacity to incur only voidable contractual duties until the beginning of the day before the person's eighteenth birthday" (*id.*).

71. Restatement (Second) of Contracts § 15(1) (1981) (Mental Illness or Defect): "A person incurs only voidable contractual duties by entering into a transaction if by reason of mental illness or defect (a) he is unable to understand in a reasonable manner the nature and consequences of the transaction, or (b) he is unable to act in a reasonable manner in relation to the transaction and the other party has reason to know of his condition."

72. Restatement (Second) of Contracts § 15(1) (1981) (Mental Illness or Defect), comment b, the standard of competency.
73. See, for example, Topheavy Studios, Inc.. v. Doe, 2005 WL 1940159 (Tex. App. 2005) (unpublished): "In Texas, a contract between an adult and a minor is voidable at the option of the minor...A minor who fraudulently misrepresents her age to induce another to enter into a contract cannot void the contract," citations omitted.
74. Restatement (Second) of Contracts § 261 (1981) (Discharge by Supervening Impracticability).
75. Restatement (Second) of Contracts § 262 (1981): "If the performance of a duty is made impracticable by having to comply with a domestic or foreign governmental regulation or order, that regulation or order is an event the non-occurrence of which was a basic assumption on which the contract was made."
76. Restatement (Second) of Contracts § 263 (1981): "If the existence of a specific thing is necessary for the performance of a duty, its failure to come into existence, destruction, or such deterioration as makes performance impracticable is an event the non-occurrence of which was a basic assumption on which the contract was made."
77. Restatement (Second) of Contracts § 264 (1981): "If the performance of a duty is made impracticable by having to comply with a domestic or foreign governmental regulation or order, that regulation or order is an event the non-occurrence of which was a basic assumption on which the contract was made."
78. Restatement (Second) of Contracts § 261 (1981) (Discharge by Supervening Impracticability), comment d, impracticality.
79. Restatement (Second) of Contracts § 261 (1981) (Discharge by Supervening Impracticability), comment d, impracticality: "A severe shortage of raw materials or of supplies due to war, embargo, local crop failure, unforeseen shutdown of major sources of supply, or the like, which either causes a marked increase in cost or prevents performance altogether may bring the case within the rule stated in this Section."
80. Restatement (Second) of Contracts § 261 (1981) (Discharge by Supervening Impracticability), comment d, impracticality.
81. Example: "A, who owns a hotel, and B, who owns a country club, make a contract under which A is to pay $1,000 a month and B is to make the club's membership privileges available to the guests in A's hotel free of charge to them. A's building is destroyed by fire without his fault, and A is unable to remain in the hotel business. A refuses to make further monthly payments. A's duty to make monthly payments is discharged, and A is not liable to B for breach of contract." Restatement (Second) of Contracts § 265 (1981) (Discharge by Supervening Frustration), illustration 3.
82. Matter of Fontana D'Oro Foods (Agosta), 472 N.Y.S.2d 528, 532 (N.Y. Supreme Court, 1983).
83. "That the parties anticipated the possibility that a fire could destroy their warehouse and inventory is not in doubt" (id.).

84. "Every contract or duty within this Act imposes an obligation of good faith in its performance or enforcement." UCC § 1-203.

85. UCC § 1-201(20): "'Good faith,' except as otherwise provided in Article 5, means honesty in fact and the observance of reasonable commercial standards of fair dealing." And from the 2008 Official Comments: "Thus, the definition of 'good faith' in this section merely confirms what has been the case for a number of years as Articles of the UCC have been amended or revised-the obligation of 'good faith,' applicable in each Article, is to be interpreted in the context of all Articles except for Article 5 as including both the subjective element of honesty in fact and the objective element of the observance of reasonable commercial standards of fair dealing. As a result, both the subjective and objective elements are part of the standard of 'good faith,' whether that obligation is specifically referenced in another Article of the Code (other than Article 5) or is provided by this Article." *Id.* (2008 electronic Pocket Part).

86. UCC § 1-201(20), Official Comments (2008 electronic Pocket Part).

87. Restatement (Second) of Contracts § 205 (1981) (Of Good Faith and Fair Dealing), comment d, Good faith performance.

88. Lorin Brennan et al. 1 The Complete UCITA, 102–129 (2004) (Glasser LegalWorks). See also Chaney v. Shell Oil Co., 827 P.2d 196, 204 (Or. App., 1992): "That definition [referring to Oregon's adoption of UCC § 1-203] includes a 'subjective' (honesty in fact) and an 'objective' component (observance of reasonable commercial standards)."

89. Raymond T. Nimmer and Jeff C. Dodd, Modern Licensing Law, § 11:3 (database updated in Westlaw, November 2011).

90. Restatement (Second) of Contracts § 241 (1981) (Circumstances Significant in Determining Whether a Failure Is Material), a. Nature of significant circumstances: "Contrast the situation where the parties have, by their agreement, made an event a condition . . . This Section therefore states circumstances, not rules, which are to be considered in determining whether a particular failure is material."

91. Restatement (Second) of Contracts § 241 (1981) (Circumstances Significant in Determining Whether a Failure Is Material).

92. Sahai Pty. Ltd. v. Sassy, Inc., 2010 WL 3781018, *5 (N.D. Ill. 2010) (slip copy): "Likewise, the materiality of a breach involves questions of fact"; Steve Silveus, Inc. v. Goshert, 873 N.E. 2d 165, 175 (Ill. App. 2007): "A material breach is one that goes to the heart of the contract, and whether a breach is material is generally a question of fact to be decided by the trier of fact"; and Hastings Associates, Inc. v. Local 369 Building Fund, Inc. 675 N.E.2d 403, 411 (Mass. App. Ct. 1997): "A material breach of contract by one party excuses the other party from performance as matter of law. Whether there is such a material breach is a question for the jury."

93. As stated by Horton v. Horton, 487 S.E.2d 200, 203 (Va. 1997), a "'material breach' is a failure to do something that is so fundamental to the contract that the failure to

perform that obligation defeats an essential purpose of the contract."

94. See, for example, Joseph P. Wright and Thomas B. Aquino, *The Right to Cure a Contract Breach*, Wisconsin Lawyer, October 2010, at 14, 17, for the application by Wisconsin courts.

95. See also Restatement (Second) of Contracts § 261 (1981) (Discharge by Supervening Impracticability), comment d, impracticality: "The difference has been described as that between 'the thing cannot be done' and 'I cannot do it,' and the former has been characterized as 'objective' and the latter as 'subjective.' This Section recognizes that if the performance remains practicable and it is merely beyond the party's capacity to render it, he is ordinarily not discharged, but it does not use the terms 'objective' and 'subjective' to express this. Instead, the rationale is that a party generally assumes the risk of his own inability to perform his duty."

96. Restatement (Second) of Contracts § 253 (1981) (Effect of a Repudiation as a Breach and On Other Party's Duties), comment a, breach.

97. Tosco Corp. v. Hodel, 611 F. Supp. 1130, 1186 (D.C. Colo., 1985): "The rationale for imposing the burden of proof on the one attacking the validity of the claim for failure to perform assessment work may also be explained in terms of *conditions precedent* and *subsequent*. Briefly, a *condition subsequent* is a provision or condition which cuts off an existing legal right, entitlement or benefit. Upon its occurrence, a *condition subsequent* operates to defeat or annul a right or benefit. On the other hand, a *condition precedent* requires certain performance or condition which must take place before a legal right can vest. The condition must occur or be performed before a right, entitlement or benefit comes into existence and becomes binding" (italics in original).

98. Ewell v. Those Certain Underwriters of Lloyd's, London, 2010 WL 3447570, *3 (Del. Super., 2010) (unpublished), footnotes omitted: "Although common in the law of property, examples of true conditions precedent in contracts are rare. The distinction between conditions precedent and conditions subsequent is only important procedurally. The burden of allegation and proof of a condition precedent is on the plaintiff, while the burden of proof and allegation of a condition subsequent is on the defendant."

99. Raymond T. Nimmer and Jeff C. Dodd, Modern Licensing Law, 2008–2009 Edition, § 11:17 at 701 (2008).

100. Stone Forest Industries, Inc. v. U.S., 26 Cl.Ct. 410, 416-417 (1992), internal quotation and citations omitted. Concluding "that, because the time limitation provision is a condition, and not a covenant, compliance with the time limitation was required before plaintiffs could enforce their refund rights under the contract" (*id.*).

101. Black's Law Dictionary, *supra* note 8, defines the "implied covenant of good faith and fair dealing" as an "implied covenant to cooperate with the other party to an agreement so that both parties may obtain the full benefits of the agreement; an implied covenant to refrain from any act that would injure a contracting party's right to receive the benefit of the contract. Breach of this covenant is often termed *bad faith*" (italics in original).

102. See, for example, Brown v. Superior Court in and for Los Angeles County, 212 P.2d 878, 881 (Cal. 1949): "In every contract there is an implied covenant of good faith and fair dealing that neither party will do anything which injures the right of the other to receive the benefits of the agreement"; Palisades Properties, Inc. v. Brunetti, 207 A.2d 522, 531 (N.J. 1965): "In every contract there is an implied covenant that neither party shall do anything which will have the effect of destroying or injuring the right of the other party to receive the fruits of the contract; in other words, in every contract there exists an implied covenant of good faith and fair dealing" (citing WILLISTON ON CONTRACTS); and RICHARD A. LORD, 2 WILLISTON ON CONTRACTS § 63:22 (4th ed. 2008, database updated in Westlaw, May 2012): "Every contract imposes an obligation of good faith and fair dealing between the parties in its performance and its enforcement, and if the promise of the defendant is not expressed by its terms in the contract, it will be implied. The duty embraces, among other things, an implied obligation that neither party shall do anything to injure or destroy the right of the other party to receive the benefits of the agreement" (footnotes omitted).

103. Matter of 5300 Memorial Investors, Ltd., 973 F.2d 1160, 1170 (5th Cir. 1992), internal quotations and citations omitted. Applying these rules and holding "that, as a matter of law, the 30 day response provision in the agreement is a covenant or a promise by Purchaser that it will respond to Seller's applications for refund within 30 days, but it is not a condition precedent to Purchaser's right to withdraw designated funds, upon invoice and notice to Seller" (id.).

104. James Klein Ins., Inc. v. Select Office Solutions, 2003 WL 22245999, *3 (Cal. App. 4 Dist., 2003) (unpublished): "There are three types of conditions, and the one at issue was not only a condition but also a covenant. A covenant is a promise to render some performance. The practical distinction between a condition and a covenant may be illustrated as follows: (1) If B agrees to render some performance to A, provided a condition happens, and the condition does not happen, A's duty of performance is excused, but A cannot recover damages from B. (2) On the other hand, if no condition is stated, and B merely makes a promise, his breach of covenant will give rise to a right of action for damages, but will not necessarily excuse A's performance. (3) However, if the condition is stated, and in addition B promises that the condition will happen, upon the failure of the condition to occur not only is A's duty excused, but A can also recover damages for the breach of covenant or promise," quotation marks to B. E. WITKIN, SUMMARY OF CALIFORNIA LAW (10th ed. 2005) omitted.

105 James Klein Ins., Inc. v. Select Office Solutions, 2003 WL 22245999, *4 (Cal. App. 4 Dist., 2003) (unpublished).

106. PAJ, Inc. v. Hanover Insurance Co.,170 S.W.3d 258, 260-261 (Tex. App. 2005). See also Summit Investors II, L.P. v. Sechrist Industries, Inc., 2002 WL 31260989, *7 (Del. 2002) (unpublished): "There are several cases that recognize the distinction between covenants and conditions. These cases all hold that, although failure of a condition may excuse a party's performance, it does not give rise to money damages. And, while

Sechrist Industries argues the notice provision at issue here is a covenant and not a condition, both the case law and common sense are to the contrary. Sechrist Industries did not bargain to receive notice as an end in itself. It bargained for notice before its obligations were triggered . . . The notice provision at issue here can only be viewed as a condition" (footnotes omitted).

107. Brookside Mills, Inc. v. William Carter Co., *4, 1994 WL 665376 (Tenn. App. 1994) (unpublished opinion), citations omitted.

108. BLACK'S LAW DICTIONARY, *supra* note 8, defines novation as the "act of substituting for an old obligation a new one that either replaces an existing obligation with a new obligation or replaces an original party with a new party."

109. NIMMER ON COPYRIGHT § 10.15 (2008) (Consequences of Violation of Assignment or License Provisions), footnotes omitted. But see H. WARD CLASSEN, A PRACTICAL GUIDE TO SOFTWARE LICENSING FOR LICENSEES AND LICENSORS 27 (3d ed. 2008): "Subject to the terms and conditions of the particular license, a copyright owner who grants a licensee a nonexclusive license to use the copyrighted material generally may not sue for copyright infringement and is limited to bring a claim for breach of contract," citing Sun Microsystems, Inc. v. Microsoft Corporation, 188 F.3d 115, 1121 (9th Cir. 1999).

110. "A copyright owner who grants a non exclusive, limited license ordinarily waives the right to sue licensees for copyright infringement, and it may sue only for breach of contract." MDY Industries, LLC v. Blizzard Entertainment, Inc., 629 F.3d 928, 939 (9th Cir. 2010) (citation and quotation marks omitted). If the licensee acts outside the license scope (breaching a condition), the licensor may sue for copyright infringement (*id.*).

111. "Also note that an oral exclusive license creates an implied nonexclusive license." H. WARD CLASSEN, A PRACTICAL GUIDE TO SOFTWARE LICENSING FOR LICENSEES AND LICENSORS 27 (3d ed. 2008), citing 17 U.S.C. § 204(a) and Gracen v. Bradford Exchange, 698 F.2d 300, 303 (7th Cir. 1983).

112. This is what happened to one institution regarding its access to the JSTOR database. In response to the activities of one Jason Swartz, JSTOR "began blocking a much broader range of IP addresses. As a result, legitimate JSTOR users at MIT were denied access to JSTOR's archive." U.S. v. Swartz, Criminal Complaint, at ¶ 18b, No. 1:11-cr-10260-NMG (Dist. Mass., filed July 7, 2011). Slowed but not stopped, Swartz devised a spoofing program and resumed his downloading in earnest. Within a couple of weeks the "ghost laptop" and "ghost macbook" were "systematically and rapidly access[ed] . . . The Pace was so fast that it brought down some of JSTOR's servers. In response, JSTOR blocked the entire MIT computer network's access to JSTOR for several days, beginning on or about October 9, 2010." U.S. v. Swartz, Criminal Complaint, at ¶ 23–24, No. 1:11-cr-10260-NMG (Dist. Mass., filed July 7, 2011).

113. MacLean Associates, Inc. v. Wm. M. Mercer-Meidinger-Hansen, Inc., 952 F.2d 769, 779 (3d Cir. 1991).

114. Graham v. James, 144 F.3d 229 (2d Cir. 1998).
115. *Id.* at 233: "CD-ROM disks containing compilations of computer programs known as 'Shareware,' 'Freeware,' and 'Public Domain software.'"
116. *Id.* at 235.
117. *Id.* at 236.
118. Raymond T. Nimmer and Jeff C. Dodd, Modern Licensing Law, § 11:27 (database updated in Westlaw, November 2011).
119. See also Sun Microsystems, Inc. v. Microsoft Corp., 188 F.3d 1115, 1121 (9th Cir. 1999): "If, however, a license is limited in scope and the licensee acts outside the scope, the licensor can bring an action for copyright infringement."
120. Graham v. James, 144 F.3d 229, 236 (2d Cir. 1998).
121. *Id.* at 237.
122. *Id.*, citing Grand Union Co. v. Cord Meyer Development Co., 761 F.2d 141, 147 (2d. Cir. 1985): "In the absence of more compelling evidence that the parties intended to create a condition, the negotiation provision must be construed as a promise or covenant"; and Warth v. Grief, 106 N.Y.S. 163, 165 (2d Dept. 1907): "The law favors covenants, rather than conditions precedent," aff'd, 193 NY. 661 (1908). See also MDY Industries, LLC v. Blizzard Entertainment, Inc., 629 F.3d 928, 939 (9th Cir. 2010): "A covenant is a contractual promise, i.e., a manifestation of intention to act or refrain from acting in a particular way, such that the promisee is justified in understanding that the promisor has made a commitment. A condition precedent is an act or event that must occur before a duty to perform a promise arises. Conditions precedent are disfavored because they tend to work forfeitures" (citations omitted).
123. Falcon Enterprises, Inc. v. Publishers Service, Inc., 2011 WL 2356788, *1 (9th Cir., 2011) (unpublished): "As Publishers owed Falcon payment only after it published Falcon's copyrighted images, its obligation to pay constituted a covenant, rather than a condition precedent that would give rise to a copyright infringement lawsuit."
124. "Generally, provisions in a contract are presumed to be covenants rather than conditions precedent because the alternative often results in a forfeiture against one party or another... In this case, the language of the July 27, 2005 agreement makes it clear that the new terms are covenants, not conditions precedent. The agreement explicitly stated that reproduction of non-complying disks is a violation' of the agreement, rather than the failure to fulfill a condition precedent. Therefore, the appropriate remedy for a breach of the covenants is a breach of contract action brought by Mosfilm, not a copyright infringement action." Russian Entertainment Wholesale, Inc. v. Close-Up International, Inc., 767 F. Supp. 2d 392, 408-409 (E.D.N.Y., 2011). "The issue is simple to state but difficult to resolve. Close-Up has an exclusive license to distribute certain Russian films in their original Russian language. The Ruscico defendants, and through them, Image, have an exclusive license from the same licensor to distribute the same films—but with subtitles. The problem is that neither the licensor nor the two licensees, when they granted and obtained their respective rights, considered an obvious fact—

a viewer can turn off the subtitles unless special protection is built into the films to prevent that. I hold that because Close-Up never obtained the right to enforce its license against a distributor of subtitled films without a 'no shut off' switch, and because the Ruscico defendants are distributing exactly the films that their license permitted them to distribute, Close-up cannot prevail in this action" (*id.* at 395).

125. Sun Microsystems, Inc. v. Microsoft Corp., 188 F.3d 1115 (9th Cir. 1999).

126. *Id.* at 1117.

127. *Id.* at 1118.

128. *Id.* at 1118.

129. *Id.* at 1122: "We must decide an issue of first impression: whether, where two sophisticated parties have negotiated a copyright license and dispute its scope, the copyright holder who has demonstrated likely success on the merits is entitled to a presumption of irreparable harm. We hold that it is, but only after the copyright holder has established that the disputed terms are limitations on the scope of the license [i.e., conditions] rather than independent contractual covenants. In other words, before Sun can gain the benefits of copyright enforcement, it must definitively establish that the rights it claims were violated are copyright, not contractual, rights."

130. Video Trip Corp. v. Lightning Video, Inc., 866 F.2d 50 (2d Cir. 1989).

131. S.O.S., Inc. v. Payday, Inc., 886 F.2d 1081 (9th Cir. 1989).

132. Sun Microsystems, *supra* note 125, at 1122.

133. Sun Microsystems, Inc. v. Microsoft Corp., 81 F. Supp. 2d 1026, 1032 (N.D. Cal. 2000), same language in, Sun Microsystems, Inc. v. Microsoft Corp., 2000 WL 33223397, at *3 (N.D. Cal. 2000) (unpublished); "The license grants in sections 2.1 ('Source Code and Development License to Technology') and 2.2 ('Distribution License to Technology') allow Microsoft to distribute the Technology and Derivative Works of the Technology as part of a Product but say nothing about the license grants being subject to, conditional on, or limited by compliance with the compatibility obligations set forth in Section 2.6 ('Compatibility')" (*id.*).

134. The rules against circumvention apply only to works protected under the copyright law, title 17 of the U.S. Code: "No person shall circumvent a technological measure that effectively controls access to a work protected under this title." 17 U.S.C. § 1201(a)(1)(A).

135. RealNetworks, Inc. v. DVD Copy Control Association, 641 F. Supp. 2d 913, 934 (N.D. Calif. 2009). "That Real may have initially gained lawful access to the CSS keys by entering into a CSS license Agreement does not mean the Real is thereby exculpated from DMCA liability forever more" (*id.*).

136. *Id.* at 925.

137. *Id.* at 934.

138. *Id.* at 935.

139. BLACK'S LAW DICTIONARY, *supra* note 8, describes replevin as "an action for the repossession of personal property wrongfully taken or detained by the defendant,

whereby the plaintiff gives security for and holds the property until the court decides who owns it."

140. Restatement (Second) of Contracts § 344 (1981) (Purposes of Remedies).

141. *Id.* at comment a., Three interests: "Although it [restoration interest] may be equal to the expectation or reliance interest, it is ordinarily smaller because it includes neither the injured party's lost profit nor that part of his expenditures in reliance that resulted in no benefit to the other party."

142. H. WARD CLASSEN, A PRACTICAL GUIDE TO SOFTWARE LICENSING FOR LICENSEES AND LICENSORS 275 (3d ed. 2008); "Any provision for liquidated damages should be mutual" (*id.*).

143. RAYMOND T. NIMMER AND JEFF C. DODD, MODERN LICENSING LAW § 11:37 (database updated in Westlaw, November 2011).

144. *Id.* at § 11:43 (footnote omitted).

145. *Id.* at § 11:56 (and cases cited therein).

146. See BRYAN M. CARSON, THE LAW OF LIBRARIES AND ARCHIVES 34 (2007).

147. Restatement (Second) of Contracts § 235(1) (1981) (Liquidated Damages and Penalties): "Damages for breach by either party may be liquidated in the agreement but only at an amount that is reasonable in the light of the anticipated or actual loss caused by the breach and the difficulties of proof of loss. A term fixing unreasonably large liquidated damages is unenforceable on grounds of public policy as a penalty"; "Finally, the licensee should carefully word the liquidated damages provision and limit the liquidated damages to a reasonable level to avoid the appearance of a penalty. Liquidated damages that are out of proportion to the probably loss or grossly in excess of the actual damages may be considered a penalty and thus unenforceable" H. WARD CLASSEN, A PRACTICAL GUIDE TO SOFTWARE LICENSING FOR LICENSEES AND LICENSORS 97 (3d ed. 2008), citing Gordonsville Energy L.P. v. Virginia Electric & Power Co., 512 S.E.2d 811 (Va. 1999).

148. RAYMOND T. NIMMER AND JEFF C. DODD, MODERN LICENSING LAW, § 11:58. This is opposed to terms indicating that the amount is based on some percentage of remaining fees (*id.*).

149. H. WARD CLASSEN, A PRACTICAL GUIDE TO SOFTWARE LICENSING FOR LICENSEES AND LICENSORS 97 (3d ed. 2008).

150. Restatement (Second) of Contracts § 235 (1981) (Liquidated Damages and Penalties), comment a, liquidated damages or penalty: "The central objective behind the system of contract remedies is compensatory, not punitive. Punishment of a promisor for having broken his promise has no justification on either economic or other grounds and a term providing for such a penalty is unenforceable on grounds of public policy."

BROADER LEGAL AND POLICY ISSUES IN LICENSING

Read this chapter to gain an understanding of public policy's role in determining the validity of license agreements in these scenarios:
► Presence of unconscionability or adhesion in nonnegotiated licenses
► Application of the doctrine of copyright misuse with copyrighted and public domain content
► Application of the doctrine of copyright preemption to licensing terms
► Recharacterization of licenses as sales and its effect on the first-sale doctrine
► How licenses can affect first-sale rights

Now that the previous two chapters have provided a general overview of contract law and application of that law to licensing, this chapter discusses several topics that are receiving increased judicial attention. Moreover, this attention occurs in the specific context of licensing and so the potential application to library, archive, and other settings is relevant. Finally, these developments involve scenarios questioning the validity or otherwise effect of the license agreement. A license can go too far, in a sense, with one or more of its terms being rule unconscionable or otherwise unenforceable. Recent case law also suggests that where a license is used to leverage rights of an owner under the copyright law, the ability to enforce those rights is suspended under the doctrine of copyright misuse. Copyright preemption can in rare circumstances be used to suspend or supersede the effect of a license. Finally, there is growing debate in the courts and elsewhere regarding whether some so-called licenses (often a label imposed by the licensor) are actually sales under the law. Issues of first-sale and other use rights under copyright are often at the heart of the "license versus sale" cases. This underscores once again the legal and practical significance of a transaction being a license or a sale.

A common theme among concepts such as unconscionability, copyright misuse, copyright preemption, and recharacterization of a license as a sale is that where the concepts are applicable the law intervenes to limit the rights of the licensor-copyright holder, to the benefit of the library or other user. The first concept is an old one, as far as the copyright law is concerned, but in recent years, courts have applied the principles of unconscionability to evaluate the nature of mass-market or consumer contracts. These are licenses where the licensee has no ability to bargain over the terms, so-called nonnegotiated agreements. The next two concepts, misuse and preemption, are established doctrines in patent law that have seen recent translation into the copyright jurisprudence. Application may be relegated to unique facts, but when the doctrine operates, it can be a powerful ally in the struggle against overaggressive vendors. The last concept is not a true concept or doctrine at all but is drawn from several recent cases that have tremendous implications for public distribution rights of users under the copyright law. These rights, found in section 109 of the copyright law, are ones that libraries, archives, educational entities, and so forth, rely upon daily to make use of physical material protected by copyright.

Each concept, when applicable, may prevent the contract from having legal impact. Moreover, each concept has important implications in the world of licensing, especially when vendors attempt to push the envelope, so to speak, of the reach of license terms. Given the proper circumstances, the law intervenes to in essence halt the legal effect of the contract, as if to say that this contract is not a valid use of the legal principles underlying the freedom to contract.[1]

PUBLIC POLICY, UNCONSCIONABILITY, AND CONTRACTS OF ADHESION IN LICENSE AGREEMENTS

The idea of a contract with terms so abhorrent that existing societal interests in preserving the obligations imposed by the contract can be nonetheless disavowed is well established in contract law. This concept is becoming more important with the ever-increasing number of transactions occurring online, where the licensee does not have the ability to bargain over terms. Such scenarios of nonnegotiated licenses set the stage for review by courts because such online contracts may be more susceptible to producing unfair results, though similar results can occur offline for that matter. Often these circumstances occur where one party to the contract is also a consumer. An adhesion contract[2] is one example where there is no opportunity for bargaining. Many online contracts, such as the website end user license agreements (EULAs) prominent on various social networking sites or other click-to-agree mechanisms, offer little or no opportunity to bargain. The same could be said of contracts associated with downloads for software upgrades or cell phone applications. The licensee may be a consumer, a library patron, or the library (through its staff) itself. Given the proper circumstances, courts could (and some in fact do) conclude that these contracts are adhesion contracts. As discussed later, this is often the first part of a determination that such contracts are unconscionable. Unconscionable contracts are voidable or their provisions may be severed as void.

Adhesion contracts are common. Licensees in such contracts are not always consumers, patrons, students, or other individuals. Yet, "a contract between merchants is rarely found to be unconscionable."[3] However, a court concluded not too long ago that the CSS (Content Scrambling System) license agreement between RealNetworks, Inc. and the DVD Copy Control Association (DVD CCA) was a contract of adhesion: "Though Real may be a large company, its interaction with DVD CCA was in the capacity of an entity seeking to build a product that implements CSS technology and Real had no choice but to accept the CSS License Agreement in order to make a DVD product that interacts with CSS-protected DVDs...Thus, the courts finds that the Agreement was a contract of adhesion."[4] When a contract is so abhorrent to a notion of fairness that courts assess whether the contract should be enforced or not, this assessment, if the result is in the affirmative, is given the legal name of unconscionability. First introduced in UCC section 2-302 and adopted in the second edition of the Restatement of Contracts, the concept of unconscionability continues to evolve. Today, the concept reaches beyond the UCC Article 2 environs and is no longer limited to "sales of goods" but can apply to all contracts regardless of subject matter. UCITA (Uniform Computer Transactions Act), discussed briefly in Chapter 11, adopts the UCC Article 2 language.[5] Looking beyond the unfairness of the contract to one party alone, other circumstances may cause the law to view the enforcement of the clause or the entire contract as "unfair" to society at large—in other words, contrary to public policy. Where the negative effects of contract enforcement outweigh the positive impacts, unconscionability may be present.

Public Policy and Contracts

The assessment of whether a contract is against public policy involves a balancing of competing interests; those interests associated with the freedom to contract (our free market disposition) and the sanctity of contracts (a sense of societal obligation to honor promises and promote reasonable reliance on such promises)[6] are balanced against interests associated with the right of the public to be free from the fallout of unwise bargains, especially when the party on the short end of the bargain has little recourse or power to alter its position relative to the dominant party. The Restatement identifies the competing interests to be weighed: those factors in favor of enforcement of the suspect term, such as the parties' justified expectations, any forfeiture that would result if enforcement were denied, and any special public interest in the enforcement of the particular term are evaluated in light of those factors weighing against enforcement of the suspect provision, such as the strength of the policy against enforcement as manifested by legislation or judicial decisions, the likelihood that a refusal to enforce the term will further that policy, the seriousness of any misconduct involved and the extent to which it was deliberate, and the directness of the connection between this misconduct and the term.[7] "The terms 'contrary to public policy' and 'illegal' often are used interchangeably in published opinions. There is, however, a distinction between the two. The term 'illegal' ought to be limited to contracts the very making of which is prohibited—contracts for murder, for example. Conversely, 'contrary to public policy' ought to be used to refer to contracts which are not per se contrary to public policy, but the execution of which is so—such as imperfect fee-splitting agreements."[8] Examples of contracts against public policy are wagers on the outcome of sporting events or loan agreements above the legal maximum allowable interest,[9] whereas a murder-for-hire contract is plainly illegal.[10] So, too, the legal principles involved in consideration of whether a contract is against public policy[11] or is unconscionable[12] are distinct, though these often are present in the same agreement.[13] Unconscionability is the more typical situation in the license environment, which is not to say that every unconscionable license is so because it is against public policy. For example, and depending on the circumstances, a choice of forum clause may be found contrary to public policy,[14] though the general rule appears to be that such clauses are not unconscionable per se.[15] The concept of unconscionability is, to an extent, a further refinement of the basic freedom to contract idea inherent in our market economy. An unconscionable contract undermines that basic freedom. Where a contract offers no opportunity for negotiation, there is no meaningful choice about its terms (as opposed to allowing a decision to enter into the contract or not based on the terms). Where a contract, in addition to the inability to bargain, has terms that are harsh or one-sided,[16] unconscionability may be present.

The possibility that a license might contain a provision or provisions that a court would conclude are unenforceable as being against public policy is growing in importance for two reasons. First, some licensors are pushing the envelope of licensee obligations by including ever-more-restrictive terms that can affect public policy (e.g., see discussion under Confidential Information and Nondisclosure in Chapter 14, note 65, regarding DeWitt clauses). Second, there is increased interest by commentators—and in one instance a court—in use of the doctrine to evaluate the palpability of such restrictive terms. An example related to both reasons involves the concept of gag-wrap provisions (see discussion under Confidential Information or Nondisclosure in Chapter 14), license terms that limit or in some cases prohibit altogether public comment about the license subject (e.g., a service or good) or that limit some other right (e.g., right of privacy). Commentators such as Belmas and Larson,[17] as well as the more conservative Nimmer and Dodd, who tend to side on the side of licensors and the right to contract advocates, suggest that such terms might be assessed under a public policy analysis. Nimmer and Dodd offer the example of a gag-wrap clause, more or less, but without naming it as such: "Almost invariably, licensing terms survive fundamental public policy challenges, though, in some limited cases (e.g., *proposed restraint on free speech in a public forum*), incursion on other fundamental interests may rise to such a level that the contract terms must give way."[18] The extent to which future courts might be receptive to contract reformation of the offending terms or a total reneging of the contract containing restraints relating to speech rights (e.g., posting of product reviews on a library blog) or privacy rights (e.g., monitoring of patron use of the licensed content and referring violators to the licensor) remains to be seen. Nonetheless, the concept has the potential to be an important weapon in the arsenal against offensive, overreaching contract terms. Of course, in circumstances where terms are negotiated, such excesses should not become part of the bargain in the first place. Likewise, courts are far less to be receptive of challenges in a climate of give-and-take negotiation. Chapter 6 will help readers identify these clauses and understand their potential legal impact.

Unconscionability

The determination of unconscionability is a matter of law for the court to decide and is made on a case-by-case basis.[19] A court can void the entire agreement (if the entire contract is unconscionable), strike a particular clause or clauses and leave the remainder of the contract sans the offending language intact and in force, or leave the language as drafted but limit the application of the clause(s) so as to rectify the unconscionable effect.[20] Most contracts, including licenses as discussed in Chapters 6–8 and exampled in Chapter 15, contain severability provisions to ensure that, in such circumstances, the remainder of the contract remains intact and in force.

Courts remain active in the development of the law in this area. Nimmer and Dodd suggest that the increased judicial activism regarding the licensing arena in general may for some licenses result in dramatic outcomes, as "information and informational rights are not goods and the relevant balance is likely to be very different."[21] This implies that courts may view the factors against enforcement with greater weight when information is involved, which may result in more terms being struck as unconscionable. In other words, a contract involving an unfair bargain over software, access to a database, or other computer information merits increased scrutiny versus an unfair bargain involving a dining room set or laptop, at least in terms of unconscionability.

The doctrine is particularly applicable with standard form contracts (this is not the same as a contract that uses standardized language, as it is a rare scenario, even in a so-called negotiated contract, that every term is "dickered over"[22] or arises from scratch) where the prejudiced party is a member of a protected class (e.g., consumers in a class-action suit). So, too, the contract may involve issues that courts have historically considered sensitive or prone to abuse, such as arbitration provisions, choice of forum clauses, and limitation of remedies.[23] Litigation often occurs in states with strong consumer rights legislation, such as California.

There are two aspects to the concept of unconscionability: procedural unconscionability and substantive unconscionability. A number of courts require that both elements be present before a provision or an entire contract is deemed unconscionable. While certain courts have indicated that substantive unconscionability alone can suffice, still others use a sliding scale whereby significant presence of one factor can balance out the bare minimum of the other element.[24] The leading case to apply the "sliding scale" notion in the context of licensing is *Comb v. PayPal, Inc.*, where the court stated, "The procedural component is satisfied by the existence of unequal bargaining positions and hidden terms common in the context of adhesion contracts. The substantive component is satisfied by overly harsh or one-sided results that 'shock the conscience.' The two elements operate on a sliding scale such that the more significant one is, the less significant the other need be."[25] Other courts have concluded likewise: "There is a good deal of sense to the adoption of such an approach [i.e., the sliding scale]. The clear import of the doctrine of unconscionability has been its flexibility... That being so, this court fails to see why such a claim should be barred if some unknown barrier for both factors is not surpassed instead of allowing such a claim to succeed when one factor is greatly exceeded, while the other only marginally so."[26] Whether assessment determines the presence of both aspects of unconscionability, the procedural or substantive alone, or an interplay (sliding scale) of the two elements, the concept of unconscionability is "characterized by bargaining power so disproportionate to preclude any meaningful choice and by terms unreasonably favorable to one party."[27] Such circumstances work to undermine that all-important market economy goal of freedom to contract, and so courts have seen it fit to intervene.

Nimmer and Dodd insist that both aspects (procedural and substantive) should be present before a court finds unconscionability, and they view a case such as *Brower v. Gateway 2000, Inc.*,[28] where the court invalidated potions of the a mandatory arbitration clause on the basis of substantive unconscionability alone after concluding that procedural unconscionability was not present, as an anomaly.[29] Nonetheless, several courts adhere to the minority position that substantive unconscionability alone would suffice:

> We agree with the Arizona Supreme Court. In some instances, individual contractual provisions may be so one-sided and harsh as to render them substantively unconscionable despite the fact that the circumstances surrounding the parties' agreement to the contract do not support a finding of procedural unconscionability. Accordingly, we now hold that substantive unconscionability alone can support a finding of unconscionability. However, since Adler has yet to prove a valid claim of procedural unconscionability, we decline to consider whether it alone will support a claim of unconscionability.[30]

The majority position requires both elements.

Paralleling the two-pronged approach, courts have observed that an unacceptable, unconscionable contract may result from external as well as internal factors. Factors can be external to the contract itself, resulting from the circumstances of contract formation (e.g., bargaining), or factors may relate to the contract's terms and conditions and the impact wrought by the shortsighted bargaining. These are the concepts of procedural and substantive unconscionability, respectively: "Procedural unconscionability involves impropriety during the process of forming a contract, whereas substantive unconscionability pertains to those cases where a clause or term in a contract is allegedly one-sided or overly harsh."[31] Unconscionability in the process of contract formation in essence deprives the other party of meaningful choice (so there can be no meeting of the minds). This can arise from superior bargaining power and the oppressive terms that may result from abuse of such power. Courts also look for the surprise factor that can result on the part of the lesser party when such terms are applied in the contract, for example, when during execution of the contract a dispute arises and the lesser-positioned party seeks redress.[32]

So what exactly is an unconscionable provision such that a court would reach the extreme conclusion of severing it from the agreement or otherwise limiting its effect? Clauses that tend to relieve someone from responsibility (legal liability), such as those which are exculpatory, are often unconscionable; likewise are clauses that limit the impact of legal responsibility for damages or other remedies. Disclaimers for harms caused by intentional conduct and often by negligence where personal injury is involved are often held to be unconscionable. "Some types of terms are not enforced, regardless of context; examples are provisions for unreasonably large liquidated damages, or limitations on a debtor's right to redeem collateral."[33] Clauses waiving remedy for economic loss are often upheld, however. In the licensing arena, recent cases have involved clauses waiving consumer remedies, such as the ability to pursue class-action suits, as previously noted, in states with strong consumer laws such as California.[34] Unreasonable arbitration clauses have also been found unconscionable where the cost of arbitration would be more expensive than the product itself.[35] Such a clause prevents a person from receiving his or her proverbial "day in court," and so such provisions have received increased judicial scrutiny.

Contracts of Adhesion: Establishing Procedural Unconscionability

Potential for unconscionability can be found in an adhesion contract.[36] An adhesion contract exists in a "take it or leave it" bargaining climate, where one party has no opportunity to bargain and no option but to accept the terms—in other words, no other place to obtain the product.[37] This is not to say that all adhesion contracts are per se unconscionable but that, in a climate of adhesion contracting, the stage is set for an unconscionability analysis to commence—with several courts concluding that adhesion contracts are procedurally unconscionable.[38]

The Restatement explains: "In many of the cases cited contracts of adhesion were involved. It is to be emphasized that a contract of adhesion is not unconscionable per se, and that all unconscionable contracts are not contracts of adhesion. Nonetheless, the more standardized the agreement and the less a party may bargain meaningfully, the more susceptible the contract or a term will be to a claim of unconscionability."[39] Courts have struck down clauses in licenses or entire licenses when significant consumer/user rights are denied in a nonnegotiated license (discussed in Chapter 6) setting. A cluster of such cases has involved unreasonable mandatory arbitration clauses and waiver of rights to pursue class actions and other remedies in nonnegotiated contracts. Courts have concluded that these terms result in substantive unconscionability, thus satisfying, for those jurisdictions which require it, that both elements of unconscionability have been established. While a recent U.S. Supreme Court decision limits the impact of such decisions, the concept of unconscionability remains intact.

Examples from Case Law: Applying the Law to the Terms of License Agreements in the Web and Other Environments

One commentator suggests that shrink-wrap licenses, discussed in greater detail in Chapter 7, satisfy both unconscionability arguments (procedural and substantive) or least have the potential to do so.[40] Of course, there is a difference between terms and conditions that are merely unfavorable and those which are unconscionable. As Judge Easterbrook observed in *Hill v. Gateway 2000, Inc.,* "[a] contract need not be read to be effective; people who accept take the risk that the unread terms may in retrospect prove unwelcome."[41] His opinion the year before in *ProCD, Inc. v. Zeidenberg*[42] validated so-called click-wrap (also discussed in Chapter 7) agreements and led to the conclusion that the form alone of these contracts is not per se suspect.

Commentators agree:

> An equally important aspect of the *ProCD* holding for electronic boilerplate is Judge Easterbrook's determination that the pop-up presentation style of clickwrap terms constitutes reasonable notice of the terms contained therein. A contrary determination would have meant that clickwrap terms are procedurally unconscionable. Courts following *ProCD* will treat clickwrap terms as functionally identical to boilerplate in the paper world, and will presume that the consumer has read the terms and agreed to them.[43]

People enter into these sorts of agreements all the time. Results may depend on the particular jurisdiction and the facts (the actual language of the agreement under review by the court), but courts have found some terms unconscionable and others not. For example, the 6th Circuit concluded that the following clauses found in an online dating website were not unconscionable: "a clause limiting damages to the amount of the contract [and] a clause allowing SexSearch [the licensor] to cancel the contract at any time."[44] Likewise, arbitration clauses, often the subject of unconscionability claims, were enforceable in two recent Washington cases, even where in one case the venue of arbitration was London.[45] Reasonable terms coupled with the potential for an unreasonable outcome from the provisions often result in enforceable provisions.[46]

Excessive Arbitration Clauses

In numerous cases, courts have found terms unconscionable. Again, the point is made that not all arbitration clauses are unconscionable, especially in light of a recent U.S. Supreme Court decision: class-action/arbitration waivers in consumer (nonnegotiated) contracts cannot be ruled unconscionable per se and will no longer be unconscionable merely because the agreement in question replaces litigation with arbitration and includes a class-action waiver to accomplish that end. Courts have concluded that unconscionability existed regarding the terms surrounding the arbitration, for example, excessive and noncoverable escrow payments, and courts may continue to do so in the future. Under the recent *AT&T Mobility LLC v. Concepcion*[47] decision referenced throughout this chapter, such broad per se unconscionability conclusions are now suspect or at least limited to a smaller subset of arbitration clauses. For example, where the terms can be viewed and understood ahead of time (locatable, readable, etc., so that there is no surprise), the effect of the terms can still be so outrageous that a court will nonetheless deem the provisions and the contract unconscionable. Again, the terms of the arbitration clause in the PayPal agreement regarding the circumstances surrounding the operation of the arbitration provision are an infamous example:

> However, Plaintiffs present evidence that PayPal has frozen customer accounts and retained funds that it alone determined were subject to dispute without notice to the named Plaintiffs. The User Agreement expressly authorizes PayPal to engage in such conduct unilaterally. While in theory a customer may seek provisional relief in the courts, including presumably an order to unfreeze an account, the cost of doing so would be prohibitive in relation to the amounts typically in dispute. For all practical purposes, a customer may resolve disputes only after PayPal has had control of the disputed funds for an indefinite period of time. Although PayPal alone may amend the User Agreement without notice or negotiation, a customer is bound to any and all such amendments for the duration of the customer's relationship with PayPal. PayPal has not shown that "business realities" justify such one-sidedness.[48]

Arbitration clauses are common in mass-market and end user (web environments) license agreements. In the *AT&T Mobility LLC v. Concepcion* decision, the Court indicated that arbitration is not per se unconscionable but that if it is part of an oppressive iteration of conditions and circumstances, the contract can be struck as unconscionable. For example, in a post–*AT&T Mobility LLC v. Concepcion* case decided in November 2011, a California court found an arbitration provision in a used-car contract unconscionable:

> We conclude that four clauses in the arbitration provision are unconscionable. First, a party who loses before the single arbitrator may appeal to a panel of three arbitrators if the award exceeds $100,000. Second, an appeal is permitted if the award includes injunctive relief. Third, the appealing party must pay, in advance, "the filing fee and other arbitration costs subject to a final determination by the arbitrators of a fair apportionment of costs." Fourth, the provision exempts repossession from arbitration while requiring that a request for injunctive relief be submitted to arbitration. Although these provisions may appear neutral on their face, they have the effect of placing an unduly oppressive burden on the buyer. In assessing unconscionability, we focus on the practical effect of a provision, not a facial interpretation.[49]

Relying on the earlier *Comb v. PayPal* but also consistent with the post–*AT&T Mobility* precedent,[50] a Pennsylvania court reached a similar conclusion regarding an arbitration clause in the Second Life user agreement, finding evidence of both procedural and substantive unconscionability:

> Here, although the TOS [terms of service] are ubiquitous throughout Second Life, Linden buried the TOS's arbitration provision in a lengthy paragraph under the benign heading "GENERAL PROVISIONS"... Linden also failed to make available the costs and rules of arbitration in the ICC by either setting them forth in the TOS or by providing a hyper-link to another page or website where they are available.[51]

As a result, the court found "surprise" requirements of substantive unconscionability present.[52] With terms similar to those found unconscionable in *Comb v. PayPal*, the one-sided impact of the clause satisfied the substantive element of unconscionability:

> In effect, the TOS provide Linden with a variety of one-sided remedies to resolve disputes, while forcing its customers to arbitrate any disputes with Linden. This is precisely what occurred here. When a dispute arose, Linden exercised its option to use self-help by freezing Bragg's account, retaining funds that Linden alone determined were subject to dispute, and then telling Bragg that he could resolve the dispute by initiating a costly arbitration process. The TOS expressly authorized Linden to engage in such unilateral conduct.[53]

Even fee-splitting or -sharing provisions can be unconscionable when the result is to render the process cost-ineffective in terms of the potential remedy or recovery.[54] This is a common theme in the cases that find unconscionability present in the terms of an arbitration provision.[55] The process is designed to be so cost-ineffective that no customer ever pursues it. As the *Bragg v. Linden Research, Inc.* court explained after doing the math:

Here, even taking Defendants characterization of the fees to be accurate, the total estimate of costs and fees would be $7,500, which would result in Bragg having to advance $3,750 at the outset of arbitration. The court's own estimates place the amount that Bragg would likely have to advance at $8,625, but they could reach as high as $13,687.50. Any of these figures are significantly greater than the costs that Bragg bears by filing his action in a state or federal court. Accordingly, the arbitration costs and fee-splitting scheme together also support a finding of unconscionability.[56]

Looking to elements of oppression (whether an adhesion contract exists) and surprise, a California district court found the arbitration provision in an eBay agreement procedurally unconscionable and the appearance of terms near useless to consumers:

> This oppression was coupled with surprise. The format in which the Terms and Conditions were presented to the plaintiff only allowed for a few single-spaced lines of block text to be visible at any given time. Furthermore, there were no paragraph, section or heading breaks that would aid in reading comprehension or allow the user to navigate to a particular section. This single-spaced massive block of impenetrable text looked the same when printed out...Accordingly, since both oppression and surprise were present, the court is satisfied that the agreement was procedurally unconscionable.[57]

As unconscionability is case specific, it is difficult to state a uniform rule. However, where the terms are difficult to determine, they exist in a mass-market, nonnegotiated license, and the impact of the arbitration provision is to preclude any meaningful remedy, the case of unconscionability can be made, or at least contemplated.

Limitation on Remedies and Class-Action Waivers in General

Substantive unconscionability (which looks to a lack of mutuality or bilateral indifference in impact) was also present in the eBay litigation in part because the arbitration provision precluded remedy through class action, often the only cost-effective way for some customers to seek relief:

> Further, the clause is especially egregious because individual damages are likely to be small and class actions are thus the only effective way to litigate such disputes...In contrast, there are no rules here save plaintiff having one hour in which to personally make all arguments regarding the merits of her own claims and the claims of her class-members. This makes it de facto impossible to litigate a class action and thus case law that holds de jure class action waivers to be substantively unconscionable is instructive here.[58]

The Cingular arbitration provision also contained a prohibition on class action and was likewise substantively unconscionable.[59] Again, the point is made that not all class-action waiver clauses are per se unconscionable and thus invalid but are instead circumstance dependent, based on who the parties are, the particular terms of the agreement, and so forth. This point was emphasized by a California court also reviewing a Cingular Wireless arbitration provision.[60] Often, when the aggrieved party is also a like-situated business and the damage limitation bears some reasonable relationship to the particulars of the business, industry, trade, or practice, the provision will be upheld. For example, in *Hebert v. Rapid Payroll, Inc.*, the district court concluded the limitation of liability provision was not unconscionable:

> With respect to procedural unconscionability, the License was the product of arms-length negotiations, and there is no indication that either side had any significant leverage. OCS was a fledgling company operating in a competitive marketplace, and Plaintiff makes no claim that it was dependent upon OCS at that time. Indeed, in its Opposition, Plaintiff asserts no arguments regarding its bargaining power at the time it entered the License Agreement. As for substantive unconscionability, it must be based on more than simple unfairness or unreasonableness; there must be a finding that the contract was a bargain "no man in his sense and not under delusion would make on the one hand, and as no honest and fair man would accept on the other."[61]

Most recent cases of unconscionable contract terms have involved disputes between businesses and consumers over nonnegotiable or mass-market agreements—the take-it-or-leave-it context of adhesion contracts.

> There have been few reported decisions in the past decade in which a court invalidates a term on this basis and virtually none in cases involving a transaction between two businesses...the core presumption holds that parties are able to make contractual arrangements or not depending on their own bargaining power and skill. The case law is replete with language denying unconscionability challenges in the business-to-business transactional environment on grounds that business representative are expected to read and live by their agreements.[62]

Again, the question would be whether a library or related entity would be considered a consumer, as courts have often concluded that in business-to-business settings the alleged aggrieved party was "not an inexperienced retail consumer"[63] or "not unwitting members of the general public."[64] Although not a business per se, is a library an inexperienced consumer or an unwitting member of the public? The library may be so when it obtains products under circumstances where it is in no better position than any other consumer. In certain transactions, the library may assume the status of a consumer: "Though plaintiff may be a business owner herself, her interaction with Live Auctions was in the capacity of an ordinary consumer— she did not have a relationship with HJA that allowed her to negotiate the Terms and Conditions. Thus, this agreement was unquestionably an oppressive contract of adhesion."[65] In circumstances of negotiated contracts, such as database service contracts, this may not be the case, but a library that obtains content from a website in the same manner as every other consumer might be deemed, for purposes of this transaction, a consumer.

Supreme Court, the Federal Arbitration Act, and Class-Action Waivers

In spring 2011, the U.S. Supreme Court ruled that a *California Supreme Court decision (Bank v. Superior Court*[66]) holding arbitration clauses in contracts prohibiting class-action lawsuits unconscionable was preempted by the Federal Arbitration Act (FAA).[67] "The question in this case is whether § 2 [of the FAA] preempts California's rule classifying most collective-arbitration waivers in consumer contracts as unconscionable."[68] The Court answered in the affirmative: "The conclusion follows that class arbitration, to the extent it is manufactured by *Discover Bank* rather than consensual, is inconsistent with the FAA"[69] and that "California's *Discover Bank* rule is preempted by the FAA."[70] In the view of the majority, "[a]rbitration is a matter of contract, and the FAA requires courts to honor parties' expectations."[71] The case law in California on this issue was well developed, as cited, with the state Supreme Court concluding under the *Discover* rule[72] that such clauses are unconscionable.

One reason the California court as well as others scrutinize arbitration clauses is that the processes commanded by such clauses oftentimes make arbitration very unwieldy and costly in terms of time and money, so much so that the likely consequence is that claims are never pursued, in essence making such mechanisms meaningless or useless from the standpoint of the consumer. Countering this rationale when considering the term of the arbitration agreement in question, the U.S. Supreme Court observed:

> The dissent claims that class proceedings are necessary to prosecute small-dollar claims that might otherwise slip through the legal system. But States cannot require a procedure that is inconsistent with the FAA, even if it is desirable for unrelated reasons. Moreover, the claim here was most unlikely to go unresolved. As noted earlier, the arbitration agreement provides that AT&T will pay claimants a minimum of $7,500 and twice their attorney's fees if they obtain an arbitration award greater than AT&T's last settlement offer. The District Court found this scheme sufficient to provide incentive for the individual prosecution of meritorious claims that are not immediately settled, and the Ninth Circuit admitted that aggrieved customers who filed claims would be essentially guaranteed to be made whole. Indeed, the District Court concluded that the Concepcion's were *better off* under their arbitration agreement with AT&T than they would have been as participants in a class action, which could take months, if not years, and which may merely yield an opportunity to submit a claim for recovery of a small percentage of a few dollars.[73]

Does such a holding preclude that an onerous arbitration clause could never be found unconscionable in the future? No. As the Court observed, such clauses remain able to be "invalidated by generally applicable contract defenses, such as fraud, duress, or unconscionability, but not be defenses that apply only to arbitration or that derive their meaning from the fact that an agreement to arbitrate is as issue."[74] In the future, unconscionability must be found from the terms of the arbitration or surrounding the arbitration, or from other contract terms altogether, and not from the mere requirements to arbitrate instead of litigate and to waive the right to litigate as part of a class-action suit.

Lower courts are still assessing the impact of the Supreme Court decision. A New Jersey court made the following observation the summer after the Supreme Court decision was issued:

> Nevertheless, the Court in *AT&T Mobility* acknowledged that the FAA does not require an arbitration provision to be enforced if the provision is defective for reasons other than public policy or unconscionability. Other contract principles under state law, such as those governing the formation and interpretation of an agreement, may still pertain, subject to the overarching objectives of the FAA.[75]

For example, a Colorado district court observed:

> Because Colorado's test for unconscionability of a contract provision does not explicitly disfavor arbitration (class or otherwise), the degree to which *Concepcion* changes the legal landscape in Colorado is unclear. There does not appear to be any reason why the *Davis* factors are not still good law. Thus, the Court will consider the facts of this case under that structure, keeping in mind the Supreme Court's statements and observations in *Concepcion*.[76]

Likewise, other courts have held other aspects of arbitration provisions unconscionable.[77]

Congress may ultimately have the last word on the subject, introducing legislation that would not necessarily restore the pre-*Concepcion* landscape to jurisdictions such as California but would ensure that such class-action waivers contain an array of procedural safeguards to ensure adequacy in terms of an opportunity for realistic remedy to consumers.[78] Even without such legislation, unconscionability remains a viable doctrine, as post–*AT&T Mobility LLC v. Concepcion* cases have demonstrated. However, the likelihood of its application to a particular license is better where the contract involves a nonnegotiated, mass-market licensing scenario. This would not apply to negotiated licenses, such as a database agreement, but as more libraries enter the consumer-oriented marketplace for new technologies (e.g., e-book readers and other handheld devices) and/or purchase media via online stores (e.g., iTunes), such contracts will govern. Despite the more limited application of the doctrine to arbitration clauses (a focus of recent licensing case in the area), the doctrine remains available for courts to use when assessing other license provisions, and the jurisprudence associated with it may likewise continue to evolve.

COPYRIGHT MISUSE AND LICENSING INFORMATION CONTENT

The doctrine of copyright misuse is recognized by a number of courts, but not all courts or jurisdictions have had the opportunity to consider the concept of misuse in the context of copyright. The doctrine of copyright misuse is adopted from similar principles in patent law relating to antitrust.[79] The concept of misuse relates to circumstances where a valid intellectual property right exists, but the owner of the right attempts to use this right to leverage some other benefit unrelated to the right.[80] Courts view this as unfair, and because the rights of copyright owners are granted by law, courts respond by holding in abeyance, or suspending in a sense, those rights during the time of misuse, at least with respect to enforcing those rights against infringers. When applicable, applying the doctrine of copyright misuse prevents the copyright owner from suing for infringement, not only the person or entity upon which the unfair leverage is thrust, but also other nonleveraged infringers as well. In other words, the owner's right to enforce the copyright is suspended during the course of the misuse.

Application of the doctrine does not confer an independent cause of action for damages. Rather, it operates as a bar to the opposing party's suit for infringement. In addition, the bar is effective only during the period of misuse. Once the misuse of copyright ceases, the plaintiff is free to pursue legal remedy (a suit for infringement of copyright), assuming the infringement continues.

> The doctrines of patent and copyright misuse provide potentially significant limitations on licensing and have no analogue in other fields of contract law or practice. Misuse doctrine is unclear, however. In practice, the doctrine reflects a judgment, often idiosyncratic, that some conduct by an intellectual property rights owner goes too far in exploiting the property right and that this wrongful conduct creates a defense to a claim of infringement by that rights owner against the licensee and against any other party.[81]

Like the concept of unconscionability, the doctrine of misuse is rooted in equitable aspects of public policy.[82] In the patent area as well as the copyright area, courts consider whether the leverage the rights holder is attempting to exert is contrary to the public policy underlying the intellectual property law in question. For example, older Supreme Court precedent indicates that using a contract to extend the duration of the patent property right beyond the number of years statutorily established by Congress by extending the period during which royalty payments are made is per se patent misuse.[83] It is hoped that a similar argument could be made under the copyright law,[84] or for any provision that attempts to extend the limited monopoly granted by the copyright law to the rights holder.[85] Courts are particularly sensitive where attempt is made to extend the period of economic return through contractual obligations.

Public Policy, the Public Domain, and Copyright Misuse

While the 7th Circuit has not had the opportunity to address the doctrine of copyright misuse, a recent decision indicated a receptive attitude to the application of the doctrine in copyright or copyright-like scenarios under the proper circumstances. Furthermore, the discussion occurred in the circumstance of a license involving both copyright and public domain content, a context common to many database license agreements. The decision could offer a window into how the court might view a database vendor that attempts to leverage or use a license agreement to push the envelope of legitimate rights under the copyright law into the illegitimate arena of misuse. As discussed in this section, in the context of licensing public domain content, for misuse to be applicable, the vendor would need to be the sole source of the public domain contracts, through an exclusive government contract to make the content available to the public, for example. Nonetheless, the decision is encouraging, as it presents a legal limit to the use of the contract law, when the circumstance relates to public domain content and the license attempts to restrict access to or use of the public domain content.

Assessment Technologies [AT] of WI, LLC v. Wiredata, Inc. involved a dispute between competing content vendors. One vendor (the one with the government contract to do so) designed a collection tool (the Market Drive program) for property assessment data. The data the program collected was factual information regarding real estate parcels, such as location, tax, and other government assessments—all of which is in the public domain. The vendor attempted several strategies to prohibit other vendors (its potential competitors) from using the public domain data collected with its protected (in terms of the copyright law) collection tool (a software program), as it feared such extraction would lead to the creation of competing commercial sources of the data. Writing for the 7th Circuit, Judge Posner observed:

> Similarly, if the only way WIREdata could obtain public-domain data about properties in southeastern Wisconsin would be by copying the data in the municipalities' databases as embedded in Market Drive, so that it would be copying the compilation and not just the compiled data only because the data and the format in which they were organized could not be disentangled, it would be privileged to make such a copy, and likewise the municipalities. For the only purpose of the copying would be to extract noncopyrighted material, and not to go into competition with AT by selling copies of Market Drive. We emphasize this point lest AT try to circumvent our decision by reconfiguring Market Drive in such a way that the municipalities would find it difficult or impossible to furnish the raw data to requesters such as WIREdata in any format other than that prescribed by Market Drive. If AT did that with that purpose it might be guilty of copyright misuse...[86]

The use of a copyright interest in combination with license, in the court's view, made the conduct of Assessment Technologies suspect: "AT is trying to use its copyright to sequester uncopyrightable data, presumably in the hope of extracting a license fee from WIREdata."[87] The defendant was not seeking the data in the same form in which AT's software program collected it. Yet, the court suggested that AT was not suing the municipalities for breach of the license agreement each entity had with it. This would not be the logical legal route to pursue to influence the behavior of a third party—as the third party here, WIREdata, is not a party to the original contract. Rather, action against a third party might proceed along some other grounds, such as intentional interference with the contract.

The court hypothesized that such legal strong-arm maneuvers, or pushing the envelope of copyright protection by forcing a settlement or even achieving an outright victory in various lawsuits, would be an abuse of process and suggested that in the future it would support the adoption of the copyright misuse doctrine in the 7th Circuit. Likewise, the court expressed skepticism at the use of the license in a later breach of contract suit, one to prevent the municipalities under the terms of the license from releasing the assessor data to others:

> WIREdata is not a licensee of AT, and AT is not suing to enforce any contract it might have with WIREdata. It therefore had no cause to drag the licenses before us. But since it did, we shall not conceal our profound skepticism concerning AT's interpretation. If accepted, it would forbid municipalities licensed by AT to share the data in their tax-assessment databases with each other even for the purpose of comparing or coordinating their assessment methods, though all the data they would be exchanging would be data that their assessors had collected and inputted into the databases. That seems an absurd result.[88]

The 7th Circuit anticipated the information owner's next move as well. Here the vendor-plaintiff did not create the database; rather,

> it created only an empty database, a bin that the tax assessors filled with the data. It created the compartments in the bin and the instructions for sorting the data to those compartments, but those were its only innovations and their protection by copyright law is complete. To try *by contract* or otherwise to prevent the municipalities from revealing their own data, especially when, as we have seen, the complete data are unavailable anywhere else, might constitute *copyright misuse.*[89]

Though stopping short of applying the misuse doctrine to circumstances without the presence of antitrust (or limited to facts where the data is not available elsewhere), Judge Posner appeared receptive to that possibility given the proper facts. While the developing case law of copyright misuse may hold hope for invalidating restrictive license agreements, the circumstances are limited to the unique situation where the licensor is the only source of the information and the information constitutes what would otherwise be public domain data.

Another case involving fact-based geographic information system (GIS) data likewise demonstrated the interface of contract and copyright. In *County of Santa*

Clara v. Superior Court, the copyright license protection issue for such data was again multifaceted. The court described one of the arguments forwarded by the government: "The County also asserts a public safety interest in guarding against terrorist threats, based on its contention that the GIS basemap contains sensitive information that is not publicly available, such as the exact location of Hetch Hetchy reservoir components."[90] The court concluded that the public interest in access outweighed any competing interest.[91] The court also rejected the county's argument that it could protect such information by copyright.[92] The county attempted to control release of such information through a license that the court concluded was contrary to California law: "As a matter of first impression in California, we conclude that end user restrictions are incompatible with the purposes and operation of the CPRA [California Public Records Act]."[93] While not using the term copyright misuse, the case nonetheless stands for the proposition that courts will impose limits to the use of license agreements, especially where public domain information is involved,[94] and view such attempts as misuse of copyright or otherwise contrary to law or public policy.

Copyright Misuse in Other Circuits

Other circuits, such as the 4th, 5th, and 9th, have accepted the application of the misuse doctrine to copyright. Again, when the doctrine applies, it does not mean that the owner's copyright is somehow invalidated; rather, the ability to enforce the copyright against a defendant during the period of misuse is suspended.[95] It operates as a defense to what otherwise would be a valid claim of infringement. The gravamen of the misuse claim is whether the plaintiff, against whom the defense is charged, is engaging in activity that undermines the public policy inherent in the copyright law, the constitutional goal of promoting creative expression. This often occurs when the plaintiff is using the copyright law to leverage an advantage in another area.[96] Further, copyright is often described as a limited monopoly, and use of copyright in this way pushes the owner's rights beyond its intended contours.[97] The resulting anticompetitive advantage is deemed a misuse of the copyright law. However, there must be "sufficient nexus between the alleged anti-competitive leveraging and the policy of the copyright laws."[98] Not all circuits have adopted the misuse doctrine from the patent law into the copyright repertoire,[99] and the expansion of the doctrine is not without detractors.[100] Of greater importance to the subject matter of this book is that several circuits have applied the doctrine to situations where the copyright owner leveraged a copyright through restrictive licensing agreements.

The 4th Circuit was the first to adopt the misuse concept into the copyright law. In *Lasercomb America, Inc. v. Reynolds*,[101] the defendants did not

> dispute that they copied Interact [the infringed software program], but they contend that Lasercomb is barred from recovery for infringement by its concomitant culpability.

They assert that, assuming Lasercomb had a perfected copyright, it impermissibly abused it. This assertion of the "misuse of copyright" defense is based on language in Lasercomb's standard licensing agreement, restricting licensees from creating any of their own CAD/CAM die-making software.[102]

While an issue of first impression, the 4th Circuit was "persuaded, however, that a misuse of copyright defense is inherent in the law of copyright just as a misuse of patent defense is inherent in patent law."[103] The anticompetitive and counterproductive impact, in terms of the licensee's potential for future creative activity, convinced the court that the copyright in the Interact program was unfairly leveraged (misused) through the terms of the licensee agreement:

> The language employed in the Lasercomb agreement is extremely broad. Each time Lasercomb sells its Interact program to a company and obtains that company's agreement to the noncompete language, the company is required to forego [*sic*] utilization of the creative abilities of all its officers, directors and employees in the area of CAD/CAM die-making software. Of yet greater concern, these creative abilities are withdrawn from the public. The period for which this anticompetitive restraint exists is ninety-nine years, which could be longer than the life of the copyright itself.[104]

As in the earlier referenced patent cases, extending through contract the duration of economic viability of the intellectual property is counterproductive to the incentive structure (economics returns during a defined period of legal right) of the intellectual property laws.

The abusive leverage was apparent from the terms of the license agreement. To obtain use of the software program now—while it was still governed by copyright protection—the licensee had to agree not to develop competing products during the current term of protection as well as during a later period beyond the period of copyright duration—for a period of 99 years from the date of the license. The court found problematic that Lasercomb attempted through its license agreement to do what the copyright law could not: prevent all derivative as well as other uses during and potentially beyond the likely duration of the copyright. While such uses during the period of copyright would impinge on the copyright owner's exclusive right under section 106, any use would otherwise be subject to the user's right of fair use, as well as other users' rights. The court held that Lasercomb could not sue to enforce its copyright in the Interact program since it engaged in copyright misuse through the use of such far-reaching (in terms of the time period) anticompetitive clauses in its licensing agreement.[105] Moreover, the defendants never signed the license agreement provided by Lasercomb.[106]

This is an important point, and one that can benefit the library, archive, and other educational communities. The benefit of the misuse defense is available not only to those who are a party to the offending activity (i.e., the institution, the licensee of the "egregious" license terms) but to nonparties or third parties as well.[107] Patrons of a library or archive or students of a school, college, or university would be a third party as far as the vendor-licensor and the library-licensee are concerned. Given the proper circumstances (where the doctrine of copyright misuse applied), a nonparty to the contract-license could bring a copyright misuse defense should the vendor-licensor attempt suit against the patron for infringement of the protected (in terms of copyright) nature of the licensed content.

The 5th Circuit has also had opportunity to consider applying the doctrine of copyright misuse in the software licensing setting and favorably endorsed the concept in *DSC Communications Corp. v. DGI Technologies, Inc.*[108] The dispute arose between two telecommunications companies:

> DSC manufactures the entire phone switch system, and has a copyright on the software used in the phone switch. DSC sells phone switches, but does not sell the software necessary to operate them. Instead, it licenses the software to its customers . . . DGI is attempting to develop a microprocessor card that can be used in DSC phone switches. Customers would use this card instead of using a DSC-manufactured card. DSC contends that DGI engaged in several acts of copyright infringement in its attempt to develop a microprocessor card.[109]

The 5th Circuit relied heavily upon the discussion of the 4th Circuit in *Lasercomb America, Inc. v. Reynolds*, agreeing that its rationale was sound[110] and affirming the grant of an injunction by the lower court.[111]

The appellate court again found that the use of anticompetitive or restrictive license agreements between the copyright owner and a third party in essence foreclosed innovation by the defendant, that is, the party now asserting the misuse defense against the plaintiff copyright owner. (In these scenarios, it is not the licensee who asserts the defense, as the license provides for, or allows, the uses it makes of the plaintiff's content protected by copyright, so the plaintiff is not concerned with then suing the licensee.)[112] This is counterproductive to the goal of the copyright law, which is designed to encourage the creation of more copyrightable works:

> DGI may well prevail on the defense of copyright misuse, because DSC seems to be attempting to use its copyright to obtain a patent-like monopoly over unpatented microprocessor cards. Any competing microprocessor card developed for use on DSC phone switches must be compatible with DSC's copyrighted operating system software. In order to ensure that its card is compatible, a competitor such as DGI must test the card on a DSC phone switch. Such a test necessarily involves making a copy of DSC's copyrighted operating system, which copy is downloaded into the card's memory when the card is booted up. If DSC is allowed to prevent such copying, then it can prevent anyone from developing a competing microprocessor card, even though it has not patented the card.[113]

Again, it could be argued that in the absence of such a restrictive license, such reproduction as part of a computer boot-up is allowed by section 117.[114] In a subsequent review of the case, the 5th Circuit observed: "A reasonable juror could conclude, based on the licensing agreement, that DSC has used its copyrights to indirectly gain commercial control over products DSC does not have copyrighted, namely, its microprocessor cards. The facts on which we based our misuse prediction in DSC I [*DSC Communications Corp. v. DGI Technologies, Inc.*[115]] have not changed substantially."[116] While some aspects of the initial injunction were amended in the later decision, the appellate court found misuse evident from the acts of DCS, now known as Acatel USA, Inc.[117]

In a scenario of related interest to libraries, the defendant publisher asserted the copyright misuse defense against the American Medical Association (AMA) when it failed to obtain what it felt was a competitive volume discount on the purchase of an AMA publication containing the coding system CPT (Current Procedural Terminology),[118] a system that the federal Health Care Financing Administration (HCFA) agreed to use to the exclusion of other coding systems in conjunction with identifying physicians' services for use in completing Medicare and Medicaid claim forms. "Practice Management argues that the AMA misused its copyright by negotiating a contract in which HCFA agreed to use the CPT exclusively."[119] The 9th Circuit reviewed the developing case law regarding copyright misuse, citing both *Lasercomb America, Inc. v. Reynolds* and *DSC Communications Corp. v. DGI Technologies, Inc.*, among other cases, and agreed to "now adopt that rule."[120]

Again, the restrictive and exclusive nature of the terms of the license agreement whereby the HCFA could use no other coding system in essence precluded competitors from attempting to devise a competing and possibly superior coding system. With the restrictive agreement in place forbidding the federal agency from adopting any other coding mechanism, there would be little point in a third party (e.g., another publisher or medical informatics firm) investing the capital needed to devise an alternative system. The original roots of antitrust and the stifling of competition present in the patent misuse case law permeate the application of the misuse doctrine in the copyright arena, at least in the views of the various courts that have considered such cases. If the HCFA would be precluded from adopting any other system, any new system that would be developed would be useless from a market standpoint because no one could use it. "The adverse effects of the licensing agreement are apparent. The terms under which the AMA agreed to license use of the CPT to HCFA gave the AMA a substantial and unfair advantage over its competitors."[121] Such results are inconsistent with the climate of creativity that copyright law attempts to foster. Notice also that the misuse claim was brought by a third party again, one that desired to develop an alternative and hopefully competing medical coding system. As with the 7th Circuit decision, where copyright owners attempt to create through use of a license a sort of information singularity (in either the source of or need for the content), courts will not hesitate to consider the application of the copyright misuse doctrine.

Likewise, the court here concluded that the restriction imposed by the AMA constituted misuse:[122]

> Taken together, and short of any rule of reason analysis such as the Federal Circuit required in patent misuse cases, *Lasercomb* and *Practice Management* create a troubling risk for copyright licensors. In both cases, license conditions precluding competition were held, in context, to constitute copyright misuse. One assumes that the doctrine does not invalidate all non-competition conditions in copyright licenses, however, the cases do not give guidance on how to gauge which contract terms of this sort are permitted and which are not. Of course, both *Lasercomb* (99 year term) and *Practice Management* (governmental agency control) involved unique and uniquely egregious limitations, but absent guidance on where the line will be drawn leaves one with small comfort given the draconian potential of a finding of misuse.[123]

Looking at both the *Assessment Technologies [AT] of WI, LLC* and *Practice Management Information Corp.* decisions, there is consistency: in the former case the public agency was the sole source of the data others could use, and in the latter case the agency was the arbiter in a sense of the content that all others (though filing claims with it) could use as well.

A valid claim of copyright misuse must then extend the exclusive rights of the rights holder beyond the limits articulated by Congress in the copyright law. "Put simply, our Constitution emphasizes the purpose and value of copyrights and patents. Harm caused by their misuse undermines their usefulness. Anti-competitive licensing agreements may conflict with the purpose behind a copyright's protection by depriving the public of the would-be competitor's creativity."[124] On the few occasions where courts have considered the intersection of copyright and free speech rights, courts often side with free speech.[125] However, a restrictive provision that impacts some other right, such as free speech, would not constitute copyright misuse (though as discussed earlier it might constitute an unconscionable term). This distinction was made by another circuit in a case subsequent to the *Lasercomb America, Inc. v. Reynolds*, *DSC Communications Corp. v. DGI Technologies, Inc.*, and *Practice Management Information Corp. v. American Medical Association* decisions. Though the court was not opposed to the concept of copyright misuse in principle, the facts of the case did not constitute copyright misuse.

In *Video Pipeline, Inc. v. Buena Vista Home Entertainment, Inc.*,[126] the restrictive license term did not prevent or limit competition in copyrightable content but rather criticism:

> Video Pipeline further contends that Disney has misused its copyright and, as a result, should not receive the protection of copyright law. Video Pipeline points to certain licensing agreements that Disney has entered into with three companies and sought to

enter into with a number of other companies operating web sites...As Video Pipeline sees it, such licensing agreements seek to use copyright law to suppress criticism and, in so doing, misuse those laws, triggering the copyright misuse doctrine.[127]

More important, while the 3rd Circuit rejected the misuse claim in affirming the grant of preliminary injunction by the district court, it nonetheless approved of the misuse doctrine as an affirmative defense to a copyright infringement suit.[128] The dispute again arose in the context of licensing:

> The licensing agreements in this case do seek to restrict expression by licensing the Disney trailers for use on the internet only so long as the web sites on which the trailers will appear do not derogate Disney, the entertainment industry, etc. But we nonetheless cannot conclude on this record that the agreements are likely to interfere with creative expression to such a degree that they affect in any significant way the policy interest in increasing the public store of creative activity.[129]

However, the appellate court suggested that if the agreement did foreclose the ability to engage in any criticism of Disney whatsoever, such a blanket gag clause might indeed constitute misuse: "The licensing agreements do not, for instance, interfere with the licensee's opportunity to express such criticism on other web sites or elsewhere. There is no evidence that the public will find it any more difficult to obtain criticism of Disney and its interests, or even that the public is considerably less likely to come across this criticism, if it is not displayed on the same site as the trailers."[130] So, a license agreement that prohibits all negative comments about the licensor and its products or services might also constitute copyright misuse? This is the implication of such developments. This result is significant, as a number of license agreements have provisions that purport to do just this (see discussion of gag-wrap provisions under Confidential Information and Nondisclosure in Chapter 14). Any such restrictive license agreement will be evaluated in light of the public policy behind both the copyright law and the concept of free speech, with the overreaching principle that more information is better than less information. Said in a different way, would applying the misuse doctrine result in an increase or decrease in the flow of information products? Would it allow fair use and other user rights to result in a more robust flow of information, creative (read: copyrighted) works, and free speech? To quote the *Video Pipeline, Inc. v. Buena Vista Home Entertainment, Inc.* court:

> Moreover, if a critic wishes to comment on Disney's works, the fair use doctrine may be implicated regardless of the existence of the licensing agreements. Finally, copyright law, and the misuse doctrine in particular, should not be interpreted to require Disney, if it licenses its trailers for display on any web sites but its own, to do so willy-nilly regardless of the content displayed with its copyrighted works. Indeed such an application of the misuse doctrine would likely decrease the public's access to Disney's works because it might as a result refuse to license at all online display of its works.[131]

While the misuse doctrine is still nascent, with only several circuits recognizing its application in the copyright-licensing arena, it may develop into a valuable tool in combating overly restrictive license terms.

What sort of language might qualify in a library, archive, or educational scenario for a misuse claim is difficult to conceive, as there is a dearth of case law.[132] In patent misuse cases, the following provisions have been deemed abusive:

> conditioning grant of a license upon the use of unpatented materials, supplies or components, license requiring a party not to deal in products that compete with the patented products, mandatory package licensing where patent owner refuses to license patents separately, patent license providing for payment of royalties after expiration of patent, conditioning license upon licensee's agreement to pay royalties based on sales regardless of actual use of the patent, some attempts to contractually restrain use or disposition of a patented product after the first authorized sale, and agreements for exclusive grant backs of newly developed technology.[133]

The list compiled by Nimmer and Dodd, in conjunction with the cases discussed, suggests that misuse might apply where a license contains provisions that attempt to leverage excessive rights beyond that of the copyright law or to extend payment obligations beyond the duration of the license, and in scenarios where the information is public domain data and the licensor is the sole source of the data or, through other mechanisms, creates a similar kind of information singularity, and perhaps where all public criticism of the vendor is foreclosed.

THE DOCTRINE OF COPYRIGHT PREEMPTION AND ITS IMPACT ON LICENSING

Another doctrine within copyright has found application in licensing scenarios in recent years and may likewise suggest opportunity for questioning the application of a license or its provisions. The copyright preemption doctrine, codified in section 301 of the copyright law,[134] reflects the supremacy of federal law (here the copyright law) over state law (here the law of contracts including licenses) vis-à-vis the Supremacy Clause of the U.S. Constitution.[135] In its simplest form, the doctrine reflects this supremacy by indicating that if a claim is merely equivalent to the rights granted to owners by the copyright law, then the federal copyright law overrides or preempts the application and enforcement of the state law. In the context of the discussion in this book, the claim would be made pursuant to the license agreement, though a claim could arise under other state law, for example, tort law, such as misappropriation.[136] In the context of contracts and licenses, copyright preemption means enforcing a right under the contract that is equivalent to the owner's exclusive right under the copyright law, which is preempted by the federal copyright law, and thus the offending equivalent provision has no effect.

As with the concept of misuse discussed previously, the doctrine of preemption exists in the patent law as well, though the doctrine there is not made express by statute, as it is in the copyright law. There is some discussion among commentators about whether the doctrine of copyright preemption limits or should limit the reach of license provisions.[137] The rationale provided by several courts for not applying preemption to license terms is based upon the fundamental differences between contract and copyright and relates to the subject matter of the license, or the "stuff" or property that is licensed: "Contract law deals with relationships and rights voluntarily created between contracting parties...In contrast, property rights are the set of legal relations among one person (the property owner) and an indefinite set of third parties with respect to a subject matter (or corpus)."[138] Nimmer and Dodd[139] observe three scenarios where preemption can occur: express preemption, where a federal statute expressly calls for all other laws to be preempted (e.g., section 301 of the copyright law); field preemption, where federal law exclusively covers the field or area of law; and conflict preemption,[140] where in the absence of express or field preemption (which also reflects a sense of "conflict") the state law is nonetheless inconsistent with the federal law and the policy goals behind the federal law. An example of the latter in the contract arena would be the conflict between exceptions to the statute of frauds "writings" requirement and the copyright law that requires all transfers of copyright be in writing.[141] Because the licenses of concern in this book often relate to use of content protected by copyright, it is the express preemption of section 301 that is the focus of the present discussion.

In the patent law, but equally applicable to copyright (and underlying the doctrine of misuse as well), the "federal policy favoring bringing information into the public domain"[142] underlies the preemption analysis: "The test for preemption by copyright law, like the test for patent law preemption, should be whether the state law 'substantially impedes the public use of the otherwise unprotected' material."[143] As copyright preemption is based on an express statutory expression found in section 301, the provision will "not preempt a state law claim that requires proof of a qualitatively relevant, additional element as compared to a claim for copyright infringement, including state law that enforces contract."[144] The goal of preemption is also efficiency; where the rights protected by the law (contract and copyright) are redundant, the federal law will prevail and preempt the state-based contract law. "The Copyright Act preempts state laws that attempt to protect rights exclusively protected by federal law. Conversely, the Copyright Act does not preempt state law from enforcing non-equivalent legal or equitable rights."[145] Nimmer and Dodd call this a form of "negative policy preemption."[146] "Courts and commentators have described this preemption analysis as encompassing a 'subject matter requirement' and a 'general scope' or 'equivalency' requirement."[147] Courts generally view an enforceable contract provision, even if a copyright infringement claim could also be brought under the circumstances, as nonetheless positing the required additional or extra element. "Congress used Section 301 to implement policy of preventing state laws from going beyond the scope of rights granted in the Copyright Act."[148] For a contract provision to survive a claim of preemption under section 301 of the copyright law, the provision must go to some right beyond those granted to the rights holder by the copyright law, or as the courts have expounded, the contract provision must present a so-called additional element. In the case of a license agreement, the provisions must enforce some other right than the five exclusive rights granted to owners under the copyright law,[149] which are the rights of reproduction, making of derivative works, public distribution, public performance, and public display.[150] Courts have held that the prerequisite extra element is satisfied in a claim for tortuous interference with a contract,[151] implied in-fact contract or implied promise to pay[152] but not unjust enrichment,[153] as well as trade secret (breach of confidentiality required in addition to copying)[154] and at-will employment contracts.[155]

The test for preemption requires two considerations. Does the matter fall within the subject matter of copyright[156]—that is, is the state law attempting to usurp a policy decision made by Congress? For example, is the law attempting to protect material that Congress has deemed should be in the public domain[157] or, by state statute, prevent a use such as in *Vault* (discussed in this chapter) that Congress decided should be allowed under the copyright law (e.g., fair use)?[158] The concept of "subject matter" is interpreted by courts to encompass the content that the copyright law protects as well as the content the copyright law excludes from protection. Both sorts of content are still impacted by the copyright law.[159] Second, is the right protected by equivalent state law, or does the state claim fail to contain the so-called extra element?[160] If the answer to both questions is yes, then preemption will occur.

In contract cases, the extra element is often present:

> The extra element is the promise to pay. This extra element does change the nature of the action so that it is qualitatively different from a copyright infringement claim. The qualitative difference includes the requirement of proof of an enforceable promise and a breach thereof which requires, *inter alia*, proof of mutual assent and consideration, as well as proof of the value of the work and appellee's use thereof.[161]

Contracts that do nothing more than reiterate the section 106 exclusive rights of the copyright owner remain subject to preemption, however: "If the promise amounts only to a promise to refrain from reproducing, performing, distributing or displaying the work, then the contract claim is preempted."[162] A distinction should be made between a negotiated contract, where there is in theory meaningful choice, and a nonnegotiated contract with no meaningful choice, where there is neither an ability to bargain nor an opportunity to choose from among alternative but still nonnegotiated agreements (these contracts are also discussed in Chapter 6). The former will not be preempted, as the additional element is present in the climate of a bargained agreement; choice (other than to accept or reject the agreement in total) being lacking in the nonnegotiated agreement, the latter will be preempted.[163]

Preemption Trends in the Courts

Several significant cases have held that the copyright law did *not* preempt enforcement of a contract claim arising from a license agreement where the license prohibited additional copying,[164] commercial purposes,[165] or reverse engineering.[166] For claims arising from implied contracts (discussed in Chapter 12), there is greater likelihood that the extra element is not present, as remedy is not based on a contractual right but on an equitable theory (as explained in Chapter 12) for use of copyrighted material—use that would fall within the exclusive right of the copyright owner.[167] The doctrine of preemption may sound too technical to understand, but the concept is a simple one in its basic essence. Does the application of the federal copyright law to the subject matter of the agreement take precedence over the state law that would otherwise control the validity and thus enforceability of the contract?

The doctrine of preemption proposes that if the state law creates a right that is essentially the same as the federal law, in this case the copyright law, then the federal law should prevail or preempt any claim under the state law. "To survive preemption, the state cause of action must protect rights that are qualitatively different from the rights protected by copyright: the complaint must allege an 'extra element' that changes the nature of the action."[168] Why is this important? Because if federal copyright preempts state law like contract or tort (e.g., in misappropriation cases), then the federal copyright law applies to the case. This seems logical and simple, but the impact is significant because it means that all of the affirmative defenses, such as fair use, and damage remission provisions available to defendants under the federal copyright law apply to the case.

For example, in *Davidson & Associates v. Jung*,[169] a dispute arose over the validity of restrictions governing a computer game. Before installation of the game from a CD-ROM onto the user's computer could begin, a series of conditions or terms of use (TOU) governing the use of the game appeared on the screen. At the end of the TOU, the user was asked to assent by clicking an "I agree" button. This end user license agreement (EULA) contained, among others, a restriction on reverse engineering:

> YOU SHOULD CAREFULLY READ THE FOLLOWING END USER LICENSE AGREE-
> MENT BEFORE INSTALLING THIS SOFTWARE PROGRAM. BY INSTALLING, COPY-
> ING, OR OTHERWISE USING THE SOFTWARE PROGRAM YOU AGREE TO BE
> BOUND BY THE TERMS OF THIS AGREEMENT. IF YOU DO NOT AGREE TO THE
> TERMS OF THIS AGREEMENT, PROMPTLY RETURN THE UNUSED SOFTWARE

CUSTOMER SERVICE...FOR A FULL REFUND OF THE PURCHASE PRICE WITHIN THIRTY DAYS OF THE ORIGINAL PURCHASE. This software program (the 'Program'), any printed materials, any on-line or electronic documentation, and any and all copies and derivative works of such software program and materials are the copyrighted work of Blizzard Entertainment...Subject to that Grant of License hereinabove, you may not, in whole or in part, copy, photocopy, reproduce, translate, *reverse engineer*, derive source code, modify, disassemble, decompile, create derivative works based on the Program, or remove any proprietary notices or labels on the Program without the prior consent, in writing, of Blizzard.[170]

Observing that the case before it involved conflict preemption,[171] the 8th Circuit nonetheless concluded that unlike the leading decision in favor of preemption,[172] the copyright law did not preclude enforcement of the EULA as it did not "conflict...with the interoperability exception under 17 U.S.C. § 1201(f) nor restrict... rights given under federal law."[173] Like the right to reverse engineer under section 1201 and under fair use in section 107, these rights may be contracted away: "'Private parties are free to contractually forego [*sic*] the limited ability to reverse engineer a software product under the exemptions of the Copyright Act,' and 'a state can permit parties to contract away a fair use defense or to agree not to engage in uses of copyrighted material that are permitted by the copyright law if the contract is freely negotiated.'"[174] The court further commented that "[w]hile *Bowers* and *National Car Rental* were express preemption cases rather than conflict preemption, their reasoning applies here with equal force. By signing the TOUs and EULAs, Appellants expressly relinquished their rights to reverse engineer. Summary judgment on this issue was properly granted in favor of Blizzard and Vivendi."[175] The court observed a difference between an implied in law contract (court created contract for reasons of justice) and an implied in fact contract (a consensual agreement similar to an express contract but implied from conduct):

> For the purpose of the preemption analysis, there is a crucial difference between a claim based on quasi-contract, i.e., a contract implied in law, and a claim based upon a contract implied in fact. In the former, the action depends on nothing more than the unauthorized use of the work. Thus, an action based on a contract implied in law requires no extra element in addition to an act of reproduction, performance, distribution or display, whereas an action based on a contract implied in fact requires the extra element of a promise to pay for the use of the work which is implied from the conduct of the parties.[176]

Again, the license needs to offer rights beyond those already granted to copyright owners under the copyright law.

The leading case in favor of preemption is *Vault Corp. v. Quaid Software Ltd.*,[177] where the Louisiana Software License Enforcement Act[178] allowed a "software producer to impose a number of contractual terms upon software purchasers provided that the terms are set forth in a license agreement,"[179] including prohibitions on copying and adapting the work, such as reverse engineering, decompilation, or disassembly. In light of the statute and the facts, it appears the court may have misspoken in referring to the holders of the license as "purchasers." (Compare the next section of this chapter discussing instances where courts have recharacterized licenses as purchases, i.e., sales.) Oddly, with little discussion, the 5th Circuit concluded:

> The provision in Louisiana's License Act, which permits a software producer to prohibit the adaptation of its licensed computer program by decompilation or disassembly, conflicts with the rights of computer program owners under § 117 and clearly "touches upon an area" of federal copyright law. For this reason, and the reasons set forth by the district court, we hold that at least this provision of Louisiana's License Act is pre-empted by federal law, and thus that the restriction in Vault's license agreement against decompilation or disassembly is unenforceable.[180]

However, in the two-plus decades since *Vault* was decided, the case has failed to impact subsequent judicial decision making. This may be so for several reasons. First is its age. The decision was one of the first cases to address the issue of preemption in the context of a license. It might best be viewed as an initial foray or experiment and less a trend. Second, later courts have restricted it to its specific facts: though involving a license, the underlying rationale for the license terms in question was a state statute promoting contract terms that prohibited all copying or reverse engineering. Finally, contracting and the freedom to contract through various mechanisms, such as licensing, continues to expand; the courts are validating new business models based on licensing, such as click-wrap and web-wrap mechanisms, especially in the context of online contracting. The result is a more restrained judiciary that would rather leave the private ordering of the license in place.

Many courts have since held that copyright law does *not* preempt such agreements when the requisite extra element is present. The distinction is that in the *Vault* decision the Louisiana statute authorized license provisions that prohibited all copying for the duration of the agreement, even if that period stretched beyond the duration of copyright for the content subject to license.[181] In *Vault*, the agreement was a mass-market agreement without opportunity for negotiation. This might represent a fourth reason for the limited application of *Vault* by other circuits.[182] Notice that the district court concluded the mass-market license at issue was a contract of adhesion.[183]

In *Bowers v. Baystate Technologies, Inc.*, "Baystate contend[ed] that the Copyright Act preempts the prohibition of reverse engineering embodied in Mr. Bowers' shrink-wrap license agreements."[184] Using the law of the circuit from which the case originated, the Federal Circuit,[185] the majority held "that, under First Circuit law, the Copyright Act does not preempt or narrow the scope of Mr. Bowers' contract claim."[186] Judge Dyk dissented in *Bowers*, viewing the majority opinion's reliance on

ProCD, Inc. v. Zeidenberg as misplaced:[187] "By holding that shrinkwrap licenses that override the fair use defense are not preempted by the Copyright Act, the majority has rendered a decision [that] permits state law to eviscerate an important federal copyright policy reflected in the fair use defense, and the majority's logic threatens other federal copyright policies as well."[188] Judge Dyk, though not disagreeing in principle with the concept of copyright preemption of contract provisions, drew distinction to scenarios where the contract is not freely negotiated, that is, a mass-market license or shrink-wrap license, without opportunity to negotiate a return gain for the relinquishment (loss) of rights granted to users under the copyright law.[189] In Judge Dyk's view, the majority opinion stands for the proposition that a contract provision, regardless of the contractual context in which it is found, could take away rights granted under the copyright law. This he concluded is unacceptable. As explained by Judge Dyk:

> A state is not free to eliminate the fair use defense. Enforcement of a total ban on reverse engineering would conflict with the Copyright Act itself by protecting otherwise unprotectable material. If state law provided that a copyright holder could bar fair use of the copyrighted material by placing a black dot on each copy of the work offered for sale, there would be no question but that the state law would be preempted ... I nonetheless agree with the majority opinion that a state can permit parties to contract away a fair use defense or to agree not to engage in uses of copyrighted material that are permitted by the copyright law, if the contract is freely negotiated. A freely negotiated agreement represents the "extra element" that prevents preemption of a state law claim that would otherwise be identical to the infringement claim barred by the fair use defense of reverse engineering.[190]

As a result, Judge Dyk would presumably see no issue of preemption with a fully negotiated license but might consider the need for preemption in a mass-market or nonnegotiated license, depending on the circumstances (e.g., in a license that purported to take away a use right under the copyright law without option). However, allowing: "There is, moreover, no logical stopping point to the majority's reasoning. The amici rightly question whether under our original opinion the first sale doctrine and a host of other limitations on copyright protection might be eliminated by shrinkwrap licenses in just this fashion."[191] Judge Dyk also viewed post-*Vault* decisions such as *ProCD* as consistent as with *Vault*. While *ProCD* also involved a shrink-wrap agreement and purported to legitimize its ascendancy over copyright, consumer choice was still present in that the consumer could choose between a license that did allow for the commercial use the licensee desired to make of the content, albeit for a higher price.[192] Thus, the contract scheme in *ProCD*, while not allowing for negotiation, still offered a choice of options with differential pricing and consequently was not a contract of adhesion per se. Other commentators would endorse this distinction between negotiated and mass-market licenses and rights waiver provisions. "In general, in a negotiated contract a licensee can contractually bind itself not to undertake acts of infringement that others would be able to perform under the fair use doctrine. It is still up in the air whether waivers of fair use rights in click-wrap and shrink-wrap agreements for mass-market software would be enforceable."[193]

Putting the *Vault* (mass market, preemption), *Bowers* (mass market, no preemption), and *ProCD* (mass market with options, no preemption) decisions together implies that a statutorily endorsed clause in a shrink-wrap, click-wrap, browse-wrap, or other nonnegotiated mass-market agreement which purported to take away a right of owners or users which the copyright law allows would be preempted, unless there were retained a range of contract options from which users could select—in other words, the choice must be more than the proverbial "take it or leave it"; a negotiated agreement with clauses achieving the same result would not be preempted.[194]

Vault involved a shrink-wrap agreement as well. What was different there? In the case of contracts, whether negotiated or mass-market, such as shrink-wrap agreements, it is the mutual assent and consideration that is different. As explained by the 7th Circuit, exclusive rights

> are rights established *by law*—rights that restrict the options of persons who are strangers to the author. Copyright law forbids duplication, public performance, and so on, unless the person wishing to copy or perform the work gets permission; silence means a ban on copying. A copyright is a right against the world. Contracts, by contrast, generally affect only their parties; strangers may do as they please, so contracts do not create "exclusive rights."[195]

The important difference is that in *Vault* the rights were public rights—a state statute allowing any contract to prohibit all copying of computer programs, a right that the federal copyright law under section 106 already grants to owners. In this light, *Vault* and *ProCD* are consistent, as is the dissent in *Bowers*. It is the majority in *Bowers* that seems anomalous. *ProCD, Inc. v. Zeidenberg* is consistent with the nonnegotiated (subject to preemption) and negotiated (not subject to preemption) distinction because, although the contract in that case was a shrink-wrap license, the user nonetheless was presented with a meaningful choice, either accept the terms "as is" (nonnegotiated), including a restriction on commercial use or further public distribution, or, if such use is desired, pay a higher license fee for the right to make those uses.[196] Reading the *Bowers* majority in the best light would require a further refinement within the mass-market arena: Is the underlying provision supported or endorsed by state imprimatur? However, this would require viewing preemption as further limited to a subset of nonoptionable, nonnegotiated consumer licenses. While database or other content agreements as well as service agreements are likely negotiated, others in the library or patron setting are indeed nonnegotiated licenses, such as many software upgrades, website and social media access, and user agreements (click to agree). According to Judge Dyk and his interpretation of *ProCD, Inc.*, as well as other decisions, preemption may not apply in situations where the terms are subject to negotiation.

WHEN IS A LICENSE NOT A LICENSE? RECHARACTERIZING LICENSES AS SALES AND THE PRACTICAL EFFECT OF THE FIRST-SALE DOCTRINE

This chapter concludes with a discussion of an albeit rare but no less important situation where a court might recharacterize a license as a sale. Recall the discussion of sales versus licenses in Chapter 1 and the different rights of sellers/licensors versus buyers/licensees along that continuum of transactions. In a license transaction, there are no perpetual rights, unless of course the license terms grant such rights. Once the term of the license is over, the licensee-library loses all rights to access the licensed content. In fact, some licenses include provisions requiring the licensee to take reasonable steps to ensure that the previously licensed content is not archived or remains in any form within the institution. For database or other content licenses, this is to be expected, though perhaps not desired. However, the characterization of a transaction as a license or sale when it involves other discrete content, such as a media product from iTunes or Amazon.com or a device such as a iPad or e-book reader, is becoming more important as libraries venture into these emerging areas of content acquisition with the hopes of bringing such content and items into traditional library distribution schemes. Such transactions do not fit the scenarios in which licenses first arose, the business-to-business transfer of software, where in fact the licensing business did return the software when the term of the license ended. While database agreements offer a similar (in most instances) non-permanent access to content, content that is the subject of purchased downloads or software that accompanies such handheld devices is not often subject to a terminable date nor does it require return of the device. As discussed in this section, these transactions appear to be sales rather than licenses, as the transactions are labeled. If it is a sale, then first-sale rights apply, as do other copyright use rights.

A library that circulates such a device acquired by sale along with the software embedded in the device is authorized under section 109 of the copyright law to make a public distribution of this device, including its accompanying software: "the owner [the library] of a particular copy or phonorecord lawfully made under this title, or any person authorized by such owner, is entitled, without the authority of the copyright owner, to sell or otherwise dispose of the possession of that copy or phonorecord."[197] This covers the device itself. There is also a provision allowing public distribution by nonprofit libraries for nonprofit purposes of a computer program that might be embedded in the device "if each copy of a computer program which is lent by such library has affixed to the packaging containing the program a warning of copyright in accordance with requirements that the Register of Copyrights shall prescribe by regulation."[198] This subsection of section 109 would cover the public distribution of the accompanying software. As previously discussed, this right of distribution and the policy underlying it known as the first-sale doctrine (i.e., that the copyright owner's control over subsequent distributions ends after the first sale) reveals the connection to the problem at hand. This public distribution right attaches only to the owner of content protected by copyright. In a license or other transaction where ownership is retained by the seller/licensor/vendor, the buyer/licensee/possessor obtains no first-sale rights. The transaction is not governed by the copyright law but by contract law, with any distribution rights dictated by the terms of the agreement. Often in the case of cell phones, e-book readers, and other handheld devices, as well as products from iTunes and Amazon.com and other such products, further distribution is specifically prohibited by the license and use is limited in some fashion to the personal use of the actual licensee.

Why would a copyright owner desire to have transactions treated with the legal impact of a license rather than a sale?

> Because of the Copyright Act's "first sale doctrine," it is in the best interest of the software vendor to characterize the transaction as a "license" rather than as the "sale" of a software copy. Under the federal copyright laws and the first sale doctrine, the "owner of a particular copy or phonorecord ... is entitled, without the authority of the copyright owner, to sell or otherwise dispose of the possession of that copy or phonorecord." By characterizing the transaction as a license, the purchaser is considered a "licensee" and not an "owner." Therefore, the provision denies purchasers the rights granted to an owner under the first sale doctrine.[199]

In an educational setting, this would include not only staff computers but student computers, network servers, and so on. With a sale, a purchase of content, the library is able to do with the content as it wishes. The copyright owner must rely on the copyright law (as expressed in the exclusive rights granted to owners and the limitations on those rights listed in sections 107 to 122 of the copyright law) alone to control uses such as fair use. Under the first-sale doctrine, codified in section 109, the purchaser or other possessor of a lawfully made copy may make a public distribution of the content. "Thus, once a publisher sells a valuable, vellum-bound volume, for example, it forfeits its exclusive distribution privilege and enables the buyer, the new owner of the volume, to resell the copy to another buyer."[200] It should be obvious that if content obtained through a license transaction should actually be treated as if it were a sale, the implications for the library-licensee are enormous: The transaction is treated as a single event. Rights of possession, for example, survive the transaction, as do rights of first sale; for example, the library-licensee can make subsequent public distributions of that content. (As observed in previous chapters, the section 109 limitation on the exclusive right of the copyright owner to control public distributions is the provision of the copyright law that libraries rely upon when circulating or otherwise making available items in their collections.)

Thus far, few district and appellate courts have considered challenges to the characterization of licenses as in fact sales. While the decisions involved software licenses, the cases nonetheless stand for the proposition that there are limits to the freedom of contract principle, that there are some interactions for which a license is not appropriate. This proposition is critical to the survival of copyright and ensures, similar to the doctrine of preemption, that in the proper circumstances copyright is ascendant over contract. Moreover, the U.S. Copyright Office raised this issue in regard to another handheld technology, the cell phone. While it is doubtful that the concept would ever be adopted by a court in a situation where information content is licensed, such as a database subscription, where there is the ability to negotiate, libraries are acquiring more and more content and services through nonnegotiated agreements. At the moment, these developments present more questions than answers, as the Supreme Court declined the opportunity to review the appeal of one such case from the 9th Circuit in fall 2011.

An early case to consider this bold action (recharacterizing a license as a sale), though not the first case,[201] was *SoftMan Products Company, Inc. v. Adobe Systems, Inc.*,[202] where an online distributor of software products sold unbundled Adobe products.[203] The distributor did not deny this practice but argued that the practice was allowed under the first-sale doctrine as codified in section 109. "While SoftMan agrees that it is breaking apart various Adobe Collections and distributing the individual pieces of them as single products, SoftMan claims that it is entitled to distribute Adobe software in this manner. There is no direct contractual relationship between Adobe and SoftMan."[204] By making this statement, the company in essence argued that the terms of the shrink-wrap license that accompanied the software package did not apply to it.

A license agreement, in the form of an EULA (discussed in Chapter 8 in the context of website agreements), accompanied each piece of software. In a typical installation of the Adobe product suite, the program would prompt the user to assent to the terms and conditions of the EULA.[205] "Once the products are distributed to the end-user, the EULA prohibits the individual distribution of software that was originally distributed as part of a Collection."[206] The problem for Adobe was that SoftMan never installed the software; it simply took apart (unbundled) the suite products before selling them individually, and thus SoftMan never accessed (loaded onto its computers) any Adobe product, so no EULA could pop up to which SoftMan could then assent.

> In short, the terms of the Adobe EULA at issue prohibit licensees from transferring or assigning any individual Adobe product that was originally distributed as part of a

Collection unless it is transferred with all the software in the original Collection. This license provision conflicts with the first sale doctrine in copyright law, which gives the owner of a particular copy of a copyrighted work the right to dispose of that copy without the permission of the copyright owner.[207]

The fact that SoftMan was never a party to the EULA was not in dispute;[208] still, Adobe desired to characterize the transaction as a license and bind SoftMan Products to its terms nonetheless.

It is unclear why the court did not simply end its discussion in reliance on the fact that SoftMan never entered into any license with Adobe, end of story. Nonetheless, the court engaged in an extensive discussion of the first-sale doctrine and the difference between sales and licenses. As a result, the case is significant because it pits the two points of the copyright-contract continuum in clear opposition to each other: "In this case, Adobe alleges that by distributing unbundled Collections, SoftMan has exceeded the scope of the EULA and has infringed Adobe's copyrights, specifically Adobe's § 106 right to distribute and control distribution. SoftMan contends that the first sale doctrine allows for the resale of Adobe's Collection software."[209] Adobe argued that the first-sale doctrine does not apply, as Adobe does not *sell* its software products; rather, it licenses its products.

The problem for Adobe is that it was impossible to figure out a way to make the physical act of opening the box and unbundling the suite of products subject to a license agreement prohibiting such unbundling. Grabbing a box of software (Adobe or otherwise) off of the shelf of the local Best Buy does not equate to a license of the program or, if packaged as a suite of products, of its individual products, unless of course the box itself is somehow shrink-wrapped. There is plastic wrapping on the package, but even if there is an indication on the box of a license inside, "acceptance" is typically conditional upon use of the products inside or upon installation. There is no language that says, "You're bound by the terms of the agreement if you walk out of the store with it," nor does Best Buy present you with a "terms of purchase" contract at the time you render payment, as would be the case in, say, a car rental or lease agreement. All the customer receives is a receipt or series of receipts in return for tender of payment. This is a sale! Adobe might have solved the problem by use of a shrink-wrap agreement on the entire physical packaging of the suite of products with the terms on the back of the box instead of using an installation mechanism, or click-wrap agreement, so that the physical act of unwrapping would have activated the license—in this situation, by SoftMan's act of unwrapping the product suite package. Or by including the actual license in print form inside the box—with appropriate notice on the outside of the package stating "License terms enclosed"—then upon keeping the products beyond the returns-allowed time stated in the agreement (30 days is often used), SoftMan would be bound by the terms not to unbundle or make further distribution of the individual suite products. Such result would be consistent with the "pay now, terms later" license agreements discussed in Chapter 2.

Nonetheless, Adobe tried to argue that the notice on the box of each software product,[210] which would be perceptible to SoftMan and which alerts the reader to the inclusion of the EULA, was sufficient to bind SoftMan to those terms. The court rebuffed this assertion as well: "However, the existence of this notice on the box cannot bind SoftMan. Reading a notice on a box is not equivalent to the degree of assent that occurs when the software is loaded onto the computer and the consumer is asked to agree to the terms of the license."[211] As a result, the court concluded "that Adobe's EULA cannot be valid without assent. Therefore, SoftMan is not bound by the EULA because it has never loaded the software, and therefore never assented to its terms of use."[212] Likewise, in the present case, "the Court finds that there is only assent on the part of the consumer, if at all, when the consumer loads the Adobe program and begins the installation process. It is undisputed that SoftMan has never attempted to load the software that it sells. Consequently, the Court finds that SoftMan is not subject to the Adobe EULA."[213] This is why the court observed that the "Adobe license compels third-parties to relinquish rights that the third-parties enjoy under copyright law... This license provision conflicts with the first sale doctrine in copyright law, which gives the owner of a particular copy of a copyrighted work the right to dispose of that copy without the permission of the copyright owner."[214] This comment suggests that third parties cannot be bound even if the contract-license is valid. Important in the library or school setting, third parties to a license would be the patrons and students.

The court then discussed the development of the licensing and evaluated whether the transaction between Adobe and SoftMan was in fact a license or a sale:

> The Court finds that the circumstances surrounding the transaction strongly suggest that the transaction is in fact a sale rather than a license. For example, the purchaser commonly obtains a single copy of the software, with documentation, for a single price, which the purchaser pays at the time of the transaction, and which constitutes the entire payment... without provisions for renewal.[215]

The court reiterated that simply calling a transaction a license is not dispositive if in fact the circumstances suggest it is a sale:

> Ownership of a copy should be determined based on the actual character, rather than the label, of the transaction by which the user obtained possession. Merely labeling a transaction as a lease or license does not control. If a transaction involves a single payment giving the buyer an unlimited period in which it has a right to possession, the transaction is a sale.[216]

As a result, the transfer of software from Adobe to SoftMan was a sale, not a license, and so first-sale rights applied. So the next time the library enters into an agreement or reviews its existing agreements—regardless of label—it should determine whether there is a single item involved. If so, is the item fixed, or does its contents, like those of a database, change over time? Is the cost set without need for renewal, or does the cost fluctuate depending upon the number of users? Even if the content is in digital format, is there a physical transfer of an object embodying the content, for example, the words of a book (a literary work), the series of zeros and ones of a computer program on a disc, or the software that accompanies an e-reader or cell phone?

Nonetheless, Adobe argued the terms and conditions of the EULA applied and limited the use SoftMan could make of the software. However, the court was quick to point out that the EULA was never assented to by SoftMan. The EULA that accompanies each Adobe software product is entered into by the end user licensee of the software, who agrees to the terms upon installation of the product on his or her own personal computer. SoftMan never uses (installs) the software in this way and so can make no assent to the EULA terms and conditions, including the restrictions on subsequent transfer.

Contrary results, of course, occur. In *Adobe Systems, Inc. v. One Stop Micro, Inc.*, for example, a dispute arose between an intermediate distributor and again Adobe Systems, Inc.; the facts are familiar:

> Adobe initially distributes the educational versions to an Adobe-authorized educational distributor, who then transfers the software to an Adobe-authorized educational reseller. The educational reseller's relationship with Adobe is governed by the "Off Campus Reseller Agreement" or the "On Campus Reseller Agreement" ("OCRA"). Under the OCRA, an educational reseller is "to make the Educational Software Products available to certain of Reseller's customers who are Educational End Users." Defendant One Stop buys and sells computer hardware and software on the open market. Adobe alleges that One Stop improperly acquired educational versions, which it then adulterated and sold as full retail versions to non-educational end users.[217]

Looking to the terms of the agreement, which included provision for Adobe to "repurchase" unsold units after termination of the agreement, the court concluded a license governed the transfer of the software packages to One Stop Micro, Inc.: "Thus, under the EULA the end user is only granted a license to use the software. Adobe's specific incorporation of the EULA indicates that the reseller obtains a license. It would be incongruous to conclude that educational resellers are owners of the Adobe educational versions, while the end users who the resellers distribute to are granted a mere license."[218] The court quoted and found convincing testimony from Adobe's expert witness, Raymond T. Nimmer, professor of law at the University of Houston, that the terms, including use of the word *purchase*, nonetheless reflected industry practice of transfer pursuant to a license and not a sale.[219] Why the difference? Same plaintiff, same expert witness for the licensor, but different district courts within California and slightly different facts, to be sure—but in *Soft-Man Products Company, Inc.* the defendants came prepared with an expert of their own to combat the Nimmer juggernaut, David A. Rice, professor of law at Roger Williams University's School of Law and longtime critic of the increased use of licenses to govern information access. The district court in Northern California, quoting his statement and citing his works, found his testimony more convincing than that of Nimmer.[220]

It is difficult to know whether the rationale underlying *SoftMan Products Company, Inc.* is limited to first-sale rights alone and in the absence of assent, or if followed by other courts, would serve to support restoration of other rights under the copyright that a license might take away. The court suggested this would be the case if some other right that the copyright law grants users were attempted through license to be usurped. "The Adobe license compels third-parties to relinquish rights that the third-parties enjoy under copyright law."[221] However, it was unclear if the court was making this assertion based on SoftMan (who was not even a party to the license in the first instance) or to any party to a license. Nonetheless, where the user is indeed a party to the agreement and not a third party, the resulting facts would be the same in the *SoftMan Products Company, Inc.* list of transaction as sale factors: the possessor of the mass-market software typically is not subject to any duration on the length of the agreement, makes a one-time payment, and does not return the software at the end of its use.[222]

Though the court's discussion would not limit the proposition (that a nonparty to a license or a nonlicense purchaser could not be bound by such restrictive terms) to scenarios involving first-sale rights alone, the more important and unanswered question is whether the court would resolve the copyright and contract conflict in favor of copyright. The court's comment appears restricted to true third parties, which a true licensee would *not* be, whereas the Professor Lemley quote it references suggests a broader category of conflicts—"software vendors . . . that compel their customers"; in other words, the "customers" would be licensees, a true party to the license. Nonetheless, the decision stands for the proposition that the term of a license agreement accompanying software will not bind the purchaser unless there is specific assent to those terms. Second, assented terms by a party cannot bind a nonparty. Regardless of the designation of party to the contract or third party, some licenses may be sales in spite of the label used to characterize the transaction by the initial holder and transferor of the software.

In a recent and closely watched litigation raising similar issues as *SoftMan Products*, the 9th Circuit posed the same question as have other courts before it. Is the acquisition of the software from the publisher-vendor (here Autodesk) subject to sale or license? The courts established the significant domino effect of licensing. If the initial transaction is a license, then that licensee does not possess first-sale rights or other rights under the copyright law. If the licensee does not have these rights, then any subject parties that it transfers the licensed content to also do not possess these rights; the rights were not the initial licensee's to transfer:

> This case requires us to decide whether Autodesk sold Release 14 copies to its customers or licensed the copies to its customers. If CTA owned its copies of Release 14, then both its sales to Vernor and Vernor's subsequent sales were non-infringing under the first sale doctrine. However, if Autodesk only licensed CTA to use copies of Release 14, then CTA's and Vernor's sales of those copies are not protected by the first sale doctrine and would therefore infringe Autodesk's exclusive distribution right.[223]

In determining whether a transaction was a sale or a license, the court looked to the following factors: "We may consider (1) whether the agreement was labeled a license and (2) whether the copyright owner retained title to the copy, required its return or destruction, forbade its duplication, or required the transferee to maintain possession of the copy for the agreement's duration."[224] Unlike the set of factors used by the *SoftMan Products Company, Inc.* court, those employed by the 9th Circuit are arguably meaningless, as most software licenses, at least those agreements purporting to be licenses reviewed by the author, include these basic elements. With this simple test in place, the 9th Circuit could hardly fail to find that the agreement in question between Autodesk and CTA was a license and not a sale:

> We hold today that a software user is a licensee rather than an owner of a copy where the copyright owner (1) specifies that the user is granted a license; (2) significantly restricts the user's ability to transfer the software; and (3) imposes notable use restrictions. Applying our holding to Autodesk's SLA, we conclude that CTA was a licensee rather than an owner of copies of Release 14 and thus was not entitled to invoke the first sale doctrine or the essential step defense.[225]

Without the initial transaction being a sale, without being an owner, CTA did not have rights under the copyright law; that is, the first-sale doctrine under section 109 does not apply, nor does the essential step doctrine under section 117 that allows the "*owner* of a copy of a computer program to make or authorize the making of another copy or adaptation of that computer program"[226] under certain conditions.[227] Worse for Vernor, without such rights CTA could not confer those rights upon Vernor.[228] As CTA was not an owner, Vernor could not be either, even though the copy or phonorecord at issue remained lawfully made.

Explaining how the chain of a nonsale affects the licensee and any subsequent transferees, the 9th Circuit commented:

> CTA was a licensee rather than an "owner of a particular copy" of Release 14, and it was not entitled to resell its Release 14 copies to Vernor under the first sale doctrine. Therefore, Vernor did not receive title to the copies from CTA and accordingly could not pass ownership on to others. Both CTA's and Vernor's sales infringed Autodesk's exclusive right to distribute copies of its work.[229]

The statute does not state that the copy or phonorecord must be lawfully acquired, only lawfully made. Even if the unlawful acquisition was due to breach of contract, such claim would lie against CTA, who transferred the software to Vernor, who in a sense is an innocent reliance party. This is the second time in as many years that the 9th Circuit offered a controversial interpretation of section 109(a), requiring in another case that "under this title" means that the copy or phonorecord must either be manufactured in the Unites States[230] or, if made elsewhere, imported and sold here with the authority of the copyright owner.

As the initial transaction is not a sale, any subsequent transaction cannot likewise be executed under the first-sale doctrine. "Therefore, when they install Release 14 on their computers, the copies of the software that they make during installation infringe Autodesk's exclusive reproduction right because they too are not entitled to the benefit of the essential step defense."[231] When the 9th Circuit examined the language of section 109, while not reading a lawfully acquired component into the lawfully made proviso, the court did see a distinction between an owner (as the statute requires) and one who is in mere possession of the lawfully made copy or phonorecord. To be sure, Vernor possessed the software in question, but he did not own it, as title was not his to acquire; because CTA was a licensee, it did not own the software—it was not CTA's to give. As discussed throughout this book, the distinction between a licensee and a purchaser is just this! Therefore, while Vernor, or any other third party for that matter, could be in possession of the software, he could not acquire ownership of it.

It could be said that this argument is circular and makes moot any investigation into whether a transaction could ever be recharacterized as a sale instead of a license. It is true that licensees are not owners, but some "licensees" are in fact owners because the true nature of the agreement is a sale. Does Amazon.com expect a customer to return an earlier generation Kindle when the customer upgrades to the next generation reader or tablet? Acquisition of the reader or tablet is not in the nature of a bailment, discussed in conjunction with the issues surrounding desk copies in Chapter 2. In some so-labeled licenses, possession and ownership is indeed acquired and in those instances the license is in legal reality a sale, so first-sale and other rights would apply. This is the situation of many terminal software transactions, like the one involved in *Vernor*. If a possessor could never be an "owner" when the label claims "license," then the licensee or any other possessor will never be able to cry "sale" and challenge the true nature of agreement and invoke first-sale rights under section 109. The three-part test employed by the court is less than helpful, as licenses would be unlikely *not* to specify that the user is granted a license, which significantly restricts the user's ability to transfer the software and imposes notable use restrictions. Without any meaningful judicial review, licensors will be free to label any software transaction a license and foreclose first-sale rights.

More important, under the 9th Circuit's interpretation, what is to prevent any copyright owner from extending its control (via use of a license) to every point, every possession in the chain of transfer of the copy or phonorecord? Commentators have had other questions regarding the opinion:

> The Ninth Circuit left some questions unanswered. For example, it did not explain how to weigh the three factors in its test, or whether any additional factors may be considered in determining whether a transaction is a license or sale. It also explicitly declined to decide the issue of which party bears the burden of proving the applicability of the first sale doctrine or the absence thereof, since the facts in the case were undisputed.[232]

Unfortunately, any final word on the license versus sale problem will not be forthcoming in the near term, as the Supreme Court declined to accept the 9th Circuit decision for review.[233]

License versus Sale and Handheld Devices

Vernor may not be the end of the license versus sale debate, as other stakeholders are commenting on the matter in related fact circumstances. The Register of Copyright recently had opportunity to discuss the software sale versus license issue in its recent rule making, granting an exemption from the prohibition of circumvention of copyright access controls and regarding wireless telephone handset operability, so-called jailbreaking.[234] The Register concluded that the state of the law is far from settled:

> [T]he state of the law with respect to the determination of ownership is in a state of flux in the courts. Both proponents and opponents cited case law in support of their respective positions, but the Register finds it impossible to determine how a court would resolve the issue of ownership on the facts presented here [firmware on iPhones] ... However, the Register does find that the proponent's fair use argument is compelling and consistent with the congressional interest in interoperability. The four fair use factors tend to weigh in favor of a finding of fair use.[235]

A similar question and comment was made in the same rule making regarding the granting of an exemption for firmware or software on cell phones that allows a user to switch wireless providers:

> The Register has reviewed the appropriate case law with respect to who is the "owner" of a copy of a computer program for purposes of Section 117 when a license or agreement imposes restrictions on the use of the computer program and has concluded that the state of the law is unclear. The Register cannot determine whether most mobile phone owners are also the owners of the copies of the computer programs on their mobile phones. However, based on the record in this proceeding, the Register finds that the proponents of the class have made a prima facie case that mobile phone owners are the owners of those copies. While the wireless networks have made a case that many mobile

phone owners may not own the computer program copies because the wireless network's contract with the consumer retains ownership of the copies, they have not presented evidence that this is always the case even if their interpretation of the law governing ownership is correct. The record therefore leads to the conclusion that a substantial portion of mobile phone owners also own the copies of the software on their phones. The Register also concludes that when the owner of a mobile makes RAM copies of the software in order to operate the phone—even if she is operating it on another network— she is making a noninfringing use of the software under Section 117 because the making of that copy is an essential step in the utilization of that software in conjunction with a machine. Similarly, the making of modifications in the computer program in order to enable the mobile phone to operate on another network would be a noninfringing act under Section 117.[236]

These comments suggest the old adage "possession is nine-tenths of the law"—or at least that possession means one is an owner when applying ownership concepts to cell phone software. If this is true, then by logic such ownership would apply to the customers of other handheld devices like e-book readers or tablets and to the software programs contained on such devices.

In light of the recent *AT&T Mobility* decision discussed earlier in this chapter, the best that could perhaps have been hoped for was the denial of the writ of certiorari in the *Vernor* decision. It is hoped that other circuits will not see the issue the same way. For a Court that believes many questions should be left to the states to decide, the decision in *AT&T Mobility* represents a newfound attraction to federalism. Whether the Court would be as aggressive in finding preemption in a copyright decision is unclear. Whether the Court would embrace license over sale in a future post-*Vernor* case it would decide to review remains to be seen, but recent cases like *AT&T Mobility* and past precedent such as the *Carnival Cruise Lines* suggest that the Court embraces and accepts licensing terms as written, suggesting a reluctance for judicial meddling into the superiority of the contract-license. Of course, the meddling could be good or bad for libraries, depending on what the Supreme Court might say in the future or, as the *Vernor* court observed, if such issues remain the realm of Congress.[237] The worry is that *Vernor* stands for the ascendency of contract over copyright, but unlike the primary market for digital content in *ProCD* or the fear of shrink-wrapped books, a license may in the future reach into secondary markets for used copies (like books) or phonorecords (CDs) as well.[238]

Books with Computer Programs: License Restrictions or First-Sale Rights

How does the contract-license versus purchase issue apply to books or other items that are accompanied by computer programs—when a disc is included at the back of the book, for example? Does the first-sale doctrine apply such that the library may circulate the book and disc? What if the disc is wrapped in shrink-wrap, where-upon unwrapping the librarian discovers that terms of use are enclosed—can the library still circulate the item? What is the result if the license and its terms become apparent only upon installation of the accompanying computer program or upon access and use of other content on the disc? Based on the concepts discussed so far regarding valid contract formation, title or ownership of a copy or phonorecord of a work protected by copyright versus mere possession of this copy or phonorecord, several observations can be made in answer to these questions. The analysis may be applicable to other physical items purported to be governed by licenses as well, such as e-readers, tablets, and so on.

The first question that needs to be decided is whether the item (the disc) is a computer program.[239] If the disc, CD-ROM, and so forth, is a computer program, then rights of public distribution apply, but circulation by a library is further con-ditioned by the copyright law: the item can be loaned but must conform to section 109 and its implementing regulatory requirements.[240]

If the item is not a computer program but just a disc of, say, forms that open in Word, a collection of images that open in some other program, or a disc of geographic information that runs on a software program the library or its patron already possesses, then first-sale rights under section 109 as well as other user rights under the copyright law apply. There are no additional requirements but for those which govern works protected by copyright.

If the disc is a phonorecord,[241] then section 109 again vests the library with certain rights of public distribution: "Nothing in the preceding sentence shall apply to the rental, lease, or lending of a phonorecord for nonprofit purposes by a nonprofit library or nonprofit educational institution." There are no additional statutory or regulatory conditions.

However, if the computer program, the phonorecord, or other item is subject to a license agreement, then the license agreement trumps any first-sale rights (as well as obligations) under the copyright law and section 109—unless of course the library desires to argue that the transaction is actually a sale and not a license. It is likely that a computer program is accompanied by language (either in print or in digital form, visible when the content is accessed) that purports to cast the acquisition transaction by the library as a license. It is unlikely that such language is found in an accompanying phonorecord, book, or other item; at least this is not yet the common practice. If documentation is present in print, inside of the shrink-wrap, on the jacket or covering of the disc, or appears on the screen when the data is accessed, and this language attempts to provide terms of use in the guise of a license, then the question becomes: is the license valid? Shrink-wrap and click-wrap agreements are valid contracts and can bind the library if the con-ditions of assent are met (see the discussions in Chapters 2 and 5). If the library, for example, had 30 days in which to decide whether to keep the item and be bound by the terms of the license regarding the disc and the library kept the item in excess of that decision period, then a valid contract exists and the terms apply to the disc.[242]

What about situations where the license and its terms are contained within the computer program or other disc content such that the license and terms would not be apparent until installation, access, or other use occurs? In such cases, the library never knows of the license or terms, as it acquired the items for patron use, not for its own internal use, and so would never have occasion to identify or otherwise view the license and its terms. Or does the book or disc indicate somewhere on the packaging "Warning: Disc contents governed by license"? As discussed here (and again in Chapter 7), if the notice added "Warning: Disc contents governed by license. Licensee has 30 days to return item for refund," then the "pay now, terms later" precedent suggests such terms can be binding. This is different from when changes to the initial terms appear later.[243] While the author would argue that such alert to the presence of a license is not the same as assent to it (at least in the instance of the warning example just discussed), the *Vernor* decision suggests that when the possessor of the licensed content is aware of the license, while the party might not be a licensee, this party is certainly not an owner of the content either. It is likely that if any disc were shrink-wrapped the license would apply to it, and not to the book it accompanied, unless the book too was shrink-wrapped.

While such transactions, license and terms upon installation or other use, for example, do not make the library a licensee, the downside is that under cases such as *Vernor* the library, while a possessor of the disc and its content, is not an owner, with the result that under *Vernor* the library would possess no first-sale rights. While in a technical sense the library might not be a licensee, it did not acquire ownership of the disc, with the result being it has no first-sale rights, as it is not the "owner of a particular copy or phonorecord lawfully made under this title."[244] The library would not possess public distribution rights with respect to the disc and the software on it, as it did with the book, unless of course these rights were included in the license. While there is legal support to the contrary, as discussed previously, these facts and results are indeed parallel to those in *Vernor*: "Vernor has sold more than 10,000 items on eBay. In May 2005, he purchased an authentic used copy of Release 14 at a garage sale from an unspecified seller. He never agreed to the SLA's terms, opened a sealed software packet, or installed the Release 14 software. Though he was aware of the SLA's existence, he believed that he was not bound by its terms. He posted the software copy for sale on eBay."[245] Nonetheless, the 9th Circuit concluded that "CTA was a licensee rather than an 'owner of a particular copy' of Release 14, and it was not entitled to resell its Release 14 copies to Vernor under the first sale doctrine. Therefore, Vernor did not receive title to the copies from CTA and accordingly could not pass ownership on to others. Both CTA's and Vernor's sales infringed Autodesk's exclusive right to distribute copies of its work."[246] The Supreme Court declined the opportunity to disturb the result. Similarly, under this decision, a library that acquired a disc subject to a click-wrap agreement would not be an owner of the disk, even if it never installed the software on the disc or assented to the click-wrap: "Because Vernor was not an owner, his customers are also not owners of Release 14 copies. Therefore, when they install Release 14 on their computers, the copies of the software that they make during installation infringe Autodesk's exclusive reproduction right because they too are not entitled to the benefit of the essential step defense."[247] Likewise, the library would possess no other use rights under the copyright law. Of course, a library in a circuit other than the 9th would be free to challenge the application of *Vernor* in its jurisdiction. So, too, a library in the 9th Circuit could attempt to argue that *Vernor* does not apply to its particular set of facts.[248] The author would of course like to see another result, but the case law appears to be tilting in favor of license over sale, and until another circuit concludes differently, creating a split among circuits which in theory would prompt reconsideration by the Supreme Court, there is risk that courts in other circuits will follow the result in *Vernor*. If *Vernor* becomes the rule, then a library might want to consider installing or otherwise accessing the license and terms upon initial acquisition to determine whether the use permitted under it allows for the sorts of uses the library desires to make of it—and, if not, return it for a refund or consider acquisition, if available, of an institutional or educational version of the license that contains those terms.

If the items in question are subject to a valid license, then the license provision would direct what use the library could make of the item. It may be that such a license agreement, as is very typical with computer programs, contains a prohibition against further public distributions. The last time the author checked, a similar prohibition was in the iTunes agreement.[249] Some handheld device licenses contain similar restrictions. However, as discussed, some courts may view such permanent transfers not as licenses but as sales, more so when the transfer is of a device. Some device licenses, at least for the content accessed through such devices, have terminable access points, such as the OverDrive Media Console Version 3.2 license,[250] suggesting the transaction is a license and possession of content is not permanent but somehow transitory. However, content may not be so conditioned, and devices certainly do not fall under this pattern, unless, for example, as in the case of cell phones, it is clear that the user is not the owner of the phone if at the end of the subscription the user returns the phone. This may be less true of device scenarios where an actual object (e-reader, e-tablet, cell phone, etc.) is acquired with software embedded in the device and perhaps less so when the entire item consists of a computer program. Case law, as well as other commentary, supports a position of device ownership, but the library must be prepared to litigate to enforce this interpretation. Where a license purports to govern the content of discs, again, an argument can be made in favor of sale, but the library must again be willing to litigate this position and expect challenge from the licensor.

SUMMARY POINTS

▶ Some contracts or provisions of contracts may be invalid based on public policy reasons. For example, some contracts unreasonably restrict one's trade or livelihood and are known as noncompetition agreements. It is possible to construct an argument, based on a public policy argument, that some license clauses which restrict speech, privacy, or other personal rights might be challenged as being contrary also to public policy.

▶ There are two elements to a claim of unconscionability in contract law: procedural and substantive. Some courts require both elements, with others accepting substantive unconscionability alone. Still other courts use a sliding scale, where the existence of an element to a varying degree can be offset by a large negative presence of the other element. Procedural unconscionability relates to the process of contract formation where there is superior bargaining power and thus no opportunity for meaningful choice. Substantive unconscionability relates to the impact of the unfair terms on the disadvantaged party, which is so extreme that the result shocks the conscience.

▶ Adhesion contracts exist in a take-it-or-leave-it climate. As a result, the adhesion contract can set the stage for an unconscionability inquiry, as the procedural element of unconscionability is often found in a climate of adhesion.

▶ Not all circuits have adopted the doctrine of copyright misuse. A license agreement that extends the nonexclusive rights of the copyright holder beyond those contemplated by Congress (e.g., a license term far in excess of the duration of copyright) in the copyright law and where the result is to stifle competition of compatible or competing products can satisfy requirements for a claim of copyright misuse.

▶ In contrast to the concept of unconscionability, when applicable, the doctrine of copyright misuse prevents the plaintiff-licensor rights holder from seeking remedy for infringement during the misuse, rather than the defendant claiming the contract-license is invalid. A claim of copyright misuse can be brought by a third party, a nonparty to the license agreement.

▶ The copyright law can preempt the enforcement (claim for breach) of a contract term. To avoid preemption, the contract must contain a so-called additional element, for example, protections beyond those of the exclusive rights (section 106). In the opinion of some courts, preemption would be more likely to apply in a nonnegotiated situation such as a shrink-wrap license or where there is no opportunity to choose from among alternative nonnegotiated licenses.

▶ There is case law to suggest that some transactions involving transfers of lawfully made software packages are sales and not licenses, as so labeled by the licensor. Factors suggesting a sale are whether possession of the copy or phonorecord is obtained for a single payment made at the time of acquisition, and where possession is for an unlimited period with no requirement to return the software at the cessation of the agreement.

▶ Alternative precedent suggests that software or other content distributed through license is not a sale and any possessor of the software, even if this party did not assent (i.e., is not a licensee), nonetheless is not an owner of that copy of software, and, thus, under decisions like *Vernor*, this party does not possess first-sale or other rights under the copyright law.

▶ A legal argument can be made in support of the position that software accompanying a device like a cell phone, tablet, e-book reader, and so forth, actually constitutes a sale even though such a transaction is also purported to be a license.

LEARNING EXAMPLES

▶ **Example 4.1**

Situation: A library is presented with a license from a content vendor. The license would allow the library and its patrons to access the vendor's website to obtain the content. There is no opportunity to bargain over the terms. Under the terms of the agreement, the licensee has no right to sue for breach. Rather, all disputes under the license are resolved through arbitration. The arbitration provision requires that arbitration take place in the state of Hawaii and that both parties must be present. The licensee must pay a nonrefundable fee of $5,000 to begin the process and additionally all costs, including those of the licensor, must be borne by the licensee. Once a request for arbitration is made, the vendor can suspend access to its website until the dispute is resolved, but the licensee must continue paying the monthly subscription price.

Legal Analysis: This license, especially the provisions relating to arbitration, is likely unconscionable. As a nonnegotiated license with such harsh terms regarding arbitration, the provision is likely procedurally unconscionable as a contract of adhesion. Substantive unconscionability is likely also present because the high cost ($5,000 initial fee plus all additional costs of both parties) of arbitration operates as a penalty rather than a true remedy.[251] In addition, the practical result from the excessive arbitration costs and the suspension of access is that no licensee will ever pursue arbitration. Recent Supreme Court precedent suggests that a license provision requiring the licensee to forgo the right to participate in class-action litigation with disputes aired through arbitration alone is not unconscionable per se as long as the process of arbitration could result in meaningful remedy.

▶ **Example 4.2**

Situation: Suppose a vendor, under government contract, designs a data tool for the collection of public domain information. A clause in the contract prohibits the governmental unit from making the public domain information that the data tool collects available to the public, as the vendor intends to develop a retrieval and content product of its own and market that to the general public.

Legal Analysis: At least one circuit court suggested that such leveraged use of a valid copyright (in the data tool, i.e., a software program) to control otherwise unprotected content (public domain information) would constitute copyright misuse.

▶ **Example 4.3**

Situation: A library is presented with a nonnegotiated license that includes a provision limiting the library's right to make a fair use of the content. When the library objects, the vendor indicates it does not bargain over terms in its license agreement. However, the vendor does offer the library a choice of alternative contracts, each with variable levels of use rights differentially priced according to the scope of rights granted, with rights similar to those of fair use allowed but of course at a higher fee.

Legal Analysis: A number of circuits would view the first contract preempted by the federal copyright law, as the agreement does not contain the "additional element" as required but rather attempts to alter the landscape of the copyright law enacted by Congress. Without an opportunity to bargain for additional use rights in return for fair-use restrictions, the required additional element is missing. In the absence of the ability to bargain for the additional element, it could be argued that a non-negotiated series of contract options containing a meaningful choice of different use rights would survive preemption.

▶ **Example 4.4**

Situation: A library receives an unopened package (in a box enclosed in a layer of shrink-wrap) of software from a patron as a donation. The library does not need the software and, as is typical with many donated items, the library decides to include the unopened package of software as part of its monthly sale of "used books," using the proceeds for collection development. Unbeknownst to both the donor-patron and the library, the software contains a license agreement that forbids transfers of the program to any other person than the original purchaser-owner. However, the back of the box clearly states that use is subject to the terms of the license agreement contained inside. The terms of the license appear upon installation and are assented to by the licensee by clicking through various "I agree" prompts.

Legal Analysis: The library and patron are not licensees. Neither party had the opportunity to review or assent to the terms of the click-wrap license. However, the question is whether the library is an owner of the unopened software package. The *Vernor* decision would answer this question in the negative, so no first-sale rights rest in the donor or library. If contrary precedent prevails, then the first-sale doctrine as codified by section 109 of the copyright law would apply to the transaction of the patron who donated the software package to the library and the library in reselling it.[252] Each party would have first-sale rights relating to the further public distribution of the software program, assuming the copy of the software package is a lawfully made copy. Yet, recent precedent by the 9th Circuit suggests that neither the patron nor the library has proper title to the software and so neither is an "owner" under statute, and so neither party has first-sale rights to make the transfer. It is possible to argue that even if a party did assent to the terms of the license upon installation, such transaction is better characterized as a sale rather than a license, as the transaction is terminal, with possession of the software program being permanent (i.e., there is no future obligation to return the software).

▶ **Example 4.5**

Situation: A library would like to begin circulating e-book readers, not just the content but the actual devices. The readers are acquired through a transaction deemed a license by the accompanying documentation. A provision in that license indicates that the devices are for personal use only and no further distribution can be made of the devices. Can the library still lend them to readers?

Legal Analysis: While there is no definitive answer from the courts on this issue, a valid argument can be made that the library actually owns the devices and the operating software embedded in the devices. If so, then as lawfully made software owned by the library, further public distribution would be subject to the rules of section 109. The most significant requirement being that the "lending of a computer program for nonprofit purposes by a nonprofit library... [requires affixing] to the packaging containing the program a warning of copyright in accordance with requirements that the Register of Copyrights shall prescribe by regulation."[253] While not without some legal risk, the library could circulate the device until the courts or Congress clarifies the law.

ENDNOTES

1. See, for example, Jennifer R. Knight, *Comment: Copyright Misuse v. Freedom of Contract: And the Winner Is...*, 73 Tennessee Law Review 237 (2006).

2. BLACK'S LAW DICTIONARY (9th ed.) (Bryan A. Garner ed., St. Paul, MN: West Publishing, 2009) defines an adhesion contract as "A standard-form contract prepared by one party, to be signed by another party in a weaker position, usually a consumer, who adheres to the contract with little choice about the terms" (no pagination in Westlaw).

3. H. WARD CLASSEN, A PRACTICAL GUIDE TO SOFTWARE LICENSING FOR LICENSEES AND LICENSORS 71–72 (3d ed. 2008), citing D.S. Am. (East), Inc. v. Chromaggrafix Imaging Systems, Inc., 873 F. Supp. 786 (S.D.N.Y. 1995).

4. RealNetworks, Inc. v. DVD Copy Control Association, 641 F. Supp. 2d 913, 947 (N.D. Calif. 2009). "Even though the Agreement between Real and DVD CCA is standardized or adhesive does not in and of itself mean it is unenforceable. Absent clear evidence of other factors, such as undue oppression or unconscionability, which has not been put forth here, the Agreement must be enforced according to its terms" (*id.* at 947–948).

5. UCITA § 111 (2000 Official Text).

6. Hodnick v. Fidelity Trust Co., 183 N.E. 488, 491 (Ind. App. 1932): "Whether or not a contract is against public policy is a question of law for the court to determine from all of the circumstances in a particular case. The courts will keep in mind the principle that it is to the best interest of the public that persons should not be unnecessarily restricted in their freedom of contract and that their agreements are not to be held void as against public policy, unless they are clearly contrary to what the Constitution, the Legislature, or the judiciary have declared to be the public policy, or unless they clearly tend to the injury of the public in some way."

7. Restatement (Second) of Contracts § 178(2)(a)–(c) and (3)(a)–(d) (1981) (When a Term Is Unenforceable On Grounds of Public Policy).

8. Daynard v. Ness, Motley, Loadholt, Richardson & Poole, P.A., 188 F. Supp. 2d 115, 124, at note 8 (D. Mass. 2002).

9. Restatement (Second) of Contracts § 178(2)(a)–(c) and (3)(a)–(d) (1981) (When a Term Is Unenforceable On Grounds of Public Policy), illustrations 1 and 3, respectively.

10. See, for example, Oubre v. Energy Operations, Inc., 522 U.S. 422, 432 (1998): "To determine whether a contract is voidable or void, courts typically ask whether the contract has been made under conditions that would justify giving one of the parties a choice as to validity, making it voidable, e.g., a contract with an infant; or whether enforcement of the contract would violate the law or public policy irrespective of the conditions in which the contract was formed, making it void, e.g., a contract to commit murder."

11. Marvin N. Benn & Associates, Ltd. v. Nelsen Steel and Wire, Inc., 437 N.E.2d 900, 903 (Ill. App. 1 Dist. 1982): "An agreement is against public policy if it is injurious to the interests of the public, contravenes some established interest of society, violates some public statute, is against good morals, tends to interfere with the public welfare or safety, or is at war with the interests of society or is in conflict with the morals of the time."

12. Zerjal v. Daech & Bauer Const., Inc., 939 N.E.2d 1067, 1073 (Ill. App. 5 Dist. 2010): "The term 'unconscionable' encompasses the absence of meaningful choice by one party, as well as contract terms that are unreasonably favorable to the other party"; and Smith v. Mitsubishi Motors Credit of America, Inc., 247 Conn. 324, 349 (1998): "The classic definition of an unconscionable contract is one which no man in his senses, not under delusion would make, on the one hand, and which no fair and honest man would accept, on the other."

13. See, for example, Vintage Health Resources, Inc. v. Guiangan, 309 S.W.3d 448, 459 (Tenn. Ct. App. 2009): "From our examination of the trial court's order, it appears that the trial court held that Mr. Guiangan's employment agreement with Vintage was unenforceable because (1) it was unconscionable and (2) it violated public policy."

14. Chong v. Friedman, 2005 WL 2083049, at *4 (Cal. App. 2005) (unpublished): "Because Nevada law does not have a comparable franchise disclosure law, it fails to further the public policy interest that California has recognized in enacting the CFIL—namely, the interest in protecting franchisees from fraud or the likelihood that a franchisor's promises would not be fulfilled. Accordingly, the choice of law provision of the license agreement is invalid as contrary to public policy."

15. See Carnival Cruise Lines v. Shute, 499 U.S. 585, 594 (1991): "It bears emphasis that forum-selection clauses contained in form passage contracts are subject to judicial scrutiny for fundamental fairness. In this case, there is no indication that petitioner set Florida as the forum in which disputes were to be resolved as a means of discouraging cruise passengers from pursuing legitimate claims. Any suggestion of such a bad-faith motive is belied by two facts: Petitioner has its principal place of business in Florida, and many of its cruises depart from and return to Florida ports. Similarly, there is no evidence that petitioner obtained respondents' accession to the forum clause by fraud or overreaching. Finally, respondents have conceded that they were given notice of the forum provision and, therefore, presumably retained the option of rejecting the contract with impunity. In the case before us, therefore, we conclude that the Court of Appeals erred in refusing to enforce the forum-selection clause." See also Koch v. America Online, Inc., 139 F. Supp. 2d 690, 694 (D. Md. 2000): "Use of a form contract...even by the party with superior bargaining power, does not necessarily make a forum selection clause enforceable"; and Fi-Med Management Inc. v. Clemco Medical Inc., 2011 WL 2133345, *2 (E.D. Wis. 2011) (slip copy): "The forum selection clause here is unambiguous and thus expresses the intent of the parties, and as such, it is valid and enforceable under federal and Wisconsin law...Absent unconscionability, fraud, or a violation of public policy, the forum selection clause will be enforced. None of the foregoing is argued here by defendants."

16. D'Antuono v. Service Road Corp., 789 F. Supp. 2d 308, 327 (D. Conn. 2011): "In other words, the party usually must show both that there was an absence of meaningful choice on the part of that party, and that the terms of the agreement were unreasonably favorable toward the other party."

17. See Genelle I. Belmas and Brian N. Larson, *Clicking Away Your Speech Rights: The Enforce-ability of Gagwrap Licenses*, 12 COMMUNICATIONS LAW AND POLICY 37, 88 (2007): "The public policy framework proposed here uses settled contract law and long-standing First Amendment jurisprudence to evaluate gagwrap promises... Under the public policy framework, many gagwrap clauses will be held unenforceable, but other promises of silence that have important commercial or social benefits, such as source confidentiality, non-disclosure, and settlement agreements, will remain intact." See, for example, People v. Network Associates, Inc., 758 N.Y.S.2d 466 (N.Y. Sup. 2003), use of restrictive clause prohibiting purchasers from disclosing results of benchmark tests or publishing reviews of its products constituted enjoined as a deceptive trade practice under New York law.

18. RAYMOND T. NIMMER AND JEFF C. DODD, MODERN LICENSING LAW § 12:29 (database updated in Westlaw, November 2011; emphasis added).

19. Restatement (Second) of Contracts § 208 (1981) (Unconscionable Contract or Term), comment f, law and fact: "A determination that a contract or term is unconscionable is made by the court in the light of all the material facts." See also Hubbert v. Dell Corp., 835 N.E.2d 113, 123 (Ill. App. 2005), citations omitted: "Unconscionability is a question of law and is determined on a case-by-case basis."

20. Restatement (Second) of Contracts § 208 (1981) (Unconscionable Contract or Term): "If a contract or term thereof is unconscionability at the time the contract is made a court may refuse to enforce the contract, or may enforce the remainder of the contract without the unconscionability term, or may so limit the application of any uncon-scionability term as to avoid any unconscionability result."

21. Nimmer and Dodd, *supra* note 18, at 12:5.

22. See Dawn Davidson, *Click and Commit: What Terms Are Users Bound to When They Enter Web Sites?* 26 WILLIAM MITCHELL LAW REVIEW, 1171, 1195–1196 (2000), footnotes omitted: "Mere inequality in bargaining power does not render a contract unenforceable, nor are all standardized contracts unenforceable. In fact, one of the purposes of standardized agreements is to eliminate bargaining over details, and parties are not necessarily expected to understand or even read the standard terms. In order for an adhesion contract to be held invalid, the plaintiff must allege both a lack of meaningful choice about whether to accept the provision in question, and that the disputed provisions are so one-sided as to be oppressive."

23. Nimmer and Dodd, *supra* note 18, at § 12:3: "Nonetheless, in the minds of some, the proper goal is to impose limitations on the enforceability of terms in standard form contracts, especially when the transactions involves a consumer and the dispute centers on sensitive substantive issues."

24. See cases discussed in Chrstina L. Kunz, et al., *Browse-Wrap Agreements: Validity of Implied Assent in Electronic Form Agreements*, 59 THE BUSINESS LAWYER 279 (November 2003): In California, unconscionability must be both procedural and substantive yet operate on a shifting or sliding scale where the more egregious the one the less need be, whereas in New York an egregious clause could satisfy the unconscionability test on the basis of the

substantive element alone. In Washington and Illinois, substantive unconscionability and procedural unconscionability are separate defenses and need not both be proven.

25. Comb v. PayPal, Inc., 218 F. Supp. 2d 1165 (N.D. Cal. 2002), citing Blake v. Ecker, 113 Cal. Rptr. 2d 422 (2001). See also Funding Systems Leas. Corp. v. King Louie Intern., 597 S.W.2d 624, 634 (Mo. Ct. App. 1979): "if there exists gross procedural unconscionability then not much be needed by way of substantive unconscionability, and that the same 'sliding scale' be applied if there be great substantive unconscionability but little procedural unconscionability"; Tacoma Boatbuilding, Inc. v. Delta Fishing Co., 1980 WL 98403, at n. 20 (W.D. Wash. 1980): "The substantive/procedural analysis is more of a sliding scale than a true dichotomy."

26. Sitogum Holdings, Inc. v. Ropes, 800 A.2d 915, 923 (N.J. Super. Ch. 2002), citation omitted.

27. Kublan v. Hasbro Toy Division of Hasbro, 50 U.S.P.Q. 2d 1539 (S.D.N.Y. 1999), citation omitted. See also Bragg v. Linden Research, Inc., 487 F. Supp. 2d 593, 605 (E.D. Pa. 2007), citations to Comb v. PayPal, Inc. omitted: "The procedural component can be satisfied by showing (1) oppression through the existence of unequal bargaining positions or (2) surprise through hidden terms common in the context of adhesion contracts. The substantive component can be satisfied by showing overly harsh or one-sided results that 'shock the conscience.' The two elements operate on a sliding scale such that the more significant one is, the less significant the other need be"; and Desiderio v. National Association of Securities Dealers, Inc., 191 F.3d 198 (2d Cir. 1999), cert. denied, 531 U.S. 1069 (2001).

28. Brower v. Gateway 2000, Inc., 676 N.Y.S.2d 569, 574 (N.Y. App. Div. 1 Dept. 1998): "While it is true that, under New York law, unconscionability is generally predicated on the presence of both the procedural and substantive elements, the substantive element alone may be sufficient to render the terms of the provision at issue unenforceable."

29. Nimmer and Dodd, *supra* note 18, at § 12:12. Compare Maxwell v. Fidelity Financial Services, Inc., 907 P.2d 51, 59 (Ariz. 1995): "The cases that require a showing of both procedural and substantive unconscionability appear to be rather fact-specific, based more on the historical reluctance of courts to disturb contracts than on valid doctrinal underpinning," and citing J. White and Robert S. Summers, 1 UCC 220, for a position opposite to that which Nimmer and Dodd forward.

30. Adler v. Fred Lind Manor, 153 Wash.2d 331, 103 P.3d 773, 782 (Wash. 2004), citation to Restatement (Second) of Contracts omitted, referring to Maxwell v. Fidelity Financial Services, Inc., 907 P.2d 51, 59 (Ariz. 1995): "Therefore, we conclude that under A.R.S. [Arizona Revised Statute] § 47-2302, a claim of unconscionability can be established with a showing of substantive unconscionability alone, especially in cases involving either price-cost disparity or limitation of remedies. If only procedural irregularities are present, it may be more appropriate to analyze the claims under the doctrines of fraud, misrepresentation, duress, and mistake, although such irregularities can make a case of procedural unconscionability."

31. In re RealNetworks Privacy Litigation, 2000 U.S. Dist. LEXIS 6584, *14 (N.D. Ill. 2000). See also Robert A. Hillman and Jeffrey J. Rachlinski, *Standard-Form Contracting in the Electronic Age*, 77 NEW YORK UNIVERSITY LAW REVIEW 429, 456 (2002), footnotes omitted: "In searching out procedural unconscionability, courts examine the transaction to ascertain whether businesses have taken undue advantage of the rational and social factors that hamper consumers from identifying the meaning of terms contained in the boilerplate. Substantive unconscionability encompasses manifestly unjust terms, such as terms that are immoral, conflict with public policy, deny a party substantially what she bargained for, or have no reasonable purpose in the trade."

32. See, for example, King v. Fox, 851 N.E.2d 1184, 1191 (N.Y. 2006): "In general, an unconscionable contract has been defined as one which is so grossly unreasonable as to be unenforcible [*sic*] because of an absence of meaningful choice on the part of one of the parties together with contract terms which are unreasonably favorable to the other party."

33. Restatement (Second) of Contracts § 208 (1981) (Unconscionable Contract or Term), comment e, Unconscionable terms.

34. Douglas v. Talk America, Inc., 495 F.3d 1062, 1068 (9th Cir. 2007): "A class action waiver provision thus may be unconscionable in California. Whether it is depends on the facts and circumstances developed during the course of litigation. The district court clearly erred in holding that the clauses (assuming that they are part of the contract at all) are consistent with California policy and therefore enforceable as a matter of law." See also America Online, Inc. v. Superior Court, 108 Cal. Rptr. 2d 699 (Ct. App. 2001), stay and dismissal of class-action suit by American Online subscribers denied, though while based on a choice of law and choice of forum clause, the provision was unenforceable because (i) enforcement of it would be the functional equivalent of a contractual waiver of consumer protection under the California Consumers Legal Remedies Act and (ii) the designated Virginia law, which does not permit class actions and has more limited remedies, would diminish plaintiffs' rights in violation of California public policy.

35. See, for example, Brower v. Gateway 2000, Inc., 676 N.Y.S.2d 569, 574 (N.Y. App. Div. 1 Dept. 1998): "We do find, however, that the excessive cost factor that is necessarily entailed in arbitrating before the ICC is unreasonable and surely serves to deter the individual consumer from invoking the process. Barred from resorting to the courts by the arbitration clause in the first instance, the designation of a financially prohibitive forum effectively bars consumers from this forum as well; consumers are thus left with no forum at all in which to resolve a dispute," citation omitted; and Comb v. PayPal, Inc., 218 F. Supp. 2d 1165 (N.D. Cal. 2002), arbitration clause found "procedurally unconscionable" where the provision froze the customer's account pending resolution of the dispute, prohibited consolidation of claims among customers, excessive cost of the arbitration in relation to the average amount in dispute, and a choice of venue provision. See also British Columbia Law Institute, Unfair Contract Terms: An Interim Report (February 2005), *BCLI Report No. 35.*

36. Robert Lee Dickens, *Finding Common Ground in the World of Electronic Contracts: The Consistency of Legal Reasoning in Clickwrap Cases*, 11 MARQUETTE INTELLECTUAL PROPERTY LAW REVIEW 379, 401 (2007): "A contract of adhesion is generally defined as a standardized contract, imposed by a party of superior bargaining strength, that provides the other party only the ability to reject or accept it. Clickwrap agreements, by definition, fall into such a category. Clickwrap agreements are, after all, typically standardized contracts that are executed with no negotiation between the parties."

37. See I-Systems, Inc. v. Softwares, Inc., 2005 WL 1430323, at *2 (D. Minn. 2005) (unpublished), citations omitted: "Adhesion contracts generally are not bargained for, but are imposed on the public for a necessary service on a 'take it or leave it' basis. However, the mere fact that a contract is on a printed form or inserted into a software program, and offered on a 'take it or leave it' basis does not necessarily cause it to be an adhesion contract. Similarly, the simple fact that the terms of a contract were not explicitly negotiated does not, alone, make a contract one of adhesion. Instead, there must be a showing that the parties were greatly disparate in bargaining power, that there was no opportunity for negotiation and that the services could not be obtained elsewhere."

38. Mazur v. eBay, Inc., 2008 WL 618988, at *7 (N.D. Cal. 2008) (slip copy); Bragg v. Linden Research, Inc., 487 F. Supp. 2d 593, 605 (E.D. Pa. 2007).

39. Restatement (Second) of Contracts § 208 (1981) (Unconscionable Contract or Term), Reporter's Note on comment a, Unconscionable terms.

40. L. J. KUTTEN, 2 COMPUTER SOFTWARE, § 9:60 (database updated in Westlaw, April 2012), footnote omitted (Are EULAs enforceable?—Are they unconscionable?): "It is arguable that tear open license agreements have both types of unconscionability. The procedural aspects arise from the fact that (1) there is deception in that the transaction looks like a sale but the drafter claims it is not a sale and (2) it is impossible to negotiate the terms of the contract. Substantive unconscionability arises from the fact that the contract gives the developer all of the benefits, while it gives the user all the obligations."

41. Hill v. Gateway 2000, Inc., 105 F.3d 1147, 1148 (7th Cir. 1997).

42. ProCD, Inc. v. Zeidenberg, 86 F.3d 1447 (7th Cir. 1996).

43. Hillman and Rachlinski, *supra* note 31, at 488. See also ROBERT A. HILLMAN, PRINCIPLES OF CONTRACT LAW 225–226 (2004), concluding such pay now, terms later "rolling contracts" are not procedurally unconscionable but should be evaluated as to substantive unconscionability. But see Honey Goodman, *I Shrink-Wrapped the Consumer: The Shrinkwrap Agreement as an Adhesion Contract*, 21 CORDOZO LAW REVIEW 319 (1999).

44. Doe v. SexSearch.com, 551 F.3d 412, 419 (6th Cir. 2008). "Limitation-of-liability clauses are viewed critically, but may be freely bargained for in Ohio and will be enforced" (*id.*). See also Dollar Rent A Car Systems, Inc. v. P.R.P. Enterprises, Inc., 2006 WL 1266515, at *28 (N.D. Okla. 2006) (unpublished): "The Corporate Defendants are contractually precluded from recovering lost profits or consequential damages from Dollar...The Defendants have failed to meet their burden to prove that the limitation of damages clauses in the License Agreements are unconscionable."

45. Hauenstein v. Softwrap Ltd., 2007 WL 2404624, at *5 (W.D. Wash. 2007) (unpublished): "But Plaintiff has not cited any legal authority suggesting that a foreign forum clause renders an arbitration clause unenforceable. And although Mr. Hauenstein states in his declaration that it is 'unduly oppressive' for him to have to arbitrate in London, he does not state that he is unable to arbitrate there, for financial or other reasons... The Court concludes that the written terms of the contract govern, and that the contract provision requiring arbitration in London is not substantively unconscionable." See also Riensche v. Cingular Wireless, LLC, 2006 WL 3827477, at *9 (W.D. Wash. 2006) (slip copy): "[T]he Court concludes that Mr. Riensche had a meaningful choice. Although the provision was a standard form agreement in small print, several factors militate against procedural unconscionability: the arbitration provision was mentioned early in the agreement; the provision began with the word 'ARBITRATION' in all capital letters; Mr. Riensche had a heightened awareness of the possibility of arbitration. Therefore, the arbitration agreement is not unenforceable on the basis of procedural unconscionability."

46. Hubbert v. Dell Corp., 835 N.E.2d 113, 126 (Ill. App. 2005): "The defendant provided evidence to the trial court that in a three-year period, 5 disputes out of 20 went to arbitration. Of the five disputes that were arbitrated, the defendant won two and lost three of the disputes. These do not appear to be results favorable to the defendant on an inordinate basis. The trial court's finding that the defendant's arbitration agreement was unconscionable was error."

47. AT&T Mobility LLC v. Concepcion, 131 S.Ct. 1740 (2011).

48. Comb v. PayPal, Inc., 218 F. Supp. 2d 1165, 1175 (N.D. Cal. 2002). Arbitration costs: "By allowing for prohibitive arbitration fees and precluding joinder of claims (which would make each individual customer's participation in arbitration more economical), PayPal appears to be attempting to insulate itself contractually from any meaningful challenge to its alleged practices" (*id.* at 1176). Venue: "The record in this case shows that PayPal serves millions of customers across the United States and that the amount of the average transaction through PayPal is $55.00" (*id.* at 1177).

49. Sanchez v. Valencia Holding Co., LLC, 2011 WL 5865694, *21 (Cal. App. 2 Dist. 2011): "Accordingly, we conclude the arbitration provision is procedurally and substantively unconscionable. The provision is permeated by unconscionability that cannot be removed through severance or restriction. The trial court properly denied the motion to compel arbitration."

50. Rivera v. American General Financial Services, Inc., 259 P.3d 803, 819 (N.M. 2011), determining that arbitration provisions in car title loan contract which permitted lender to seek judicial redress of its likeliest claims, while forcing borrower to arbitrate any claim was unconscionable: "We therefore determine that the arbitration provisions are unfairly one-sided and void under New Mexico law... the arbitration provisions in this case are so substantively unconscionable that we need not consider whether the provisions are also procedurally unconscionable. See also In re Checking Account

Overdraft Litigation, 2011 WL 4454913, *9 (S.D. Fla. 2011), finding arbitration provision in dispute over excessive overdraft debit card fees where the practice was coupled with an unbounded right to simply seize fees and costs directly from a plaintiff's bank account unconscionable.

51. Bragg v. Linden Research, Inc., 487 F. Supp. 2d 593, 606-607 (E.D. Pa. 2007), footnote omitted.

52. Compare, Net Global Marketing v. Dailtone, Inc., 217 Fed. Appx. 598, 601 (9th Cir. 2007), finding procedural unconscionability where "the arbitration clause is listed in the midst of a long section without line breaks under the unhelpful heading of 'Miscellaneous'"; and Higgins v. Superior Court, 45 Cal. Rptr. 3d 293, 297 (2006), holding arbitration agreement unconscionable where "[t]here is nothing in the Agreement that brings the reader's attention to the arbitration provision"; with Boghos v. Certain Underwriters at Lloyd's of London, 115 P.3d 68, 70 (Calif. 2005), arbitration clause was enforceable where it was in bolded font and contained the heading "BINDING ARBITRATION."

53. Bragg v. Linden Research, Inc., 487 F. Supp. 2d 593, 608 (E.D. Pa. 2007).

54. Ting v. AT&T, 319 F.3d 1126, 1151 (9th Cir. 2003), unconscionability exists where the terms "impose . . . on some consumers costs greater than those a complainant would bear if he or she would file the same complaint in court." See also Ferguson v. Countrywide Credit Industry, 298 F.3d 778, 785 (9th Cir. 2002): "[A] fee allocation scheme which requires the employee to split the arbitrator's fees with the employer would alone render an arbitration agreement substantively unconscionable."

55. See, for example, In re Checking Account Overdraft Litigation, 2011 WL 4454913, *9 (S.D. Fla. 2011), in denying a bank's motion to compel arbitration in a dispute over excessive overdraft debit card fees the court concluded: "This Court has already explained why a fee-shifting provision, coupled with an unbounded right to simply seize fees and costs directly from a plaintiff's bank account, is unreasonably favorable to the Bank. The Court now finds that these terms are so unreasonably favorable to BB&T that it turns out that one side is to be penalized by the enforcement of the terms of a contract so unconscionable that no decent, fair-minded person would view the ensuing result without being possessed of a profound sense of injustice. Accordingly, the Court finds the arbitration provisions in BB&T's Agreement are unconscionable under North Carolina law" (citations and quotation omitted).

56. Bragg v. Linden Research, Inc., 487 F. Supp. 2d 593, 609-610 (E.D. Pa. 2007).

57. Mazur v. eBay, Inc., 2008 WL 618988, at *5 (N.D. Cal. 2008) (slip copy), footnote omitted.

58. Id. at *7.

59. Riensche v. Cingular Wireless, LLC, 2006 WL 3827477, *12-*13 (W.D. Wash. 2006) (slip copy): "Here, the class action prohibition does not affect Cingular, because there is no circumstance under which Cingular would bring a class action against consumers. But it deprives consumers of an important means for enforcing their rights under the CPA [Washington Consumer Protection Act, RCW 19.86 et seq.]. The class action prohibition

is unilateral and excessively favors Cingular, and is therefore substantively uncon-scionable... The limitation on injunctive relief is one-sided and overly harsh to con-sumers, because it limits a remedy available to consumers under the CPA, which Cingular would never seek. In the event that an arbitrator found that Cingular violated the rights of an individual consumer under the CPA, the arbitrator would be barred from enjoining Cingular from continuing the violative practice as to other consumers. The Court concludes that the limitation excessively favors Cingular and is therefore substantively unconscionable."

60. Winig v. Cingular Wireless LLC, 2006 WL 2766007, at *4 (N.D. Cal. 2006) (slip copy): "We do not hold that all class action waivers are necessarily unconscionable. But when the waiver is found in a consumer contract of adhesion in a setting in which disputes between the contracting parties predictably involve small amounts of damages, and when it is alleged that the party with the superior bargaining power has carried out a scheme to deliberately cheat large numbers of consumers out of individually small sums of money, then... the waiver becomes in practice the exemption of the party 'from responsibility for [its] own fraud, or willful injury to the person or property of another.' [Citing California Civil Code § 1668] Under these circumstances, such waivers are unconscionable under California law and should not be enforced."

61. Hebert v. Rapid Payroll, Inc., 2005 WL 6172659, at *6 (C.D. Cal. 2005) (unpublished), quoting California Grocers Association v. Bank of America, 27 Cal. Rptr. 2d 396, 402 (1994).

62. RAYMOND T. NIMMER, 2 INFORMATION LAW § 12.47 (database updated in Westlaw, November 2011).

63. M.A. Mortenson Co., Inc. v. Timberline Software Corp., 998 P.2d 305 (Wash. 2000).

64. Davidson & Associates, Inc. v. Internet Gateway, Inc., 334 F. Supp. 2d 1164, 1179 (E.D. Mo. 2004), aff'd sub. nom. Davidson & Associates v. Jung, 422 F.3d 630 (8th Cir. 2005).

65. Mazur v. eBay, Inc., 2008 WL 618988, at *5 (N.D. Cal. 2008) (slip copy). Compare Prescription Counter v. AmerisourceBergen Corp., 2007 WL 3511301, at *12 (D.N.J. 2007) (unpublished): "Consideration of these factors indicates that the contract was not procedurally unconscionable under Georgia law. Mr. Calabrese, who signed the contract, is a well-educated businessperson. He is a licensed pharmacist, since 1975 he has been the owner and operator of Prescription Counter, and he also served as mayor of South Orange...Although Prescription Counter argues this was a take-it-or-leave-it contract, Prescription Counter has not offered any evidence in support of its argument that NDCHealth was in a far-superior bargaining position. The record indicates that NDCHealth is not the only business that offers such a service...Additionally, Prescrip-tion Counter offers no legal excuse for Mr. Calabrese not having read the terms of the contract. It appears that he simply chose not to do so. Accordingly, it does not appear that the contract provision is procedurally unconscionable under Georgia law."

66. "Nevertheless, relying on the California Supreme Court's decision in Discover Bank v. Superior Court, 36 Cal. 4th 148, 113 P. 3d 1100 (2005), the court found that the

arbitration provision was unconscionable because AT&T had not shown that bilateral arbitration adequately substituted for the deterrent effects of class actions." AT&T Mobility LLC v. Concepcion, 131 S.Ct. 1740, 1745 (2011).

67. See 9 U.S.C. § 1, et seq.

68. AT&T Mobility LLC v. Concepcion, 131 S.Ct. 1740, 1746 (2011).

69. *Id.* at 1750–1751.

70. *Id.* at 1753.

71. *Id.*

72. "We refer to this rule as the Discover Bank rule." AT&T Mobility LLC v. Concepcion, 131 S.Ct. 1740, 1746 (2011). "California courts have frequently applied this rule [the Discover rule] to find arbitration agreements unconscionable. See, for example, Cohen v. DirecTV, Inc., 142 Cal. App. 4th 1442, 1451–1453, 48 Cal. Rptr. 3d 813, 819–821 (2006); Klussman v. Cross Country Bank, 134 Cal. App. 4th 1283, 1297, 36 Cal Rptr. 3d 728, 738–739 (2005); Aral v. EarthLink, Inc., 134 Cal. App. 4th544, 556–557, 36 Cal. Rptr. 3d 229, 237–239 (2005)." AT&T Mobility LLC v. Concepcion, 131 S.Ct. 1740, 1746 (2011).

73. AT&T Mobility LLC v. Concepcion, 131 S.Ct. 1740, 1753 (2011), internal references and quotations court omitted, emphasis in original.

74. AT&T Mobility LLC v. Concepcion, 131 S.Ct. 1740, 1746 (2011), quotation marks omitted. "Although Concepcion is unlikely to settle with finality the validity of arbitration provisions including class-action waivers, its broad holding signals the expectations of the U.S. Supreme Court that courts must carefully question the notion that mandatory arbitration agreements containing a ban on class actions are inherently unfair to consumers." Andrew L. Sandler, *Supreme Court and Congress Focus on Mandatory Pre-Dispute Arbitration Agreements: The Debate Continues*, 29 WESTLAW JOURNAL OF COMPUTER AND INTERNET 1 (July 29, 2011), no pagination in Westlaw.

75. NAACP of Camden County East v. Foulke Management Corp., 2011 WL 3273896, *12 (N.J. Super. A.D. 2011). "The fact that the arbitration provisions in AT&T Mobility may have been more generous to consumers than the provisions here does not affect the force of the Supreme Court's preemption analysis…Applying, as we must, the governing precedent of AT&T Mobility to this record, we sustain the trial court's conclusion that the dealership's class action waiver was not per se invalid. However, that discrete ruling still does not make the waiver provisions, as they were drafted here, enforceable. As we have already shown, the provisions before us are simply too convoluted and inconsistent to be enforced" (*id.* at *20).

76. Daugherty v. Encana Oil & Gas (USA), Inc., 2011 WL 2791338 (D. Colo. 2011) (slip copy) (July 15, 2011), referring to Davis v. M.L.G. Group, 712 P.2d 985, 991 (Colo. 1986): "Colorado courts consider several factors in determining whether a contractual provision is unconscionable, including: (1) the use of a standardized agreement executed by parties of unequal bargaining power; (2) the lack of an opportunity for the customer to read or become familiar with the document before signing it; (3) the use of fine

print in the portion of the contract containing the provision in question; (4) the absence of evidence that the provision was commercially reasonable or should reasonably have been anticipated; (5) the terms of the contract, including substantive fairness; (6) the relationship of the parties, including factors of assent, unfair surprise, and notice; and (7) the circumstances surrounding the formation of the contract, including setting, purpose, and effect." Accord, Bernal v. Burnett, 793 F. Supp. 2d 1280, 1287 (D. Colo. 2011): "There does not appear to be any reason why the Davis factors are not still good law. Thus, the Court will consider the facts of this case under that structure, keeping in mind the Supreme Court's statements and observations in Concepcion."

77. See In re Checking Account Overdraft Litigation, 2011 WL 4454913 (S.D. Fla. 2011), arbitration clause including ability to seize customer account unconscionable; Sanchez v. Valencia Holding Co., LLC, 2011 WL 5865694, *12 (Cal. App. 2 Dist. 2011): "We conclude that four clauses in the arbitration provision are unconscionable. First, a party who loses before the single arbitrator may appeal to a panel of three arbitrators if the award exceeds $100,000. Second, an appeal is permitted if the award includes injunctive relief. Third, the appealing party must pay, in advance, "the filing fee and other arbitration costs subject to a final determination by the arbitrators of a fair apportionment of costs." Fourth, the provision exempts repossession from arbitration while requiring that a request for injunctive relief be submitted to arbitration. Although these provisions may appear neutral on their face, they have the effect of placing an unduly oppressive burden on the buyer. In assessing unconscionability, we focus on the practical effect of a provision, not a facial interpretation"); and Rivera v. American General Financial Services, Inc., 259 P.3d 803 (N.M. 2011), arbitration provisions in car title loan contract which permitted lender to seek judicial redress of its likeliest claims, while forcing borrower to arbitrate any claim she might have, were unreasonably one-sided and substantively unconscionable.

78. Andrew L. Sandler, *Supreme Court and Congress Focus on Mandatory Pre-Dispute Arbitration Agreements: The Debate Continues* 29 WESTLAW JOURNAL OF COMPUTER AND INTERNET 1 (July 29, 2011), no pagination in Westlaw.

79. For a thorough discussion of antitrust applied to intellectual property and licensing see, Nimmer, *supra* note 62, at §§ 11.15–11.35.

80. See Lateef Mtima, *Protecting and Licensing Software: Copyright and Common Law Contract Considerations*, INTELLECTUAL PROPERTY LICENSING TODAY, American Law Institute–American Bar Association Continuing Legal Education ALI-ABA Course of Study (SM049 ALI-ABA 81, 92 October 5–6, 2006): "Finally, an infringing party who cannot claim the benefit of Fair Use may argue that the copyright holder should not be allowed to recover because she has misused or abused her copyright to obtain benefits not intended by the copyright law. The defense of copyright misuse bars a culpable plaintiff from prevailing on an action for the infringement of the misused copyright. The copyright law provides only specific property rights to the copyright holder, and competitors and the general public retain the right to challenge any over-reaching in connection with those rights.

Thus the copyright law forbids the use of the copyright law to secure an exclusive right or limited monopoly not granted by the Copyright Office and which is contrary to public policy to grant," internal quotations to Lasercomb American Inc. v. Reynolds, 911 F.2d 970, 972 and 977 omitted.

81. Nimmer, *supra* note 62, at § 11.36.

82. See, for example, Victoria Smith Ekstrand, *Protecting the Public Policy Rationale of Copyright: Reconsidering Copyright Misuse*, 11 COMMUNICATION LAW AND POLICY 565 (2006).

83. Brulotte v. Thys Co., 379 U.S. 29, 30 (1964): "One defense was misuse of the patents through extension of the license agreements beyond the expiration date of the patents. ...We conclude that the judgment below must be reversed insofar as it allows royalties to be collected which accrued after the last of the patents incorporated into the machines had expired." See also, as the Federal Circuit explained in Virginia Panel Corp. v. MAC Panel Co., 133 F.3d 860, 869 (Fed. Cir. 1997), certain practices constitute per se patent misuse, including "arrangements in which a patentee effectively extends the term of its patent by requiring post-expiration royal-ties." In addition, "there are patent-to-product arrangements, the so-called tying arrangements in which a patentee conditions a license under the patent on the purchase of a separable, staple good." David W. Van Etten, *Note: Everyone in the Patent Pool: U.S. Philips Corp. v. International Trade Commission*, 22 BERKELEY TECHNOLOGY LAW JOURNAL 241, 248 (2007), citing Virginia Panel Corp. v. MAC Panel Co. See also Michael Koenig, *iBRIEF/PATENTS & TECHNOLOGY: Patent Royalties Extending Beyond Expiration: An Illogical Ban from Brulotte to Scheiber*, 2003 DUKE LAW AND TECHNOLOGY REVIEW 5 (2003).

84. Commenting on Lasercomb America, Inc. v. Reynolds, 911 F.2d 970 (4th Cir. 1990), discussed in detail below, Nimmer and Dodd observe that the case involved "a contract term in a license...not to develop software technology products in the same general field over the term of a 99-year license. This extended the no-compete control beyond the term of the copyright." Nimmer and Dodd, *supra* note 18, at § 13:33.

85. Alcatel USA, Inc. v. DGI Technologies, Inc., 166 F.3d 772, 793 (5th Cir. 1999): "But the public policy which includes original works within the granted monopoly excludes from it all that is not embraced in the original expression. It equally forbids the use of the copyright to secure an exclusive right or limited monopoly not granted by the Copyright Office and which is contrary to public policy to grant."

86. Assessment Technologies of WI, LLC v. Wiredata, Inc., 350 F.3d 640, 645 (7th Cir. 2003).

87. *Id.*

88. *Id.* at 647.

89. *Id.* at 646–647, emphasis added. See also Wiredata, Inc. v. Village of Sussex, 729 N.W.2d 757 (Wis. App. 2007): "The municipalities and their independent assessors argue that the PDF provided to WIREdata satisfied the requirements of WIREdata's open records request...the public policy underpinning the open records law require more. They require access to the source material—the material as it is both inputted and stored in

the database, regardless of its physical form or characteristics... The imputed data, maintained at public expense in the Microsoft Access database, is as much a part of the public record as if it were written on paper property cards and organized and stored in a file cabinet... These municipalities must provide WIREdata access to the computer database so that it may examine and copy the property assessment information it seeks," affirmed in part, reversed in part, by WIREdata, Inc. v. Village of Sussex, 751 N.W.2d 736 (Wis. 2008).

90. County of Santa Clara v. Superior Court, 89 Cal.Rptr.3d 374, 393 (Cal. App. Dist. 6 2009).

91. *Id.* at 395: "Independently weighing the competing interests in light of the trial court's factual findings, we conclude that the public interest in disclosure outweighs the public interest in nondisclosure."

92. "In its substantive arguments, the County maintains that copyright law protects its compilation of data as a 'unique arrangement.' The County seeks the right to demand an end user agreement upon disclosure of the GIS basemap, to protect its rights as the 'rightful owner' of copyrightable intellectual property in the map" (*id.* at 395). "In sum, while section 6254.9 [California Government Code] recognizes the availability of copyright protection for software in a proper case, it provides no statutory authority for asserting any other copyright interest" (*id.* at 399).

93. *Id.* at 399. See also Microdecisions, Inc. v. Skinner, 889 So.2d 871, 876 (2004): "The Florida public records law, on the other hand, requires State and local agencies to make their records available to the public for the cost of reproduction."

94. County of Santa Clara v. Superior Court, 89 Cal.Rptr.3d 374 (Cal. App. Dist. 6 2009). "The CPRA contains no provisions either for copyrighting the GIS basemap or for conditioning its release on an end user or licensing agreement by the requester. The record thus must be disclosed as provided in the CPRA, without any such conditions or limitations" (*id.* at 400, relying on Microdecisions, Inc. v. Skinner, 889 So.2d 871, 876 (2004)).

95. Lasercomb America, Inc. v. Reynolds, 911 F.2d 970, 972 (4th Cir. 1990): "A successful defense of misuse of copyright bars a culpable plaintiff from prevailing on an action for infringement of the misused copyright."

96. *Id.* at 978: "So while it is true that the attempted use of a copyright to violate antitrust law probably would give rise to a misuse of copyright defense, the converse is not necessarily true-a misuse need not be a violation of antitrust law in order to comprise an equitable defense to an infringement action. The question is not whether the copyright is being used in a manner violative of antitrust law (such as whether the licensing agreement is 'reasonable'), but whether the copyright is being used in a manner violative of the public policy embodied in the grant of a copyright."

97. "Moreover, although dissemination of creative works is a goal of the Copyright Act, the Act creates a balance between the artist's right to control the work during the term of the copyright protection and the public's need for access to creative works. The copyright term is limited so that the public will not be permanently deprived of the fruits of an

artist's labors . . . the limited monopoly conferred by the Copyright Act is intended to motivate creative activity of authors and inventors by the provision of a special reward, and to allow the public access to the products of their genius after the limited period of exclusive control has expired." Stewart v. Abend, 495 U.S. 207, 228–229 (1990), citation and quotation marks to Sony Corporation of America v. Universal City Studios, Inc., 464 U.S. 417, 429 (1984) omitted.

98. MGM Studios, Inc. v. Grokster, Ltd., 454 F. Supp. 2d 966, 995 (C.D. Cal. 2006). "StreamCast primarily alleges that Plaintiffs have restrained competition in the market for digital distribution of music and movies by collectively refusing to deal with StreamCast and other file-sharing services . . . StreamCast's argument is unpersuasive. Concerted boycotts may violate the antitrust laws, but the existence of an antitrust violation is a separate question from the applicability of the copyright misuse defense. Even if Plaintiffs did act in concert to refuse licenses to StreamCast and restrict competition in the market for digital media distribution, that would not have extended Plaintiffs' copyrights into ideas or expressions over which they have no legal monopoly" (*id.* at 997).

99. See, for example, Broadcast Music, Inc. v. Hampton Beach Casino Ballroom, Inc., 1995 WL 803576, at *5, n. 7 (D.N.H. 1995): "The First Circuit has not addressed the issue of copyright misuse."

100. Meg Dolan, *Misusing Misuse: Why Copyright Misuse Is Unnecessary*, 17 DEPAUL-LCA JOURNAL OF ART AND ENTERTAINMENT LAW 207 (2007).

101. Lasercomb America, Inc. v. Reynolds, 911 F.2d 970 (4th Cir. 1990).

102. *Id.* at 972, footnote omitted. The offending language in the license consisted of two clauses: "D. Licensee agrees during the term of this Agreement that it will not permit or suffer its directors, officers and employees, directly or indirectly, to write, develop, produce or sell computer assisted die making software. E. Licensee agrees during the term of this Agreement and for one (1) year after the termination of this Agreement, that it will not write, develop, produce or sell or assist others in the writing, developing, producing or selling computer assisted die making software, directly or indirectly without Lasercomb's prior written consent. Any such activity undertaken without Lasercomb's written consent shall nullify any warranties or agreements of Lasercomb set forth herein" (*id.* at 973). The term of the agreement was 99 years.

103. *Id.* at 973. "The origins of patent and copyright law in England, the treatment of these two aspects of intellectual property by the framers of our Constitution, and the later statutory and judicial development of patent and copyright law in this country persuade us that parallel public policies underlie the protection of both types of intellectual property rights. We think these parallel policies call for application of the misuse defense to copyright as well as patent law" (*id.* at 974).

104. *Id.* at 978, footnote omitted.

105. *Id.* at 979: "Holding that Lasercomb should have been barred by the defense of copyright misuse from suing for infringement of its copyright in the Interact program, we reverse the injunction and the award of damages for copyright infringement."

106. *Id.* at 973: "Defendants were not themselves bound by the standard licensing agreement. Lasercomb had sent the agreement to Holiday Steel with a request that it be signed and returned. Larry Holliday, however, decided not to sign the document, and Lasercomb apparently overlooked the fact that the document had not been returned. Although defendants were not party to the restrictions of which they complain, they proved at trial that at least one Interact licensee had entered into the standard agreement, including the anticompetitive language" (footnotes omitted).

107. *Id.* at 979: "Therefore, the fact that appellants here were not parties to one of Lasercomb's standard license agreements is inapposite to their copyright misuse defense. The question is whether Lasercomb is using its copyright in a manner contrary to public policy, which question we have answered in the affirmative."

108. DSC Communications Corp. v. DGI Technologies, Inc., 81 F.3d 597 (5th Cir. 1996).

109. *Id.* at 599.

110. *Id.* at 601: "We concur with the Fourth Circuit's characterization of the copyright misuse defense," affirmed in part and reversed in part by, vacated by, in part, remanded by, in part, sub nom. by Alcatel USA, Inc. v. DGI Technologies, Inc., 166 F.3d 772 (5th Cir. 1999).

111. *Id.* at 601–602: "Of course, we do not hold that DGI will successfully avail itself of the copyright misuse defense. After a trial on the merits, the district court may well decide that DSC did not commit copyright misuse, or that DGI cannot avail itself of the defense because it has 'unclean hands.' We simply hold that the district court did not abuse its discretion in implicitly holding that DSC did not have a substantial likelihood of success on the merits because-based on the evidence before the district court-DGI may prevail on its misuse to the defense," affirmed in part and reversed in part by, vacated by, in part, remanded by, in part, sub nom. by Alcatel USA, Inc. v. DGI Technologies, Inc., 166 F.3d 772 (5th Cir. 1999).

112. DSC Communications Corp. v. DGI Technologies, Inc., 81 F.3d 597, 599 (5th Cir. 1996): "Because DSC did not sell its operating system software on the open market, the only way to gain access to the software was to license it from DSC. DGI needed to gain access to DSC's operating system software in order to develop a microprocessor card, because the microprocessor card had to be able to download the software into RAM, and had to be compatible with the software. To obtain access to the operating system software, DGI obtained access to a DSC phone switch owned by NTS. NTS gave DGI permission to use its phone switch to test microprocessor cards," affirmed in part and reversed in part by, vacated by, in part, remanded by, in part, sub nom. by Alcatel USA, Inc. v. DGI Technologies, Inc., 166 F.3d 772 (5th Cir. 1999). "Because the licensing agreement between DSC and NTS only allows the software to be booted up on DSC equipment, this copying is not authorized. Therefore, DSC argues, booting up a microprocessor card violates its copyright. DGI does not dispute that a copy is made when the microprocessor cards are booted up. Instead, DGI argues, *inter alia*, that it is entitled to the defense of copyright misuse" (*id.* at 600).

113. DSC Communications Corp. v. DGI Technologies, Inc., 81 F.3d 597, 601 (5th Cir. 1996), affirmed in part and reversed in part by, vacated by, in part, remanded by, in part, sub nom. by Alcatel USA, Inc. v. DGI Technologies, Inc., 166 F.3d 772 (5th Cir. 1999).

114. See 17 U.S.C. 117(a)(1): "Notwithstanding the provisions of section 106, it is not an infringement for the owner of a copy of a computer program to make or authorize the making of another copy or adaptation of that computer program provided that such a new copy or adaptation is created as an essential step in the utilization of the computer program in conjunction with a machine and that it is used in no other manner."

115. DSC Communications Corp. v. DGI Technologies, Inc., 81 F.3d 597 (5th Cir. 1996).

116. Alcatel USA, Inc. v. DGI Technologies, Inc., 166 F.3d 772, 793 (5th Cir. 1999).

117. Id. at 794, footnote omitted: "Hence, without the freedom to test its cards in conjunction with DSC's software, DGI was effectively prevented from developing its product, thereby securing for DSC a limited monopoly over its uncopyrighted microprocessor cards...By misusing its software copyright, DSC sullied its hands, barring itself from obtaining the equitable reward of injunction on grounds of copyright infringement."

118. Practice Management Information Corp. v. American Medical Association, 121 F.3d 516, 517–518 (9th Cir. 1997), cert. denied 522 U.S. 933 (1997): "Over thirty years ago, the AMA began the development of a coding system to enable physicians and others to identify particular medical procedures with precision. These efforts culminated in the publication of the Physician's Current Procedural Terminology ('the CPT'), on which the AMA claims a copyright...The AMA revises the CPT each year to reflect new developments in medical procedures...Practice Management, a publisher and distributor of medical books, purchases copies of the CPT from the AMA for resale. After failing to obtain the volume discount it requested, Practice Management filed this lawsuit seeking a declaratory judgment that the AMA's copyright in the CPT was invalid for two reasons: (1) the CPT became uncopyrightable law when HCFA adopted the regulation mandating use of CPT code numbers in applications for Medicaid reimbursement, and (2) the AMA misused its copyright by entering into the agreement that HCFA would require use of the CPT to the exclusion of any other code. The district court granted partial summary judgment for the AMA and preliminarily enjoined Practice Management from publishing the CPT. Practice Management appeals," amended opinion, 133 F.3d 1140, cert. denied 524 U.S. 952 (1998).

119. Practice Management Information Corp. v. American Medical Association, 121 F.3d 516, 520 (9th Cir. 1997), cert. denied 522 U.S. 933 (1997), amended opinion, 133 F.3d 1140, cert. denied 524 U.S. 952 (1998).

120. Id.

121. Id. at 521.

122. Id. at 520–521: "On the undisputed facts in the record before us, we conclude the AMA misused its copyright by licensing the CPT to HCFA in exchange for HCFA's agreement not to use a competing coding system...However, the plain language of the AMA's

licensing agreement requires HCFA to use the AMA's copyrighted coding system and prohibits HCFA from using any other. The controlling fact is that HCFA is prohibited from using any other coding system by virtue of the binding commitment it made to the AMA to use the AMA's copyrighted material exclusively What offends the copyright misuse doctrine is not HCFA's decision to use the AMA's coding system exclusively, but the limitation imposed by the AMA licensing agreement on HCFA's rights to decide whether or not to use other forms as well. Conditioning the license on HCFA's promise not to use competitors' products constituted a misuse of the copyright by the AMA," cert. denied 522 U.S. 933 (1997), amended opinion, 133 F.3d 1140, cert. denied 524 U.S. 952 (1998).

123. Nimmer, *supra* note 62, at § 11.38, footnote omitted.

124. Video Pipeline, Inc. v. Buena Vista Home Entertainment, Inc., 342 F.3d 191, 204 (3d Cir. 2003), cert. denied 540 U.S. 1178 (2004).

125. See, for example, NXIVM Corp. v. Ross Institute, 364 F.3d 471, 482 (2d Cir. 2004): "It is plain that, as a general matter, criticisms of a seminar or organization cannot substitute for the seminar or organization itself or hijack its market. To be sure, some may read defendants' materials and decide not to attend plaintiffs' seminars. Indeed, the record reflects that soon after the dissemination of defendants' material, actress Goldie Hawn cancelled a visit with NXIVM's leader, Keith Raniere. But that sort of harm, as the district court properly recognized, is not cognizable under the Copyright Act. If criticisms on defendants' websites kill the demand for plaintiffs' service, that is the price that, under the First Amendment, must be paid in the open marketplace for ideas."

126. Video Pipeline, Inc. v. Buena Vista Home Entertainment, Inc. 342 F.3d 191 (3d Cir. 2003), cert. denied 540 U.S. 1178 (2004).

127. *Id.* at 203, footnote omitted. The text of the restrictive clause is as follows: "The Website in which the Trailers are used may not be derogatory to or critical of the entertainment industry or of [Disney] (and its officers, directors, agents, employees, affiliates, divisions and subsidiaries) or of any motion picture produced or distributed by [Disney] . . . [or] of the materials from which the Trailers were taken or of any person involved with the production of the Underlying Works. Any breach of this paragraph will render this license null and void and Licensee will be liable to all parties concerned for defamation and copyright infringement, as well as breach of contract" (*id.*).

128. *Id.* at 206: "Thus, while we extend the patent misuse doctrine to copyright, and recognize that it might operate beyond its traditional anti-competition context, we hold it inapplicable here. On this record Disney's licensing agreements do not interfere significantly with copyright policy (while holding to the contrary might, in fact, do so). The District Court therefore correctly held that Video Pipeline will not likely succeed on its copyright misuse defense."

129. *Id.* at 206.

130. *Id.*

131. *Id.*

132. See Nimmer and Dodd, *supra* note 18, at § 13:33: "Misuse doctrine in its copyright form suffers from a maddening and hopefully terminal incompleteness. The theory rests on an equitable doctrine. But what equities are involved and in what manner a court balances them remains unclear and largely ad hoc."

133. *Id.* at § 13:28, footnotes to cases cited in support omitted. Nimmer and Dodd observe that the Patent Misuse Reform Act of 1988, codified at 35 U.S.C. § 271, limits the current application of the misuse doctrine in patent law, but also observe: "That result may not, however, apply to copyright licensing where Section 271 does not govern" (*id.* at § 13.29). This suggests that in the absence of Congressional limitation to the contrary courts are free to expand the application of the doctrine in copyright licensing scenarios. Under current law Nimmer and Dodd view the cases standing for three areas of patent misuses: misuse per se (payment of a patent royalty beyond the duration of the patent), anti-competitive conduct that misuses the patent power in one market to obtain or leverage power in another market (traditional anti-trust behavior), and patent scope or field of use scenarios (*id.* at § 13.30).

134. "[A]ll legal or equitable rights that are equivalent to any of the exclusive rights within the general scope of copyright as specified by section 106 in works of authorship that are fixed in a tangible medium of expression and come within the subject matter of copyright as specified by section 102 and 103 . . . are governed exclusively by this title. Thereafter, no person is entitled to any such right or equivalent right in any such work under the common law or statutes of any State . . . Nothing in this title annuls or limits any rights or remedies under the common law or statutes of any State with respect to activities violating legal or equitable rights that are not equivalent to any of the exclusive rights within the general scope of copyright as specified by section 106," per 17 U.S.C. § 301(a) and (b)(3).

135. United States Constitution, Article VI, Clause 2 states: "This Constitution, and the Laws of the United States which shall be made in Pursuance thereof; and all Treaties made, or which shall be made, under the Authority of the United States, shall be the supreme Law of the Land; and the Judges in every State shall be bound thereby, any Thing in the Constitution or Laws of any State to the contrary notwithstanding."

136. See, for example, Laws v. Sony Music Entertainment, Inc., 448 F.3d 1134, 1136 (9th Cir. 2006), federal copyright law preempted a state-based misappropriation claim by Debra Laws against Sony after it used a sample of one of her recordings in a recording by Jennifer Lopez and LL Cool J.

137. Viva R. Moffat, *Super-Copyright: Contracts, Preemption, and the Structure of Copyright Policy-making*, 41 U.C. Davis Law Review 45, 71 (2007): "As a general matter, courts rarely hold that federal statutes preempt the operation of state contract law, and, more specifically, contractual restrictions on baseline copyright principles have generally been upheld over preemption challenges. This approach has been misguided and the results skewed, however, because courts have failed to engage in the interpretive preemption task." But see AT&T Mobility LLC v. Concepcion, 131 S.Ct. 1740 (2011) (Federal Arbitration Act can preempt state contract unconscionability law), discussed earlier in Chapter 4.

138. Nimmer and Dodd, *supra* note 18, at § 13:2.
139. *Id.* at § 13:3; see also §§ 13.4–13.8.
140. See Viva R. Moffat, *Super-Copyright: Contracts, Preemption, and the Structure of Copyright Policy-making*, 41 U.C. DAVIS LAW REVIEW 45, 80–81 (2007), observing two forms of preemption, express and implied, and characterizing field and conflict (or obstacle) preemption as two forms of implied preemption.
141. See 17 U.S.C. § 204(a): "(a) A transfer of copyright ownership, other than by operation of law, is not valid unless an instrument of conveyance, or a note or memorandum of the transfer, is in writing and signed by the owner of the rights conveyed or such owner's duly authorized agent."
142. Nimmer and Dodd, *supra* note 18, at § 13:14.
143. Bowers v. Baystate Technologies, Inc., 320 F.3d 1317, 1335 (Fed. Cir. 2003) (Dyk, J., concurring in part, dissenting in part), citing Bonito Boats, Inc. v, Thunder Craft Boats, Inc. 489 U.S. 141, 157 (1989).
144. Nimmer and Dodd, *supra* note 18, at § 13:4.
145. Davidson & Associates v. Jung, 422 F.3d 630, 638 (8th Cir. 2005), citing National Car Rental Systems, Inc. v. Computer Associates International, Inc., 991 F.2d 426, 428 (8th Cir. 1993). See also "The extra element takes the claim out from the scope of federal property law and places it within some other areas of law because the extra element signifies that different rights or relationships are being protected. In a contract breach claim, the extra element consists of the enforceable contract, the contractual promise and its terms" (Nimmer and Dodd, *supra* note 18, at § 13:12, discussing patent preemption, but the concept applies in the area of copyright as well).
146. Nimmer and Dodd, *supra* note 18, at § 13:19.
147. Wrench LLC v. Taco Bell Corp., 256 F.3d 446, 453 (6th Cir. 2001), citations omitted.
148. Nimmer and Dodd, *supra* note 18, at § 13:19.
149. 17 U.S.C. § 106: "Subject to sections 107 through 121, the owner of a copyright under this title has the exclusive rights to do and to authorize any of the following: (1) to reproduce the copyrighted work in copies or phonorecords; (2) to prepare derivative works based upon the copyrighted work; (3) to distribute copies or phonorecords of the copyrighted work to the public by sale or other transfer of ownership, or by rental, lease, or lending; (4) in the case of literary, musical, dramatic, and choreographic works, pantomimes, and motion pictures and other audiovisual works, to perform the copyrighted work publicly; (5) in the case of literary, musical, dramatic, and choreographic works, pantomimes, and pictorial, graphic, or sculptural works, including the individual images of a motion picture or other audiovisual work, to display the copyrighted work publicly; and (6) in the case of sound recordings, to perform the copyrighted work publicly by means of a digital audio transmission."
150. See Data General Corp. v. Grumman Systems Support Corp., 36 F.3d 1147, 1164 (1st Cir. 1994), quoting Gates Rubber Co. v. Bando Chemical Industries, 9 F.3d 823, 847 (10th Cir. 1993): "This would require the license to protect some interest beyond the

copyright owner's exclusive rights, 'beyond mere copying, preparation of derivative works, performance, distribution or display.'" See also Gates Rubber Co. v. Bando Chemical Industries, 9 F.3d 823 (10th Cir. 1993), copyright preemption is foreclosed if "if a state cause of action requires an extra element, beyond mere copying, preparation of derivative works, performance, distribution or display, then the state cause of action is qualitatively different from, and not subsumed within, a copyright infringement claim and federal law will not preempt the state action" (*id.* at 847).

151. Telecom Technical Services, Inc. v. Rolm Co., 388 F.3d 820, 833 (11th Cir. 2004): "If, however, the state law involves different or additional elements for recovery, then it is not preempted because it is not the same action. The district court found, and we agree, that the tortious interference claim involves an additional element. The tortious interference claim requires Siemens to demonstrate that the ISOs violated the terms of Siemens's software license for third parties, which is an element beyond federal copyright law that prohibits unauthorized copying" (citation omitted).

152. Grosso v. Miramax Film Corp., 383 F.3d 965, 968 (9th Cir. 2004).

153. *Id.*: "In Del Madera we held that a claim for unjust enrichment was equivalent to a claim for copyright infringement, and thus preempted, because the claim lacked an extra element-the bilateral expectation of compensation." See Del Madera Props. v. Rhodes & Gardner, Inc., 820 F.2d 973, 976 (9th Cir. 1987), overruled on other grounds by Fogerty v. Fantasy, Inc. 510 U.S. 517 (1994).

154. Data General Corp. v. Grumman Systems Support Corp., 36 F.3d 1147, 1165 (1st Cir. 1994). See also Computer Associates International, Inc. v. Altai, Inc., 982 F.2d 693, 716 (2d Cir. 1992).

155. Walthal v. Rusk, 172 F.3d 481 (7th Cir. 1999).

156. 17 U.S.C. § 102(a)(1)–(8): "Copyright protection subsists, in accordance with this title, in original works of authorship fixed in any tangible medium of expression, now known or later developed, from which they can be perceived, reproduced, or otherwise communicated, either directly or with the aid of a machine or device. Works of authorship include the following categories: (1) literary works; (2) musical works, including any accompanying words; (3) dramatic works, including any accompanying music; (4) pantomimes and choreographic works; (5) pictorial, graphic, and sculptural works; (6) motion pictures and other audiovisual works; (7) sound recordings; and (8) architectural works."

157. "As other circuits have recognized, one function of § 301(a) is to prevent states from giving special protection to works of authorship that Congress has decided should be in the public domain, which it can accomplish only if 'subject matter of copyright' includes all works of a *type* covered by section 102 and 103, even if federal law does not afford protection to them." Lipscher v. LRP Publications, Inc., 266 F.3d 1305, 1311 (11th Cir. 2001), emphasis in original, citing ProCD, Inc. v. Zeidenberg, 86 F.3d 1447, 1453 (7th Cir. 1996); and National Basketball Association v. Motorola, Inc., 105 F.3d 841, 849-850 (2d Cir. 1997): "Law Bulletin filed suit against LRP and Fiore, alleging

that LRP surreptitiously obtained subscriptions to Law Bulletin's verdict reporters by posing as a Florida law firm named 'Fiore and Cohen' and then used the information from the newsletters as its basis for reporting jury verdicts from Illinois" (*id.* at 1308).

158. Whether protected or not, both copyrightable and noncopyrightable content is nonetheless within the subject matter of copyright, as the law addresses its status or disposition. As the 4th Circuit observed: "In other words, Berge wants to argue that ideas embodied in a work covered by the Copyright Act do not fall within the scope of the Act because the Act specifically excludes them from protection. But scope and protection are not synonyms. Moreover, the shadow actually cast by the Act's preemption is notably broader than the wing of its protection." U.S. ex rel. Berge v. Board of Trustees of the University of Alabama, 104 F.3d 1453, 1463 (4th Cir. 1997). See also Wrench LLC v. Taco Bell Corp., 256 F.3d 446, 455 (6th Cir. 2001): "The Second, Fourth, and Seventh Circuits have held that the scope of the Copyright Act's subject matter extends beyond the tangible expressions that can be protected under the Act to elements of expression which themselves cannot be protected," citing National Basketball Association v. Motorola, Inc. (2d Cir.), U.S. ex rel. Berge v. Board of Trustees of the University of Alabama (4th Cir.), and ProCD, Inc. v. Zeidenberg (7th Cir.).

159. Wrench LLC v. Taco Bell Corp., 256 F.3d 446, 455 (6th Cir. 2001): "We join our sister circuits [Second, Fourth and Seventh] in holding that the scope of the Copyright Act's subject matter is broader than the scope of the Act's protections."

160. For example, the 11th Circuit observed that "this court recognized a two-part test to be applied in copyright preemption cases. Preemption occurs if the rights at issue (1) 'fall within the "subject matter of copyright" set forth in sections 102 and 103' and (2) 'are "equivalent to" the exclusive rights of section 106.'" Lipscher v. LRP Publications, Inc., 266 F.3d 1305, 1311 (11th Cir. 2001), citing Crow v. Wainwright, 720 F.2d 1224, 1225-1226 (11th Cir. 1983).

161. Wrench LLC v. Taco Bell Corp., 256 F.3d 446, 456 (6th Cir. 2001). See also Lipscher v. LRP Publications, Inc., 266 F.3d 1305, 1318-1319 (11th Cir. 2001): "LRP further contends that the district court should have dismissed the contract claim based on public policy grounds. This argument fails as well. The subscription agreements do not remove any information from the public domain, and the rights created by the agreements are not exclusive rights. The rights sought to be enforced in Law Bulletin's breach of contract claim are not equivalent to the exclusive rights of §106, and, in order to succeed on its claim, Law Bulletin needed to show an extra element, the existence of a valid contract between the parties. The district court was correct in holding that Law Bulletin's breach of contract claim was not preempted."

162. Wrench LLC v. Taco Bell Corp., 256 F.3d 446, 457 (6th Cir. 2001).

163. See, for example, Ryan J. Casamiquela, *Contractual Assent and Enforceability in Cyberspace*, 17 Berkeley Technology Law Review 475, 492 (2002): "Because producers use shrinkwrap and clickwrap licenses in mass-market transactions, courts would be giving

Broader Legal and Policy Issues in Licensing ▶ 217

producers the opportunity to re-write copyright law if federal law did not preempt private contracts."

164. National Car Rental System, Inc. v. Computer Associates International, Inc., 991 F.2d 426 (8th Cir. 1993).

165. ProCD, Inc. v. Zeidenberg, 86 F.3d 1447 (7th Cir. 1996)

166. Bowers v. Baystate Technologies, Inc., 320 F.3d 1317 (Fed. Cir. 2003), applying the law of the 1st Circuit.

167. Nimmer and Dodd, *supra* note 18, at § 10:8, identifying four types of implied licenses, implied-in-fact, estoppel-based, implied-by-construction, and implied-in-law but nonetheless observing: "The Types of implied licenses are more like hues that sharply distinct colors and relate to bases for creating the license, not to its effect. Fairness, fidelity to the supposed intension of the parties, and fealty to expectations built on commercial and legal background rules are the stuff of which implied licenses are made" (*id.* at 612–613).

168. Grosso v. Miramax Film Corp., 383 F.3d 965, 968 (9th Cir. 2004), citation omitted.

169. Davidson & Associates v. Jung, 422 F.3d 630 (8th Cir. 2005).

170. *Id.* at 635, note 4, emphasis in original.

171. *Id.* at 638, citations omitted: "This case concerns conflict preemption. Conflict preemption applies when there is no express preemption but (1) it is impossible to comply with both the state and federal law or when (2) the state law stands as an obstacle to the accomplishment and execution of the full purposes and objectives of Congress."

172. Vault Corp. v. Quaid Software Ltd., 847 F.2d 255, 270 (5th Cir. 1988): "The Fifth Circuit held that the Louisiana [Software] License Enforcement Act, which permitted a software producer to impose contractual terms upon software purchasers conflicted with the rights of purchasers of the computer program under the Copyright Act, specifically 17 U.S.C. § 117, which permits a computer program owner to make an adaptation of a program provided that the adaption is either created as an essential step in the utilization of the computer program in conjunction with a machine or is for archival purpose only."

173. Davidson & Associates v. Jung, 422 F.3d 630, 639 (8th Cir. 2005).

174. *Id.* at 638, quoting Bowers v. Baystate Technologies, Inc., 320 F.3d 1317, 1325–1326 and 1337 (Dyk, J., concurring in part, dissenting in part) (Fed. Cir. 2003).

175. Davidson & Associates v. Jung, 422 F.3d 630, 639 (8th Cir. 2005).

176. Wrench LLC v. Taco Bell Corp., 256 F.3d 446, 459 (6th Cir. 2001).

177. Vault Corp. v. Quaid Software Ltd., 847 F.2d 255 (5th Cir. 1988).

178. Louisiana Revised Statutes Annotated 5§ 1:1961.

179. Vault Corp. v. Quaid Software Ltd., 847 F.2d 255, 268 (5th Cir. 1988).

180. *Id.* at 270.

181. "Terms of which shall be deemed to have been accepted . . . in an accompanying license agreement . . . may include any or all of the following: . . . the prohibition or limitation of rights to modify and/or adapt the copy of the computer software in any way, including without limitation prohibitions on translating, reverse engineering, decompiling,

disassembling, and/or creating derivative works based on the computer software." LA. REV. STAT. ANN. § 51:1964 (3).

182. Bowers v. Baystate Technologies, Inc., 320 F.3d 1317, 1325 (Fed. Cir. 2003): "Moreover, while the Fifth Circuit has held a state law prohibiting all copying of a computer program is preempted by the federal Copyright Act, [citation to *Vault* omitted] no evidence suggests the First Circuit would extend this concept to include private contractual agreements supported by mutual assent and consideration."

183. Vault Corp. v. Quaid Software Ltd., 655 F. Supp. 750, 761 (E.D. La. 1987).

184. Bowers v. Baystate Technologies, Inc., 320 F.3d 1317, 1323 (Fed. Cir.), cert. denied 539 U.S. 928 (2003).

185. Bowers v. Baystate Technologies, Inc., 320 F.3d 1317, 1325 (Fed. Cir.) ("The First Circuit recognizes contractual waiver of affirmative defenses and statutory rights."), cert. denied 539 U.S. 928 (2003).

186. Bowers v. Baystate Technologies, Inc., 320 F.3d 1317, 1323 (Fed. Cir.), cert. denied 539 U.S. 928 (2003).

187. Bowers v. Baystate Technologies, Inc., 320 F.3d 1317, 1335 (Fed. Cir. 2003) (Dyk, J., concurring in part, dissenting in part), citation omitted: "The case before us is different from ProCD. The Copyright Act does not confer a right to pay the same amount for commercial and personal use. It does, however, confer a right to fair use, which we have held encompasses reverse engineering. ProCD and the other contract cases are also careful not to create a blanket rule that all contracts will escape preemption," cert. denied 539 U.S. 928 (2003).

188. Bowers v. Baystate Technologies, Inc., 320 F.3d 1317, 1335 (Fed. Cir. 2003) (Dyk, J., concurring in part, dissenting in part), citation omitted, cert. denied 539 U.S. 928 (2003).

189. Bowers v. Baystate Technologies, Inc., 320 F.3d 1317, 1336 (Fed. Cir. 2003), Dyk, J., concurring in part, dissenting in part: "I nonetheless agree with the majority opinion that a state can permit parties to contract away a fair use defense or to agree not to engage in uses of copyrighted material that are permitted by the copyright law, *if the contract is freely negotiated*" (emphasis added), cert. denied 539 U.S. 928 (2003).

190. Bowers v. Baystate Technologies, Inc., 320 F.3d 1317, 1336–1337 (Fed. Cir.) (Dyk, J., concurring in part, dissenting in part) (citation omitted), cert. denied 539 U.S. 928 (2003).

191. Bowers v. Baystate Technologies, Inc., 320 F.3d 1317, 1337 (Fed. Cir. 2003) (Dyk, J., concurring in part, dissenting in part).

192. Bowers v. Baystate Technologies, Inc., 320 F.3d 1317, 1338 (Fed. Cir. 2003) (Dyk, J., concurring in part, dissenting in part): "The case before us is different from ProCD. The Copyright Act does not confer a right to pay the same amount for commercial and personal use. It does, however, confer a right to fair use, 17 U.S.C. § 107, which we have held encompasses reverse engineering," cert. denied 539 U.S. 928 (2003).

193. Classen, *supra* note 3, at 32.

194. Bowers v. Baystate Technologies, Inc., 320 F.3d 1317, 1337 (Fed. Cir. 2003) (Dyk, J., concurring in part, dissenting in part): "However, state law giving effect to shrinkwrap licenses is no different in substance from a hypothetical black dot law. Like any other contract of adhesion, the only choice offered to the purchaser is to avoid making the purchase in the first place. State law thus gives the copyright holder the ability to eliminate the fair use defense in each and every instance at its option," citation omitted, cert. denied 539 U.S. 928 (2003).

195. ProCD, Inc. v. Zeidenberg, 86 F.3d 1447, 1454 (7th Cir. 1996). The 7th Circuit cited three other circuits that likewise found right based in contract to possess the requisite additional element: National Car Rental Systems, Inc. v. Computer Associates International, Inc., 991 F.2d 426, 433 (8th Cir. 1993); Taquino v. Teledyne Monarch Rubber, 893 F.2d 1488, 1501 (5th Cir. 1990); and Acorn Structures, Inc. v. Swantz, 846 F.3d. 923, 926 (4th Cir. 1988). See also the Federal Circuit interpreting the 1st Circuit case law in Bowers v. Baystate Technologies, Inc., 320 F.3d 1317, 1325 (Fed. Cir. 2003): "This court believes that the First Circuit would follow the reasoning of ProCD and the majority of other courts to consider this issue. This court, therefore, holds that the Copyright Act does not preempt Mr. Bowers' contract claims."

196. ProCD, Inc. v. Zeidenberg, 86 F.3d 1447, 1449 (7th Cir. 1996): "ProCD decided to engage in price discrimination, selling its database to the general public for personal use at a low price (approximately $150 for the set of five discs) while selling information to the trade for a higher price."

197. 17 U.S.C. § 109(a).

198. 17 U.S.C. § 109(b)(2)(A). See also implementing regulations 37 C.F.R. § 201.24.

199. Apik Minassian, *The Death of Copyright: Enforceability of Shrinkwrap Licensing Agreements*, 45 U.C.L.A. LAW REVIEW 569, 572 (1997), quoting 17 U.S.C. § 109(a).

200. Apple Inc. v. v. Psystar Corp., 658 F.3d 1150, 1155 (9th Cir., 2011).

201. Novell, Inc. v. Network Trade Center, Inc., 25 F. Supp. 2d 1218, 1230–1231 (D. Utah 1997): "This Court holds that transactions making up the distribution chain from Novell through NTC to the end-user are 'sales' governed by the U.C.C. Therefore, the first sale doctrine applies. It follows that the purchaser is an 'owner' by way of sale and is entitled to the use and enjoyment of the software with the same rights as exist in the purchase of any other good. Said software transactions do not merely constitute the sale of a license to use the software. The shrinkwrap license included with the software is therefore invalid as against such a purchaser insofar as it purports to maintain title to the software in the copyright owner. Based upon the foregoing, this Court rules that NTC's customers who obtained legally copyrighted materials from NTC did not violate the law and are therefore entitled to use the software in accordance with its intended use, including unrestricted copying of the software onto their hard drives."

202. SoftMan Products Company, Inc. v. Adobe Systems Inc., 171 F. Supp. 2d 1075 (C.D. Calif. 2001).

203. The "'[c]ollections' are sets of individual Adobe products, such as Adobe Photoshop or Illustrator on separate CD's, that are sold together in a larger Adobe Retail Box. These Collections are offered by Adobe at a discount from the individual retail products comprising the Collection" (*id.* at 1080, at note 2).

204. *Id.* at 1080.

205. *Id.*: "Each piece of Adobe software is also accompanied by an End User License Agreement ('EULA'), which sets forth the terms of the license between Adobe and the end user for that specific Adobe product. The EULA is electronically recorded on the computer disk and customers are asked to agree to its terms when they attempt to install the software."

206. *Id.* at 1082.

207. *Id.* at 1083. "The parties have made much of the change to Adobe's EULA that occurred in April 2000. The Court finds that, under the current language of the EULA, Adobe's clear intent is to prohibit the unbundling activity. Therefore, assuming arguendo that the prior agreement did not prohibit the conduct at issue, the current EULA does clearly state that the 'unbundling activities' are barred" (*id.* at 1083, at note 7).

208. *Id.* at 1082–1083: "It is not disputed that SoftMan has no licensing agreement with Adobe."

209. *Id.* at 1082.

210. "The Adobe Collections boxes state: 'NOTICE TO USERS: This product is offered subject to the license agreement included with the media.'" (*id.* at 1087).

211. *Id.*

212. *Id.* at 1088.

213. *Id.* at 1087.

214. *Id.* at 1083.

215. *Id.* at 1085.

216. *Id.* at 1086.

217. Adobe Systems Inc., v. One Stop Micro, Inc. 84 F. Supp. 2d 1086, 1088 (N.D. Cal. 2000).

218. *Id.* at 1091."In conclusion, the Court holds that based upon the undisputed evidence submitted by Adobe regarding the intent of the parties in entering into the agreement, trade usage, the unique nature of distributing software, as well as the express restrictive language of the contract, the OCRA is a licensing agreement" (*id.* at 1092).

219. Adobe Systems Inc., v. One Stop Micro, Inc. 84 F. Supp. 2d 1086, 1091–1092 (N.D. Cal. 2000).

220. SoftMan Products Company, Inc. v. Adobe Systems Inc., 171 F. Supp. 2d 1075, 1082–1088 (C.D. Calif. 2001).

221. *Id.* at 1083, citing at note 9, Mark A. Lemley, *Intellectual Property and Shrinkwrap Licenses*, CALIFORNIA LAW REVIEW 1239 (1995), and quoting *id.* at 1239: "Software vendors are attempting en masse to 'opt out' of intellectual property law by drafting license provisions that compel their customers to adhere to more restrictive provisions than copyright law would require."

222. Accord, Krause v. Titleserv, Inc., 402 F.3d 119, 124 (2d Cir. 2005): "We conclude that Titleserv owned copies of the disputed programs within the meaning of § 117(a). We reach this conclusion in consideration of the following factors: Titleserv paid Krause substantial consideration to develop the programs for its sole benefit. Krause customized the software to serve Titleserv's operations. The copies were stored on a server owned by Titleserv. Krause never reserved the right to repossess the copies used by Titleserv and agreed that Titleserv had the right to continue to possess and use the programs forever, regardless whether its relationship with Krause terminated. Titleserv was similarly free to discard or destroy the copies any time it wished. In our view, the pertinent facts in the aggregate satisfy of § 117(a)'s requirement of ownership of a copy."

223. Vernor v. Autodesk, Inc., 621 F.3d 1102, 1107 (9th Cir. 2010), cert. denied 132 S.Ct. 105 (Oct. 3, 2011), footnote to note 6: "If Autodesk's transfer of Release 14 copies to CTA was a first sale, then CTA's resale of the software in violation of the SLA's terms would be a breach of contract, but would not result in copyright liability."

224. Vernor v. Autodesk, Inc., 621 F.3d 1102, 1109 (9th Cir. 2010), cert. denied 132 S.Ct. 105 (Oct. 3, 2011), citation omitted.

225. *Id.* at 1111.

226. 17 U.S.C. § 117(a) (emphasis added).

227. Vernor v. Autodesk, Inc., 621 F.3d 1102, 1105 (9th Cir. 2010), cert. denied 132 S.Ct. 105 (Oct. 3, 2011): "Autodesk distributes Release 14 pursuant to a limited license agreement in which it reserves title to the software copies and imposes significant use and transfer restrictions on its customers. We determine that Autodesk's direct customers are licensees of their copies of the software rather than owners, which has two ramifications. Because Vernor did not purchase the Release 14 copies from an owner, he may not invoke the first sale doctrine, and he also may not assert an essential step defense on behalf of his customers."

228. Vernor acquired his copies at a garage sale and from CTA directly: Vernor v. Autodesk, Inc., 621 F.3d 1102, 1105 and 1106 (9th Cir. 2010): "In May 2005, he purchased an authentic used copy of Release 14 at a garage sale from an unspecified seller. He never agreed to the SLA's terms, opened a sealed software packet, or installed the Release 14 software... In April 2007, Vernor purchased four authentic used copies of Release 14 at CTA's office sale," cert. denied 132 S.Ct. 105 (Oct. 3, 2011).

229. Vernor v. Autodesk, Inc., 621 F.3d 1102, 1112 (9th Cir. 2010) (references to 17 U.S.C. § 109(a) and 17 U.S.C. § 106(3) omitted), cert. denied 132 S.Ct. 105 (Oct. 3, 2011).

230. Omega S.A. v. Costco Wholesale Corp., 541 F.3d 982, 986 (9th Cir. 2008): "The statute would not apply because Omega made copies of the Omega Globe Design in Switzerland and Costco sold the copies without Omega's authority in the United States," judgment affirmed by an equally divided court without opinion, Costco Wholesale Corp. v. Omega S.A., 131 S.Ct. 565 (2010). See also Katherine A. Chamberlain, *"Lawfully Made under This Title": The Implications of "Costco v. Omega" and the First Sale Doctrine on Library Lending,* 37

JOURNAL OF ACADEMIC LIBRARIANSHIP 291 (2011 Vernor v. Autodesk, Inc., 621 F.3d 1102, 1112 (9th Cir. 2010) (references to 17 U.S.C. § 106(1) and 17 U.S.C. § 117(a)(1) omitted), cert. denied 132 S.Ct. 105 (Oct. 3, 2011).).

231. Section 117 confers the right to make a copy of a computer program as an essential step in its use, but restricts the reproduction to the "owner of a copy of a computer program" alone. A licensee nor someone who is not an owner, even though arguably a lawful possessor as was Vernor or his would-be customers, do not have this section 117 reproduction right. "Our conclusion that those who rightfully possess, but do not own, a copy of copyrighted software are not entitled to claim the essential step defense is also supported by the legislative history... Without explanation, Congress substituted 'owner' for 'rightful possessor.' This modification suggests that more than rightful possession is required for § 117 to apply—i.e., that Congress did not intend licensees subject to significant transfer and use restrictions to receive the benefit of the essential step defense" (*id.* at 1112, footnote omitted).

232. Marcelo Halpern, Yury Kapgan, and Kathy Yu, *Vernor v. Autodesk: Software and the First Sale Doctrine Under Copyright Law*, 23 INTELLECTUAL PROPERTY AND TECHNOLOGY LAW JOURNAL 3, 7 (March 2011).

233. On April 13, Vernor received an extension of time to petition the U.S. Supreme Court for certiorari, to May 18, 2011. Timothy Vernor v. Autodesk Inc., letter to Clerk, U.S. Court of Appeals for the Ninth Circuit, no. 09-3596, Order (9th Cir. Jan. 18, 2011), retrieved from Ninth Circuit Case Management/Electronic Case Filing system, April 28, 2011. A petition for writ of certiorari was filed with the U.S. Supreme Court on May 20, 2011 (Dkt. No. 10-1421). The American Library Association filed an amici curiae brief on June 20, 2011. Prior to these filings, Vernor filed a petition for the case to be reheard en banc on October 1, 2010. Autodesk filed its reply on November 10, 2010. The Ninth Circuit denied the request on January 18, 2011. Vernor v. Autodesk Inc., no. 09-3596, Order (9th Cir. Jan. 18, 2011), retrieved from Ninth Circuit Case Management/Electronic Case Filing system, April 28, 2011. In October the U.S. Supreme Court declined to review the decision, Vernor v. Autodesk Inc., 132 S.Ct. 105 (Oct. 3, 2011), declining a writ of certiorari in Vernor v. Autodesk, Inc., 621 F.3d 1102, 1112 (9th Cir. 2010).

234. Exemption to Prohibition on Circumvention of Copyright Protection Systems for Access Control Technologies, Final Rule, 75 FEDERAL REGISTER 43825, 43829 (July 27, 2010) (amending 37 C.F.R. § 201.40): "Moreover, the Register cannot clearly determine whether the various versions of the iPhone contracts with consumers constituted a sale or license of a copy of the computer programs contained on the iPhone."

235. Exemption to Prohibition on Circumvention of Copyright Protection Systems for Access Control Technologies, Final Rule, 75 FEDERAL REGISTER 43825, 43829 (July 27, 2010) (amending 37 C.F.R. § 201.40).

236. Exemption to Prohibition on Circumvention of Copyright Protection Systems for Access Control Technologies, Final Rule, 75 FEDERAL REGISTER 43825, 43831 (July 27, 2010) (amending 37 C.F.R. § 201.40).

237. "The ALA fears that the software industry's licensing practices could be adopted by other copyright owners, including book publishers, record labels, and movie studios. These are serious contentions on both sides, but they do not alter our conclusion that our precedent...requires the result we reach. Congress is free, of course, to modify the first sale doctrine and the essential step defense if it deems these or other policy considerations to require a different approach." Vernor v. Autodesk, Inc., 621 F.3d 1102, 1115 (9th Cir. 2010), cert. denied 132 S.Ct. 105 (Oct. 3, 2011).

238. Marcelo Halpern, Yury Kapgan, and Kathy Yu, *Vernor v. Autodesk: Software and the First Sale Doctrine Under Copyright Law*, 23 INTELLECTUAL PROPERTY AND TECHNOLOGY LAW JOURNAL 3, 7 (March 2011): "The results in Vernor, Blizzard, and UMG [UMG v. Augusto (9th Cir. 2011) and discussed in the previous chapter] suggest that license restrictions on transfer and use of software are likely to be more prevalent and powerful. The decision also could affect conduct in the secondary markets for all copyrighted works, not just secondhand software. It's not difficult to imagine software-style licensing terms being attached to other kinds of works. Indeed, many copyright owners who distribute their works electronically already use technological measures to restrict transfer and use by anyone other than the original purchaser, and these measures may be backed by license agreements that also limit transfer and use, and explicitly state that the purchaser does not own the copy of the purchased work. Vernor may bolster such agreements and weaken markets for resale of secondhand copies of all types of copyrighted works, particularly those distributed electronically, whether software, music, movies, or books."

239. The copyright law defines a computer program as a "set of statements or instructions to be used directly or indirectly in a computer in order to bring about a certain result" (17 U.S.C. § 101).

240. The library remains able to circulate or make other public distribution of the computer program in the nature of lending "if each copy of a computer program which is lent by such library has affixed to the packaging containing the program a warning of copyright in accordance with requirements that the Register of Copyrights shall prescribe by regulation." 17 U.S.C. § 109(b)(2)(A). Implementing regulations are found at 37 C.F.R. § 201.24.

241. "'Phonorecords' are material objects in which sounds, other than those accompanying a motion picture or other audiovisual work, are fixed by any method now known or later developed, and from which the sounds can be perceived, reproduced, or otherwise communicated, either directly or with the aid of a machine or device. The term phonorecords' includes the material object in which the sounds are first fixed" (17 U.S.C. § 101). The copyright law uses the term phonorecord to distinguish such reproductions from copies. "'Copies' are material objects, other than phonorecords, in which a work is fixed by any method now known or later developed, and from which the work can be perceived, reproduced, or otherwise communicated, either directly or with the aid of a machine or device. The term 'copies' includes the material object, other than a phonorecord, in which the work is first fixed" (17 U.S.C. § 101).

242. See Vernor v. Autodesk, Inc., 621 F.3d 1102, 1104 (9th Cir. 2010), cert. denied 132 S.Ct. 105 (Oct. 3, 2011): "Since at least 1986, Autodesk has offered AutoCAD to customers pursuant to an accompanying software license agreement ('SLA'), which customers must accept before installing the software. A customer who does not accept the SLA can return the software for a full refund. Autodesk offers SLAs with different terms for commercial, educational institution, and student users. The commercial license, which is the most expensive, imposes the fewest restrictions on users and allows them software upgrades at discounted prices."

243. See Douglas v. Talk America, Inc., 495 F.3d 1062, 1065 (9th Cir. 2007). Facts: "Joe Douglas contracted for long distance telephone service with America Online. Talk America subsequently acquired this business from AOL and continued to provide telephone service to AOL's former customers. Talk America then added four provisions to the service contract: (1) additional service charges; (2) a class action waiver; (3) an arbitration clause; and (4) a choice-of-law provision pointing to New York law. Talk America posted the revised contract on its website but, according to Douglas, it never notified him that the contract had changed. Unaware of the new terms, Douglas continued using Talk America's services for four years." New terms are not part of the agreement: "Even if Douglas had visited the website, he would have had no reason to look at the contract posted there. Parties to a contract have no obligation to check the terms on a periodic basis to learn whether they have been changed by the other side. [footnote 1]" (*id.* at 1066). Footnote 1: "Nor would a party know *when* to check the website for possible changes to the contract terms without being notified that the contract has been changed and how. Douglas would have had to check the contract every day for possible changes. Without notice, an examination would be fairly cumbersome, as Douglas would have had to compare every word of the posted contract with his existing contract in order to detect whether it had changed" (*id.*).

244. 17 U.S.C. § 109(a).

245. Vernor v. Autodesk, Inc., 621 F.3d 1102, 1105 (9th Cir. 2010), cert. denied 132 S.Ct. 105 (Oct. 3, 2011).

246. *Id.* at 1112, citations to sections 109 and 106 omitted.

247. *Id.*, citations to section 106 and 117 omitted. "We hold today that a software user is a licensee rather than an owner of a copy where the copyright owner (1) specifies that the user is granted a license; (2) significantly restricts the user's ability to transfer the software; and (3) imposes notable use restrictions. Applying our holding to Autodesk's SLA, we conclude that CTA was a licensee rather than an owner of copies of Release 14 and thus was not entitled to invoke the first sale doctrine or the essential step defense" (*id.* at 1111).

248. The software owner in Vernor offered several options to potential licensees: "Autodesk offers SLAs with different terms for commercial, educational institution, and student users. The commercial license, which is the most expensive, imposes the fewest restrictions on users and allows them software upgrades at discounted prices." Vernor v.

Autodesk, Inc., 621 F.3d 1102, 1104 (9th Cir. 2010), cert. denied 132 S.Ct. 105 (Oct. 3, 2011). A choice of license options may not be the precise situation in futures cases. Though if an institutional or "library" license is available, albeit at a higher price, and a library chooses a less expensive version and attempts to circulate the software claiming first-sale rights a court would likely be unsympathetic to its claim that it was anything other than a licensee.

249. See iTunes Store, Terms and Conditions, http://www.apple.com/legal/itunes/us/terms.html#SERVICE (accessed December 6, 2011): "USAGE RULES (i) You shall be authorized to use iTunes Products only for personal, noncommercial use."

250. See OverDrive Media Console Version 3.2 (November 2011), section titled "Important Notice about Copyrighted Materials" includes the following: "For Content downloaded from a library services, at the end of the lending period, your license to the Content terminates, and ou may no longer use or access the Content. At the end of the lending period, you are required to delete and/or destroy any and all copies of the Content."

251. See Classen, *supra* note 3, at 276, suggesting an amount equal to two month's service or subscription fee as a "termination fee" when termination is without cause by the licensee.

252. Though it could be argued that the restriction of first-sale rights in the statute does not apply to sales in the first instance: "unless authorized by the owners of copyright in the sound recording or the owner of copyright in a computer program (including any tape, disk, or other medium embodying such program), and in the case of a sound recording in the musical works embodied therein, neither the owner of a particular phonorecord nor any person in possession of a particular copy of a computer program (including any tape, disk, or other medium embodying such program), may, for the *purposes of direct or indirect commercial advantage,* dispose of, or authorize the disposal of, the possession of that phonorecord or computer program (including any tape, disk, or other medium embodying such program) by rental, lease, or lending, or by any other act or practice in the nature of rental, lease, or lending" (17 U.S.C. § 109(b)(1)(A)). Such use limits apply to "rental, lease, or lending, or by any other act or practice in the nature of rental, lease, or lending," but not to sales.

253. See 7 C.F.R. § 201.24 (Warning of copyright for software lending by nonprofit libraries).

▶ PART II

THE RANGE AND NATURE OF INFORMATION RESOURCE LICENSES THAT LIBRARIES ENCOUNTER

◀

▶ 5

ELECTRONIC SIGNATURES IN GLOBAL AND NATIONAL COMMERCE ACT AND THE UNIFORM ELECTRONIC TRANSACTIONS ACT

Read this chapter to understand the nature and legality of these license situations:
▶ Online contracting in various forms
▶ Federal legislation paving the way for online contracting
▶ State legislation that further legitimizes the use of contracts online

In addition to the license that a database or service vendor may present to the library, there may be occasions where library staff—or patrons, for that matter—come face-to-face with a license agreement. This is not to say that staff or patrons will negotiate for products and services with a vendor but, rather, that in the course of the workday (or, for patrons, during the information-seeking process), these individuals may encounter a website that requests users to agree to certain terms of use before entering or using the site. In a similar situation, staff members may be faced with this while downloading routine software upgrades that are again subject to acceptance of terms before installation can commence. These are all examples of the sorts of licenses that might be present in the daily interactions of the library. This chapter reviews the recent legislative developments that paved the way for the nature, scope, and occurrences of such licenses, as well as their legality.

In the past several decades, as online contracting has increased, questions were raised as to whether the statute of frauds concepts (discussed in Chapter 3) would prevent such transactions from having legal effect. For example, courts reviewing whether exchanges of e-mail correspondence could constitute a valid contract (offer, acceptance, consideration, assent, etc.) reached inconsistent results.[1] Uncertainty is a dangerous condition in the legal universe and never as important as in the galaxy of contracts. For example, use of consistent terms across contracts as well as consistent application of those terms offers predictability, which in turn results in some amount of efficiency.[2] This goal drove the development of early software licensing:

> Historically, the purpose of "licensing" computer program copy use was to employ contract terms to augment trade secret protection in order to protect against unauthorized copying at a time when, first, the existence of a copyright in computer programs was doubtful, and later, when the extent to which copyright provided protection was uncertain.[3]

With the advent of online contracting, concerns were only heightened, and as a response, both uniform and federal legislation was proposed and adopted that validates the online form of contracting by, in essence, codifying certainty—in other words, an online contract is not deemed invalid simply by its mere existence in that form, as some earlier cases had ruled. The goal of such efforts is to place formation practices in e-commerce on the same legal footing as the analog universe.[4] As a result, electronic records and signatures can have the same legal force as a paper record of the meetings of the minds and mutual assent (signatures).[5] This nondiscrimination concept is found in both state expressions through the Uniform Electronic Transactions Act (UETA), which was finalized and approved by the National Conference of Commissioners on Uniform State Laws (NCCUSL), and by federal so-called stop-gap legislation for those jurisdictions which have not adopted some form of UETA,[6] the Electronic Signatures in Global and National Commerce Act (ESIGN).[7] Similar legislation is also in effect in Europe.[8] There are differences between the state-based UETA, which contains more substantive rules regarding online contract formation, and the federal ESIGN, "rais[ing] significant interpretive issues as determinations must be made as to which state law provisions on electronic signatures and records are preempted (see that pre-emption issue again) by E-Sign, and which state-enacted UETA provisions 'supersede' federal law."[9] The state legislative route is preferred, with the federal ESIGN provisions operating as a stop-gap measure in the subject state (federal laws apply to all jurisdictions) until UETA is enacted in that state.

ELECTRONIC SIGNATURES IN GLOBAL AND NATIONAL COMMERCE ACT

The ESIGN federal statute indicates the circumstances under which an electronic contract should be presumed valid. In other words, the statute establishes a default presumption of validity for electronic transactions, contracts, records,[10] and signatures. The federal ESIGN statute prevents "a signature, contract, or other record relating to such transaction" from "be[ing] denied legal effect, validity, or enforceability solely because it is in electronic form. [A] contract relating to such transaction may not be denied legal effect, validity, or enforceability solely because an electronic signature or electronic record was used in its formation."[11] Even though ESIGN was enacted after UETA was proposed by NCCUSL, Congress chose to act "largely in response to urging by the high-tech and financial services industries, who were concerned by the amount of time it was likely to take before UETA could be truly adopted nationwide and by the continued problem of laws widely divergent from UETA."[12] A uniform law, to be truly effective, must be uniform across the states—and it must be enacted by all of the states.

ESIGN leaves other requirements of "writings" statutes, such as the statute of frauds or the substantive law of contract, untouched,[13] thus obviating the need to rewrite state statutes to achieve harmonization or make resort to principles of comity.[14] The legislation is broad in application, reaching all electronic transactions other than those specifically excluded.[15] The exclusions do not mean that such areas of law cannot be the subject of an electronic transaction, but that the federal law will not extend the presumption of validity to transactions "governed by" extant state law.

ESIGN does not require anyone to use electronic signatures or electronic records[16] "other than a governmental agency with respect to a record other than a contract to which it is a party."[17] In consumer transactions, use of electronic trans-actions is acceptable if the consumer consents through an affirmative act; that is, nonaction cannot constitute acceptance (e.g., "If you do not object, an electronic signature may be used" is not acceptable; rather, "Your submittal of this request indicates your acceptance to conduct this transaction in electronic form").[18] For the consent to be effective, the consumer must be informed of the option to refuse to use electronic modes and have the option to withdraw his or her consent (the procedure for exercising withdrawal and any fees that might be due if withdrawal is exercised), whether the consent applies to the immediate transaction at hand or to a group of related transactions, and the process for requesting a hard copy of the transaction and any fees associated with that request.[19] A library would not be a consumer (limited to products or services for "personal, family, or household purposes") under ESIGN; rather, acquisition transactions would be evaluated in the climate of business-to-business environs.[20] As a result, if the transaction is governed by UETA because the controlling jurisdiction has enacted the uniform law, "UETA will govern nonetheless because no provisions of UETA that are incon-sistent with E-Sign are implicated."[21]

ESIGN will preempt state contract law unless a particular state enacts qualifying legislation and UETA is so stated within that legislation as so qualifying.[22] Whether a state enacts UETA or some other form of electronic transaction legislation "consistency with E-Sign is the general requirement for states wishing to avoid federal preemption by E-Sign."[23] Though, oddly, and instead of stating that ESIGN preempts inconsistent statutes as does typical preemption statutes, such as section 301 of the copyright law discussed in Chapter 4, "E-Sign approaches the subject from the opposite direction setting forth the limited circumstances in which state laws will not be preempted."[24] The concept of state contract law preemption by federal law was introduced in Chapter 4.

There is a dearth of case law interpreting and applying ESIGN. An early circuit decision involving e-mail communication observed that the application of ESIGN would have resulted in a valid contract formation had the electronic communication occurred after the effective date of the legislation, but that ESIGN should not be applied retroactively.[25] In a somewhat more recent case, another circuit considered the "enforceability of a mandatory arbitration agreement, contained in a dispute resolution policy linked to an e-mailed company-wide announcement."[26] In discussing whether the e-mail announcement could be an effective vehicle for contract formation, the court observed that ESIGN "likely precludes any flat rule that a contract to arbitrate is unenforceable under the ADA [Americans with Disabilities Act] solely because its promulgator chose to use e-mail as the medium to effectuate the agreement."[27] The court concluded that the embedded link to the policy rendered the new policy unenforceable, yet the flaw was not due to the method of communication (electronic mail) but to the lack of reasonableness as to what would be the expected content of that electronic communication.[28] A similar result was reached in *In re Cafeteria Operators, L.P.*, where the court concluded that e-mails constituted writings as a result of ESIGN but the content of those writings was insufficient to establish the necessary meeting of the minds over the terms in dispute.[29] Other decisions reached similar results, concluding that e-mails, as would be arguably any other electronic means of communication, constitute a valid writing for purposes of the contract law.[30]

UNIFORM ELECTRONIC TRANSACTIONS ACT

Like the Uniform Commercial Code (UCC), UETA is another uniform law drafted by NCCUSL and promoted to state legislatures for adoption. Unlike the Uniform Computer Information Transactions Act (UCITA), which is discussed in more depth in Chapter 11, UETA received a warmer reception. Most states,[31] the District of Columbia, and the U.S. Virgin Islands have adopted UETA. The few remaining states often have adopted some legislation regulating electronic signatures. States are, of course, free to tinker with the proposed language of UETA, and several did. As a result, there is less uniformity than one might be led to believe,[32] though the underlying principle of removing the legal bias against electronic transactions is nonetheless present.[33] UETA does not require the use of electronic contracts but sets standards for validity and enforcement when parties choose to enter into an electronic contract.

Finding the Library as "Party" in UETA Transactions

As the scope note explains, "coverage is inherently limited by the definition of 'transaction.' The Act does not apply to *all* writings and signatures, but only to electronic records and signatures relating to a transaction, defined as those interactions between people relating to business, commercial and governmental affairs."[34] The law, as proposed by NCCUSL, does not impact substantive provisions of commercial law. Like ESIGN, its purpose is to remove barriers to online contract formation, but it does not attempt to influence in a legal way the nature or content of that contract; therefore, UETA is "minimalist and procedural."[35]

After section 1 indicating the title, section 2 (the body of the act) defines a series of terms. Again, for the library, finding its place in the company of either consumers or business is often an important categorization in contract law. Unfortunately, UETA does not define or treat a consumer any differently from any other party in its subsequent substantive sections. Under section 2(12), a person is "an individual, corporation, business trust, estate, trust, partnership, limited liability company, association, joint venture, governmental agency, public corporation, or any other legal or commercial entity,"[36] and a variety of transactions between those persons are covered: "an action or set of actions occurring between two or more persons relating to the conduct of business, commercial, or governmental affairs."[37] As a result, a library is treated as a person for the purposes of the enumerated transactions covered by UETA. Similar to ESIGN, UETA does not apply to the creation and execution of wills, codicils, or testamentary trusts, UCITA, and the UCC except for sections 1-107 and 1-206, article 2, and article 2A governing sales and leases and licenses.[38] States remain free to designate other exceptions.[39]

As with ESIGN, UETA does not require that electronic means be used in a given transaction.[40] Further, like ESIGN, parties under UETA must agree to the electronic nature of the transaction.[41] Parties under UETA remain free to refuse to consent, even if an initial transaction was undertaken in electronic form with consent. Moreover, this choice cannot be waived, for example, by a clause in a license agreement that requires the licensee to conduct all future transactions by electronic means.[42] Unless there is a specific limitation, the effect of other provisions may be varied by agreement.[43]

As with the application of basic contract concepts of consent, consent to contract through electronic means can be inferred by conduct, such as past practice, or by specific assent.[44] However, UETA recognizes that electronic agents can replace one of the parties. For example, when a person purchases goods from a website, the other party is not present but the seller's computing system processes the transaction at its various stages; it retrieves information about the product in which the buyer was interested, collects information from the buyer that allows purchase and delivery of the product, and offers mechanisms such as a click-wrap agreement for the buyer to assent to the terms of the transaction.

The same general statement for presuming electronic contracts and signatures to those contracts is expressed in section 7: "A record or signature may not be denied legal effect or enforceability solely because it is in electronic form. A contract may not be denied legal effect or enforceability solely because an electronic record was used in its formation. If a law requires a record to be in writing, an electronic record satisfies the law. If a law requires a signature, an electronic signature satisfies the law."[45] As the comment to section 7 expounds, the goal of UETA is to give credibility to transactions or to give parts of transactions, such as signatures, validity.[46]

Once the parties have agreed to conduct a transaction through electronic means, if the law requires "a person to provide, send, or deliver information in writing to another person, the requirement is satisfied if the information is provided, sent, or delivered, as the case may be, in an electronic record capable of retention by the recipient at the time of receipt."[47] Some sort of password mechanism for returning customers or patrons would be an acceptable example.[48] However, other provisions of substantive law remain unaffected.[49] Section 8, however, requires attribution—in other words, it requires that the parties can know one another's identity.

When errors occur, either person to person or between a person and an electronic agent, an "individual may avoid the effect of an electronic record that resulted from an error made by the individual" if there was no opportunity to correct the error and the individual gives prompt notice of the error and takes reasonable action regarding return or destruction of any consideration received in the absence of use or receipt of any benefit from the consideration.[50] This provision may not be varied by the agreement.[51] Where the error is not that of the individual but of the electronic agent, then "the conforming party may avoid the effect of the changed or erroneous electronic record."[52]

Use of Websites with Click-to-Agree Controlled Access

Where a transaction is conducted between electronic agents, there is likewise a presumption of validity: "A contract may be formed by the interaction of electronic agents of the parties, even if no individual was aware of or reviewed the electronic agents' actions or the resulting terms and agreements."[53] In a provision reaching the issue of assent in "click" scenarios between an electronic agent and an individual, such assent is valid if the "individual performs actions that the individual is free to refuse to perform and which the individual knows or has reason to know will cause the electronic agent to complete the transaction or performance."[54] The comment to section 14 reinforces the applicability (read: a valid contract is formed) of UETA to online click scenarios:

> On the other hand it may be possible that A's actions indicate agreement to a particular term. For example, A goes to a website and is confronted by an initial screen which advises her that the information at this site is proprietary, that A may use the information

for her own personal purposes, but that, by clicking below, A agrees that any other use without the site owner's permission is prohibited. If A clicks 'agree' and downloads the information and then uses the information for other, prohibited purposes, should not A be bound by the click? It seems the answer properly should be, and would be, yes.[55]

The comments suggest that UETA would apply to scenarios where there is no money exchanged but consideration comes in the form of access to information alone. The comment continues:

If the owner can show that the only way A could have obtained the information was from his website, and that the process to access the subject information required that A must have clicked the "I agree" button after having the ability to see the conditions on use, A has performed actions which A was free to refuse, which A knew would cause the site to grant her access—in other words, "complete the transaction." The terms of the resulting contract will be determined under general contract principles, but will include the limitation on A's use of the information, as a condition precedent to granting her access to the information.[56]

Websites that a librarian or patron accesses, clicking through a series of "click-to-agree" prompts to get the desired content as quick as he or she can, nonetheless represent agreement to be bound by the terms of use governing that information, even where the access is not presented within the trappings of an online purchases of physical products or other services.

Receipt of Notice and Other Rules of Process

Section 15 of UETA appears to adopt the mailbox rule: when an electronic record is sent that is properly addressed to an information-processing system the recipient has so designated for receipt of records, the record is capable of being processed by that system, and the record so sent enters that information-processing system.[57] An example would be the inbox of a recipient's e-mail account.[58] It is preferable to have notice effective upon receipt, not mailing, and to indicate the person and office where such notices shall be sent, the form of notice, and that a second copy of the notice be sent as well, often to the general counsel or legal department. An electronic record is deemed "sent" when the record in accessible form "enters an information processing system that the recipient has designated or uses for the purpose of receiving electronic records or information of the type sent and from which the recipient is able to retrieve the electronic record."[59] Another example of such a system would the e-mail server of a library.

As discussed, UETA is not necessarily "process" legislation alone. When enacted into state law, UETA may alter the existing contract law of particular states, creating, in some instances, two sets of rules for contract formation and substantiation: one for online transactions (UETA) and one for offline transactions (UCC, common law contract, etc.). Although the UCC, statutes of fraud provision or the common law in theory determines contract formation, including online transactions, certain aspects of UETA may impact the application of those formation rules. UETA section 8(a)—remember that as each state enacts UETA, the UETA section of the state will be assigned a numbering identifier consistent with the state's existing numbering mechanism—requires content be capable of retention at the time of receipt through printing out, downloading, and so on, by the recipient before the content can qualify as an electronic record. Content that was available on the website of the sender as "read only" without the ability to print or save would not be an electronic record.[60] An e-mail system would qualify; even a mass mailing to a list of identified recipients would qualify, but a bulk mailing to a system would not.[61] Under UETA section 15(a), a record is sent when received in the system of the recipient, assuming it is properly addressed or directed, the record is in a form that the recipient's system can process, and the record moves into a processing system that the recipient designates or uses and from which the recipient is able to retrieve the record.[62] Messages sent within an institution would not qualify because the record never left the sender's system.[63] Under UETA section 15(b), a record is received when the record is in a form that the recipient's system can process and the record enters an information-processing system the recipient designates or uses and from which the recipient is able to retrieve the record.[64]

Parties may agree upon different definitions of what constitutes "sending" as well as "receipt."[65] Barring no alteration in the definition, UETA makes clear that "an electronic record is received under subsection (b) even if no individual is aware of its receipt."[66] Further, receipt of an electronic acknowledgment of receipt does not mean the specific record has been received and read; in other words, the acknowledgment does not serve as a verification, but, rather, the receipt of the acknowledgment only "establishes that a record was received but, by itself, does not establish that the content sent corresponds to the content received."[67] In general, "the record will be considered sent once it leaves the control of the sender, or comes under the control of the recipient... the critical element when more than one system is involved is the loss of control by the sender."[68] As a result, parties may desire to determine the precise process for acknowledgment and the conditions under which one party may rely upon receipt or not.

THE IMPACT OF ESIGN AND UETA IN PRACTICE

Several cases demonstrate the interplay between enacted UETA provisions and existing contract law. In *Alliance Laundry Systems, LLC v. Thyssenkrupp Materials*,[69] the court observed that the UCC controls the substantive contract formation issue:

> The UCC, not the UETA, provides the substantive law that determines whether parties form contract... Thus, in the present case, if the jury determines that the parties' e-mails

were sufficient to form a contract, the UETA will not prevent its enforcement... Whether an e-mail signature constitutes the signature called for by the UCC is a question to which the UETA might be relevant...absent a statute of frauds defense, a contract formed by electronic means will be enforceable under the UCC even if for some reason the UETA does not apply to the transaction.[70]

Recall that UETA applies only if the parties have agreed to contract through electronic means.[71] In the absence of such acquiescence, a contract may nonetheless have been formed under existing principles of contract law, where that law alone would apply. For example, in *Crestwood Shops, LLC v. Hilkene*,[72] the court, in applying UETA to various electronic communications between the parties, observed: "The offer conveyed by email, and the acceptance conveyed by certified mail, constituted a valid contract to terminate the lease. The two documents satisfy the requirements of the Statute of Frauds. The March 17, 2005, email from Ms. Hilkene to Mr. Padon satisfied the requirements of the Uniform Electronic Transactions Act. Ms. Hilkene's email was a valid written offer."[73] As online "click to agree" transactions are now given presumptive validity, another result is that UETA may also place shrink-wrap and click-wrap licenses on a "firmer footing."[74] As this chapter discusses, different states have moved at different paces in validating online click, browse, and other forms of agreement. So, to this extent, the ESIGN legislation may place federal and state requirements in conflict. This would at least be true for those few jurisdictions that have not enacted UETA. ESIGN resolves this conflict in terms of its preemption provision. As with the copyright law, federal law preempts state law.[75] The impact for libraries and other online shoppers and website visitors is that federal ESIGN or state UETA will not prevent (or prevent such shoppers or visitors from dealing with the consequences of) contract formation in "click to agree" scenarios. The significant message of online contracting is to be "careful what you click for."

Unintended consequences may also result because within two other federal laws, ESIGN and the 1976 Copyright Act, there may be a conflict. Another unintended consequence of ESIGN, or UETA where enacted, occurs where, through online signature validation and subsequent contract formation, the terms of website use are enforceable and a website's terms condition use on the relinquishment of copyright ownership over content posted. This is not an uncommon requirement in some content aggregator websites. As explained by one commentator:

> E-Sign substantially alters the circumstances under which copyright ownership may be transferred. Previously, a purported transfer was invalid unless there was a piece of paper signed with wet ink by the owner of the rights being transferred. Under E-Sign, a "writing" need no longer be in paper form, but rather can be an electronic record such as an e-mail or a Web page on the Internet.[76]

While the concern for the library in online contracting is that the library or its patrons can now be bound by online click and other contracting principles underlying ESIGN and UETA, these laws can be useful to the library when its role is one of licensor. What's good for the goose is good for the gander, as the saying goes. The impact on libraries may be good or bad depending on the goal of a particular circumstance. Is the library establishing an online repository of scholarly writing by faculty or by presenters at lectures, workshops, conferences, and so on, hosted by it over the years? Does the library desire to facilitate patron interlibrary loan requests, e-reader downloads, or other transfer of content, and to allow patrons to access services such as the Internet or online catalogs (which may include the ability for patrons to contribute contents, e.g., reviews of items in the collection) through its website or other online interfaces? If so, ESIGN or UETA might facilitate the permissions processes surrounding the content or access, including patron click-to-agree services that describe the library's terms of use for such content or services.

SUMMARY POINTS

► UETA does not require the use of an electronic contract for transactions but sets standards for validity and enforcement when parties choose to enter into an electronic contract.
► As with ESIGN, UETA does not require that electronic means be used in a given transaction but indicates that such transactions are not invalid merely because the agreement is not in writing.

LEARNING EXAMPLES

► Example 5.1

Situation: The state in which your library is located has adopted UETA. Does ESIGN still apply?

Legal Analysis: No, ESIGN does not apply, as it is stop-gap legislation, applying or preempting state law only if the state has failed to adopted UETA or a statute that otherwise qualifies.

► Example 5.2

Situation: A librarian goes to a website and orders several items for the collection of the library using a click-to-agree purchase mechanism and submitting the proper payment documentation. Afterward, the library thinks better of the acquisition and recalls having browsed through the first few chapters of this book about contract requirements and the meeting of the minds. Since this transaction was conducted without a person on the other end of the order request, can the librarian claim that there is no contract and the library is not obligated to accept and pay for the items ordered?

Legal Analysis: No, this is a valid contract. This is the point of enacting ESIGN or UETA legislation: one cannot claim the contract is void or voidable merely because it takes place online or uses an automated agent. In a provision regarding the issue of assent in "click" scenarios between an electronic agent and an individual, such agreements are valid if the "individual performs actions that the individual is free to refuse to perform and which the individual knows or has reason to know will cause the electronic agent to complete the transaction or performance."[77] Of course, the librarian may be able to return the items depending on the terms of the transactions. (Remember to read the terms of purchase before you "click to agree to these terms" or "click to indicate you have reviewed our terms of purchase and return policy"!)

ENDNOTES

1. Compare, Shattuck v. Klotzbach, 14 Mass. L. Rptr. 360, at *9 (Mass. Super. Ct. 2001): "Finally, the multiple e-mails demonstrate the parties to the sale, to wit the plaintiff and the defendants. Thus, a reasonable trier of fact could conclude that the parties had formed an agreement as to the essential terms of a land sale contract; the parties, the locus, the nature of the transaction, and the purchase price"; Rosenfeld v. Zerneck, 4 Misc. 3d 193, 194 and 195–196 (Sup. Ct. 2004): "A great deal can be accomplished over the Internet: A few well placed keystrokes can send us to exotic places, requisition goods and services, find employment and educate us. Is it possible to make a contract for the sale of real property via e-mail? . . . This court holds that the sender's act of typing his name at the bottom of the e-mail manifested his intention to authenticate this transmission for statute of frauds purposes and the copy of the e-mail in question submitted as evidence by the defendant constitutes a sufficient demonstration of same"; and Bazak International Corp. v. Tarrant Apparel Group, 378 F. Supp. 2d 377, 382 (S.D.N.Y. 2005): "First, Tarrant contends that the alleged contract violates the Statute of Frauds. Specifically, Tarrant argues both that the October 3 e-mail does not fulfill the 'merchant's exception' requirements and that the Exhibit 3 letter cannot be admitted as evidence of an alternative writing. The Court disagrees, and finds that the October 3 e-mail satisfies the New York Uniform Commercial Code Statutory requirements that present questions of law"; with Hugh Symons Group v. Motorola, Inc., 292 F.3d 466, 470 (5th Cir. 2002): "Read in full, the email does not confirm any such agreement. At best, it can be read as preliminary information being exchanged between parties, one of whom is developing a product not yet in production. There is no language expressing or contemplating a final agreement or settling on terms; it is an overture to further joint discussion or ongoing negotiations, not a binding agreement," cert. denied, 537 U.S. 950 (2002).

2. But see Ryan J. Casamiquela, *Contractual Assent and Enforceability in Cyberspace*, 17 BERKELEY TECHNOLOGY LAW JOURNAL 475, 491 (2002): "Arguably, allowing parties to fashion the

terms and conditions of their transactions is more efficient and desirable than using the government to estimate the expectations of the parties." Contrast Niva Elkin-Koren, *What Contracts Cannot Do: The Limits of Private Ordering in Facilitating a Creative Commons*, 74 FORDHAM LAW REVIEW 375, 380 (2005) (Symposium, Law and the Information Society, Panel 1: Intellectual Property and Public Values): "Yet, identifying and locating the rights holder, and then negotiating a license with her is likely to be prohibitively expensive."

3. SoftMan Products C. v. Adobe Systems, Inc., 171 F. Supp. 2d 1075, 1083 (C.D. Cal. 2001).

4. Robert A. Wittie and Jane K. Winn, *Electronic Records and Signatures under the Federal E-SIGN Legislation and the UETA*, 56 BUSINESS LAWYER 293, 297 (2000), (the legislation achieves "legal parity" by "plac[ing] electronic records and signatures on a legal par with their paper and ink counterparts).

5. Andrew D. Stewart, *Navigating the E-Sign Nebula: Federal Recognition of Electronic Signatures and Impact*, 24 UNIVERSITY OF HAWAII LAW REVIEW 309, 312 (2001): "The law's primary effect is that it creates a nationwide standard which grants electronic records and signatures the same legal validity as paper documents and hand-written signatures."

6. Wittie and Winn, *supra* note 4, at 296: "By the time E-Sign was enacted in June 2000, eighteen states had enacted UETA and it was under consideration in eleven more."

7. Pub.L. 106-229, Title I, § 101, June 30, 2000, 114 Stat. 464.

8. See Directive of European Parliament and Council, on Certain Legal Aspects of Electronic Commerce in the Internal Market, Directive 2000/31/EC,-OJ-(2000); and Directive of European Parliament and Council, on Community Framework for Electronic Signatures, Directive 1999/-/EC,-OJ-(1999).

9. Wittie and Winn, *supra* note 4, at 297.

10. Mike Watson, *E-Commerce and E-Law: Is Everything E-Okay? Analysis of the Electronic Signatures in Global and National Commerce Act*, 53 BAYLOR LAW REVIEW 803, 809 (2001): "One of the most critical issues surrounding electronic transactions is the retention or records and their originality and integrity."

11. 15 U.S.C. § 7001(a). A detailed discussion of ESIGN is found in F. LAWRENCE STREET AND MARK P. GRANT, LAW OF THE INTERNET § 1.05[2], at 1-61–1-68 (2001, updated through release #19, December 2011). See also Jay M. Zitter, Construction and Application of Electronic Signatures in Global and National Commerce Act (E-Sign Act), 15 U.S.C.A. §§ 7001–7006, 29 A.L.R. Fed. 2d 519 (2008, updated weekly online).

12. Wittie and Winn, *supra* note 4, at 296: "In 1999, California became the first state to enact UETA, but only after making very substantial amendments to the official text of UETA" (*id.*).

13. 15 U.S.C. § 7001(b)(1): "This subchapter does not limit, alter, or otherwise affect any requirement imposed by a statute, regulation, or rule of law relating to the rights and obligations of persons under such statute, regulation, or rule of law *other than a requirement that contracts or other records be written, signed, or in nonelectronic form*."

14. Comity is a "practice among political entities (as nations, states, or courts of different jurisdictions), involving especially mutual recognition of legislative, executive, and

judicial acts." BLACK'S LAW DICTIONARY 502 (9th ed.) (Bryan A. Garner ed., St. Paul, MN: West Publishing, 2009), no pagination in Westlaw.

15. 15 U.S.C. § 7003(a) excepts wills, codicils, testamentary trusts, family law including divorce and adoption, UCC except for sections 1-107 and 1-206 and articles 2 and 2A. Subsection (b) indicates an additional list of exceptions including cancellation notices of utilities services or insurance (health and life), foreclosure, and product recall. One commentator has concluded that the legislative intent of the subsection (b) listing "was to prevent states from allowing electronic notices to suffice for [such] transactions . . . until Congress decides otherwise" (Watson, *supra* note 10, at 818).

16. See Prudential Insurance Co. of America v. Prusky, 413 F. Supp. 2d 489, 494 (E.D. Pa. 2005): "E-Sign Act does not require Prudential to accept electronic signatures."

17. 15 U.S.C. § 7001(b)(2). "This strongly suggests that governmental agencies are required to accept electronic records for filing and other non-contractual purposes," per Wittie and Winn, *supra* note 4, at 315, but later concluding, based on the legislative history as well as contrary provisions within ESIGN, that "the balance [is] in favor of concluding that electronic files maybe precluded by regulatory 'standards or formats' requirements."

18. 15 U.S.C. § 7001(c)(a)(A).

19. 15 U.S.C. § 7001(c)(1)(B)(i)–(iv).

20. 15 U.S.C. § 7006(1).

21. Watson, *supra* note 10, at 836. Using the example of a business purchasing office supplies online: "UETA will govern the entire transaction because all relevant provisions of UETA are consistent with E-Sign and thus avoid federal preemption" (*id.*).

22. 15 U.S.C. § 7002(a)(1). See Watson, *supra* note 10, at 822–824, arguing that, based on legislative history, adoption of UETA would still need to be supplemented by increased consumer protections contained in ESIGN though absent in UETA, discussing the "shall be preempted to the extent such exception is inconsistent with" proviso.

23. Watson, *supra* note 10, at 833: "UETA [Section 8] as approved and recommended is inconsistent with Section 7001(c) of E-Sign and thus UETA will be preempted with respect to the requirement for consumers to consent to electronic transactions that are otherwise required to be in writing."

24. Wittie and Winn, *supra* note 4, at 325.

25. Cloud Corp. v. Hasbro, Inc., 314 F.3d 289, 295 (7th Cir. 2002), referring to 15 U.S.C. § 7001: "That would be conclusive in this case-had the e-mails been sent after the Act took effect in 2000. But they were sent in 1996. The Act does not purport to be applicable to transactions that occurred before its effective date, and, not being procedural, compare, it is presumed not to apply retroactively," citation omitted.

26. Campbell v. General Dynamics Government Systems Corp., 407 F.3d 546, 547 (1st Cir. 2005).

27. *Id.* at 556.

28. *Id.* at 559: "Under the peculiar circumstances of this case, we cannot say that the e-mail announcement would have apprised a reasonable employee that the Policy was a contract

that extinguished his or her right to access a judicial forum for resolution of federal employment discrimination claims."

29. In re Cafeteria Operators, L.P., 299 B.R. 411, 418 (Bankr. N.D. Tex. 2003).

30. See, for example, Medical Self Care, Inc. ex rel. Development Specialists, Inc. v. National Broadcasting Co., 2003 WL 1622181, at *6 (S.D.N.Y. 2003): "Defendant has offered no reason as to why an e-mail should not be considered a writing for the purposes of enforcing a 'written consent' clause of a contract . . . Moreover, a decision not to consider an e-mail a writing is arguably foreclosed by 15 U.S.C. section 7001." Compare Seagate US LLC v. Cigna Corp., 2006 WL 1071881 (N.D. Cal. 2006), (denying motion for summary judgment), observing that in spite of 15 U.S.C. section 7001, "the phrase ['written notice'] at issue is ambiguous in the context of the [insurance] Policies," and as a result the "record should be further developed to determine the meaning of the phrase 'written notice'" (*id.* at *3).

31. The following list is compiled from Uniform Laws Annotated, Uniform Electronic Transactions Act, References, updated and available on Westlaw: Ala. Code 1975, §§ 8-1A-1–8-1A-20; Alaska Statutes 09.80.010–09.80.195; Ariz. Rev. Statutes §§ 44-7001–44-7051; West's Ark. Code Ann. §§ 25-32-101–25-32-121; West's Ann. Cal. Civil Code §§ 1633.1–1633.17; West's Colo. Rev. Statutes Ann. §§ 24-71.3-101–24-71.3-121; Conn. Gen. Statutes Ann. §§ 1-266–1-286; 6 Del. Code Ann. §§ 12A-101–12A-117; D.C. Official Code §§ 28-4901–28-4918; West's Fla. Statutes Ann. § 668.50; Hawaii Rev. Statutes §§ 489E-1–489E-19; Idaho Code Ann. §§ 28-50-101–28-50-120; West's Ann. Ind. Code §§ 26-2-8-101–26-2-8-302; West's Iowa Code Ann. 554D.101–554D.125; Kan. Statutes Ann. §§ 16-1601–16-1620; Baldwin's Ken. Rev. Statutes Ann. 369.101–369.120; West's Louisiana Rev. Statutes Ann. 9:2601–9:2620; 10 Maine Rev. Statutes Ann. §§ 9401–9507; West's Ann. Code of Maryland, Commercial Law §§ 21-101–21-120; Mass. Gen. Laws Ann. Ch. 110G, §§ 1–18; Mich. Compiled Laws Ann. §§ 450.831–450.849; Minn. Statutes Ann. §§ 325L.01–325L.19; Mississippi Code 1972 Ann. §§ 75-12-1–75-12-39; Vernon's Ann. Missouri Statutes §§ 432.200–432.295; Mont. Code Ann. 30-18-101–30-18-118; Rev. Statutes of Neb. §§ 86-2101–86-2116, Nev. Revised Statutes 719.010–719.350; New Hampshire Rev. Statutes Ann. 294-E:1–294-E:20; New Jersey Statutes Ann. 12A:12-1–12A:12-26; West's New Mexico Statutes Ann. §§ 14-16-1–14-16-19; Gen. Statutes of North Carolina §§ 66-308–66-308.17; North Dakota Century Code 9-16-01–9-16-18; Page's Ohio Code Rev. Code Ann. §§ 1306.01–1306.23; 12A Oklahoma Statutes Ann. §§ 15-101–15-121; Oregon Rev. Statutes 84.001–84.061; 73 Pennsylvania Statutes Ann. §§ 2260.101–971, No. 69 2260.903; General Laws of Rhode Island §§ 42-127.1-1–42-127.1-20; Code of Laws of South Carolina §§ 26-6-10–26-6-210; South Dakota Codified Laws 53-12-1–53-12-50; Tenn. Code Ann. §§ 47-10-101–47-10-123; Texas Bus. and Com. Code Ann. §§ 322.001–322.021; Utah Code Ann. 46-4-101–46-4-503; 9 Vermont Statutes Ann. §§ 270–290; 11 Virgin Islands Code Ann. 101–120; Code of Virginia §§ 59.1-479–59.1-497; West Virginia Code, 39A-1-1–39A-1-17; Wis. Statutes Ann. 137.01–137.26; Wyoming Statutes Ann. §§ 40-21-101–40-21-119.

32. The legal publication containing information on uniform laws indicates in the notes

to Arizona, California, and Wisconsin this caution: "While the Wisconsin [or Arizona or California] act is a substantial adoption of the major provisions of the Uniform Act, it departs from the official text in such manner that the various instances of substitution, omission, and additional matter cannot be clearly indicated by statutory notes." Uniform Laws Annotated, Uniform Electronic Transactions Act, References and Annotations, General Statutory Notes (2002), updated and available on Westlaw.

33. MICHAEL RUSTAD, INTERNET LAW IN A NUTSHELL 118 (St. Paul, MN: West Publishing, 2009): "UETA validates electronic signatures and records in order to remove barriers to electronic commerce."

34. Uniform Laws Annotated, Uniform Electronic Transactions Act, References and Annotations, Prefatory Note A: Scope of the Act and Procedural Approach (2002), emphasis in original; updated and available on Westlaw.

35. Uniform Laws Annotated, Uniform Electronic Transactions Act, References and Annotations, Prefatory Note B: Procedural Approach (2002), updated and available on Westlaw. See also F. LAWRENCE STREET AND MARK P. GRANT, LAW OF THE INTERNET § 1.05[1], at 1-51 (2001, updated through release #19, December 2011): "UETA is not intended to change the substantive legal rules that apply to commercial and governmental transactions, but instead, to promote the use of these transactions through electronic media. UETA sets forth only procedural requirements and does not affect substantive rules of law or general statutory contract law."

36. Uniform Laws Annotated, Uniform Electronic Transactions Act, § 2, Definitions (2002), updated and available on Westlaw.

37. Uniform Laws Annotated, Uniform Electronic Transactions Act, § 2(16), Definitions (2002), updated and available on Westlaw; see also § 2(16), Definitions, Comment to § 2 (2002), updated and available on Westlaw: "The term includes all interactions between people for business, commercial, including specifically consumer, or governmental purposes."

38. Uniform Laws Annotated, Uniform Electronic Transactions Act, § 3, Scope, Comment 7 to § 2 (2002), updated and available on Westlaw: "Finally, it is in the area of sales, licenses and leases that electronic commerce is occurring to its greatest extent today. To exclude these transactions would largely gut the purpose of this Act."

39. Uniform Laws Annotated, Uniform Electronic Transactions Act, § 3, Scope (2002), updated and available on Westlaw.

40. Uniform Laws Annotated, Uniform Electronic Transactions Act, § 5(a), Use of Electronic Records and Electronic Signatures; Variation by Agreement (2002), updated and available on Westlaw.

41. Uniform Laws Annotated, Uniform Electronic Transactions Act, § 5(b), Use of Electronic Records and Electronic Signatures; Variation by Agreement (2002): "applies only to transactions between parties each of which has agreed to conduct transactions by electronic means"; updated and available on Westlaw.

42. Uniform Laws Annotated, Uniform Electronic Transactions Act, § 5(c), Use of Electronic Records and Electronic Signatures; Variation by Agreement (2002): "A party that agrees

to conduct a transaction by electronic means may refuse to conduct other transactions by electronic means. The right granted by this subsection may not be waived by agreement"; updated and available on Westlaw.

43. Uniform Laws Annotated, Uniform Electronic Transactions Act, § 5(d), Use of Electronic Records and Electronic Signatures; Variation by Agreement (2002): "the effect of any of its provisions may be varied by agreement"; updated and available on Westlaw.

44. Uniform Laws Annotated, Uniform Electronic Transactions Act, § 5(b), Use of Electronic Records and Electronic Signatures; Variation by Agreement, Comment 4 (2002): "the Act expressly provides that the party's agreement is to be found from all circumstances, including the parties' conduct. The critical element is the intent of a party to conduct a transaction electronically. Once that intent is established, this Act applies"; updated and available on Westlaw.

45. Uniform Laws Annotated, Uniform Electronic Transactions Act, § 7(a)–(d), Legal Recognition of Electronic Records, Electronic Signatures, and Electronic (2002), updated and available on Westlaw.

46. Uniform Laws Annotated, Uniform Electronic Transactions Act, § 7, Legal Recognition of Electronic Records, Electronic Signatures, and Electronic Transactions, Comment 1 (2002): "the fundamental premise of this Act: namely, that the medium in which a record, signature, or contract is created, presented or retained does not affect it's legal significance"; updated and available on Westlaw. In addition, "evidence of a record or signature may not be excluded solely because it is in electronic form" (*id.* at § 13, Admissibility in Evidence).

47. Uniform Laws Annotated, Uniform Electronic Transactions Act, § 8, Provision of Information in Writing; Presentation of Records (2002), updated and available on Westlaw.

48. Rustad, *supra* note 33, at 120: "Passwords, for example, are a well-established attribution method . . . The attribution of messages between sender and receiver is a key feature of the infrastructure of online contracting."

49. Uniform Laws Annotated, Uniform Electronic Transactions Act, § 8, Provision of Information in Writing; Presentation of Records, Comment 1 (2002): "This section is a savings provision, designed to assure, consistent with the fundamental purpose of this Act, that otherwise applicable substantive law will not be overridden by this Act. The section makes clear that while the pen and ink provisions of such other law may be satisfied electronically, nothing in this Act vitiates the other requirements of such laws"; updated and available on Westlaw. In a similar vein, section 20 offers a severability clause: "If any provision . . . is held invalid, the invalidity does not affect other provisions or applications . . . and to this end the provisions . . . are severable."

50. Uniform Laws Annotated, Uniform Electronic Transactions Act, § 10(2), Effect of Change or Error (2002), updated and available on Westlaw.

51. Uniform Laws Annotated, Uniform Electronic Transactions Act, § 10(4), Effect of Change or Error (2002), updated and available on Westlaw.

52. Uniform Laws Annotated, Uniform Electronic Transactions Act, § 10(1), Effect of Change or Error (2002), updated and available on Westlaw. "If the error results from

the electronic agent, it would constitute a system error. In such a case the effect of that error would be resolved under paragraph (1) if applicable, otherwise under paragraph (3) and the general law of mistake" (*id.*, Comment 4).

53. Uniform Laws Annotated, Uniform Electronic Transactions Act, § 14(1), Automated Transaction (2002), updated and available on Westlaw.

54. Uniform Laws Annotated, Uniform Electronic Transactions Act, § 14(2), Automated Transaction (2002), updated and available on Westlaw.

55. Uniform Laws Annotated, Uniform Electronic Transactions Act, § 14, Automated Transaction (2002), Comment 2, updated and available on Westlaw.

56. Uniform Laws Annotated, Uniform Electronic Transactions Act, § 14, Automated Transaction (2002), Comment 2, updated and available on Westlaw.

57. Uniform Laws Annotated, Uniform Electronic Transactions Act, § 15(a)(1)–(3), Time and Place of Sending Receipt, (2002), updated and available on Westlaw.

58. "For example, within a university or corporate setting, e-mail sent within the system to another faculty member is technically not out of the sender's control since it never leaves the organization's server. Accordingly, to qualify as a sending, the e-mail must arrive at a point where the recipient has control. This section does not address the effect of an electronic record that is thereafter 'pulled back,' e.g., removed from a mailbox . . . the recipient's ability to receive a message should be judged from the perspective of whether the sender has done any action which would preclude retrieval." Uniform Laws Annotated, Uniform Electronic Transactions Act, § 15, Time and Place of Sending Receipt, Comment 2 (2002), updated and available on Westlaw.

59. Uniform Laws Annotated, Uniform Electronic Transactions Act, § 15(b)(1), Time and Place of Sending Receipt, (2002), updated and available on Westlaw.

60. "An electronic record is not capable of retention by the recipient if the sender or its information processing system inhibits the ability of the recipient to print or store the electronic record." Uniform Laws Annotated, Uniform Electronic Transactions Act, § 8(a), Provision of Information in Writing; Preservation of Records (2002), updated and available on Westlaw.

61. Uniform Laws Annotated, Uniform Electronic Transactions Act, § 15, Time and Place of Sending Receipt, Comment 2 (2002), updated and available on Westlaw.

62. Uniform Laws Annotated, Uniform Electronic Transactions Act, § 15(a)(1)–(3), Time and Place of Sending Receipt (2002), updated and available on Westlaw.

63. Uniform Laws Annotated, Uniform Electronic Transactions Act, § 15, Time and Place of Sending Receipt, Comment 2 (2002), updated and available on Westlaw: "For example, within a university or corporate setting, e-mail sent within the system to another to another faculty member is technically not out of the sender's control since it never leaves the organization's server."

64. Uniform Laws Annotated, Uniform Electronic Transactions Act, § 15(b)(1) and (2), Time and Place of Sending Receipt (2002), updated and available on Westlaw.

65. Uniform Laws Annotated, Uniform Electronic Transactions Act, § 15(a) and (b), Time and Place of Sending Receipt, (2002), updated and available on Westlaw.

66. Uniform Laws Annotated, Uniform Electronic Transactions Act, § 15(e), Time and Place of Sending Receipt, (2002), updated and available on Westlaw. "[R]eceipt is not dependent on a person having notice that the record is in the person's system" (*id.* at Comment 5).

67. Uniform Laws Annotated, Uniform Electronic Transactions Act, § 15(f), Time and Place of Sending Receipt, (2002), updated and available on Westlaw.

68. Uniform Laws Annotated, Uniform Electronic Transactions Act, § 15, Time and Place of Sending Receipt, Comment 2 (2002), updated and available on Westlaw.

69. Alliance Laundry Systems, LLC v. Thyssenkrupp Materials, 570 F. Supp. 2d. 1061 (E.D. Wis. 2008).

70. *Id.* at 1067, note 3.

71. Uniform Laws Annotated, Uniform Electronic Transactions Act, § 5(b), Use of Electronic Records and Electronic Signature; Variation by Agreement (2002), updated and available on Westlaw: "This [Act] applies only to transactions between parties each of which has agree to conduct transaction by electronic means."

72. Crestwood Shops, LLC v. Hilkene, 197 S.W.3d 641 (Mo. App. 2006).

73. *Id.* at 648, quoting the trial court. "Ms. Hilkene's March 17, 2005, email to Crestwood was a signed writing comporting with the Statute of Frauds. The UETA gives legal effect to contracts formed by electronic record, but its application is limited to transactions where all the parties to the agreement have agreed to conduct transactions by electronic means" (*id.* at 651).

74. See also F. Lawrence Street and Mark P. Grant, Law of the Internet § 1.03[4], at 1-37 (2001, updated through release #19, December 2011).

75. See Andrew D. Stewart, *Navigating the E-Sign Nebula: Federal Recognition of Electronic Signatures and Impact*, 24 University of Hawaii Law Review 309, 310 (2001): "The most controversial aspect of E-Sign so far has been its preemption mechanism . . . does not specify in detail the type of state law it preempts nor does it sufficiently identify its own provisions which may be preempted by state law . . . E-Sign only preempts state laws that impose writing requirements or limit legal recognition to electronic signatures created by a specific type of technology. Thus, E-Sign preempts state law to the extent necessary for accomplishing its goal of achieving nationwide legal recognition of electronic signatures" (footnotes omitted).

76. Jason J. Poston, *Upsetting a Delicate Balance: E-Sign's Effect on the Copyright Act of 1976*, 26 Entertainment and Sports Lawyer 1, 21 (2009). Using the example of a person who desires to post a short subject film on a content aggregator's website and agrees to the terms and conditions of the website: "Thus, pursuant to E-Sign, the statutory requirements under section 204 (a) of the Copyright Act are satisfied, and Jim's client transfers to the Web site her entire copyright ownership in the short film she created. She caused this result, probably unwittingly, by clicking 'I Agree' to the Web site's Terms of Use" (*id.* at 24).

77. Uniform Laws Annotated, Uniform Electronic Transactions Act, § 14(2), Automated Transaction (2002), updated and available on Westlaw.

▶ 6

NEGOTIATED AND NONNEGOTIATED LICENSES

Read this chapter to understand the nature of and differences between negotiated and nonnegotiated licenses:
- ▶ The array of nonnegotiated licenses used in personal and professional practice
- ▶ The positives and negatives of negotiated and nonnegotiated licenses

A distinction is made in the present discussion regarding licenses that are negotiable and those which are nonnegotiable. Nonnegotiable licenses are often called mass-market or consumer licenses. Software—including updates, whether obtained from a box at the store or downloaded from a website—is often subject to a nonnegotiated license. To an extent, this distinction is somewhat nebulous, as a license presented from a vendor or copyright holder might at first appear to be nonnegotiable but after inquiry turns out to be negotiable. Although the opportunity for an individual to negotiate a nonnegotiable license is almost nil (good luck contacting someone at iTunes to ask a question about a clause in its license, much less have the opportunity to negotiate over it), at times institutional- or consortia-level actors may have success broaching what initially appears to be a nonnegotiated license. In contrast, a typical negotiated license in a library setting is one that comes from a database or service vendor.

The most common content distributed through a nonnegotiated license is software and web sales of products or services, like airline tickets, hotel packages, and concert and theater tickets. The software can be obtained either by purchasing a physical package containing the software at a store (brick-and-mortar or online) or by ordering downloadable content online, in which case the user agrees to download the software over the Internet as a file attachment or from a website. If the item is obtained in physical form (regardless of the form of the store), the transaction is likely subject to a shrink-wrap agreement, where the terms are found inside the packaging of the physical "copy or phonorecord," to use the words of the copyright law in section 109, for example. For downloaded content, the terms may appear upon installation of the software, which courts have referred to as a click-wrap agreement, where assent is acknowledged by the user-installer clicking some sort of "I agree" prompt or icon. If the software is obtained through download, a click-wrap agreement may also be used to indicate assent with contract formation, the result subject to the terms so agreed or "clicked" to, whether read or not. This is typical in web sales of products or services. Online environments may also be governed by what some courts have deemed a browse-wrap agreement. This is a form of contract that courts have scrutinized, concluding on occasion that assent, and thus valid contract formation, did not occur. Shrink-wrap, click-wrap, and browse-wrap agreements are all forms of non-negotiated licenses. These various permutations and the implications of each are discussed in Chapter 7. Finally, though not a distinct sort of license, some agreements, and the uses the content or product is subject to, are what some commentators have termed as gag-wrap agreements.

In addition, access to a website may be subject to the terms of a license. In the specific context of website access, there may be no sale, but access is nonetheless conditioned on assent to terms of use, such as access to a social networking site. Though not used exclusively in the website context, the term end user license agreement (EULA) is used in this book to describe this context but is modified by the word *website*, indicating its specific application here (website EULA) and to distinguish it for those readers who might be more familiar with its general use in a variety of other licensing contexts, especially that of software.[1] For more detailed information on EULAs, see Chapter 8.

ADVANTAGES AND DISADVANTAGES OF NONNEGOTIATED LICENSES

The following Chapters 7, 8, and 9 discuss a number of nonnegotiated licenses that the library or its users may encounter. These nonnegotiated or so-called mass-market or consumer licenses can also be characterized as standardized licenses, in that the vendor offers its product (e.g., software) or service (e.g., access to a website) on the same terms to every taker. There is no opportunity for negotiation. This is not the same as a license with standardized provisions; even a negotiated license may have standard-ized clauses in it. As a result, such nonnegotiable licenses, depending on the circum-stances, may be viewed as adhesion contracts (discussed in Chapter 4). Recall, however, that this status alone does not make the contract void or voidable. Rather, the presence of an adhesion contract may mean that the circumstances are ripe for further analysis. A contract of adhesion might satisfy the procedural element of un-conscionability, depending on the jurisdiction (the other element being substantive unconscionability). Having said this, licensing standardization, whether part of a nonnegotiated or negotiated license, can have advantages as well as disadvantages.

Advantages of Nonnegotiated Contracts

There are several significant advantages of standardized, mass-market licenses. "[S]tandard-form contracting has advantages, even for consumers. Standard forms are ubiquitous precisely because they provide significant economics to businesses and consumers."[2] The first advantage is efficiency, from both licensor and licensee perspectives. If the time or other effort that would be expended in a given transaction is not expended by negotiating, drafting, and so forth, of terms, then that time and effort is available to be used elsewhere. Consistency is another advantage, as the licensor may use the same terms horizontally, across its other products and services, and vertically, over time, and of course with every customer. It is also possible that the terms may be further consistent across licensors, reflecting industry standards.

> Extra time and greater access to information are of no value to a consumer who is not inclined to use them. Despite the rational benefits to the consumer of the electronic world, and the elimination of social pressures, in the main, e-consumers are as unlikely to investigate and to understand the importance of the standard terms as their paper-world counterparts. Thus, courts must continue to be concerned that consumers unwittingly will enter into standard-form agreements that are primarily exploitative rather than mutually beneficial.[3]

Moreover, mass-market licenses often appear as shrink-wrap or click-wrap agreements, and the general enforceability of such agreements is also a benefit to commerce as both licensor and licensee proceed in the security of such legality.[4] At least from the licensor's perspective, certainty in terms of legal risk may be another benefit, as the agreement presented by the licensor has likely survived some measure of legal scrutiny, at least by the licensor's legal counsel.[5] "Yet, two things are clear. The first is that few contracts today entail elaborate bargaining over detailed terms. Second, enforcing standard forms is central to sustaining ordinary efficient business practice, a fact documented if by no other proof by the recurrent use of this format throughout all areas of business and commerce."[6] Many licenses in this category require that the disputes be settled by arbitration instead of what can at times be lengthy legal proceedings. From the licensor's perspective, and perhaps less so for the licensee, this may offer additional certainty of process. The legal construction of the agreement may also reflect the past experiences of the licensor or other licensors; in other words, the agreement reflects the current state of the law. These advantages can also represent the benefit garnered by use of standardized clauses in negotiated agreements as well.

Of course, the big issue is whether the terms as presented are at least as advantageous to the licensee who receives the terms "as is" as to the licensor who drafted and presents those terms. If this is so, then the standardization of such terms across agreements can result in significant efficiency, certainty, and so on. To an extent, this is found in negotiated licenses as well, in the use of boilerplate provisions. For example, most contracts contain a force majeure provision, suspending the performance obligations of parties for acts of God, yet such provisions may vary greatly from license to license. Chapter 3 provides examples of this, as do the sample licenses in Chapter 15. However, in this reality or possibility, as the case may be, lies the disadvantage of standardization, especially when found in nonnegotiated licenses. The mass-market license is characterized by a lack of flexibility through the inability to bargain over questionable or unwanted terms, and "[t]he cognitive perspective that consumers tend to adopt with respect to contractual risks makes it unlikely that many will take advantage of these new tools."[7] However, there may be occasions where a licensee may possess some degree of market power (e.g., a consortium or system of libraries or educational entities) so that what is presented as a nonnegotiable license to individual consumers is nonetheless negotiable.

Disadvantages of Nonnegotiated Contracts

With contract of license terms presented on a "take it or leave it" basis, without the ability to negotiate for changes, pure logic explains why licensors often present terms favorable to the licensor. "Mass-market licensors typically disclaim warranties, offering only the repair or replacement of the software disk or other media as the sole or exclusive remedy."[8] It may also be that a licensor using a standardized license at the outset may allow for amendments that nonetheless provide for some tailoring to the licensee's particular needs or concerns. Nonnegotiable licenses, as mentioned, may be ripe for abuse as adhesion contracts containing unconscionable terms.[9] Through one-sided drafting, the legal team of the licensor may attempt to minimize the permitted and maximize the prohibited uses, licensee obligations, and other terms to its advantage. Nonnegotiated or mass-market licenses often take away rights that the copyright law grants to users, such as those of the first-sale doctrine.[10] Licenses are not sales, so while access is allowed or possession of a physical item might be transferred, ownership of the item remains with the licensor—so section 109 does not apply, as discussed in Chapter 4. As a result, the use of browse-wrap agreements involves, from the licensee perspective, a weighing of the costs and benefits.[11] More interesting, a recent study of 500 online contracting agreements found that while it would be a costless measure to include terms favoring the licensor, because many consumers never bother to read the terms before clicking to agree, most agreements did not include a majority of what the investigator called the "negative nine": disclaimer of implied warranties, limitation of damage types (often excluding consequential damages), choice of law, choice of forum, limitation of damages (caps, often limited to cost of merchandise purchased), arbitration, class waiver, contractual statute of limitations, and waiver of jury trial.[12]

SUMMARY POINTS

► A distinction is made in the present discussion regarding licenses that are negotiable and those that are nonnegotiable. Nonnegotiable licenses are often call mass-market or consumer licenses.

▶ Nonnegotiated licenses have advantages: efficiency, in terms of time saved from drafting or negotiating, and legal consistency, in that the terms are the same from licensee to licensee. Thus, nonnegotiated licenses help to facilitate online commerce.

▶ Nonnegotiated licenses have disadvantages. An obvious one is the lack of ability to negotiate what is likely an agreement that favors the licensor. Many nonnegotiated licenses often also take away use rights that would exist under the copyright law if the item were purchased or limit remedies.

LEARNING EXAMPLES

▶ **Example 6.1**

Situation: A librarian is acquiring a software program to help with budgeting. The program is available for download from a vendor website. During the acquisition process, a screen of click-to-agree terms and conditions appears indicating the transaction is a license and that the software cannot be loaded on multiple work-stations. The librarian would like to have the program on both her desktop and her laptop. If the librarian calls the number on the website, will she be able to negotiate for both desktop and laptop rights?

Legal Analysis: Not likely. Such online click-to-agree transactions and downloads are nonnegotiated transactions. It is possible that if the library is part of a consortium representing a critical mass of users, this might persuade the vendor to negotiate, as this would still allow for a certain transaction efficiency (see previous Summary Points), but surely not with everyone who desired to obtain a copy of the software program.

ENDNOTES

1. L. J. KUTTEN, 2 COMPUTER SOFTWARE § 9:55 (database updated April 2012): "An End-User License Agreement (EULA), also known as 'tear open,' or 'box top' or 'shrink-wrap' license agreement is the document that purports to form a contract between the mass market software developer and end-user. Before the development of software distribution via the Internet, it was typically a preprinted form on the outside of the packing or on the envelope that contained the software."

2. Robert A. Hillman and Jeffrey J. Rachlinski, *Standard-Form Contracting in the Electronic Age*, 77 NEW YORK UNIVERSITY LAW REVIEW 429, 437–438 (2002), footnotes omitted. "In short, businesses standardize their risks and reduce bargaining costs by offering one set of terms to all consumers" (*id.* at 439, footnote omitted).

3. *Id.* at 485 (2002), footnotes omitted.

4. William J. Condon, Jr., *Comments and Notes: Electronic Assent to Online Contracts: Do Courts Consistently Enforce Clickwrap Agreements?*, 16 REGENT UNIVERSITY LAW REVIEW 433, 454 (2003): "The better view of this apparent conflict is that clickwrap agreements are prima facie valid when the user clicks 'I Agree.' Online vendors and consumers are generally bound by clickwraps. This general enforceability fosters online commerce by allowing both parties to properly arrange their online business affairs" (footnotes omitted).

5. See Rachel S. Conklin, *Be Careful What You Click For: An Analysis of Online Contracting*, 20 LOYOLA CONSUMER LAW REVIEW 325, 331 (2008): "online contracts can increase transaction costs as well, primarily in the form of uncertainty."

6. RAYMOND T. NIMMER, 2 INFORMATION LAW § 11.145 (database updated in Westlaw, November 2011).

7. Hillman and Rachlinski, *supra* note 2, at 495, footnotes omitted.

8. MICHAEL L. RUSTAD, INTERNET LAW IN A NUTSHELL 108 (St. Paul, MN: West Publishing, 2009).

9. Blaze D. Waleski, *Enforceability of Online Contracts: Clickwrap vs. Browse Wrap*, 7 E-COMMERCE LAW AND STRATEGY 19 (November 2002): "The end user has no bargaining power. With terms drawn by one side, there is a potential to favor the drafting party over the end user. While one-sided terms will not necessarily be unenforceable, terms that are unconscionable will not be enforced."

10. See Rustad, *supra* note 8, at 109: "Standard form licenses agreements not only reallocate the risk of software failure to the licensee, but usually also bypass the first sale doctrine of federal copyright law."

11. Hillman and Rachlinski, *supra* note 2, at 436, footnote omitted: "The consumer, engaging in a rough but reasonable cost-benefit analysis of these factors, understands that the costs of reading, interpreting, and comparing standard terms outweigh any benefits of doing so and therefore chooses not to read them carefully or even at all." See Conklin, *supra* note 5, at 341: "If the speed and efficiency provided by browsewrap outweighs the uncertainty it also instills, net transactions costs will fall and consumers will continue to demand online contracts at the same or increased rate."

12. Ronald J. Mann and Travis J. Siebeneicher, *Just One Click: The Reality of Internet Retail Contracting*, 108 COLUMBIA LAW REVIEW 984, 998 (2008): "Thus, we expected, retailers would almost always include the kinds of pro-seller terms that are standard for boilerplate contracts with consumers in other contexts. We were surprised to find that none of the nine clauses that we collected appeared in more than half of the contracts." Distribution of the nine clauses were as follows: disclaimer of implied warranties (49 percent), limitation of damage types (often excluding consequential damages) (49 percent), choice of law (40 percent), choice of forum (42 percent), limitation of damages (caps, often limited to cost of merchandise purchased) (22 percent), arbitration (9 percent), class waiver (7 percent), contractual statute of limitations (6 percent), and waiver of jury trial (1 percent) (*id.* at 999).

▶ 7

SHRINK-WRAP, CLICK-WRAP, AND BROWSE-WRAP LICENSES

Read this chapter to understand the nature and legality of these license situations:
- ▶ Items that are acquired by the library for its collection that are encased in shrink-wrap with the terms of use inside or on the cover
- ▶ Click-to-agree, or click-wrap, contracts that pop up during installation or before use of a product or service online
- ▶ Browse-wrap contracts that regulate access to website content

SHRINK-WRAP AND CLICK-WRAP

A nonnegotiated or mass-market license might govern the transaction when a person obtains a product where the item is packaged in a box or some sort of container. The box or container is literally wrapped by a thin plastic covering that is shrunk tight to fit snugly around the box or container,[1] thus the term *shrink-wrap* is used. Software licenses are often conveyed in this fashion. The significant characteristic is that the licensee does not see the terms until the plastic packaging around the box is unwrapped and the contents opened.[2] Of course, if the would-be licensee does not desire the product (or service) under the now-revealed terms, the item may be returned. These were the circumstances of the licenses in numerous cases involving the purchase of computers from Gateway, Inc.,[3] where the terms found inside the box upon arrival at the purchaser's home indicated that keeping the item beyond a certain time period or making a particular use of the item constituted acceptance of the terms.[4] "The main policy reason not to enforce shrinkwrap or clickwrap is to require producers to disclose their material terms before payment or delivery, if they want them to be part of the contract."[5] The cases suggest that unreasonable terms may be challenged on public policy or unconscionability grounds, should the licensor push the envelope of unfavorable licensee terms too far.[6]

A variation on shrink-wrap is a scenario where, rather than viewing the terms upon the opening of the box or container, the terms appear upon installation (of software, e.g., after it is taken out of the box and its discs, etc., are inserted into the computer of the licensee to begin use). This was the case in *ProCD, Inc. v. Zeidenberg*, the first decision to enforce a shrink-wrap license if not in fact by implication,[7] although the agreement in question might more accurately be called click-wrap, as the terms appeared upon installation, not by merely opening the package.[8] Some courts and commentators reserve the phrase *click-wrap* for circumstances of online contracting alone. Courts prior to *ProCD, Inc. v. Zeidenberg* had refused to enforce shrink-wrap licenses.[9] Since *ProCD, Inc. v. Zeidenberg*, courts have ruled shrink-wrap licenses enforceable.[10] However, there are still exceptions for those courts who view the contract as formed when the item is first ordered, considering the sale ("pay now") as completed, with the accessible-only-after-opening shrink-wrapped terms ("terms later") constituting an amendment for additional terms rather than initial terms that are merely provided later, as would be the sequence in a true "pay now, terms later" or rolling contract.

Courts have found the rationale of *ProCD, Inc. v. Zeidenberg* convincing,[11] but not all have found the event of contract formation over a sequence of events with terms available later. When the contract is complete upon order, then terms appearing later are not the original terms (as would be the case if contract formation occurred á la sequence, i.e., when the box was opened, terms viewed, and then the item kept for a specified time period) but are additional terms that do not become part of the agreement unless assented to by some express means or conduct. For example, in *Wachter Management Co. v. Dexter & Chaney, Inc.*, the Kansas Supreme Court, over dissent, viewed the software transaction as sale of goods under the Uniform Commercial Code (UCC) and the applicable Kansas provision requiring express consent of additional terms: "DCI argues that Wachter expressly consented to the shrinkwrap agreement when it installed and used the software rather than returning it. However, continuing with the contract after receiving a writing with additional or different terms is not sufficient to establish express consent to the additional or different terms."[12] However, the court distinguished the prior case law validating shrink-wrap by observing that those cases involved "consumers who did not enter into negotiations with the vendors prior to their purchases...the last act indicating acceptance of DCI's offer to sell software to Wachter occurred when Wachter signed DCI's proposal. Thus, the contract was formed before DCI shipped the software and Wachter had an opportunity to consider the licensing agreement."[13] Here, it was the interpretation the majority gave to the sequence of negotiations before the software and license was shipped that resulted in a different conclusion, that is, that the terms included in the shipment were additional terms, than that reached in *ProCD, Inc. v. Zeidenberg*[14] and not necessarily on the principle that "pay now, terms later" contracts approved in the *ProCD, Inc.* decision and its prodigy is not good law.

Ascendency and Development of Click-Wrap or Click-to-Agree Contracting

As transactions moved online so did licensing, where terms may appear during completion of the transaction or as the product or service is obtained, such as through download. Prompts appear that allow the licensee to view the terms of the agreement and to assent to those terms by clicking "I agree" or affirming some other prompt.[15] Thus, the term *click-wrap* is used to describe such agreements, whereas with shrink-wrap the licensee, without opportunity to bargain, finds the transaction wrapped in the terms offered by the licensor, and assent is found by a click-to-agree or other similar affirmative act, for example, click to process your request and then be bound by the price you find.[16] The legal analysis used in shrink-wrap scenarios is applied by courts assessing click-wrap as well.[17] Various courts have upheld click-wrap agreements as valid.[18] As will be discussed, "UCITA [Uniform Computer Information Transactions Act, covered in Chapter 11] seems to validate shrinkwrap and clickwrap terms first presented after payment and delivery."[19] For example, in *Adsit Co., Inc. v. Gustin*, the court observed that in order "[t]o complete a transaction, a user must accept the policy, the text of which is immediately visible to the user. The user is required to take affirmative action by clicking on the 'I Accept' button; if the user refuses to agree to the terms, she cannot engage in the transaction. The entire policy is essentially three short paragraphs—one-half of a page."[20] Suppose library staff, while compiling a series of bookmarked links to various reference sites or before cutting and pasting various background texts related to readers' advisory pages of the library website, clicked various "I agree" buttons before accessing and evaluating the pages. Is the library bound by these agreements? Some of the websites prohibit linking or deep linking or reposting of information contained on the site. Yes, the library must honor these agreements. "It is possible that your library is legally liable for any such contracts. A prudent approach for any library is to ensure that its staff members are fully aware of the library's rights and obligations with regard to entering into online agreements. Also, it is helpful to inform staff members that they may bear responsibility when online agreements are entered into by a staff member who has no authority from the library to do so."[21] Such clicks result in valid contracts not only in scenarios where items are purchased but also in other nontransactional web settings.

Law, including contract law, is a two-way street, in a sense, with its rules equally applicable to licensor and licensee, regardless of which role the library happens to fill in a particular circumstance. As a result, the positive implications of click-wrap agreements for libraries might occur in situations regarding patron access to network services and the codes of behavior that the library establishes to govern use of such services. These are often presented as a list of acceptable uses in cases where the policy listing such acceptable uses is presented in the form of a contract:

"I the patron agree to do the following...and not to engage in the following..." Where the terms of the policy are the "offer," the consideration for abiding by the terms is the access granted by the library to the computer workstation or the Internet. Where the assent to such terms is a "click to agree" button or other affirmative act, then it is arguable that an enforceable contract results. The library may then have termination rights whereby it can disable the patron's access to such services. As discussed in this chapter, these cases suggest that submission of a patron's library card number into an online screen box can also constitute assent if it is clear to the patron that "by submitting your library card number you agree to the terms listed," or words to that effect, making evident the consequences of such submission and providing an opportunity to review the terms. This scenario is discussed in Chapter 8 on website end user license agreements (EULAs).

BROWSE-WRAP (ONLINE)

A key component in an enforceable click-wrap is the availability of the terms prior to the click and a specific indication that clicking equals agreement to those terms.[22] The *Adsit Co., Inc. v. Gustin* court did not see this as a contract of adhesion, given both the brevity and simplicity of the terms in the click-wrap before it: "We also find that the contract was not an impermissible contract of adhesion because she was capable of understanding its terms, consented to them, and could have rejected the agreement with impunity."[23] Courts apply basic contract principles of notice of terms and assent to those terms. For example, where subscribers were required to scroll through the terms of an agreement section by section, with the prompt, "Please read the following agreement carefully" at the beginning and an "I agree" click required at the end before proceeding, a court concluded that proper notice was provided.[24] However, in some instances, terms were not as readily available and assent was not conditioned on a specific click. Courts developed a new concept to apply to these tenuous online variations of shrink-wrap and click-wrap agreements.[25]

If a party is not aware of a term or had no opportunity to become aware of the term and does not undertake any act of assent, there is no contract. "As we have seen, standards for forming a contract concentrate on whether there are objective indicia (manifestations) of assent. In the typical online environment, assent to a contract entails assent to terms of a standard form set out by the site owner or product vendor. The assent issue involves whether the site user or product purchaser assented to the terms."[26] Where there is no manifestation of assent, courts will not hold the party to terms to which it did not agree. In *A.V. v. iParadigms, Ltd.*, the court commented that "the Usage Policy is not binding on Plaintiffs as an independent contract because Plaintiffs did not assent to the Usage Policy...In this case, there is no evidence that Plaintiffs assented to the terms of the Usage Policy. There is no evidence that Plaintiffs viewed or read the Usage Policy and there is no evidence that Plaintiffs ever clicked on the link or were ever directed by the Turnitin system to view the Usage Policy. There is no evidence to impute knowledge of the terms of the Usage Policy to Plaintiffs."[27] A similar result was reached in *Williams v. America Online, Inc.* where the terms could not be viewed until after the agreement click, and the court concluded that meaningful assent could not be given to terms that could not be viewed.[28] This reasoning sounds logical, but some licensors have attempted to push the envelope of the concept of meeting of the minds by disguising the consequences of clicks that are less obvious than "I agree" but nonetheless have sought to read agreement to enter into a contract by that click. Courts conclude that these scenarios do not result in valid contracts. The incidence of the contractual prerequisites of offer and acceptance of terms are simply too tenuous. Such attempts at valid licensing are termed by the courts as browse-wrap agreements.

One characteristic of a browse-wrap agreement is its occurrence exclusively in website settings. More important, browse-wraps are characterized by obscurity regarding the terms of the agreement—not because the terms are incomprehensible but because the terms are hard to locate or the site visitor did not think the terms should be consulted as an impending agreement was not apparent. Obscurity then is present not only in the location of the terms but also in the mechanism of assent.[29] Often the terms do not appear in conjunction with an assent mechanism. Unlike a scenario of "click here to see the terms" together with "click here to agree to the terms," the visitor (and prospective licensee) is required to move to some other portion of the website without an indication that in fact there are terms to view, or that use of the site is governed by such terms, or that the terms appear only after the user scrolls several screens forward. Second, the assent mechanism itself is obscure. Rather than a precise pronouncement of assent ("To agree to these terms, click here"), the licensor conditions assent on some other act, such as some use of the website ("By continuing to the next page you agree to be bound by the terms"), but there is no acknowledgment mechanism for the site user to indicate that he or she is aware of that condition. It should be no surprise that the validity of browse-wrap agreements has been met with great scrutiny by the courts.

One of the earliest cases to use the term *browse-wrap* was *Pollstar v. Gigmania Ltd.*,[30] where the court identified the common trait of a browse-wrap, the disassociation of the terms from the place of assent:

> This license agreement is not set forth on the homepage but is on a different web page that is linked to the homepage. However, the visitor is alerted to the fact that "use is subject to license agreement" because of the notice in small gray print on gray background. Since the text is not underlined, a common Internet practice to show an active link, many users presumably are not aware that the license agreement is linked to the

homepage. In addition, the homepage also has small blue text which when clicked on, does not link to another page. This may confuse visitors who may then think that all colored small text, regardless of color, do not link the homepage to a different web page.[31]

Where terms appear on another part of the website without a clear indication of assent to those terms, other courts have found incomplete contract formation.

The 2nd Circuit came to a similar result in *Specht v. Netscape, Inc.*:

> Principally, we are asked to determine whether plaintiffs-appellees ("plaintiffs"), by acting upon defendants' invitation to download free software made available on defendants' webpage, agreed to be bound by the software's license terms (which included the arbitration clause at issue), even though plaintiffs could not have learned of the existence of those terms unless, prior to executing the download, they had scrolled down the webpage to a screen located below the download button.[32]

Under these circumstances, the court concluded that "a reasonably prudent Internet user in circumstances such as these would not have known or learned of the existence of the license terms before responding to defendants' invitation to download the free software, and that defendants therefore did not provide reasonable notice of the license terms. In consequence, plaintiffs' bare act of downloading the software did not unambiguously manifest assent to the arbitration provision contained in the license terms."[33] In contrast, a scenario where the website visitor is forced to scroll through text, even if several screens' worth, and then click on an "I agree" button would constitute adequate notice:

> However, the record demonstrates that the forum selection clause was stated clearly in the registration agreement. By the very nature of the electronic format of the contract, Barnett had to scroll through that portion of the contract containing the forum selection clause before he accepted its terms. Therefore, he had an adequate opportunity to read and understand the forum selection clause. Parties to a written contract have the obligation to read what they sign; and, absent actual or constructive fraud, not shown to be present here, they are not excused from the consequences attendant upon a failure to read the contract. The same rule applies to contracts which appear in an electronic format. It was Barnett's responsibility to read the electronically-presented contract, and he cannot complain if he did not do so.[34]

Likewise, in *Defontes v. Dell Computer Corp.*, the licensee was provided "the opportunity to read the terms and conditions on three separate occasions, one of which was in the form of a browsewrap agreement. Specifically, Plaintiffs could have viewed the terms via a hyperlink, inconspicuously located at the bottom of the webpage. [The court observed that as] in *Specht*, this was not sufficient to put Plaintiffs on notice of the terms and conditions of the sale of the computer. As a result, the browsewrap agreement found on Dell's webpage cannot bind the parties to the arbitration agreement."[35] And in *Pollstar v. Gigmania, Ltd.*, the inconspicuous, almost purposeful disguising of the terms provided insufficient notice to users of the website: "Gigmania contends that the breach of contract claim fails as a matter of law because Pollstar cannot allege the required contract element of mutual consent. Viewing the web site, the court agrees with the defendant that many visitors to the site may not be aware of the license agreement. Notice of the license agreement is provided by small gray text on a gray background."[36] A similar comment was offered in *Ticketmaster Corp. v. Tickets.com, Inc.*[37]

According to Nimmer, *Specht* is not the trend but the anomaly:

> *Specht* was a unique setting in many respects, including in the fact that the free availability of the software without charge failed to suggest any reason to expect that contractual assent was being required. In contrast to the unique situation in *Specht*, many cases have held that contracts are formed by clicking on a screen item indicated to show assent to a contract and that, when the circumstances clearly indicate that contract terms are being required, mere downloading without any further explicit indications of assent suffice.[38]

Nonetheless, courts find browse-wrap agreements problematic because the basic requirement of contract (mutual assent, which requires terms and clear assent to those terms) is stretched to the limits of legal reason.

In *Jesmer v. Retail Magic, Inc.*, the court concluded:

> Nonetheless, the DLA [Digital Licensing Agreement governing a computer system] is not enforceable here because Jesmer did not have the opportunity to read or assent to it. Although the fact that Jesmer did not actually read the DLA is not necessarily dispositive, an end user must be given the opportunity to view the DLA, a circumstance which was not established here. The DLA never appeared on First Americans' computer screens either before or after Auto-Star's POS system was installed. First Americans never expressly agreed to the DLA, never authorized Magic to agree to the DLA on its behalf, and did not know of its existence until raised by Auto-Star in this action.[39]

The significant characteristic of browse-wrap, which makes such agreements problematic from a contract-formation perspective, is that unlike a click-wrap, where the licensee cannot proceed without clicking "I have read the terms and I agree" or words to that effect, under browse-wrap, the licensee can proceed without ever having the opportunity to view the terms, much less agree to those terms once viewed. Disputes arise when the licensor nonetheless claims the other party is bound by the terms through contract formation. While some might consider it overkill, the clearest form of online contract requires two clicks (consider, e.g., typical sites for purchasing airline or theater tickets): one acknowledging that the user has read the terms ("I have read the terms"), and the second confirming that the user wants to make a purchase or otherwise proceed subject to those terms.

As the concept of a browse-wrap is still developing, there is no definition that fits all scenarios. Some courts use the term in the pejorative, while others appear to adhere to the characteristics of hidden terms and imprecise assent. In *Fiser v. Dell Computer Corp.*, the court offered a good assessment of variation within the browse-wrap concept, placing those browse-wrap scenarios with less conspicuous terms on the unenforceable end (in terms of contract formation and binding terms) and those browse-wrap scenarios with conspicuous terms on the other, enforceable end of the continuum:

> In a browse-wrap agreement, a potential customer has the terms and conditions available, but is never required to indicate acceptance of such terms by any positive action. In a click-or shrink-wrap agreement, there is the requirement of positive action. While the courts in *Specht*[40] would not allow the virtually hidden hyperlink to indicate assent to the terms and conditions contained therein, other courts have affirmed the existence of a contract based on terms and conditions contained in hyperlinks that it found to be more conspicuous and that were repeated multiple times.[41]

Unfortunately for the licensee, the online component of the transaction was accompanied by superseding print terms so, in the end, adequate notice of terms and assent were present nonetheless.[42] A similar pattern of repeat use doomed Tickets.com, Inc. in a dispute over use of concert and other event information on the Ticketmaster Corporation and Ticket Online-CitySearch, Inc. website.[43]

Feldman v. Google, Inc. is an example of a browse-wrap (the court contrasted the agreement under review with that of the agreement from *Specht v. Netscape, Inc.*, and oddly referred to the *Specht v. Netscape, Inc.* agreement as a click-wrap) where the terms were conspicuous—or, at least in the court's view, conspicuous enough to be binding:

> The facts in *Specht*, however, are easily distinguishable from this case. There, the internet users were urged to click on a button to download free software. There was no visible indication that clicking on the button meant that the user agreed to the terms... The only reference to terms was located in text visible if the users scrolled down to the next screen, which was "submerged." Even if a user did scroll down, the terms were not immediately displayed. Users would have had to click onto a hyperlink, which would take the user to a separate webpage entitled "License & Support Agreements"... Through a similar process, the AdWords Agreement gave reasonable notice of its terms. In order to activate an AdWords account, the user had to visit a webpage which displayed the Agreement in a scrollable text box. Unlike the impermissible agreement in *Specht*, the user did not have to scroll down to a submerged screen or click on a series of hyperlinks to view the Agreement. Instead, text of the AdWords Agreement was immediately visible to the user, as was a prominent admonition in boldface to read the terms and conditions carefully, and with instruction to indicate assent if the user agreed to the terms. That

the user would have to scroll through the text box of the Agreement to read it in its entirety does not defeat notice because there was sufficient notice of the Agreement itself and clicking "Yes" constituted assent to all of the terms.[44]

The mechanism in *Feldman v. Google, Inc.* would not let the licensee proceed until he or she had acknowledged assent to the terms: "Unlike the impermissible agreement in *Specht*, the user here had to take affirmative action and click the 'Yes, I agree to the above terms and conditions' button in order to proceed to the next step. Clicking 'Continue' without clicking the 'Yes' button would have returned the user to the same webpage. If the user did not agree to all of the terms, he could not have activated his account, placed ads, or incurred charges."[45] Based on the description of the mechanism in *Feldman*, the case appears to be more a click-wrap, with the click coming after the user scrolled or browsed through the terms. The majority of browse-wrap cases appear to be those where it is not clear that terms of use are available, much less that a contract might be formed involving those terms.

In *Hotels.com, LP v. Canales*, the court observed that the circumstances did not meet characterization as a click-wrap or browse-wrap:

> The reservation page on the Hotels.com website, included as part of the record, required consumers to click on a button that said "I Agree to the Terms and Conditions Book Reservation" to reserve their room. Right above the button, the terms and conditions specifically provided, "By proceeding with this reservation you agree to all Terms and Conditions, [including] and all terms and conditions contained in the User Agreement." The User Agreement phrase was hyperlinked to the User Agreement pages. Additionally, the reservation page referenced the User Agreement three different times. The Hotels.com User Agreement cannot be neatly characterized as either a "click-wrap" or "browse-wrap" agreement.[46]

The court offered the following comment related to the notice of terms:

> In the present case, although the website does not require the consumer to actually open and view the User Agreement, the consumer must click "I Agree to the Terms and Conditions" which specifically state "by proceeding with this reservation, you agree to all Terms and Conditions, which include … all terms contained in the User Agreement." A consumer continuing the transaction had a choice to continue with or without reviewing the additional terms and conditions. By clicking "I Agree to the Terms and Conditions," the consumer presumably selected to follow through with the contract, consciously aware of the additional terms and conditions and their availability. If the link is sufficient notice of the arbitration provision for even part of the internet consumers, then Canales is arguably not a typical plaintiff of the entire class. If however, Hotels.com's User Agreement is found to be insufficient notice to the consumer, the User Agreement would be inapplicable and Canales would likely satisfy the typicality requirement.[47]

Because the trial court never undertook this analysis, the appellate had no choice but to reverse and remand.[48]

Likewise, in *Register.com, Inc. v. Verio, Inc.*, the court viewed the browse-wrap label as not quite appropriate: "While there are some similarities between Register.com's arrangement and a browsewrap license, we find the browsewrap label does not fit. Unlike the situation in Pollstar, no hyperlink is provided where one could view the proposed license terms. Instead, only upon receiving the WHOIS query results from Register.com's database is an end-user exposed to Register.com's proposed terms."[49] Where there is no opportunity even by browsing the website to view the terms, some courts have noted these instances do not involve browse-wrap. Unfortunately, courts have no new label for these cases. Nonetheless, a contract may still be deemed formed depending on the circumstances. "Verio does not argue that it was unaware of these terms, only that it was not asked to click on an icon indicating that it accepted the terms. However, in light of this sentence at the end of Register.com's terms of use, there can be no question that by proceeding to submit a WHOIS query, Verio manifested its assent to be bound by Register.com's terms of use, and a contract was formed and subsequently breached."[50] Here the repeat use of the website on numerous occasions contributed to the court's conclusion that Verio knew of the terms, though a first-time visitor would not be aware of the terms.[51] How many visits are necessary before such terms would be binding the court did not indicate.[52] Nonetheless, the 2nd Circuit concluded that even though Verio knew of the terms after repeated use, Verio rejected those terms, making no affirmative act to assent to the terms.[53]

Repeated commercial use of a website was also at issue in *Southwest Airlines Co. v. BoardFirst, L.L.C.*, where the court concluded: "This case resembles *Verio* more than *Specht*. There is no dispute that BoardFirst has had actual knowledge of Southwest's Terms at least since Kate Bell received from Southwest the December 20, 2005 cease-and-desist letter in which Southwest informed Bell that the Terms forbid the use of the Southwest website for commercial purposes. Despite having actual knowledge of the Terms, BoardFirst has continued to use the Southwest site in connection with its business. In so doing BoardFirst bound itself to the contractual obligations imposed by the Terms."[54] The lesson of these cases is awareness. Some websites may bury their terms of use or the terms may not be readily apparent. Be sure to seek out terms and, where difficult to locate, be more wary of submitting queries or performing other functions, as these cases demonstrate that some website purveyors seek to connect such processes with assent. Of course, the track record of these purveyors as litigants is not successful, but if zero risk or very low risk is a goal, it is better to be safe and avoid potential issues later. However, a message to view terms by accessing them through a hyperlink, if the message is clear, can suffice.[55] The implication for the library as licensor is that, when using click agreements, it is important to make sure the terms of use are readily available—and to make sure it is clear to users that by clicking "I agree" they are deemed to have agreed to those terms.

See Table 7.1 for a comparison of the elements of the different nonnegotiated licenses.

▶ **TABLE 7.1** **Comparison of Nonnegotiated (Mass-Market) Licenses**

License Type	Shrink-Wrap	Click-Wrap	Browse-Wrap
Legal definition	"The term 'shrinkwrap' license is used to describe the box-top license generally provided with the sale of software. Once the software package is opened the purchaser is presented with the license, and is supposed to then read and understand it. Once read the purchaser then has the option of accepting the conditions within the license by proceeding to use or install the software, or the purchaser may choose to reject the license and return the un-used software for a refund. The purported license attempts to limit the rights of possessors of the software by prohibiting copying and distribution of the software, and retains ownership of the software with the copyright holder." *Novell, Inc. v. Network Trade Center, Inc.*, 25 F. Supp. 2d 1218, 1230, at note 16 (D. Utah 1997).	"The type of contract at issue here is commonly referred to as a 'clickwrap' agreement. A clickwrap agreement appears on an internet webpage and requires that a user consent to any terms or conditions by clicking on a dialog box on the screen in order to proceed with the internet transaction." *Feldman v. Google, Inc.*, 513 F. Supp. 2d 229, 263 (E.D. Pa. 2007). "A click-wrap license presents the user with a message on his or her computer screen, requiring that the user manifest his or her assent to the terms of the license agreement by clicking on an icon. The product cannot be obtained or used unless and until the icon is clicked." *Specht v. Netscape, Inc.*, 150 F. Supp. 2d 585, 593–594 (S.D.N.Y. 2001), footnote omitted, aff'd. 306 F.3d 17 (2d Cir. 2002).	Compare *Hotels.com, Inc. L.P. v. Canales*, 195 S.W.3d 147, 155 (Tex. App. 2006): "[W]hat has been defined as a 'browse-wrap' agreement, that being an agreement whereby the user can download the software prior to manifesting assent to any licensing terms, and before being given an opportunity to view any terms or actually receiving notice of the terms"; with *Recursion Software, Inc. v. Interactive Intelligence, Inc.*, 425 F. Supp. 2d 756, 782, at note 14 (N.D. Tex. 2006), citation omitted: "Browsewrap licenses, however, are distinguishable from clickwrap licenses. A 'browsewrap' license is typically part of a web site—its terms may be posted on the site's home page or may otherwise be accessible via a hyperlink."
Negotiated or nonnegotiated	Nonnegotiated, visible terms.	Nonnegotiated, visible terms.	Nonnegotiated, available terms (but see "Format of presentation or delivery of terms").

(continued)

► **TABLE 7.1**   Comparison of Nonnegotiated (Mass-Market) Licenses *(Continued)*

License Type	Shrink-Wrap	Click-Wrap	Browse-Wrap
Format of presentation or delivery of terms	Terms may appear outside but more typically are inside the physical packaging (see "Event of contract formation" and "Legal interpretation by the courts").	Terms appear on screen during installation or online as the transaction progresses (see "Event of contract formation" and "Legal interpretation by the courts").	Terms often are not apparent or do not appear until after assent or other affirmative act (see "Event of contract formation" and "Legal interpretation by the courts") when the user continues browsing the site.
Event of contract formation	Contract formation occurs after payment is rendered and after some event occurs or conduct undertaken, e.g., using the product or service beyond some reasonable length of time: "Generally, in the shrinkwrap context, the consumer does not manifest assent to the shrinkwrap terms at the time of purchase; instead, the consumer manifests assent to the terms by later actions." *Register.com, Inc. v. Verio, Inc.*, 356 F.3d 393, 428 (2d Cir. 2004).	Contract formation occurs when the user clicks the "I agree" button or expresses a similar act of assent: "In short, i.LAN explicitly accepted the clickwrap license agreement when it clicked on the box stating 'I agree'." *i.Lan Systems, Inc. v. Netscout Service Level Corp.*, 183 F. Supp. 2d 328, 338 (D. Mass. 2002). See also *A.V. v. iParadigms, Ltd.*, 544 F. Supp. 2d 473, 480 (E.D. Va. 2008): "The Court finds that the parties entered into a valid contractual agreement when Plaintiffs clicked 'I Agree' to acknowledge their acceptance of the terms of the Clickwrap Agreement." Other acts can constitute assent if clearly labeled, e.g., "by submitting this request you agree to be bound by the terms . . . to see the terms click here." See *Register.com, Inc. v. Verio, Inc.*, 356 F.3d 393, 430 (2d Cir. 2004): "there can be no question that by proceeding to submit a WHOIS query, Verio manifested its assent to be bound by Register.com's terms of use, and a contract was formed and subsequently breached."[a]	Contract may not be formed as licensee was not aware of terms or did not understand that a particular course of conduct constituted assent to the terms. "Besides the fact that querying Register.com's WHOIS database is not a 'pay now, terms later' transaction or even a consumer purchase, access to Register.com's database, which is the 'product' that Register.com provides to end-users, is given *prior* to notice of proposed terms and an opportunity to review them." *Register.com, Inc. v. Verio, Inc.*, 356 F.3d 393, 429 (2d Cir. 2004), emphasis original, footnotes omitted.[b]

(continued)

▶ **TABLE 7.1**   Comparison of Nonnegotiated (Mass-Market) Licenses *(Continued)*

License Type	Shrink-Wrap	Click-Wrap	Browse-Wrap
Legal interpretation by the courts	"The recent weight of authority is that 'shrink-wrap' licenses which the customer impliedly assents to by, for example, opening the envelope enclosing the software distribution media, are generally valid and enforceable." *Peerless Wall and Window Coverings, Inc. v. Synchronics, Inc.*, 85 F. Supp. 2d 519, 527 (W.D. Pa. 2000), citations omitted. Contrast *Novell, Inc. v. Network Trade Center, Inc.*, 25 F. Supp. 2d 1218, 1230, at note 16 (D. Utah 1997), citations and footnote omitted: "Most courts that have addressed the validity of the shrinkwrap license have found them to be invalid, characterizing them as contracts of adhesion, unconscionable, and/or unacceptable pursuant to the U.C.C. A minority of courts have determined that the shrinkwrap license is valid and enforceable."	"A reasonably prudent internet user would have known of the existence of terms in the AdWords Agreement. Plaintiff had to have had reasonable notice of the terms. By clicking on 'Yes, I agree to the above terms and conditions' button, Plaintiff indicated assent to the terms. Therefore, the requirements of an express contract for reasonable notice of terms and mutual assent are satisfied. Plaintiff's failure to read the Agreement, if that were the case, does not excuse him from being bound by his express agreement." *Feldman v. Google, Inc.*, 513 F. Supp. 2d 229, 238 (E.D. Pa. 2007). See also *Register.com, Inc. v. Verio, Inc.*, 356 F.3d 393, 429 (2d Cir. 2004): "Essentially, under a clickwrap arrangement, potential licensees are presented with the proposed license terms and forced to expressly and unambiguously manifest either assent or rejection prior to being given access to the product."	Compare *Pollstar v. Gigmania, Ltd.*, 170 F. Supp. 2d 974, 982 (E.D. Cal. 2000): "Taking into consideration the examples provided by the Seventh Circuit—showing that people sometimes enter into a contract by using a service without first seeing the terms—the browser wrap license agreement may be arguably valid and enforceable"; with *Register.com, Inc. v. Verio, Inc.*, 356 F.3d 393, 430 (2d Cir. 2004): "In this case, submission of a single query does not manifest assent to be bound by the terms of use even though the terms themselves say otherwise. A party cannot manifest assent to the terms and conditions of a contract prior to having an opportunity to review them; a party must be given some opportunity to reject or assent to proposed terms and conditions prior to forming a contract."
Significant advantages	"There are many advantages of software shrinkwrap licenses. First, ultimate control and copy prevention are important benefits of shrinkwrap licenses. Warranties can also be readily limited or excluded under a	Same as "Shrink-Wrap."	"Speed and efficiency are particular advantages of browsewrap. The user can form a binding contract without spending any time proceeding through multiple screens or acknowledging contract terms. This is particularly

(continued)

▶ **TABLE 7.1** Comparison of Nonnegotiated (Mass-Market) Licenses *(Continued)*

License Type	Shrink-Wrap	Click-Wrap	Browse-Wrap
Significant advantages *(continued)*	shrinkwrap license. Retailers gain transaction efficiency and contractual predictability from using boilerplate license terms. Compared with other forms of protecting software, license contracts are quick, easy, and inexpensive. However, license contracts alone cannot protect the functional aspects of software from independent competition." Frank J. Pita, *Reconciling Reverse Engineering and Conflicting Shrinkwrap License Terms Under U.C.C. Article 2b: A Patent Law Solution*, 14 SANTA CLARA COMPUTER AND HIGH TECHNOLOGY LAW JOURNAL 465, 479 (1998). See also Robert W. Gomulkiewicz and Mary L. Williamson, *A Brief Defense of Mass Market Software License Agreements*, 22 RUTGERS COMPUTER & TECHNOLOGY LAW JOURNAL 335, 341–361 (1996): efficiency through standardization, informative of rights and restriction to those unfamiliar with rights under the copyright law, among others.		useful if the Internet user is familiar and comfortable with a website. If a consumer makes frequent purchases on a particular website, she may prefer not to scroll through the same terms and conditions before each purchase." Rachel S. Conklin, *Be Careful What You Click For: An Analysis of Online Contracting*, 20 LOYOLA CONSUMER LAW REVIEW 325, 330–331 (2008).
Significant disadvantages	"The disadvantage for consumers and competitors is that software vendors combine trade secret and license agreement protections to create rights far beyond those granted under patent and copyright	Same as "Shrink-Wrap."	"Because online users are notoriously impatient, one of the disadvantages of a clickwrap approach is the number of extra steps required in order to conclude an agreement and get to the point of sale." David F.

(continued)

▶ **TABLE 7.1**   Comparison of Nonnegotiated (Mass-Market) Licenses *(Continued)*

License Type	Shrink-Wrap	Click-Wrap	Browse-Wrap
Significant disadvantages *(continued)*	law. Additionally, typical license agreements impose restraints on software use that are not freely bargained for by the consumer." Frank J. Pita, *Reconciling Reverse Engineering and Conflicting Shrinkwrap License Terms Under U.C.C. Article 2b: A Patent Law Solution*, 14 SANTA CLARA COMPUTER AND HIGH TECHNOLOGY LAW JOURNAL 465, 479 (1998).		Scranton, *"Clickwrap" or "Browsewrap": Enforceable Website Agreements*, 119 BANKING LAW JOURNAL 290 297 (2002). "However, online contracts can increase transaction costs as well, primarily in the form of uncertainty. If an Internet user is wary of inadvertently accepting a hidden contract, or if the user knows contract terms are available but has difficulty finding them, the added outlay of time and effort could actually exceed that of driving to a store and forming a paper contract for a good or service. Asymmetric information between the parties also adds to transaction costs. This situation occurs when one party has significantly more information than the other, or when one party does not understand the information presented to it by the other party." Rachel S. Conklin, *Be Careful What You Click For: An Analysis of Online Contracting*, 20 LOYOLA CONSUMER LAW REVIEW 325, 331 (2008), footnotes omitted.

[a] *Register.com, Inc. v. Verio, Inc.*, 356 F.3d 393, 430 (2d Cir. 2004).
[b] Distinguishing a "query-first, terms later" scenario from a true "browse-wrap" license where terms are reviewable before assent: "While there are some similarities between Register.com's arrangement and a browsewrap license, we find the browsewrap label does not fit. Unlike the situation in *Pollstar*, no hyperlink is provided where one could view the proposed license terms." *Register.com, Inc. v. Verio, Inc.*, 356 F.3d 393, 429–430 (2d Cir. 2004).

SUMMARY POINTS

▶ There are several significant advantages of standardized, mass-market licenses, including efficiency, certainty of process, and equal rights for all users.

▶ There are several significant disadvantages, including a greater benefit to the licensor and no ability for the licensee to negotiate terms.

▶ Shrink-wrap: The box or container is literally wrapped by a thin plastic covering that is shrunk tight to fit snugly around the box or container, and, thus, the term *shrink-wrap* is used.

▶ One key component in an enforceable click-wrap is the availability of the terms prior to the click—acknowledgment that one has read the terms and a specific indication that clicking constitutes agreement to those terms.

▶ A characteristic of so-called browse-wrap agreements is their occurrence exclusively in website settings. More important, browse-wraps are characterized by obscurity regarding the terms of the agreement—not because the terms are incomprehensible but because they are difficult to locate or the site visitor did not think the terms should be consulted. Obscurity is present not only in the location of the terms but also in the mechanism of assent.[56]

LEARNING EXAMPLES

▶ **Example 7.1**

Situation: The library acquires a software package with the box wrapped in plastic. Other than a general description and promotional wording, there are no terms visible on the outside. Upon opening the box to remove and load the discs onto a public computer workstation, the librarian finds a license agreement inside with a provision indicating that keeping the software more than 30 days constitutes acceptance of the remaining terms of the agreement. An additional term indicates that the software is to be used for "personal use only" by "the purchaser" and may not be "further distributed." The library typically donates its used software to the local day care center after a period of use. What is the result?

Legal Analysis: If the library keeps the software longer than 30 days, the contract is valid, an example of "pay now, terms later" or rolling contracting. Use on a public workstation is prohibited by the personal use restriction. Further, the library on whose behalf the individual librarian purchased the software would not be able to use the public distribution rights granted to nonprofit libraries under section 109(b)(A)(1).[57] This is because section 109 applies only when the possessor of the item is also "owner of a particular copy or phonorecord lawfully made under this title" and recent case law reiterates that a license does not transfer ownership of the item.

▶ **Example 7.2**

Situation: Assume the same facts as in Example 7.1, except that instead of the terms printed on a piece of paper inside the box, the terms appear on the screen during installation along with a "click-to-agree" mechanism for acceptance of those terms.

Legal Analysis: This produces the same result as in Example 7.1; the contract is valid and prohibits the intended course of actions by the library.

▶ **Example 7.3**

Situation: A librarian uses a website with search capabilities. Next to the search box is the phrase "By processing your search, you agree to be bound by the terms of use for this site," with an additional phrase of "Click here to see our terms." The librarian does not click to see the terms but processes/submits a search nonetheless. One of the terms indicates that the website could download spyware and monitor certain future searching on the computer where the librarian was working.

Legal Analysis: The contract is valid and the spyware can be lawfully added to the library computer without seeking additional permission.

ENDNOTES

1. JONATHAN D. ROBBINS, ADVISING E BUSINESSES, § 8.6 (database updated in Westlaw, November 2011). Acceptances on the Internet: Click-wrap, shrink-wrap, and browse-wrap agreements (2006): Shrink-wrap "[s]oftware is commonly packaged in a container or wrapper that advises the purchaser that the use of the software is subject to the terms of the license agreement contained inside the package. The license agreement generally explains that, if the purchaser does not wish to enter into a contract, he must return the product for a refund. Failure to return the product within a certain period constitutes assent to the license terms." See also Robert Lee Dickens, *Finding Common Ground in the World of Electronic Contracts: The Consistency of Legal Reasoning in Clickwrap Cases*, 11 MARQUETTE INTELLECTUAL PROPERTY LAW REVIEW 379, 381 (2007): "The term 'clickwrap' evolved from the use of 'shrinkwrap' agreements, which are agreements wrapped in shrinkwrap cellophane within computer software packaging, and that, by their terms, become effective following the expiration of a predefined return period for the software (typically thirty days)" (footnote omitted).

2. Arizona Cartridge Remanufacturers Association v. Lexmark International, Inc., 421 F.3d 981, 987, at note 6 (9th Cir. 2005), emphasis in original: "Another variant involves 'shrinkwrap licenses' on software, which impose restrictions that a consumer may discover only after opening and installing the software."

3. Hill v. Gateway, Inc., 105 F.3d 1147 (7th Cir. 1996), cert. denied 522 U.S. 808 (1997), shrink-wrap license within shipping box is valid when activated by close of 30-day return

policy; Contra, Klocek v. Gateway, Inc., 104 F. Supp. 2d 1332 (D. Kan. 2000). shrink-wrap license within shipping box activated by expiration of 5-day return policy not valid; and Licitra v. Gateway 2000, Inc., 734 N.Y.S. 2d 389 (N.Y. Civ. Ct. 2001), refused to uphold arbitration clause on notice and public policy grounds.

4. See Licitra v. Gateway 2000, Inc., 734 N.Y.S. 2d 389, 390–391 (N.Y. Civ. Ct. 2001): "A contract results when the package is opened and the consumer uses the equipment for a specified period of time which is set forth in the written agreement. Courts have held that such a practice results in a binding contract between the parties."

5. Jean Braucher, *UCITA and the Concept of Assent*, 175, 184, in UNIFORM COMPUTER INFORMATION TRANSACTIONS ACT: A BROAD PERSPECTIVE (Stephen Y. Chow and Riva F. Kinstlick eds., 2001) PLI Intellectual Property Course Handbook #G-673. "Competition is impaired when buyers cannot easily compare deals before making purchase decisions" (*id.*).

6. Robert W. Gomulkiewicz and Mary L. Williamson, *A Brief Defense of Mass Market Software License Agreements*, 22 RUTGERS COMPUTER AND TECHNOLOGY LAW JOURNAL 335, 345 (1996): "Rather than relying on their own negotiating skills or knowledge of the relevant law, most users are better served by relying on the contract doctrine of unconscionability, the contract principle that agreements should be construed against the drafter, the copyright doctrine of misuse, consumer protection laws, and the intense competition within the software market to obtain advantageous terms in acquiring software." See also discussion in Chapter 4.

7. ProCD, Inc. v. Zeidenberg, 86 F.3d 1447, 1449 (7th Cir. 1996): "Shrinkwrap licenses are enforceable unless their terms are objectionable on grounds applicable to contracts in general (for example, if they violate a rule of positive law, or if they are unconscionable)."

8. See, for example, i.Lan Systems, Inc. v. Netscout Services Level Corp., 183 F. Supp. 2d 328, 329 (D. Mass. 2002): "You plunk down a pretty penny for the latest and greatest software, speed back to your computer, tear open the box, shove the CD-ROM into the computer, click on 'install' and, after scrolling past a license agreement which would take at least fifteen minutes to read, find yourself staring at the following dialog box: 'I agree.' Do you click on the box? . . . Is that 'clickwrap' license agreement enforceable? Yes, at least in the case described below."

9. See, for example, Step-Saver Data Systems., Inc. v. Wyse Technology, 939 F.2d 91, 102–103 (3d Cir. 1991); Vault Corp. v. Quaid Software Ltd., 847 F.2d 255, 268–270 (5th Cir. 1988); Arizona Retail Systems, Inc. v. Software Link, Inc., 831 F. Supp. 759, 763–766 (D. Ariz. 1993).

10. See, for example, Davidson & Assocs. v. Jung, 422 F.3d 630, 638–639 (8th Cir. 2005); Bowers v. Baystate Techs., Inc., 320 F.3d 1317, 1323–1325 (Fed. Cir. 2003); Meridian Project Systems, Inc. v. Hardin Construction Co., 426 F. Supp. 2d 1101, 1106–1107 (E.D. Cal. 2006); Information Handling Services, Inc. v. LRP Publications, Inc., No. Civ.A. 00-1859, 2000 WL 1468535, at 2 (E.D. Pa. Sept. 20, 2000); Peerless Wall & Window Coverings, Inc. v. Synchronics, Inc., 85 F. Supp. 2d 519, 527 (W.D. Pa. 2000); Adobe Systems, Inc. v. One Stop Micro, Inc., 84 F. Supp. 2d 1086, 1090–1091 (N.D. Cal. 2000); M.A. Mortenson Co. v. Timberline Software Corp., 998 P.2d 305, 311–313 (Wash. 2000).

11. Meridian Project Systems, Inc. v. Hardin Const. Co., 426 F. Supp. 2d 1101, 1107 (E.D.Cal. 2006): "The EULA is not rendered invalid merely because defendant purchased the Prolog software and then received the EULA after opening the package. There is no dispute that defendant purchased licenses to use various versions of plaintiff's Prolog software. Defendant had notice of the EULA, and the EULA was included in the box containing the software and the user manual. Defendant does not dispute that it had an opportunity to return Prolog to Meridian if it did not agree to the EULA, but did not do so. Further, defendant never objected or sought an amendment to the terms of the EULA. Under these facts, this is not an unconscionable contract or a contract of adhesion. Therefore, Meridian's EULA may be an enforceable contract."

12. Wachter Management Co. v. Dexter & Chaney, Inc., 144 P.3d 747, 752 (Kan. 2006).

13. *Id.* at 754.

14. *Id.* at 755: "Because the contract was formed before DCI shipped the software with the enclosed license agreement, the Software Licensing Agreement must be treated as a proposal to modify the terms of the contract."

15. Robbins, *supra* note 1, at § 8.6, Acceptances on the Internet: Click-wrap, shrink-wrap and browse-wrap agreements: "A click-wrap license presents the user with a message on their computer screen, requiring that the user manifest his consent to the terms of the agreement by clicking on an icon. The user cannot continue to view the website or buy the particular product unless and until the icon is clicked," footnote omitted. See also Dickens, *supra* note 1, at 381: "In such transactions, sellers have increasingly begun utilizing clickwrap agreements, whereby standard terms and conditions are displayed on the computer screen when the user attempts to access the seller's services. In a clickwrap agreement, the seller's terms typically pop up before a purchased software disc can be installed (CD clickwrap) or while a service is being requested on the Internet" (footnotes omitted).

16. See Rachel S. Conklin, *Be Careful What You Click For: An Analysis of Online Contracting*, 20 LOYOLA CONSUMER LAW REVIEW 325, 327 (2008): "Clickwrap agreements required the user to ask some manifestation of his or her intent to be bound by a contract after being present with that contract's terms, for instance by clicking a button labeled 'I agree' after viewing the terms." See also Scott J. Lochner, *A Legal Primer on Software Shrink-Wrap: Click Wrap or Click-to-Accept and Browse-Wrap License Agreements*, INTELLECTUAL PROPERTY TODAY (December 2003): "Generally, click-wrap license agreements are either (i) online (i.e., over the internet) license agreements that are used when copies of software are marketed and delivered electronically, or (ii) license agreements that are part of the initialization process that occurs during the loading of software on a computer. These license agreements for software are referred to as 'click-wrap' or 'click-to-accept' license agreements because the initialization procedure requires the customer to click on an 'enter' or 'approved' icon in order to signify acceptance to the terms of the software license agreement."

17. Lateef Mtima, *Protecting and Licensing Software: Copyright and Common Law Contract Considerations*, INTELLECTUAL PROPERTY LICENSING TODAY, SM049 ALI-ABA 81, 96 (October 5–6,

2006), American Law Institute, American Bar Association Continuing Legal Education Program, citations to cases omitted: "Currently the courts remain divided on the issue of the enforceability of shrinkwrap licenses. Some courts continue to find them unenforceable...In general, however, it seems that a shrinkwrap license is more likely to be held enforceable where (i) there is evidence that the user is aware of the license, (ii) there is concrete manifestation of assent to the license terms or a reasonable period of time upon which assent will be inferred, and (iii) it contains commercially reasonable terms, particularly where consumers are involved. In contrast to shrinkwraps, the courts have had less difficulty upholding clickwraps, primarily because these agreements typically require the user to indicate assent to the terms of the license before she can obtain or use the software. Whether a shrinkwrap or a clickwrap, however, a court could find an enforceable license overall but nonetheless make independent rulings as to the enforceability and/or commercial reasonableness of a specific standardized term."

18. Compare In re RealNetworks Privacy Litigation, 2000 U.S. Dist. LEXIS 6584, *6 (N.D. Ill. 2000): "The user can then click on the License Agreement, listed separately as either 'RealJukeBox License Agreement' or 'RealPlayer License Agreement,' depending on the product, and easily print out either agreement from the file pull down menu"; with Comb v. PayPal, Inc., 2002 U.S. Dist. LEXIS 16364 (N.D. Cal. 2002), arbitration clause found "procedurally unconscionable": freeze funds, prohibition of consolidation, $5,000 cost of arbitration, venue unreasonable. See also DeJohn v. The .TV Corporation International, 245 F. Supp. 2d 913, 915-916 (N.D. Ill. 2003): "The electronic format of the contract required DeJohn to click on a box indicating that he had read, understood, and agreed to the terms of the contract in order to accept its provisions and obtain the registration or reject the provisions and cancel the application. This type of online contract is known as a click-wrap"; Koresko v. RealNetworks, Inc., 291 F. Supp. 2d 1157, 1163 (E.D. Cal. 2003): "Plaintiff accepted the terms by clicking 'I agree' to the terms and conditions of the contract including the forum selection clause"; Stomp, Inc. v. NeatO, LLC, 61 F. Supp. 2d 1074, 1081 (C.D. Cal. 1999); and Regency Photo & Video, Inc. v. American Online, Inc., 214 F. Supp. 2d 568, 573 (E.D. Va. 2002).

19. Jean Braucher, *supra* note 5.

20. Adsit Co., Inc. v. Gustin, 874 N.E.2d 1018, 1023 (Ind. App. 2007).

21. LESLEY ELLEN HARRIS, LICENSING DIGITAL CONTENT: A PRACTICAL GUIDE FOR LIBRARIANS 107 (2d ed. 2009).

22. See Ronald J. Mann and Travis J. Siebeneicher, *Just One Click: The Reality of Internet Retail Contracting*, 108 COLUMBIA LAW REVIEW 984, 995 (2008). Mann and Siebeneicher place shrink- and browse-wrap agreements on a continuum. Starting with "pure browsewrap" and little likelihood of enforceability to "highest level of enforceability": "1) Pure browsewrap, with no language on any of the order pages that suggests agreement [88.0 percent]. 2) Statement that a transaction involves consent to a document that is neither displayed nor linked. [1.8 percent] 3) Statement, not adjacent to the "place order" button, that a transaction involves consent to a specified document that is not displayed

but is linked. [1.2 percent] 4) Statement immediately adjacent to "place order" button that transaction involves consent to a specified, linked document. [3.6 percent] 5) Pre-checked radio button that acknowledges acceptance of terms and conditions. [0.6 percent] 6) Radio button that must be affirmatively checked to acknowledge acceptance of terms and conditions. [3.0 percent] 7) Scrolling through contract terms required before purchase, with radio button. [1.2 percent] 8) Documents pushed to user at time of entering site or when registering, with registration being a condition to entering the order placement process. [0.8 percent]" (*id.*; percentages from Table 5, *id.* at 998).

23. Adsit Co., Inc. v. Gustin, 874 N.E.2d 1018, 1023 (Ind. App. 2007): "The entire policy is essentially three short paragraphs—one-half of a page. Moreover, the paragraph that contains the forum selection clause begins with the following heading, which is bolded and in all capital letters: 'AGREEMENT ON JURISDICTION TO DAMAGES.'"

24. Forest v. Verizon Communications, Inc., 805 A.2d 1007, 1010 (D.C. Ct. Ap. 2002): "Many consumers, though, presumably read the Agreement in a scroll box on their computer monitors, where only a small portion of the document is visible at any one time."

25. Robbins, *supra* note 1, at § 8.3, Acceptances on the Internet: Click-wrap, shrink-wrap and browse-wrap agreements): "As a general rule, courts are most likely to enforce click-wrap agreements, less likely to enforce shrink-wrap contracts, and less likely still to enforce browse-wrap agreements." See also Chrstina L. Kunz et al., *Browe-Wrap Agreements: Validity of Implied Assent in Electronic Form Agreements*, 59 The Business Lawyer 279 (2003): "Taken together, the decisions specifically addressing browse-wrap agreements do not provide a clear answer to the question of the validity of users' assent to the proposed terms... The shortfall in the browse-wrap case law and the lack of consensus among scholars has left attorneys in a quandary as to how to advise clients who want to rely upon—or already are relying upon—browse-wrap agreements to contractually bind the users of their Web sites or software, or clients who need to know whether they are bound by the terms of a Web site they may have viewed"; Drew Block, *News: Caveat Surfer: Recent Developments in the Law Surrounding Browse-Wrap Agreements, and the Future of Consumer Interaction with Websites*, 14 Loyola Consumer Law Review 227, 228 (2002): "Browse-wrap agreements are of questionable enforceability... because of their lack of one of the traditional elements of a contract, namely mutual assent between the contracting parties"; and Jennifer Femminella, *Note: Online Terms and Conditions Agreements: Bound by the Web*, 17 St. John's Journal of Legal Commentary 87, 91 (2003): "It is clear that [browse-wrap] agreements should be held invalid and unenforceable." Compare Robert A. Hillman and Jeffrey J. Rachlinski, *Standard-Form Contracting in the Electronic Age*, 77 N.Y.U. Law Review 429, 493 (2002): "Courts, therefore, should be willing to consider enforcing browsewrap"; and Dan Streeter, *Comment: Into Contract's Undiscovered Country: A Defense of Browse-Wrap Licenses*, 39 San Diego Law Review 1363, 1389 (2002): "Browse-wrap, when done properly, is no different than any other sort of mass market license, or any contract for that matter. If users are given proper notice that they are entering into a license, and if the terms are available for review, the license should be enforced."

26. RAYMOND T. NIMMER, 2 INFORMATION LAW § 12.33 (database updated in Westlaw, November 2011).

27. A.V. v. iParadigms, Ltd., 544 F. Supp. 2d 473, 485 (E.D. Va. 2008), affirmed 562 F.3d 630 (4th Cir. 2009).

28. Williams v. America Online, Inc., 2001 WL 135825, *3 (Mass. Super. 2001) (unpublished), AOL motion to dismiss denied: "Cass, who has more than 20 years' experience with mainframe and personal computers, owns and operates Cass, Inc., a provider of database and computer support services. In his affidavit, Cass describes in detail the AOL 5.0 installation process. He states that the alleged harm occurs before the user clicks 'I Agree.' He describes a complicated process by which subscribers 'agree' to the TOS after configuration of the computer has been altered. AOL sets the default for reviewing the TOS to 'I Agree.' A customer who merely clicks 'I Agree' is instantly bound by the terms of a TOS she has never seen. The customer's only other option is to click off the default and select 'Read Now.' That option also fails to provide a customer with an opportunity to read the TOS. A customer who selects 'Read Now' is presented with another choice between the default 'OK, I Agree' and 'Read Now'. Thus, the actual language of the TOS agreement is not presented on the computer screen unless the customer specifically requests it by twice overriding the default... Therefore, the fact that plaintiffs may have agreed to an earlier TOS or the fact that every AOL member enters into a form of TOS agreement does not persuade me that plaintiffs and other members of the class they seek to represent had notice of the forum selection clause in the new TOS before reconfiguration of their computers."

29. See Conklin, *supra* note 16, at 327: "On the other hand, the terms of a browsewrap contract are often inconspicuous or even unavailable to a consumer online; a contract is accepted by performance as the consumer continues to navigate the website or uses a product or service found on the site."

30. Pollstar v. Gigmania Ltd., 170 F. Supp. 2d 974, 981 (E.D. Cal. 2000): "No reported cases have ruled on the enforceability of a browse wrap license."

31. *Id.* The court was reluctant to declare by rule the invalidity of browse-wrap agreements: "While the court agrees with Gigmania that the user is not immediately confronted with the notice of the license agreement, this does not dispose of Pollstar's breach of contract claim. The court hesitates to declare the invalidity and unenforceability of the browse wrap license agreement at this time. Taking into consideration the examples provided by the Seventh Circuit—showing that people sometimes enter into a contract by using a service without first seeing the terms—the browser wrap license agreement may be arguably valid and enforceable" (*id.* at 982).

32. Specht v. Netscape, Inc., 306 F.3d 17 (2d Cir. 2002).

33. Specht v. Netscape, Inc., 306 F.3d 17 (2d Cir. 2002). "We conclude that in circumstances such as these, where consumers are urged to download free software at the immediate click of a button, a reference to the existence of license terms on a submerged screen is not sufficient to place consumers on inquiry or constructive notice of those terms" (*id.* at 38).

34. Barnett v. Network Solutions, 38 S.W.3d 200, 204 (Tex. App. 2001), citations omitted.

35. Defontes v. Dell Computers Corp., 2004 R.I. Super. LEXIS 32, at *17 (2004).

36. Pollstar v. Gigmania, Ltd., 170 F. Supp. 2d 974, 980–981 (E.D. Cal. 2000). "In the present case, Pollstar alleges that users of the concert information are bound by the license agreement. This license agreement is not set forth on the homepage but is on a different web page that is linked to the homepage. However, the visitor is alerted to the fact that 'use is subject to license agreement' because of the notice in small gray print on gray background. Since the text is not underlined, a common Internet practice to show an active link, many users presumably are not aware that the license agreement is linked to the homepage. In addition, the homepage also has small blue text which when clicked on, does not link to another page. This may confuse visitors who may then think that all colored small text, regardless of color, do not link the homepage to a different web page" (*id.* at 981).

37. Ticketmaster Corp. v. Tickets.com, Inc., 54 U.S.P.Q.2d 1344, 1346 (C.D. Cal. 2000): "Many web sites make you click on 'agree' to the terms and conditions before going on, but Ticketmaster does not. Further, the terms and conditions are set forth so that the customer needs to scroll down the home page to find and read them. Many customers instead are likely to proceed to the event page of interest rather than reading the 'small print.' It cannot be said that merely putting the terms and conditions in this fashion necessarily creates a contract with any one using the web site. The motion is granted with leave to amend in case there are facts showing Tickets' knowledge of them plus implied agreement to them."

38. Nimmer, *supra* note 26, at § 12.32, footnote omitted.

39. Jesmer v. Retail Magic, Inc., 863 N.Y.S.2d 737, 745 (2008), citations omitted.

40. Specht v. Netscape, Inc., 150 F. Supp. 2d 585 (S.D.N.Y. 2001), aff'd. 306 F.3d 17 (2d Cir. 2002).

41. Fiser v. Dell Computer Corp., 165 P.3d 328, 334 (New Mexico Ct. App. 2007), reversed and remanded by 188 P.3d 1215 (New Mexico 2008).

42. Fiser v. Dell Computer, Corp., 165 P.3d 328, 334–335 (New Mexico Ct. App. 2007): "In this case, we need not decide the outer reaches of what type of notice and assent is necessary to form a contract in a transaction consummated solely over the internet. That is because we hold that Fiser's conduct in keeping the computer after receiving the written terms and conditions constitutes acceptance of the terms contained therein . . . A consumer who purchases goods and is informed of the contractual terms when the product is delivered, and is given a specified number of days in which to return the product, is deemed to have accepted the terms unless the product is returned within the specified time period"; reversed and remanded by 188 P.3d 1215, 1220 (New Mexico 2008): "Thus, we conclude that Defendant's prohibition on class action relief, when applied to small claims plaintiffs, is contrary to New Mexico's fundamental public policy to provide a forum for relief for small consumer claims."

43. Ticketmaster Corp. v. Tickets.com, Inc., 2003 WL 21406289, *7–*8 (C.D. Cal. 2003): "Earlier in this case (and at the time of the motion for preliminary injunction) the notice

was placed at the bottom of the home page of the TM web site, so that a user without an especially large screen would have to scroll down the page to read the conditions of use. Since then, TM has placed in a prominent place on the home page the warning that proceeding further binds the user to the conditions of use. As one TX executive put it, it could not be missed. At the time of the preliminary injunction motion, the court commented that there was no evidence that the conditions of use were known to TX. Since then, there has been developed evidence that TX was fully familiar with the conditions TM claimed to impose on users, including a letter from TM to TX which quoted the conditions (and a reply by TX stating that it did not accept the conditions). Thus, there is sufficient evidence to defeat summary judgment on the contract theory if knowledge of the asserted conditions of use was had by TX, who nevertheless continued to send its spider into the TM interior web pages, and if it is legally concluded that doing so can lead to a binding contract."

44. Feldman v. Google, Inc., 513 F. Supp. 2d 229, 237 (E.D. Pa. 2006).

45. *Id.*

46. Hotels.com, LP v. Canales, 195 S.W.3d 147, 154 (Tex. App. 2006).

47. *Id.* at 156.

48. *Id.* at 157.

49. Register.com, Inc. v. Verio, Inc., 356 F.3d 393, 429–430 (2d Cir. 2004).

50. *Id.* at 430.

51. *Id.*: "In this case, submission of a single query does not manifest assent to be bound by the terms of use even though the terms themselves say otherwise. A party cannot manifest assent to the terms and conditions of a contract prior to having an opportunity to review them; a party must be given some opportunity to reject or assent to proposed terms and conditions prior to forming a contract."

52. *Id.* at 431: "Although the first (or first few) query submissions are clearly insufficient to create a contract for the reasons discussed above, repeated exposure to the terms and conditions (via repeated submissions) would have put Verio on notice of both the general terms and the specific term."

53. *Id.*: "We do not believe that one can reasonably infer that Verio assented to Register.com's proposed terms simply because Verio submitted multiple queries with knowledge of those terms. Verio (and every other end-user) may repeatedly submit WHOIS queries to Register.com based on an (accurate) understanding that Register.com does not own WHOIS information and that such information must be made freely and publicly available (with two specified restrictions) pursuant to the ICANN Agreement. Viewed in this manner, Register.com's repeated proposals that terms not authorized by the ICANN Agreement be adopted could reasonably have been repeatedly rejected by Verio. There is no basis to infer that Verio in fact assented to Register.com's mass marketing restriction."

54. Southwest Airlines Co., v. Boardfirst, L.L.C., 2007 U.S. Dist. LEXIS 96230, at *20–*21 (N.D. Texas 2007), reference to pleadings omitted.

55. Christina L. Kunz, *Browse-Wrap Agreements: Validity of Implied Assent in Electronic Form Agreements*, 59 BUSINESS LAWYER 279, 305–306 (2003): "Assuming that the terms are reasonably legible and presented on a timely basis, does the practice of disclosing contractual terms behind a hyperlink satisfy the 'adequate notice' test? Our conclusion, drawing from precedent addressing click-through and browse-wrap agreements and from analogous practices in the paper world, such as terms incorporated by reference, is that using a hyperlink to disclose electronic standard terms can satisfy the proposed requirement of 'opportunity to review.'"

56. See Conklin, *supra* note 16, at 327: "On the other hand, the terms of a browsewrap contract are often inconspicuous or even unavailable to a consumer online; a contract is accepted by performance as the consumer continues to navigate the website or uses a product or service found on the site."

57. See 17 U.S.C. § 109(b)(A)(1): "The transfer of possession of a lawfully made copy of a computer program by a nonprofit educational institution to another nonprofit educational institution or to faculty, staff, and students does not constitute rental, lease, or lending for direct or indirect commercial purposes under this subsection."

▶ 8

END USER LICENSE AGREEMENTS (WEBSITES)

Read this chapter to understand the nature and legality of access conditions in these situations:
- ▶ Enforceability of terms and conditions for use of websites in the absence of any monetary transaction
- ▶ Use agreements for social networks, chat rooms, blogs, virtual worlds, and massively multiplayer online gaming
- ▶ Click-to-agree mechanisms that can govern library or campus network facilities and services

WHAT IS AN END USER LICENSE AGREEMENT?

A library may be the provider as well as the user (along with its patrons) of online forums or other website spaces where there is no payment made, the service is not purchased, nor is a product bought. Rather, what is acquired is access alone and not in return for payment. Social network websites are often arranged this way. There may be no payment required to join or participate but nonetheless the membership and/or access to and use of the site and/or its contents are governed by terms and conditions. As one court observed regarding the use of MySpace:

> [I]t cannot be considered a stretch of the law to hold that the owner of an Internet website has the right to establish the extent to (and the conditions under) which members of the public will be allowed access to information, services and/or applications which are available on the website. [Citations omitted.] Nor can it be doubted that the owner can relay and impose those limitations/restrictions/conditions by means of written notice such as terms of service or use provisions placed on the home page of the website.[1]

Under what circumstances are the terms binding because a contract exists? The website or forum offers access to its online or otherwise virtual space[2] in return for an agreement (an acceptance of the terms offered) to abide by the use restrictions accompanying that access. Consideration can be found in the benefit of access to the content or service, and if some of the terms are covenants (promises), those terms can operate as consideration as well. Thus, all three requirements for contract formation are present; add assent to those terms through a click-wrap or click-to-agree mechanism and the site licensor is in business, so to speak. Thus, libraries, or educational entities for that matter, can be both licensors (offering access to their network or computing services) and licensees. Some virtual-world websites operate in this climate.[3] Governing the terms of use of such sites are end user license agreements (EULAs). Massively multiplayer online gaming is one example: "These EULAs allow too much developer discretion in enforcing their terms, preventing players from predicting what they can or cannot do and endangering player investments in time and money. These EULAs also fail to conform to players' reasonable expectations surrounding their rights in virtual property. To tap the potential of virtual worlds, developers should create EULAs that strike a better balance between their own needs and player expectations."[4]

It should be obvious that if a fee is involved, there is sufficient consideration. The more interesting situations and the litigation some disputes have generated are found in circumstances where consideration comes in the form of access alone. Is this consideration adequate? Recall from discussion in Chapter 2 that consideration can come in many nonmonetary forms, such as a promise or something else of value. It may also be the case that these sorts of EULAs are the kind of agreements that libraries and educational entities most often employ when assuming the role of licensor. It may also be that for the constituents of these organizations, for patrons and students, these agreements are the most problematic, as these users may not be aware that such click-to-agree/click-to-access agreements can be just as binding as other contracts, online or otherwise, and can contain the same unfavorable terms as other contracts. For this reason, some time is spent here discussing the legality and use of these agreements in both library as licensor and library as licensee situations. EULAs come in a variety of forms and arise in a variety of circumstances. The common thread is that the agreement is intended to cover the terms and conditions of use of content or, more common, of a service, such as a website, chat room, other online forums, or virtual spaces or worlds.

As in the application of EULAs in the software arena, scrutiny in the website environment is made with a similar set of concerns.[5] In the website environment, the visitor may not necessarily be seeking the acquisition of a product or service through sale or license but rather simply use of website contents. Use of the website may still be governed by terms of use. The mechanism of entry may in addition require the website visitor to assent through clicking "I agree," similar to a click-wrap, or through some other course of conduct representing assent, similar to a browse-wrap, such as continued use of the website.[6] The question is whether these terms coupled with such assent represent an enforceable contract. Recall that "[w]hat contract law looks for are indicia that the actual or likely existence of terms or of contractual relationships being sought sufficiently appears so that one can conclude that the actor should know or have had reason to know that its conduct (e.g., downloading, using the site) would objectively manifest assent."[7] The question is not whether the website licensor allows a user access to the website or allows the user to use the services provided by the website or allows the user to copy content found on the website. Rather, the question is, under what circumstances (terms) does the website allow that access, use of service, copying, or other use, such as posting? Was access, use, copying, or other use conditioned on acceptance of certain terms that prohibit certain uses? And where are those terms of use presented to the website visitor? Was agreement to those terms acknowledged by the visitor through some particular conduct, such as clicking an "I accept" button? This conditioning conduct could include clicking something else, such as a "search" or "submit" icon, or continued use of the website, when under the circumstances it could be concluded that the visitor had sufficient opportunity to understand that such conduct would be interpreted by the website owner as acceptance of the terms. "Nothing prevents a party from conditioning access to its information or location on agreement to a contract. A provider who indicates that access constitutes acceptance, or that a right of access is conditional on acceptance of a contract for access has made an offer. Conduct, writings, or words from the other party consistent with acceptance of that offer do accept in law so long as that party had an alternative—e.g., to simply sign off and leave the offered site or information."[8] As a result, there is no absolute right to use information on the Internet because the user thinks it should be so available: "Non-lawyers and, indeed, some lawyers may wrongly believe that [having] an alternative means that they should have the right to use the site without accepting the contract. That is not true, of course. The fact that I offer to sell my car to you under stated terms does not mean that a contract exists only if you accept while having had the choice to decline and still take my car. The alternative referred to as making the contract choice voluntary and negotiated is the alternative of walking away from the deal."[9] In another example more akin to the "free" or public use of website information, it would be as if a hunter argues that simply because a property owner lets the hunter cross his property to hunt, such permitted access includes the right for the hunter to harvest and keep the landowner's crops as well. This would appear to be a ridiculous argument, and some argue similar faulty logic is being employed in the virtual environment as well—for example, when a user thinks, "Well, the content was just sitting there on the website. Nothing stopped me from copying it, so I thought I was authorized to copy and send it to whomever I choose." Some website users would like to believe that clicking "I accept" somehow includes the right to do anything with the website and its content. It may be that what the website grants is access alone, even if the right to copy or perform some other act is not specifically prohibited by the terms.[10]

The focus of this discussion is contract, so these fact scenarios are understood to occur in circumstances where access, use, copying, or other use is subject to terms. It may be that website users (librarians or patrons) are inclined to click and click and click again, without bothering to read any terms associated with those clicks and without much care or concern about what the actual clicks may represent. The point is that visitors to websites need to realize what these steps to access or use the site may in fact represent. So, in our previous analogy, it would be as if the hunter were faced with a sign posted on the gate of some forest property, the contents of which included the conditions of entrance to and use of the property and concluded with the following: "By opening the gate and entering the property, you agree to abide by these conditions." The terms indicate what the hunter may do, and it could be that these terms allow what might otherwise be unlawful conduct— for example, the terms might allow the hunter to pick apples on the property in addition to using the land to hunt. What is different about contract scenarios versus examples offered in the absence of contract (a truly open website, not governed by any agreement whatsoever, where only the rules of copyright, as well as other laws, apply) is that when a contract such as a EULA is involved, the terms may restrict users from otherwise engaging in what might be lawful. In the website scenario, terms may prohibit any copying whatsoever, even of fair-use portions.[11] Of course, some websites may not contain content subject to copyright protection, or the purpose of use by the website visitor is not to copy but to use the site; in these cases, the unlawful act to which the contract (EULA) grants permission is based in trespass as applied to virtual spaces,[12] unauthorized use of a computer,[13] or some other legal concept.[14] What if the website consists of public domain or content otherwise not subject to copyright protection—can such terms still lawfully restrict the uses a site visitor can make of such content?

Building upon previous discussion, many EULAs come in the form of what might be called browse-wrap, in that "[n]otice of the agreement usually appears on the home page (often in the form of a link). Clicking on the notice links the user to a separate web page containing the full text of the license agreement. The user is not required to click on an icon expressing agreement to the terms of the agreement (as in the case of click-wrap agreements), nor is the user ever required to view the terms (as in the case of shrink-wrap agreements). The agreement is simply there for them to view if they wish to, and if they can find it."[15] What consistently characterizes the website EULA is that the agreement is not undertaken in conjunction with any purchase of a product or service but regards use of the site and its content alone.[16] "In the online context, this may require some indication that access to, or use of the site, or downloading of information from it, is conditional on assent to a contract or at least that a contract is offered for some purpose."[17] There may, of course, be some websites that appear truly free and open for anyone to use; even a thorough search of their pages reveals no terms and/or assent mechanisms. However,

Nimmer cautions that such sites may nonetheless be subject to restrictions: "A large number of Internet sites are *public or free sites* without any requirement of contractual permission for use. The same is true for large amounts of Internet information. It is not true that no contract ever arises from use of such sites, but an appearance of unrestricted access and use may vitiate any intent to contract or, as more properly stated, any reason to expect that mere use or downloading manifests assent to a contract...Of course, in some cases at least, the very nature of the site and what one must go through to access it communicates the same thing without there necessarily being any explicit statement about a contract being offered."[18] Whether explicit or implicit, restrictions governing the use of webspace are here to stay.[19]

While the acronym *EULA* and the term *end user license agreement* are both used by courts in product acquisition scenarios, such as those governing software,[20] the acronym is used herein to distinguish those license scenarios where the subject of the license is mere access to the site or use of some feature contained within the site (e.g., data search or data processing) from those EULAs which govern acquisition of a product (e.g., software, airline tickets, or concert tickets) or services (e.g., hotel or car rental reservations). The former would include website EULAs that govern access to various social networking sites or proprietary information sites. These pose the more interesting cases compared to traditional software EULAs unless, as discussed, there are contract formation issues due the software EULA being presented in the context of shrink-, click-, or browse-wrap agreements. Often the website EULA poses some of the same problems that browse-wrap scenarios do, perhaps compounded by the fact that most website visitors are not expecting, in the absence of an actual commercial transaction, that an agreement would nonetheless govern their use of the website, but it can and often does. In the words of one web commentator, the website purveyor, like the landowner, can view things a bit differently: "Users should expect that web site publishers will want to control the manner in which the service they provide and information that they post is used."[21] In addition, the contractual mechanisms of notice of terms and assent in the more questionable sites are like the browse-wrap scenario—less than conspicuous when compared to the click-wrap scenarios previously discussed.[22] When the EULA is presented in the context of a clear click-wrap, the analysis is more in line with click-wrap scenarios.

THE LEGAL THEORY PROTECTING WEBSITES AND THE VALIDITY OF WEBSITE EULAs

Some of the same issues regarding unconscionability that are present in shrink-wrap, click-wrap, and browse-wrap agreements are present in the website EULA environment as well. As case law suggests, most are likely valid,[23] although the basis for enforcement may not rest in copyright, as the website content may not be protected by copyright in those situations where the website consists of public domain content or noncopyrightable content (e.g., fact-based information such as statistics, dates, times, venues and places of concerts), where access to the site is nonetheless restricted. As noted earlier, the right of interest in these scenarios, the right underlying the "misuse" of website content, would not rest in copyright but in some quasi-property theory, such as virtual trespass, misappropriation, and, of course, breach of contract.

Are such website EULAs valid contracts? Yes, if there is an available statement of the terms, the user understands that by clicking "I agree" or taking some other affirmative act, such as submitting a query or proceeding to the next page of the website, he or she is indeed agreeing to be bound by those terms in using the website and its content. In the case of public domain or other content, the analogy might be: it is as if there is a park on public land, but park visitors must still agree to abide to some conditions of use. The consideration, the thing of value, is the mutual promises exchanged between the website owner and website visitor: "I promise not to sue you for..." by the website owner and "I promise not to make commercial use of the content of your website or..." by the website visitor, for example. As explained by Nimmer:

> One can describe a license as a contract-based defense to infringement or trespass claims because complying with it absolves the licensee from liability for a claim of property-rights infringement for its conduct. The limiting terms in the license reserve rights to the licensor in that they do not give permission to act in a way that infringes the property rights. Most licenses operate in both ways—as mutual promises and as waivers or permissions.[24]

These concepts are also at play when considering the enforceability of the Creative Commons license. Several cases illustrate these problems.

Disputes Involving EULAs

The issue in *People v. Direct Revenue, LLC* arose from complaints from consumers that the defendant had installed ad-generating software on their computers without their consent. The New York attorney general's office investigated and found that "[i]n each of the seven cases, the investigator was presented with a computer hyperlink which specifically referred to Direct Revenue's end-user license agreement ('EULA'). A dialog box labeled 'Security Warning' appeared each time, offering the user the option of accepting the terms of the EULA by clicking 'Yes' or declining it by clicking 'No.' The accompanying message explained that by clicking on 'Yes,' the user acknowledged that he or she had read the EULA and agreed to be bound by its terms."[25] The EULA made it clear that by clicking "Yes" the website user agreed to allow information regarding the other websites the user visited to be collected, and that target advertisements would display on their computer screens automatically as a result of the installation of software that the EULA also indicated would be installed on the user's computer. The EULA also made clear that the user could uninstall the software. The website did not offer any products or services for sale or any other transaction; rather, "it receives compensation from the companies whose products and services it advertises. To induce consumers to view the ads, the company offers them popular software applications, such as screensavers or games, free."[26] In dismissing the complaint, the court observed that even though the "Yes" click did not specifically acknowledge a user had read the terms—though the terms were available for review—a contract was nonetheless formed: "In each case that the AG's investigators successfully installed respondents' advertising client, they first clicked on the 'Yes' button on a dialog box to assent to the terms of the EULA. This conduct created a binding 'click-wrap' agreement which bars any claim for deceptive or unlawful conduct. Under New York law, such contracts are enforced so long as the consumer is given a sufficient opportunity to read the EULA, and assents thereto after being provided with an unambiguous method of accepting or declining the offer."[27] As in most disputes, the moral of the story is "Look before you leap" or, in such cases, "Look before you click."

Disputes can arise between businesses or competitors as well, not just between the business/website purveyors and consumers. In *Ticketmaster L.L.C. v. RMG Technologies, Inc.*, a dispute arose over the automated extraction by ticket brokers of ticket information from the Ticketmaster website. The defendant developed an automated program that could read and enter the words that appeared in a security dialogue box on the Ticketmaster site, a feature that otherwise requires a human being to read the word on a shaded or disguised background and enter it into another dialogue box before proceeding. The instructions indicated that automated programs or other technologies could not be used to access the subsequent website ordering pages. "First, visitors to ticketmaster.com are required to accept contractual provisions set forth in the website's 'Terms of Use.' These terms permit viewers to use ticketmaster.com for personal use only, prohibit commercial use, prohibit the use of automatic devices, prohibit users from accessing ticketing pages more than once during any three second interval, and prohibit consumers from purchasing more than a specific number of tickets in a single transaction."[28] There was no issue with obscure or inconspicuous terms; rather, the defendant argued that the simple conditions or "terms of use" did not constitute an enforceable agreement.[29] The EULA granted users the right to engage in what would otherwise be copyright infringement: each successive page of the Ticketmaster website viewed by the visitor would be copied into the RAM of the visitor, and for purposes of copyright law, this is a "copy."[30] This provided the additional legal leverage to enforce the agreement—under copyright as well as contract principles—and avoid any issue of preemption: "Thus, by the Terms of Use, Plaintiff grants a nonexclusive license to consumers to copy pages from the website in compliance with those Terms. Inasmuch as Defendant used the website, Defendant assented to the terms."[31] For similar reasons, the court found Ticketmaster likely to succeed on its breach of contract claims as well:

> that Plaintiff is highly likely to prove that use of ticketmaster.com is governed by the Terms of Use; that Defendant was on notice of, and assented to, the Terms of Use; and that Defendant violated the Terms of Use by using automated devices to access the website, using an application that makes several requests per second (in violation of the provision limiting the frequency of requests to no more than one every three seconds), and by using an application designed to thwart Plaintiff's access controls (which breaches the user's agreement to "not use any device, software or routine that interferes with the proper working of the Site nor shall you attempt to interfere with the proper working of the Site."). The Court therefore finds that Plaintiff is therefore likely to prevail on its breach of contract claim.[32]

As the defendant continued to use the website, it was under an obligation to make sure its use conformed to the terms and conditions of the EULA that Ticketmaster presented.[33]

In another dispute regarding Ticketmaster, this time involving a consumer who, instead of using robots to extract ticket information or purchase tickets, legitimately accessed the ticket-ordering mechanism but took issue with developments in the aftermath of the purchase of her tickets.[34] Again, the website was governed by a "terms of use" statement that predicated further use of the website on assent to those terms.[35] The plaintiff claimed the terms were not conspicuous, but the court, citing previous cases, observed: "courts have consistently held that the use of a website for such purposes as purchasing a ticket manifests the user's assent to the Terms of Use, and that such terms constitute a binding contract as long as the terms are sufficiently conspicuous."[36] The plaintiff also argued that e-mail updates concerning the status of the contract did not alter the agreement and did not constitute new terms.

> Under the terms of her contracts with Ticketmaster, plaintiff has no right at all to be notified by Ticketmaster in the event of a Concert's cancellation or rescheduling by individuals or entities other than Ticketmaster. The court cannot imply such a right into the plaintiff's contracts. Plaintiff's allegation that "the e-mail activity and communications to plaintiffs" modified or amended her contract with Ticketmaster or constituted some "course of conduct" apart from the contract is frivolous. The simple fact is that plaintiff consented to receive daily email alerts about the Concert from Ticketmaster when she purchased her tickets. They were part and parcel of her contract, and nothing more.[37]

The Ticketmaster cases stand for the proposition that use of a website (submitting a query or processing a request, proceeding to view subsequent pages, etc.) can constitute assent when the website indicates that such use does indeed constitute this assent. These cases are contrasted with websites that merely have the site's "code of conduct" or other listing of acceptable uses posted without any mechanism of assent whatsoever.[38] A statement or other policy posted on a website without such a mechanism does not offer any enforceable promise.[39]

An online forum, such as a list, board, chat, blog, or other service, may condition forum access and use of the service on participants agreeing to various terms and conditions of use. The researcher as participant must likewise assent to these terms and conditions. In the online context, users are given the opportunity to read the terms and conditions of use before joining the list or board, logging into the chat or blog, and so forth, and to acknowledge their assent by clicking on an "I agree" button before proceeding. One possible provision in the click-wrap EULA agreement governing an online forum may limit use of forum content to personal purposes or prohibit further dissemination of forum content without the permission of the participant who posted it. Such a clause would prohibit the researcher from using the content in the classroom or including the content in a scholarly publication.

Assuming that a forum is governed by click-wrap or another agreement, the terms and conditions of the agreement are available for review by the researcher or other participant, and users are aware that, by clicking "I agree" or undertaking some other affirmative act, their use of the forum is bound by those terms and conditions: the developing precedent regarding online licensing as well as existing contract law suggest that these agreements are indeed enforceable contracts, as conduct can also constitute assent. Consider the following sequence of notices and prompts: "By entering the chat room you agree to be bound by the terms and conditions governing the forum"; "Click here to view the terms and conditions"; "If you want to enter the chat room, click here." When there is an opportunity to review the terms and conditions and it is made clear that by engaging in a particular act the user is assenting to the terms and conditions, courts have concluded that a valid contract can be formed.[40]

It is irrelevant that the researcher or other participants click away without bothering to read the terms and conditions of service. The Restatement (Second) of Contracts comments on the general rule of responsibility: "Generally, one who assents to a writing is presumed to know its contents and cannot escape being bound by its terms merely by contending that he did not read them; his assent is deemed to cover unknown as well as known terms."[41] This rule applies in the context of mass-market or standardized agreements, even where the common practice is to assent before reading or assent without ever reading. "Customers do not in fact ordinarily understand or even read the standard terms. They trust to the good faith of the party using the form and to the tacit representation that like terms are being accepted regularly by others similarly situated. But they understand that they are assenting to the terms not read or not understood, subject to such limitations as the law may impose."[42] The responsibility is on the participant to read the terms and conditions of use even where the user may need to "click here" to bring up a pop-up window to view the terms and conditions or visit another part of the online forum to access the terms and conditions. As long as it is made clear to the participant that by clicking "I agree" he or she will be bound by the terms and conditions of use (i.e., acknowledging those are the terms and conditions which apply to this particular forum), acknowledges that the terms and conditions were read ("I have read the accompanying terms and conditions"), even though in reality this may not be the case, and proceeds to click the final "I agree" button, the contract is completed. As discussed in a previous chapter, factors may exist to diminish the capacity of a participant to understand the terms and conditions of an agreement. The Restatement (Second) of Contracts states the general rule: "Unless a statute provides otherwise, a natural person has the capacity to incur only voidable contractual duties until the beginning of the day before the person's eighteenth birthday."[43] Different jurisdictions may set an older age of majority. While contracts entered into by minors may be voidable, not all contracts involving minors are unenforceable.[44]

Many of the cases regarding the validity of wrap and web agreements relate to enforceability of arbitration or choice of forum clauses in transactions, such as the sale of goods and services[45] or the download of software without cost.[46] Challenges to arbitration clauses may be foreclosed in some instances or limited in others in the future due to federal preemption as a result of the Supreme Court[47] decision in spring 2011, as discussed in Chapter 4. "The focus was on public policy and unconscionability, with the issue of the enforceability of shrink-wrap and click-wrap agreements being a secondary concern or consideration. Nonetheless, it appears these decisions were influenced by the act that the forum-selection or arbitration clause was expressed in the shrink-wrap or click-wrap agreement form. In those unusual cases in which click-wrap and shrink-wrap agreements were not enforced, other factors were involved."[48] But, can such terms and conditions be enforceable in noncommercial settings, such as access to and use of an online forum without a fee or other cost? Consider the neighbors in this example: The first neighbor asks, "Can I use your new outdoor grill this summer?" The second neighbor responds, "Okay, but you have to clean the grill and fill the gas cylinder when you are done." The authorized use of the grill by the first neighbor binds him to those two tasks (clean the grill and fill up the gas) as the terms and conditions of use offered by the second neighbor, with the cleaning and filling the consideration in return for grill use. A similar situation exists in the case of a list, board, chat room, blog, or other online forum that asks a participant, "Would you like to use the forum?" and the participant responds yes by clicking the "I agree" button. Where compliance with the terms and conditions and use by the participant constitute adequate consideration, an enforceable contract will result.

The forum selection clause was at issue in a case involving use of a website service. "The Court finds the present situation to be analogous to the use of a website where terms and conditions of use are imposed...Like the website users in these cases Fru-Con made the decision to submit its prequalification application for the County's review after having the opportunity to review the terms governing the County's review of such applications and Fru-Con's correlating rights. Further, Fru-Con made representations as to its understanding of those terms. Accordingly, the forum selection clause is binding on Fru-Con."[49] In an appellate decision considering the validity of website user agreements where the object of the "contract" is access to the information on the website, the *Register.com, Inc. v. Verio, Inc.* concluded: "As we see it, the defendant in *Ticketmaster* [*Ticketmaster Corp. v. Tickets.com, Inc.*] and Verio in this case had a similar choice. Each was offered access to information subject to terms of which they were well aware. Their choice was either to accept the offer of contract, taking the information subject to the terms of the offer, or, if the terms were not acceptable, to decline to take the benefits...We find that the district court was within its discretion in concluding that Register showed likelihood of success on the merits of its contract claim."[50] Likewise, where the forum participant does not desire to purchase any particular good or service but rather seeks access to the information the forum contains, and the researcher-participant and acknowledges this desire by acceptance of the applicable terms and conditions of use, a court would conclude that a valid contract exists.

EULAs have tremendous application in libraries of all sorts. Libraries are using them daily, likely without realizing it in some cases. Libraries may expect patrons to honor the terms and conditions of a series of statements that appear on a log-in screen or are linked on a separate page before accessing a library computer network and to agree to those terms and conditions by "clicking here," and libraries rely on the enforcement of EULAs—contracts that purport to control conditions under which access is granted to website content, services, and so on (or in this case the ability to search the library catalog, use the library Internet access to surf the web, enter the virtual reference desk and receive online assistance, etc.) when the access is offered for free. Unlike a click-wrap (which can be offline or online) or browse-wrap (which entails agreements to purchase or otherwise obtain some actual goods or services online, e.g., airline tickets, furniture, car rental or hotel reservations, books, DVDs), a EULA is generally used for access to information or services without delivery of goods or a product at the end of it. Rather, what is offered to the user is access, that is, being able to browse a website or use the network access to send e-mail or participate in chat rooms, blogs, and so forth. There is no charge for this access—only the requirement that the user promises to comply with the terms and conditions of service (access) presented. The user (or patron) delivers nothing of value (does not submit a credit card number nor promise to "buy now, pay later" when the goods are delivered) but merely promises to use the free access in compliance with the rules established by the site owner.

It is as if no fee is paid to access the woods of a landowner, but the hikers agree not to pick any flowers along the trails they walk. Is this an enforceable contract? Translate the facts to the virtual world: Can a website purveyor, such as a library, enforce similar use restrictions? When mechanisms exist such that patrons are made aware that their use is subject to certain terms, the terms are readily available, and by proceeding each user is bound to the terms, case law suggests that a valid contract is created and the library can hold the patron to those terms.

SUMMARY POINTS

▶ Libraries, or educational entities, for that matter, can be both licensors (offering access to their network or computing services) and licensees. The library or other public institution can employ the use of enforceable terms of use or an end user license agreement to govern the use of its website, to control patron behavior or conduct regarding use of its services, for example.

▶ Some websites may not contain content subject to copyright protection or the purpose of the use by the website visitor is not to copy content or purchase a product or service but merely to access and use the site. In these situations, the EULA grants permission under the stated terms without fear of legal reprisal, where such reprisal would then be based not in copyright but rather in trespass[51] as applied to virtual spaces,[52] unauthorized use of a computer,[53] or some other legal concept.

LEARNING EXAMPLES

▶ **Example 8.1**

Situation: A librarian accesses a website of possible useful information in answering a patron query, but before the deeper pages of the site can be explored, the librarian is asked to "click to agree" before proceeding; one restriction is that the information must be for personal use only and may not be further distributed to the public. Are the terms enforceable or can the librarian copy and further distribute the content of the site to the patron?

Legal Analysis: The EULA governing the site is a valid contract, and the terms and conditions are enforceable—practical issues in policing and enforcing those terms and conditions notwithstanding!

▶ **Example 8.2**

Situation: A library patron accesses an online chat room from a computer at the library; the chat room is designed for teenagers but the patron is an adult. The patron moves through the online prompts to become a member of the chat, including a click-to-agree EULA that requires the patron to be between the ages of 12 and 17. Another term indicates that any violation of the EULA can result in termination and loss of any content posted on the chat log by the user. Later, the website running the chat room determines that the patron is indeed an adult. What is the result?

Legal Analysis: The EULA agreement is enforceable. The adult patron can be terminated from the chat and no longer able to access any content he or she posted. Furthermore, if damage or harm results, the patron might be subject to a claim of unauthorized access to a computer system under relevant federal or state law.[54]

ENDNOTES

1. U.S. v. Drew, 259 F.R.D. 449, 461–462 (C.D. Cal., 2009).
2. RAYMOND T. NIMMER, 2 INFORMATION LAW § 12.33 (database updated in Westlaw, November 2011): "Nothing prevents a party from conditioning access to its information or location on agreement to a contract. A provider who indicates that access constitutes acceptance, or that a right of access is conditional on acceptance of a contract for access has made an offer."
3. See Jamie J. Kayser, *Note and Comment: The New New-World: Virtual Property and the End User License Agreement,* 27 LOYOLA OF LOS ANGELES ENTERTAINMENT LAW REVIEW 59 (2006/2007).
4. Bobby Glushko, *Tales of the (Virtual) City: Governing Property Disputes in Virtual Worlds,* 22 BERKELEY TECHNOLOGY LAW JOURNAL 507, 508 (2007).
5. See L. J. KUTTEN, 2 COMPUTER SOFTWARE, § 9:59 (database updated April 2012) (Are EULAs enforceable?—Are they valid contracts?—The reality): "Until approximately 1995, this author would have argued that the validity of a EULA was an open question: there were cases both in directions. However, the recent trend has been that such agreements are, for the most part, valid contracts. They are deemed valid for a variety of reasons. These include: (a) course of conduct; (b) failure to object to the terms; and (c) actions which indicate acceptance of the terms. Courts that have disapproved of EULA have also used a variety of rationales. These include: (a) failure of adequate notice; (b) conflict between a previous contract and the EULA; (c) finding that the user was not required to agree to the terms; and (d) finding that the terms of the EULA contradicted federal copyright law."
6. Blaze D. Waleski , *Enforceability of Online Contracts: Clickwrap vs. Browse Wrap,* 19 E-COMMERCE LAW AND STRATEGY 7 (2002), no pagination in Westlaw: "Clickwrap agreements have become the norm for software license agreements and are also frequently used in web site user agreements . . . Web site clickwrap agreements operate similarly to clickwrap

software license agreements. When the user attempts to access an activity or service on the web site (e.g., set up an e-mail account or access streaming audio or video), the relevant terms are displayed and the user must acknowledge his or her assent by clicking 'I agree.' The user may be redirected to a different web page, or presented with a pop-up window, displaying the terms, in either case with the option of clicking 'I agree' or 'I don't agree.' The operation may be designed so that the user must click the 'I agree' button more than once to confirm the action, bolstering the user's affirmative demonstration of assent and evidencing that the user did not inadvertently or mistakenly click the button."

7. Raymond T. Nimmer, Law of Computer Technology § 13.27 (database updated in Westlaw, September 2011) (Contract formation online).

8. *Id.* at note 8 (Contract formation online—Access contracts and use of site or data). "As a general matter, the offeror (site operator of provider of the information) has a right to indicate how acceptance can occur...Entering a site and using it manifests assent if it should have been reasonably clear that this step would do so" (*id.*).

9. Nimmer, *supra* note 2, at note 8 (database updated in Westlaw, November, 2011).

10. *Id.* at note 6: "Since much of the informational material on the Internet is copyrighted and access to a computer of a third party is illegal unless authorized, even in free public sites, something more is occurring than simply giving information or access away. At minimum, one would rely on implied license (under copyright) or implied authorization (criminal and trespass law). These could be implied in fact and, thus, somewhat similar to simple contractual relationships...In effect, one could suggest, a contract arose when the user accepted the offer to copy the information or use the site" (footnote omitted).

11. See, for example, eBay, Inc. v. Bidder's Edge, Inc., 100 F. Supp. 2d 1058 (N.D. Cal. 2000) (Trespass to real property versus trespass to chattels or conversion); *Register.com v. Verio, Inc.*, 126 F. Supp. 2d 238 (S.D.N.Y. 2000) (Injunction issued, likelihood of harm demonstrated, if others allowed to replicate Verio's actions of using robot to extract data, system operability would suffer); Ticketmaster, Corp. v. Tickets.com, 2000 U.S. Dist. LEXIS 12987 (C.D. Calif. 2000) (Tacit acceptance of digital trespass, but no evidence of harm demonstrated in this instance).

12. See David P. Sheldon, *Claiming Ownership, but Getting Owned: Contractual Limitations on Asserting Property Interests in Virtual Goods*, 54 UCLA Law Review 751, 764–768 (2007), discussing the use of property concepts to exclude users as the basis for control of virtual world sites. See also Daniel C. Miller, *Notes: Determining Ownership in Virtual Worlds: Copyright and License Agreements*, 22 Review of Litigation 435 (2003).

13. See 18 U.S.C. § 1030. See also Ticketmaster L.L.C. v. RMG Technologies, Inc., 507 F. Supp. 2d 1096,1113 (C.D. Cal. 2007): "It appears likely that Plaintiff will be able to prove that Defendant gained unauthorized access to, and/or exceeded authorized access to, Plaintiff's protected computers, and caused damage thereby. Based on the statute and the cases Plaintiff cites, the Court also agrees that the required $5,000 of harm may consist of harm to a computer system, and need not be suffered by just one computer during one particular intrusion."

14. See, for example, Fred Wehrenberg Circuit of Theatres, Inc. v. Moviefone, Inc., 73 F. Supp. 2d 1044 (E. D. Mo. 1999) (Website of movie listings not "hot news" under *Motorola* [NBA v. Motorola, 105 F.3d 841 (2d Cir. 1997)] standard that requires the following elements be present: high cost, time sensitive, commercial free-riding, parties in direct competition, reduce incentive to collect, i.e., missing the incentive element); Pollstar v. Gigmania, Ltd., 170 F. Supp. 2d 974 (E.D. Cal. 2000) (Extraction by competing website of concert ticket information, the court "declines to decide this issue at the present time" but observes that the "claim was pled with sufficiency as a "hot news" claim").

15. JONATHAN D. ROBBINS, ADVISING E BUSINESSES, § 8.6 (database updated in Westlaw, November 2011), Acceptances on the Internet: Click-wrap, shrink-wrap and browse-wrap agreements, available in Westlaw. See also Scott J. Lochner, *A Legal Primer on Software Shrink-Wrap: Click Wrap or Click-to-Accept and Browse-Wrap License Agreements*, INTELLECTUAL PROPERTY TODAY (December 2003): "Another internet standard form contract is the 'browse-wrap' license. 'Browse-wrap' refers to a notice placed on a web page indicating that the user of the software is subject to a license agreement which is typically viewable on a separate webpage. A 'browse-wrap license does not require the user to click an icon in order to signify acceptance before downloading, installing or using the software"; and Blaze D. Waleski, *Enforceability of Online Contracts: Clickwrap vs. Browse Wrap*, 19 E-COMMERCE LAW AND STRATEGY 7 (no pagination in Westlaw): "The term 'browse wrap' is used to describe terms that are viewable only if the user searches them, for example, by clicking a link at the bottom of the home page on a web site that redirects the user to another page displaying the terms." See discussion in Chapter 7.

16. See Genelle I. Belmas and Brian N. Larson, *Clicking Away Your Speech Rights: The Enforceability of Gagwrap Licenses*, 12 COMMUNICATIONS LAW AND POLICY 37 (2007), discussing the two forms of browse-wrap. "A browsewrap agreement may take one of two general forms: (1) a document appearing to the consumer that is obviously intended to be a license agreement, to which the consumer is not required to assent before the transaction is consummated; and (2) a statement somewhere on a Web page that viewing the page is subject to terms of use or a license agreement appearing elsewhere. Both types are typically held unenforceable unless the terms are displayed in such a conspicuous way as to ensure the consumer's knowledge of the terms and to infer the consumer's assent to them" (*id.* at 50).

17. Nimmer, *supra* note 7, at § 14.27. Nimmer adds that "even in free public sites, something more is occurring than simply giving information or access away. At minimum, one would rely on implied license (under copyright) or implied authorization (criminal and trespass law). These could be implied in fact and, thus, somewhat similar to simple contractual relationships" (*id.* at note 7).

18. Nimmer, *supra* note 2, at § 12.33, footnotes omitted, italics in original.

19. See F. LAWRENCE STREET AND MARK P. GRANT, LAW OF THE INTERNET § 1.02[4], at 1–8 (2001, updated through release #19, December 2011), advocating the use of contracts to protect website content: "If copyright protection [or] some other form of intellectual

property protection... [is] not available then contract provision and license restrictions are the main sources of protection. For example, innovative Web sites should ask users to agree to specified and reuse restrictions before they are allowed access to the materials."

20. See, for example, Collin County v. Siemens Business Services, 250 Fed. Appx. 45, 47 (5th Cir. 2007): "March 2004, after an earlier meeting with Siemens and SAP representatives, the County entered into two contracts: a software end user license agreement with SAP and a services agreement with Siemens"; Kloth v. Microsoft Corp., 444 F.3d 312, 318 (4th Cir. 2006): "To use Microsoft software, the end-users were required to agree to the EULAs, which provided, among other things, a Microsoft-funded refund to the end-user if the end-user declined to enter into the EULA"; and Faulkner v. National Geographic Enterprises, 409 F.3d 26, 32 (2d Cir. 2005): "In addition, in some copies of the CNG marketed by Encore Software, an End User License Agreement."

21. Dawn Davidson, *Click and Comment: What Terms Are Users Bound to When They Enter Web Sites*, 26 WILLIAM MITCHELL LAW REVIEW 1171, 1196 (2000). "[C]ourts should require at a minimum that links to the agreements be conspicuous so that Web site users are likely to distinguish them from the other information on the page. In addition, courts should require some sort of statement alerting users that their use of the site constitutes acceptance of terms and conditions that can be found through the link" (*id.*).

22. *Id.*, footnotes omitted. "The problem is that the terms and conditions often are written in the form of a contract, the existence of which is not easily known to Web site users. The only way to find the contacts is through a line at the bottom of the home page or elsewhere. These links are usually one word or a short phrase among several other links" (*id.* at 1175–1176).

23. *Id.* at 1201, concluding that standardized website user agreements are likely to be enforced; in spite of the absence of meaningful choice, most are not "unreasonably favorable" to the website owner; while procedurally unconscionable, most website user agreements are not substantively unconscionable; and while warranty waiver clauses may be suspect, forum selection clauses are not. See also Robert W. Gomulkiewicz, *Getting Serious about User-Friendly Mass Market Licensing for Software*, 12 GEORGE MASON LAW REVIEW 687, 688–787 (2004), footnotes omitted: "The issues have been talked to death. Despite all the scholarly debate, one important reality remains: EULAs are here to stay for the foreseeable future. Courts, by and large, have enforced EULAs, provided the software publisher gives the user a reasonable opportunity to review and the user makes a meaningful manifestation of assent. Given this reality, it is crucial to address an issue that scholars have thus far ignored: what can be done to make licensing more user-friendly? Specifically, what can be done to help people better understand the terms and conditions of EULAs, and what can be done to encourage software publishers to craft simpler, fairer, more understandable licenses?"

24. Nimmer, *supra* note 2, at § 11.3.

25. People v. Direct Revenue, LLC, 2008 WL 1849855, at *2 (Sup. Ct. 2008) (unreported disposition, slip opinion).

26. *Id.* at *1.

27. *Id.* at *4, citations omitted. "It is not necessary that it be made impossible for the consumer to signal assent or proceed to installation without being first forced to read the EULA; rather, it is sufficient that a separate hyperlink leading to the agreement is available" (*id.*, citations omitted).

28. Ticketmaster L.L.C. v. RMG Technologies, Inc., 507 F. Supp. 2d 1096, 1102 (C.D. Cal. 2007).

29. *Id.* at 1107.

30. *Id.* at 1106: "Thus, copies of ticketmaster.com webpages automatically stored on a viewer's computer are 'copies' within the meaning of the Copyright Act."

31. *Id.* at 1108. "Because the Court finds that Plaintiff has a strong likelihood of proving that Defendant violated ticketmaster.com's Terms of Use by using automated devices, making excessive requests, and interfering with the proper working of the website when it used and/or designed applications that access ticketmaster.com, the Court finds that Plaintiff has a strong likelihood of succeeding on the merits of its claim for direct copyright infringement" (*id.* at 1110).

32. *Id.* at 1112–1113.

33. *Id.* at 1108: "Thus, by the Terms of Use, Plaintiff grants a nonexclusive license to consumers to copy pages from the website in compliance with those Terms. Inasmuch as Defendant used the website, Defendant assented to the terms."

34. The terms on a ticket are enforceable: "It is likewise well-established that the terms of the plaintiff's ticket constitute an enforceable contract. Bickett v. Buffalo Bills, Inc., 122 Mics.2d 880, 472 N.Y.S.2d 245, 247 (N.Y. Cup. Ct. 1983) (enforcing statement on football ticket providing that 'admission may be refunded or terminated at any time'); Barnett v. Madison Square Garden Center, Inc., 227 A.D.2d 178, 641 N.Y.S. 669 (1st Dept. 1996) (ruling that ticket to New York Rangers' game constituted a 'valid written contract between the parties' that precluded any claim for recovery beyond a refund of the ticket purchase price)."

35. Druyan v. Jagger, 508 F. Supp. 2d 228, 234 (S.D.N.Y. 2007): "Those statements including Ticketmaster's Terms of Use, which provide as follows: 'By using or visiting the Site, you expressly agree to be bound by these Terms and follow these Terms, and all applicable laws and regulations governing the Site.' The Terms of Use themselves expressly notify all users (including the plaintiff) that events such as the Concert occasionally 'are cancelled or postponed by the promoter, team, band or venue.' The Terms of Use further provide that in the event of any such cancellation 'Ticketmaster will not be liable for travel or any other expenses that [plaintiff] or anyone else incurs.'"

36. *Id.* at 237, citing Ticketmaster Corp. v. Tickets.com, Inc., 2003 WL 21406289 (C.D. Cal. 2003) and Register.com v. Verio, 126 F. Supp. 2d 238 (S.D.N.Y. 2000).

37. *Id.* at 238.

38. A.V. v. iParadigms, Ltd., 2008 WL 728389, *9 (E.D. Va. 2008): "Second, the Usage Policy is not binding on Plaintiffs as an independent contract because Plaintiffs did not assent

to the Usage Policy…In this case, there is no evidence that Plaintiffs assented to the terms of the Usage Policy. There is no evidence that Plaintiffs viewed or read the Usage Policy and there is no evidence that Plaintiffs ever clicked on the link or were ever directed by the Turnitin system to view the Usage Policy. There is no evidence to impute knowledge of the terms of the Usage Policy to Plaintiffs."

39. See, for example, Dyer v. Northwest Airlines, 334 F. Supp. 2d 1196, 1199 (D.N.D. 2004): "First, broad statements of company policy do not generally give rise to contract claims. As such, the alleged violation of the privacy policy at issue does not give rise to a contract," citation omitted. See also EF Cultural Travel BV v. Zefer Corp., 318 F.3d 58, 63 (1st Cir. 2003): "the public website provider can easily spell out explicitly what is forbidden and, consonantly, that nothing justifies putting users at the mercy of a highly imprecise, litigation-spawning standard like 'reasonable expectations.' If EF wants to ban scrapers, let it say so on the webpage or a link clearly marked as containing restrictions."

40. See Pollstar v. Gigamania, Ltd., 170 F. Supp. 2d 974, 980–981 (E.D. Cal. 2000); Register.com v. Verio, Inc., 356 F.3d 393 (2d Cir. 2004).

41. Restatement (Second) of Contracts (1981), § 157, Effect of Fault of Party Seeking Relief, comment b.

42. Restatement (Second) of Contracts (1981), § 211, Standardized Agreements, comment b.

43. Restatement (Second) of Contracts (1981), § 14, Infants.

44. See A.V. v. iParadigms, Ltd., 2008 WL 728389 (E.D. Va. 2008), high school students click agreement to be bound by terms and conditions of use of a plagiarism detection system enforceable. "However, the infancy defense cannot function as 'a sword to be used to the injury of others, although the law intends it simply as a shield to protect the infant from injustice and wrong,'" quoting, MacGreal v. Taylor, 167 U.S. 688, 701 (1897) (*id.* at *4).

45. Caspi v. The Microsoft Netowrk, LLC, 732 A.2d 528 (N.J. Super. Ct. 1999).

46. Specht v. Netscape Communications Corp., 150 F. Supp. 2d (S.D.N.Y. 2001).

47. A&T Mobility LLC v. Concepcion, 131 S.Ct. 1740 (2011). "Supreme Court ruled that a California Supreme Court decision [Discover Bank v. Superior Court, 36 Cal. 4th 148, 113 P. 3d 1100 (2005),] holding that arbitration clauses in contracts prohibiting class action lawsuits unconscionable was pre-empted by the Federal Arbitration Act [FAA], the Ninth Circuit concluding that the arbitration provision was unconscionable because AT&T had not shown that bilateral arbitration adequately substituted for the deterrent effects of class actions" (*id.* at 1745).

48. Scott J. Lochner, *A Legal Primer on Software Shrink-Wrap: Click Wrap or Click-to-Accept and Browse-Wrap License Agreements*, INTELLECTUAL PROPERTY TODAY (December 2003), referring to the "AOL cases": 204 F. Supp. 2d 178 (D. Mass. 2002); 2001 WL 135825 (Mass Super. 2001); 108 Cal. Rptr. 2d 699 (2001). See also Erez Reuveni, *On Virtual Worlds: Copyright and Contract Law at the Dawn of the Virtual Age*, 82 INDIANA LAW JOURNAL 261, 289–290 (2007): "While a minority of courts have refused to uphold shrinkwrap and clickwrap licenses, these courts have relied on factors unique to each case, rather than general contract principles."

49. Fru-Con Const. Corp. v. County of Arlington, 2006 WL 273583, *2 (E.D. Va., 2006), citing Cairo, Inc. v. Crossmedia Services., Inc., 2005 U.S. Dist. LEXIS 8450 (N.D. Cal. Apr. 1, 2005); Register.com v. Verio, Inc., 356 F.3d 393 (2d Cir. 2004).

50. Register.com v. Verio, Inc., 356 F.3d 393, 403–404 (2d Cir. 2004).

51. Nimmer, *supra* note 2, at § 11.145: "Given this Restatement standard [Contracts 2d §19], arguments that deny that assent can be shown by opening a package or clicking on an 'I agree' button on a computer screen seem disingenuous. So long as preceded by a chance to review the terms and in a context where there is reason to know that the act will reflect assent, no conceptual problem exists with this form of manifesting assent in general. These preconditions, however, must be met."

52. See David P. Sheldon, *Claiming Ownership, but Getting Owned: Contractual Limitations on Asserting Property Interests in Virtual Goods*, 54 UCLA LAW REVIEW 751, 764–768 (2007), discussing the use of property concepts to exclude users as the basis for control of virtual world sites. See also Daniel C. Miller, *Notes: Determining Ownership in Virtual Worlds: Copyright and License Agreements*, 22 REVIEW OF LITIGATION 435 (2003).

53. See 18 U.S.C. § 1030. See also Ticketmaster L.L.C. v. RMG Technologies, Inc., 507 F. Supp. 2d 1096, 1113 (C.D. Cal. 2007): "It appears likely that Plaintiff will be able to prove that Defendant gained unauthorized access to, and/or exceeded authorized access to, Plaintiff's protected computers, and caused damage thereby. Based on the statute and the cases Plaintiff cites, the Court also agrees that the required $5,000 of harm may consist of harm to a computer system, and need not be suffered by just one computer during one particular intrusion."

54. "In an interesting case that expands the scope of a federal computer crime statute, the Computer Fraud and Abuse Act of 1986, a computer hacking statute codified as 18 U.S.C. § 1030, a federal jury convicted a Missouri mother of what essentially amounted to 'cyberbullying.' The jury found Lori Drew guilty of three misdemeanor charges of computer fraud for her involvement in creating a phony account on MySpace in order to trick a teenager, who later committed suicide. Drew created a fictitious MySpace account under the name 'Josh Evans' and sent several mean-spirited messages to Megan Meier, a girl who was 13 years old and had a history of depression and suicidal tendencies . . . on August 28, 2009, the court granted the defendant's motion for acquittal and set aside her conviction . . . the court focused its analysis on whether Lori Drew accessed a computer without authorization or exceeded her authorized access . . . the court concluded that the CFAA might arguably encompass contractual violations of terms of use such as those of MySpace." GEORGE B. DELTA AND JEFFREY H. MATSUURA, LAW OF THE INTERNET § 12.03, at *12-98–*12-99 (2012, updated in Westlaw through the 2012-2 Supplement). See U.S. v. Drew, 259 F.R.D. 449 (C.D. Cal. 2009). The terms of the agreement Drew agreed to included the following: "By using the Services, you represent and warrant that (a) all registration information you submit is truthful and accurate; (b) you will maintain the accuracy of such information; (c) you are 14 years of age or older; and (d) your use of the Services does not violate any applicable law or regulation" (*id.* at 454). The court

also observed that under a "breach of contract approach, most courts that have considered the issue have held that a conscious violation of a website's terms of service/use will render the access unauthorized and/or cause it to exceed authorization" (*id.* at 460, citations omitted). See also Indictment, United States v. Drew (C.D. Cal. May 15, 2008), available at https://ecf.cacd.uscourts.gov/doc1/03102934740 (last visited July 17, 2009); Docket, United States v. Drew (C.D. Cal. May 15, 2008), available at https://ecf.cacd .uscourts.gov/cgi-bin/DktRpt.pl?386201967319426-L_801_0-1 (last visited July 17, 2009).

▶ 9

GENERAL PUBLIC LICENSES, OPEN SOURCE AGREEMENTS, AND CREATIVE COMMONS AGREEMENTS

Read this chapter to understand the nature and legality of these license situations:
▶ Creative Commons agreements such as Attribution Noncommercial No Derivatives (BY-NC-ND), Attribution Noncommercial Share Alike (BY-NC-SA), Attribution Noncommercial (BY-NC), Attribution No Derivatives (BY-ND), Attribution Share Alike (BY-SA), and Attribution (BY)
▶ Open source licenses such as General Public License, Free Documentation License, and Lesser General Public License

The question of enforceability of open source[1] or Creative Commons (CC) licenses is also controversial and unsettled.[2] This again relates to the nature of licenses being promises not to sue, in other words, promises not to enforce other rights such as copyright, misappropriation, trespass, and so on, if you use the content consistent with the terms provided. In the case of open source or CC licensing, this also relates to the manner in which the transfer of content is accomplished, that is, without the click-to-agree of an installation, download, or website access mechanism.

> There are those who believe that a restricted transfer does not require assent to the terms of the restriction. Thus, for example, some advocates of the open-source software movement believe that terms under which they distribute software need not be contractual, but are notices or permissions that, if violated, expose the violator to an infringement claim ... To be effective, control of use by a mere notice would seem to require that there be notice in fact, or at least reason to know that the limiting terms are present whenever they reach beyond the terms that arise from mere property rights law restrictions.[3]

This is important for libraries for obvious reasons central to the concepts of this book. First, libraries and their patrons, as consumers of licensed content, may prefer to license content subject to such licenses because the restrictions may be

fewer, the permitted uses are often greater, and the use requires little or no monetary cost. Further, the duration of the agreement can be perpetual. From the
opposite side of the equation, when licensing content under its control, the library
may desire to employ open source or CC licenses to ensure the maximum level
of access to patrons and the wider public, while at the same time prohibiting
commercialization or dominion of such content by private interests. Finally, open
source and CC agreements have a certain cachet among many users of information.
Thus, understanding the nature of such agreements and assessing the legal standing
of such agreements and the terms such agreements contain are critical for the
library both as consumer and producer of such licenses.

> [S]ome advocates of the open-source software movement believe that terms under
> which they distribute software need not be contractual [i.e., based in contract law], but
> are notices or permissions that, if violated, expose the violator to a claim of unauthorized
> use. There is some appeal to the argument, at least where the terms of the notice or
> permission are focused on primary rights (copying under the copyright law or access in
> reference to laws protecting a computer system from unauthorized access).[4]

The unauthorized access to which Nimmer refers would be based on a trespass
theory[5] or other unauthorized taking or misappropriation[6] or unauthorized
access.[7] As with the website EULA discussed in Chapter 8, the legal foundation for
such claims is not a contract but a property right.

> A property owner can, seemingly, give a limited permission to use its property the
> enforcement of which does not depend on it proving that a contract was created.
> Ultimately, however, where the restrictive terms involve elaborate controls on users of the
> copyrighted software and limitations of warranty in the case of open source based pro-
> grams for example, it is difficult to visualize elaborate terms being enforced without the
> benefit of an agreement. Indeed, at least with respect to warranties, the articulation and
> disclaimer of which typically must come through the force of an agreement (contract).[8]

For example, all of the six CC license options indicate that if (and it is a big "if")
the license will be interpreted as a contract, then the acceptance of the terms is
the consideration.[9] The same problem that plagues consideration of whether a
website end user license agreement (EULA) is enforceable is also present when
considering open source or CC licensing schemes.[10]

> To determine whether a promise should be enforced, a court must determine whether
> the promisor reasonably expected to induce action by the promisee, and whether such
> action was in fact induced. The doctrine applies to any promise that lacks consideration
> and that induced the type of reliance required. In the license of intellectual property,
> the license is operates as a promise not to sue for what would otherwise be infringing
> use of the content.[11]

The significant legal question is whether these agreements are enforceable and, if so, is the nature of the legal right enforced one of contract, property, or both?

OPEN SOURCE AND CREATIVE COMMONS LICENSES

It may be more a matter of semantics whether the general public license (GPL) or the CC license is a form of public domain designation (or affirmation)[12] or a separate form of permission (license) or agreement (contract). "The key element in open source is making source code publicly available under license with broad rights to modify and a general obligation to redistribute."[13] According to the Open Source Institute, by definition an open source license should contain the following elements: free distribution, availability of source code, allowance for derivative works and modifications, identification of modifications, antidiscrimination (persons or subjects), distribution of the license in downstream (viral) environments, absence of product tying, and anticontamination provisions.[14] While the phrase "open source" is used to refer to computer or software programs, CC licenses can be found in a variety of circumstances. "It has been humorously noted that the difference between open source and proprietary licenses is simple. Open source licenses allow everything except that which is forbidden, while proprietary licenses prohibit everything except that which is allowed."[15] This is a telling observation. The open source movement gave rise to what is now termed the "copyleft" movement, which is not the same as the opposite or absence of copyright. In fact, an open source license uses copyright not to restrict access or control the use of protected content but instead to ensure that the content (i.e., the software) remains available for use. The concept is not without its critics.[16] Often this is equated with "free" software, but it is not quite the same. Available or "free" means freedom to use, study, distribute, and modify the program—again, the pillars of traditional open source, distribution and derivatives—but you cannot do whatever you please with true open source content. In this sense, such software or other content is not free or without any burden. In open source, the terms of the license or permission promote the open source copyleft agenda, as defined previously. How does the licensor of such software get others to agree? By threatening enforcement through copyright infringement![17] For example, permission is granted to make derivative uses of the software—uses that would otherwise be infringing, actionable uses, such as the right to prepare derivative works, is a right of the copyright owner under section 106.[18] (Again, knowing a little bit about the copyright law is essential to understanding licensing—in this instance, knowing what a derivative use is so one can assess whether that right of use is one now granted by the open source agreement or whether it is some subset of it.[19]) Under a typical open source agreement, any derivative work must also be distributed for free. This is the so-called serial (share alike) and perpetuating nature of the open source concept: one has the right to make use of the software or other content, but any property right created with it, such as a derivative work, must likewise remain available for the next user as well. (Of course, a CC license may prohibit the creation of derivative works.) If users do not comply with the restrictions or conditions, the original licensor can sue the licensee-derivative creator, for example, for copyright infringement, claiming that an unauthorized derivative work was made.[20]

GOALS OF CREATIVE COMMONS LICENSING

Creative Commons is as much social movement as it is legal development, perhaps more so the former than the latter. It is an attempt to alter the default rules of the current copyright regime, where protection is the default. The CC license places reliance on the proverbial "kindness of strangers" to allow extended use of works by third parties on condition that those third parties in turn allow the same level of use of their works, and so on. Once a critical mass of content is subject to such conditions, an alternative landscape to copyright will exist, a commons of creative content upon which others can draw or, as one commentator suggested, a semi-commons.[21] Some commentators are doubtful that the CC license can achieve the necessary critical mass of acceptance.[22] Others observe that the serial nature may have unintended consequences.[23] To be sure, there may be millions of works subject to one of the CC licenses,[24] but it may be quality not quantity that matters. Like the GPL, the CC scheme envisions an interdependent world of legal responsibilities and obligations in the form of serial rights (not in the periodical sense but in the sense of pervasive obligations being self-perpetuating). This is "share alike" (SA) serial licensing:

> By requiring any derivative works based on the original work to be licensed on the same terms as the original work, SA provisions help create an intellectual property commons that resists appropriation, forcing anyone making derivative works to perpetuate the same sharing-based regime the original licensor has chosen. There is tension between NC [noncommercial] and SA [share alike] provisions, because including an NC term in an SA license cuts against the primary purpose of SA—growing an intellectual property commons that resists efforts to appropriate creative works—by excluding those who wish to profit from creative works without exerting exclusive control over intellectual property.[25]

In other words, foreclosure of all possibility for profit may appeal to some, but others, with all opportunity for gain removed, may avoid those works. Under the current copyright scheme, many derivative as well as other uses of content protected by copyright are justified under fair use; that is, the majority of fair-use cases are commercial uses.[26] With such use now subject to an NC-CC license instead of copyright, the contract law (or least some legal concept to enforce the license) governs and such uses would be prohibited, though potentially fair use under the copyright law.

The author knows of no legal way to designate something a work in the public domain,[27] in other words, the legal equivalent of donating it to the government or to the world.[28] Other commentators suggest this is possible[29] or assume it is so.[30] Though the effect may be the same, as such public disclaimer would surely lead a court to estop the reneging owner from later enforcing the copyright or other property right.[31]

> Although works covered by the GPL or Creative Commons licenses are not technically in the public domain (at least as narrowly defined to include only those works that are not subject to any intellectual-property-based restrictions), they are available to the public for many uses that copyright law would otherwise forbid, just as works covered by conservation easements may be open to the public—or at least dedicated to purposes that ultimately benefit the public—in ways that private property typically is not.[32]

Such designations or dedications are available for software but not for other works.[33] This mechanism was enacted as part of the Computer Software Rental Amendments Act of 1990.[34] The House Report describing the provision made the following comment:

> For purposes of this section, shareware is computer software which meets the standard of originality in the Copyright Act but for which the author sets certain conditions for its use and distribution. The Committee is aware that the terms "computer shareware" and "public domain computer shareware" are not found in the Copyright Act, and are susceptible of different meanings in the computer and legal communities. It is apparent that there is a lack of a central clearinghouse for information about shareware, and that such a clearinghouse would aid in wider dissemination of such works. The Register is given wide latitude to promulgate practices and procedures that fulfill the purposes of this section and also to obtain information—prior to the "sunset" of this Title—about an important manifestation of the creative computer community. Because of the different interpretations of the term shareware in the computer industry, it will be left up to the individual author submitting the document to designate it as pertaining to shareware. Failure to so designate the document will result in the document being recorded with the general copyright records.[35]

Congress has not added a provision that would allow the recording of such designations for other works. As explained by one commentator:

> Congress has enumerated the rights of copyright holders but has left protections for the public domain largely dependent upon holders respecting the limits on those enumerated rights. The Copyright Act provides no civil remedy against publishers who improperly claim copyright over materials that are part of the public domain. A federal Copyright Office registers copyrighted works, but there exists no federally supported Public Domain Office to catalog publicly owned materials. While the © designates what is copyrighted, there is no corresponding mark to indicate public domain works.[36]

But even this discussion posits that such work would not achieve that status by operation of law (lapse of copyright duration, ruling by court that the work is not subject to copyright protection, etc.) but would be available under, at best, circumstances indicating the owner's intent that it be available for anyone to use.[37] (Such designated works would not be in the public domain in a legal sense, unless one could execute a valid transfer of copyright to a successive copyright entity or owner known as the public domain.) While the effect may be the same, through other legal concepts such as estoppel, the result is a sort of shadow or other-dimensional public domain that exists parallel to the legal public domain of works not subject to copyright protection or of works no longer protected by copyright. "It is well settled that rights gained under the Copyright Act may be abandoned. But abandonment of a right must be manifested by some overt act indicating an intention to abandon that right."[38] The effect of abandonment was easy to accomplish when the law required published works to contain a notice of copyright.

Abandonment is still possible, but it is still based on the estoppel of rights enforcement based on the owner's conduct, not on the otherwise changed legal status of the work. "Abandonment of copyright protection provides a defense to a claim of copyright infringement. In copyright, waiver or abandonment of copyright occurs only if there is an intent by the copyright proprietor to surrender rights in his work."[39] The legal foundation for that "public" status might then lie in some concept of estoppel or implied license as a defense to a later claim of infringement. This can be a dangerous proposition, however, as it is not at all clear that mere appearance on a website is sufficient. For estoppel to apply, there must be reasonable reliance. Simply posting on a website under the assumption that such posting is the equivalent of "free" or "without any protection" is a dangerous proposition, considering how much protected content is posted without consent of the owner. Such content does not become public domain content just because it is posted on the web.

The assumption is that content accompanied by a clear statement of this intent, such as a CC license, would accomplish the property circumstances of reasonable reliance, but it is far from clear that such a license changes the legal status of such content.

The best would be a promise never to sue someone for use in conflict with the owner's exclusive right, or in the absence of articulated standards, depending on the circumstances, a court could conclude an implied license exists. This is because the protection under the copyright law is automatic, in a sense; there are no formal requirements of registration, and thus modern copyright law is an opt-out system. The right springs by operation of law once the three requirements for copyright are met.[40] The owner need do no more to preserve the right.[41] In contrast, an owner would need to take affirmative steps to renege his or her right to exercise dominion under the copyright or other property law.

UNDERSTANDING THE CREATIVE COMMONS SCHEMA
AND ITS POTENTIAL IMPACT

Each of the six CC licenses requires attribution and uses the symbol of a person inside a circle. This replaces the previous symbol of "BY:" in a circle (instead of a "c" in a circle as with the familiar ©, which is a bit of a misnomer, as it was supposed to indicate that the copyright owner is not necessarily the same entity as the creator).[42] However, "by" is still used in the letter coding of the license. Typically, attribution is a right of the creator, who of course may also be the owner of the work—but because it is a right that remains with the creator it is considered less of a copyright and more of a moral right. The use of the person icon is a bit more accurate, though a copyright owner need not be a person but could be a corporation, organization, or amalgam, such as a copyright collective. Other options include indicating that only noncommercial use may be made of a work. This symbol is a dollar sign in a circle crossed with the familiar "universal no" or prohibition slash. This designation allows others to make use that might otherwise step on the exclusive rights of the copyright owner. Section 106 establishes the exclusive rights of the copyright owner.[43] Two rights—to reproduce and make derivative use—do not require public use in order to trigger the owner's rights, but the following three rights do: the right to distribute, to display, and to perform the work. However, the CC license does not condition use on its private as opposed to public nature; as long as the use is noncommercial, under this provision it is acceptable, whether private or public.

A third option is to prohibit derivative uses,[44] whether commercial or noncommercial. The symbol here is an equals sign in a circle, though, again, since the symbol's appearance means that you cannot make a derivative use, a more accurate symbol would be the equals sign in a circle but with a prohibition slash. The CC-ND (No Derivative work, used in one-third of the license types) prohibits making derivative works based upon content subject to this provision. The SA (Share Alike, used in half of the license types) restrictions also may prevent combinations of other works unless they are covered by the same license. Contrary to popular belief, instead of creating a creative commons from which all can draw (recall that a license trumps copyright, so basic defenses such as fair use are not available), the CC license may in some cases be creating information islands where the only works accessible are accessible by like license (share alike) and from a CC license alone (serial or viral nature). For some users, this might result in actually a smaller universe of works from which to draw. While a work subject to copyright protection alone is still available for fair use (and commercial exploitation by others), if subject to a license, including a CC license, such uses may be foreclosed. "SA works spread the SA license virally; any derivative work that uses an SA-licensed work as an input must itself be licensed under SA. Compatibility issues arise when two 'viruses' meet, that is, when a follow-on innovator seeks to create and distribute a derivative work based on multiple preexisting works subject to different licenses. As with all CC licenses, in determining what restrictions apply to a derivative work, licenses to input works with more restrictive terms trump licenses to input works with less restrictive terms."[45] The restrictions on creating derivative works are the major impediment, in the eyes of some commentators for CC and other licenses, to supporting innovation.[46]

The prohibition prevents you from writing your own adventure involving characters from your favorite novel, television show, and so forth. Even though you do this as a hobby and show the stories to no one, in theory you are violating the terms and conditions of the license, as your story is derivative of the original. If Harry Potter were subject to a CC license with this restriction, such enthusiast uses would be prohibited. It might a safe bet to say that at least one reader, if not many readers, of J. K. Rowling's stories has done this, and that without any further distribution, reproduction, and so on, this derivative use is likely fair use. Creating a lexicon of the Potter world is not derivative,[47] but if the books were also subject to a noncommercialization condition, the lexicon that was eventually published could not have been,[48] nor could any other works such as *The Reader's Guide to Harry Potter and the Philosopher's Stone.*[49] As one commentator reflects:

> To the extent that the creation of information and cultural goods is a personally, politically, and economically significant activity, restricting the availability of inputs to the creative process by regulating the derivative works right is of substantial importance. Additionally, the regulation of derivative works will likely be the broadest and longest-term effect of a CC license because of the viral nature of SA provisions, which spread through the creation of derivative works. Moreover, the creation of derivative works involves the most complex interactions between CC licenses and raises the specter of license choices giving rise to unexpected consequences. Derivative works are inherently synthetic, often resulting from the combination of one creative work with one or more other works. The creation of derivative works is thus likely to involve combining works subject to different CC licenses, which has the potential to systematically produce outcomes neither expected nor desired by the original licensors of input works.[50]

Though the text of the "Attribution-NonCommercial-NoDerivs 3.0 Unported" Creative Commons license, clause 2, "Fair Dealing Rights," suggests that such rights are preserved in other instances,[51] the license operates as an exception to derivative-based fair uses:

> Because ND licenses do not grant licensees the right to make derivative works, ND works cannot be combined with other works and are thus per se incompatible with other CC works. While ND is a popular CC provision, included in approximately one-third of CC licenses, ND works constitute an infertile species that will never self-populate—no derivative works can be made from ND works—or breed with other content types—no derivative works can be made from a combination of ND works and non-ND works.[52]

A fourth option allows you to make derivative uses but to distribute the derivative only if it is subject to "a license identical to the license that governs your work."[53] This is represented by the familiar © symbol except with the "c" facing the opposite direction, with the letter's opening to the left, representing "copyleft" as opposed to copyright. As a result then, in combination there are several options, each with its own license and set of symbols: Attribution Noncommercial No Derivatives (BY-NC-ND),[54] Attribution Noncommercial Share Alike (BY-NC-SA),[55] Attribution Noncommercial (BY-NC),[56] Attribution No Derivatives (BY-ND),[57] Attribution Share Alike (BY-SA),[58] and Attribution (BY).[59] To attract more contributors to the "commons," options are offered that allow owners to retain different sets of rights while contracting others away, that is, to offer a promise not to sue but only for certain uses, prohibiting others. "One of the unintended consequences of such choice is the dilution of the signaling effect of a licensing scheme."[60] The variety may also confuse some contributors.[61]

While it is true that a license can alter what otherwise would be the result under the copyright law, the point of the CC license is to create a commons of works as if copyright did not apply, but this requires a positive act. However, the licenses, in making these designations, fail repeatedly to use definitions consistent with the copyright law, so the carve-outs from copyright are not done with legal precision. This may leave some rights still under protection or may at least lead to further confusion. For example, compare "work" under the CC license[62] with the categories of authorship in the copyright law;[63] or "publicly perform" under the CC license[64] with section 101's concept of public display or performance;[65] or collection[66] under the CC license with a collective work or compilation under the copyright law.[67]

Again, there is nothing odd about a license agreement altering the copyright landscape by alternative definitions; in fact, that is often the purpose of the license agreement. But where the purpose of a CC license agreement is to take work that would otherwise be subject to copyright restrictions and place such works into an implied (to borrow a contract law concept) public domain, it would appear that a more accurate way to do this would be to use markers that identify the work within the copyright law protection scheme so it can be taken out of that protection.

Each of the six CC licenses contains a disclaimer of warranties but no indemnification clause. So, users beware! If content is presented for use by an owner subject to a CC license, but in reality that licensor had no authority to license the content, and the reader makes what he or she thought was a permitted use under the CC license, but it isn't because the licensor really did not have the permission to grant this use in the first place, the reader's use could be infringing. With the indemnification, the erroneous licensor is off the hook. While the author knows of no reported case of a CC license where a licensor did not have the proper authority to license and a licensee made a reliance on the grant to his or her detriment, it is quite possible, given the misconceptions that often exist about copyright use rights, that such misinformation might also carry over into ownership rights. Given the nature of the CC license, where individuals without access to legal advice license works, this may be a common occurrence, especially when the licensed work is based on an unauthorized derivative work.

THE LEGALITY (VALIDITY) OF CREATIVE COMMONS LICENSES

Is the open source license agreement enforceable, in contract and/or under a theory of copyright infringement? Is the open source agreement more akin to a promise not to sue for copyright infringement—a lawsuit that could then be estopped under some theory of implied, if not in fact, license, or under an equitable concept of reliance? Or is it an enforceable contract based on consideration? Remember, a promise can constitute consideration. If it is a valid contract, can rights of noncompliance with its terms and conditions proceed under copyright theory as well as contract? A recent circuit decision appears to answer both the contract and copyright questions in the affirmative.

In *Jacobson v. Katzer*, a district court denied plaintiff Jacobson's motion for preliminary injunction to stop the use made of it by Katzer (commercial development of the Jacobson software for use by the model railroading industry and hobbyists) because it reasoned that the license granted by the open source agreement was too broad to leave Jacobson with any rights left to enforce under the copyright law. It is the possibility of being sued that ensures the terms and conditions which implement the goals of the open source are fulfilled, in other words, open access but with attribution requirements or prohibitions on commercial use unless the same open source mechanisms are in place. "The District Court found that Jacobsen had a cause of action only for breach of contract, rather than an action for copyright infringement based on a breach of the conditions of the Artistic License. Because a breach of contract creates no presumption of irreparable harm, the District Court denied the motion for a preliminary injunction."[68] The license Jacobson used contained a restriction common to open source systems:

> By requiring that users copy and restate the license and attribution information, a copyright holder can ensure that recipients of the redistributed computer code know the identity of the owner as well as the scope of the license granted by the original owner. The Artistic License in this case also requires that changes to the computer code be tracked so that downstream users know what part of the computer code is the original code created by the copyright holder and what part has been newly added or altered by another collaborator.[69]

Based on these circumstances, the appellate court articulated the precise question, capturing both the intent of the CC license (to designate works in the "public domain") and whether the terms effecting that designation were enforceable under a theory of copyright (assuming the work was otherwise protected by copyright and such designation was indeed necessary): "We consider here the ability of a copyright holder to dedicate certain work to free public use and yet enforce an 'open source' copyright license to control the future distribution and modification of that work."[70]

The author warned the reader that some of the discussion in the basic contract chapter would become important in later chapters. Recall the discussion regarding covenants or promises in contracts and conditions and the impact each has when interpreting the contract? This distinction is critical to the decision and to CC licensing. "The heart of the argument on appeal concerns whether the terms of the Artistic License are conditions of, or merely covenants to, the copyright license."[71] Again, the difference between a condition and a covenant is important. Recall that breach of a covenant (or promise) may give rise to damages if the breach is material (e.g., a promise to pay for access to a database). However, if the provision is a condition, there is no breach, and no right to claim damages, but if the condition is not met, it releases the other party from its obligation; in other words, the triggering event requiring a return act has not occurred. (For example, the obligation to pay for the database is conditioned on the vendor providing access to it. If the vendor does not provide this access, the library cannot sue the vendor for damages, but it does not have to pay for the database either, as the condition of access was not fulfilled so the promise to pay did not arise.)

The license of an exclusive right under the copyright law leaves no rights left to enforce other than contract. (Licenses in the library world typically offer nonexclusive rights.) However, if the owner retains effective rights and the license is limited in scope, then the unauthorized use of the content can be answered by a claim for copyright infringement. "Thus, if the terms of the Artistic License allegedly violated are both covenants and conditions, they may serve to limit the scope of the license and are governed by copyright law. If they are merely covenants, by contrast, they are governed by contract law."[72] (Recall from a previous chapter that license provisions in the library world can be both covenants and conditions. "We promise to report noncompliance by our patrons using your database" can also be a condition because if the licensor believes you are not complying, it might have the right to suspend access.) Looking to the case law from within the boundaries of the 9th Circuit, the jurisdiction from which the case arose (as an issue in the case involved patent law, the Federal Circuit assumed appellate jurisdiction for the initial appeal of the California district court decision), the Federal Circuit observed the rule "[u]nder California contract law [but again remember that contract is state law, even the court trying the case is a federal one], 'provided that' typically denotes a condition."[73] The rights granted by Jacobson were indeed prefaced by the "provided that" clause.[74] In one of the strongest statements in support of the enforceability of open source license agreements, the court commented: "Copyright holders who engage in open source licensing have the right to control the modification and distribution of copyrighted material."[75] In the very next breath, the Federal Circuit implied that the agreements are valid contractually because the necessary consideration is rendered in the form of a promise not to undertake ("provided that") certain uses: "Copyright licenses are designed to support the right to exclude; money damages alone do not support or enforce that right. The choice to exact consideration in the form of compliance with the open source requirements of disclosure and explanation of changes, rather than as a dollar-denominated fee, is entitled to no less legal recognition."[76] That the owner retained rights under the copyright law is further revealed in the conditions themselves. For example, inviting the user to "make other distribution arrangements with the Copyright Holder" for uses that exceed those granted by the license, for example, "use the modified Package only within [the user's] corporation or organization."[77] The court concluded that the restrictions in the CC license were conditions as well as covenants, meaning that a claim against the licensee could rest in copyright as well as contract.

> The Artistic License states on its face that the document creates conditions...The conditions set forth in the Artistic License are vital to enable the copyright holder to retain the ability to benefit from the work of downstream users...The District Court interpreted the Artistic License to permit a user to "modify the material in any way" and did not find that any of the "provided that" limitations in the Artistic License served to limit this grant. The District Court's interpretation of the conditions of the Artistic License does not credit the explicit restrictions in the license that govern a downloader's right to modify and distribute the copyrighted work. The copyright holder here expressly stated the terms upon which the right to modify and distribute the material depended and invited direct contact if a downloader wished to negotiate other terms. These restrictions were both clear and necessary to accomplish the objectives of the open source licensing collaboration, including economic benefit.[78]

In light of this misinterpretation by the district court, the circuit court reversed the decision and remanded the case for further proceedings.[79] The case is significant because "[p]rior to this, there have been no rulings on the enforceability of open-source copyright."[80]

Is open source a good thing, as the court in *Jacobson v. Katzer* observed? "Open source licensing has become a widely used method of creative collaboration that serves to advance the arts and sciences in a manner and at a pace that few could have imagined just a few decades ago."[81] When used with full understanding of the implications of the CC license options from both licensor and licensee perspectives, it can be. The value of the CC license for patrons is that you can structure your resources to include only those resources subject to a particular CC license that meets the needs of your patrons.[82] For example, if teachers would like to make a variety of uses (e.g., reproduce, derivative, public distribution, display or performance) that might step on exclusive rights, if use is made of only those CC licensed works which allow for such uses except when for commercial purposes (i.e., noncommercial), then the only concern teachers need have is to remember to make proper attribution of the work; they need not worry about whether a use is fair or falls under the educator provision of section 110. Despite a positive decision such as the *Jacobson* case, there are still unanswered questions regarding the legal nature of the CC license that only future disputes will resolve.[83]

UNDERSTANDING THE GENERAL PUBLIC LICENSE

Version 3 of the GNU General Public License (GPL) was released on June 29, 2007.[84] A GNU Free Documentation License, Version 1.3, is dated November 2008. Like the CC license, its intent is to offer an alternative to the present default of the copyright law (e.g., "This work is protected and not available for use unless..."), offering a copyleft option (the work is protected but is available for use under the following terms)[85] and employing a licensing scheme to accomplish that goal: the GPL "is intended to guarantee your freedom to share and change all versions of a program—to make sure it remains free software for all its users... use the GNU General Public License for most of your software; it applies also to any other work released this way by its authors. You can apply it to your programs, too."[86] The GPL is part manifesto—as the document contains an extensive preamble—and part legal document. Like the CC license, the GPL uses copyright to enforce its goal of software that is forever free—or, perhaps more accurately, "forever available"—as long as users abide by certain terms.

As is typical in software agreements, content subject to the GPL is not subject to any warranty,[87] and any modifications must be identified "so that their problems will not be attributed erroneously to authors of previous versions."[88] As is also typical of disclaimers, the "program is [provided] 'as is' without warranty of any kind, either expressed or implied, including, but not limited to, the implied warranties of merchantability and fitness for a particular purpose."[89] Liability is also limited without recourse to "damages, including any general, special, incidental or consequential damages arising out of the use or inability to use the program."[90] Open agreements contain very broad disclaimer provisions, essentially offering no warranty whatsoever. "One of the major liability risks with regard to use of open sources software is that code contributed by third parties is of unknown origin and consequently constitutes an intellectual property risk."[91] This reality, coupled with the absence of warranties and the presence of broad disclaimers, may make it unattractive as a building block for an institution's programming.

The definition of "to modify" does not parallel the statutory language in the copyright law of "derivative work" but does make clear reference to the copyright law and what would otherwise be a use requiring permission of the copyright owner-licensor.[92] Like the CC license, the rights granted extend for the duration of copyright of the content "and are irrevocable provided the stated conditions are met," with the main grant of rights being the "unlimited permission to run the unmodified program."[93] Copies of the source code may be conveyed as long as the licensee "conspicuously and appropriately publishes on each copy an appropriate copyright notice."[94] Another provision states that "[n]o covered work shall be deemed part of an effective technological measure."[95] This clause is significant because, under section 1201, a protection circumvention of technological protection measures is prohibited, but the provision applies only to a control that "effectively controls access to" that work.[96] Since a GPL is deemed to be unprotected in this manner, section 1201 does not apply and circumvention could be undertaken. Likewise, when a work covered by the GPL is conveyed, the conveyor agrees to "waive any legal power to forbid circumvention of technological measures" and "disclaim any intention to limit operation or modification of the work as a means of enforcing...your or third parties' legal rights to forbid circumvention of technological measures."[97]

The viral or perpetual nature of the license is guaranteed by section 10: "Each time you convey a covered work, the recipient automatically receives a license for the original licensors. To run, modify and propagate that work, subject to this License."[98] The viral nature is also supported by provision for termination unless works are propagated or modified under the terms and conditions, one of which is to license serially any content subject to the license.[99] There are instructions on how best to effect the goals of the GPL and ensure that subsequent users are aware that their use of the program or any modification to it is also subject to the terms of a GPL.[100] There are also instructions to have employees secure a "copyright disclaimer" from their employers for works that might be subject to the work-made-for-hire doctrine.[101]

Another characteristic is that derivative programs must also be subject to the same initial GPL conditions of ability to copy, modify, or redistribute. These rights are the core rights of copyright owners and offer the requisite commercial incentive to develop and distribute new (including derivative) works. The GPL attempts to circumvent this commercial incentive mechanism of the copyright law; thus, it is deemed copyleft and is "a key legal innovation of the GPL."[102] Contrary to popular sentiment, the GPL may hurt innovation in certain circumstances.[103] "The more controversial GPL terms, however, are those that apply to derivative works based upon GPL-licensed works...It is because of these terms [identification of changes, changes subject also to GPL, and redistribution under GPL] that the GPL is often referred to as 'viral,' because it 'infects,' or subjects all modified works to the GPL, which in turn subjects all modified works of modified works to the GPL, and so on."[104] Professor Determann concludes that most new preparations of software subject to a GPL will not result in a prohibited derivative work; as a result, the alleged negative impact on innovation will not occur.[105] Another commentator reaching a similar result[106] argues for a broader reading of derivative works in the application of the GPL, an unlikely result, as the commentator admits.[107]

Finally, there is a prompt that the GNU GPL "does not permit incorporating of your program into proprietary programs," instead recommending the GNU Lesser General Public License for this program.[108] Other documentation, while indicating that "most GNU libraries are covered by the Lesser GPL," urges consideration of the GPL unless there is a case where "a free library's features are readily available for proprietary software through other alternative libraries. In that case, the library cannot give free software any particular advantage, so it is better to use the Lesser GPL for that library... using the GPL for ours would have driven proprietary software developers to use another—no problem for them, only for us."[109]

To accompany the GPL, because "free software needs free documentation," a second GNU license, the Free Documentation License is available. The preamble offers a clearer statement of the viral or serial nature of the copyleft goal: "This License is a kind of 'copyleft,' which means that derivative works of the document must themselves be free in the same sense. It complements the GNU General Public License, which is a copyleft license designed for free software."[110] Combinations ("with other documents released under this License") and collections of documents ("consisting of the Document and other documents released under this license") are allowed, as is the extraction of "a single document from such a collection."[111] Content subject to the Free Documentation License "or its derivative" may be combined with works not subject to the Free Documentation License, but then these works are deemed aggregates.[112] Translations are considered modifications.[113] The Free Documentation License is intended "to make a manual, textbook, or other functional and useful document 'free' in the sense of freedom: to assure everyone the effective freedom to copy and redistribute it, with or without modifying it, either commercially or noncommercially... But this License is not limited to software manuals; it can be used for any textual work, regardless of subject matter or whether it is published as a printed book. We recommend this License principally for works whose purpose is instruction or reference."[114]

On condition (remember from the previous discussion that contract clauses introduced by the words "provided that" are generally construed to be conditions) relating to the use of notice, rights of reproduction—though the license uses the term *copy*—public display, and distribution (whether public or private) are granted. Prohibitions on the use of technical measures are included, though both rights and limitations are contained in a provision titled Verbatim Copying.[115] Section 2 also prohibits use of technological protection measures that would "obstruct or control the reading or further copying of the copies you make or distribute."[116] Though not a right of the copyright owner, the Free Documentation License, like the CC license, incorporates the concept of attribution.[117] As with the GPL, similar provision is made for terminations[118] and future revisions.[119]

THE LEGAL STATUS OF THE GPL AND OTHER OPEN SOURCE SOFTWARE

As with the CC license, the important question is whether the GPL Documentation License (or the Lesser General Public License) is enforceable.[120] As explained by Professor Moglen, a GPL is enforceable, at least against those who make a distribution of software subject to the GPL scheme:

> Because there's nothing complex or controversial about the license's substantive provisions, I have never even seen a serious argument that the GPL exceeds a licensor's powers. But it is sometimes said that the GPL can't be enforced because users haven't "accepted" it. This claim is based on a misunderstanding. The license does not require anyone to accept it in order to acquire, install, use, inspect, or experimentally modify GPL'd software. All of those activities are either forbidden or controlled by proprietary software firms, so they require you to accept a license, including contractual provisions outside the reach of copyright, before you can use their works. The free software movement thinks all those activities are rights, which all users ought to have; we don't even *want* to cover those activities by license. Almost everyone who uses GPL'd software from day to day needs no license, and accepts none. The GPL only obliges you if you distribute software made from GPL'd code, and only needs to be accepted when redistribution occurs. And because no one can ever redistribute without a license, we can safely presume that anyone redistributing GPL'd software intended to accept the GPL. After all, the GPL requires each copy of covered software to include the license text, so everyone is fully informed.[121]

In this sense, the GPL is a nonlicense. Users are granted rights under certain conditions of use, in other words, that the subsequent distribution or derivative version will also be subject to the GPL. In this way, the seriality of the content is what is licensed. The use rights promised are irrevocable, but the legal essence of the license is an agreement not to sue. As there is no remedy available to the licensee should the licensor withdraw the permission, the mechanism appears less of a contract with enforceable rights going to each party.

According to Nimmer, "On the other hand, treating an FOSS [Free Software and Open Source] license as a contract dependent on contractual rights for enforceability requires consideration of each transaction to answer whether or not, in that transaction, there were adequate indicia of assent to the contract or, as stated in UCITA and in common law, whether the licensee manifested assent to the license after having had an opportunity to review its terms. Because of this contextual aspect of contract-making (a contract is, after all, an agreement between two parties), asking noncontextual questions such as, 'is the GPL an Enforceable contract?' is nonsensical. The question is, rather, whether as used in a particular transaction, did the FOSS license come to represent the terms of contract of the parties?"[122] Under this view, the licensor makes an offer defined by the terms of the GPL, and the licensee accepts by incorporating and distributing the GPL-licensed code. The burdens that the licensor undertakes constitute consideration. Many copyright attorneys and scholars believe that the GPL is a contract and hold this view despite the Free Software Foundation's (FSF) assertions to the contrary.[123] "A license is a unilateral abrogation of rights. The licensor has, by law, the ability to enforce certain rights against the licensee, and the license functions as a promise not to enforce those rights. A 'conditional license'—if such a creature exists— is a license that can be revoked if the conditions are violated, which essentially makes it a contract."[124] Another commentator suggests that, as a contract, the GPL would raise preemption issues (discussed in Chapter 4).[125] However, Determann concludes that in jurisdictions where courts construe terms more narrowly issues of enforceability may arise, not necessarily related to contract formation but related to "copyright misuse doctrines, competition laws, and unfair contract terms."[126]

What is missing from the GPL is the meeting of the minds. There may be consideration in the promises made but no assent by subsequent, serial users. If this is true, then, as with the CC license, when the promise not to sue induces reasonable reliance one commentator argues that the GPL, while not a contract, is nonetheless enforceable under the guise of promissory estoppel.[127]

Though no court has addressed the specific enforceability of the GPL as a contract, it is implicit in several decisions. "That the software had been distributed pursuant to a GNU General Public License does not defeat trademark ownership, nor does this in any way compel a finding that Darrah abandoned his rights in trademark. Appellants misconstrue the function of a GNU General Public License. Software distributed pursuant to such a license is not necessarily ceded to the public domain and the licensor purports to retain ownership rights, which may or may not include rights to a mark."[128] Other scholars, such as Kumar, appear to support enforceability of the GPL but have no definitive precedent on which to rely: "Scholars and advocates struggle to articulate the legal groundwork that makes the license enforceable. Hindering this work is a chicken-and-egg problem, where the lack of related precedent causes parties to settle lawsuits, and frequent settlement prevents the generation of precedent."[129] Professor Kumar argues for the enforceability of the GPL as a contract, as opposed to the "noncontract" theory of validity that is forwarded by the proponent-founders of GPL: "The second theory holds that the GPL is a contract. This theory is plausible, because traditional software licenses are generally interpreted as contracts. But such licenses also have cash consideration. Contract proponents argue that consideration does exist under the GPL. But ultimately, they are unable to show that there is a meeting of minds between the licensor and licensee, thus failing the requirements of contract formation."[130]

The *Jacobsen v. Katzer* decision discussed previously involved software under a CC license, but its holding would be directly applicable to the GPL, L-GPL, or any other open source software program. Such licenses are enforceable. This is a positive for proponents of such regimes. However, if the terms of such licenses are enforceable in one context, such terms might very well be enforceable in another. Provisions that take away fair-use rights to reverse engineer or otherwise create derivative works would be enforceable as well.[131] Tacit acceptance of the GPL was made in *Wallace v. International Business Machines Corp. et al.*[132] While the decision involved the antitrust law, there could be no consideration of whether use of the GPL violates antitrust law (which the court concluded it does not) if the terms of the GPL were not in some way enforceable or otherwise valid in the first instance.

In *Wallace v. International Business Machines Corp. et al.*,[133] a competing developer challenged the validity of the GPL as unfair restraint on trade; in other words, with the GPL provision that all derivative uses of Linux remain free in force, he cannot develop a commercially viable product.[134] The issue of whether the restriction violated the federal antitrust laws could be relevant only if in fact the provision could be enforced or had the desired effect:

> Intellectual property can be used without being used up; the marginal cost of an additional user is zero (costs of media and paper to one side), so once a piece of intellectual property exists the efficient price of an extra copy is zero, for that is where price equals marginal cost. Copyright and patent laws give authors a right to charge more, so that they can recover their fixed costs (and thus promote innovation), but they do not require authors to charge more. No more does antitrust law require higher prices. Linux and other open-source projects have been able to cover their fixed costs through donations of time; as long as that remains true, it would reduce efficiency and consumers' welfare to force the authors to levy a charge on each new user.[135]

Planetary Motion, Inc. v Techplosion, Inc.[136] involved a trademark dispute relating to the name of a Unix-based e-mail program that was initially distributed subject to a GPL[137] but later purchased by the plaintiff from the developer.[138] In discussing the legal significance of the GPL, the 11th Circuit, much like the 7th Circuit in *Wallace v. International Business Machines Corp. et al.*, implied that the agreement could at least convey an otherwise valid promise of use rights: "That the Software had been distributed pursuant to a GNU General Public License does not defeat trademark ownership, nor does this in any way compel a finding that Darrah abandoned his rights in trademark. Appellants misconstrue the function of a GNU General Public License. Software distributed pursuant to such a license is not necessarily ceded to the public domain and the licensor purports to retain ownership rights, which may or may not include rights to a mark."[139]

Computer Associates International v. Quest Software, Inc.[140] raised the issue of whether the inclusion of 22 lines of code from an existing software program subject to a GPL in the creation of a "parser" code that was then used to create another program[141] violated the terms of the GPL. The court explained the restrictions the GPL placed on subsequent users:

> One publicly available program used in the creation of EDBA [Enterprise Database Administrator] was Bison, a program distributed by the Free Software Foundation (FSF). The EDBA code contains a string indicating that it uses "GNU Bison version 1.25." Bison is open source code, meaning that it is distributed by the FSF at no cost. Any user of that code is, however, bound by the terms of the GNU General Public License (GPL). The GPL puts restrictions on the modification and subsequent distribution of freeware programs. Essentially, once the programs are freely released into the public domain, the creators intend for them to stay free. Defendants claim that plaintiff's are violating the GPL by attempting to claim a copyright in a program that contains Bison source code.[142]

Implicit in this comment is the recognition that the GPL will have some legal effect, that its restrictions on subsequent users are valid. The court went on to explain that the GPL restrictions, while valid, applied only to the code which was derived from it, not independent code that was later created with it. A critical distinction: "Defendants' argument fails because plaintiff is not attempting to claim a copyright in the Bison source code. Instead, the creators of EDBA used the Bison utility program to create the parser source code. While doing so, they made modifications to the Bison program to suit the specific task of creating a parser to use in database administration software. The GPL would prevent plaintiff from attempting to claim a copyright in that modified version of Bison."[143] However, in this case, the GPL specifically allowed the creation and commercialization of output programs like the parser program.[144] In a similar dispute involving whether a subsequent program was derivative or independent, another federal district court appeared also to assume the validity of the GPL and its restrictions on derivative uses.[145]

THE LESSER GPL

The Lesser GPL is designed for scenarios where a user desires to retain a proprietary interest or as the terms of the license indicate is an "application," defined as "any work that makes use of an interface provided by the Library, but which is not otherwise based on the Library."[146] The opening but otherwise unlabeled sentence of the Lesser GPL indicates that the license "incorporates the terms and conditions of version 3 of the GNU General Public License, supplemented by the additional permission listed below."[147] This section then allows a user to "convey a work under section 3 and 4 of this license without being bound by section 3 of the GNU GPL," those sections being the provisions requiring viral or serial licensing of all software based on content subject to a GNU GPL.[148] Sections 3 and 4 of the Lesser GPL allow a user to "convey such object code [from an application that "incorporate[s] material from a header file that is part of the Library"] under terms of your choice" or to "convey a Combined work ["combining or linking an Application with the Library"[149]] under terms of your choice"[150] subject to conditions of notice and inclusion of the GPL and Lesser GPL documentation.

In deciding between GPL and L-GPL and in the context of higher education, the following statement is made: "Free software contributes to human knowledge, while non-free software does not. Universities should therefore encourage free software for the sake of advancing human knowledge, just as they should encourage scientists and other scholars to publish their work."[151] This statement expresses the worldview of the proponents of open source. While a "free" content system certainly accomplishes the goal of access to knowledge to a greater extent than does a system based on proprietary interests (assuming equal or equitable access to the tools to access that knowledge), there is debate as to whether it results in more knowledge creation per se. The reality is that knowledge is created under both open source (as recent decades have shown) and proprietary systems (as history has shown).

SUMMARY POINTS

▶ When the underlying content of a CC license is protected by copyright, then the terms of the license can be both conditions and covenants and, as covenants, can be enforced both in copyright and contract.

▶ As the decision in *Jacobson v. Katzer* reveals, CC licenses are valid contracts.

▶ The GPL, L-GPL, and accompanying documentation licenses, as well as the CC licenses, would appear to be enforceable either as a contract or, if not a contract, as a license based on the concept of estoppel. When rights are reserved by the license an open source or CC license may be enforced like other licenses if the use exceeds the scope of the permission through copyright infringement claims.

▶ Recent court decisions tacitly accept the enforceability of such agreements under a contract theory. This is good for open source proponents, but the same case law can be used by proprietary-aggressive licensors to enforce similar restrictions, such as no derivatives, even if that use would otherwise be a fair one under the copyright law, in the absence of the license. Further, such licenses could include terms that extend restrictions beyond the concept of derivative to all modifications or adaptations or sourcing.

LEARNING EXAMPLES

▶ **Example 9.1**

Situation: A library digitizes a collection of letters and photographs for which it has determined the copyright protection is expired. The library desires to make the collection available on its website subject to a Creative Commons license and, as a part of that license, prohibit commercial use of any item in the collection without further permission. A locally based national corporation uses several of the photographs and letters in an upcoming nationwide advertising campaign.

Legal Analysis: Creative Commons or similar licenses are enforceable under contract principles. If the underlying works were still protected by copyright, then an action to enforce the license could rest in both copyright and contract. The important requirement is to ensure that use rights take the form of a covenant and a condition; with a condition being present, the terms are enforceable under both copyright and contract.

ENDNOTES

1. For a listing and discussion of other open source licenses, such as the MPL (Mozilla Public License), see F. Lawrence Street and Mark P. Grant, Law of the Internet § 14.04 at 14-10–4-12 (2001, updated through release #19, December 2011). See also Kennedy, *A Primer on Open Source Licensing Legal Issues; Copyright, Copyleft and Copyfuture*, 20 St. Louis University Public Law Review 345 (2001).

2. Sapna Kumar, *Enforcing the GNU GPL*, 2006 University of Illinois Journal of Law, Technology, and Policy 1, 13 (2006): "Hammering the GPL into a contract-shaped mold for legal stability is very tempting. Contract law is more developed then licensing law and offers a wide range of legal remedies that are not available under the Copyright Act. Judges and intellectual property attorneys have little experience in dealing with non-contractual licenses."

3. Raymond T. Nimmer, Information Law § 12:40 (Notices as a Non-Contractual Relationship) (database updated in Westlaw, November 2011).

4. Raymond T. Nimmer, Law of Computer Technology § 13.37 (Effect of contract not being formed—Notices as a noncontractual relationship) (database updated September 2011).

5. eBay, Inc. v. Bidder's Edge, Inc., 100 F. Supp. 2d 1058 (N.D. Cal. 2000) (trespass to real property versus trespass to chattels or conversion discussed); Register.com v. Verio, Inc., 126 F. Supp. 2d 238 (S.D.N.Y. 2000), injunction issued, likelihood of harm demonstrated, if others allowed to replicate Verio's actions of using robot to extract data, system operability would suffer; and Ticketmaster, Corp. v. Tickets.com, 2000 U.S. Dist. LEXIS 12987 (C.D. Calif. 2000), tacit acceptance of digital trespass, but no evidence of harm demonstrated.

6. Pollstar v. Gigmania, Ltd., 170 F. Supp. 2d 974 (E.D. Cal. 2000): court "declines to decide this issue at the present time" but observes that the "claim was pled with sufficiency as a 'hot news' claim"; and Fred Wehrenberg Circuit of Theatres, Inc. v. Moviefone, Inc., 73 F. Supp. 2d 1044 (E. D. Mo. 1999): movie listings not "hot news" under Motorola standard (high cost, time sensitive, commercial free-riding, parties in direct competition, reduce incentive to collect, i.e., missing the incentive element). See NBA v. Motorola, 105 F.3d 841 (2nd Cir. 1997): articulating a genus of modern misappropriation law: "hot news."

7. See, for example, the Computer Fraud and Abuse Act (CFAA), 18 U.S.C. § 1030, offering a civil right of action for those who access a computer "without authorization or exceeding authorized access." The statute has been used in website settings. Ticketmaster L.L.C. v. RMG Technologies, Inc., 507 F. Supp. 2d 1096, 1113 (C.D. Cal. 2007): "It appears likely that Plaintiff will be able to prove that Defendant gained unauthorized access to, and/or exceeded authorized access to, Plaintiff's protected computers, and caused damage thereby. Based on the statute and the cases Plaintiff cites, the Court also agrees that the required $5,000 of harm may consist of harm to a computer system, and need not be suffered by just one computer during one particular intrusion." See also Creative Computing v. Getloaded .com LLC, 386 F.3d 930, 934–935 (9th Cir. 2004) (interpreting the CFAA). "However, because Plaintiff has not quantified its harm as required by the statute or even attempted to show what portion of the harm is attributable to Defendant, the Court cannot find that Plaintiff has affirmatively shown that its harm caused by Defendant exceeds the $5,000 minimum. Thus, the CFAA claim does not provide a basis for a preliminary injunction."

8. Nimmer, *supra* note 4.

9. "By exercising any rights to the work provided here, you accept and agree to be bound by the terms of this license. To the extent this license may be considered to be a contract, the licensor grants you the rights contained herein consideration of your acceptance of such terms and conditions" (http://creativecommons.org/licenses/by/3.0/legalcode).

10. Compare Jason B. Wacha, *Taking the Case: Is the GPL Enforceable?*, 21 SANTA CLARA COMPUTER AND HIGH TECHNOLOGY LAW JOURNAL 451, 455–456 (2005), footnotes omitted: "Whether the GPL is a contract at all is a subject for a longer discussion, and does not, for purposes of this analysis, affect the validity of the document. It may, however, affect the remedies available for a violation of the GPL. A pure copyright license would be enforceable under U.S. federal copyright law. A contract, on the other hand, would be enforceable under state contract law, which may vary from state to state. Additionally, enforcement as a pure license would eliminate certain defenses available to an alleged infringer under contract law. The Free Software Foundation, which authored the GPL, claims that document is a copyright license, not a contract. Others have stated that the GPL is a 'conditional license,' while many others simply believe that the GPL is a contract" with Kumar, *supra* note 2, footnote omitted: "The GPL's validity does not rest upon exotic forms of property or upon the manipulation of the license into a contract.

Rather, the license is enforceable by the licensor through federal copyright law and by the licensee through a state promissory estoppel action."

11. Kumar, *supra* note 2, at 25, footnotes omitted. See also Nimmer, *supra* note 3, at § 11.4: "The stated tradition in intellectual property law fields holds that a license is a permission, waiver or release of rather than an affirmative grant."

12. See Niva Elkin-Koren, *What Contracts Cannot Do: The Limits of Private Ordering in Facilitating a Creative Commons*, 74 FORDHAM LAW REVIEW 375, 376 (2005) (Symposium, Law and the Information Society, Panel 1: Intellectual Property and Public Values): "Could, however, the copyright opposition use contracts for strengthening the public domain? Creative Commons seeks to do exactly that. Creative Commons is a nonprofit U.S. based organization that operates a licensing platform promoting free use of creative works. The idea is to facilitate the release of creative works under generous license terms that would make works available for sharing and reuse" (footnote omitted).

13. Street and Grant, *supra* note 1, § 14.01 at 14-2.

14. See http://www.opensource.org/docs/definition.html.

15. Street and Grant, *supra* note 1, § 14.01 at 14-2, note 2.

16. See Zachary Kats, *Pitfalls of Open Licensing: An Analysis of Creative Commons Licensing*, 46 IDEA: THE INTELLECTUAL PROPERTY LAW REVIEW 391, 393 (2006): "License proliferation also raises a second concern. In at least two instances, CC licenses have led to incompatibility problems, where conflicting license provisions inhibited the creation of new works, contrary to the apparent wishes of the creators of the original works . . . this Article concludes that CC license proliferation could create systematic and unexpected incompatibilities between licenses. These incompatibilities could result in islands of CC-licensed works that cannot be combined with other types of works" (footnote omitted).

17. Street and Grant, *supra* note 1, at Appendix 14-A, 14-A-11: "The first thing to keep in mind is that a license can only have an effect if what you are doing would, without the license, infringe an intellectual property right owned by the licensor."

18. The right "to prepare derivative works based upon the copyrighted work" is one of the exclusive rights of the copyright owner (17 U.S.C. § 106(2)).

19. "A 'derivative work' is a work based upon one or more preexisting works, such as a translation, musical arrangement, dramatization, fictionalization, motion picture version, sound recording, art reproduction, abridgment, condensation, or any other form in which a work may be recast, transformed, or adapted. A work consisting of editorial revisions, annotations, elaborations, or other modifications which, as a whole, represent an original work of authorship, is a 'derivative work'" (17 U.S.C. § 101).

20. Open source theory may not work for patent. The GPL may not be valid where patent is concerned, as "a patent is infringed by anything that falls with the claims of the patent, even if there has been no copying of any kind. If software covered by the PGL were held to infringe patent, the patent owner could impose restrictions on the use and distribution of that software and the GPL could not prevent this" (Street and Grant, *supra* note 1, at Appendix 14-A, 14-A-16).

21. Lydia Pallas Loren, *Building a Reliable Semicommons of Creative Works: Enforcement of Creative Commons Licenses and Limited Abandonment of Copyright*, 14 GEORGE MASON LAW REVIEW 271, 296–297 (2007): "The Creative Commons notice acts as a boundary marker indicating that the copyright owner has decided to 'place' a work within the semicommons. The deed and the symbols it contains are the sign posts of the use rights the public has been granted to this 'piece' of 'property.' These clear words and simple symbols seek to notify the public that these works have common use rights on which the public should be able to confidently rely. The dynamic interaction between the public use rights and the private use rights are an important aspect of a semicommons."

22. Elkin-Koren, *supra* note 12, at 377 (Symposium, Law and the Information Society, Panel 1: Intellectual Property and Public Values). "Creative Commons' strategy presupposes that minimizing external information costs is critical for enhancing access to creative works. It seeks to reduce these costs by offering a licensing platform. Yet, facilitating an alternative to copyright *through* contracts requires that licenses be made enforceable against third parties. Such licenses may increase the external information cost carried by those seeking to avoid copyright infringement. The lack of standardization further increases the cost of determining the duties and privileges related to any specific work. Each licensing format, which binds third parties, would dramatically increase the cost of avoidance, thus enhancing the chilling effect of copyright law," suggesting that the greatest benefit may accrue to the individual creator versus an "industrial" creator that views these barriers as a cost of production (*id.* at 384–385). "While the current copyright regime serves the needs of intermediaries, Creative Commons focuses on the needs of individual creators" (*id.* at 385).

23. Severine Dusollier, *Contract Options for Individual Artists: Master's Tools v. The Master's House: Creative Commons v. Copyright*, 29 THE COLUMBIA JOURNAL OF LAW AND THE ARTS 271, 271 (2006): "This Article, which is the result of that reflection, explores some unintended, potential effects of the Creative Commons licensing regime on culture and creation, due to the project's somewhat ambiguous ideology and its hidden agenda"; and Joseph Scott Miller, *Allchin's Folly: Exploding Some Myths about Open Source Software*, 20 CARDOZO ARTS AND ENTERTAINMENT LAW JOURNAL 491, 496–497 (2002): "In sharp contrast to placing a piece of software into the public domain by utterly disclaiming copyright protection, using a free software license such as the GPL prevents downstream recipients from using the software to create new programs for distribution under a closed source approach. The GPL demonstrates that one can harness the control that copyright law provides to make a piece of software fully and indefinitely accessible, or free, to its users. The carefully crafted license terms do all the work. In other words, open source software, far from forswearing copyright protection, relies centrally on the basic rights that copyright law gives to authors."

24. Data on distribution of license among the six options is available at http://creative commons.org/weblog/entry/5293 (Neeru Paharia, entry dated February 25, 2005): "Last week we mentioned there were over 5 million web pages linking to Creative

Commons licenses. This week, it has come to our attention that Yahoo! has updated their index to find well over 10 million web pages that link to our licenses."

25. Zachary Katz, *Pitfalls of Open Licensing: An Analysis of Creative Commons Licensing*, 46 IDEA: THE INTELLECTUAL PROPERTY LAW REVIEW 391, 396–397 (2006).

26. See Tomas A. Lipinski, *A Functional Approach to Understanding and Applying Fair Use*, in 45 ANNUAL REVIEW OF INFORMATION SCIENCE AND TECHNOLOGY (ARIST) 525 (Blaize Cronin, ed. 2010) (pp. 525–621).

27. Computer Assocs. Int'l v. Quest Software, Inc., 333 F. Supp. 2d 688, 697 (N.D. Ill. 2004), reference to GPL-licensed code as being in the public domain.

28. See, for example, Dennis W. K. Khong, *Orphan Works, Abandonware and the Missing Market for Copyrighted Goods* 15 INTERNATIONAL JOURNAL OF LAW AND INFORMATION TECHNOLOGY 54, 62 (2007): "With the abolishment of registration and the automatic subsistence of copyright based on inter alia the nationality of the author, copyright was transformed from an opt-in system to a theoretical opt-out system. It is 'theoretical' because although authors and copyright owners may dedicate his copyright to the public domain, there is no system, until recently, to declare or register such intention. It was only recently when the appearance of open access and public licenses that a copyrighted work may be offered to the public under a pre-consented licence. Even then, it is doubtful whether there is a mechanism under law or contract which may transfer a copyrighted work absolutely to the public domain"; and Christopher Sprigman, *Reform(aliz)ing Copyright*, 57 STANFORD LAW REVIEW 485, 518 (2004): "There is one final observation (not exactly an objection) related to the filtering function of registration and notice. It might be argued that, even in our current unconditional system, authors are free to dedicate their works to the public domain, and therefore rather than reinstall formalities, we should encourage public domain deeding as a method of filtering commercially valueless works out of copyright. But dedication to the public domain is not a substitute for the filtering function that formalities provide in a conditional copyright system. First, there is no provision in our current unconditional regime establishing rules for how dedication may be accomplished, and it has never been conclusively determined under current law that one may irreversibly dedicate a work to the public domain (though dedication has been judicially enforced under pre-1976 law).

29. Street and Grant, *supra* note 1, § 14.05[1] at 14-12–14-13: Discussing the application of public domain concepts to software modifications: "If a developer does not want to own the copyright...he/she would have to place the code changes in the public domain because the copyright ownership vests automatically by law. This could be done by posting the source code on the Internet with no license agreement to restrict use or protect against liability."

30. Jay P. Kesan and Rajiv C. Shah, *Shaping Code*, 18 HARVARD JOURNAL OF LAW AND TECHNOLOGY 319, 377, note 340 (2005): "A work in the public domain is not protected by copyright and is free to use by anyone. The work may enter the public domain in a number of ways, such as the term for the copyrighted work expiring, Congress passing

an act, and the copyright holder expressly disclaiming copyright protection for the work. Legal ambiguity regarding how to disclaim a copyright has led organizations like Creative Commons to issue a sample disclaimer for copyright holders who wish to place their work into the public domain."

31. Estoppel is a form of defense, a response to claim of unlawful conduct: "A bar that prevents one from asserting a claim or right that contradicts what one has said or done before or what has been legally established as true." BLACK'S LAW DICTIONARY 502 (9th ed.) (Bryan A. Garner ed., 2009) (no pagination in Westlaw).

32. Molly Shaffer Van Houweling, *Cultural Environmentalism and the Constructed Commons* 70 LAW AND CONTEMPORARY PROBLEMS 23, 25–26 (2007), footnote omitted.

33. 37 C.F.R. § 201.26 (Recordation of documents pertaining to computer shareware and donation of public domain computer software): "This section prescribes the procedures for submission of legal documents pertaining to computer shareware and the deposit of public domain computer software under section 805 of Public Law 101-650, 104 Stat. 5089 (1990). Documents recorded in the Copyright Office under this regulation will be included in the Computer Shareware Registry. Recordation in this Registry will establish a public record of licenses or other legal documents governing the relationship between copyright owners of computer shareware and persons associated with the dissemination or other use of computer shareware."

34. Pub. L. No. 101-650 (Title VIII), § 805 (Recordation of Shareware), 104 Stat. 5134, 5135 (1990) (Computer Software Rental Amendments Act of 1990).

35. H.R. Rep. No. 101-735, 101st Cong. 2d Sess. 15 (1990).

36. Jason Mazzone, *Copyfraud*, 81 NEW YORK UNIVERSITY LAW REVIEW 1026, 1035–1036 (2006).

37. See Loren, *supra* note 21, at 327–328 (2007): "Enhancing confidence in the semi-commons status of Creative Commons-licensed works will encourage more individuals to use those works in the manners authorized. Providing reliable public use rights requires recognizing the irrevocable nature of a copyright owner's decision to grant the public certain clearly-defined rights to use his copyrighted work. Adopting a doctrine of limited copyright abandonment would best achieve these goals. Limited abandonment, as proposed and defined in this article, would result in the copyright owner retaining the ability to enforce the copyright rights that have not been granted to the public, while at the same time allowing the public to rely on the copyright owner's clear expressions of intent to permit certain uses."

38. Micro Star v. Formgen Inc., 154 F.3d 1107, 1114 (9th Cir. 1998).

39. Melchizedek v. Holt, 792 F. Supp. 2d 1042, 1051 (D. Ariz. 2011), quoting A&M Records, Inc. v. Napster, Inc., 239 F.3d 1004, 1026 (9th Cir. 2001).

40. The work must be within the subject matter of copyright, fixed and original. See 17 U.S.C. § 102(a): "Copyright protection subsists, in accordance with this title, in original works of authorship fixed in any tangible medium of expression, now known or later developed, from which they can be perceived, reproduced, or otherwise communicated, either directly or with the aid of a machine or device."

41. Though enforcing that right (suing someone for infringement) requires additional steps, such as registration. See 17 U.S.C. § 411: "[N]o action for infringement of the copyright in any United States work shall be instituted until registration of the copyright claim has been made in accordance with this title."

42. The description on the Creative Commons website uses the possessive "your work" to suggest this: "This license lets others distribute, remix, tweak, and build upon your work, even commercially, as long as they credit you for the original creation. This is the most accommodating of licenses offered. Recommended for maximum dissemination and use of licensed materials" (http://creativecommons.org/licenses/).

43. The exclusive rights listed in 17 U.S.C. § 106 are as follows: to reproduce the work, to prepare derivative works, to distribute copies of the work to the public, to perform or display the work publicly, and in the case of sound recordings to perform the work publicly by means of a digital audio transmissions. Understanding the nuances of these rights and the terms the law uses to define the parameters of the rights, for example, public performances versus private performances is important but beyond the scope of this book. An explanation in the context of the library is found in KENNETH D. CREWS, COPYRIGHT LAW FOR LIBRARIANS AND EDUCATORS: CREATIVE STRATEGIES AND PRACTICAL SOLUTIONS (3d ed. 2012).

44. The creative license uses the less legal, in terms of the copyright statute, term *adaptation* to mean "a work based upon the Work, or upon the Work and other pre-existing works, such as a translation, adaptation, derivative work, arrangement of music or other alterations of a literary or artistic work, or phonogram or performance and includes cinematographic adaptations or any other form in which the Work may be recast, transformed, or adapted including in any form recognizably derived from the original, except that a work that constitutes a Collection will not be considered an Adaptation for the purpose of this License. For the avoidance of doubt, where the Work is a musical work, performance or phonogram, the synchronization of the Work in timed-relation with a moving image ('synching') will be considered an Adaptation for the purpose of this License" (http://creativecommons.org/licenses/by-nc-nd/3.0/legalcode). Compare with the definition of derivative work under the copyright law: "A 'derivative work' is a work based upon one or more preexisting works, such as a translation, musical arrangement, dramatization, fictionalization, motion picture version, sound recording, art reproduction, abridgment, condensation, or any other form in which a work may be recast, transformed, or adapted. A work consisting of editorial revisions, annotations, elaborations, or other modifications which, as a whole, represent an original work of authorship, is a 'derivative work'" (17 U.S.C. § 101).

45. Katz, *supra* note 25, at 401.

46. *Id.* at 393: "Incompatibility problems arise when licenses block would-be creators from making derivative works based on two or more original works released under different CC licenses." "Moreover, the creation of derivative works involves the most complex interactions between CC licenses and raises the specter of license choices giving rise to

unexpected consequences. Derivative works are inherently synthetic, often resulting from the combination of one creative work with one or more other works. The creation of derivative works is thus likely to involve combining works subject to different CC licenses, which has the potential to systematically produce outcomes neither expected nor desired by the original licensors of input works" (*id.* at 400).

47. Warner Brothers Entertainment, Inc. v. RDR Books, 575 F. Supp. 2d 513 (S.D.N.Y. 2008). "By condensing, synthesizing, and reorganizing the preexisting material in an A-to-Z reference guide, the Lexicon does *not recast* the material in another medium to retell the story of *Harry Potter*, but instead gives the copyrighted material another purpose ... Under these circumstances, and because the Lexicon does *not fall under any example of derivative works listed in the statute*, Plaintiffs have failed to show that the Lexicon is a derivative work" (*id.* at 539, emphasis added).

48. See STEVE VANDER ARK, THE LEXICON: AN UNAUTHORIZED GUIDE TO HARRY POTTER FICTION AND RELATED MATERIALS (2009).

49. STEVE VANDER ARK, THE READER'S GUIDE TO HARRY POTTER AND THE PHILOSOPHER'S STONE (The Harry Potter Lexicon Reader's Guide Series) (2001).

50. Katz, *supra* note 25, at 399–400: "As derivative works are created, SA licenses increase their prevalence while the prevalence of other CC licenses remains unchanged. ND and non-ND, non-SA works' share of total CC works thus decreases over time. Because SA provisions are included in half of CC licenses, this could represent a significant effect in the future. In the model, the key driver of this effect is the ratio of entirely new (non-derivative) woks created in a time period to derivative works created in that time period. As this ratio shrinks, SA's viral spread increases" (*id.* at 408).

51. "Nothing in this License is intended to reduce, limit, or restrict any uses free from copyright or rights arising from limitations or exceptions that are provided for in connection with the copyright protection under copyright law or other applicable laws" (http://creativecommons.org/licenses/by-nc-nd/3.0/legalcode).

52. Katz, supra note 25, at 401.

53. Creative Commons Licenses, http://creativecommons.nuvvo.com/lesson/183-licenses/: "This license lets others remix, tweak, and build upon your work even for commercial reasons, as long as they credit you and license their new creations under the identical terms. This license is often compared to open source software licenses. All new works based on yours will carry the same license, so any derivatives will also allow commercial use."

54. "Attribution-NonCommercial-NoDerivs" license, http://creativecommons.org/licenses/by-nc-nd/3.0/legalcode.

55. "Attribution-NonCommercial-ShareAlike" license, http://creativecommons.org/licenses/by-nc-sa/3.0/legalcode.

56. "Attribution-Noncommercial" license, http://creativecommons.org/licenses/by-nc/3.0/legalcode.

57. "Attribution-NoDerivs" license, http://creativecommons.org/licenses/by-nd/3.0/legalcode.

58. "Attribution-ShareAlike" license, http://creativecommons.org/licenses/by-sa/3.0/legalcode.

59. "Attribution" license, http://creativecommons.org/licenses/by/3.0/legalcode.

60. Elkin-Koren, *supra* note 12, at 392 (2005).

61. *Id.* at 396 (Symposium, Law and the Information Society, Panel 1: Intellectual Property and Public Values): "The licensing scheme is designed to enable the licensing of works under a wide range of terms: from minimalist authorization, such as sampling a musical composition, to a broad waiver of all rights. It is exactly this diversity of licensing options that makes Creative Commons' licensing scheme less effective for promoting access by individuals to creative works."

62. See Definitions 1.f.: "'Work' means the literary and/or artistic work offered under the terms of this License including without limitation any production in the literary, scientific and artistic domain, whatever may be the mode or form of its expression including digital form, such as a book, pamphlet and other writing; a lecture, address, sermon or other work of the same nature; a dramatic or dramatico-musical work; a choreographic work or entertainment in dumb show; a musical composition with or without words; a cinematographic work to which are assimilated works expressed by a process analogous to cinematography; a work of drawing, painting, architecture, sculpture, engraving or lithography; a photographic work to which are assimilated works expressed by a process analogous to photography; a work of applied art; an illustration, map, plan, sketch or three-dimensional work relative to geography, topography, architecture or science; a performance; a broadcast; a phonogram; a compilation of data to the extent it is protected as a copyrightable work; or a work performed by a variety or circus performer to the extent it is not otherwise considered a literary or artistic work."

63. 17 U.S.C. § 102: "Copyright protection subsists, in accordance with this title, in original works of authorship fixed in any tangible medium of expression, now known or later developed, from which they can be perceived, reproduced, or otherwise communicated, either directly or with the aid of a machine or device. Works of authorship include the following categories: (1) literary works; (2) musical works, including any accompanying words; (3) dramatic works, including any accompanying music; (4) pantomimes and choreographic works; (5) pictorial, graphic, and sculptural works; (6) motion pictures and other audiovisual works; (7) sound recordings; and (8) architectural works."

64. "Publicly Perform" means to perform public recitations of the Work and to communicate to the public those public recitations, by any means or process, including by wire or wireless means or public digital performances; to make available to the public Works in such a way that members of the public may access these Works from a place and at a place individually chosen by them; to perform the Work to the public by any means or process and the communication to the public of the performances of the Work, including by public digital performance; to broadcast and rebroadcast the Work by any means including signs, sounds or images.

65. 17 U.S.C. § 102: "To perform or display a work 'publicly' means—(1) to perform or display it at a place open to the public or at any place where a substantial number of persons outside of a normal circle of a family and its social acquaintances is gathered; or (2) to transmit or otherwise communicate a performance or display of the work to a place specified by clause (1) or to the public, by means of any device or process, whether the members of the public capable of receiving the performance or display receive it in the same place or in separate places and at the same time or at different times."

66. Clause 1.b: "'Collection' means a collection of literary or artistic works, such as encyclopedias and anthologies, or performances, phonograms or broadcasts, or other works or subject matter other than works listed in Section 1(f) below, which, by reason of the selection and arrangement of their contents, constitute intellectual creations, in which the Work is included in its entirety in unmodified form along with one or more other contributions, each constituting separate and independent works in themselves, which together are assembled into a collective whole. A work that constitutes a Collection will not be considered an Adaptation (as defined above) for the purposes of this License" (http://creativecommons.org/licenses/by-nc-nd/3.0/legalcode).

67. "A 'collective work' is a work, such as a periodical issue, anthology, or encyclopedia, in which a number of contributions, constituting separate and independent works in themselves, are assembled into a collective whole. A 'compilation' is a work formed by the collection and assembling of preexisting materials or of data that are selected, coordinated, or arranged in such a way that the resulting work as a whole constitutes an original work of authorship. The term 'compilation' includes collective works" (17 U.S.C. § 101).

68. Jacobson v. Katzer, 535 F.3d 1373 at 1377 (Fed. Cir. 2008).

69. *Id.* at 1379.

70. *Id.* at 1375.

71. *Id.* at 1380.

72. *Id.*

73. *Id.* at 1382.

74. *Id.* at 1380: "*provided that* [the user] insert a prominent notice in each changed file stating how and when [the user] changed that file, and provided that [the user] do at least ONE of the following: a) place [the user's] modifications in the Public Domain or otherwise make them Freely Available, such as by posting said modifications to Usenet or an equivalent medium, or placing the modifications on a major archive site such as ftp.uu.net, or by allowing the Copyright Holder to include [the user's] modifications in the Standard Version of the Package. b) use the modified Package only within [the user's] corporation or organization. c) rename any non-standard executables so the names do not conflict with the standard executables, which must also be provided, and provide a separate manual page for each nonstandard executable that clearly documents how it differs from the Standard Version, or d) make other distribution arrangements with the Copyright Holder" (emphasis added).

75. Jacobson v. Katzer, 535 F.3d 1373 at 1381 (Fed. Cir. 2008).

76. *Id.* at 1381–1382.

77. *Id.* at 1382.

78. *Id.* at 1381.

79. *Id.* at *6: "Having determined that the terms of the Artistic License are enforceable copyright conditions, we remand to enable the District Court to determine whether Jacobsen has demonstrated (1) a likelihood of success on the merits and either a presumption of irreparable harm or a demonstration of irreparable harm; or (2) a fair chance of success on the merits and a clear disparity in the relative hardships and tipping in his favor."

80. Victoria K. Hall, as quoted in Pamela A. MacLean, *Landmark Ruling Backs Key Software Copyright*, THE NATIONAL LAW JOURNAL, August 25, 2008, at 6.

81. Jacobson v. Katzer, 535 F.3d 1373 at *3 (Fed. Cir. 2008).

82. "Creative Commons licenses facilitate a rebalancing that frees libraries to better perform their traditional roles as well as new ones called for by the digital environment." Michael W. Carroll, *Creative Commons and the New Intermediaries*, 2006 MICHIGAN STATE LAW REVIEW 45, 51 (2006) (Symposium: W(h)ither the Middleman: The Role and Future of Intermediaries in the Information Age), Discussing new intermediaries: search engines, archives and libraries, producers and publishers, creative commons communities ("as community norms"), and education (*id.* at 49–59). "Creative Commons licenses can be complemented by new licensing intermediaries who can facilitate transaction under the rights reserved to the copyright owner under a Creative Commons license" (*id.* at 48).

83. Elkin-Koren, *supra* note 12, at 402: "The first major challenge for Creative Commons is therefore to ensure that license provisions, and particularly Share Alike provisions, would be enforceable against third parties. The fact that licenses are enforceable against their immediate contracting parties is simply insufficient . . . If subsequent users of the original work were not subject to the terms of the original license, the licensing scheme would shortly become meaningless."

84. The GNU General Public License is available at http://www.gnu.org/copyleft/gpl .html. The license is analyzed in Street and Grant, *supra* note 1. Appendix 14-A offers analysis of Version 2 (June 1991) of the GPL at 14-A-8–14-A-20, and Version 2.1 (February 1999) of the LGPL at 14-A-26–14-A-34.

85. Tennille M. Christensen, *Note: The GNU General Public License: Constitutional Subversion?*, 33 HASTINGS CONSTITUTIONAL LAW QUARTERLY 397, 398 (2006): "The GPL is often described as 'copyleft' because where typical copyright licenses vest control over the creation in the creator, the GPL requires that, when copyrighted works are distributed, it is without limitation on who can use them, and who can see how they work."

86. Preamble, paragraph 2, GNU General Public License, Version 3, 29 June 2007, http://www.gnu.org/copyleft/gpl.html.

87. Paragraph 15, GNU General Public License, Version 3, 29 June 2007.

88. Preamble, paragraph 7, GNU General Public License, Version 3, 29 June 2007. Terms and Conditions, section 5, Conveying Modified Source Versions, GCN General Public License, Version 3, 29 June 2007, requiring notice of modification, notice of license, requirement of license and "Appropriate Legal Notices" regarding interactive user interfaces (*id.* at subparagraphs 5a–5d).

89. Terms and Conditions, Section 15, Disclaimer of Warranty, GNU General Public License, Version 3, 29 June 2007.

90. Terms and Conditions, Section 16, Limitation of Liability, GNU General Public License, Version 3, 29 June 2007.

91. Street and Grant, *supra* note 1, at 14-18. "Open source licenses do not provide warranties to the risk is on the licensee" (id. at § 14.07 at 14-19).

92. Terms and Conditions, Section 0, Definitions, GNU General Public License, Version 3, 29 June 2007: "To 'modify' a work means to copy from or adapt all or part of the work in a fashion requiring copyright permission, other than the making of an exact copy, The resulting work is called a 'modified version' of the earlier work or a work 'based on' the earlier work."

93. Terms and Conditions, Section 2, Basic Permissions, GNU General Public License, Version 3, 29 June 2007.

94. Terms and Conditions, Section 4, Conveying Verbatim Copies, GCN General Public License, Version 3, 29 June 2007.

95. Terms and Conditions, Section 3, Protecting Users' Legal Rights From Anti-Circumvention Law, GNU General Public License, Version 3, 29 June 2007.

96. 17 U.S.C. § 1201(a)(1)(A).

97. Terms and Conditions, Section 3, Protecting Users' Legal Rights From Anti-Circumvention Law, GNU General Public License, Version 3, 29 June 2007.

98. Terms and Conditions, Section 10, Automatic Licensing of Downstream Recipients, GNU General Public License, Version 3, 29 June 2007.

99. Terms and Conditions, Section 8, Termination, GNU General Public License, Version 3, 29 June 2007: "You may not propagate or modify a covered work except as expressly provided under this License. Any attempt otherwise to propagate or modify it is void, and will automatically terminate your rights under the License."

100. How to Apply These Terms to Your New Programs, GNU General Public License, Version 3, 29 June 2007: notices that should be attached "to the start of each source file" include identifying information, disclaimer of warranty and URL direction to the text of the license on the GNU GPL, and a notice indicating the viral nature of the licensed content: "This program is free software: you can redistribute it and/or modify it under the terms of the GNU General Public License as published by the Free Software Foundation, either version 3 of the License, or (at your option) any later version."

101. How to Apply These Terms to Your New Programs, GNU General Public License, Version 3, 29 June 2007.

102. Mitchell L. Stoltz, *Note: The Penguin Paradox: How the Scope of Derivative Works in Copyright Affects the Effectiveness of the GNU GPL*, 85 BOSTON UNIVERSITY LAW REVIEW 1349, 1441 (2005).

103. Douglas A. Hass, *The Myth of Copyleft Protection: Reconciling the GPL and Linux with the Copyright Act*, 25 INTELLECTUAL PROPERTY LAW NEWSLETTER, 1, 2006, at 22; and Lothar Determann, *Dangerous Liaisons—Software Combinations as Derivative Works? Distribution, Installation, and Execution of Linked Programs under Copyright Law, Commercial Licenses, and the GPL*, 21 BERKELEY TECHNOLOGY LAW JOURNAL 1421 (2006).

104. Tennille M. Christensen, *Note: The GNU General Public License: Constitutional Subversion?*, 33 HASTINGS CONSTITUTIONAL LAW QUARTERLY 397, 403 (2006), footnotes omitted. See also Street and Grant, *supra* note 1, Appendix 14-A, 14-A-11, commenting on the "any works" derivative clause "sometimes referred to as the 'GNU virus,' which infects all derivative software with the free software license terms and causes problems in the commercial world."

105. Determann, *supra* note 103, at 1497: "Most software combinations fail to meet one or more of these requirements and thus constitute compilations, collective works, or non-copyrightable arrangements, none of which implicate copyright owners' adaptation rights under Section 106 of the U.S. Copyright Act."

106. Stoltz, *supra* note 102, at 1349. "If copyright law does not recognize a derivative work where two programs interact in common ways, the GPL copyleft regime may contain an enormous loophole for proprietary exploitation" (*id.* at 1442). "If the Sega line of cases applies in the same way to GPL-licensed software, then most dynamically linked modules, such as Linux kernel modules, will not be derivative works. These modules can be released under proprietary licenses and without disclosing the corresponding source code. For the reasons described above, this creates a substantial loophole in the GPL" (*id.* at 1464).

107. Stoltz, *supra* note 102, at 1349. "The solution proposed by this Note is that courts could broaden the definition of a derivative work in GPL-related cases in light of the GPL's purpose" (*id.* at 1477). "Asking for a different derivative works test for FOSS would be much more difficult than asking for a denial of fair use, because the 'equitable' doctrine of fair use leaves more discretion to judges than does the basic definition of a derivative work" (*id.* at 1476).

108. How to Apply These Terms to Your New Programs, GNU General Public License, Version 3, 29 June 2007.

109. Why You Shouldn't Use the Lesser GPL for Your Next Library, 2011, http://www.gnu .org/philosophy/why-not-lgpl.html, giving the example of GNU Redline and cautioning against the commodification of university projects: "By releasing libraries that are limited to free software only, we can help each other's free software packages outdo the proprietary alternatives." There may be another problem: "Such a work in isolation falls outside the copyright in the Library and therefore is not covered by the license. The problem is that linking such a work to the Library creates an executable that contains

portions of the Library and therefore may be a derivative work if legally significant portion is used" Street and Grant, *supra* note 1, Appendix 14-A, 14-A-26–14-A-27, reviewing GPL, Version 2.1. See also Determann, *supra* note 103, at 1421.

110. GNU Free Documentation License, Version 1.3, 3 November 2008, Section 0, Preamble, paragraph 2, http://www.gnu.org/licenses/fdl.html.

111. GNU Free Documentation License, Version 1.3, 3 November 2008, Sections 5 and 6, Combining Documents and Collections of Documents.

112. GNU Free Documentation License, Version 1.3, 3 November 2008, Section7, Aggregation with Independent Works.

113. GNU Free Documentation License, Version 1.3, 3 November 2008, Section 8, Translation: "Translation is considered a kind of modification, so you may distribute translations of the Document under the terms of section 4 [Modifications]."

114. GNU Free Documentation License, Version 1.3, 3 November 2008, Section 0, Preamble, paragraphs 1 and 3. See also GNU Free Documentation License, Version 1.3, 3 November 2008, Section 4, Modifications; "You may copy and distribute a Modified Version of the Document under the conditions of sections 2 and 3 above, provided that you release the Modified Version under precisely this License." In addition, Section 4, Modification, subsections A through O list 15 additional conditions regarding required notices, identification of various parties and content, and inclusions and deletions.

115. GNU Free Documentation License, Version 1.3, 3 November 2008, Section 2, Verbatim Copying: "You may copy and distribute the Document in any medium, either commercially or noncommercially, provided that this License, the copyright notices, and the license notice saying this License applies to the Document are reproduced in all copies, and that you add no other conditions whatsoever to those of this License."

116. GNU Free Documentation License, Version 1.3, 3 November 2008.

117. GNU Free Documentation License, Version 1.3, 3 November 2008, Section 0, Preamble, paragraph 1: "Secondarily, this License preserves for the author and publisher a way to get credit for their work, while not being considered responsible for modifications made by others." See also GNU Free Documentation License, Version 1.3, 3 November 2008, Section 4, Modifications, B and C: "B. List on the Title Page, as authors, one or more persons or entities responsible for authorship of the modifications in the Modified Version, together with at least five of the principal authors of the Document (all of its principal authors, if it has fewer than five), unless they release you from this requirement. C. State on the Title page the name of the publisher of the Modified Version, as the publisher."

118. GNU Free Documentation License, Version 1.3, 3 November 2008, Section 9, Termination.

119. GNU Free Documentation License, Version 1.3, 3 November 2008, Section 10, Future Revisions of this License (Verbatim Copying).

120. See Kumar, *supra* note 2, and Wacha, *supra* note 10, concluding the GPL is enforceable.

121. Eben Moglen, *Free Software Matters: Enforcing the GPL*, I, http://emoglen.law .columbia .edu/publications/lu-12.html.

122. Nimmer, *supra* note 4, at § 10:15, footnote omitted. "When the terms of GPL are examined, the only reasonable conclusion is that GPL contains language consistent both with an attempted contract and with a non-contractual release (restrictive notice)" (*id.* at § 10:19).

123. See Kumar, *supra* note 2, at 14, footnotes omitted.

124. Wacha, *supra* note 10, at 456; evaluating ad seriatim the various rationales forwarded unenforceability of the GPL (*id.* at 459).

125. Tennille M. Christensen, *Note: The GNU General Public License: Constitutional Subversion?*, 33 HASTINGS CONSTITUTIONAL LAW QUARTERLY 397, 404 (2006): "Accordingly, when it [GPL] functions as a bare license, the GPL is a constitutional, conditional grant of rights from the copyright holder. However, attempts to enforce the GPL as a contract under state law would be null and void because the GPL is preempted by federal copyright law under Article VI of the United States Constitution."

126. Determann, *supra* note 103, at 1498: "It seems possible, however, that courts may interpret the GPL in a broader way, which would increase concerns regarding the validity of the GPL under copyright misuse doctrines, competition laws, and unfair contract terms laws. Such concerns can be greater or lesser depending on the circumstances of the licensing parties and jurisdictions involved. If such broad interpretations prevail, the software industry might move more generally to GPL-like restrictive licensing practices that permit and prohibit certain software combinations. Such interpretations and ensuing practices would potentially have a serious impact on interoperability and cause software combinations to become dangerous liaisons."

127. Kumar, *supra* note 2, at 6: "The GPL's validity does not rest upon exotic forms of property or upon the manipulation of the license into a contract. Rather, the license is enforceable by the licensor through federal copyright law and by the licensee through a state promissory estoppel action." BLACK'S LAW DICTIONARY, *supra* note 31, defines "promissory estoppel" as the "principle that a promise made without consideration may nonetheless be enforced to prevent injustice if the promisor should have reasonable expected the promise to rely on the promise and if the promise did actually rely on the promise to his or her detriment."

128. Planetary Motion, Inc. v Techplosion, Inc., 261 F.3d 1188, 1198 (11th Cir. 2001).

129. Kumar, *supra* note 2, at 5, footnote omitted.

130. *Id.* at 6. "Propos[ing] that the GPL is a failed contract, which lacks only consideration. It advocates enforcing the license through state promissory estoppel law and the Copyright Act" (*id.*).

131. Benjamin I. Narodick, *Note: Smothered by Judicial Love: How Jacobsen v. Katzer Could Bring Open Source Software Development to a Standstill*, 16 BOSTON UNIVERSITY JOURNAL OF SCIENCE AND TECHNOLOGY LAW 264, 277 (2010): "The Federal Circuit decision in Jacobsen, while granting a long-awaited recognition of the rights of open-source software distributors,

also includes an important and overlooked expansion of the legal idea that licensing agreements can confer intellectual property rights upon the copyright holder that might not be supported by the Copyright Act."

132. Wallace v. International Business Machines Corp. et al., 467 F.3d 1104, 1105 (7th Cir. 2006): "Authors who distribute their works under this license, devised by the Free Software Foundation, Inc., authorize not only copying but also the creation of derivative works-and the license prohibits charging for the derivative work. People may make and distribute derivative works if and only if they come under the same license terms as the original work. Thus the GPL propagates from user to user and revision to revision: neither the original author, nor any creator of a revised or improved version, may charge for the software or allow any successor to charge. Copyright law, usually the basis of limiting reproduction in order to collect a fee, ensures that open-source software remains free: any attempt to sell a derivative work will violate the copyright laws, even if the improver has not accepted the GPL. The Free Software Foundation calls the result 'copyleft.'"

133. *Id.* at 1106: "Daniel Wallace would like to compete with Linux — either by offering a derivative work or by writing an operating system from scratch — but maintains that this is impossible as long as Linux and its derivatives are available for free. He contends that IBM, Red Hat, and Novell have conspired among themselves and with others (including the Free Software Foundation) to eliminate competition in the operating system market by making Linux available at an unbeatable price."

134. *Id.* at 1105: "Does the provision of copyrighted software under the GNU General Public License ('GPL') violate the federal antitrust laws?" Judge Easterbrook answering that "[t]he GPL and open-source software have nothing to fear from the antitrust laws" (*id.* at 1108).

135. *Id.* at 1107–1108.

136. Planetary Motion, Inc. v. Techplosion, Inc., 261 F.3d 1188 (11th Cir. 2001).

137. *Id.* at 1191: "In late 1994, Byron Darrah ('Darrah') developed a UNIX-based program (the 'Software') that provides e-mail users with notice of new e-mail and serves as a gateway to the users' e-mail application. Darrah had named the Software 'Coolmail' and this designation appeared on the announcement sent to the end users on Sunsite as well as on the Software user-manual, both of which accompanied the release. The Software was distributed without charge to users pursuant to a GNU General Public License that also accompanied the release...After the release of the Software, Darrah received correspondence from users referencing the 'Coolmail' mark and in some cases suggesting improvements. In 1995, Darrah released two subsequent versions of the Software under the same mark and also pursuant to the GNU General Public License."

138. *Id.* at 1192: "In July of 1999, Planetary Motion purchased from Darrah all rights, title, and interest to the Software including all copyrights, trademarks, patents and other intellectual property rights."

139. *Id.* at 1198.

140. Computer Associates International v. Quest Software, Inc., 333 F. Supp. 2d 688 (N.D. Ill. 2004).

141. *Id.* at 691: "This program [Enterprise Database Administrator (EDBA)] allowed database administrators to automate numerous tasks that would previously have been extremely time-consuming."

142. *Id.* at 697–698.

143. *Id.* at 698.

144. *Id.*: "The output of that program (the parser source code), however, is not subject to the restrictions of the GPL—it is the creation of plaintiff. FSF explicitly allowed for such commercial use of the output by adopting the following exception to the GPL: 'As a special exception, when this file is copied by Bison into a Bison output file, you may use that output file without restriction. This special exception was added by the Free Software Foundation in version 1.24 of Bison.' There is no indication that Mackowiak, or any other Platinum or CA employee, used a version of Bison older than 1.24. Therefore, even though the output lines contain some of the utility source code, CA is free to use the output files without restriction, as allowed by the exception to the GPL."

145. Progress Software Corporation v. MySQL AB, 195 F. Supp. 2d 328, 329 (D. Mass. 2002): "With respect to the General Public License ('GPL'), MySQL has not demonstrated a substantial likelihood of success on the merits or irreparable harm. Affidavits submitted by the parties' experts raise a factual dispute concerning whether the Gemini program is a derivative or an independent and separate work under GPL P 2. After hearing, MySQL seems to have the better argument here, but the matter is one of fair dispute. Moreover, I am not persuaded based on this record that the release of the Gemini source code in July 2001 didn't cure the breach."

146. GNU Lesser General Public License, Version 3, 29 June 2007, Section 0, Additional Definitions, http://www.gnu.org/licenses/lgpl.txt.

147. GNU Lesser General Public License, Version 3, 29 June 2007.

148. GNU Lesser General Public License, Version 3, 29 June 2007, Section 1, Exception to Section 3 of the GNU GPL.

149. GNU Lesser General Public License, Version 3, 29 June 2007, Section 0, Additional Definitions. A library "refers to a covered work governed by this license" (*id.*).

150. GNU Lesser General Public License, Version 3, 29 June 2007, Section 3, Object Code Incorporating Material from Library Header Files and Section 4, Combined works.

151. Releasing Software if you work at a University, http://www.gnu.org/philosophy/university.html, encouraging users to resist the current trend in higher education of "grasping," that is, developing and commercially exploiting the institution's intellectual property portfolio, urging faculty to base their position on ethical values: "Whatever approach you use, it helps to approach the issue with determination and based on an ethical perspective, as we do in the free software movement. To treat the public ethically, the software should be free—as in freedom—for the whole public."

► 10

BASIC MUSIC AND MEDIA LICENSES

Read this chapter to understand the nature and legality of these license situations:
► Reproduction and distribution of the work on a physical medium such as a CD
► Public performance of dramatic and nondramatic musical works
► Inclusion of a musical work or sound recording in an audiovisual work such as a documentary
► When a performance license is needed for a musical work or sound recording and when the copyright law allows for the use without a license

◄

In the realm of music,[1] there are several types of media licenses[2] for public performance, reproduction (copying the sheet music, copying a previous sound recording of the musical work, or recording a new version of the musical work), and public distribution of a musical work or sound recording, or inclusion of either in an audiovisual work, such as use of a musical work or sound recording in a soundtrack to a motion picture. A musical work is the musical composition itself: the music and words, if there are words, are often expressed in sheet music.[3] While a sound recording is a "work...that result[s] from the fixation of a series of musical, spoken, or other sounds, but not including the sounds accompanying a motion picture or other audiovisual work, regardless of the nature of the material objects, such as disks, tapes, or other phonorecords, in which they are embodied."[4] Musical work and sound recording copyright issues can compound very quickly, especially in live performances involving performance by musicians or use of prerecorded music in dramatic performances, and even more so with cover, tribute, or reverence bands, for example, involving other intellectual property rights such as trademark.[5]

> Most songs played on the radio, sold on CDs in music stores, or digitally available on the Internet through services like iTunes embody two distinct copyrights—a copyright in the "musical work" and a copyright in the "sound recording." The musical work is the musical composition—the notes and lyrics of the song as they appear on sheet music. The sound recording is the recorded musical work performed by a specific artist. Although almost always intermingled in a single song, those two copyrights are

legally distinct and may be owned and licensed separately. One party might own the copyright in the words and musical arrangement of a song, and another party might own the copyright in a particular artist's recording of those words and musical notes.[6]

This discussion only scratches the surface, though it does review the significant rights and corresponding licenses that are available and introduces circumstances in the copyright law where, for certain uses, including those by nonprofit entities such as libraries and educational institutions, a license or other permission may not be necessary because such uses are granted statutory exemption. The area of musical works and sound recording use (performance) is a prime example of how important an understanding of copyright law is to licensing or, in the examples of library and educational uses of musical works and sound recordings offered in this chapter, knowing whether copyright would allow for such use (and therefore no license would be needed) or if a license must be obtained.

Depending on the circumstances, reproducing or performing one or both of these works could trigger the exclusive rights of the copyright owner. However, to make more efficient the process of requesting permission to use such works, the copyright codified mechanisms known as statutory licensing facilitate such use. Unlike some other licensing scenarios discussed in this book, this form of license is particular in that no negotiations need occur. So, too, is the process peculiar in that the copyright owner has no ability to refuse the licensee. The right to obtain a license is set forth in the statute. Moreover, the rate of the license is set by regulatory process. This type of license is also referred to as a compulsory license. Depending upon the work and its use, the license may have a more specific and descriptive name. Sometimes a user still contacts the copyright owner to negotiate a more favorable license rate than that established by the law (through statute and regulatory process), but the default or statutory rate is always available, assuming the use fits within the licensing scheme the law has established.

Reproduction and performance rights in musical works are historically governed by separate licenses. Reproduction of the musical work in a sound recording is governed by a mechanical license. Mechanical licenses do not apply to musical works that have yet to be distributed. Reproducing a sound recording involves two potential copyrights: one in the underlying music and the other in the performance of the music, or the sound recording. The reproduction of the underlying music embodied in a recording is also subject to mechanical licensing if the source phonorecord (the "copy" of the sound recording) is lawfully made and a license or permission was obtained from the owner of the sound recording.

Some uses of a musical work might be covered by fair use. If this is the situation, then there is no infringement of the musical work owner's right to reproduce the work or make a public performance or display of it or to make a derivative work or a public distribution of the reproduction. Some uses of musical works have been held to be fair. For example, use of excerpts from a rap song in a documentary film was deemed fair use,[7] as was similar use of the John Lennon song "Imagine."[8] Use of part of a musical work in another song was held to be a fair-use parody in *Campbell v. Acuff-Rose Music*[9] and in *Bourne v. Twentieth Century Fox Film Corp.*[10] However, the reproduction of music and lyrics in home karaoke machines was not fair use,[11] nor is the use of song segments in ringtones and related markets.[12] However, when fair use does not apply or there is no other statutory exception,[13] copyright law has created a statutory licensing mechanism.[14] A recent case involving the sampling of a sound recording led the court to review the scope and range of licensing options:

> The question then is whether there was a question of fact concerning the existence and scope of the license. In the context of music sampling, clearance from a music composition copyright holder generally takes one of three forms: a flat-fee buy-out agreement under which no future payments are owed; an adjusted mechanical license fee requiring payment of a sum for each record sold; or a co-publishing arrangement under which the copyright owner of the sampled composition shares an interest in the copyright of the new work.[15]

The mechanism includes preset rates and in a sense creates an automatic permission (the owner cannot say no, thus the license is referred to as a compulsory license[16]) as long as statutory requirements are followed. For example, the work must be performed as written and the lyrics must not be changed.[17] "Because the requirements of the mechanical compulsory license can be burdensome (e.g., it requires a monthly accounting to copyright owners), reproduction or musical works in phonorecords is usually done pursuant to agreement."[18]

MECHANICAL LICENSES

The license mechanism in place to reproduce the work and then to distribute the phonorecord,[19] or the copies of the work, is known as a mechanical license.[20]

> So-called "mechanical licenses" refer only to licenses in musical compositions, not in sound recordings. Compulsory licenses for the use of musical compositions are often referred to as "mechanical licenses" as the provision of the Copyright Act that provides for them, 17 U.S.C. § 115, allows the act of "mechanically" recording a song on fixed media, such as a phonograph record or piano roll.[21]

This is the license used when a recording of a song is made and distributed in album, tape, CD, and other such audio formats. It is essential to the recording industry as we know it.[22] The Harry Fox Agency is a major player in licensing mechanical music rights.

PERFORMANCE RIGHTS AND STATUTORY EXCEPTIONS

To undertake a public performance of a musical work also requires a form of license. Examples include the neighborhood garage band doing a live cover performance and playing songs from a jukebox in the local diner. The American Society of Composers, Artists, and Publishers (ASCAP) and Broadcast Music, Inc. (BMI) are major players in this license arena. For teachers and students, significant privileges to perform an entire musical work (whether nondramatic or dramatic) are available (so no license is needed) in section 110(1) for face-to-face instructional sessions[23] and in section 110(2) for performance of an entire nondramatic work or "reasonable and limited portions" of a dramatic work, including musical works, in distance education sessions.[24] In public library and school scenarios outside the formal class session, a performance can also qualify as the use of nondramatic musical works under section 110(4).[25] Singing a song (performance of a nondramatic musical work) or playing a recording of someone else's recording of it during a library story hour or performing a review of show tunes at the school's spring concert would qualify for this exception, subject to the other requirements of section 110(4). Fair use may also apply, but likely only for performances of less than the entire work. In the example of using (playing, performing) someone else's recording of the musical work during class or story hour, recall that doing so represents use of two copyrights: the musical work and the sound recording. Various subsections of section 110 allow for performance of the underlying nondramatic musical work, but what about performance of the sound recording? No worries—a performance right in a sound recording is *not* one of the exclusive rights of the copyright law under section 106, unless the performance is "by means of a digital audio transmission."[26]

SYNCHRONIZATION RIGHTS

Suppose that, rather than simply record a musical work or make an anthology of other previously made recordings, the musical work is used in conjunction with another work, such as a film. The musical work is synchronized in some fashion, enhancing the other work.[27] "A synchronization license is required if a copyrighted musical composition is to be used in 'timed-relation' or synchronization with an audiovisual work."[28] The mechanical license does not include these rights. "Though it is not explicit in the Copyright Act, courts have recognized a copyright holder's right to control the synchronization of musical compositions with the content of audiovisual works and have required parties to obtain synchronization licenses from copyright holders."[29] Whereas the "mechanical license allows the licensee to use a song in the manufacture and sale of phonorecords...a synchronization license authorizes the licensee to include a song in a motion picture in synchronism with the on-screen image."[30] There is no statutory licensing for such uses. Instead, as explained by the Supreme Court, "where ASCAP's blanket-license scheme does not govern, competitive markets do. A competitive market for 'synch' rights exists, and after the use of blanket licenses in the motion picture industry was discontinued, such a market promptly developed in that industry. In sum, the record demonstrates that the market at issue here is one that could be highly competitive, but is not competitive at all."[31] This "soundtrack" right is known as a synchronization license but applies beyond motion pictures to other films, such as documentaries and other audiovisual works. "'Synchronization licensing' describes a license for use of a composition in a film, pre-recorded radio or television program, or radio or television."[32] Even with a licensing mechanism in place, disputes do arise.

The facts of one dispute involved a short documentary film made and used by ABC Sports during its coverage of the 1984 Winter Olympics held in Sarajevo:

> The specific claims in this suit arise out of the airing of a three-minute documentary created by ABC entitled "*Ski Jump—Evolution of Style*," shown in connection with ABC's coverage of the 1984 Winter Olympics in Sarajevo, Yugoslavia (the "Documentary"). To depict the evolution in ski-jumping style from 1920 to the present, ABC assembled clips from each decade and filmed or videotaped selected portions of each. ABC then recorded music from the relevant time periods onto the soundtrack of the film or videotape in synchronization with the visual images of the ski-jumping. The film clip representing the ski-jumping styles of the 1950's was accompanied by nineteen seconds of a musical composition entitled "Walkin' With Mr. Lee," (the "composition"), a copyrighted song owned by Angel Music.[33]

While some uses in a documentary film of music might be fair, as previously seen, others are not.[34] Although this does not happen often in the library or school or other educational setting, the possibility exists—along with the potential for licensing issues to arise. For example, the school's library might decide to do a similar "history of" audiovisual work or make a short promotional film as part of a capital campaign or voter referendum for a new building.

Using a piece of prerecorded music in a soundtrack involves use of a work with layered rights, the underlying musical composition (e.g., "Blister in the Sun" by The Violent Femmes in the 1997 movie *Grosse Pointe Blank*), and the original sound recording of it. Often the musical work copyright and the sound recording copyright are owned by two different entities. "Under copyright law, an entity wishing to synchronize music with visual images in a video, motion picture, etc., must obtain a synchronization license from the musical composition copyright holder and must also obtain a license from the sound recording copyright holder."[35] The musical work synchronization right was just discussed; the license to use the sound recording is known as a master license, which is discussed later in this section. When both of these licenses are granted, they allow the use of sound recordings in synchronization with their underlying musical work, to copy and to distribute the synchronized version or copy at a later time.

In one example of these concepts, synchronization rights were not required by the company producing karaoke machines to display the lyrics. The company obtained the necessary lyric reprint rights, and displaying the lyrics on the machine's screen during playback of the music did not constitute an audiovisual use, for which synchronization rights would have been required. Showing the lyrics was a display, but such display is authorized by section 109(c) of the copyright law:[36] "Notwithstanding the provisions section 106 (5) [the exclusive right to display a work], the owner of a particular copy lawfully made under this title, or any person authorized by such owner, is entitled, without the authority of the copyright owner, to display that copy publicly, either directly or by the projection of no more than one image at a time, to viewers present at the place where the copy is located."[37] Likewise, beaming the lyrics to a popular song used as the theme of a high school graduation ceremony on a large screen in the school auditorium (so the audience can sing along) would not require synchronization rights, at least as suggested by the *Leadsinger, Inc. v. BMG Music Publishers* decision,[38] assuming the school had a lawfully made copy of the sheet music and was using a device that could project this copy of the sheet music without making additional copies of it (sheet music reproduction rights are handled by the Harry Fox Agency). Use of lyrics in a karaoke machine would require synchronization rights, as the lyrics are "fixed" or synchronized in sequence with the music.[39] If the school wanted each person in attendance to have his or her own copy of the words and music, this would be another story, but the section 109(c) right allows the "owner of a particular copy lawfully made . . . to display that copy publicly, either directly or by the projection of no more than one image at a time, to viewers present at the place where the copy is located."[40] Reprinting the lyrics alone in the graduation program would still raise copyright issues because "lyrics are copyrightable as a literary work and, therefore, enjoy separate protection under the Copyright Act."[41] The performance of the musical work, or singing and playing the song in public, is allowed by section 110(4), so no license is necessary for the school choir and band to perform it. For example, in *In re Cellco Partnership*, the court concluded: "playing of a ringtone by any Verizon customers in public is thus exempt under 17 U.S.C. § 110(4) and does not require them to obtain a public performance license."[42] Making a copy of the musical work in the reproduction of the sound-recording clip to create a ringtone is not a fair use, however, and does require performance licensing from ASCAP.[43] If the band is lousy and the school would rather just play the actual recording, a license is not needed either, as there is no performance right in a sound recording, whether public or private, or whether the use is commercial or noncommercial. However, performance rights in sound recordings arise when the performance is streamed or transmitted by some other digital means, per section 106(6), exclusive right.

SOUND RECORDINGS

Sound recordings are protected by federal copyright law if fixed or recorded on or after February 15, 1972. Prior to this time, there was no federal protection for sound recordings. Works created prior to this time were protected (and still are protected) under state law or common law copyright.[44] However, under the copyright restoration provisions of section 104A, a qualifying foreign sound recording may be nonetheless protected under federal copyright law.[45] One condition of restoration is that the work still be under copyright protection in its source country on the triggering date of "restoration," which was January 1, 1996.[46] For works under federal copyright protection either due to the time of creation or fixation or qualification under restoration, rights of reproduction and performance can be involved in the use of these works by libraries and in educational settings.

Under present copyright law (since the effective date of the 1976 Copyright Act, January 1, 1978), there is no exclusive right to perform a sound recording, unless it is by means of a digital audio transmission.[47] Assuming a CD of music is subject to both a musical work copyright and a sound recording copyright, and the musical work copyright is squared by reference to one of the performance exceptions discussed previously, the public or school librarian, teacher, or student need not worry about any copyright issues in merely playing the music to a live or face-to-face audience. If the underlying musical work is in the public domain and the library or teacher possesses a recent CD of it, librarians or teachers could play (perform) it in public (library meeting room, classroom, etc.) to their hearts' content as far as the copyright law is concerned, as there is no public performance in a sound recording.

The situation is not quite as easy for reproduction of sound recordings as it is for performance. "Since no compulsory license system is in place for sound recordings, I must enter into a 'master use license' with the copyright owner of the sound recording to lawfully copy the recording."[48] For example, if the synchronization rights to use, say, Johnny Cash songs (mechanical license of the musical works) in the movie *Walk the Line* were obtained, there would still be the need to obtain the rights from the sound recording copyright holder. While it might be more aesthetic to have actors do their own singing, as Val Kilmer did for the film *The Doors*, filmmakers often have the actors do their own singing because it is also likely less expensive than acquiring another set of rights to use the actual sound recording. "T-Bone Burnett, the music producer of *Walk the Line*, opted to re-record the Johnny Cash classic songs using the vocals of the film's lead actors. However, if producers wanted to use the actual Johnny Cash and June Carter recordings in the movie, they would have to acquire permission from both the music publisher [the underlying musical work copyright owner or licensor] and the owner of the sound recording, which is usually the record company."[49]

DRAMATIC PERFORMANCES AND GRAND RIGHTS

Dramatic performing rights in plays or operas are known as grand rights, as these works are not the nondramatic musical works discussed previously. Moreover, many of the statutory exceptions do not apply. Whether a librarian chooses to sing a song during story hour (perform a nondramatic work) or chooses instead to sing a song from an opera (a dramatic work), the section 110(4) exception previously discussed would still cover the performance. However, if the librarian decides to act out the song in costume as part of a dramatic scene (i.e., a dramatic performance of a nondramatic work) or perform the entire opera, a performance of a dramatic work would result and a license would likely be needed.

Dramatic works require further considerations, as do "dramatic" performances of a nondramatic work. An example of the latter would be a pop song (a nondramatic musical work) that, instead of just singing (a nondramatic performance), the library or school wants to build into a spring musical (making this a dramatic performance of the song, now part of a story line, similar to ABBA songs in the musical *Mama Mia*.[50] As explained by Lindey and Landau:

> ASCAP members do not grant ASCAP the right to license dramatic performances of their works. While the line between dramatic and non dramatic is not clear and depends on the facts, a dramatic performance usually involves using the work to tell a story or as part of a story or plot. Dramatic performances, among others, include: (i) performance of an entire "dramatico-musical work." For example a performance of the musical play *Oklahoma* would be a dramatic performance. (ii) performance of one or more musical compositions from a "dramatico-musical work" accompanied by dialogue, pantomime, dance, stage action, or visual representation of the work from which the music is taken. For example a performance of "People Will Say We're In Love" from *Oklahoma* with costumes, sets or props or dialogue from the show would be dramatic. (iii) performance of one or more musical compositions as part of a story or plot, whether accompanied or unaccompanied by dialogue, pantomime, dance, stage action or visual representation. For example, incorporating a performance of "If I Loved You" into a story or plot would be a dramatic performance of the song. (iv) performance of a concert version of a "dramatico-musical work." For example, a performance of all the songs in *Oklahoma* even without costumes or sets would be a dramatic performance.[51]

So, for example, if the library staff decided instead to perform the entire score or dialogue from *The Lion King*, this would be a performance (albeit a dramatic performance, as the work being performed is dramatic) of a dramatic work (a Broadway play), and the section 110(4) right would not apply.

However, a teacher or student could perform the play in a qualifying live, face-to-face class session under section 110(1) or perform a "reasonable and limited" portion in a qualifying distance-education class session under section 110(2), as the section 110 classroom rights include both sorts of works seemingly without regard to the sort of performance (nondramatic or dramatic), but requiring that the performance be related to the subject and teaching of the class and not for mere entertainment. Furthermore, rendering a song or two from a dramatic work would not appear to require a license but would fall under the statutory exception for nondramatic works.[52] It appears, then, that a dramatic work (which could be musical) can be performed dramatically, as that is its nature, but it could also be performed in a nondramatic fashion by a simple vocal rendition without costumes or acting and otherwise outside its dramatic context. Likewise, a nondramatic work can be either performed non-dramatically, as was its initial design, or interpreted or interposed in a dramatic setting for dramatic purpose, thus making its performance dramatic. The case law, as the commentators point out, is not as clear as it could be, as Table 10.1 indicates.

▶ **TABLE 10.1   Rights and Licenses in Musical Works and Sound Recordings**

Work Rights/Users	License/Permission Statutory Source	Examples of the Work or Its Use	Comment
Musical work: the initial composition (i.e., the music and lyrics if extant)	The composer maintains all the exclusive rights listed in § 106: the right to reproduce, perform, or display the musical work in public, make public distribution of the work, or make a derivative use of it.	A librarian composes by scribbling the words and music (notes and guitar chords) for a sing-a-long on a napkin during lunch before the afternoon book talk with kindergartners.	Composers often contract their rights to music publishers, who become the copyright owners in exchange for royalties.
Musical work: as sheet music or embodied in a sound recording Reproduction of a musical work subject to compulsory license	*Mechanical license* (the musical work in sound recording form): terms and compensation rates are established by statute and regulation. Requires prior recordation and distribution (as a sound recording) in the United States, where the purpose of the recording is for private home consumption. 17 U.S.C. § 115(a)(1). Once recordation and distribution occurs, others are free to record their version of the work subject to mechanical license. The current rates are as follows: "For every phonorecord made and distributed on or after	Each of the staff members at the library records a cover version of his or her favorite popular song for a CD, with sales to be used as a library fundraiser. The library desires to create an audio compilation of songs with library or book themes, like "Marian the Librarian" from *The Music Man* as a fundraising idea. A librarian wants to download (reproduce a musical work as embodied in the sound	Music publishers often license the rights to use the work, to reproduce and distribute the work (a) as a sound recording or (b) as sheet music. The Harry Fox Agency is the largest agency of musical compositions. See http://www.harryfox .com/index.jsp. Hal Leonard Publishing, Warner/Chappell Music, Cherry Lane Music Company, Music Sales Corporation, and Warner Bros. are well-known publishers/licensors of sheet music.

(continued)

▶ **TABLE 10.1** **Rights and Licenses in Musical Works and Sound Recordings** *(Continued)*

Work Rights/Users	License/Permission Statutory Source	Examples of the Work or Its Use	Comment
Musical work: as sheet music or embodied in a sound recording Reproduction of a musical work subject to compulsory license *(continued)*	after January 1, 2006, the royalty rate payable with respect to each work embodied in the phonorecord shall be either 9.1 cents, or 1.75 cents per minute of playing time or fraction thereof, whichever amount is larger." 37 C.F.R. § 255.3(m) (2011) (current through 76 FEDERAL REGISTER 52145 (August 19, 2011)). This would include a "permanent digital download." Effective March 1, 2009, "the rate to be paid under section 115 for ringtones is 24¢." 74 FR 4510, 4510 (January 26, 2009) (Mechanical and Digital Phonorecord Delivery Rate Determination Proceeding). A mechanical license is also available to reproduce a sound recording of the musical work already in existence in an anthology recording, for example.	recording) a ringtone for use on her personal cell phone. See *U.S. v. American Soc. of Composers, Authors and Publishers*, 599 F. Supp. 2d 415, 434 (S.D.N.Y. 2009): "all four fair use factors favor a finding against fair use, and there are no other factors that weigh in favor of fair use, applicant's motion for summary judgment is denied . . . The parties may proceed with discovery as this rate court proceeding moves forward." All of these uses require permission, but a mechanical license is readily available.	
Musical work: performing a musical work in public Nondramatic performance of musical work	*Small rights*, such as a performance license to make a nondramatic performance of a musical work under permission from the publisher or owner, are administered through performing rights organizations, e.g., ASCAP, BMI, etc. Statutory exceptions exist. For example, for teachers and students under § 110(1) and (2), where performances made "in the course of services at a	A librarian covers a song written by The Beatles during the annual holiday party at a local restaurant. The children's librarian sings "Puff the Magic Dragon" during a library story hour. A teacher covers "Blowing in the Wind" during a session on the 1960s' peace movement in a course on American	The rights here and for the two previous rows relate to the copyright/ license in the musical work, not the sound recording copyright, that might be involved when reproducing and distributing or performing a sound recording of a musical work. For performances of the sound recording this is not an issue as there is

(continued)

▶ **TABLE 10.1** Rights and Licenses in Musical Works and Sound Recordings *(Continued)*

Work Rights/Users	License/Permission Statutory Source	Examples of the Work or Its Use	Comment
Musical work: performing a musical work in public Nondramatic performance of musical work *(continued)*	place of worship or other religious assembly," under § 110(3), and for qualifying noncommercial performances under § 110(4): "On occasions when Verizon customers have activated their ringtones, the telephone rings in the presence of a broader audience, and it rings at a level to be heard by others, that playing of a musical work satisfies all of the requirements of the § 110(4) exemption . . . The playing of a ringtone by any Verizon customers in public is thus exempt under 17 U.S.C. § 110(4) and does not require them to obtain a public performance license." *In re Cellco Partnership*, 663 F. Supp. 2d 363, 375 (S.D.N.Y. 2009).	culture, society, and media. The performance at the local establishment is likely not covered by § 110(4) and a license may be needed, but many establishments possess such a license. The library story hour rendition is covered by § 110(4), assuming the requirements of that section are met. The teacher performance is covered by § 110(1). In these two latter examples, a license is not needed.	no exclusive right in the performance of sound recording under § 106, unless the performance is by means of a digital audio transmission per § 106(6). As for performance of a nondramatic musical work by the librarian in a noncommercial public library or school setting like the story hour, the performance is likely exempt by § 110(4), so there is no need for a license (see second column discussion). The karaoke performance at the local bar is likely not subject to the statutory exception in § 110, as the context is commercial, i.e., it is not made "without any purpose of direct or indirect commercial advantage." 17 U.S.C. § 110(4). See *Lorimar Music A. Corp. v. Black Iron Grill Co.*, 2010 WL 3022962, *5 and *8 (W.D. Mo. 2010) (slip copy): "the Court flatly rejects defendants' argument that a karaoke rendition of the copyrighted songs is a parody that constitutes fair use . . . Based on the foregoing, the Court finds defendants Black Iron Grill Company, Richard DeBuhr and Kim DeBuhr jointly and severally liable for eight acts of copyright infringement for the public performance of eight copyrighted musical compositions."

(continued)

► **TABLE 10.1**   Rights and Licenses in Musical Works and Sound Recordings *(Continued)*

Work Rights/Users	License/Permission Statutory Source	Examples of the Work or Its Use	Comment
Dramatic performance of a musical work: performing the musical work in public as part of another work	*Grand rights* are obtained from the music publisher.	The music of Green Day used in the Broadway musical *American Idiot*. As with the discussion in the previous row, it could be argued that a dramatic performance of a nondramatic work is also subject to the statutory exceptions of § 110(4) as those exceptions relate the work's nature, i.e., nondramatic, not the fashion (nondramatic or dramatic) of its rendering. Subsection (1), classroom use for example, also does not make this distinction. Songs like a Beatles tune, "Puff the Magic Dragon," "Blowing in the Wind," and tracks on Green Day albums or CDs are nondramatic musical works. However, rendering the songs in a dramatic fashion according to the case law is outside the nondramatic "small right" license generally granted and likewise the statutory exemption as well. See, e.g., *Robert Stigwood Group Ltd. v. Sperber*, 457 F.2d 50, 56 (2d Cir. 1972) (preliminary injunction issued against defendants from "performing any songs accompanied by dramatic action, scenic accessory or costumes" where defendants possessed only nondramatic rights and did not have grand rights). In the alternative, if a work is arguably dramatic, say "Do You Hear the People Sing?" or "Bring Him Home" from the musical *Les Miserables,* and the local high school honors chorus decides to	If a librarian were to take a Green Day song and perform it during a children's program while acting it out with a dance routine, this would arguably be a dramatic performance of a nondramatic work (a musical work, i.e., a song from a Green Day album), but the author argues it could nonetheless be covered by the statutory exceptions for performances of nondramatic works in § 110(4). (There is a difference between a dramatic performance of a nondramatic musical work and a performance of a dramatic musical work, the librarian scenario being an example of the former not the latter; the exemption does not distinguish in the rendering, only in the nature of the work: "performance of a nondramatic literary or musical.") Moreover, unlike the *American Idiot* production, the librarian is making a qualifying noncommercial performance under § 110(4); a Broadway production by the show's producers does not qualify for this exemption due to its commercial nature. But see *Johnson v. Radio City Productions, Inc.*, 1998 WL 171463 (S.D.N.Y. 1998) (unpublished), in which the songwriter claimed that performance of his

(continued)

▶ **TABLE 10.1   Rights and Licenses in Musical Works and Sound Recordings** *(Continued)*

Work Rights/Users	License/Permission Statutory Source	Examples of the Work or Its Use	Comment
Dramatic performance of a musical work: performing the musical work in public as part of another work *(continued)*		include one of the numbers in the upcoming spring concert, is a grand right required? Does it fall outside the section 110(4) exemption? Professor Abrams argues that the nondramatic rendering does indeed share in the rights that users of other nondramatic works possess: "What then is the difference between a dramatic and a nondramatic musical work? The classification of a musical composition as dramatic or nondramatic turns, initially at least, on the purpose for which it was composed. Musical compositions written as an integral part of a dramatic work would be considered dramatic while musical compositions written to be used as individual compositions without being part of a dramatic work would be deemed nondramatic . . . The trickier question arises when a musical composition written as an integral part of a dramatic work is taken out of the dramatic work and performed or embodied in a phonorecord as if it were a nondramatic work. To phrase the issue in more concrete terms, if a song that was originally written and performed as an integral part of a musical play is recorded as part of a sound recording that contained none of the other songs from the play, should that song become subject to the compulsory licenses and exemptions that apply to nondramatic musical works? This question should be answered affirmatively . . . Thus once the copyright owner has decided to	composition in the annual Radio City Music Hall holiday show was beyond the nondramatic performance right granted by the ASCAP license: "In particular, the 1977 and 1995 license agreements authorized only 'nondramatic performances,' and defined a 'dramatic performance' to include, among other things, 'performance of one or more musical compositions as part of a story or plot, whether accompanied or unaccompanied by dialogue, pantomime, dance, stage action or visual representation'" (*id*. at *3). An example of a dramatic performance would be a "performance of one or more musical compositions as part of a story or plot, whether accompanied or unaccompanied by dialogue, pantomime, dance, stage action or visual representation." ALEXANDER LINDEY AND MICHAEL LANDAU, LINDEY ON ENTERTAINMENT, PUBLISHING, AND THE ARTS § 8.51 (3d ed. 2004) (updated in Westlaw, July 2011).

(continued)

► **TABLE 10.1**   Rights and Licenses in Musical Works and Sound Recordings *(Continued)*

Work Rights/Users	License/Permission Statutory Source	Examples of the Work or Its Use	Comment
Dramatic performance of a musical work: performing the musical work in public as part of another work *(continued)*		treat the work as if it were a nondramatic work, it would distort the balances drawn by Congress to permit the work to enjoy the rights and be commercially exploited as a nondramatic musical work but not subject to the limitations that are imposed on such works. In sum, the copyright owner should not expect to gain the benefits of using the work as a nondramatic musical work without being subject to the limitations that Congress has placed on the use of nondramatic musical works." HOWARD B. ABRAMS, 1 THE LAW OF COPYRIGHT § 2:39 (database updated in Westlaw, November 2011).	
Reproduction of a musical work as part of motion picture (an audiovisual work) soundtrack	Another form of grand rights, *synchronization rights* are obtained from the music publisher. 17 U.S.C. § 114(b): "The exclusive right of the owner of copyright in a sound recording under clause (1) of section 106 [exclusive right to reproduce a work] is limited to the right to duplicate the sound recording in the form of phonorecords or copies that directly or indirectly recapture the actual sounds fixed in the recording. The	The songs used in the soundtrack to the motion picture *Party Girl*. Suppose the film class group project results in a movie that uses prerecorded music in its soundtrack or records the musical review of songs with themes related to work ("Nice Work if You Can Get It," "Sixteen Tons," etc.) that includes dances, pantomime, story line, etc. Synchronization rights would be required to include the songs (musical work) in the film. *Note:* The educator rights in § 110 do not include reproduction (in the soundtrack) but relate to	See *Maljack Productions, Inc. v. GoodTimes Home Video Corp.*, 81 F.3d 881, 884–885 (9th Cir. 1996) (recognizing the concept of synchronization rights); and *ABKCO Music Inc. v. Stellar Records, Inc.*, 96 F.3d 60, 63 (2d Cir. 1996): "A synchronization license is required if a copyrighted musical composition is to be used in 'timed-relation' or synchronization with an audiovisual work." See also *EMI Entertainment World, Inc. v. Priddis Music, Inc.*, 505 F. Supp. 2d 1217, 1221 (D. Utah 2007): "Under copyright law, an

(continued)

► **TABLE 10.1** Rights and Licenses in Musical Works and Sound Recordings *(Continued)*

Work Rights/Users	License/Permission Statutory Source	Examples of the Work or Its Use	Comment
Reproduction of a musical work as part of motion picture (an audiovisual work) soundtrack *(continued)*	exclusive right of the owner of copyright in a sound recording under clause (2) of § 106 [exclusive right to prepare a derivative work] is limited to the right to prepare a derivative work in which the actual sounds fixed in the sound recording are rearranged, remixed, or otherwise altered in sequence or quality."	performance or display alone.	entity wishing to synchronize music with visual images in a video, motion picture, etc., must obtain a synchronization license from the musical composition copyright holder and must also obtain a license from the sound recording copyright holder."
Sound recording: performance in public implicating an exclusive right only if by means of digital audio transmission, per § 106(6)	Analog transmission exempt from performance right, e.g., traditional AM or FM radio. Digital audio transmission subject to *compulsory license* with rates established by the Copyright Royalty Board. See Summary of the Determination of the Librarian of Congress on Rates and Terms for Webcasting and Ephermeral Recordings, http://www.copyright.gov/carp/webcasting_rates_final.html. "Interactive stream means a stream of a sound recording of a musical work, where the performance of the sound recording by means of the stream is not exempt under 17 U.S.C. § 114(d)(1) and does not in itself or as a result of a program in which it is included qualify for statutory licensing under 17 U.S.C. § 114(d)(1)." 37 C.F.R. § 385.11 current through 76 FEDERAL REGISTER 52145 (August 19, 2011).	Playing a CD to a face-to-face class. Statutory exception is not required here as there is no exclusive right of the copyright owner implicated by the performance of a sound recording other than by means of a digital audio transmission. Streaming tracks from various music CDs as part of an Irish "trad" podcast on St. Patrick's Day. This is likely covered by the section 114(d)(1) exemption: "The performance of a sound recording publicly by means of a digital audio transmission, other than as a part of an interactive service, is not an infringement . . . if the performance is part of a nonsubscription broadcast transmission." Streaming prerecorded music as part of an on-demand web-based subscription service or	There is no exclusive right to merely play a CD or other sound recording, even in public. The exclusive right is triggered only upon "digital audio transmission" of the sound recording.

(continued)

▶ **TABLE 10.1** **Rights and Licenses in Musical Works and Sound Recordings** *(Continued)*

Work Rights/Users	License/Permission Statutory Source	Examples of the Work or Its Use	Comment
Sound recording: performance in public implicating an exclusive right only if by means of digital audio transmission, per § 106(6) *(continued)*	Digital audio transmission not covered by the compulsory license must be negotiated with the copyright owner.	allowing patrons to access music from the library's e-bank of music is not exempt under § 114(d)(1) and would likely be subject to statutory licensing per the regulatory rate. See section 114(d)(2): "The performance of a sound recording publicly by means of a subscription digital audio transmission not exempt under paragraph (1)...shall be subject to statutory licensing, if the transmission is not part of an interactive service."	
Sound recording: reproduction of the sound recording under § 114 the exclusive right of the owner and not subject to compulsory license	*Master use license*: "A master use license permits the use of a sound recording in an audiovisual work, in synchronization with the images of the audiovisual work. The 'master' refers to the first or second generation of the recording, which offers a high sound quality. The master use license generally will also grant all of the rights necessary for the audiovisual work to be exploited as a feature film or television program, such as reproduction, public performance, and public distribution." ROBERT LIND ET AL., ENTERTAINMENT LAW: LEGAL CONCEPTS AND BUSINESS PRACTICES (3d ed.) § 9.93 (updated in Westlaw, May 2011). *Synchronization rights: Agee v. Paramount Communications, Inc.*, 59 F.3d 317, 324 (2d Cir. 1995): "producers of movies,	A small portion of a sound recording is included as background to public television documentary airing on its local affiliate, or snippets of sound recordings are included in a video yearbook made by the high school senior class. See *Agee v. Paramount Communications, Inc.*, 59 F.3d 317, 322 (2d Cir. 1995): "the Copyright Act specifically permits certain entities to reproduce sound recordings in soundtracks, provided that copies of the programs containing those recordings are not distributed to the public. For example, Congress provided in section 114(b) that noncommercial broadcasting entities have the right to include sound recordings in educational radio and television broadcasts, and may distribute and transmit copies	It is typical to negotiate such rights to reproduce the sound recording. These rights are obtained directly from the copyright owner.

(continued)

▶ **TABLE 10.1** Rights and Licenses in Musical Works and Sound Recordings *(Continued)*

Work Rights/Users	License/Permission Statutory Source	Examples of the Work or Its Use	Comment
Sound recording: reproduction of the sound recording under § 114 the exclusive right of the owner and not subject to compulsory license *(continued)*	television shows, and commercials often obtain master use licenses from sound recording copyright owners that allow them to synchronize sound recordings with visual images, as well as to copy and distribute the audiovisual work." See *Copyright Law Revision* (H. Rpt. No. 94-1476, 94th Cong. 2d Sess. 106 (1976)), reprinted in 5 UNITED STATES CODE CONGRESSIONAL AND ADMINISTRATIVE NEWS 5659, 5721 (1976): Exclusive right is triggered "whenever all or any substantial portion of the actual sounds that go to make up a copyrighted sound recording are reproduced in phonorecords . . . by reproducing them in the soundtrack or audio portion of a motion picture or other audiovisual work"; see also *Agee v. Paramount Communications, Inc.*, 59 F.3d 317, 324 (2d Cir. 1995): "In short, Paramount purchased Agee's sound recording but made no attempt to obtain a license for its reproduction in the soundtrack of its program. It therefore infringed Agee's sound recording at the moment it put portions of his recording on tape to make a segment of *Hard Copy.*"	or phonorecords as long as 'copies or phonorecords of said programs are not commercially distributed by or through public broadcasting entities to the general public.' 17 U.S.C. § 114(b). The plain implication of section 114(b) is that commercial entities like Paramount may not reproduce sound recordings on soundtracks of audiovisual works, whether or not the reproduction involves synchronization." These uses are therefore likely exempt, not covered by the § 114 right, or fair use. There is a split among the circuits as to whether very small excerpts for commercial use would be fair use or not. See *Bridgeport Music, Inc. v. Dimension Films*, 410 F.3d 792 (6th Cir. 2005): Analysis of a sound recording infringement is different than infringement of a musical work composition. Sampling part of a sound recording is a derivative use under § 114(b). "That leads us directly to the issue in this case. If you cannot pirate the whole sound recording, can you 'lift' or 'sample' something less than the whole. Our answer to that question is in the negative" (*id.* at 800). Court rejects use of substantial similarity or de minimis test: "a sound recording owner has the	

(continued)

▶ **TABLE 10.1** **Rights and Licenses in Musical Works and Sound Recordings** *(Continued)*

Work Rights/Users	License/Permission Statutory Source	Examples of the Work or Its Use	Comment
Sound recording: reproduction of the sound recording under § 114 the exclusive right of the owner and not subject to compulsory license *(continued)*		exclusive right to 'sample' his own recording" (*id*. at 801). "This means that the world at large is free to imitate or simulate the creative work fixed in the recoding so long as an actual copy of the sound recording itself is not made" (*id*. at 398). Not all circuits agree with this result. See *Newton v. Diamond*, 388 F.3d 1189, 1196 (9th Cir. 2004), cert. denied 545 U.S. 1114 (2005): "We hold that Beastie Boys' use of a brief segment of that composition, consisting of three notes separated by a half-step over a background C note, is not sufficient to sustain a claim for infringement of Newton's copyright in the composition 'Choir.'" See also *Saregama India Ltd. v. Mosley*, 687 F. Supp. 2d 1325, 1341 (S.D. Fla. 2009) (rejecting the interpretation of section 114 made by the *Bridgeport Music Inc.* court).	In sum, section 114(b) does not seem to support the distinction between sound recordings and all other forms of copyrightable work that the *Bridgeport* court imposes. Apart from its reading of the statute, the *Bridgeport* court proffers a variety of policy-based arguments for treating sound recordings differently from other copyrightable works.

REVIEW: PERFORMING A MUSICAL WORK IN THE LIBRARY

In the simplest scenario, suppose the library or its parent educational or other nonprofit institution desires to host the performance of a singing group, perhaps its own band and glee club. Does it need licenses to have the groups perform at graduation or a free seasonal concert? The answer is no, if the performance complies with section 110(4): "the performance of a nondramatic literary or musical work otherwise than in a transmission to the public, without any purpose of direct or indirect commercial advantage and without payment of any fee or other compensation for the performance to any of its performers, promoters, or organizers."[53] The use is deemed an allowed "privilege" against the owner's exclusive right to perform that music "if there is no direct or indirect admission charge" or, if there is a charge, "the proceeds, after deducting the reasonable costs of producing the performance, are used exclusively for educational, religious, or charitable purposes and not for private financial gain."[54] However, in cases where there is a direct or indirect admission charge, the section 110 limitation on the owner's exclusive right does not apply; in other words, the performance triggers the owner's exclusive right to perform the work "where the copyright owner has served notice of objection to the performance under certain circumstances."[55] It could be argued that the performance of a musical work, dramatic or nondramatic (dramatization), is derivative of the underlying work. As a result, there is the potential to trigger another set of rights.[56] The right to make derivate works is an exclusive right of the copyright owner.[57] However, performances of these works do not become derivative unless the performance is somehow fixed in a tangible medium, which is one of the requirements that has to be fulfilled for copyright protection to exist; refer to the discussion in the following section. So be careful about recording exempt (under the statute) performances, as such recordings may trigger additional rights of the copyright owner that the performance exemption is not designed to cover.

REVIEW: PERFORMING RECORDED MUSIC (MUSICAL WORK EMBODIED IN A SOUND RECORDING) IN THE LIBRARY

What if, instead, the library or institution desires to play prerecorded music? Is a license needed? No. First, understand that when prerecorded music is performed (e.g., playing a CD on a portable stereo), two categories of protected works may be at play: a musical work (the underlying song) and the recording of it (the sound recording). So there are potentially two sets of rights to consider. One problem is quickly solved by a close reading of section 106(4), the provision relating to the performance right. Sound recordings are not listed there. There is no exclusive right in the performance of a sound recording, unless the work is performed "publicly by means of a digital audio transmission."[58]

Under section 106(6), the performance right in a sound recording could be triggered when a library makes available to the public a web-based repository of sound recordings, digitized from vinyl records, cassette tapes, and so forth, that it collected over the years. Without discussing the copyright issues involved in the digitization process, when a patron listens to a recording from the repository online from his or her home computer, a performance by means of digital audio transmission is made every time that patron listens to any of these sound recordings. Depending on the circumstances, a statutory license may be available.[59] However, since the playlist, so to speak, could arguably appear as part of the online library catalog from which the patron could obtain digital audio on-demand transmissions, the performance would likely not be exempt or qualify for the compulsory license but would be subject to the full exclusive right of the copyright owner.[60]

This leaves the musical work to consider. Here again, section 110(4) can cover the performance of the CD, subject to the same considerations as the band and glee club performance.[61]

REVIEW: PERFORMING AND TRANSMITTING A DRAMATIC WORK (LITERARY OR MUSICAL) IN THE LIBRARY

Instead of performing a single song from a musical play at the graduation or seasonal concert, is a license or other permission needed to perform an entire play, such as *West Side Story*? Yes, a performance license is needed. Section 110(4) would not apply to a dramatic literary or musical work such as a play or opera. Performance of these works would require a license or some form of permission. As discussed, such works could be performed in qualifying classroom encounters. There is no such restriction in the teaching provisions. Such works could be performed in a face-to-face setting under section 110(1) and a "reasonable and limited portion" could be performed in a distance-education setting under section 110(2). Of course, one requirement of section 110 is that the content be related to the course being taught, such as History of American Theater.

In a slightly complicating variation, what if the library or institution desires to air the performance of the graduation or seasonal concert on a local cable channel? Section 110(4) states "otherwise than in a transmission." As a result, such broadcasts, analog or digital, do not fall under the nonprofit performance provisions of section 110. The broadcast will require a license or other form of permission.

SUMMARY POINTS

► Reproducing a musical work beyond fair use would require a license. Reproduction of the musical work in a sound recording (recording your playing of the song) is subject to the statutory so-called mechanical licensing scheme. Reproducing the sheet music requires licensing as well. Harry Fox Agency as well as such music publishers as Hal Leonard Publishing, Warner/Chappell Music, Cherry Lane Music Company, Music Sales Corporation, and Warner Bros. are well-known publishers/licensors of sheet music.

► Performing a musical work is also subject to licensing administered by ASCAP and BMI. Dramatic performance rights are known as grand rights and need to be negotiated. Fair use can again apply.

► Teachers and students would have performance rights for all categories of copyrighted works, including musical works, under sections 110(1) and 110(2), that is, play and sing the score of a song, or to make a public display .of the sheet music in a classroom setting or in the course of a class session online, subject to the conditions of these subsections. Section 112(b) allows for the reproduction of work in anticipation of its use in an online class session, subject to the conditions of section 112(f).

▷ There is no performance right in a sound recording unless by means of a digital audio transmission.

▷ Public library and other qualifying nonprofit, noncommercial performances of nondramatic literary or musical works are allowed under section 110(4).

▷ Performance of dramatic works, or dramatic renderings of nondramatic works, beyond a fair use requires a grand performance right.

▷ Reproduction of a sound recording beyond fair use requires a license as well. However, at least one appellate court does not approve of even a *di minimus* reproduction of a sound recording in a commercial setting.

▷ Recording a musical work to movement (producing a music video), reproducing the words along with a recording (selling karaoke machines), or using songs in a soundtrack of a motion picture require a synchronization license.

LEARNING EXAMPLES

▷ **Example 10.1**

Situation: A librarian sings a song from the *Lion King* during a library story hour sing-a-long. In the alternative, the librarian plays a song from the library's copy of the *Lion King* soundtrack CD. What is the result?

Legal Analysis: The sing-a-long is allowed under section 110(4)—no license is needed. Likewise, playing the CD is also covered under section 110(4) regarding the musical work, and there is no performance right triggered by playing the sound recording, as there is no exclusive right of the copyright to perform a sound recording unless done by means of a digital audio transmission.

▷ **Example 10.2**

Situation: The high school drama club decides to perform the music of U2 and build a play (scenes, costumes, stage movement, etc.) around it, telling the history and resolution of the conflict in Northern Ireland. What is the result?

Legal Analysis: This is a dramatic performance of arguably nondramatic works. Copyright owners and some commentators would argue a grand performance right is required, as the exemption falls outside section 110(4).

▷ **Example 10.3**

Situation: The high school glee club would like to take a series of songs from various operas (which are dramatic works) and perform them in a concert as a series of individual numbers. What is the result?

Legal Analysis: While the works are dramatic, given the nondramatic nature of the performance, assuming there is no acting out, costumes, and so on, associated with the rendering of the performances, some commentators would argue that the section 110(4) exemption regarding noncommercial performance of nondramatic literary or musical works applies and no license is needed.

▶ **Example 10.4**

Situation: Students include snippets of sound recordings in a multimedia work as part of a final project presentation on the last day of the semester.

Legal Analysis: The students' performance of the musical work underlying the sound recording should be covered by section 110(1) as long as the performance of the musical work underlying the sound recording is related to class and satisfies the other requirements of this section. There is case law to suggest that reproducing small excerpts of the musical work and sound recording to set a historical context, social commentary, example, or illustration is fair use.[62]

▶ **Example 10.5**

Situation: In a public library setting, teenagers create and present a 60-second book talk using a few seconds of various songs to emphasize, underscore, or contrast elements of their presentation. What is the result?

Legal Analysis: While the section 110 performance right does not apply, as this is not a class session, under the explanation in Legal Analysis for Example 10.4, a fair-use argument could be made for the use of small excerpts of sound recordings and underlying musical works embodied in those sound recordings to underscore, highlight, comment, or otherwise complement the critique, review, or promotion of the book.

ENDNOTES

1. A definitive source on the topic is AL KOHN AND BOB KOHN, KOHN ON MUSIC LICENSING (3d ed. 2002).

2. For additional information, see ROBERT LIND ET AL., ENTERTAINMENT LAW 3D: LEGAL CONCEPTS AND BUSINESS PRACTICES: (updated in Westlaw, December 2011); JAMES G. SAMMATARO, FILM AND MULTIMEDIA AND THE LAW (updated in Westlaw, July 2011); and MARK S. LEE, ENTERTAINMENT AND INTELLECTUAL PROPERTY LAW (updated in Westlaw, November 2011).

3. See also Shapiro, Bernstein & Co. v. Jerry Vogel Music Co., 161 F.2d 406, 409 (2d Cir. 1947): "The words and music of a song constitute a 'musical composition' in which the two contributions merge into a single work to be performed as a unit for the pleasure of the hearers; they are not a 'composite' work, like the articles in an encyclopedia, but are as little separable for purposes of the copyright as are the individual musical notes which constitute the melody."

4. 17 U.S.C. § 101.

5. Brent Giles Davis, *Identity Theft: Tribute Bands, Grand Rights, and Dramatico-Musical Performances*, 24 CARDOZO ARTS AND ENTERTAINMENT LAW JOURNAL 485 (2006).

6. Recording Industry Association of America, Inc. v. Librarian of Congress, 608 F.3d 861, 863 (D.C. Cir. 2010).

7. Higgins v. Detroit Educational Television Foundation, 4 F. Supp. 2d 701 (E.D. Mich. 1998).

8. Lennon v. Premise Media Corp., 556 F. Supp. 2d 310 (S.D.N.Y. 2008), use of segment from song "Imagine" in documentary message film fair use.

9. Campbell v. Acuff-Rose Music, 510 U.S. 569 (1994), use of signature guitar riff from Roy Orbison song "Pretty Woman" in rap song fair use. See also Abilene Music, Inc., et al. v. Sony Music Entertainment, Inc., et al., 320 F. Supp. 2d 84 (S.D.N.Y. 2003), use of song "What a Wonderful World" in a rap song fair use.

10. Bourne v. Twentieth Century Fox Film Corp., 602 F. Supp. 2d 499 (S.D.N.Y. 2009), parody of Disney song "When You Wish Upon a Star" in *Family Guy* episode fair use.

11. Leadsinger, Inc. v. BMG Music Publishing, 429 F. Supp. 2d 1190 (C.D. Cal. 2005).

12. U.S. v. American Soc. of Composers, Authors and Publishers, 599 F. Supp. 2d 415 (S.D.N.Y. 2009).

13. For example, a so-called "ephemeral recording" provision in section 110 allows qualifying educational entities to make transitory copies of works (including musical works) that will be performed or displayed in the course of a qualifying transmission under section 110 (2) (distance education): "For purposes of paragraph (2), no governmental body or accredited nonprofit educational institution shall be liable for infringement by reason of the transient or temporary storage of material carried out through the automatic technical process of a digital transmission of the performance or display of that material as authorized under paragraph (2)" (17 U.S.C. § 110).

14. 17 U.S.C. § 115: "In the case of nondramatic musical works, the exclusive rights provided by clauses (1) [exclusive right to reproduce a work] and (3) [exclusive right to make public distribution of a work] of section 106, to make and to distribute phonorecords of such works, are subject to compulsory licensing under the conditions specified by this section."

15. Bridgeport Music, Inc. v. DJ Yella Muzick, 99 Fed. Appx. 686, 691 (6th Cir. 2004).

16. See 17 U.S.C. § 115.

17. 17 U.S.C. § 115(a)(2) provides: "A compulsory license includes the privilege of making a musical arrangement of the work to the extent necessary to conform it to the style or manner of interpretation of the performance involved, but the arrangement shall not change the basic melody or fundamental character of the work, and shall not be subject to protection as a derivative work under this title, except with the express consent of the copyright owner." Since 2 Live Crew desired to mock the sentiment and story line of the original Orbison song, it could not qualify for the mechanical, statutory license available to other singers that might cover the song. When it asked for permission and was told

no, the group proceeded anyway, spawning the subsequent litigation. See Campbell v. Acuff-Rose Music, 510 U.S. 569 (1994).

18. June M. Besek, Copyright Issues Relevant to Digital Preservation and Dissemination of Pre-1972 Commercial Sound Recordings by Libraries and Archives 17 (2005).

19. 17 U.S.C. § 101 defines phonorecords as "material objects in which sounds, other than those accompanying a motion picture or other audiovisual work, are fixed by any method now known or later developed, and from which the sounds can be perceived, reproduced, or otherwise communicated, either directly or with the aid of a machine or device. The term 'phonorecords' includes the material object in which the sounds are first fixed."

20. "'Mechanical licensing' is a music industry term that describes a license from the copyright holder for use of its composition in a sound recording in return for payment of a royalty; royalties are usually paid each time a copy of the sound recording is sold." Bridgeport Music, Inc. v. Agarita Music, Inc., 182 F. Supp. 2d 653, 657, note 4 (M.D. Tenn. 2002), citation omitted.

21. Allegro Corp. v. Only New Age Music, Inc., 2003 WL 23571745, *16, note 4 (D. Or., 2003) (unpublished).

22. "A compulsory mechanical license permits a third party to manufacture and distribute for sale to the public phonorecords of musical compositions that have previously been manufactured and distributed by the originator of the copyright." Electronic Realty Associates, L.P. v. Paramount Pictures Corp., 935 F. Supp. 1172, 1175, n. 1 (D. Kan. 1996).

23. 17 U.S.C. § 110(1) allows the "performance or display of a work by instructors or pupils in the course of face-to-face teaching activities of a nonprofit educational institution, in a classroom or similar place devoted to instruction, unless, in the case of a motion picture or other audiovisual work, the performance, or the display of individual images, is given by means of a copy that was not lawfully made under this title, and that the person responsible for the performance knew or had reason to believe was not lawfully made."

24. 17 U.S.C. § 110(2) allows "the performance of a nondramatic literary or musical work or reasonable and limited portions of any other work."

25. 17 U.S.C. § 110(4) allows for qualifying "performance of a nondramatic literary or musical work otherwise than in a transmission to the public, without any purpose of direct or indirect commercial advantage and without payment of any fee or other compensation for the performance to any of its performers, promoters, or organizers."

26. 17 U.S.C. § 106(6).

27. Agee v. Paramount Communications, Inc., 59 F.3d 317, 235 (2d Cir. 1995): "producers of movies, television shows, and commercials often obtain master use licenses from sound recording copyright owners that allow them to synchronize sound recordings with visual images, as well as to copy and distribute the audiovisual work."

28. ABKCO Music, Inc. v. Stellar Records, Inc., 96 F.3d 60, 63 note 4 (2d Cir. 1996).

29. Leadsinger, Inc. v. BMG Music Publishing, 512 F.3d 522, 527 (9th Cir. 2008).

30. Fred Ahlert Music Corp. v. Warner/Chappell Music, Inc., 155 F.3d 17, 19, note 1 (2d Cir. 1998).

31. Broadcast Music, Inc. v. Columbia Broadcasting System, Inc., 441 U.S. 1, 33 (1979), footnotes omitted.
32. Bridgeport Music, Inc. v. Agarita Music, Inc., 182 F. Supp. 2d 653, 657, note 5 (M.D. Tenn. 2002), citation omitted.
33. Angel Music, Inc. v. ANC Sports, Inc., 631 F. Supp. 429, 430 (S.D.N.Y. 1986). This is not the first time ABC Sports has been involved in copyright disputes. See Iowa State University Research Foundation, Inc. v. American Broadcasting Companies, Inc., 621 F.2d 57 (2d Cir. 1980), use of film clip from a documentary on Olympic wrestler Dan Gable in broadcast of Olympic games is not a fair use.
34. House of Bryant Publications, LLC v. A&E Television Networks, 2009 WL 3673055, *1 (M.D. Tenn. 2009) (slip copy). "For the next six to seven seconds, the UT band (with no vocal accompaniment) can clearly be heard to be playing 'Rocky Top' as scenes from the game and the crowd are displayed. In the five to six seconds after that, an interviewee discusses that UT football is 'nuts,' while images of a football game continue to be displayed and 'Rocky Top' can still be heard in the background, although less clearly than in the 6–7 preceding seconds. 'Rocky Top' is not played at any other time in the Episode, which runs about 47 minutes and, for the most part, focuses on an attempted contract killing that, as far as the court can tell, had nothing to do with UT, 'Rocky Top,' or football." The court concluded that three of the fair use factor weighed against a finding of fair use and only one factor, the amount and substantiality weighed slightly in favor of fair use (*id.* at *5–*9).
35. Bridgeport Music, Inc. v. Still N The Water Publishing, 327 F.3d 472, 481, note 8 (6th Cir. 2003).
36. EMI Entertainment World, Inc. v. Priddis Music, Inc., 505 F. Supp. 2d 1217, 1224 (D. Utah 2007). "Concerning the necessity or applicability of a synchronization license for karaoke recordings in which the text of lyrics is displayed in timed relation to Priddis' sound recordings of EMI's musical works, Priddis' motion shall be granted for the same reasons that EMI's motion was denied" (*id.* at 1225).
37. 17 U.S.C. § 109(c).
38. The beaming of lyrics on a screen under section 109(c) is different from the use of lyrics in a karaoke machine, and the lyrics in the sing-along device are tied to the music that is played. This is not so with beaming of lyrics to the school audience. See Leadsinger, Inc. v. BMG Music Pub. 512 F.3d 522, 528, n. 2 (9th Cir. 2008): "The images of song lyrics for the purpose of karaoke differ from song lyrics printed on a sheet of paper. Song lyrics printed on paper are not a series of images, have no relationship to a machine, and are not capable of indicating to the consumer when the lyrics are to be sung. On the other hand, images of song lyrics embedded in a karaoke device are part of a series of images, and must be shown by a machine so that the consumer knows when to sing each lyric."
39. This is the majority opinion, although one court found to the contrary. See EMI Entertainment World, Inc. v. Priddis Music, Inc. 505 F. Supp. 2d 1217, 1226 (D. Utah 2007): "Concerning the necessity or applicability of a synchronization license for karaoke

recordings in which the text of lyrics is displayed in timed relation to Priddis' sound recordings of EMI's musical works, Priddis' motion shall be granted for the same reasons that EMI's motion was denied." Contra, Leadsinger, Inc. v. BMG Music Pub. 512 F.3d 522, 528, n. 2 (9th Cir. 2008): "The only court to hold that a karaoke device is not an audiovisual work is the District Court for the District of Utah, in EMI Entertainment World, Inc. v. Priddis Music, Inc., which concluded that synchronization licenses are not necessary to sell a product that displays lyrics in timed relation with music. In essence, the *EMI Entertainment World, Inc. v. Priddis Music, Inc.* court did not view the use of song lyrics for karaoke as different from the production of printed copies of song lyrics. We are not persuaded by the court's reasoning in *EMI Entertainment World, Inc. v. Priddis Music, Inc.* That case failed to consider the use of song lyrics in context."

40. 17 U.S.C. § 109(c).

41. Leadsinger, Inc. v. BMG Music Publishing, 512 F.3d 522, 527 (9th Cir. 2008). "We hold that Leadsinger's [karaoke] device falls within the definition of an audiovisual work. As a result, in addition to any § 115 compulsory licenses necessary to make and distribute phonorecords and reprint licenses necessary to reprint song lyrics, Leadsinger is also required to secure synchronization licenses to display images of song lyrics in timed relation with recorded music" (*id.* at 529, citations omitted).

42. In re Cellco Partnership, 663 F. Supp. 2d 363, 375 (S.D.N.Y. 2009).

43. U.S. v. American Soc. of Composers, Authors and Publishers, 599 F. Supp. 2d 415 (S.D.N.Y. 2009).

44. Capital Records, Inc. v. Naxos of America, Inc., 4 N.Y. 540, 560 (Court of Appeals 2005): "The musical recordings at issue in this case, created before February 15, 1972, are therefore entitled to copyright protection under New York common law until the effective date of federal preemption—February 15, 2067."

45. See, for example, Peter B. Hirtle, *Copyright Renewal, Copyright Restoration, and the Difficulty of Determining Copyright Status*, D-LIB MAGAZINE, July/August 2008.

46. Besek, *supra* note 18: "Foreign sound recordings published before 1946 were already in the public domain in their source countries on the restoration date and were not eligible for restoration. Thus, virtually all pre-1946 foreign sound recordings are in the public domain as far as U.S. federal copyright law is concerned."

47. 17 U.S.C. § 106(6): "in the case of sound recordings, to perform the copyrighted work publicly by means of a digital audio transmission."

48. Joseph Gratz, *Note, Reform in the "Brave Kingdom": Alternative Compensation Systems for Peer-to-Peer File Sharing*, 6 MINNESOTA JOURNAL OF LAW, SCIENCE, AND TECHNOLOGY 339, 403 (2004).

49. Howell O'Rear, *Pay Me My (Licensing) Money Down: Legal and Practical Aspects of Karaoke Licensing*, 6 VIRGINIA SPORTS AND ENTERTAINMENT LAW JOURNAL 361, 367 (2007), footnote omitted.

50. See, for example, the discussion of section 110(2) as enacted in 1976, which was limited to nondramtatic musical or literary works. The comment from the House Reports suggests

that dramatizations of nondramatic works would not be included: "The clause is not intended to limit in any way the copyright owner's exclusive right to make dramatizations, adaptations, or other derivative works under section 106(2). Thus, for example, a performer could read a nondramatic literary work aloud under section 110(2), but the copyright owner's permission would be required for him to act it out in dramatic form." H.R. Rep. No. 94-1476, at 83 (1976), as reprinted in 1976 UNITED STATES CODE CONGRESSIONAL AND ADMINSTRATIVE NEWS 5659, 5697.

51. ALEXANDER LINDEY AND MICHAEL LANDAU, LINDEY ON ENTERTAINMENT, PUBLISHING, AND THE ARTS § 8.51 (3d ed. 2004) (database updated in Westlaw, October 2011).

52. See HOWARD B. ABRAMS, 1 THE LAW OF COPYRIGHT § 2:39 (database updated in Westlaw, November 2011): "The trickier question arises when a musical composition written as an integral part of a dramatic work is taken out of the dramatic work and performed or embodied in a phonorecord as if it were a nondramatic work. To phrase the issue in more concrete terms, if a song that was originally written and performed as an integral part of a musical play is recorded as part of a sound recording that contained none of the other songs from the play, should that song become subject to the compulsory licenses and exemptions that apply to nondramatic musical works? This question should be answered affirmatively." See also "In some instances, the musical work itself may be categorized as 'dramatic.' But excerpts of those dramatic works may be performed nondramatically. Most popular songs are written as nondramatic works, but virtually any might be performed in a dramatic fashion." Bernard Korman and I. Fred Koenigsberg, *Performing Rights in Music and Performing Rights Societies*, in PATENTS, COPYRIGHTS, TRADEMARKS, AND LITERARY PROPERTY COURSE HANDBOOK SERIES, *39, *43 (1987) (Practising Law Institute, 238 PLI/Pat 9) (footnotes omitted; text of n. 12 reads as follows: "For example, a single song from a musical comedy sung in a nightclub." *Id.* at *).

53. 17 U.S.C. § 110(4). Notice the statute requires that there be no "purpose of direct or indirect commercial advantage." Purpose goes to intent or design of the performance and the institution responsible for it; this is not the same as an act that produces such result. "This provision expressly adopts the principle established by the court decisions construing the 'for profit' limitation: that public performances given or sponsored in connection with any commercial or profit-making enterprises are subject to the exclusive rights of the copyright owner even though the public is not charged for seeing or hearing the performance." H.R. Rep. No. 94-1476, at 85 (1976), as reprinted in 1976 UNITED STATES CODE CONGRESSIONAL AND ADMINISTRATIVE NEWS 5659, 5699.

54. 17 U.S.C. § 110(4)(A)(B). A direct admission charge would be an obvious entrance fee paid in the form of a ticket. An indirect admission charge might be an annual student activity fee which gives each student ten coupons to attend throughout the academic year the ten events of his or her choosing, which would otherwise require a paid ticket.

55. The statute prescribes the conditions of a valid notice: "(i) the notice shall be in writing and signed by the copyright owner or such owner's duly authorized agent; and (ii) the notice shall be served on the person responsible for the performance at least seven days

before the date of the performance, and shall state the reasons for the objection; and (iii) the notice shall comply, in form, content, and manner of service, with requirements that the Register of Copyrights shall prescribe by regulation." 17 U.S.C. § 110(4)(B)(i)–(iii).

56. A derivative work is defined as "a work based upon one or more preexisting works, such as a translation, musical arrangement, dramatization, fictionalization, motion picture version, sound recording, art reproduction, abridgment, condensation, or any other form in which a work may be recast, transformed, or adapted." 17 U.S.C. § 101.

57. 17 U.S.C. § 106(2).

58. 17 U.S.C. § 106(6).

59. United States Copyright Office, *Report on Copyright and Digital Distance Education* 95–96 (1999): "In its current form, section 114 divides the types of transmissions that carry performances of sound recoding into three categories. Depending on the category into which the digital transmission falls, the performance of the sound recording could be subject to no right at all, a statutory license, or full exclusive right." See also Table 10.1.

60. "The third tier...require negotiating a license with the copyright owner. These performances...include interactive digital audio services (on-demand streaming)." Besek, *supra* note 18: An online library music catalog from which patrons select what to listen to would be considered on-demand. See also UNITED STATES COPYRIGHT OFFICE, REPORT ON COPYRIGHT AND DIGITAL DISTANCE EDUCATION 97 (1999): "For either a subscription or eligible nonsubscription transmission to qualify for the statutory license, however, it must be interactive and meet a series of criteria set out in section 114, including not publishing the titles of the sound recordings in advance and not transmitting too many selections from the same phonorecord or by the same performer...Because many asynchronous distance education activities are interactive, they will likely fall into this category."

61. The legislative history also indicates that "exemption would be limited to public performances given directly in the presence of an audience whether by means of living performers, the playing of phonorecords, or the operation of a receiving apparatus." H.R. Rep. No. 94-1476, at 85 (1976), as reprinted in 1976 UNITED STATES CODE CONGRESSIONAL AND ADMINISTRATIVE NEWS 5659, 5699.

62. See, for example, Lennon v. Premise Media Corp., 556 F. Supp. 2d 310 (S.D.N.Y. 2008) (use of segment from song "Imagine" in documentary message film fair use); and Higgins v. Detroit Educational Television Foundation, 4 F. Supp. 2d 701 (E.D. Mich. 1998) (rap song excerpt in documentary film fair use).

11

THE UNIFORM COMPUTER INFORMATION TRANSACTIONS ACT

Read this chapter to understand the nature and legality of these license situations:
▶ Expansion of licensing
▶ Digital information transactions
▶ Licensing of other intangibles

LICENSING ON STEROIDS

After digesting the previous chapters, from basic contract concepts to emerging and evolving issues in licensing through the nuts and bolts of licenses in practice (and there is more applied information in Part III), it is time to consider the future of licensing, whether it will change, and if so how dramatically. Two targets—one, for the moment at least, is stationary (Uniform Computer Information Transactions Act, or UCITA), the other still moving (continued developments and changes in licensing terms and conditions presented by vendors/licensors)—need be considered. Lessons can be learned from recent attempts at making uniform across the states a law for information contracting, or UCITA.

As economies evolve, so, too, do their commercial laws, from exchanges of horses and grain to production of manufactured goods to the law of sales and consumer transactions. In the United States, this evolution led to the development of article 2 of the Uniform Commercial Code (UCC) in the second half of the twentieth century to provide a uniform statutory law from which courts could evaluate particular circumstances: sales of goods. Our economy continued to evolve from one based in goods to one based in services. The library community knows this only too well: "Transactions in online information are clearly different from transactions for acquiring tangible copies of information and the same rules cannot apply. A contract with Westlaw for access to its database is simply not the same as a contract for purchase of a copy of the West reporter service in print form."[1] However, some would argue that a distinct treatment between goods and information or information and software was due more to the existing statute, given the layout and organization of the UCC, than to variation in the inherent nature of such products.[2] Nonetheless, digital information is a key element to many of those services. In addition, the methods of distribution of those services differed from goods-based transactions. Thus, a need for a body of code targeting the uniqueness of digital information transactions, as opposed to tangible goods, was according to some needed. "UCITA was drafted in response to this fundamental economic change and need for clarity in the law."[3] However, the certainty through uniformity is undermined by the poor drafting within UCITA, at least in the minds of some commentators.[4]

While UCITA is the law in only two states, its significance cannot be underestimated for several reasons. The development of UCITA represented evidence that when libraries and other user communities desire to mobilize and call out the troops, so to speak, the result can be quite effective in facilitating change or, in the specific instance of UCITA, in curtailing or preventing questionable change. Nonetheless, when one discusses UCITA, one is discussing a law designed for licensing. There is no need to resort to makeshift or improvised approaches in applying the law of tangible goods to information transactions, as demonstrated in several of the shrink-wrap and click-wrap decisions noted in previous examples and in Chapter 7. At the time, the practices of software licensing, intellectual property rights, and licensing of other intangibles were not new, but UCITA attempted to capture the law thus far and direct (as model and uniform laws do) where that law might head or should head (in the opinion of its drafters) in the future. For that reason alone, UCITA is worth a look,[5] even if one desires to characterize the aftermath of its development and current adoption by only two states as a legal anomaly or curiosity. In truth, "UCITA applies to a wide range of Internet-related contracts and is the single most comprehensive body of contract law for cyberspace."[6] Even where enacted, its provisions are default, allowing the parties the freedom, with some exception, to alter the application of a particular provision or to (in theory) opt in or out of UCITA entirely.[7] It is the defaults UCITA establishes that to some are controversial, or at least not without issue. While UCITA may not represent an accurate or complete picture of the future of licensing, it is a future that some desire. In the historical context, we understand what might have been, learn proverbially from history in determining what could be in the future, and take measures to prepare for a future we desire, not dread.[8]

Case law awarded early victories to licensees by indicating that transactions were not governed by the UCC or otherwise found its rules inapplicable.[9] Again, as previous discussions indicate, this prevented uniformity in the law applicable to such transactions, though it did not prevent licensors from using language or agreements that seemed uniform at times. Commerce does not like uncertainty. Moreover, even when article 2 ("transactions in goods") applied, the result produced unwanted consequences. For example, article 2 transactions are governed by a perfect tender rule that requires the goods—which in an article 2 transaction would mean that the software—be provided in total conformity with the terms of the contract. Software is notoriously imperfect. As a result, some licensors did not want article 2 to apply and incorporated contractual language to exclude it. Article 2 became less and less useful, even though some courts have indicated that the UCC does govern software transactions.[10]

In 1990, a committee of the Massachusetts Bar Association drafted a new part B to article 2 that proposed to revise those provisions of the existing article which did not appear to fit quite right with software transactions. Nothing ever became of part B, but it generated discussion and pointed a direction to pursue. The National Conference of Commissioners on Uniform State Laws (NCCUSL) took up the matter but decided to create a new article 2B from the ground up and, in August 1990, undertook revision of article 2B, again with the thought of creating a uniform body of law applicable to software licensing. With draft in hand, in September 1995, the NCCUSL board began discussing its revision with the American Law Institute (ALI). However, after revisions, discussion, and a healthy dose of concern and criticism from various stakeholders regarding the impact that the proposed article 2B might have on contract, consumer, and copyright law, NCCUSL in 1999 decided not to pursue the matter further. Revision of article 2 was thought less useful than a law dedicated to "tailoring digital information to the modern marketplace,"[11] and so UCITA was born.

Abandoning the UCC offshoot approach, NCCUSL concocted a new stand-alone law that would apply not only to software but to all information transactions. NCCUSL released UCITA in 1999. In response to criticism from the American Bar Association as well as other stakeholders, including the library community, NCCUSL in 2002 modified a number of provisions, clarifying the applicability to and impact on licensees and consumers. Prior to that, in spring 2000, Virginia enacted UCITA (effective July 2001)[12] and Maryland followed suit later that fall (effective October 1, 2000).[13] While UCITA was introduced in a number of other states' legislatures and progressed toward enactment with various level of success, the overall reception was underwhelming. As a result, NCCUSL withdrew UCITA from its list of active legislation.

UCITA in a sense validates the license as the preferred form of transaction involving computer information. As the Prefatory Note observes in a telling example: "[I]n a sale of goods, the buyer owns ... someone that acquires a copy of computer information may or may not own ... rights acquired or withheld depend[ing] on what the contract says ... implicit in Article 2 for goods such as books; UCITA makes it explicit for the information economy where, unlike in the case of a book, the contract (license) is the product."[14] According to section 103, UCITA applies to "computer information transactions." This does not mean all digital or online communications covered by UCITA but does include computer programs, multimedia product transfers, or development contracts as well as contracts to obtain information in a program, accessing content of a multimedia product.[15] "A contract for an airline ticket is not a computer information transaction simply because the ticket may be represented in digital form."[16]

As stated, Virginia and Maryland are the only two states that adopted UCITA. It could be argued the mobilization of opponents, including libraries, and attempts to assuage the negative impact of UCITA at the state level in the passages of UCITA in Maryland and Virginia raised awareness of UCITA's deficiencies and unintended consequences so that other state legislatures became less receptive to blind adoption.[17] In fact, in July 1999, half of all the nation's state attorneys general signed a letter openly opposing UCITA.[18] "The greatest 'user' support for UCITA has come from the mass market software and database publishing businesses, who wish to codify their practices which may or may not have become established in the marketplace."[19] At the same time, "there has been some significant disagreement within the legal community as to the effectiveness of the Act in meeting all the concerns of the various constituencies."[20] Other public interest groups voiced their objections as well.[21] A revision process in 2002, which generated 19 changes, also met with resistance; as a result, in July 2003, NCCUSL discharged the adoption committee, which had been charged with promoting adoption of UCITA by the states. It should be observed that no state has enacted the 2002 version of UCITA. There was no exemption for libraries or educational entities from mass-market licenses, whereby any clause that contravened fair use or other rights was void. Such legislation has been proposed at the national level with little interest.[22]

A number of states reacted to adoption of UCITA by enacting anti-UCITA laws or so-called bomb-shelter legislation. "The source of much of the controversy surrounding the uniform law is that it both validates shrinkwrap licenses and sets forth what many believe are unfair default rules governing those licenses... especially when used in larger purchases, commercial transactions, or for services such as Internet access provision."[23] Bomb-shelter legislation operates by insulating the citizens of the enacting state from the legal effects of UCITA by making its provisions void and unenforceable in that state's courts. The legislation accomplishes this in specific by voiding any choice of law provision in a contract that happens to occur in a jurisdiction where UCITA is in effect, in other words, Maryland or Virginia. As a result, the law of either state, in essence UCITA, cannot apply to the contract at hand. So far several states have taken this additional step, in addition to simply not enacting UCITA.[24]

A few comments can be made regarding the substance of UCITA.[25] This is done not to favor those readers from the two states where UCITA is the law but to understand that the basics of UCITA offer several advantages. First, should there arise once again interest in UCITA adoption, the reader will be prepared. Unlikely as that might be, UCITA represents a significant development in recent contract law—a contract law designed with information-based products and services in mind. One reason perhaps such renewed interest is unlikely to resurface is related to a second benefit that is available with an understanding of UCITA. Some of its provisions may become more prevalent in contracts in the twenty-first century. Understanding the impact of such provisions will help you with the licenses you do have. UCITA was never meant to be the final word on software or information transactions but was intended to serve as an intermediate step.[26] UCITA may not be the last such law, proposed or enacted, governing information-based transactions.[27] However, UCITA does represent a free-market approach to contracting; though it recognizes public policy imprimaturs and concepts such as unconscionability, there is a decided deference to the decisions of the parties vis-à-vis the contract terms chosen.[28] Thus, it is imperative that the library and other user communities remain vigilant, not only with an eye to future developments and lessons learned but to the current practices of licensors. "Libraries are significant transferees (licensees) and libraries and universities are significant licensors of information... UCITA did not create the digital world or its effect on libraries, but the library community seems to insist at times that the states through UCITA must *solve* their market and technological problems."[29] It may also be that in the future some alternative to UCITA is proposed, likely with many of the same attitudes that UCITA reflected, and again understanding the basics will help assess any future such proposals.

UCITA AND THE MODERN LICENSE FOR INFORMATION CONTENT AND SERVICES

As its subtitle implies, touted as a "commercial contract code for the computer information transactions,"[30] UCITA applies to all computer information transactions, whether licenses or sales.[31] A computer information transaction is defined as "an agreement of the performance of it to create, modify, transfer or license computer information or informational rights in computer information," per UCITA § 103(a) and § 102(11). Computer information is "information in electronic form which is obtained from or through the use of a computer or which is in a form capable of being processed by a computer."[32] Fortunately for libraries, UCITA does not apply to transactions involving print, such as "books, magazines, newspapers," and so forth, or to goods, such as "televisions, VCRs, DVD players or similar goods."[33]

A consumer contract is a "contract between a merchant and a consumer."[34] Mass-market transactions include consumer contracts as well as qualifying end user agreements.[35] Mass-market transactions are determined by the market, the terms, and the type of information involved.[36] "An end user is a licensee that intends to use the information or information rights in its own business or personal affairs."[37] This passage suggests that a merchant, the other type of party, can enter into mass-market transactions. However, the Official Comment indicates that "business to business transactions are not" mass-market transactions.[38] Similar to the UCC definition, a merchant is defined as a person "that deals in information or information rights of the kind involved in the transaction," or who by "occupation holds itself out as having knowledge or skill peculiar" to the "circumstances or substance of the transaction," or in situations where such attribution is made because one uses an agent or other intermediary and the agent or intermediary holds itself out to be similarly schooled, skilled, or so endowed.[39] A library dealing in transactions involving databases, for example, would likely be deemed a merchant as "an organization is charged with the expertise of it employees."[40] "The definition distinguishes between profit-making, professional, or business use, from non-business of family use. Only when a contract is primarily for the latter is there a consumer contract."[41] However, some transactions are not mass market and are excluded by section 102: "any transaction intended for redistribution of the information by further license, loan or sale, or for public performance of a copyrighted work. Such transactions involve no attributes of a retail market. For purposes of this Act, public performance or display does not include use by a library patron of software acquired by the library in the mass market."[42]

UCITA defines receipt in terms of electronic notice with a delivery concept: "coming into existence in an information processing system or at an address in that system in a form capable of being processed by or perceived from a system of that type by recipient, if the recipient uses, or otherwise has designated or holds out, that place or system for receipt of notices of the kind to be given and the sender does know that the notice cannot be accessed from that place."[43] So if you designate e-mail for this purpose, the notice is received when it enters your server's or system's inbox, even though unbeknownst to the sender your e-mail server crashed last Friday and will be inaccessible by you the better part of the week following.[44] "In UCITA, there is a crucial difference between knowledge and notice. Knowledge means actual knowledge. Notice, however, includes receipt of notification of a fact"[45] even if not known at the time of receipt. "Whether the message actually is processed is not relevant to receipt."[46] The definition of "send" mirrors a similar "in a form capable of being processed by or perceived from a system" but adds that "[r]eceipt within the time in which it would have arrived if properly sent, has the effect of a proper sending."[47]

While executory obligations are discharged upon termination of a contract, UCITA lists 11 rights and obligations that survive, in other words, need not be stated in the agreement. Licenses often indicate what terms survive the agreement, often including restrictions on use and disclaimer (of warranties) indemnifications, and UCITA makes these implicit in the agreement. The impact of such structure is that when a party desires the right or obligation to *not* continue after termination, it must be specifically released in the agreement or the UCITA default rule of right or obligation will exist. The following rights survive in a UCITA license: a right based on a previous breach or performance of the contract; an obligation of confidentiality, nondisclosure, or noncompetition to the extent enforceable under other law; a contractual-use term applicable to any licensed copy or information received from the other party or copies made of it, which are not returned or returnable to the other party; an obligation to deliver or dispose of information, materials, documentation, copies, records, or the like to the other party; an obligation to destroy copies; a right to obtain information from an escrow agent; a choice of law or forum; an obligation to arbitrate or to otherwise resolve disputes by alternative dispute resolution; a term limiting the time for commencing an action or for giving notice; an indemnity term or a right related to a claim of a type described in section 805(d)(1) ("a breach of warranty against third-party claims for: (a) infringement or misappropriation; or (b) libel, slander, or the like"); a limitation of remedy or modification or disclaimer or warranty; an obligation to provide an accounting and make any payment due under the accounting; and any term that the agreement provides will survive.[48] The point is that when a UCITA contract is silent, the default rules apply.

So what lessons does the UCITA controversy import for the state of licensing and its future? Courts will continue to develop a body of law and apply this law to disputes involving contracts, at times interpreting a codified law of contract such as the UCC, where applicable—though UCC is less likely to be relevant when discussing content or service licenses. To an extent, UCITA attempted to codify court trends as well as industry desires, developments with which consumers and other user groups were less than pleased. UCITA offered such expressions as a stationary target of sorts at which criticism could be aimed. Rather than disparate judicial decision across numerous jurisdictions or individual examples of heavy-handed licensing that varied from licensor to licensor, UCITA funneled unsettling developments (at least in the opinion of some) as well as criticism to a single point. In this sense, licensees sought and won a victory in halting the initial spur of UCITA. However, what UCITA represents will not go away but has in a sense gone underground. No longer in the public eye as proposed legislation (or enacted in Virginia and Maryland), some licensors will continue to push the envelope of obligations, prohibitions, and other terms favorable to their interests. Consumers and other users of licenses need therefore to be aware of how such developments are articulated in license agreements and be prepared to respond. It is hoped that the discussions in this book have positioned library-licensees to do this well.

SUMMARY POINTS

▶ UCITA represents an attempt to codify on a state-by-state basis a law for information contracting. The law would apply to software as well as content, such as databases. Only two states (Maryland and Virginia) have enacted UCITA, while other states have enacted legislation making its provisions void.

LEARNING EXAMPLES

▶ **Example 11.1**

Situation: In a situation where UCITA is the law, a library enters a contract to have a number of historically significant out-of-print titles reprinted for its collection. Does UCITA apply?

Legal Analysis: Even in the two states that have adopted UCITA, it would not apply, as UCITA does not apply to transactions involving print, such as "books, magazines, newspapers," and so on, or to goods, such as "televisions, VCRs, DVD players or similar goods."[49]

ENDNOTES

1. REPORT OF UCITA STANDBY COMMITTEE, 19 (December 17, 2001), emphasis added, http://www.law.upenn.edu/bll/archives/ulc/ucita/UCITA_Dec01_Proposal.pdf.

2. See, for example, Amelia Boss, *Taking UCITA on the Road: What Lessons Have We Learned?*, 121, 132, in UNIFORM COMPUTER INFORMATION TRANSACTIONS ACT: A BROAD PERSPECTIVE (Stephen Y. Chow and Riva F. Kinstlick eds., 2001) PLI Intellectual Property Course Handbook #G-673 ("on the logistics of restructuring Article 2" of the UCC).

3. UCITA, Prefatory Note. "[A] body of law based on images of the sale of manufactured goods ill fits licenses and other transactions in computer information" (*id.*).

4. Jean Braucher, *UCITA and the Concept of Assent*, 175, 186, in UNIFORM COMPUTER INFORMATION TRANSACTIONS ACT: A BROAD PERSPECTIVE (Stephen Y. Chow and Riva F. Kinstlick, eds., 2001) PLI Intellectual Property Course Handbook #G-673: "The technical quality of UCITA, in its structure and in many individual provisions, is poor, and UCITA thus will not produce certainty."

5. Boss, *supra* note 2, at 127: "Should UCITA be an international model... And if one views UCITA as a 'checklist' of issues that must be confronted... the answer is still yes... if one views UCITA as a specific body of law, to be enacted substantially as is with little reevaluation, reexamination and reassessment of its provisions... then the answer is no."

6. MICHAEL RUSTAD, INTERNET LAW IN A NUTSHELL 122 (St. Paul, MN: West Publishing, 2009).

7. Section 104 of UCITA, Mixed Transactions; Agreement to Opt In or Opt Out, was deleted from a revised UCITA in 2002.

8. In the end, UCITA became larger than itself. As one commentator phrased it: "This evolution—from contract issues to information policy issues—increased the visibility of the product in industry and contributed to the growing dissatisfaction with its provisions." Boss, *supra* note 2, at 131.

9. See discussion in Specht v. Netscape, Inc., 306 F.3d 17 (2d Cir. 2002).

10. See Wachter Management Co. v. Dexter & Chaney, 144 P.3d 747, 750 (Kan. 2006).

11. UCITA, Prefatory Note. "UCITA is the first uniform contract law designed to deal specifically with the new information economy" (*id.*).

12. Virginia Code Annotated § § 59.1–501.1, et seq.

13. Maryland Code Annotated § § 22–101, et seq.

14. UCITA, Prefatory Note (2000), http://www.law.upenn.edu/bll/archives/ulc/ucita/ucita200.htm.

15. UCITA, § 102, Definitions, Official Comment, 9: "An agreement to use e-mail to communicate about a contract for the shipment of petroleum or to files an application in digital form does not bring the transaction within this definition."

16. *Id.* "The subject matter of that agreement is not the computer information, but the service—air transportation" (*id.*).

17. James A. Meal, *The Fight Against UCITA*, LIBRARY JOURNAL, September 15, 2000, at 36, 35: "American Libraries are at war... UCITA has moved the confrontation to our state governments... With the introduction of UCITA, the historical balance preserved in our federal copyright law between the interests of copyright producers and the legitimate needs of our users from effective access to information has never been more threatened." See also this source at 37 for a brief discussion of efforts by the library to insert an amendment into the Maryland UCITA that would preserve library and user rights under the copyright law.

18. Letter from the National Association of Attorneys General to Carlyle C. Ring, Commissioner, National Conference of Commissioners on Uniform State Laws (November 13, 2000), http://www.affect.ucita.com/pdf/Nov132001_Letter_from_AGs_to_Carlyle_Ring.pdf.

19. Stephen Y. Chow, *Effects on Traditional Technology Licensing*, 7, 17 (2001), in UNIFORM COMPUTER INFORMATION TRANSACTIONS ACT: A BROAD PERSPECTIVE (Stephen Y. Chow and Riva F. Kinstlick, eds., 2001), PLI Intellectual Property Course Handbook #G-673.

20. INTERNET LAW AND PRACTICE § 23:14 (2006), chapter author Keith Witek (*Online IP Licensing*).

21. See, for example, the mission statement of AFFECT: "AFFECT, Americans for Fair Electronic Commerce Transactions, is a broad-based national coalition of consumers, retail and manufacturing businesses, financial services institutions, technology professionals and librarians opposed to the Uniform Computer Information Transactions Act (UCITA). AFFECT has been dedicated to educating the public and policy makers about the dangers of UCITA" (http://www.ucita.com/).

22. See, for example, H.R. 1066, 108th Cong., 1st Sess. (Benefit Authors without Limiting Advancement or Net Consumer Expectations (BALANCE Act of 2003)), § 123(b): "When a digital work is distributed to the public subject to nonnegotiable license terms, such terms shall not be enforceable under the common laws or statutes of any State to the extent that they restrict or limit any of the limitations on exclusive rights under this title." See, for example, H.R. 5522, 107th Cong., 2nd Sess., Digital Choice and Freedom Act of 2002, § 4 granting digital first-sale rights.

23. Riva F. Kinstlick, *Overview of UCITA*, 59, 67 and 68 (2001), in UNIFORM COMPUTER INFORMATION TRANSACTIONS ACT: A BROAD PERSPECTIVE (Stephen Y. Chow and Riva F. Kinstlick eds. 2001) PLI Intellectual Property Course Handbook #G-673.

24. See, for example, N.C. General Statutes § 66-329: "A choice of law provision in a computer information agreement which provides that the contract is to be interpreted pursuant to the laws of a state that has enacted the Uniform Computer Information Transactions Act, as proposed by the National Conference of Commissioners on Uniform State Laws, or any substantially similar law, is voidable and the agreement shall be interpreted pursuant to the laws of this State if the party against whom enforcement of the choice of law provisions is sought is a resident of this State or has its principal place of business located in this State"; and West Virginia Code § 55-8-15, identical language adopted.

25. For another brief review of UCITA, see, F. LAWRENCE STREET AND MARK P. GRANT, LAW OF THE INTERNET § 1.04, at 1-38–1-47 (2001; updated through release #19, December 2011); for a thorough review of UCITA, see LORIN BRENNAN ET AL., THE COMPLETE UCITA, 2 vols. (Glasser Legal Works, 2004). Also the text of UCITA, as approved in September 2000 with Prefatory Notes and Comments, is quite lengthy and useful as well. Reprinted in Appendix B, RAYMOND T. NIMMER AND JEFF C. DODD, MODERN LICENSING LAW, pp. 1077–1260 (ed. 2008–2009).

26. See H. WARD CLASSEN, A PRACTICAL GUIDE TO SOFTWARE LICENSING FOR LICENSEES AND LICENSORS 206 (3d ed.) (Chicago, American Bar Association, 2008).

27. "UCITA is the first uniform contract law designed to deal specifically with the new information economy" (UCITA, Prefatory Note).

28. See UCITA, Prefatory Note: "Whether specific terms are appropriate for a given transaction or set of parties is fundamentally a marketplace issue."

29. REPORT OF UCITA STANDBY COMMITTEE, 19 (December 17, 2001), emphasis added, http://www.law.upenn.edu/bll/archives/ulc/ucita/UCITA_Dec01_Proposal.pdf.

30. UCITA, Prefatory Note, italicized caption within quotation marks under heading.

31. UCITA, Prefatory Note: "UCITA does not require that computer information products and services be licensed; it covers sales as well."

32. UCITA § 102(10).

33. UCITA § 103, Official Comment 3.

34. UCITA § 102(16) (defining consumer contract).

35. UCITA § 102(45) (defining mass-market transaction) which can be "any other transaction" in "information or informational rights directed to the general public as a

whole . . . in a retail transaction . . . consistent with an ordinary transaction in a retail market."

36. UCITA § 102, Official Comment 39, mass-market license and mass-market transaction.

37. *Id.*

38. *Id.*

39. UCITA § 102(46) (defining merchant).

40. UCITA § 102, Official Comment 40, merchant. See also Stephen Y. Chow, *Effects on traditional Technology Licensing*, 7, 49 (2001), in UNIFORM COMPUTER INFORMATION TRANSACTIONS ACT: A BROAD PERSPECTIVE (Stephen Y. Chow and Riva F. Kinstlick eds., 2001), PLI Intellectual Property Course Handbook #G-673: "A university or a hospital likely would be considered a merchant relative to licensing technology, and, on the face of section 401(a), would be held to provide a warranty of noninfringement for 'information' that it delivers."

41. UCITA § 102, Official Comment 13, consumer and consumer contract.

42. UCITA § 102, Official Comment 39, mass-market license and mass-market transaction.

43. UCITA § 102(53) (defining receipt).

44. UCITA § 102, Official Comment 47, receive. "Similarly [to receipt in a post office box], arrival at an appropriate electronic mail address is receipt by the addressee." Id.

45. Brennan et al., *supra* note 25, at vol. 1, 102–180.

46. UCITA § 102, Official Comment 47, receive.

47. UCITA § 102(60) (defining send).

48. UCITA § 616(b)(1)–(11).

49. UCITA § 103, Official Comment 3.

▶ 12

THE DEVELOPING LAW OF IMPLIED LICENSES

Read this chapter to understand the nature and legality of these license situations:
- ▶ Use of content posted on the Internet, including online discussion boards, blogs, social networking sites, and distance-education Internet course management systems
- ▶ Circumstances under which an implied license to use content protected by copyright arises
- ▶ When inaction on the part of an aggrieved copyright owner can create an implied license to use the work in question

Remember that a license is like a promise (a promise to allow use of content, a promise not to sue for use of that content, etc.). There may be times when a user would wish that such promises were given, such as for use of content posted on a website. While there is no license per se, the law nonetheless views the situation as one in which the parties should operate as if there were a license. Recent case law points to new ways to think about licensing in the context of content available on the Internet.[1] So when is a license not really a license but still called a license? When the law for reasons of fairness or equity of circumstances construes that the parties should be held to a course of behavior as if an actual agreement were in place, as if both parties had agreed upon and assented to the terms of an agreement. There may be times when there is no license governing the use of content in a library setting but the librarians on staff wish there were. The developing law of implied license may assist in determining that the use of protected content by a librarian or patron is indeed lawful under the concept of an implied license.[2]

Determining when the concept of implied license might apply and when it might not is critical. Misread conclusions can be disastrous, leading to claims of infringement leveled at users who proceeded to use protected content under the mistaken impression that the content was available for use. For example, many users of content posted on the Internet, including online discussion boards, blogs, social networking sites, and distance-education Internet course management systems, may believe that as long as content is posted without obvious restrictions—such as a lack of "If you agree to our terms and you click here you can use our website" mechanisms—then the person responsible for posting such content is in essence saying, "You can use this content in any way you see fit." It should be obvious that such assessment contains a tremendous assumption and a potentially dangerous one in terms of the copyright law. The problem is that the person who posted the content may not be the owner of the content or may not otherwise have the authority to post the content. Given the frequency with which the author encounters this opinion in the classroom, it is valuable to spend a few pages discussing when an implied license might actually arise and when it might not. If there can be any legal basis for assuming that content a user encounters on a website, for example, is accompanied by the permission to use that content, it would rest on a claim that the content owner has somehow granted permission to use the content. This "permission" is the essence of a claim based on implied license.

UNDERSTANDING THE CONCEPT OF IMPLIED LICENSE

The law of implied license is different than a typical, actual license governing the use of copyrighted content. The typical license is a contract, where one party makes an offer ("I'll paint your house for $500"), the other accepts the offer ("Okay, you can start anytime you like"), and consideration ("Here's $250; I'll pay you the balance when you're done") binds the parties. Of course, consideration can occur in the absence of an exchange of money ("I'll paint your house if you cut down my tree" or "I'll paint your house if you let me use your new outdoor grill this summer"). With an implied license, there are no terms and conditions to which the parties acknowledge and agree to as binding. Rather, courts construe its terms, conditions, and assent by the conduct of the parties alone.

We have already discussed how websites, blogs, and other Internet forums can dictate through contract the terms under which access and use of content can be granted (see Chapter 8). But in the absence of such agreement, are there circumstances where such permission can nonetheless be implied and, more important, with legal effect? Many users would like to think so. While merely placing or posting content on a website, blog, and the like, might not be the proper circumstance from which a court would conclude that it was reasonable for users to assume permission was granted, other factors might lead a court to conclude this is indeed the case.

The law of implied license in the courts is less than consistent, with courts concluding that some form of obligation exists based on a variety of concepts, such as a license implied-in-fact (based on the otherwise unauthorized use of the work coupled with evidence of a promise regarding that use), or other courts basing the obligation on the equitable concept of estoppel;[3] still other courts use the quasi-contractual concept of unjust enrichment (a contract implied-in-law based upon the unauthorized use of the work alone).[4] The latter implied-in-law license is not a true contract but, rather, like estoppel, is an equitable concept that courts use to impart a sense of justice into the relationship of the parties. An implied license-in-fact is more aligned with contract concepts discussed thus far, that is, some evidence of assent though executed imperfectly. The two categories of implied license, estoppel and implied-in-fact, constitute the majority of decided cases in the area. Across the cases, these distinctions may be less useful as there is often no consistent bright line of jurisprudence, but both concepts may help readers understand why courts would imply licensing in the absence of a four-corner document purporting to do so.

For the purposes of this discussion, focus is upon a narrower subset of cases where courts are asked to imply the existence of a license (read: permission) to use material protected by copyright or other law-protected information. True, the number of cases are not large, but given the rationalized belief shared by many Internet users that all accessible content on the web is available for use ("If it's posted on the web, it must have been done with the intent that it be used"), understanding when a court would support this belief through law and what circumstances fall outside the realm of legal reason is important. Several cases involving the application of implied license, especially in the context of extending the duration or impact of an existing and often current or previous licensed relationship, are discussed. As a result, the implied-in-fact genus is of particular interest in the library or other information setting.

Courts use the term *implied license* in conjunction with the concept of estoppel, previously referenced and defined, whereby one party is prevented or barred from doing something. For the purposes of importance to this book, the estoppel concept often takes the form of a defense to a claim of infringement or other unlawful use of content or service and prevents one party from suing the other party because the courts imply a license granting permission to do what would otherwise be infringing or unlawful. "Such an implied license, a species of contract implied in fact, does not transfer ownership of the copyright; rather, it simply permits the use of the copyrighted work in a particular manner. While federal copyright law recognizes an implied license from the parties' course of dealing, state contract law determines its existence and scope."[5] Often the conduct of one party prompts this remedy from the court, as conduct and circumstances induced the other party to rely (now to their detriment in being sued for copyright infringement) on said conduct and circumstances such that it would be unfair to allow the suit for infringement to proceed.

The existence of an implied nonexclusive license in a particular situation turns on three factors: (1) whether the parties were engaged in a short-term discrete transaction as opposed to an ongoing relationship; (2) whether the creator utilized written contracts providing that the copyrighted materials could be used only with the creator's future involvement or express permission; and (3) whether the creator's conduct during the creation or delivery of the copyrighted material indicated that the use of the material without the creator's involvement or consent was permissible.[6] Lack of objection can also create an implied license, but the reliance must be reasonable under the circumstances. Further, as the relationship is implied, there is unlikely consideration on which to base a firm commitment; thus, an implied license without consideration is revocable. Moreover, as "a nonexclusive license does not transfer ownership of the copyright from the licensor to the licensee, the licensor can bring suit for copyright infringement if the licensee's use goes beyond the scope of the nonexclusive license."[7] A user can, in theory, exceed the scope of a nonexclusive implied license or the "license" may be reworked.[8]

THE DEVELOPING LAW OF IMPLIED LICENSE IN THE COURTS

The implied license is by nature a cautious proposition by courts—a proposition that is not invoked without careful consideration of the surrounding circumstances. An implied license is often found in a situation where one hires another to create some work and dispute later arises over use of that work by the requisitioning party.[9] A basic concept of copyright contracts sets the stage for the concept of implied license: "While an exclusive license to use copyrighted material must be written, a nonexclusive license can be granted orally or can be implied from the conduct of the parties."[10] In *Korman v. HBC Florida, Inc.*, the court concluded that the plaintiff offered the defendant radio station an implied nonexclusive license to use jingles she had written for the station: "Korman wrote jingles for WQBA for seven years, and during that time she allowed the station to air those jingles, including the one at issue in this case. Given that conduct, she 'cannot reasonably deny' that she granted WQBA a nonexclusive license to use her jingle."[11] The concept developed decades ago to deal with the unfairness that arose when patent (another area of the intellectual property law, from which the misuse doctrine was also borrowed) owners aware of infringing conduct of their patents chose to do nothing until it was more advantageous to claim infringement. The U.S. Supreme Court in *De Forest Radio Telephone & Telegraph Co. v. U.S.*[12] observed:

> No formal granting of a license is necessary in order to give it effect. Any language used by the owner of the patent or any conduct on his part exhibited to another, from which that other may properly infer that the owner consents to his use of the patent in making or using it, or selling it, upon which the other acts, constitutes a license, and a defense to an action for a tort.[13]

Again, the equities are critical in determining the existence of an implied license. Courts conclude it unfair that the property owner, aware of the infringing use by the defendant, does nothing to prevent the use or makes no other indication of its disfavor. The defendant relies on the acquiescence only later to be sued by the property owner. (As discussed in Chapter 14 and exampled in Chapter 15, many licenses now include a waiver provision indicating that the failure to pursue a breach under the agreement does not waive, or a court could not estop, the aggrieved party from enforcing a similar breach on another occasion.)

The concept has since been applied to the copyright law as well. In the online context, again there is a tendency to believe that everything on the web is there "for free." Whether users know it or not, and with the caveat that it is not true in all cases or perhaps not even in many cases, when such belief is true, the legal argument supporting this attitude is that of implied license. Simply because content is offered for free does not mean that in every instance an implied license accompanies the content, however. As Palfrey observes: "In the really simple syndication space, which is the mode of aggregating Web blogs and replaying them, this is a dominant argument, which says: If you put something out there on a blog and you put it in an XML format that lets other people re-aggregate it, of course you are implying that they can use it. Now, I am not sure that is sustainable, but it is clearly one of the arguments."[14] Think of an analog analogy. Consider a free community newspaper that is placed in a public kiosk for distribution. While there is an implied license to take and read a copy of the newspaper, there is no attendant implied license to use the protected content contained within the newspaper, such as photographs or an essay on the state of the local political scene, to reproduce, repost, or resell such content. In other words, the concept of implied license is not without limit.

THE INTERNET, COURTS, AND IMPLIED LICENSE

As cases developed, a common characteristic was the existence of a prior relationship between the parties. In the typical case, it is the prior formal relationship coupled with subsequent "assenting" conduct that is significant. The courts in essence imply an extension of the agreement with its terms modified to reflect the parties' respective, subsequent conduct. Rather than "imply" a contract in the first instance, the court implies by license an extension of the previous and express but now modified agreement based upon the conduct of the one to be estopped. This implied license is revocable. However, if there is proper consideration, the license is irrevocable.[15] Courts proceed with caution in this area, as courts are often reluctant to hold unenforceable a contract or void its terms and conditions in existence; courts are even more reluctant to create a contract, in other words, imply that a nonexclusive license has been granted by the plaintiff to the defendant. A federal appellate court refused to find an implied license in the since seminal peer-to-peer litigation involving Napster: "Napster also argues that plaintiffs granted the company an implied license by encouraging MP3 file exchange over the Internet. Courts have found implied license only in 'narrow' circumstances where one party 'created a work at [the other's] request and handed it over, intending that [the other] copy and distribute it.'"[16] In the online context, a common circumstance where courts do conclude that an implied license exists is when a developer designs a website under contract and then challenges the right of the contracting party to use or alter the site. Courts conclude that the contracting party has an implied license to use the website it paid the other party to develop. This represents an extension of the rationale behind the existing precedent of requisition cases where one party contracts another to provide a particular product, with courts concluding that along with the initial requisition to create the product there is an implied license to use the product once created. While the right to use a requisitioned work might appear obvious, some developers have argued and sued, claiming that a right to use the work after it is created is distinct. It would be a ridiculous result to allow one party to claim, in essence, "You hired me to create this specialized inventory form for your business, but now you have to pay me extra if you actually want to use the form for your ordering needs." Likewise, in the website design market, courts conclude an implied license exists for the contracting or requisitioning party to use the website after it is created.[17] As an implied license can have harsh practical consequences for the parties involved (a contract is imposed), courts are reluctant to identify the existence of such a license in the absence of obvious and justifying facts and circumstances.

The more typical case of implied license occurs where one party is making an infringing use of the material but the aggrieved other party, fully aware of the conduct, does nothing. For example, in *Video Pipeline, Inc. v. Buena Vista Home Entertainment, Inc.*, the court refused to find an implied license was created. In spite of a prior business relationship, the aggrieved party did not engage in any conduct that would lead the court to conclude that Buena Vista Home Entertainment approved of the infringing conduct; in fact, quite the opposite occurred: "plaintiff was informed that streaming of such trailers or previews online was unauthorized, there can be no finding that defendant created an implied license for plaintiff to continue such use."[18] Moreover, the "defendant had demanded all of its in-store trailers back."[19] In an instructive comment involving the use of content in an online discussion board—arguably another environment where common sense dictates an assumed permission to quote from or include a prior post in one's follow-up comment or response—another district court suggested that an implied license would allow the inclusion of such previous postings in the responses made by subsequent participants. Of course, an important assumption is that the initial post is made lawfully and is not infringing: "Erlich argues that it is common practice on the Internet to repeat large portions of a previous posting verbatim, which is necessary to add context for those who are late in joining a discussion. While this would perhaps justify the copying of works that were previously posted by their authors on the basis of an *implied license* or *fair use* argument, these defenses would not apply where the first posting made an unauthorized copy of a copyrighted work."[20] It is critical that the court in *Religious Technology Center v. Netcom On-Line Communication Services, Inc.* conditioned the implied license on the assumption that the initial posting was not infringing, as many controversies arise in the Internet context because the post in question is unlawful in the first instance. Subsequent use by others cannot qualify for the application of the concept of implied license, as the "permission" to use the infringing content is not the original poster's to give.

In Internet environments, courts have looked at whether the cessation of infringement was easily within the plaintiff's—the alleged copyright violation victim—purview:

> The scope of the implied license is a question of fact. The facts here could lead a reasonable jury to find that Veterans Society's implied license allows the current use of the images in question on Veterans Society's own website. Under plaintiffs' theory of the case, they could revoke at any time the implied license to Veterans Society, whatever its terms might be. Plaintiffs could use that power to insist that Veterans Society revise its website in a way that satisfies plaintiffs. Plaintiffs have not taken either step, presumably for business reasons, such as maintaining good relationships with their dealers in general and with this dealer in particular. Regardless of their reasons, plaintiffs' failure to take those steps is evidence that tends to prove that Veterans Society is not violating the terms of its implied license by allowing Funeral Depot to display its telephone number on the web pages with the licensed images.[21]

When such self-correcting measures are available but not taken, an implied license can be found, underscoring that the concept of implied license is an equitable doctrine whereby the plaintiff is not allowed to succeed in a claim of infringement where the infringement could easily have been prevented or mitigated by the plaintiff's conduct.

The choice not to undertake self-help when readily available may have led a recent district court to issue what is to date the most expansive application of the implied license concept to the Internet. In *Field v. Google, Inc.*, the district court observed: "Consent to use the copyrighted work need not be manifested verbally and may be inferred based on silence where the copyright holder knows of the use and encourages it."[22] Recall that this 2006 Google case involved a challenge to the caching of web content by Google. The court found determinative the plaintiff's failure to include in the metatag to his website instructions that would have prevented Google's robots from crawling, indexing, and caching his website.

In light of the ease with which this could be done and the industrywide knowledge of this bypass protocol, the court found that the requisite awareness and acquiescence constituted an implied license:

> Field concedes he was aware of these industry standard mechanisms, and knew that the presence of a "no archive" meta-tag on the pages of his Web site would have informed Google not to display "Cached" links to his pages. Despite this knowledge, Field chose

not to include the no-archive meta-tag on the pages of his site. He did so, knowing that Google would interpret the absence of the meta-tag as permission to allow access to the pages via "Cached" links. Thus, with knowledge of how Google would use the copyrighted works he placed on those pages, and with knowledge that he could prevent such use, Field instead made a conscious decision to permit it. His conduct is reasonably interpreted as the grant of a license to Google for that use.[23]

While there was no prior formal relationship between Field and Google, the court interpreted the industrywide well-known protocol as sufficient to place Field on notice of what would be the likely course of conduct by Google. This case does not stand for the proposition that anyone can copy content from any site from which the no-archive metatag is absent, but one could cache it for purposes of archiving. The scenario would be limited to situations of archiving or preservation of some fashion, which the court found to be a socially important purpose.

A court might construe an implied license in online peer-to-peer forums. As Nimmer observes:

> Merely posting a work on the Internet does not relinquish the copyright owner's rights in that work. It may create an implied authorization to do something with the information thus made available, but the scope of such implied license is very uncertain and has not been addressed by the court. In any event, a contractually greater permission may be important *for the user*. For example, posting information without restriction may imply that a user has a right to download a copy, but almost certainly does *not* authorize making and distribution of copies to other persons. While a concept of implied authority (license) may protect the downloading, any such idea of implied authority does not extend very far in this environment especially in light of the protective approach courts often take with respect to rights owners.[24]

Whether defendants will continue to enjoy expanded rights of implied license in Internet environments is unclear, but the argument in defense of such use exists. It may depend on whether social network users, forum participants, or other Internet users could easily indicate that their postings were not available for use beyond the forum in which initially posted, or whether other technological protection similar to that available to the plaintiff in *Field v. Google Inc.* were available and participants failed to take advantage of those protections. An example would be a process whereby a participant could select a simple icon, much the same way participants can select the font and color of their text postings, that would appear next to the user's name and associated posting indicating whether the participant allows his or her content to be posted for other uses. Even in the absence of such mechanisms or in the absence of the traditional context of implied license (existing relationship), there is at least commentator support for the suggestion that personal use could be made of such content, but not necessarily public use, such as further public display, performance, or distribution.

SUMMARY POINTS

▶ Implied license can be found in Internet contexts. The "do not cache" protocol is one example, where website creators who do not want Google (or other search engines) to cache their site content can easily make such an indication. In the absence of such designation, one court concluded that an implied license to cache existed. It may also apply in other online forums where the protocol is to use previous posts in subsequent comments.

▶ An implied license is an equitable doctrine whereby a court concludes that conduct otherwise infringing should be allowed because of the circumstances. Borrowed from the patent law it developed, the concept is more common in circumstances where a prior relationship exists between the parties in dispute.

▶ Another likely scenario of implied license is a discussion board or chat room post where a court might construe an implied license to excerpt the original post to which a reply is made on the condition that the original posting is not itself infringing of another's copyright.

LEARNING EXAMPLES

▶ **Example 12.1**

Situation: The library contracts with a web developer to design a new website for the library. The developer is likely an independent contractor of the library rather than an employee. After the website is "delivered," the developer claims the library does not have the authority to use the website.

Legal Analysis: If the contract is silent on the matter, as there exists a contract to create the website in the first place, a court would likely construe an implied license exists for the library to use the website it contracted to have created once the website is so constructed.

ENDNOTES

1. Orit Fischman Afori, *Implied License: An Emerging New Standard in Copyright Law*, 25 SANTA CLARA COMPUTER AND HIGH TECHNOLOGY LAW JOURNAL 275 (2009); and John S. Sieman, *Comment, Using the Implied License to Inject Common Sense into Digital Copyright*, 85 NORTH CAROLINA LAW REVIEW 885 (2007).

2. RAYMOND T. NIMMER AND JEFF C. DODD, MODERN LICENSING LAW, § 10:8 (database updated in Westlaw, November 2011). Identifies four types of implied licenses: implied-in-fact, estoppel-based, implied-by-construction, and implied-in-law but nonetheless observing: "The types of implied licenses are more like hues than sharply distinct colors and relate to bases for creating the license, not to its effect. Fairness, fidelity to the supposed intension

of the parties, and fealty to expectations built on commercial and legal background rules are the stuff of which implied licenses are made" (*id.*)

3. The essence of the legal concept of estoppels is one of fairness, of not allowing people to say one thing and do another: "A bar that prevents one from asserting a claim or right that contradicts what one has said or done before or what has been legally established as true." BLACK'S LAW DICTIONARY 502 (9th ed.) (Bryan A. Garner ed., 2009) (no pagination in Westlaw).

4. Nimmer and Dodd, *supra* note 2, at § 10:2.

5. Lowry's Reports, Inc. v. Legg Mason, Inc., 271 F. Supp. 2d 737, 749 (D. Md. 2003), citation omitted.

6. John G. Danielson, Inc. v. Winchester-Conant Properties, Inc., 322 F.3d 26, 41 (1st Cir. 2003). See also Nelson-Salabes, Inc. v. Morningside Development, LLC, 284 F.3d 505, 516 (4th Cir. 2002): "(1) whether the parties were engaged in a short-term discrete transaction as opposed to an ongoing relationship; (2) whether the creator utilized written contracts, such as the standard AIA [American Institute of Architects] contract, providing that copyrighted materials could only be used with the creator's future involvement or express permission; and (3) whether the creator's conduct during the creation or delivery of the copyrighted material indicated that use of the material without the creator's involvement or consent was permissible."

7. Teter v. Glass Onion, Inc.,723 F. Supp. 2d 1138, 1149 (W.D. Mo. 2010).

8. *Id.* at 1150: "Where no consideration is given, a nonexclusive implied license is revocable . . . Neither party argues that GOI paid money or gave legal consideration for the license—that is, consideration for the specific licensing right to display images of Teter's works on its website; therefore, Teter was free to revoke his consent at any time. The Court finds Teter revoked the license with the May 20, 2008, letter from SFFA to the Walpoles, which unequivocally revoked."

9. See Effects Associates v. Cohen, 908 F.2d 555, 558-559 (9th Cir. 1990): "While the particular facts of each case are most relevant, an implied license may be granted when (1) a person (the licensee) requests the creation of a work, (2) the creator (the licensor) makes that particular work and delivers it to the licensee who requested it, and (3) the licensor intends that the licensee-requestor copy and distribute his work."

10. Korman v. HBC Florida, Inc., 182 F.3d 1291, 1293 (11th Cir. 1999).

11. *Id.*

12. De Forest Radio Telephone & Telegraph Co. v. U.S., 273 U.S. 236 (1927).

13. *Id.* at 241.

14. John G. Palfrey Jr., *Fair Use: Its Application, Limitations, and Future*, 17 FORDHAM INTELLECTUAL PROPERTY, MEDIA AND ENTERTAINMENT LAW JOURNAL 1017, 1041 (2007).

15. I.A.E., Inc. v. Shaver, 74 F.3d 768, 772 (7th Cir. 1996): "The [district] court also rejected Mr. Shaver's argument that he later revoked any implied nonexclusive license he may have granted; it followed the position of *Nimmer on Copyright* that 'when, as here, consideration is paid for a license, it is irrevocable.'" Reply number 78 at 16, citing

Melville B. Nimmer & David Nimmer, 3 *Nimmer on Copyright* §§ 10.01(C)(5), 10.02(B)(5) (1995).

16. A&M Records, Inc. v. Napster, Inc., 239 F.3d 1004, 1026 (9th Cir. 2001), quoting SmithKline Beecham Consumer Healthcare, L.P. v. Watson Pharmaceuticals, 211 F.3d 21, 25 (2d Cir. 2000), cert. denied 531 U.S. 872 (2000), further quoting Effects Associates, Inc. v. Cohen, 908 F.2d 555, 558 (9th Cir. 1990).

17. Attig v. DRG, Inc., 2005 WL 730681 (E.D. Pa. 2005) (unpublished); Holtzbrinck Pub. Holdings, L.P. v. Vyne Communications, Inc., 2000 WL 502860 (S.D.N.Y. 2000) (unpublished).

18. Video Pipeline, Inc. v. Buena Vista Home Entertainment, Inc., 275 F. Supp. 2d 543, 558–559 (D.N.J. 2003), affirmed 342 F.3d 191 (3d Cir. 2003), cert. denied 540 U.S. 1178 (2004).

19. *Id.* at 559.

20. Religious Technology Center v. Netcom On-Line Communication Services, Inc., 923 F. Supp. 1231, 1247, note 18 (N.D. Cal., 1995), citation omitted.

21. Batesville Services, Inc. v. Funeral Depot, Inc., 2004 WL 2750253, *6 (S.D. Ind. 2004) (unpublished).

22. Field v. Google Inc., 412 F. Supp. 2d 1106, 1116 (D. Nev., 2006), citation omitted.

23. *Id.*

24. Raymond T. Nimmer, 2 Information Law § 12.39, footnote omitted (database updated in Westlaw, November 2011).

▶13

THE FUTURE LOOK OF LICENSES

To some extent, writing a conclusion for a book on licensing is difficult, as the end of this book is really the beginning. The use of licensing is sure to continue, if not expand. The terms and conditions in licenses will evolve as well, as licensors (or at least their legal counsel) expand the universe of contractual language to respond to perceived new opportunities and threats. In response, licensees will challenge or push back against these efforts, either in concerted effort or by specific scenario. The law of licensing will continue to evolve, and litigants will test or challenge the application of existing contract and license principles to the licensing environment. This book offers a preparation for all of these developments. (Remember to consult Part III for chapters that include discussion of dozens of licensing terms or provisions with examples from actual licenses, a walk-through commentary of four complete licenses, a list of 125 questions that can be used as an audit or checklist of important provisions, and a summary of important license provisions with sample language upon which alternative or library-friendly language can be used.)

While some may have only browsed the initial chapters discussing contract law, the discussion there laid the foundation for later concepts and their application in licensing scenarios. Early chapters also set a theme running throughout this book: the difference between a sale of an item to the library and a license, and the legal significances of this difference, as well as other contrasts between the contract law (applicable to licenses) and the copyright law. Licenses do not confer title or ownership over the content, so the provisions of the copyright law that condition use rights on ownership (as opposed to possession of an item) do not apply.

Chapter 4 built upon this foundation by introducing more advanced concepts that highlighted the controversial or problematic side of contracts and how such concepts or doctrines can apply in the world of licensing—at times in order to challenge the validity of a term or the entire license. Some readers may not be interested in such details, but comments made in the later chapters build upon these explanations. The range of license types was discussed in Chapters 6 through 10 and a review of dozens of types of license terms and conditions is provided in

Chapter 14. Numerous cases and examples were discussed to demonstrate the application of the contract and other law to licensing, the variety of approaches reflected across licenses, and how to assess the good and bad of the terms in a license.

Libraries and their staffs must be able to take on some of this work themselves. The librarian, rather than legal counsel, will know best both the needs of his or her constituency and the impact that a particular provision can have on that constituency. This book, of course, is not a substitute for legal advice or for communication about a license with the library's legal counsel, but it can signal the direction of such communication and make more effective the path this communication might take.

WHAT IS THE FUTURE OF LICENSING?

There is a track record of campaigns against the encroachment of the owner's rights into the user's spaces. Involvement by library organizations and library professionals and educators is critical to ensuring that the precious balance of the copyright law is maintained—or at least is not slanted too much in the owner's direction. Recent mobilizations regarding the Digital Millennium Copyright Act[1] (DMCA)[2] and the Sonny Bono Copyright Term Extension Act[3] (CTEA),[4] both enacted in 1998, and in the formation process of the Technology and Copyright Harmonization Act[5] (TEACH),[6] enacted in 2002, and, more specific to licensing, state-by-state adoption of the Uniform Computer Information Transactions Act[7] (UCITA),[8] the unresolved issue of orphan works,[9] and the ongoing discussion over reform of the main library and archive provision in the copyright law, section 108,[10] and the work of the Section 108 Study Group[11] are some of the more notable examples. It is hoped that this book gives the legal and intellectual ammunition necessary to stand up for the rights of libraries and library patrons when licensing is involved.

It is unclear what impact digital rights management (DRM) may have upon licensing processes in the future.[12] DRM consists of two components: technological protection measures (TPM), which can be used in tandem to enforce owners'/licensors' rights and desires and likewise further control user rights/behavior, and copyright management information (CMI), which can be used to embed licensing terms in the licensed content.

The use of DRM to some extent warps the contract-copyright continuum, giving new tools of enforcement to licensors. However, the use of TPM and CMI applies only to content protected by copyright and arguably to works of mixed nature. TPM can further uses—except for statutory exceptions—to the desires of the licensor. However, contracts can extend the curtailment beyond the limits of statute and its regulatory exceptions.[13] On the other hand, where the licensed content is subject to DRM protection, such protection can be extended beyond that of what is legally permissible under contract law.

DRM can be used to enforce EULA clauses or even policies that are not legally enforceable. Generally, the use of technological protection measures could increase the power of rights-holders to set excessive conditions on the users. The combination of a contract and technological protection measures could represent a powerful mixture for a fully automated system of secure distribution, rights management, monitoring, and payment of protected content. So, DRM, de facto, could also be seen as the imposition of "unilaterally contractual terms and conditions." When users access content protected by a technological protection measure, the content provider, in practice, imposes a contractual provision by a click-through or click-wrap agreement.[14]

For example, early disputes litigated under the DMCA (section 1201) over access to protected digital content "foretell troubled days for educational fair use."[15] Three cases are demonstrative of this threat. In the first appellate decision to apply section 1201 and pit fair use and free speech concepts squarely against the rights of copyright owners under the section, the copyright owners came out ahead. The 2nd Circuit offered the following observation of these competing interests and the fair-use rights that nonetheless still exist in a world of content subject to TPM:

> One example is that of a school child who wishes to copy images from a DVD movie to insert into the student's documentary film. We know of no authority for the proposition that fair use, as protected by the Copyright Act, much less the Constitution, guarantees copying by the optimum method or in the identical format of the original. Although the Appellants insisted at oral argument that they should not be relegated to a "horse and buggy" technique in making fair use of DVD movies, [footnote omitted] the DMCA does not impose even an arguable limitation on the opportunity to make a variety of traditional fair uses of DVD movies, such as commenting on their content, quoting excerpts from their screenplays, and even recording portions of the video images and sounds on film or tape by pointing a camera, a camcorder, or a microphone at a monitor as it displays the DVD movie. The fact that the resulting copy will not be as perfect or as manipulable as a digital copy obtained by having direct access to the DVD movie in its digital form, provides no basis for a claim of unconstitutional limitation of fair use.[16]

A similar sentiment was expressed by a district court on the opposite side of the country: "Thus to the extent the DMCA impacts a lawful purchaser's 'right' to make a backup copy, or to space shift that copy to another computer, the limited impairment of that one right does not significantly compromise or impair the First Amendment rights of users so as to render the DMCA unconstitutionally overbroad."[17] The district court likewise suggested the sort of mechanics involved in making fair use of protected content now subject to TPM: "For example, nothing in the DMCA prevents anyone from *quoting from a work or comparing texts for the purpose of study or criticism*. It may be that from a technological perspective, the fair user may find it more difficult to do so—*quoting may have to occur the old fashioned way, by hand or by re-typing*, rather than by 'cutting and pasting' from existing digital media. Nevertheless, the fair use is still available."[18]

The same district court made a similar pronouncement two years later in *321 Studios v. Metro Goldwyn Mayer Studios, Inc.*: "*Fair use is still possible under the DMCA*, although such copying will not be as easy, as exact, or as digitally manipulable as plaintiff desires."[19] While fair use is still possible, of course, the efficiency of the use is compromised. The content is digital, and yet the use suggested by all three cases is analog. A compounding problem is that as access and use controls (section 1201 not only prohibits circumvention of access TPMs but also prohibits trafficking in either access or use TPMs) merge, it can be argued that an access control in essence controls use as well. In any space that may exist within the statutory structure, circumventing a use control is not prohibited, as copyright owners "may be closing the token crack in the fair use window completely as they merge access and rights controls."[20] This is also why section 1201(a)(1)(D) contains a three-year cycle of an administrative de novo rule making that allows for exemption from the prohibition on circumventing an access TPM or control where "noninfringing uses by persons who are users of a copyrighted work are, or are likely to be, adversely affected." In a telling criticism, Sharp observes of the present administration that "the Librarian of Congress becomes the Fair Use Czar under the DMCA."[21] Further, prohibitions on removal of CMI content ensure that the terms of use are always present, embedded in the digital content: "No person shall, without the authority of the copyright owner or the law, intentionally remove or alter any copyright management information."[22] It is clear from the plain language of the statute that CMI includes the "terms and conditions for use of the work."[23] The extent to which DRM is used in combination with licensing is unknown, though it is likely more widely at play in mass-market and consumer licensing. What can be said is that when employed by a licensor, DRM allows for a greater potential to ensure that license terms are imposed through and embedded in digital content and, moreover, that those terms are enforced through extra-legal technological measures.

ENDNOTES

1. Pub. L. No. 105-304, 112 Stat. 2860 (1998).
2. See Brief of Amici Curiae American Civil Liberties Union, American Library Association, Association for Research Libraries, Music Library Association, National Association of Independent Schools, Electronic Privacy Information Center, and Computer and Communications Industry Association in Support of Appellants and Reversal of the Judgment below, 2001 WL 34105522 (Feb. 1, 2001), in support of the position that the DMCA places an unconstitutional burden on free speech. The argument did not persuade the court. Universal Studios, Inc. v. Corley, 273 F.3d 429 (2d Cir. 2001).
3. Pub. L. No. 105-298, 112 Stat. 2827 (1998).

4. See Brief Amici Curiae of The American Association of Law Libraries, American Historical Association, American Library Association, Art Libraries Society of North America, Association for Recorded Sound Collections, Association of Research Libraries, Council on Library and Information Resources, International Association of Jazz Record Collectors, Medical Library Association, Midwest Archives Conference, Music Library Association, National Council on Public History, Society for American Music, Society of American Archivists, and Special Libraries Association in Support of Petitioners, 2002 WL 1059710 (May 20, 2002), arguing the copyright term extension unconstitutional and that the library, archive and educational entity provision of section 108(h) did not mitigate the unconstitutional burden. The constitutionality of CTEA was upheld in Eldred v. Ashcroft, 537 U.S 186, 193 (2003): "In accord with the District Court and the Court of Appeals, we reject petitioners' challenges to the CTEA. In that 1998 legislation, as in all previous copyright term extensions, Congress placed existing and future copyrights in parity. In prescribing that alignment, we hold, Congress acted within its authority and did not transgress constitutional limitations."

5. Pub. L. No. 107-273, 116 Stat. 1758 (2002), tit. III, subtitle C, sec. 13301 (21st Century Department of Justice Appropriations Authorization Act).

6. See UNITED STATES COPYRIGHT OFFICE, REPORT ON COPYRIGHT AND DIGITAL DISTANCE EDUCATION (1999), Prepared Comments in volume II and Testimony in volume III of various library advocates in support of a balanced revision of the copyright provisions affecting distance education. The actual report and recommendation of the U.S. Copyright Office is in volume I.

7. Uniform Computer Information Transactions Act, http://www.law.upenn.edu/bll/ archives/ulc/ucita/2002final.htm. "The Uniform Computer Information Transactions Act represents the first comprehensive uniform computer information licensing law. This act uses the accepted and familiar principles of contract law, setting the rules for creating electronic contracts and the use of electronic signatures for contract adoption—thereby making computer information transactions as well-grounded in the law as traditional transactions." UCITA Legislative Fact Sheet, http://www.nccusl.org/Update/ uniformact_factsheets/uniformacts-fs-ucita.asp. The NCCUSL has since removed this page, but see the Computer Information Transactions Act Summary at http://uniformlaws .org/ActSummary.aspx?title=Computer%20Information%20Transactions%20Act for more information.

8. See UCITA, Impact on Libraries (how UCITA could impact libraries, including ILL services), http://www.ala.org/ala/issuesadvocacy/copyright/ucita/impact.cfm.

9. U.S. COPYRIGHT OFFICE, REPORT ON ORPHAN WORKS (2006). The report defines orphan works as "a term used to describe the situation where the owner of a copyrighted work cannot be identified and located by someone who wishes to make use of the work in a manner that requires permission of the copyright owner." U.S. COPYRIGHT OFFICE, REPORT ON ORPHAN WORKS 15 (2006) and H.R. 5439, the Orphan Works Act of 2006. H.R. 5439 was combined with other amendments to title 17, U.S. Code, and reintroduced as title

2 of H.R. 6052, Copyright Modernization Act of 2006, on September 18, 2006. Neither bill passed before the 109th Congress ended.

10. United States Copyright Office Public Roundtables, United States Copyright Office and the Office of Strategic Initiatives, Library of Congress, Docket No. 06-10801, Section 108 Study Group: Copyright Exceptions for Libraries and Archives, 71 FEDERAL REGISTER 70434 (Dec. 4, 2006) and 7999 (Feb. 15, 2006). This discussion includes participation (public comments and written comments) by various stakeholders. Transcripts and written comments are available at http://www.section108.gov/.

11. More information on the work of the Section 108 Study Group is available at http://www.section108.gov/.

12. See Gerald R. Faulhaber, *File Sharing, Copyright, and the Optimal Production of Music: "Music for Nothin' and the Flicks Are Free,"* 13 MICHIGAN TELECOMMUNICATIONS AND TECHNOLOGY LAW REVIEW 77, 85 (2006): "In fact, music sold with DRM and the accompanying end user license agreement (EULA) constitutes a contract (the EULA) together with a mechanism to enforce that contract (the DRM). The combination of the EULA and an effective DRM scheme renders the music sold copyable only under the terms of the EULA, thereby circumventing the consumer's fair use rights."

13. See 17 U.S.C. § 1201(d)–(j) and 37 C.F.R. § 201.40.

14. Nicola Lucchi, *The Supremacy of Techno-Governance: Privatization of Digital Content and Consumer Protection in the Globalized Information Society,* 15 INTERNATIONAL JOURNAL OF LAW AND INFORMATION TECHNOLOGY 192, 215–216 (2007), footnotes omitted.

15. Jeff Sharp, *Coming Soon to Pay-per-View: How the Digital Millennium Copyright Act Enables Digital Content Owners to Circumvent Educational Fair Use,* 40 AMERICAN BUSINESS LAW JOURNAL, 1, 33 2002 at *44.

16. Universal City Studios, Inc. v. Corley, 273 F.3d 429 (2d Cir. 2001).

17. United States v. Elcom, Ltd., 203 F. Supp. 2d 1111, 1135 (N.D. Cal. 2002).

18. *Id.* at 1131, emphasis added.

19. 321 Studios v. Metro Goldwyn Mayer Studios, Inc., 307 F. Supp. 2d 1085, 1102 (N.D. Cal. 2004).

20. Neil J. Conley, *Circumventing Rights Controls: The Token Crack in the Fair Use Window Left Open by Congress in Section 1201 May Be Open Wider Than Expected—Technically Speaking,* 8 CHICAGO-KENT JOURNAL OF INTELLECTUAL PROPERTY 297, 316 (2009).

21. Sharp, *supra* note 15, at 42.

22. 17 U.S.C. § 1202(b)(1).

23. 17 U.S.C. § 1202(c)(6).

▶ PART III
A LICENSING REFERENCE TOOLKIT FOR EVERYDAY USE

▶ 14

A BASIC LICENSING GLOSSARY

The focus of this chapter is on the variety of terms or provisions that are common to most content agreements. Some provisions are standard to most, if not all, such agreements, and many are common in service or software licenses as well, such as choice of forum or law provisions. Other provisions are common across content agreements but vary from license to license. One analysis or even the analysis of several variations cannot fit all agreements. Therefore, it is impossible to include every variation or nuance, but this chapter provides a good beginning. Entries offer examples drawn from actual agreements, discuss the pitfalls or issues from the library or user side that each provision may contain, as well as offer consideration of preferable alternatives. (Actual sample language for a number of provisions is also found in Chapter 16). Some comment is made where applicable on the legal context of each provision (i.e., reference to case law involving the term or provision as an example), especially where a court has defined the term or provision or commented upon its validity and/or legal effect.

Readers are likely aware of other such listings or checklists of licensing resources.[1] A number of licensing principles or guidelines can also be used as a checklist of terms and issues even if such content does not label or discuss specific provisions per se.[2] However, this discussion is independent of that content and is built from the bottom up: dozens of content license agreements were reviewed and this glossary is compiled from those reviews. Comments, observations, and examples of various license terms are drawn from an examination of approximately 60 license agreements collected from a variety of for-profit and nonprofit publishers of online content and library service providers.[3]

Why is an understanding of license terms important? There are two reasons: one practical, the other legal. First, if the librarian does not understand how the principles, concepts, and warnings discussed in this book thus far are applied in practice, in other words, the form such principles, concepts, and warnings take in an actual agreement, then some pieces of the puzzle (and an understanding of that puzzle) remain missing. Second, a licensee is bound to the terms of the contract to which he or she assents, and such assent can have consequences for the library and its patrons or other constituents. The distinction between the scope of the license (i.e., an articulation of those uses that would otherwise be copyright infringement but are now allowed by the license) and covenants is important. Scope-of-use provisions often operate in combination with other terms (e.g., payment of the license fee) as conditions of the license that must be met before such use is allowed. In the instance of the former (covenant and scope permission), remedy would be under contract and copyright theories (or other intellectual property areas), and in the instant of covenant, remedy would be under contract alone. Nimmer offers the following example:

> In many cases, the distinction between scope and promise (covenant) is clear. Thus, if I give you permission to use my software for one hour, using it for a longer period in a way that involves making a copy infringes my copyright because you have exceeded the license permission. The theory is simple: you are only permitted to do the contracted for actions if you perform the relevant preconditions. On the other hand, if I license you to use my motion picture and you agree to pay a stated royalty, your failure to pay breaches the contract but, unless payment was a precondition to the license, your breach may leave the license in force. Your use within the terms of the license may not infringe. If, because of the non-payment, I can cancel the license and I do so, your further use is not protected by the license.[4]

This can be important when considering whether or not breach occurs.

> A carefully drafted contract can establish that any type of performance to which the parties agree constitutes a condition, failure of which excludes the license. Ordinarily, however, contracts are no so clearly drafted. Modern courts generally prefer interpretations that treat contractual performance as a covenant (promise), rather than as a condition, because implementing the idea of the term being a condition can lead to forfeiture of important rights for minor problems in the contract performance.[5]

The following listing is alphabetical by the name or description of the term under discussion.

ARBITRATION

This is also known as alternative dispute resolution, or ADR. Under the recent *AT&T Mobility LLC v. Concepcion*[6] decision discussed in Chapter 4, provisions that require arbitration to settle disputes under the license in mass-market or consumer licenses (discussed in Chapter 6) are no longer per se unconscionable. One impact may be an increased use of an arbitration provision whereby the licensee waives his or her right to litigate any disputes arising under the agreement in lieu of seeking redress through arbitration. It is also common to include in such provisions a class-action waiver, again with the licensee waiving his or her rights to join in any class-action litigation, or become a member of the class, against the licensor. Prior decisions question the use of such provisions in consumer or mass-market agreements.[7] However, such provisions are rare in content license agreements where the parties have the opportunity to negotiate the terms of the agreement. Arbitration and class-action waiver provisions work in tandem with remedy limitation provisions by also restricting the path the licensee may pursue to secure those remedies which are allowable under the contract.

ARCHIVE (PERPETUAL ACCESS)

To underscore again the difference between the purchase of a copy or phonorecord (to use the phrasing of many copyright provisions[8]) of an item for the collection where both possession (licenses transfer possession alone; some do not even do that, offering only access) and title to the copy or phonorecord of the work are obtained, as opposed to possession or access alone: In a license, often the right to retain the content after the duration of the agreement ends is not included. As possession or access alone was licensed, once the license is over, the content must be returned or access to it ceases. Unlike the purchase of items for the collection, the library does not own (have legal title to) a copy of the licensed item or content; this means that once the license ends, access to the content generally ceases as well. Archive provisions are found in some content agreements, so negotiating for such a right where initially absent is not unheard of.

The Springer license indicates that the term "archive" or "archival rights" "shall mean access to the full text of the Springer Content. Archival Rights vary depending on the continuity of the relationship between the parties and the length of time following termination of this Agreement." American Physical Society Online (APSO) makes it clear that "[u]pon lapse of subscription, no additional service is provided." However, APSO does allow the "[s]ubscriber [to] be given the option to purchase a physical archive copy, for example a CD-ROM, of the content in the Online Journal, starting with the 2000 subscription year and published during the term for which a paid subscription was maintained." The American Society of Civil Engineers contains identical language. If this is a sale, the conditions of use should not apply beyond those in copyright, and yet the license agreement (though not the actual contract governing the sale of the "physical archive copy") indicates that "definitions of Authorized Users and allowed and prohibited uses as provided in this Agreement shall otherwise apply to use of the archive copy." The intent of the licensor is that the same conditions and prohibitions of use which apply to the licensed content also apply to the purchased content, though unless a separate agreement governing that sale is executed, it is difficult to understand on what legal basis the same terms and conditions would apply to some future event and or purchased content.

The Accessible Archives allows for a perpetual license except where termination occurs for cause (e.g., a material breach, as discussed in Chapter 3). If the licensee requests ("at Licensee's bequest"), the "licensor shall provide Licensee with an archival copy of the database at a minimal cost." The Accessible Archives license is one of the few reviewed that offers to provide a digital version of "purchased files, for storage in a Digital Repository" and states that "Licensee will be lawful owner of the digital copy." Though not in the character of sale, Ovid allows for archival rights "[s]olely for journal[s] subscribed to during the terms of this Agreement, Subscriber shall be entitled to the archive rights related to those journals." However, the "right is subject to change without notification to Subscriber."

JSTOR also anticipates some level of permanent access and offers a bifurcated payment schedule: "Institutional Licensees typically pay two types of fees to JSTOR, an Annual Access Fee and an Archive Capital Fee." However, this statement and the section in which it is located (titled "Archiving") are a bit of a misnomer, as the archive referenced is not the licensee's but JSTOR's. "The Archive Capital Fee is one-time fee per JSTOR collection aimed at ensuring the long term preservation, upgrading, and enhancements of the scholarly materials in the JSOTR Archive." The way it apparently works from the succeeding language is that if the licensee has paid the one-time Archive Capital Fee and then terminates, the licensee gets nothing in terms of archive rights of its own or access rights to the JSTOR Archive. However, should the licensee later resume subscription, the licensee "[m]ay resume access to that collection and all content subsequently added to that collection at any time in the future through payment only of the Annual Access Fee. It would not need to repay the Archive Capital Fee." This mechanism seems less about institutional archiving and more about a surcharge to cover the cost of adding new content to its database over time, as would likely be done anyway. There is no indication what the result would be if the licensee chose to pay only the Annual Access Fee, never receiving any updated content as newer editions or volumes of titles were added. Although this would be odd indeed, it seems that JSTOR has figured out a way to underwrite some of the cost of maintaining previous and current content in the guise of an attractive, or at least more palatable (from the customer's perspective), concept such as "archiving" or "archive."

ARCHIVING

This term is used in the sense of retaining licensed content for your own archive versus having continued access to the licensor's archive of the content. While a library may desire to retain the content after the license has expired, this may not be practical from the licensor's perspective. It defeats the point of choosing the form of transaction as a license as opposed to a sale. Purchase a book, and the nature of the transaction is a sale; you have the right to retain the book, as the purchaser obtains not only possession but ownership of the item. License a database or a specific journal, and the nature of the transaction is not a sale but a right of access.

The transaction falls short of a loan, as possession of a physical item does not occur (loans in the form of a bailment and in the context of circulation of library materials or review of a desk copy are covered in Chapter 1); the right granted is to access the content and use the content under the terms and conditions of the agreement for the duration of the license. This provision is related to but different from that described as an "archive right of access." Here, there may be limits on what the library-licensee can achieve under its own accord with the license it archives.

It is not inconceivable that some licenses might allow for this, though it may come with additional cost. The Alexander Street Press (ASP) license contemplates such ability: "If the Customer has purchased perpetual rights to the Product(s), ASP will provide Customer, upon request and when the Product(s) reach completion, the data contained in the Product(s) either on a digital storage medium or through a third-party vendor of archiving services." ASP continues: "The Customer that has purchased perpetual rights to the Product(s) may optionally load data onto a local server to be accessed by Authorized Users through the Customer's search and retrieval software. In the case of audio or video, such access must be restricted by DRM [Digital Rights Management] and be limited to one (1) simultaneous user." American Chemical Society provides the following: "Archival Rights for Reagent Chemicals Online: Upon request, a CD-ROM containing the PDFs of the currently-posted version of Reagent Chemicals Online will be supplied. Only one (1) CD-ROM will be supplied, and it may be requested at any time during the life of the posted edition."

Some licenses place other limits on the scope of archiving indirectly. The Brepolis license agreement prohibits the "re-utilization" in "any form of making available to the public all or a substantial part of the contents of the Database, by distribution of copies, by renting, by on-line or other forms of transmission." BioOne allows for continued access to the content that was "published or added to the Licensed Material within the Subscription Period." The access may be direct from BioOne, a third-party contractor, or through in-house access made possible from "supplying electronic files to the Licensee." It is not clear whether, for example, the licensee chooses the mode or the licensor makes the decision. The institution would likely desire to have the electronic files itself if it was undertaking some larger archiving and repository-building initiative. The clause would not prohibit archiving per se but might not allow the content so archived to be given to patrons (as this would be making the content available to the public, which appears prohibited), but without such access, archiving may be useless.

Some agreements offer the right to archive content, at least tacitly, through a general downloading provision that restricts such activity by amount. Marquis Who's Who uses phrasing that states it allows users to "print out or copy discrete insubstantial portions of information from the Database solely in conjunction with those uses [from the previous clause: "business information, research, and educational purposes"] and for professional writings provided that proper attribution is provided and all other copyright and other notices contained therein are maintained." Similarly, in the Springer license: "Licensee may copy and store a single copy of an insubstantial portion of individual books included within the Springer Content." SilverPlatter WebSPIRS uses the concept of insignificant, defined in the negative as follows: "You MAY: b) make a very limited number of hard copies of any search output that does not contain a significant segment of a database, which copes may be used only internally but may not be sold."

The Accessible Archive provides that "Licensee and its Users shall not download or copy all or any material portion of the Licensed Material to any media whatsoever, except small extracts for teaching, research, and scholarship." First, note the conjunctive: small extracts can be downloaded or copied only for uses that are for teaching and research and scholarship—as the phrase is not in the form A or B or C. Second, and more important, what is a "material portion" and how much is a "small extract"? Again, the Accessible Archive allows for a perpetual license except where termination occurs for cause. If the licensee requests ("at Licensee's bequest"), the "licensor shall provide Licensee with an archival copy of the database at a minimal cost." The Accessible Archive license is one of the few reviewed to offer to provide a digital version of "purchased files, for storage in a Digital Repository," and states that "Licensee will be lawful owner of the digital copy."

Personal archiving, to an extent, is allowed under the ProQuest license—but only of portions of articles, not entire articles: "The Products may be used for your internal research or educational purposes, as follows: b. Digital and Print copies. You and your Authorized Users may download or create printout of a reasonable portion of the articles or other works contained in the Products . . . for your own internal or personal use as allowed under the doctrines of 'fair use' and 'fair dealing.' Downloading of all or parts of a Product in a systematic or regular manner so as to create a collection of material comprising all or a material subset of the Product is strictly prohibited whether such collection s in electronic or print form." How much is a reasonable portion, what is a regular manner, or what constitutes a material subset?

These schema parallel the European Union database directive.[9] The agreement defines insubstantial in negative and less-than-helpful terms: "any part of the Database which cannot be considered a substantial part of the Database." A substantial part is then defined as "any part of the database that can stand on its own as a coherent body of data which can be relevant for a larger audience or that represents a considerable amount of data from the database." Without any quantitative indicators, exactly how much is considerable is unclear. Certainly an amount that could be a coherent, useful portion for use by a larger audience might in terms of an amount constitute a small percent.

Project MUSE allows for a personal archive: "Subscriber's institution may 1. download and print one copy of each article for personal use and archive contents on their own personal computers." Though Project MUSE, after termination, "will provide the Subscriber, upon request, an archival (non-searchable) file on DVD-ROM or other appropriate media as determined by Project MUSE®, containing the content of all issues published online during the 12-month subscription term." Likely this clause is intended to prevent commercial but also conceivably other large-scale uses. The American Fisheries license provides that the institution "may hold one archival copy of each journal issue." Associated Press Images states: "You may not make any archival files of the content," though storage is permitted "for no longer than 30 days," and "You may retain one copy of the work You create incorporating the Content solely as necessary for archival purposes." A different approach is taken by FirstSerach, which allows: "In addition, such copies of limited portions of such data may be transferred or sold as an incidental part of the attorney/client, consultant/client or similar relationship, or used for identifying materials to be ordered via interlibrary loan, where the principal purpose is not the distribution of data."

Other agreements prohibit automated archiving, for example, ScienceDirect: "The site may contain robot exclusion headers, and you agree that will not use any robots, spiders, crawlers or other automated downloading programs or devices to access, search, index, monitor or copy any Content." The ramifications of this restriction are discussed elsewhere in conjunction with the Swartz case, concerning an individual who attempted to download large portions of the JSTOR database in hopes of making it freely available on the Internet.[10] The point of archiving provisions is to understand the desires of the library in creating such an archive and the potential limitations, either outright or in the guise of limitations on the amount of content that can be copied, downloaded, retained (some licenses require the licensee to destroy all retained content from the database once the license ends), and so forth.

ASSENT

How does the license define assent? What act or conduct constitutes assent? While entering the initial agreement may not pose significant issues ("please sign and return the enclosed contract"), assent to renew or accept a change in terms can be critical and less obvious. Initially, a signed copy of the agreement would of course constitute assent. Euclid Prime indicates that a signature constitutes acceptance or assent: "and with the signature below the Licensee accepts these terms." Unintended consequences abound when use or continued use of the licensed content (e.g., running a search in the database) can constitute assent. Courts have held that such use can constitute valid assent.[11]

Again, as long as notice of the "use" as assent is made known, such use can then constitute agreement. There would need to be some acknowledgment (e.g., activation through a click-wrap "I agree" button) that the licensee realizes that "copying or otherwise using" the database would constitute assent. Examples of click-to-agree contracts abound: From Westlaw Campus Research: "To accept that terms and conditions, to be bound by them and to gain access to Campus Research, read the Agreement. If you agree with the terms of the Agreement, click on 'I Agree' below and click on 'Continue' to submit the Agreement." HAPI Online uses a similar click-to-agree proviso: "By clicking on the Accept button, you agree to accept these terms." The Bibliography of Asian Studies Online admonishes the licensee to "Please read the Terms and Conditions. By signing below you certify that you have read and agree to abide by all such Terms and Conditions listed below." Gartner uses a similar mechanism: "By completing the enrollment process, you agree to the terms of this agreement just as if you had signed this agreement. If you do not wish to by bound by this agreement, please do not complete the enrollment process."

The concern is whether assent can be triggered by any user's access and use of the content, for example, by running a search. Several agreements reviewed contain such "use as assent to the contract" admonition: the American Statistical Association and Institute of Mathematical Statistics ("By clicking on the 'AGREE' button and/or accessing the CIS-ED Database, or copying or otherwise using the CIS/ED Database, Licensee agrees to be bound by the terms of this Agreement"), Cengage Learning ("Any use of such web pages constitutes the user's agreement to abide by the Terms"), BioMed Central ("By using this Web Site you agree to be bound by these terms and conditions which from a binding contract"), Brepolis ("or by using one or more of the BREPOLIS databases, the user is deemed to have agreed to comply with all of the terms and conditions below"), and Cambridge Journals Online ("By using the Cambridge University Press website at http://www.cambridge.org/ and by registering to access the Cambridge Journals Online service (CJO) you are indicating that you accept the terms and conditions set out below"). These clauses may push the envelope, as there is no acknowledgment that the licensee has read terms in order to know that using the website equates to assent. Worse, use of service by patrons might constitute assent to renewal or acceptance of a change in terms. Of course, it may be that to have access to the site one must first register, and as part of that process this is made clear and the users make acknowledgment to the fact that further use equals assent. Where the licensor uses a bifurcated mechanism, acknowledgment of terms followed by use of service as assent to contract, there is less chance of unintended consequence.

Consider the EBSCOhost agreement: "By using the services available at this site or by making the services available to Authorized Users, the Authorized Users and the Licensee agree to comply with the following terms and conditions (the 'Agreement')." Not only does use or service availability constitute assent under the agreement but this act binds the authorized users as well. These may include third parties, such as members of the local community, students, and so on. Some sites appear to get the sequence not quite right: to use the site, you must first agree to the terms, as the Marquis Who's Who site infers ("To use the marquiswhos who.com web site [the 'web site'], you must agree to be bound by these terms and conditions of use"); in other words, you must first agree to be bound by the terms of use before you can use the site, but the next sentence suggests that it is possible to use the site before agreeing to all of the terms, in which case you are admonished to stop use: "If you do not agree to be bound by these terms and conditions of use, you must not use or must immediately terminate your use of this web site."

The point is that it's important to understand how the licensor views assent and the consequences such assent can have in terms of the initial contract and, more important, how renewal or agreement to a change in terms is accomplished. It is recommended that "use" or "continued use" alone should not constitute assent. It is better to incorporate a mechanism of renewal or change that separates notice of the renewal or proposed change in terms from agreement to renew or accept the new terms. Instead, offer clear notice and a separate signature or click-on notice followed by assent of agreement with that renewal or change-in-terms notice, rather than have use of the service itself (one would expect users to use the service!), in some circumstances, for example, use after an e-mail of change was sent, to also constitute assent.

ASSIGNMENT OR ASSIGNABILITY

It is common for the initial library-licensee not to be able to assign the agreement to another licensee. The Nature (Academic: Americas) agreement restricts assignment: "The Licensee may not assign, sub-license, transfer, charge or otherwise dispose of its rights under this Agreement without the prior written consent of the Licensor." Since turnabout is fair play, this prohibition should likewise apply to the licensor. If licensors have the right to assign the agreement, then the successor licensor might proceed to change the terms (which, as discussed, might lead to problems, depending on the mechanism of assent). BioOne allows for licensor assignment but provides: "If rights in all or any part of the Licensed Material are assigned to another publisher, BioOne shall use its best efforts to ensure that the terms and conditions of this License are maintained." While not a common occurrence, if it is possible that the library entity may merge with another library or somehow change legal form, then the right to assign at least to a successor legal entity should be available. Licensors do not like to grant this right: "The underlying theory originated with the proposition that a nonexclusive license is merely a promise to not sue the other party (the licensee) as long as it uses the intellectual property in a manner consistent with the license. That promise is personal in nature and limited to the particular licensee; it cannot be transferred without consent."[12]

AUTHORITY

Some licenses may have a statement acknowledging that the licensee signatory indeed has the ability to enter into the agreement. This is important as "a principal will be bound by a contract entered into by the principal's agent on his behalf only if the agent had authority to bind him."[13] With this thought in mind, the Associated Press Images agreement contains the following clause: "User represents and warrants that User has the authority to bind, and has bound, such Principal to these License Terms." The Bibliography of Asian Studies Online admonishes the licensee: "Please read the Terms and Conditions. By signing below you certify that you have read and agree to abide by all such Terms and Conditions listed below, and that you are authorized to sign this form on behalf of your institution." A straightforward example of assent and authority is found in the MathSciNet agreement: "Please read the Terms and Conditions. By signing below you certify that you have read and agree to abide by all such Terms and Conditions and that you are authorized to sign this form on behalf of your organization." Use of the word "by" when signing ("by Tomas A. Lipinski") along with the person's title indicates that the person is entering the agreement on behalf of the institution and in his or her corporate capacity and not as an individual. This limits the signatory's personal liability under the agreement. In addition, "attest" is used for a corporate signatory, "witness" for an individual. It may sound obvious, but the library should ensure that the proper person signs the license. For the library, this may be the provost or similar position in a campus setting or the library board president for a public library. The repercussion may be disastrous and the contract may be voidable by the principal, in other words, the government agency like a university or public library.[14] This is why the licensor wants to ensure that such authority is vested in the person signing the contract. "The person who signs the license may protect herself by asking her library for written documentation setting out that she does in fact have authority to sign the license. This may protect her should a content owner ever take legal action personally against the signing person."[15] The legal designation or title of each party to the agreement also should be included. This should be one of the warranties: that each party has the right to bind the organization and that the act of entering into the contract will not violate any third-party agreement, akin to the right to make the licensed content available in the first place, and that its provision is not infringing.

AUTHORIZED USERS

While it might be the rare licensor that sues a customer, one area where a licensor will pursue legal recourse is if the licensee exceeds the authority under the contract in terms of who is allowed to use the content so licensed. Most licenses restrict those who can have legitimate (authorized) access and use of the licensed content. Licenses can require also that the licensee-library or licensee-institution takes measures to ensure some level of compliance with such provisions, making users aware that only those in the proper category may access and use the licensed content; others require reasonable efforts, while some simply require the licensee to ensure ("warrant" or promise) that only such users and uses are undertaken. In the recent criminal complaint against Internet activist Aaron Swartz, the indictment notes that he "was a fellow at Harvard University's Center for Ethics. Although Harvard provided Swartz access to JSTOR's services and archive as needed for his research . . . Swartz was not affiliated with MIT as a student, faculty member, or employee or in any other manner that his and MIT's common location in Cambridge."[16] Swartz's initial access might have been as a walk-in user, but, as the complaint alleges, his subsequent extraction of significant portions (millions of articles) exceeded any authorized use, regardless of status or category of authorized user.

In a recent case, Elsevier claimed that one licensee exceeded the terms of the contract by allowing unauthorized users the ability to access and download articles from its ScienceDirect database: "Elsevier Inc. and two related entities (collectively, 'Elsevier') bring this action alleging breach of contract and contributory copyright infringement against Ingenix, Inc. ('Ingenix'), and copyright infringement and unauthorized computer access against Ingenix's parent company UnitedHealth Group, Inc. and 93 subsidiaries (collectively, 'UHG'). The identities of the UHG employees who allegedly accessed Elsevier's database are relevant to this action, but ascertaining them involves burdensome discovery. In an effort to obviate that discovery, Plaintiffs move for partial summary judgment on two test cases of copyright infringement. Elsevier contends that it can show that two of its copyrighted articles were accessed and copied by employees of two separate unauthorized, yet unidentified, UHG subsidiaries."[17] It should be obvious that defining in the license the range or scope of users desired is critical. Disputes have arisen over the number of authorized users, for example, that the number of users exceeds those authorized under the license. This is especially true in instances of software licensing.[18]

The International Federation of Library Associations and Institutions (IFLA) recommends authorized users include those "affiliated with licensee" whether on-site or off-site or at remote sites, or if not affiliated but nonetheless are on the premises.[19] A list provided by ARL offers 17 categories of user.[20] "It is important to determine in your license who is authorized to use the licensed content [e.g., will the public be authorized users?] . . . Another consideration is whether the group of authorized users is defined geographically, for instance, all faculty on campus X."[21] The point here is that other policies of the library must be coordinated with the definition or identification of authorized users in the license. For example, suppose a university runs a continuing education (CE) program whereby student services policies promise that all educational facilities, including the library, are open to CE students. Does the license agreement include these noncredit or professional "credit" students? If not, the library is obligated to administer multiple levels of access privileges. To some extent, it may be difficult to avoid this problem, but attempting to maximize uniformity makes the most sense in terms of administration and service.

How authorized users are defined varies greatly among licensors. WilsonSelect defines users differently depending on the library type. For a K–12 school it "means school staff, employees and duly enrolled students." In a public library the authorized users include "library staff, library patrons, including walk-in patrons that are not registered borrowers"; however, remote access is limited to "staff and registered borrowers" alone. In a special library the authorized users are "patrons, on-site staff and employees." The American Statistical Association and Institute of Mathematical Statistics commercial license restricts users to those "at a single corporate site and by current employees of the corporate Licensee."

ProQuest defines authorized user for a public library to include "staff, individual residents of your reasonably defined geographic area served and walk-in patrons while they are on-site." Similarly, the CSA Illumina license provides for public libraries "library staff, individual residents of your reasonably defined geographic area served and walk-in patrons while they are on site." Conflagration of clauses may result in less than clear language if read literally, though likely the intent is present: by the plain meaning of the provision, these three groups are all authorized users (staff, residents, and walk-ins), as all appear listed under that paragraph. Paragraph 3 addresses remote access and indicates: "If your subscription allows you to provide remote access to a Product, you will strictly limit such access to Authorized Users through use of passwords, IP addresses or other secure method of user verification." But if a category of authorized user is a walk-in while they are on-site, is such a user also authorized and allowed remote access?

Remote access is often a concern to educational entities. Greenwood Press, for example, indicates that students and employees are allowed remote access "regardless of the physical location of such persons." Authorized users include "full and part time students and employees (including faculty, staff, affiliated researchers and independent contractors) of Licensee and the institution of which it is a part."[22] At first blush, the clause may appear beneficial in that "affiliated researchers and independent contractors" are included. However, the problem with the formulation is that by including a parenthetical elucidation of who is included within the category of "employee" the clause may do more harm than good. First, if the intent was to include affiliated researchers such as alumni or visiting scholars within the primary user group to which remote access is extended, this is fine—but these individuals are rarely employees. Thus, some confusion arises. Are users in these categories included only if such persons are also employed by the institution? If so, including independent contractors is just as problematic because under the copyright law—the property law most relevant to licensing law—independent contractors, while likely paid by the institution, are not considered employees.[23] Under copyright law, the two terms are mutually exclusive. If such additional users are intended to be included, it would be best to indicate that such persons may have remote access even though they are not within the employ of the institution. The Alexander Street Press (ASP) license indicates such users as independent categories: "students, employees, faculty, staff, affiliated researchers, distance learners, and visiting scholars." Brepolis includes a rather broad category of "registered users of the library" that could include a wide number of associated users, such as alumni. Cambridge Journals Online could include a wide array of patrons: "via his/her affiliation with a subscribing institution as a current student, faculty member, library patron, or employee."

The American Chemical Society definition strikes at the concept of delineating a group of core users who should be extended remote access, that is, those "individuals officially affiliated with the Licensee," and then indicates "for example" that the group may include "those serving in the capacity of employees, consultants under contract with the Licensee, faculty and other teaching staff, and persons officially registered as full or part-time students." The problem with the sentence is that it concludes with "that are located at an Authorized Site and use an Authorized Terminal." Problems now abound. Must all the "individuals officially affiliated," including the exemplar groups, be at an "Authorized Site and use an Authorized Terminal" or just "officially registered . . . full or part-time students?" Second, the term "authorized terminal" is not defined, nor does it appear in any other provision of the agreement. While the concept of "authorized site" is addressed elsewhere and relates to Internet protocol (IP) addresses that the licensee must submit to ACS,[24] a common verification mechanism, there is no indication how one could have a valid IP address yet not be at an "authorized" terminal.[25]

Return to the provisions regarding on-site or walk-in users. (Not to pick on Greenwood; all the licenses discussed in this book have some flaws, in a sense. Some are flawed in the sense of rights granted versus obligations or conditions imposed; others are flawed due to poor drafting. This license might be an example of the latter. Of course, some licenses are plagued by both kinds of flaws. This exegesis demonstrates the sorts of problems licensing verbiage can cause and the value of reading carefully.) The Greenwood Press definition of authorized users contains another conundrum, regarding the remaining users—on-site or walk-in. By indicating that "library cardholders or patrons not affiliated with Licensee who are physically present at Licensee's site(s) ('walk-ins')" are also authorized users, it suggests that even those users who have library cards may be relegated to on-site or walk-in access alone. This begs the question: if a person is a library card holder, would this person not then be an "affiliated researcher"? This result would make little sense, unless of course they must also be an employee. It is possible the clause intends to exclude from remote access an alumnus who may have library borrowing privileges with respect to the physical collection yet is not allowed remote access to online resources.

The Accessible Archive appears to solve this problem, but more logically, relegating in-house, on-site, or walk-in access alone to those persons "not affiliated with Licensee who are physically present at Licensee's sites(s) ('walk-in')." The ASP agreement, using a more conversational tone, attempts the same goal, but unlike the Accessible Archive agreement that prefaces its statement with a one-word header ("Walk-ins"), the ASP license places the term "walk-in" into the operational proviso: "Walk-in patrons are also authorized to access to [*sic*] Product(s) while physically present at the Site." Are not walk-in patrons by definition "physically present"? Is this an example of poor drafting, or is the proviso attempting to suggest either that walk-in patrons can be in some state of access other than "physically present" or that perhaps there are categories of patrons other than walk-ins who also can be "physically present at the site"?

FirstSearch makes it clear that for a public library remote access is allowed "provided remote access requires the patron to first log on to the library system's local computer using a current authorized library card or other library-controlled authorization before accessing the FirstSearch service." In the ASP license, the walk-in proviso does not include walk-ins within the list of "authorized users," as did the Accessible Archive provision,[26] but rather states that walk-in patrons are also authorized to access content when present. (Of course, by operation, this may make "walk-in patrons" authorized users, but then the illogic of the "physically present" condition returns front and center.) In other words, under the Accessible Archive provision, authorized users consist of two clear groups, those "affiliated" and walk-ins (who are nonaffiliated "patrons" and physically present), while under the ASP provision its construction might best be viewed as allowing two groups of users access to content in-house or on-site: "authorized users" who also have remote access and walk-ins (those in-house or on-site users that are not otherwise "authorized." FirstSearch Academic uses the phrase "primarily affiliated with the licensed campus and authorized on-site patrons of Subscriber's library."

Might the problem be that the term *walk-in* possesses some independent meaning to the average reader when it was likely intended to mean anyone other than an authorized user? Euclid Prime uses the term on the assumption that readers know what it means: "Walk-ins are also deemed Authorized Users of the site license, but do not have remote access privileges." Read this finely, the ASP provision at least makes some sense. It might be best to simply state that walk-ins can also have access and then define who those patrons might be—for example, "anyone who is not an authorized user but is physically present." Again, this is just one of many examples indicating that slight alterations in word choice and usage can create additional legal implications, issues of interpretation, among other difficulties.

HAPI Online allows "occasional users who access HAPI either directly at the Site or via telecommunications hook-ups to computers physically located at Licensee's Site." It's not clear what "occasional" means, but apparently some third-party users who access the system via a proxy server, perhaps, would be included. For example, the American Statistical Association and Institute of Mathematical Statistics university license is "for use by faculty, staff, students, and visitors authorized to conduct research at an institution of higher education only and holding valid passwords to access the computer system or network and at a single campus of the educational institution." It is not clear who makes this authorization. If it can be made by the licensee, then alumni would arguably be included. Johns Hopkins University Press allows for "library patrons," who could be anyone, and then specifies that "[d]istance learners, alumni, and other off-campus affiliates may access the Online Reference if their internet access is through the campus network or via a secure proxy server," though there appears to be a general preference ("best feasible efforts") to enable access to the Online Reference only to these groups ("faculty, students, staff, alumni, and walk-in library patrons") "using the campus physical facilities."

Again, the use of words in a different context can complicate even the simplest provisions. Consider the statement found in the American Mathematical Society license: "Authorized users must be employees, faculty, staff, or students affiliate with the subscriber, or authorized on-site patrons of the subscriber's library facilities." Again, a dual set of users, those which are somehow "affiliate" and those on-site, but the modifying those "on-site patrons of the subscriber's library facilities" with the word "authorized" makes the phrasing less than clear, or at least clouds its meaning. Use of the word "authorized" is likely not meant to represent the same thing as "authorized users" in the first instance; rather, "authorized" in the second sense refers to patrons who are properly or legally in the library. It would be more effective not to use the word "authorized" in two senses. Perhaps it could be rephrased in this way: "or on-site patrons of the subscriber's library facilities who have permission or who otherwise have lawful access to the subscriber's library."[27]

Again, language and turn of phrase can be everything. Consider the following example from the American Meteorological Society: "Authorized Users must be employees, faculty, staff, and students officially affiliated with the Subscriber Institution and patrons of the Subscribing Institution's library facilities. This includes occasional users who access AMS journals through stations physically located on the site and under the control and administration of the Subscribing Institution." Reading each sentence in isolation, this might appear to allow all sorts of walk-ins or "occasional users." However, the first sentence indicates that authorized users come from a narrow list of "faculty, staff, and students" who are "officially affiliated" with the licensee ("Subscriber Institution") and who are also patrons ("and patrons of the Subscribing Institution's library facilities"). While an on-site or on-campus student would qualify (the person is a student, officially affiliated with the licensee and a patron of "library facilities"), a distance-education student might not because he or she, although a student officially affiliated with the licensee, is not necessarily a patron of the library facilities. Though this person is a patron of the library, albeit a remote user, the phrase "library facilities" suggests the person needs a physical connection to the library. If remote access was intended in this scenario, "library services" might have been a better choice than "library facilities." The sentence does not read: "Authorized Users must be employees, faculty, staff, and students officially affiliated with the Subscriber Institution, and patrons of the Subscribing Institution's library facilities" or "Authorized Users must be either employees, faculty, staff, or students officially affiliated with the Subscriber Institution or patrons of the Subscribing Institution's library facilities." An additional reason why the second sentence may not allow for all sorts of walk-in users, though this is likely its intent, is that beginning the sentence with the words "This includes" suggests this sentence does not offer an additional category of authorized users but rather elucidates a subset of authorized users, in other words, one that is first a faculty, staff, or student, "officially affiliated," and a patron. While inclusion of walk-ins is likely the intent, the language is less than clear in accomplishing this result.

The ARTstor license attempts to sort out visiting scholars from general members of the public. Authorized users include those "officially affiliated," such as "staff, faculty, enrolled students," but also includes "volunteer staff, and affiliated researchers," though the last phrase is rather clumsy, as it uses the term to define the term. A second category of authorized users is those "not officially affiliated" but nonetheless allowed access because they have "an educational or scholarly or similar association with Licensee (such as visiting researchers and lecturers)." A final category allows "individuals physically present in the facilities of Licensee ('Walk-in Users')." A final sentence in the definition of authorized users oddly repeats, in effect, the third categorization of authorized user, the walk-in user, though it does arguably elaborate upon the persons it intends to exclude: "Individuals who do not have an official or unofficial affiliation with License (such as alumni or persons whose only association to Licensee is that they pay fees to use the physical facilities or services [such as users of a college library]), may only access the ARTstor Digital Library as Walk-In Users."

JSTOR uses the term "affiliated and visiting researchers," while Marquis Who's Who identifies faculty and staff in a "permanent, temporary, contract, or visiting" capacity. The impact of these sentences is twofold. First, walk-in users include users like alumni and members of the general public who might have library privileges, such as circulation access, as a result of some fee payment, but as such persons are not either officially affiliated or unofficially affiliated (or to use an earlier phrase in the agreement, "not officially affiliated"), their access to the database content is relegated to on-site access. The last sentence, that some users are relegated to on-site access alone, implies that other categories, both the officially and not officially affiliated, have remote access.

EBSCOhost allows a broad range of users that might include visiting scholars or other guests and is clear to include "employees, students, registered patrons, walk-in patrons, or other persons affiliate with Licensee or otherwise permitted to use Licensee's facilities and authorized by Licensee to access Databases," though all such persons must be "authorized" to do so, but "'Authorized User(s)' do not include alumni of the Licensee." But what if the alum now works for the library or is a returning master's student? Is this individual now excluded? It might be better to express this exclusion with different language: "Alumni are not considered authorized users unless they fall into one of the above categories." Project MUSE is more generous, allowing that "distance learners, alumni, and other off-campus affiliates may access Project MUSE if their internet access is through the campus network or via secure proxy server."

The point of this extended discussion is multifold. First, there is great variation in how licensors embody the concept of authorized users in their licenses. Common inclusions, but with variation, are concepts of remote use and walk-in users. In addition, descriptions of the primary user base are also subject to variation. The best strategy is to make a list of all of the conceivable users the library would like to include and negotiate for the inclusion of those users. As explained, if the license cues "authorized" to the policy of the library regarding its own concept of authorized user, the possibility to expand the range of users is possible without additional negotiation—but the library may need to change its own policy. In other words, tie the concept of authorized user to the library's policies and procedures regarding who can use the library or its services, whether on-site or remote. Likewise, make sure that if the license conditions authorized use based on some affiliation or categorization by the library, such policy and procedures include the targeted users. If not, negotiation may be necessary with more distant (in terms of relationship as well a geographically) users. Such inclusion may also require a higher license premium.

AUTHORIZED USES: PERMITTED, RIGHTS GRANTED

See also PROHIBITED USES

Defining authorized uses in a license can be as important and as complex (comparing license to license) as defining authorized users. One strategy would be to ensure that the library and its patrons (authorized users) have the same use rights as each would under the copyright law, or more. Licensors might be interested in going beyond the scope of copyright alone, as this would be one way to ensure the license contains the extra element necessary to avoid preemption issues (discussed in Chapter 4). Unfortunately, most license agreements do not use the same language as the copyright law when they reference use rights, which limits the copyright owner's exclusive rights (section 106 rights): reproduction, derivative works and public performance, display, and distribution. The provisions of the copyright law that limit these rights also operate in reference to these rights. The sections of concern to libraries would, at a minimum, include sections 107 (fair use, library and archive reproduction and public distribution, and public distributions and displays) through 110 (public display or performance in face-to-face and distance-education classrooms and other noncommercial use of nondramatic musical and literary works), 117 (reproduction of a computer program), and 121 (use of content for the blind and other people with disabilities).

A second task is to discern or translate the uses that are mentioned in the license to the needs of your particular circumstances.[28] Understanding the scope of these uses allows the library to better assess whether the cost of the license is worth the benefit of the license. The use of some of these terms in a license may not be intended to have the same meaning as under the copyright law; in other words, if a right to reproduce the content is included, then a separate right to save or print should arguably not be necessary. The International Federation of Library Associations and Institutions (IFLA) suggests that all personal uses should be allowed,[29] and yet this ignores at least U.S. law that under fair use the concept of personal versus public use (in terms of display, performance, or distribution) may not be as important as whether the use is commercial or noncommercial.[30] In other words, a use could be personal but commercial. While this may appear a practical strategy, it requires every sort of contingency or possible use to be articulated. "Some licenses set out the grant of rights followed by a phrase such as 'and all similar uses' or 'and related uses,' and so on. This is advantageous to a library, since the license may thereby include some uses that are not specifically mentioned in its various clauses."[31] The list of authorized uses is likely the most significant term of the license. "Copyright licenses are assumed to prohibit any use not authorized."[32] If the use is not articulated in the agreement (and assuming there is an integration clause), it will be very difficult if not impossible to construe other implied uses. "As noted earlier, the language of the Agreement [between RealNetworks and DVD Copy Control Association] must be construed in accordance with the purposes underlying federal copyright law, and copyright license agreements are assumed to prohibit any use not authorized."[33] In other words, if the use is not authorized and it falls within the owner's copyright (the exclusive rights), it is not granted; uses that exceed this grant are then infringing, and if such use represents a breach of a covenant in the contract, this would also give rise to a remedy under contract law as well as copyright.

The practical consideration is whether the library gets its money's worth, so to speak, under the license when considering the additional obligations or restrictions it must assume. Each entity must assign variable, situational value (benefit and cost) to the terms, but if the uses garner little value to the library and its constituency in terms of costs, then perhaps the terms need to be revised or the license agreement not pursued. Where "the existence of a license agreement is not in dispute, and the scope of the license is the only issue, the copyright owner bears the burden of proving that the copying was unauthorized."[34] Uses that exceed those authorized can result in a claim for both copyright infringement and breach of contract, as most licenses are limited in the scope of rights (uses) granted: "If, however, a license is limited in scope and the licensee acts outside the scope, the licensor can bring an action for copyright infringement."[35] Words are important. As mentioned before, defining terms can add or take away value from a use provision.

Consider the use granted by the Alexander Street Press license: "Authorized use includes the making of a limited numbers or hard or electronic copies of texts for research, education, or other non-commercial use only; and the use of the paper format of small, insignificant portions of the Product(s) as a source of interlibrary Loan ('ILL')." So ILL is allowed but only of print copies and in "small, insignificant portions." The use of both modifiers ("small" and "insignificant") suggests perhaps both quantitative ("small" in terms of amount) and qualitative ("insignificant" in terms of significance) standards. How much is too much?

The use of content in reserves (electronic or otherwise) is another significant area in educational settings. Euclid Prime allows for use of electronic reserves on a "secure site accessible to class members only, and articles purged from the e-reserve system at the end of each semester." However, this does not mean the files might not be stored elsewhere—otherwise, this would necessitate searching for and downloading an article each semester it is used. Project MUSE requires that only the links be removed: "use a persistent URL...for courses of instruction offered by the Subscribing Institution where access is restricted to students enrolled in the course, to instructor, and to library staff maintaining the link, and such access is limited to the duration of the course...and the links to such items shall be deleted by the Subscriber when they are no longer required for such purpose." WilsonSelect is the simplest: "Use the Subject Database to create electronic reserves."

One might question use of terms such as "reasonably necessary" (ARTstor: "Authorized Users may print only that amount of ARTstor Content that is reasonably necessary for Permitted Uses and...reproduce such copies in limited quantities as reasonably necessary for Permitted Uses.") Such phrases might be open to reasonable but differing interpretations. The Accessible Archive allows users to "download small extracts only of the Licensed Materials" and "print extracts of a reasonable portion of the Licensed Materials for the purposes of study, research, inclusion in essays and papers, and inclusion in materials for course work." What about use in theses or dissertations? ARTstor allows for use in dissertation, including for deposit regardless of format, but not remote access: "use in research or a dissertation, including reproduction of the dissertation provided such reproductions are only for personal use, library deposit, and/or use solely within the institution with which the Authorized User and/or his or her faculty or curatorial readers are affiliated." Similarly, the JSTOR license allows for use "in research papers or dissertations, including reproductions of the dissertations, provided such reproductions are only for personal use, library deposit, and/or use solely within the institution(s) with which the Authorized User and/or his or her faculty readers are affiliated." This would allow an institution to digitize its collection of student theses or dissertations but not make the content available online, as this would likely be a public display, nor could the files be digitally copied for a patron at another institution, as this would entail both reproduction (which is allowed) and public distribution (which is not allowed). A similar on-premise limitation is contained in the current copyright provision regarding digitization and archiving, in section 108. Licenses should be designed to offer rights beyond that of the copyright law in the absence of an agreement. Otherwise, the value of the license to the institution is diminished. Does the license also allow for portfolio use by students, for example? (For example, JSTOR allows "use in a student, faculty, or curatorial portfolio, including non-public display thereof, if such use conforms to the customary and usual practice in the field.")

Again, language is key. Are all personal or educational uses also noncommercial? The fair-use case law would answer an emphatic no, and several license phrasings suggest the same conclusion. The result is that an authorized use under a license agreement may need to fall into one of the authorized categories and be also noncommercial—personal or educational uses could of course be commercial. A student could use the license content to fill article requests from his or her employer, or a faculty member may use licensed content to prepare for a speaking engagement or a consulting gig for which compensation or an honorarium is paid. Compare Cengage Learning ("Cengage Learning grants you a limited license to access and make personal noncommercial use of this site, subject to the Terms") with Bowker's Books in Print ("Content received through the Products may be displayed, reformatted and printed for non-commercial, scholarly or reference purposes only"). In the Cengage Learning license, the use of the phrase "personal noncommercial" suggests that the site use must be both personal and noncommercial, whereas the use of commas to separate the three purposes—"non-commercial, scholarly or reference"—suggests the disjunctive, with the result that any of the three purposes is possible, but are the three concepts mutually exclusive? In the academic world, one would hope not: as any noncommercial display, reformat, or print of the products is allowed, as should be any scholarly use, even if compensation is received, such as when the products are used to write a new textbook for which the faculty author receives royalties and in response to a reference query from a local corporation that pays an annual fee to be a library affiliate and receive such service. EBSCOhost also uses a similar "personal, non-commercial use" in its remote access provision, suggesting too that uses under this clause are allowed if the use is both personal and noncommercial. Of course, the provisions regarding authorized users must also be considered, as the local corporation may be excluded unless its staff person comes to the library-licensee on-site, but other fee-based, or commercial, reference use by authorized users is certainly conceivable.

The OverDrive Media Console Version 3.2 (November 2011) admonishes the licensee that the "digital Content" is "only for your personal, non-commercial, entertainment use and not for any redistribution of the Content or other use restricted in this Section" (in a section titled "Restrictions") and, in a later section titled "Important Notice about Copyrighted Materials," reiterates that the licensee "may use the Content only for your personal, non-commercial use. The Content and any other copyrighted material may not be modified, copied, distributed, shared, displayed, emailed, transmitted, sold or otherwise transferred, conveyed or used, in a manner inconsistent with the Agreement, or rights of the copyright owner."

In light of this discussion, the Gale license offers a perplexing combination: users "may make a single print, nonelectronic copy of a permitted portion of the content for personal, non-commercial, educational purposes only." Note that "personal, non-commercial, educational" are not in the disjunctive, there is no "or" between the three conditions. Therefore, the use is not intended to be one of personal or noncommercial or educational but rather all three modify the allowed "purpose." The use must be personal and noncommercial and educational. As discussed, the noncommercial may or may not pose problems for the nonprofit entity but arguably would mean no use for paid consulting, honoraria, or royalty-producing activity by faculty, staff, or students. In a school, college, or university setting, the "educational" restriction should pose little problem, but are all uses in a public library setting educational, where library mission statements typically include recreational pursuits alone by patrons as justification for providing content in the form of physical on-site collections or virtual online resources to patrons? Finally, for the educational entity and even the public library, the "personal" suggests the opposite of public, which would mean the content could not be brought into the nonprofit classroom or the public library meeting or program room, as these would be, at least under the copyright law, places of public performance or display.[36] It not clear whether the licensor intends as strict a definition of public as the copyright law supposes in section 101,[37] but the use of the modifier "personal" must be in contrast to some use, a nonpersonal use—for example, group use is prohibited, which arguably could be in a classroom of a public educational institution, certainly in a meeting or community room of a public library. Perhaps the licensor does not intend to be this restrictive in result, but words in a contract are not superfluous; each word or combination of words must be given meaning, and as written, such restrictions are more than conceivable. If such public space uses are anticipated by the licensor, then a different word should be used—or perhaps "noncommercial" or a concept of that beyond cost recovery for printing alone should be inserted instead of "personal" or "personal, noncommercial."

Gutenberg-e Columbia University Press confuses the personal versus public use even further by allowing "[a]ny user" to "make single printed copies of individual writings for private personal use or research." This suggests some personal uses could be something other than private and thus prohibited. Otherwise, if both words convey the same meaning, the use of one is superfluous, and words in law generally are not interpreted to be so; each must be given meaning. Is this merely poor drafting, or is there a category of use such as "public personal" that is intended to be prohibited, in other words, is not an authorized use? Is there then also a "private group" that is prohibited (as opposed to "private personal," as the actual agreement requires)? With both words in play, the use ("search, download, and save") must be both private and personal aspects, that is, for individual use in a nonpublic setting. The LexisNexis license attempts to solve this issue by using a different phrasing to restrict use "primarily for one person's exclusive use." Similarly, SPIE Digital Library restricts use "solely for the private use or research of the individual Subscriber."

Once a list of conceivable uses is compiled and compared against those granted in the license, a second strategy is to determine whether the use rights granted are phrased in such a way as to limit the rights in some way. Watch for so-called givebacks, a broad sweep of uses with some impossible conditions. For example, SCA Illumina allows use for "internal research or educational purposes" and expands in specific "for educational, scientific, or research purposes, including illustration, explanation, example, comment, criticism, teach, research or analysis" (compare these to those presented in the preamble to the list of four statutory fair use factors: "for purposes such as criticism, comment, news reporting, teaching [including multiple copies for classroom use], scholarship, or research"), but then adds "provided that in doing so you or your Authorized Users do not violate an express provision of this Agreement."[38] Getting all of your faculty, staff, students, patrons, and so on, to abide by each of the express terms might prove challenging, if not a practical impossibility (*see* IMPOSSIBLE TERMS).

BANKRUPTCY

See also TERMINATION RIGHTS

Though not a likely scenario, bankruptcy, when it occurs, can have unintended consequences for both licensor and licensee.[39] If one party goes into bankruptcy or some similar state of financial duress, or it is otherwise no longer able to carry on its business, or it must limit in some substantial way its business activities, then the other party may desire a right to terminate the license or, in the alternative, to have the license continue. It depends on how necessary the licensed content is to the licensee (and whether other sources of the content can be found or substituted for it) and to what extent the availability of the licensed content is impacted by the bankruptcy or financial downturn of the licensor. It can also depend on who desires the license to continue and if the bankruptcy is in the form of a complete cessation of business. It is understandable that a licensee might want the licensor to continue providing a service even if the licensor goes belly-up, but some obligations are difficult to fulfill if the entity no longer exists.

The unintended consequences are the result of the intersection of the federal contract and bankruptcy laws. First, if the licensor is bankrupt but the licensee desires continuation of service and contractually included such rights in its language, the bankruptcy laws may override this contractual provision because such contracts—to continue to perform a function, to continue to provide a service such as maintain a database—are executory in nature.[40] It is not the same as ordering a stack of widgets already made when bankruptcy occurs and all that remains is for the widgets to be loaded from the supply dock onto the truck and final delivery undertaken. Rather, in executor contracts, some continuing service must be rendered or some production continued. For a legal entity to continue such undertakings in the shadow of bankruptcy may not be prudent, so the law allows the executor of the bankrupt estate to make the decision whether to honor such commitments. Under section 365 of the federal bankruptcy law, the trustee of the bankrupt estate may choose which executory contracts to honor and which not to honor. Such contracts are subject to special discharge rules vested in the bankruptcy trustee, as a bankrupt entity might have difficulty surviving bankruptcy if every contractual obligation needs to be fulfilled or performed.[41]

Second, suppose the licensor goes belly-up. The licensee can terminate and chooses to do so but is due a refund. The refund might be deemed a debt that, under the bankruptcy laws, the payment of which is delineated by a statutory hierarchy of creditors and codified processes by which such creditors are paid. As the U.S. Bankruptcy Court has the authority to stay transactions within 90 days of filing for bankruptcy, for a licensor in bankruptcy, the court might order the return of the refund paid to the licensor into the bankruptcy estate if it was paid within 90 days of filing. Such monies would be aggregated into the bankrupt estate and, along with any debts still owed, shared prorated among the creditors according the statutory priority rules.[42]

Third, if the licensee is bankrupt but has paid its annual renewal fee, the bankruptcy laws may again intervene through the automatic stay in which all transactions are frozen, turned, or rolled back to a point 90 days before the date the bankrupt estate was created, if the bankruptcy filings were made with U.S. Bankruptcy Court.[43]

Further termination rights of the licensor in the case of licensee bankruptcy may be unenforceable: "Although many licensors include language in their license agreement automatically terminating the underlying license agreement in the event of the licensee's bankruptcy, such language is unenforceable. Section 365(e)(1) of the Bankruptcy Code provides that an executory contract of the debtor may not be terminated or modified at any time after a bankruptcy filing because of a provision in the license agreement that is conditioned on the insolvency of the debtor or the commencement of a bankruptcy filing."[44] This is because section 362, the automatic stay provision, freezes all transactions of the bankrupt estate, giving the trustee time to regroup financially. This holding period allows the trustee to collect outstanding monies, pull back monies paid within the stay period of 90 days of filing, and figure who should be paid and how much, what debts to reaffirm, what contracts to continue, and so forth. Any attempt to circumvent the stay order, imposing the "stay" or hold on transactions, is in essence ignoring a court order. The court has the power to assess with penalties akin to contempt. "Any attempt by the non-bankrupt party to unilaterally terminate a contract covered by the provision the bankruptcy code may expose such party to significant liability."[45] Classen proposes inclusion of the following language in an attempt to toll the operation of the bankruptcy laws: "All rights and licenses granted pursuant to any section of this Agreement are, and will otherwise be, for purposes of Section 365(n) of the U.S. Bankruptcy Code, licenses of rights to 'intellectual property,' as defined under Section 101(35A) of the U.S. Bankruptcy Code. The parties will retain and may fully exercise all of the respective rights and elections under the U.S. Bankruptcy Code."[46] It is typical for a license to allow either party to terminate upon the bankruptcy, insolvency, or receivership of the other. Some licenses allow the party in such a state of demise to terminate as well.

Another consideration occurs where the licensee has paid the subscription fee in advance. The licensor is now bankrupt and a refund is now sought. First, is a refund right articulated in the agreement? Some agreements are silent on the matter or offer a credit against future service, which in the case of bankruptcy is of little value. Second, where a refund is owed, as the bankruptcy laws suggest, even the best-worded refund provision is at the mercy of the bankruptcy laws. Moreover, the licensee is most likely an unsecured creditor, one of the lowest priorities in the bankruptcy scheme of debt. The articulation of bankruptcy or similar concept often bridges across several provisions in a license (termination, refund, etc.), so specific examples are not offered here but are discussed in the context of the several agreements exampled in Chapter 15.

BEST OR REASONABLE EFFORTS

Often licenses contains words or phrases modified by the word *reasonably*, such as "reasonably possible" or "reasonably defined geographic," or *reasonable*, as in "reasonable efforts." Another phrase that might be used is "best efforts." Some courts appear to use the terms interchangeably: "The requirement to employ reasonable efforts or 'best efforts', as it is generally expressed, in the performance of contractual obligations is deemed to be implicit in every agreement. However, to be enforceable, there must be objective criteria against which a party's efforts can be measured, whether the requirement is deemed to be implicit or explicit."[47] Other courts take a different view, with the concept of "reasonable efforts" thought to represent a somewhat lesser though implicit requirement that a party act reasonably under the situation, while the phrase "best efforts" represents a higher standard of behavior: "'Best efforts' has been found to require 'greater care and diligence than ordinary care and diligence.' It requires more than good faith, which is implied in all contracts and generally requires diligence and an elevated duty of good faith."[48]

Of course, this begs the question: if acting reasonably is implicit, an obligation upon all citizens, then why do some licenses include the phrase? "The parties can impose a true best efforts standard by contract if they choose to do so. If they do not, the licensee's obligation is to act fairly, but this does not require that it sacrifice itself for the benefit of its licensor."[49] Most courts do nonetheless see a distinction between the implicit concept of reasonableness in the performance of contractual obligations and those agreements which impose a higher best-effort standard—in other words, maybe it is reasonable that a party not be at its best in a given situation or circumstance. As explained by one commentator: "Best efforts" and "good faith" are closely aligned but are legally distinct concepts. A contract may include a specific "best efforts" clause, but "best efforts" may be implied as part of the good-faith obligation of a party to try to bring about the anticipated outcome of the contract. "While the phrase 'best efforts' is often used to describe the extent of the implied undertaking [of good faith] this has properly been termed an 'extravagant' phrase. A more accurate description of the obligation owed would be the exercise of 'due diligence' or 'reasonable efforts.'"[50] Another commentator cautions against the use of best efforts as a higher but dangerous standard: "The parties should avoid adopting a 'best efforts' standard unless it is clearly defined. By defining best efforts, the parties can ensure certainty in the interpretation of their contract. A potential definition might be: 'Reasonable diligence necessary to further the intentions of the parties hereunder.'"[51] Moreover, in the author's experience, the concept of reasonableness is far more often articulated. While uncommon in database license agreements, in other business-to-business contracts, the concept of "commercially reasonable efforts" is often found. "A common compromise is the use of a 'commercially reasonable efforts' standard. Again, the meaning of 'commercially reasonable' is ambiguous unless it is defined. General contract law, however, will impose a reasonableness standard unless it is explicitly disclaimed."[52] In any event, the concept of what is reasonable is based upon the circumstances and the position of the party upon whom the obligation is imposed.[53] Based on the discussion in Classen, the definition in a library or educational setting might be something along the following: "'Commercially Reasonable Efforts' means taking such steps and performing in such a manner as a well managed business or similarly institution of higher education would undertake where such business or institution was acting in a determined, prudent, and reasonable manner to achieve a particular desired result for its own benefit."[54] This obligation does not impose an impossible burden or contemplate that success in fulfilling the obligation will always be achieved, but it does impose a standard to do what is common, undertake available, and so on.

Of course, the parties may still debate what is reasonable. Having some sense of the possible and then assessing what is acceptable practice and documenting such efforts are crucial. A provision that authorized users comply with all use provisions of the agreement and that the licensee-institution must take reasonable steps to ensure this obligation might, when compared to other similar obligations of the licensee, signal a course of conduct. For example, institutions often fulfill obligations to ensure that users of its computing facilities not engage in infringing conduct under the copyright law or destroy all copies of the licensed content after the agreement terminates (a not uncommon provision in database licenses). Such institutions may use network monitoring or filtering mechanisms or may engage in information outreach or user awareness, such as sending reminders or updates to curtail infringement. To fulfill a similar obligation under a license agreement would suggest that similar undertakings should be made. What would be unreasonable is to expect the staff of the licensee to look over the shoulder of every authorized user to ensure compliance or to scrub the hard drives of every user. Though possible, these would be unreasonable efforts.

BIBLIOGRAPHIES, USE OF CONTENT IN COMPILATION OF

A license might restrict the use of content in what would otherwise not be a violation of copyright law. For example, simple factual description cannot be protected by copyright, such as a listing of someone's name, address, phone number, and so on.[55] The URL of a website or a citation is of similar nature. Oddly, the American Statistical Association and Institute of Mathematical Statistics prohibit the use of content to create certain bibliographies: "Bibliographies based on more that [sic] 250 records from the Database may not be distributed without the prior written consent of Licensors." It is argued that creating bibliographies and other access tools is not derivative. Further, a citation like an entry in a telephone white page directory is not protected by copyright. Bibliographies are nothing more than listings of other items, such as monographs, reports, serials, or other documents, arranged in some creative fashion. "Such a listing is in reality a compilation of publicly-available facts."[56] In theory, another researcher could extract a different set of articles into another bibliography, but not one consisting of more than 250 such items, but the license agreement restricts such uses.

BREACH

While parties may not desire to focus on the negative, defining the concept of breach is important. Often, termination, cure, and other rights are dependent upon whether the breach is material or not, with such rights triggered only if the breach is material. Having some idea of which terms are material and which terms are not is therefore useful. "The reason that a material breach is required lies in concepts about not allowing forfeiture of contractual benefits for minor flaws in performance. Especially in an ongoing relationship, minor problems are common should not be sufficient to end the relationship. For breaches that are not material, the injured party has a right to damages, but cannot cancel the contract unless specific contractual language clearly allows it to do so."[57] What sorts of terms, in the absence of specific identification in the agreement, could be considered material? The answer again relates to the underlying rationale for contract enforcement and the designs of the parties in so entering the contract: what is the underlying objective of the contract? Under New York law, for example, "a breach of a contract is material if it is so substantial as to defeat the purpose of the transaction or so severe as to justify the other party's suspension of performance."[58] There is of course a downside to articulating terms as material: if the conduct is not so listed, then conduct not included in the list cannot be deemed material.[59]

It is important for the prospective licensee to determine what rights under the contract are triggered when the breach is material and to consider what specific provisions should be identified as material or not in the agreement. "Materiality, thus, can hinge on both the cause and the effect of the breach. It involves the assumption that the allegedly injured party performed properly to enable the other's full performance."[60] If the parties cannot agree on what constitutes a material breach—for example, the licensee may consider the clause paramount, such as loss of certain content from the database—then there should at least be a requirement that notice of such loss be included in the agreement. (See Chapter 15 for examples of material breach provisions and a discussion of breach in the context of each specific agreement.)

CIRCUMVENTION

Circumvention of access controls on content protected by copyright in digital format is prohibited by section 1201.[61] The prohibition does not apply if the content is not protected by copyright. Some licenses also include such circumvention in a list of prohibited uses, potentially expanding the prohibition on circumvention to noncopyrighted content and making a violation rest in contract as opposed to quasi-copyright under section 1201. For example, the CQ Press agreement contains the following: "Accordingly, you shall not (a) circumvent or attempt to circumvent any security measure designed to control access to the Site or Services or in any way obtain or attempt to obtain unauthorized access to or use of any elements or portion of the Services." And in another provision, CQ Press alerts the licensee to the use of TPM (technological protection measures) and reminds users: "Any circumvention of such measures is strictly prohibited and subject to criminal prosecution as well as civil sanctions." Likewise, JSTOR licensees or users may not "attempt to override, circumvent, or disable any encryption features of software protections employed in JSTOR." JSTOR also prohibits systematic extraction through use of robots, spiders, scrapers, and so forth. Other licenses prohibit additional and related activities. From Johns Hopkins University Press, consider the following prohibition: users must not "burden server(s)with activities, such as computer programs, that automatically download content, commonly known as web robots, spiders, crawlers, wonderers, or accelerators." Project MUSE contains an identical prohibition. A recent criminal complaint alleged that a "major portion" (4.8 million articles) was downloaded by one JSTOR user.[62] Use of such "devices" might be considered circumventions, as some websites (e.g., ticket-ordering websites) have technological controls that attempt to ensure actual persons are ordering tickets and not a robot designed to constantly check and report ticket price and availability. Such circumvention of a website would likely also violate the federal computer crime statute.[63] For example, a prohibited use from Cambridge Journals Online: "Use this website in such a way that disrupts, interferes with or restricts the use of this website by other users." One alternative is to agree to such anticircumvention provisions but only if the circumvention would otherwise be a violation of section 1201 (the circumvention provision of the copyright law). This confines the rights of the licensor to those which would otherwise exist under the copyright law.

COMMERCIAL USE

This is often a common prohibition. Library-licensees generally are not interested in reselling content from databases. However, be careful that such prohibitions would not extend to downstream or one-step-removed commercial activity. For example, JSTOR prohibits "use of JSTOR for commercial purposes, including charging a fee-for-service for the use of JSTOR beyond reasonable printing or administrative costs." But what if the content is accessed by a faculty member who then prepares a book for publication or a seminar for presentation, services for which he or she will receive royalties or an honorarium? Is this allowed? The next sentence of the license attempts to clarify but helps little: "For purposes of clarification, 'commercial purposes or gains' shall not included research whose end-use is commercial in nature." One option is to allow for "incidental" commercial activity or to allow for "indirect financial gain." This might allow for the faculty scenario just described, as well as when there is an indirect financial gain, for example, when a patron pays a public library for guest status (so if the other provisions are done properly, the patron would be an "authorized user") as the library is the only one in the area that subscribes to a particular database, or specific exclusion from the prohibition as JSTOR does ("beyond reasonable printing or administrative costs").

CONFIDENTIAL INFORMATION OR NONDISCLOSURE

This definition focuses on gag-wrap and other restrictions on public comment or limitations on civil rights or rights in the nature of civil rights. While not as common in database license agreements, many service agreements for library automation software contain a confidentiality provision or gag order. It is typical that pricing information be subject to a nondisclosure or gag provision. Other agreements may treat the entire agreement as confidential (different from a proprietary right provision, which also contains a nondisclosure element). For example, the Springer license contains the following general prohibition: "Neither party shall disclose the terms and conditions or the subject matter of this Agreement including without limitation, the content of the attachments, fees, and any usage data compiled and supplied under Section 4.3, usage statistics or any other information about the other party's business to any third party (other than content suppliers in the case of usage data) without the prior written consent of the other." Consider the Google license: "You [the licensee] further acknowledge that the Services may contain information which designated confidential by Google and that you shall not disclose such information without Google's prior written consent." Often licensors have reason to keep fee information confidential, but it appears overkill to prohibit comment on other provisions. "Sweeping lists that include most or all business and/or technical information are often ineffective and counterproductive."[64]

As discussed in Chapter 4, some licenses contain provisions that prohibit public comment on the content of the database, how the database or service works, or the level of service provided in support of the license. Given the proper circumstances, some commentators believe that such restrictions would be against public policy or constitute copyright misuse.[65] Even Nimmer and Dodd suggest such terms might be questioned under a public policy analysis, giving the example of a so-called gag-wrap clause without so naming it as such: "Almost invariably, licensing terms survive fundamental public policy challenges, though, in some limited cases (e.g., *proposed restraint on free speech in a public forum*), incursion on other fundamental interests may rise to such a level that the contract terms must give way."[66] If there is sensitive information, such as pricing details, that the licensor does not want the licensee to share, then the information should be described with enough specificity so that the licensee may identify it and put measures in place to restrict its release. Some licenses are far too broad or leave the licensee to guess as to what might be so sensitive as to require silence.

One court has considered a license provision prohibiting the making of product reviews in the context of state fair trade laws: "Therefore, following respondent's instructions, after reading the license agreement and the Restrictive Clause, consumers may reasonably interpret that the rules and regulations enumerated in the Restrictive Clause exist independent of the license contract and are made and enforced by an entity other than the corporation itself. This language implies that limitations on the publication of reviews do not reflect the policy of Network Associates, but result from some binding law or other rules and regulations imposed by an entity other than Network Associates. Thus, the Attorney General has made a showing that the language at issue may be deceptive, and as such, the language is not merely unenforceable, but warrants an injunction and the imposition of civil sanctions."[67] Moreover, clauses that prohibit fair comment on how well the product works are overly harsh. "E-businesses realize that with a few mouse clicks, disgruntled e-consumers can broadcast their dissatisfactions to thousands of potential consumers."[68] While this might be true, what if the license contains a clause prohibiting product review or a more general clause that prohibits any conduct which might interfere with the ability of the licensor to exploit the contents of the database or software commercially? For example, the Nature (corporate) licensee may not "*undertake any activity* which may have a *damaging effect* on the Licensor's ability to *achieve revenue* through selling and marketing the Licensed Material." Making a truthful but nonetheless damaging comment on a library mailing list or blog about the glitches in a new circulation module or a software program, or about the poor customer or technical support associated with a database, can certainly harm the licensor's interest in this way.

Here again the impact of negotiated versus nonnegotiated contracts is apparent. "Contract terms that preclude comment about products and their performance are similar to terms that preclude disclosure of secrets, but are more likely to be challenged in the absence of any commercial purpose for the contract term other than to protect the reputation of the product. That being said, the better view is that, without more, a properly worded clause should be enforceable in the mass market if obtained pursuant to a reasonable commercial objective of the licensor, subject to ordinary contract law restrictions on unconscionability and the like."[69] Recent attempts at codifying the laws of information and software failed to offer any clarification. In the official comments to section 105 of UCITA, regarding fundamental public policy, is the observation that a "term that prohibits a person from criticizing the quality of software *may* raise public policy concerns if included in a shrink-wrap license for software in the mass market, [but] a similar provision included in an agreement between a developer and a company applicable to experimental or early version software not yet perfected for the marketplace would not raise similar concerns."[70] So, too, the official comments to UCITA section 111, Unconscionable Contract or Term—which for some sections go on for pages and pages—are rather brief, constituting little more than half a page and indicating little further guidance as to what might constitute an unconscionable contract or term in instances of computer information other than to note that section 2-302 of the UCC concept of unconscionability is adopted. Since there has been much case law on the concept of unconscionability, the official comment instructs that section 112, now requiring that parties be given an opportunity to review terms, "resolves many procedural issues preventing unfair surprise."[71] As Street and Grant observe: "There is a tendency by vendors and customers in drafting the scope of confidentiality clauses to use standardized form language for all transactions, and to overreach with numerous and sometimes inapplicable, particulars."[72] Such provisions may be specific or guised in general terms, or the licensee may not "undertake any activity which may have a damaging effect on the Licensor's ability to achieve revenue through selling and marketing the Licensed Material." One compromise regarding fair comment and product review is to strike such clauses that prohibit any comment whatsoever but to compromise; if comment is made public, the licensor must be given notice by the licensee of the comment and the forum where made, thus providing the licensor an opportunity to respond.

CONSIDERATION

Many agreements have language along the following lines: "In consideration of the mutual promises contained herein and other good and valuable consideration" (from the Greenwood Press agreement). This indicates that promises in addition to the monetary payment by the licensee (of the license fee) also are part of the consideration rendered for the license. Remember (from Chapter 1) that a contract can be formed where only promises are exchanged, as a promise for a promise constitutes sufficient consideration. Identical language is found in Springer: "In consideration of the mutual promises contained herein and other good and valuable consideration, the receipt and sufficiency of which are hereby acknowledged." This phrasing is an example of boilerplate language that is found in a range of license agreements, especially those involving intellectual property such as copyright.[73]

CONTENT LICENSED

Some licenses are incredibly vague as to the content licensed, and this may be especially true of database aggregators or if the database represents a family of titles or resources. For example, Westlaw Campus Research indicates that the subscription "consists of various West-owned and third party databases, services and functions (collectively 'Features')." Compare, for example, BioMed Central ("All articles published by BioMed Central on the Web Site"), Cambridge Journals

Online ("The full texts of journal articles (referred to below as 'the Materials') may be accessed"), Euclid Prime ("electronic database of the journal included in Euclid Prime"), and JSTOR ("Use of the JSTOR Archive"). The American Chemical Society license, for example, lists the specific titles and offers some indication of the sorts of content ("The entire contents of the ACS Web Editions, ACS Legacy Archives, Chemical & Engineering News Online, Reagent Chemical Online, and ACS Division Proceedings Online (hereinafter referred to as the 'ACS Products') including individual journals, articles, abstracts, book chapters, proceedings and other items within these materials"), and Ovid indicates the databases of "journals and/or books," "software," and "documentation" and then references specifics in various "schedules." MathSciNet's language is precise at first ("MathSciNet is the online version of the AMS publications *Mathematical Reviews*, from 1940 to present, and *Current Mathematical Publications*") but then follows up with this: "The AMS reserves the right to add or delete MathSciNet content at any time. While it might be unreasonable to expect an aggregator to maintain the same list of titles from year to year or to maintain the same range of years within a particular title, when the license content consists of one or a few titles, loss of a title or years within a title range may be significant. SPIE Digital Library also indicates the specific titles within the SPIE Digital Library and SPIE Online Journals are the electronic versions of the following publications published and copyrighted by SPIE"; it then lists the journals by name, for example, *Journal of Biomedical Optics*: "Subscription to SPIE Digital Library includes access to all of these titles." However, the next sentence indicates that the entire run may not be available or the range of years may change: "Access rights for a given subscription may be limited to a subset of the publications available online." Taylor and Francis Group references its list of titles in "Exhibit A and as may be added to the list of online publications from time to time and by amendment at a later date." Others make reference to what would be a definite list located elsewhere or as an attachment, for example, Accessible Archive ("The material that are the subject of the Agreement shall consist of electronic information published or otherwise made available by Licensor as described in Appendix A hereto") and CSA Illumina ("access and use the products listed on our approved Order Form, invoice or purchase"). Licensors use a variety of approaches, and problems can be found in each permutation.

It could be argued that in these singular or limited-title services, the loss of a title or years of a title is a material change and would or should, by the terms of the agreement, require notice and assent or at least a prorated return of the subscription fee. The terms can be structured so that reduction in terms of percentage of years actually offered compared to years available (offered versus not offered) is also equivalent to the reduction in subscription price. Consider ARTstor: "Should ARTstor permanently withdraw five percent or more of all ARTstor Content in the ARTstor Digital Library (excluding Local Content), ARTstor will provide Licensee with a pro rata reduction in the annual user fee for each subsequent year until ARTstor makes available an equivalent amount of ARTstor Content (whether of the same of different images) as that provided before the withdrawal of such ARTstor Content." Content may change, especially where the license agreement gives the licensor the right to do this. "You should consider a clause in your license to get out of the contract obligations or at least to obtain a reduction of license fees should the content not be available throughout the duration of the license."[74] Of course, one could argue that any reduction in titles should be offset by a reduction in price in the form of a credit or refund, but consider that turnabout is fair play. Does the licensee want to be contractually bound by the license to pay for a proportional increase every time titles and content are added?

Consider the Oxford English Dictionary (OED) license from Oxford University Press: "and as may be added to the roster of online publications from time to time and as more particularly set forth in Exhibit A to this agreement or as added by amendment at a later date." This language indicates that changes to the list of items may be added; it doesn't indicate that titles will be removed. Per the license used by Greenwood Press, the licensee understands that from time to time the licensed materials may be added to, modified, or deleted from by licensor and/or that portions of the licensed material may migrate to other formats. BioOne indicates the circumstances that will cause it to withdraw content and that notice will be given of such withdrawal: "BioOne reserves the right at any time to withdraw from the Licensed Material any item or part of an item for which it no longer retains the right to publish or which it has reasonable grounds to believe infringes copyright or is unlawful [e.g., defamatory]. BioOne shall give notice to the Licensee of such withdrawal." Springer uses almost identical language— "Springer reserves the right to withdraw from the Springer Content any item or part of an item to which it no longer retains the right to publish or it has reasonable grounds to believe infringes copyright or is otherwise unlawful"—but then adds, "If the withdrawal represents more than ten (10%) percent of the total Springer Content, Springer shall refund that portion of the license fee that is in proportion to the amount of Springer Content withdrawn and the remaining unexpired part of the term." As with downtime clauses, why set the trigger for refund or prorated addition to service at this amount? Why not compensate all losses of content or at least set the trigger at a lower percentage? CSA Illumina also anticipates giving notice of changes to the content through its mailing list service but only those which it deems are substantial: "ProQuest will announce any substantial additions, deletions or modifications of information, databases, materials, capabilities or service with the Products on its electronic mailing list service." As for CQ Press: "CQ Press may change, suspend, or discontinue any aspect of the Service at any time, including the availability of any Service Feature, database, or content."

There are two issues with these clauses. First, is the licensed content identified with sufficient detail? This is an obvious goal, but it may also be important if other clauses allow the licensor to add or delete content at any time or, in the alternative, if the loss of certain content triggers other rights or obligations, such as the right to terminate on the part of the licensee or an obligation on the part of the licensor to find reasonable replacement content. Again, if a termination right to a loss of agreed-upon content cannot be secured, then at least a notice right to that change coupled with an obligation to secure comparable replacement content should be included. A termination right might be more relevant where the list of titles is singular or small, rather than in the scenario of a database aggregator providing hundreds or thousands of title or files, or where the licensee seeks unique content; in other words, a substantial reason for choosing the particular vendor was a specific title or small cluster of titles. A reduction (refund) in subscription fees should also be considered where the change in content is significant (a qualitative measure) or substantial (a quantitative measure), correlating to the percentage loss of non-substituted titles/files. If the database in now 5 percent smaller in terms of titles or documents, why shouldn't the licensee receive a similar reduction in price? Yet if titles are added, the licensee might be expected to pay more in this scenario. If a refund is desired, it might be triggered only when some higher threshold of net change occurs.

Second, the licensee must understand that licensed content is not purchased content nor is title to the property itself obtained; in other words, the intellectual property right is not itself transferred (though a contract can be used to accomplish that too). An aggregator does possess the legal title or ownership in terms of the copyright law to content it aggregates and makes available in its license to the library. Licensors make clear that all ownership rights are retained by the licensors. Per Greenwood Press: "Greenwood and is licensors are the sole and exclusive owners of the Licensed Materials and retail title to and ownership of the copyrights, trademarks, trade secrets and other intellectual property rights vested in it." Such clauses go to the core difference between a license and a sale of content. The American Statistical Association and Institute of Mathematical Statistics: "All title and copyrights in and to the Database, the User Guide, and any copies of the Database are owned by Licensors." ProQuest extends this clause to documentation as well: "Except as expressly set forth in this Agreement, you do not acquire any intellectual property rights in the Products or any associated software, systems, documentation or other materials. All such rights and interests remain in ProQuest and its licensors." Likewise, the Cengage Learning agreement provides: "All content provided on this site is owned by or licensed to Cengage Learning and/or its affiliates . . . and protected by the United States and international copyright laws." CQ Press is more specific: "All content included on this Site, such as text, graphics, logos, button icons images, audio clips, digital downloads, data compilation, and software, the compilation of all content on this Site, and all software used on this Site are the property of CQ Press or its content suppliers and protected by the United States and international copyright laws."

COPYRIGHT: LIBRARY RIGHTS UNDER THE COPYRIGHT LAW (SECTIONS 108, 109, AND 110)

Contract law and not copyright law governs what uses may be made. It is typical to list those uses permitted and prohibited in a separate section, but at the outset, many agreements indicate that numerous uses which, depending on the context, might be fair use are prohibited. Greenwood Press: "Except as expressly set forth herein, no part of the Licensed Materials may be modified, copied or distributed in hardcopy or machine-readable form without prior written consent from Licensor." In one sentence, transformative fair uses are prohibited, along with other potential lawful uses under section 107 (fair use) or other provisions such as 112 (some reproductions known as ephemeral recordings), as well as public distribution rights under section 108 (library and archive reproduction and public distribution) or 109 (public distribution including circulation of content by libraries). At least EBSCOhost indicates that exceptions exist and these are listed in the agreement: "the Licensee and Sites may not reproduce, distribute, display, modify, transfer or transmit, in any form, or by any means, any Database or any portion thereof without the prior written consent of EBSCO, except as specifically authorized in this Agreement." The EBSCOhost agreement, touching on all five exclusive rights of the copyright owner save for the performance right (unless "transfer or transmit" includes performance?), pretty much takes away any privileges users would otherwise have under the copyright law. It also expands those rights to reach all distribution, all display, and, if performance is subsumed in "transfer or transmit," all performances, even private or personal ones, as the exclusive rights of the copyright owner apply to public distributions, public displays, and public performances alone. These sorts of prohibitions do not allow for incidental reproduction, distribution, display, modification, transfers, or transmission, beyond those "specifically authorized in this Agreement." In contrast, the Bibliography of Asian Studies Online recognizes fair uses, including a similar listing: "Recompiling, copyright, publication or republication of data beyond 'fair use,' in any form or medium whatsoever, may be done only with specific written permission from the AAS." An earlier sentence states the licensee is "allowed the 'fair use' of all information for non-commercial, education, instructional, and scientific purposes by authorized users." While use beyond those permitted would violate the terms of the agreement, such use would not necessarily be a violation of copyright; as suggested, such uses might otherwise be fair or privileged by some other provision of the copyright law. In light of this, it is rather an odd statement and an untruth that the

American Society of Civil Engineers includes: "Unauthorized copyright or redistribution of any ASCE Journal content is a violation of copyright laws." Redistributing a fair-use portion of an ASCE journal article is not infringing, so any remedy pursued by the licensor would rest in contract law alone, that is, for breach of a covenant not to make further distributions of the ASCE content. While parties to a license agreement might agree that certain conduct is impermissible, it is quite another to agree by contract that the conduct is unlawful under some noncontract regime.

There may be provisions that restrict use rights which the copyright law otherwise grants to users or institutions. As mentioned, it is important that a license not restrict these rights. Again, the fact that the content obtained by the library is licensed and not purchased impacts section 109 rights, but it need not impact the other rights. As it can be argued, the public distribution of content under this section is dependent upon the library owning a copy. There are two approaches to respond to ensure such rights are retained. First, include a general provision that grants all the rights users have under the copyright law (statutes and interpreting case law) at the time a use is made of the content. The other is to cherry-pick from among the rights, including each right in a separate provision. This can be accomplished in one of two ways. Either describe the right, for example, interlibrary loan, e-ILL, international library loan (i-ILL), and so forth, or include a provision that allows for use consistent with the copyright law (statutes and interpreting case law) at the time a use is made of the content, for example, any public distribution lawful under the copyright law.

The idea behind this entry is to remind the licensee that users of content protected by copyright law have significant rights under the law, such as fair use, right of reproduction and public distribution under section 108, rights of public distribution and display under section 109, right of public performance and display under section 110, right of reproduction under section 112 in conjunction with distance education under subsection (2) of section 110, and right to reproduce software under section 117. Any license should offer at least those rights and not take away any such rights. This requires knowing a bit of copyright law, but such intersections between copyright use rights and license restrictions have been pointed out throughout this text and are not repeated here; see Table 14.1 for examples of the effect of different license terms on copyright use rights. The point is that you should not contract away your fair use and other use rights. These have been "negotiated" in a sense for you already, through our public processes of lawmaking—through Congress when it created section 107 and other provisions—and modified each time a court decision in your jurisdiction, for example, interprets fair use provisions.

COURSE PACKS

Delineating whether licensed content can be used in course packs, anthologies, or similar readers, whether in print, included in digital physical form (CD-ROM), or

▶ **TABLE 14.1** Copyright Use Rights and License Terms

Copyright Provision and Rights Granted (See Statute for Additional Conditions)	Example of Right	Example of Restricting or Enabling Provision	Comment
17 U.S.C. § 108: Right to reproduce and distribute unpublished works, right to reproduce and distribute published works, right to reproduce and distribute for patrons	§ 108(d): The rights of reproduction and distribution under this section apply to a copy, made from the collection of a library or archives where the user makes his or her request or from that of another library or archives, of no more than one article or other contribution to a copyrighted collection or periodical issue, or to a copy or phonorecord of a small part of any other copyrighted work.	BioOne: Provide single printed or electronic copies of single articles at the request of individual authorized users. Provide interlibrary loans.	The first sentence allows for copying for patrons upon request similar to §108(d), as long as the patron is an "authorized user." There is no restriction or other condition on interlibrary loan, and as that concept is understood in libraries the content could be used to fill a request from a patron at another library who is not an authorized user.
17 U.S.C. § 109: Right to make public distributions and public displays of works	Notwithstanding the provisions of § 106(3), the owner of a particular copy or phonorecord lawfully made under this title, or any person authorized by such owner, is entitled, without the authority of the copyright owner, to sell or otherwise dispose of the possession of that copy or phonorecord (17 U.S.C. § 109(a)).	Nature (Academic: Americas): Title to, and ownership of, the licensed material (including any copies made by or on behalf of the licensee including by the authorized users) is not transferred to the licensee and remains vested in the licensor.	The right to make a public distribution of works under § 109 requires that the distributor be the owner of a particular copy of phonorecord. Because the license indicates that title or ownership is not a part of the licensing transaction, first-sale rights could not be exercised by the licensee or any downstream or subsequent possessor of the content.

(continued)

▶ **TABLE 14.1**   Copyright Use Rights and License Terms *(Continued)*

Copyright Provision and Rights Granted (See Statute for Additional Conditions)	Example of Right	Example of Restricting or Enabling Provision	Comment
17 U.S.C. § 110: Right to make public displays and public performances in the classroom, right to make noncommercial public displays and public performances of nondramatic musical and nondramatic literary, right to make temporary copies to facilitate use of works in distance-education classrooms	For purposes of paragraph (2), no governmental body or accredited nonprofit educational institution shall be liable for infringement by reason of the transient or temporary storage of material carried out through the automatic technical process of a digital transmission of the performance or display of that material as authorized under paragraph (2).	BioOne: Make temporary (less than 24 hours) local electronic copies by means of caching of all or part of the licensed material as is necessary to ensure efficient use by authorized users, provided that such use is subject to all the terms and conditions of this agreement and does not result in the making available to authorized users of duplicate copies of the licensed material.	§ 110 allows for caching or cache copies of works to be made in conjunction with a qualifying transmission, a public display, or a public performance in a distance-education classroom. The statute uses the word *temporary*, whereas the license requires the cache be kept for no more than 24 hours. However, the legislative history of the subsection suggests storage of a short-term and incidental nature. See, e.g., Conference Report, H. Rpt. No. 107–685, 107th Cong., 2d Sess. 233 (2002): "Organizations providing digital distance education will, in many cases, provide material from source servers that create additional temporary or transient copes or phonorecords of the material in storage known as 'caches' in other servers in order to facilitate the transmission . . . In addition, transient or temporary copies or phonorecords may occur in the transmission stream, or in the computer of the recipient of the transmission."

online, is an example of where a license can resolve the uncertain legality of certain practices under the copyright law. Course packs could be specifically prohibited or allowed by a license, or they may be prohibited implicitly. Consider the following sentence from the Greenwood Press license: "To request permission to make multiple copies of limited portions of the Licensed Materials for classroom or other use, contact permissions@greenwood.com." Since course packs by design involve multiple copies of content, such construction would be prohibited.

The American Chemical Society allows for course packs but only as linked entries: "Authorized Users may include (and are encouraged to provide) links to the ACS Product as part of a course pack offerings, or within an e-mail communication."

The American Society of Civil Engineers allows "Faculty at the Subscriber's institution [to] include articles from the Licensed Materials in anthologies (coursepacks) in print or digital form for distribution to Authorized Users for their use in connections with classroom instruction or in reserves (print or digital) set up by the subscribing institution for access by Authorized Users in connection with specific courses." WilsonSelect is the simplest: "Use the Subject Database to create course packs provided that the material is removed at the end of the semester." There are, however, limits to the scope of reproduction such provisions allow: In *Blackwell Publishing, Inc. v. Excel Research Group, Inc.*, the license agreement did not allow students to copy course pack masters at an off-site copy shop: "That license [governing four of thirty-three works], agreement between the University of Michigan and Elsevier, permits students to 'print' and 'download' material...does not allow students to copy and pay for material at an offsite copy shop."[75]

While not specifically referencing course packs, the BioOne license lists as one of several prohibited uses "systematically mak[ing] print or electronic copies of multiple extracts," which would seem to apply to the creation of course packs. (BioOne does, however, allow the licensee to "[i]ncorporate parts of the Licensed Material in Electronic Reserves for the use of Authorized Users in the course of instruction.") This would also appear to be the result under the Cambridge Journals Online license that prohibits "systematic copying or downloading of the Materials." Likewise, in the OED license, "You may not... [s]ystematically make printed or electronic copies of multiple extracts of the Licensed Works for any purpose." Are the practices of the reserve librarians or staff who cull the databases for reserve reading a systematic process? Are such processes written down so student workers know what to check first, next, and so on? If so, the argument could be made that repeated downloading or printing in this fashion is systematic. Using similar language, EBSCOhost would appear to prohibit course packs as well: "Downloading all or parts of the Database in a systematic or regular manner so as to create a collection of materials comprising all or part of the database is strictly prohibited whether or not such collection is in electronic or print form." If the intent is to prevent creating a companion or mirror in-house database, this language appears to sweep more broadly than is necessary, as even a use of a "part" is not allowed. It could be argued that accessing the database repeatedly in order to populate a series of e-course packs or an e-reserve system would be "systematic." JSTOR clearly prohibits use of content in course packs and reserves: "Institutions and users may not...reproduce or distribute Content in bulk in any form, such as by including Content in course packs, electronic reserves, or organizational intranets (but see Section 2.3 below)." Euclid Prime prohibits downloading as well but of the "entire database for any purpose." The point is that the library should consider what collating and incorporation rights it desires and review the permitted and prohibited use provisions to ensure that such uses are included and there is not potential to claim that such uses are excluded.

CREDIT

Oftentimes licenses will offer a credit if the database maintenance or downtime reaches some articulated threshold. The parameters of the threshold should of course be first identified and evaluated. However, the concept of credit can raise additional issues. Is a credit (or refund) if owed a dischargeable debt for purposes of bankruptcy law? (See discussion of these issues in Chapter 16.) While bankruptcy seldom occurs among vendors, it is more likely that a credit may raise issues of timing for the agreement, whereby the credit extends the period of the agreement beyond the initial subscription period, as opposed to an applicable reduction in the price of the renewal. Thus, credits can come in two forms in licenses: either a credit in time, in which the duration of the current subscription period is extended, or a credit in dollars that can be applied against the next subscription period (renewal). If the credit results in an extension of the current subscription, the renewal date shifts. This extension can have a domino effect. As the period within which notice of nonrenewal must be given, the time within which the renewal fee must then be paid is now also pushed out on the calendar. Further, the credit or refund threshold might be triggered only after some significant period of downtime within a time frame stated in terms of hours, days, and so forth.

It is common for some threshold to be reached before a credit or refund is made. For example, Street and Grant observe: "In the event the customer is down more than a certain number of times per month the entire month may be credited."[76] The author does not agree with the use of thresholds before a credit or refund is due. Why should the licensee pay for any service it did not receive? Any downtime (including maintenance, unless already factored into the subscription price) should be tracked, aggregated, and an appropriate refund—in preference to the complications that can arise with credits, as mentioned—rendered. If a credit is given, it should be usable against the next renewal period rather than extend the current term. A threshold of downtime or maintenance should be articulated but not a trigger for refund or credit, rather as a trigger for material breach for which termination is possible.

CURE, RIGHT TO

If a breach is material, the nonbreaching party may have the right to terminate the license. However, should things go awry, both parties should be aware that it is common for a cure right to exist, or a right to cure the breach is often given to the party in breach. The time within which the breach must be fixed or cured is usually 30 days. This may mean that the library has to give the licensor 30 days after receipt of notice to fix the problem; for example, the licensor has exceeded the limit on downtime for the measuring period but must allow another 30 days for the system to come back. Licensees should be wary of excessively long periods for cure, for example, 60 or 90 days. Of course, the street goes both ways: if the licensor thinks that a prohibited use has been undertaken by authorized users or that some use was made by nonauthorized users, the licensor would not have the right to terminate but would be required to give the library the chance to remedy the problem, in other words, to remind users again of terms of use or to effect additional security measures. For example, the SPIE Digital Library license provides that "SPIE, however, will not be liable for any delay, downtime . . . or other failure of performance. SPEI and/or its agents will use commercially reasonable efforts to correct any material performance problem brought to its attention and may suspend performance pending such correction."

Cure and termination is another area where often one-sided, stacked, or at least uneven rights are found, with far more flexibility on the right of the licensor to either cure or terminate or both. Consider the Greenwood Press provision on early termination: "In the event that either party believes that the other materially has breached any obligations under this Agreement, or if Licensor believes that Licensee has exceeded the scope of the License, such party shall so notify the breaching party in writing. The breaching party shall have 30 days from the receipt of notice to cure the alleged breach and to notify the non-breaching party in writing that cure has been effected. If the breach is not cured within the 30 days, the non-breaching party shall have the right to terminate the Agreement without further notice. Upon Termination of this Agreement for cause online access to the Licensed Materials by Licensee and Authorized Users shall be terminated. In the event of early termination permitted by this Agreement, Licensee shall be entitled to a refund of any fees or pro-rata portion thereof paid by Licensee for any remaining period of the Agreement from the date of termination, offset by the amount of any damages incurred by Licensor as a result of a breach by Licensee, if any." This is typical language. The Accessible Archive uses an identical provision on early termination. Notice, first, that if a party is in material breach, the other party must notify ("shall so notify") the party in breach. This notice will then trigger cure rights. Such breach must be material to trigger the notice and cure provision. However, the licensor can trigger this sequence at any time ("or if") the "Licensor believes that Licensee has exceeded the scope of the License." Once the cure right is activated by proper notice ("in writing"), the nonbreaching party must wait 30 days for the other to cure. As a result, the licensor could terminate without notice if it thought use exceeded the scope of the permitted uses or constituted a prohibited use, gave notice of such, waited 30 days without response, or perhaps even disagreed with the response (i.e., believed it was not a satisfactory cure). As discussed elsewhere, notice should also be defined in the license (i.e., when is notice, in this case notice of a material breach, effective?); otherwise, the breaching party may argue it did not realize there was a problem. Defining when notice is received establishes the date from which the cure period begins.

The party in breach must notify the other party of the occurrence of the cure. If cure does not occur, then the nonbreaching party may terminate immediately. The question the license does not address is what happens when the party in breach sends notice that is has effected a cure but the other party disagrees with the success of the cure. It might be best to define cure or use language—for example: "Breaching party shall notify the nonbreaching party in writing that cure has been effected. If the nonbreaching party disagrees that cure has been effected, then it shall notify the party in breach that further response upon a mutually agreed-upon course of action is required"—so that there is an obligation to agree upon what is a reasonable cure attempt before termination can occur. Should termination occur, the Greenwood Press agreement allows for a prorated refund, less damages incurred by the licensor. It might be best to have the prorated amount be mutually determined as well, requiring the licensor to demonstrate "damage" if claiming a reduction in the prorated amount, for example.

EBSCOhost foresees the problem of adequate response and documentation, but oddly its termination provision assumes that only the licensee would be in breach ("Licensee shall have the right to remedy... If the Licensee fails to remedy such a breach... If EBSCO becomes aware of a material breach of Licensee's obligations..."): "Within the period of such notice Licensee will make every reasonable effort and document said effort to remedy such breach and shall institute any reasonable procedures to prevent future occurrences of such breaches." EBSCOhost also reserves "the right to temporarily suspend the Licensee's access to the Product(s)" during the period of cure (30 days), and if cure occurs ("the breach of infringement has been remedied or the offending activity halted"), EBSCO shall "reinstate access to the Databases." If cure does not result within 30 days, EBSCO may terminate upon "written notice to the Licensee." Likewise, Lexis "may suspend or discontinue providing the Online Services to you without notice and pursue any other remedy legally available to it if you fail to comply with any of your obligations hereunder." Cure can be useful to the licensee as well. If suspension of service is a right granted the licensor when it suspects that, for example, authorized users like library patrons are not using the licensed content properly, where the agreement is not terminated (and refund might be possible, though many agreements deny refund where termination is for cause) but access to the service is suspended, then turnabout is indeed fair play. The licensee should have the right to cure with the attendant right to be notified of a perceived breach, which then triggers a right to cure within some reasonable time period, two weeks, for example. Otherwise, the library might be paying for something it does not receive.

CURRENCY

This might be obvious, but some other countries around the world use dollars as their currency units. Depending on where the licensor is located, the price quoted might be in terms of U.S. or Canadian or Australian dollars. Fluctuations in international currencies may matter when negotiating licenses with vendors in other countries.

CUSTOMER SUPPORT

Many agreements include a provision of support, often expressed in terms of reasonable availability. Of course, what the licensee library believes is reasonable (24/7 support) may differ from what the licensor believes is reasonable (9 a.m. to 5 p.m. Eastern Standard Time). This can mean that to a library in California most afternoon help is not available, as 2 to 5 p.m. at the Pasadena Public Library is 5 to 8 p.m. in New York or New Jersey, where the licensor may be located. Even if calls are handled offshore in India, the range of hours may still be cued to East Coast time. For example, the American Mathematical Society is based on the East Coast: "In addition, the AMS will provide the subscriber with email and/or telephone support service during AMS's normal business hours (Monday–Friday, 9:00 a.m. to 4:00 p.m., ET)." The American Meteorological Society has a similar statement but excludes holidays; support is offered through e-mail alone, and there is no indication of the time frame within which an e-mail response will be made to the licensee: "Technical assistance solely related to the online technical aspects of the AMS journals database can be obtained by sending e-mail to amsejt@amestoc.org or, Monday through Friday excluding holidays, from 9:00 A.M. to 4:30 P.M. ET, by calling 617-227-2426 ext. 303." What is expected should be articulated as to scope (technical support, search or query formulation, etc.) and mode (phone, e-mail, etc.). The format (e-mail, phone, etc.) and availability in time (East Coast versus West Coast time zones) and day of service should be articulated. Consider the Accessible Archive: "Licensor will offer reasonable levels of continuing support to assist Licensee in use of the Licensed Materials." Alexander Street Press (ASP) provides that "ASP will offer reasonable levels of continuing support via email, phone or fax, during normal business hours for feedback, problem-solving, or general questions. Any technical assistance that ASP may provide to the Customer is provided at the sole risk of the Customer."

Use of general phrasing may do more harm than good, raising expectations without foundation. For example, to indicate that "information technology support and maintenance services" will include or means "the support and maintenance services provided by Vendor to Customer in order to maintain the System," according to Classen, "is so broad that it is essentially meaningless. The parties should specifically set forth in detail the specific services to be provided and the time in which they will be provided."[77] In a related thought and more relevant to licenses for software systems, such as library automation, it is conceivable to request the vendor warrant that it has "not received a systematic number of customer complaints related to the product in question or one aspect of the product in question."[78] It is not unheard of to have a dispute over adequate levels of customer support.[79] In library automation or other software environments, this service is more critical.

DAMAGES

See also REMEDIES OTHER THAN DAMAGES

It is typical to limit monetary damages to the amount of the subscription price. From ARTstor: "Except as set forth in section 12.4, in no event shall ARTstor's liability exceed the fees paid to ARTstor by Licensee." The American Statistical Association and Institute of Mathematical Statistics, after disclaiming a similar range of damages, state: "In no event will licensor's liability exceed the amount paid by you for access to the database." This is a common strategy, done, depending on the license fee, to dissuade a licensee from pursuing legal remedy. The damages that are available are often limited to the price of the product or service, or the current subscription. For example, per the American Physical Society Online (in capitals): In no event shall the total aggregate liability of APS... exceed the total amount paid by institutional subscriber during the current subscription year in which such claims, loss or damage occurred." Ovid contains similar language: "Subscriber agrees that the entire liability of OVID... will in no event exceed an amount equal to the fee paid for the use of the product." The Oxford University Press (OUP) license goes the other way, limiting the damages to the equivalent of three months' worth of subscription fees: "In the event that OUP is deemed liable in any manner, then such liability... shall, in no event, exceed the amount you have paid for your use of the licensed works during the preceding three (3) month period." Bowker's Books in Print: "Subscriber agrees that the liability of Bowker... shall not exceed the amount subscriber paid to Bowker for the use of the Products in the twelve

(12) months immediately preceding the event giving rise to such claim." The Springer license contains a similar limit tied to the preceding year ("shall be limited to the aggregate amount of charges and fees paid by Licensee in the twelve (12) month period preceding the event giving rise to such claim"), as does UlrichsWeb ("shall not exceed the amount subscriber paid to ProQuest for the use of the products in the 12 months immediately preceding the event giving rise to such claim").

Another aspect is a disclaimer of specific types of damages. (Damages were discussed in Chapter 3.) Per the American Society of Civil Engineers: "ASCE shall not be liable for: exemplary, special, indirect incidental, consequential or other damage, arising out of or in connection with the subscription or licenses granted hereunder." CQ Press: "You expressly understand and agree that CQ Press shall not be liable for any direct, indirect, incidental, special, punitive, consequential or exemplary damages arising out of or in any way related to this agreement or the use of any or all of the services." Wharton Research Data Services (WRDS) goes one further, adding the intangible concept of goodwill: "Neither WRDS nor any of its third-party suppliers will be liable for: (I) special, punitive, indirect, incidental, exemplary or consequential damages or loss of data, lost profits, loss of good will in any way arising from or relating to this agreement or the service." Similar intangible elements are found in the Taylor and Francis Group license: "Taylor and Francis group will not in any way be liable . . . for any damages (whether direct or indirect, or consequential, punitive, special or exemplary, including but not limited to, loss of profits, loss of good will, loss of reputation and for any other type of special indirect, incidental or consequential loss or damage) resulting there from." Access NewspaperARCHIVE contains a broader statement of damage disclaimer: "In no case will we or our third party providers be liable for any direct, indirect, punitive, special or other damages including without limitation, lost or delay of use, lost profits, loss of data or any other damage in contract, tort, equity or any other legal theory, even if advised of the possibility thereof." At most, licensors will limit the damages (limitation of liability) to actual direct damages and disclaim all speculative or third-party damages. Licenses can also exclude certain harms from the limitation on liability, such as personal bodily harm, personal property damages, gross negligence, or intentional torts. Most licenses will disclaim liability for most damages, limiting recovery to an amount equal to the subscription fee (*see also* WARRANTIES AND DISCLAIMERS). Finally, as contract law is state law, some states may not allow the disclaimer of certain categories of damages. See Chapter 15 for examples.

DAYS: BUSINESS, CALENDAR, OR OTHERWISE

Does the licensee refer to a length of time in various provisions, such as the duration of the cure right, the time period within which an event must occur or is deemed to occur (e.g., notice is effective within ten days of posting)? If so, is the time measured in calendar days, weekdays, or business days? The difference may be significant. Even if a business day is used to define tolling periods, to whose business day does the provision refer? Different entities may have different calendaring of holidays, keeping in mind the academic calendar might be different from the state or federal government calendar or the banking calendar. Classen offers the following suggested phrasing that the author adapts to an academic calendar: "'Business Day' means any weekday other than a day designated as a holiday under the then applicable academic calendar of the licensee. Any reference herein to 'day' that is not specifically referenced as 'Business Day' means a calendar day."[80]

DEFINITIONS

When in doubt, ask. When afraid to ask, define. Good contract drafting is good anticipation. Define as many terms as possible; at the very least, define those terms and concepts, and the provisions which relate to each, that are critical to the licensee. Define as many terms as possible in one main section rather than as the terms arise.[81] Harris recommends defining at least the following terms: authorized uses, authorized users, commercial use, content, interlibrary loan, licensed content, premises, and territory.[82] When in doubt, ask, and have it explained and defined and placed into the agreement. Other provisions such as prohibited and permitted uses may sound like definitions, but if additional terms are defined, it might be useful to have them collected in one location in the agreement. Two common problems are missing terms or terms that when applied in the context of other provisions make little sense or cause more confusion.[83] Minor changes can have great impact, as in the definition of authorized users, for example, or the scope of the content. It is a good idea to define authorized users with the same definition in your access policy. This avoids having to keep track of two sets of users, users as defined by library policy and users as defined by the license agreement, or, worse, multiple concepts if the definitions of user vary across license agreements. While aligning definition of authorized library user with authorized license user may make some content providers nervous that anyone in the world could use the licensed content, most libraries do not operate this way. Services such as registration and circulation privileges attend to a well-defined, albeit changing, population, such as all students enrolled in a class in a given semester or persons living in the geographical boundaries of the municipality. The point is that the license should allow for the folks a library normally would consider patrons to have complete access to the licensed content, no more and no less.

While most licenses are for content, a service agreement, for library automation software, should pay particular attention to how satisfactory function is articulated. Libraries can take a hard lesson from the business world. Review any satisfaction or "specification" clauses in library automation software agreements to ensure that a successful and functional deliverable meets the library's needs: When does the agreement indicate the installation and operation of the software is satisfactory such that the future interaction between the licensor's technical staff would be for regular technical support or for upgrades, if the contract specifies or the libraries agrees to acquire such additionally? The "installation period" is typically one of intense training and or service provided by the licensor and typically does not continue throughout the duration of the license—thus the licensor's use of such provisions.

For a service, it is common to have an "acceptance test specification" definition that indicates what constitutes the completion of a successful test period. "From the client viewpoint, final acceptance testing is best executed online on the host server. While individual components may operate satisfactorily, the only true test is to operate the completed website in the computing environment for which it was designed."[84] The same could be said of any service the library contracts. Often there may be a test period by the licensor/developer with licensor data/conditions, then a second test by the licensee with licensor/developer data/conditions, and finally a live test by the licensee with licensee data/conditions. "Some contracts provide that the warranty period commences upon successful live testing."[85] Is the testing or installation definition adequate in terms of duration? How is the period defined, in terms of days or occurrence of an event, and scope (training and other support)? These are questions to consider.

DERIVATIVE USES

The right to prepare a derivative work[86] of a work protected by copyright is an exclusive right of the copyright owner under section 106. However, derivative uses are also subject to fair use. Some agreements may try to take away those fair-use rights, restricting all derivative uses of the licensed content. (Recall the discussion of Creative Commons licenses in Chapter 9: an option for a licensor is to prohibit all derivative uses.) Mergent allows the "Customer may use, access, copy, store display and create derivative works of (collectively "Use") the Data for its internal business purposes." In contrast, Bowker's Books in Print prohibits "use of the Content or the Products to create derivative or competitive works." The prohibition on commercial use is understandable to an extent. However, most of the fair-use case law is populated by scenarios of commercial use that is nonetheless found to be fair. It might be difficult to conceive of a derivative use of the entire listings of Books in Print. Conceivably, a library might want to make its own internal database of the listings, and this might be a derivative work. The Brepolis license anticipates and prohibits such uses: "Furthermore, neither the Licensee nor the Users are entitled to rearrange the Database or to set up derived Databases." Gale also prohibits the making of derivatives: "you may not . . . create derivative works base on, or in any other way exploit any of the Content." The phrasing "or in any other way exploit" implies that all derivative uses are exploitative, which is simply not true, and, moreover, they would be subject to fair use in the absence of the license. One example of a derivative work that might arise in an academic setting would be a translation from one language into another. If such a prohibition applied, then students, for example, could not translate an article's sources from the licensed content as part of an assignment in a foreign language class.

DISCLAIMERS

The UCC § 2-316(2) requires that any contractual warranty disclaimer related to merchantability mention the word "merchantability" and, if in writing, be conspicuous (e.g., the provisions are generally in capital script).[87] The concept of merchantability relates to common understandings of the salable quality product or service, not its perfection. "Merchantability warranties, when not disclaimed, do not give assurance that the particular product will be ideal, perfect or even optimal for particular uses, but merely that the product or program quality falls within general standards of fitness for ordinary purposes under the product description. Since the reference point is an ordinary program or product of similar type, there will ordinarily be an expectation that aspects of a program or system contain at least minor performance problems or 'bugs.' Merchantability does not assure a perfect product, but only one of ordinary quality purpose."[88] Disclaimers in license agreements are enforceable.[89]

As licensing developed in the age of software, which by design is imperfect and contains bug software, licensors got in the habit of disclaiming all sorts of warranties related to product code errors and the like. In a similar fashion, content providers realize that text, whether an article or table of statistics, might contain typos and spelling and other errors. As a result, vendors of these products disclaim those warranties. Various sorts of disclaimers may be present: accuracy or completeness where the licensed content is made available "as is,"[90] merchantability,[91] and fitness for a particular purpose.[92] "It appears, then, that the warranty of merchantability warrants that the goods sold are of average quality within the industry, whereas a warranty of fitness for a particular purpose warrants that the goods sold are fit for the purposes for which they are intended. The latter is also further qualified by the requirement that the seller must know, at the time of sale, the particular purpose for which the goods are required and also that the buyer is relying on the seller to select or furnish suitable goods."[93] In addition, Harris observes that "[m]any public institutions in the United States may not accept certain limitations of liability in the indemnity, and you may need to check your institution's position on this."[94] Being asked to waive warranty rights is significant. As a result, contract law requires that such statements be in bold or capital letters to call the licensee's attention to the disclaimers or limitation on what would otherwise be some warranty in the product. Warranties can be express, stated in specific terms of what the product or service can provide, or they may be implied from the product or service itself. Most licenses disclaim all such warranties. In content license agreements, it is typical to make no promise as to the accuracy of the content. Greenwood Press license: "NO REPRESENTATION OR WARRANTY, EXPRESS OR IMPLIED, THAT THE INFORMATION CONTAINED IN THE LICENSED MATERIALS IS COMPLETE OR FREE FROM ERROR, AND EXPRESSLY DISCLAIM ANY LIABILITY TO ANY PERSON FOR LOSS OR DAMAGE CAUSED BY ERRORS OR OMISSIONS, WHETHER THE RESULT OF NEGLIGENCE, ACCIDENT OR ANY OTHER CAUSE."

One way that some licensors accomplish the no-warranty concept regarding the content of the product and any errors or defects is to include the words "as is," in that the licensor makes no warranties or representations about anything in the product or service. The licensor may describe what is in the database, as it would be an odd way to do business if no information was forthcoming, but the licensor does not want any legal liability with respect to those representations. Consider the Access NewspaperARCHIVE: "Heritage Microfilm, Inc. and its third party suppliers provide all Content in this Service 'AS IS,' and without any warranty of any kind." The Accessible Archive also includes an "as is" clause but adds a very specific limitation: "makes no warranties respecting any harm that may be caused by the transmission of a computer virus, worm, time bomb, logic bomb, or other such computer program." Cambridge Journals Online, in addition to "as is," uses an "as available" phrase as well: "Owing to the nature of the Internet we cannot guarantee that this website or the websites to which it is linked will always be available to users." Cengage Learning, CQ Press, CSA Illumina, Wharton Research Data Services (WRDS), and ProQuest also use both "as is" and "as available." The American Mathematical Society "will make good faith efforts to ensure that AMS distributed electronic journals are complete and accurate. However, the AMS does not warrant completeness or accuracy, and does not warrant that the subscriber's use of the electronic journals will be uninterrupted or error-free."

Alexander Street Press (ASP) warrants that it has the right to offer the product but only in so far "as is," with the warranty ("as is") being "in lieu of any and all other warranties, written or oral, express or implied, including without limitation, warranties of merchantability of fitness for a particular purpose, all of which ASP disclaims."

Oral warranties were disclaimed as well. An oral warranty might arise in a common library undertaking, for example, conversations with a vendor at a convention or otherwise. Sales reps have likely been cautioned by their own management or legal counsel to make careful, truthful statements. Just in case something false slips out, this clause indicates that any such statement, which would otherwise be an enforceable representation under basic contract law, is not under this agreement.

The Ovid license makes clear that "No OVID employee or agent is authorized to make any statement that adds to or amends the warranties or limitation contained in this agreement." While disclaimers are generally not avoidable in licenses, understanding the legal significance of such disclaimers is important.

DOWNTIME AND MAINTENANCE

Many licenses indicate that a certain amount of downtime or loss of service is acceptable. These clauses are often stated as a part of the licensor obligations to use reasonable effort to provide continuous services and, short of a force majeure, recognize that unforeseen events occur and this should be expected. It is common to see the acceptable limits stated in hours per month or hours of continuous inaccessibility. Assessing these terms requires the library to ask itself, "What amount of nonservice can we live with?" Greenwood Press: "Licensor shall use reasonable efforts to provide continuous service seven (7) days a week with an average of 98% up time per month. The 2% downtime includes scheduled maintenance and repair. Scheduled downtime will be performed at a time to minimize inconvenience to Authorized Users." So downtime is expected and can constitute up to 2 percent of service time. True, nothing is perfect, but the question is whether such "acceptable" (under the license) downtime is reflected or at least assessed by the library in the context of the subscription price? A similar promise is found in the Euclid Prime license indicating that Duke University Press "shall use all reasonable endeavors to make access available on 24-hour basis. But if access is suspended or interrupted or a defect occurs that prevents access, Project Euclid's liability shall be limited to using all reasonable efforts to restore access as soon as is practicable." Are "all reasonable endeavors" the same as "all reasonable efforts"? The American Statistical Association and Institute of Mathematical Statistics reflect this acceptable downtime concept: "Licensors cannot guarantee uninterrupted access to the Database. Licensors will make reasonable efforts to maintain continuity of service but Licensors shall not be responsible for interruptions or curtailments of access to the Database for interruptions in service, power outages, network problems, service or maintenance problems or issues, or any cause beyond the reasonable control of Licensors." Alexander Street Press (ASP) uses a different measure; instead of percent, days are used, and instead of downtime, the provision indicates a promise to have the service available a certain amount of time per month: "ASP will use reasonable efforts to provide continuous service with an average of 28 days of up-time per month and will attempt to perform scheduled downtime at low-usage times." Other vendors can be far less precise: "ACS [American Chemical Society] shall use reasonable commercial efforts to provide continuous availability of the licensed material through the Internet." The American Society of Civil Engineers "will not be liable for any delay, downtime, transmission error, software or equipment incompatibilities, force majeure or other failure of performance," but it "will use commercially reasonable efforts to correct any material performance problem brought to its attention and may suspend performance pending such corrections." Elsevier refuses even this much in its Engineering Village and ScienceDirect licenses, for example: "Elsevier aims to keep the Site available twenty-four (24) hours a day, seven (7) days a week and to maintain saved information. However, due to technical failures, acts of God or routine maintenance, availability may be limited and/or information may be lost. Elsevier shall not be liable for lost information or non-availability of the services." Compare ARTstor: "If the ARTstor Digital Library fails to operate in conformance with the terms of this Agreement, Licensee shall promptly notify ARTstor, and ARTstor's sole obligation shall be to repair the nonconformity." Notice also that according to the ARTstor license the effort to supply the licensed content is not modified by a stated level of effort, such as all reasonable endeavors or efforts or words to that effect: "ARTstor shall try to provide continuous availability of the ARTstor Digital Library online." Some are far more nebulous: Springer promises ("shall") to "make all reasonable efforts to ensure uninterrupted online access to and continuous availability of the Springer Content to Licensee and the Authorized Users at the specified above as Licensee's address, in accordance with this Agreement, and to restore access to the Springer Content as promptly as possible in the event of an interruption or suspension of the SpringerLink service caused by failure of Springer's server." Again, the concept of reasonable efforts, discussed previously, does not mean extraordinary efforts but, rather, what is standard among similar vendors.

As discussed under the concept of credit, consideration of desired response beyond restoration should be made for downtime. Is a credit sufficient, and, if so, when is credit triggered (the threshold again) and how is the credit applied? According to the BioOne license, if the "interruption or suspension of service last...more than 72 consecutive hours, the Licensee's contract will be extended by an equal number of hours." This is an attempt at fair compensation, but if users conceivably might access the database 24/7, then any loss of service might make an impact. So why not make any downtime trigger contract extension, at the licensee's option, by an equal number of hours? Why set the bar at 72 hours, and why only when service has been down for three days straight? A database that is down every afternoon from lunch until dinner would not be reached by such a clause in its present form. JSTOR also uses the 72-hour benchmark—not continuous hours, but 72 hours within a continuous 30-day calendar period, so were the service down for 48 hours the last week of June and 48 hours the first week of July, it would trigger the following provision (but not 24 hours every other week): "If JSTOR fails to provide online availability to the JSTOR Archive for more than 72 hours during any period of 30 consecutive calendar days Institutional Licensee may, upon written request, (a) be granted a choice of a refund or a credit of a prorated portion of its annual access fee for each 30-day period so affected or (b) terminate its agreement by providing written notice to JSTOR." If some threshold of downtime is allowed by the license (assuming this is reflected in the overall price), the threshold should be aggregated during the subscription period and, if exceeded, a refund or credit at the option of the licensee should be offered. Consider also some higher threshold that would trigger a right to terminate the agreement as well, again with a refund right.

ENFORCEMENT

License agreements often contain language obligating the licensee to assist in enforcing the terms of the agreement and to report any suspected infringement. The American Chemical Society is an example: "Licensee is required to notify ACS of any infringements of copyrights or unauthorized use of which they become aware. Licensee will cooperate with the ACS in investigating any such unauthorized uses and taking reasonable steps to prevent a reoccurrence." While there is no obligation to monitor or seek out acts of noncompliance with the terms, the reporting of infringers raises issues of privacy. A kinder, gentler nudge in that direction is found in the American Fisheries Society license, indicating that the "subscribing institution will not be held liable for abuses of AFS Journals Online by users but institutional assistance in halting abuses will be appreciated," so there is no requirement to intervene but it sure would be nice if the library did respond, perhaps as part of its overall mission to educate. Some licenses require that the license inform users of restrictions. Bowker's Books in Print likewise expects reasonable attempts at notice and reasonable efforts at enforcement: "Subscriber will exercise reasonable efforts to inform Authorized Users of the restrictions on the use of the Products and Content and to enforce such restrictions." UlrichsWeb: "Subscriber will exercise commercially reasonable efforts to inform Authorized Users and USAS Users of the restriction on the use of the Products and Content and to enforce such restrictions." Notice that the informing proviso is subject to "commercially reasonable," but the enforcement proviso ("and to enforce such restrictions") is not. Like the Bowker's BIP license, enforcement must be complete. This is a ridiculous obligation to incur. A better option is to require the licensee to give users reasonable notice of terms regarding permitted and prohibited uses and to set enforcement obligation at a level of effort and response consistent with other institutional policies that its users might violate.

Given the number and variation among licenses, providing adequate notice to users may be no small task. It would be possible in theory to include links on the library webpage from which users access a particular database that indicate "to see important use restrictions associated with this database click here" or some similar screen notice mechanism upon login to a particular licensed resources.

Other licenses do much more. Caution should be taken when promising compliance with the terms of use by third parties such as students or patrons over which the licensee has less control than say employees such as staff or faculty. Even promises as to employee compliance can raise issues. How can the library-licensee avoid the reality that in at least some circumstances at some time the parameters of use will not be followed? Ensuring such compliance may be impractical or near impossible. It is better to promise that the library will undertake "reasonable" efforts, those in common use among similar institutions, to control user conduct such as basic notices or warnings, authorized user policy (AUP), general network traffic monitoring, and so on, to inform users of the limits or restrictions on use. The Accessible Archive offers an example: "Licensee shall make reasonable efforts to provided Authorized Users with appropriate notice of the terms and conditions under which access to the Licensed Materials is granted under the Agreement including, in particular, any limitations on access or use of the Licensed Materials as set forth in this Agreement." The Accessible Archive also requires that "[i]n the event of any unauthorized use of the Licensed Materials by an Authorized User, Licensee shall cooperate with Licensor in the investigation of any unauthorized use of the Licensed Materials of which it is made aware and shall use reasonable efforts to remedy such unauthorized use and prevent its recurrence." Licensor may also "terminate such Authorized User's access to the Licensed Materials after first providing reasonable notice to Licensee (in no event less than two (2) weeks) and cooperating with the Licensee to avoid recurrence of any unauthorized use." The same concept is in the American Society of Civil Engineers license: "brief quotations from the content of Online Journal articles with the customary acknowledgement of the source." This notice and remedy provision is perhaps similar to measures that a campus might undertake in response to allegations of unlawful file sharing or in response to section 512 take-down requests.[95]

The Taylor and Francis Group license also uses the concept of reasonableness: "The Licensee shall use reasonable efforts to ensure that only Authorized Users are permitted access to the Licensed Material and that all Authorized Users abide by the provisions of this License." More detail is not given, so it is unclear what sort of enforcement efforts must be undertaken. What is reasonable? Are best practices (assuming such exist) sufficient? Does this mean a level of effort that would be undertaken to enforce any other rule on campus or in the library, an AUP governing computer use, for example, or a code of behavior? This would suggest that turning a blind eye would be unacceptable or that deviations which never resulted in the imposition of any penalties would likewise be unacceptable. How would a campus treat a case of plagiarism or a public library treat a case of patron harassment (excessive staring at or following of other patrons)? Retaining the option to decide what compliance measures are effective and reasonable should remain with the licensee.

The next generation or level of enforcement obligation that can be found in licenses is provided by Associated Press Images (API). As with many licenses, it does not require monitoring but it does require that, when unauthorized use by third parties is known, the library must inform the licensor and divulge any relevant information (which may raise patron privacy issues), and should the licensor pursue legal recourse against the third party, the library must reasonably cooperate in that recourse (which may raise further privacy issues). In an educational setting, a student would be a third party, but the student would likely also be an authorized user, so it is unclear whether the provision is meant to reach students as third parties, and would be opposed to immediate parties such as employees, or is meant to cover only those beyond the user groups identified in the agreement. The same issue would be raised for a public library licensee and its patrons who are not immediate parties such as employees but are either or both third parties and authorized users, depending on how one interprets the concept of third parties. In the case of API, it appears that "third parties" is intended to mean beyond the authorized user group, as a preceding clause commands the licensee "[t]o take all commercially reasonable efforts to prevent third parties from misappropriating or obtaining unauthorized access, use or transmission of the Content." However, other agreements make clear that reporting of unauthorized uses applies to authorized users, or that unauthorized use by an authorized user is indeed a possibility and that cooperation in enforcement by the licensee is one of the obligations under the agreement. For example, the Accessible Archive license states: "In the event of any unauthorized use of the Licensed Materials by an Authorized User, Licensee shall cooperate with Licensor in the investigation of any unauthorized use of the Licensed Materials of which it is made aware and shall use reasonable efforts to remedy such unauthorized use and prevent its recurrence." Licensor may also "terminate such Authorized User's access to the Licensed Materials after first providing reasonable notice to Licensee (in no event less than two (2) weeks) and cooperating with the Licensee to avoid recurrence of any unauthorized use." The Bibliography of Asian Studies Online: "The Subscriber shall use reasonable efforts to protect the database from a use that is not permitted under this Agreement, and shall notify the AAS of any such use of which it learns or is notified." As with other licenses, suspension or termination of service is a possible repercussion: "In the event of a violation of the User Rules, the Subscriber agrees to consider the imposition of further restrictions on access to, and downloading and printing from, the database." Springer retains the right to "terminate the access of the Internet Protocol ('IP') address(es) from which such unauthorized use occurred" and also has the right to make such request of the licensee, "and/or (b) Licensee shall terminate such Authorized User's access to the Licensed Materials upon Springer's request," though not without first giving notice: "Springer shall take none of the steps described in this paragraph without providing reasonable notice to the licensee." BioOne also includes notice, reporting, and enforcement (at the institutional level and by the institution): "Use reasonable efforts to ensure that Authorized Users are made aware of an undertake to abide by the terms and conditions of this License; and immediately on becoming aware of any unauthorized user or other breach, inform BioOne and take reasonable steps, including appropriate disciplinary action, both to ensure that such activity cease and to prevent any recurrence." A later clause ensures that the licensee-library or institution cannot sit idly by when it is aware of breach by one of its authorized users: "Nothing is this License shall make the Licensee liable for breach of the terms of the License by an Authorized User provided that the Licensee did not cause, knowingly assist, or condone the continuation of such breach after becoming aware of an actual breach having occurred." Rather than an obligation to report all infractions, the licensee should have the option of responding to use of licensed content that deviates from the terms of the agreement without having to contact the licensor, to exercise its own attempt at a teachable moment. (This discussion is predicated on the assumption that whether an infraction has occurred is not in dispute.) Of course, the licensor may be able to detect such deviation as well, and an obligation that the licensee cooperate with enforcement efforts is reasonable.

Some licenses state such conditions rather broadly and expand the rights covered far beyond the copyright basis of most agreements. For example, Cambridge Journals Online commands: "Users undertake to ensure that the intellectual property rights of the copyright holder and the software owners and the moral rights of the authors of the Materials are not infringed." Moral rights[96] are a slightly different creature than copyright and are fully developed in the legal traditions of European countries but have limited application in U.S. law.[97]

Most agreements trigger a reporting obligation upon actual knowledge. JSTOR appears to assume the knowledge can come from others ("Institutional Licensees shall notify JSTOR of any such unpermitted uses of which they learn or are notified and shall cooperate with JSTOR in resolving problems or unpermitted use") and anticipates that suspension or termination by the licensor or licensee to the licensed content is an appropriate response: "In the event of violation of these Terms and Conditions of Use by an Authorized User, (a) JSTOR may suspend or terminate, or, where practicable, request that Institutional Licensee suspend or terminate, such Authorized User's access to the JSTOR Archive." The Kraus Curriculum Development Library (KCDL) likewise places the burden on the subscriber "for terminating any unauthorized access of which it has actual notice or knowledge." Such provisions bring up the concern: What obligations does the licensee have in assuring that uses of the licensed content by its employees as well by authorized users, like patrons and students, comply with the terms of the agreement? More important, how likely is it that such compliance can be achieved?

Many licenses, like the BioOne and JSTOR, allow the licensor to pursue so-called self-help remedies such as suspension of services when the licensor perceives significant breach is occurring and will continue to occur unless such action is taken. Would a licensor ever pursue such course of remedy? Yes, as the recent criminal indictment filed against Aaron Swartz who, according to the grand jury charges, "stole approximately 4.8 million articles, a major portion of the total archive in which JSTOR had invested."[98] The indictment indicates that as a part of attempts to stop excessive downloading by Swartz, JSTOR blocked access to the IP address Swartz was using for his systematic extraction.[99] Undaunted by this setback, Swartz obtained a new IP address.[100] As both attempts used the same stem address, JSTOR "began blocking a much broader range of IP addresses. As a result, legitimate JSTOR users at MIT were denied access to JSTOR's archive."[101] Slowed but not stopped, Swartz devised a spoofing program and resumed his downloading in earnest. Within a couple of weeks, the "ghost laptop" and "ghost macbook" were "systematically and rapidly access[ed] . . . The pace was so fast that it brought down some of JSTOR's servers. In response, JSTOR blocked the entire MIT computer network's access to JSTOR for several days, beginning on or about October 9, 2010."[102] As the *U.S. v. Swartz* complaint charges, there may be serious consequences for users, authorized or not, of egregious use of the licensed content.[103]

Privacy issues can also arise in enforcement provisions. The connection to searches performed with the licensed content, or any content for that matter, such as a Google or Bing search, raises unforeseen privacy issues in the library context. Most states have statutes that protect the privacy of qualifying library patron records where (as is common in most statutes) the library is supported in whole or in part with public monies. It is typical that the record must contain some identifying patron information and the subject or nature of the library material, service, or use made. If the qualifying library made its own content database (like a library catalog) and a patron searched it looking for books on a specific subject and the patron had logged into the system (as many systems do when a patron desires to make a request of a found item), many state statutes would protect a record of the search, prohibiting release to third parties and, again as is typical, to condition release to law enforcement upon a showing of cause through a subpoena or warrant process. When patrons search licensed content, a similar record may be generated that would connect a particular patron (this might be especially true where the access is through remote login) or at least a particular computer (located in a particular staff member's office or at a particular staff member's desk). This would certainly be true of a Google search. It may be possible to link the subject matter or trail of a particular search with a specific patron. However, it is unlikely that such searches fall under any state library statute. Google has no responsibility other than under its general terms of service to protect the privacy of anyone or anything. The database licensor is also not bound by such library privacy statutes and would be free to release such information if collected or obtained. However, because such agreements, unlike contracts with Google, are negotiated, such a clause or term could be inserted. At least, patrons should be made aware of the lack of privacy if such conditions are not included in the agreement. If after the notification or subsequent communication (because once notified of the suspect use the licensor requests additional information, e.g., the licensor desires to pursue legal action against the infringing, in terms of the copyright law, user), the licensee reveals information identifying a specific user or library patron, then the release of the patron's name or other personally identifying information coupled with the obvious fact that the patron made use of a particular library service or resource (i.e., the licensor's database) would be prohibited under some state privacy confidentiality statutes, at least in those states which protect information regarding patron use of particular services or resources. If the licensor desires such identifying information, the licensor would need to pursue this information through legal process, such as a discovery subpoena.[104] Discussion of such laws is beyond the scope of this book, but review of enforcement compliance provisions in any license agreement should be made in light of a library's governing state statute.[105] Classen discusses personal information in the context of licensing and offers the following language to include:

> "Personally Identifiable Information" shall mean any information which, alone or in combination with other information, relates to a specific, identifiable individual. Personally Identifiable Information includes individual names, social security numbers, [student or employee or other unique identifying numbers], telephone numbers home address, driver's license number, account number, email address, and vehicle registration number. Any information that can be associated with Personally Identifiable Information shall also be Personally Identifiable Information. For example, an individual's age by itself is not Personally Identifiable Information, but if such age is capable of being associated with one or more specific identifiable individuals then such age would be deemed personally Identifiable Information.[106]

Including this or similar language (perhaps taken from a library's relevant state statute) in the license agreement and ensuring that such protected information shall be excluded from the operation of the enforcement obligations is a way to ensure that patron privacy rights are protected and aligned with applicable state law as well.

ERRORS, LOSS OF SERVICE, OR OTHER FULFILLMENT ISSUES

See also WARRANTIES AND DISCLAIMERS

Licensor responsibility for errors is often limited "for correcting 'reproducible errors.' This limitation is a general trade practice and is based upon the notion that if an error cannot be reproduced for correction, the error cannot be corrected."[107] Licensors do not want to be responsible for errors that might be in the content licensed. This is true whether the licensor created the content or is an aggregator of content created by others. Licensees may wish such a promise of error-free data would be forthcoming from the licensor, but this is actually an unreasonable expectation. Perhaps in a perfect world such is obtainable, but errors are bound to occur. If licensors would be responsible and could not limit their liability, a very likely result would be that many licensors would simply choose not to make such content available—an even more undesirable result.

EXCLUSIVE VERSUS NONEXCLUSIVE RIGHTS

Content license agreements typically do not transfer exclusive rights but rather transfer nonexclusive rights (Alexander Street Press: "This Agreement constitutes a non-exclusive, non-transferable license to use the Product(s).") In other words, your library is not the only licensee. Exclusive rights might be important in licensing story rights from a novel or play to a motion picture company, as the value for Paramount is in resting assured that it and it alone has the rights to turn the next Dan Brown book or David Mamet play into a motion picture. Such is not the case with the library and the typical content it licenses.

FAIR USE

A number of licenses ensure that use consistent with fair use is allowed. Alexander Street Press (ASP) allows "use [of] the Product(s) in way that is consistent with U.S. Fair Use Provisions and international law." The American Fisheries Society license allows for "one print copy in circulation according to normal 'fair use' practices." The question is whether other clauses by operation are contradictory. A library may believe that its reserve, e-reserve, or course pack processes are within fair use, while other provisions may appear to take away these rights. Generally, specific clauses override general ones.

Consider the following provision from the American Meteorological Society license that appears to grant but at the same time limits fair use: "to share such hard copy with third parties to the same extent as the print edition or to the extent permitted under fair use provisions of the Copyright Act of 1976." The problem is that if the library's fair use of the licensed content is limited to "hard copy" alone, then fair-use rights have been restricted. Fair use applies equally to online as well as offline (print) content. The ARTstor license contains a similar pull-back, in other words, fair use or other provisions such as section 110 ("educational exceptions") restricted to print or download content alone: "Nothing in this Agreement should be construed or interpreted to limit those uses of ARTstor Content printed or downloaded from the ARTstor Digital Library that are permitted under the far use, educational exceptions, or other provisions of the US copyright or other intellectual property rights laws." At least the provision makes reference to other use rights under the copyright law, such as section 110 where the classroom rules are found, but section 110 contains other use rights that a library might want to have (see discussion of music licensing in Chapter 10) but are not referenced, or other significant provisions of the copyright law, such as section 108 (reproduction and public distribution for qualifying libraries and archives) or section 109 (rights of public distribution and public display). If anything, a license, if it requires additional obligations, such as monitoring, terms of process, including choice of forum and law, and so forth, should then also allow for rights beyond what the copyright law allows. BioOne, for example, allows for fair use without any restriction on format: "Nothing in this license shall in any way exclude, modify, or affect anything the Licensee or any Authorized User is allowed to do in respect of any of the Licensed Materials consistent with existing 'fair use' law, defined by the U.S. Copyright Code of 1976 (17 U.S.C. §§ 105–107)." Section 105 deals with the public domain status of works of the federal government, and section 106 lists the exclusive rights of the copyright owner. Both provisions might be in play during a preliminary process of determining whether fair use is even necessary—in other words, fair use would not be needed if the content was not protected by the copyright law through application of section 105 or if the use did not implicate one of the exclusive rights of the copyright owner under section 106, neither related directly to fair use. An earlier provision regarding multiple copies for classroom use also references fair use: "Create multiple copies of a discrete excerpt from the License Material for classroom instruction use, consistent with existing 'fair use' law and regulation." Of course, the license does not really clarify anything. Debate rages over what kind of multiple copying, either in terms of implicit impact through e-reserves or explicit effect through course packs or direct distribution of multiple copies for students in class, constitutes fair use and what is beyond fair use. If licenses are to have value, it should be through certainty, not the affirmation of the status quo.

A similar statutory identification faux pas is made by the Taylor and Francis Group: "Nothing in this Agreement shall limit your rights to make fair use of the Licensed Works, as that term is defined under Sections 107 and 108 of the Copyright Revision Act of 1976." Oddly, section 108 does not define fair use other than to confirm statutorily that the section does nothing to limit its application, as well as that of license provisions, in subsection 108(f)(4): "Nothing in this section in any way affects the right of fair use as provided by section 107, or any contractual obligations assumed at any time by the library or archives when it obtained a copy or phonorecord of a work in its collections." Is the concept of fair use used by the Taylor and Francis Group meant in a more general sense of uses that are legal under the copyright law under either section 107 or section 108? The better approach is to list the sections or rights the parties wish to reaffirm or retain. But this raises another question: are rights not explicitly reaffirmed then not allowed? The

ASP license states that "[a]ny rights not expressly granted in this license agreement are reserved to ASP." For example, the Westlaw Campus Research license makes clear in its license that the answer to this question is no, as "if not expressly prohibited by this Agreement, as allowed under the fair use provision of the Copyright Act (17 U.S.C.A. § 107)." Fair use, unless expressly prohibited, is preserved, but what of the other use provisions under the copyright law. Are those rights then not granted?

JSTOR reaffirms a broad range of use rights under the copyright law not tied to fair use alone, allowing for "fair use under Section 107 of the U.S. Copyright Act, educational exceptions, or other similar provisions to the copyright laws or other intellectual property right laws in the United States or in other countries," as does Project MUSE ("All Journal content is subject to 'fair use' provisions of U.S. or applicable international copyright laws"). CSA Illumina and ProQuest are more specific regarding foreign laws, adding the non-U.S. concept of "fair dealing" to its provision: "Nothing in this agreement restricts your use of the materials contained within the Products under the doctrines of 'fair use' or 'fair dealing' as defined under the laws of the United States or England, respectively." Of course, the problem with even these broad confirmations of rights is that reasonable minds (owners and users) can disagree over what uses might be "consistent with existing 'fair use' law" and what uses might fall outside of the law.

Even the extraction and posting onto an online forum of a line or two is prohibited by some licenses. Consider Bowker's Books in Print: "Subscriber agrees that it shall not: (i) copy, reproduce, modify, download, retransmit, distribute, disseminate, sell, publish, broadcast, circulate or otherwise make all or any part of the Content or the Products available in any medium or in any way, in whole or in part, to any third parties except as specifically authorized herein." Worse, library patrons or students ("Authorized Users") cannot do this either: "Subscriber and Authorized Users may not post any Content from the Products to newsgroups, mail lists or electronic bulletin boards without the prior written consent of Bowker." How will the library ensure that this does not happen? A better alternative is to allow for incidental uses. So, too, never promise to control the behavior of your patrons. A better alternative is to promise to offer notice of prohibited uses via a login screen or a linked message "Check here for usage restrictions." A general approach is to include a provision, listed among the "authorized uses," allowing any use that, under the existing copyright law at the time, would be a fair use or otherwise lawful. A sample of such language is found in Chapter 16.

FORCE MAJEURE

Force majeure clauses are typical in all contracts. The concept behind such language is that some circumstances relating to forces of nature are beyond anyone's control and the parties should not be responsible for obligations under the contract in such circumstances. The list of events often relates to natural disasters. Harris indicates the scope of such clauses: "Regarding license agreements, it is important to include additional conditions in a force majeure clause such as power failures, destruction of network facilities, and so on."[108] The legal effect of such clauses under the contract is that in the circumstance of the event so listed the affected party is excused from its obligations under the contract. In other words, such failure to fulfill the obligation shall not be considered a breach of the contract. Such clauses are enforceable and can excuse otherwise breaching conduct. As one state supreme court commented: "we disagree with the district court and find the force-majeure clause is not ambiguous...A force-majeure clause is not intended to shield a party from the normal risks associated with an agreement. Wells claims the parties to the contract did not intend the force-majeure clause to have its common meaning: thus, Wells is relieved from performing even if a strike, accident, explosion, flood, fire or the total loss of the manufacturing facilities was caused by an event within its control. Had the parties meant to change the common meaning of the force-majeure clause, the parties should have had a discussion or negotiations regarding the definition of a force-majeure event...Accordingly, as a matter of law we find the phrase 'that is beyond the reasonable control of that party' modifies all the events enumerated by the parties in the force-majeure clause."[109] Some force majeure provisions may indicate that the circumstance must last for a period of time before it will qualify under the force majeure provision. What is often absent in these clauses is an indication of when obligations would recommence under the contract (i.e., once the floodwaters recede or the nonfunctioning server is replaced) or how soon after the event the other party can expect restoration of service, for example. Perhaps use of the word *reasonable* is again justified. In the absence of such language, other licenses allow that if the condition of force majeure exists for a stated period of time, a termination right is triggered by the other party, the party that suffered the event, or either party.[110] Regardless of time period, remember to obtain the right to refund (or credit) for any loss of service, even if due to force majeure. The licensee might not have the right to sue for breach as the obligation is suspended; a licensee, as stated before and in the author's opinion, should never be required to pay for service it did not receive. The main purpose of force majeure is to indicate that such circumstances do indeed excuse performance; in other words, they do not constitute a material breach leading to termination rights. However, the clause should not be used to commit a licensee to paying for service it does not receive. Loss of service even due to force majeure should qualify for refund or credit, at the option of the licensee, even if it cannot trigger a termination right.

Often overlooked as so-called boilerplate, the parties should consider carefully what events fall within force majeure and what events do not. "For example, many licensees are hesitant to include labor strife or strikes within the list of events constituting and event of force majeure."[111] Brepolis includes a rather extensive list of force majeure events: "fire, flood, earthquake, elements of nature or Acts of God, acts of war, terrorism, riots, civil disorders, strikes, lockouts, labour [*sic*] difficulties, and any other similar cause beyond the reasonable control of a (non-performing) party." Some licenses do not include labor strikes or other events that are in a sense the result of human endeavor, even if to some extent outside the control of the party suffering the force majeure. One option would be to draft different clauses, conditions, obligations, rights, results, and so on, for different events or categories of force majeure. Natural disasters and other events that are usually termed acts of God might be one category, while events caused by man (power outages, labor problems, etc.) might be another. The impact of the event might be a third category—for example, a hurricane might not cause a city to flood immediately, but several hours or days after the storm passes, a man-made levee might fail, allowing the collected floodwaters to enter and flood the city.

FORUM: CHOICE OF OR SELECTION; IDENTIFICATION OF SPECIFIC COURT (STATE AND FEDERAL)

With a written contract, this may be indicated in the text of the agreement; where the transaction occurs online and there is no textual agreement (e.g., you purchase a used book from eBay or Amazon.com), the often confusing, complex, and variable law of jurisdiction becomes relevant. Nimmer indicates: "Where transactions occur entirely on-line, no situs exists and the applicable doctrine for applicable forum for disputes remains unclear. The better view holds that either as a matter of statutory interpretation (of the long-arm statute) or as a matter of constitutional due process concepts of fairness, an on-line provider or its licensee should not be held to account in a particular state unless something in the transaction indicates assent to and use of a particular state as an intended or, at least an expected, element of the transaction"[112] But this is an odd statement to make, as no online licensor would want to be reachable by another state's courts; no licensor would make such assent. Rather, the more recent trend is to assign jurisdiction to a state foreign to the online licensor where so-called minimum contacts have been established. Forum selection clauses can bind parties even where agreement is a nonnegotiable or mass-market consumer contract and not subject to negotiation.[113] "Use of a form contract . . . even by the party with superior bargaining power, does not necessarily make a forum selection clause enforceable."[114] Absent language in the contract, sorting out jurisdiction issues may also resolve choice of law disputes as well, again assuming the contract is silent on this issue. Forum selection clauses are "prima facie valid."[115] Depending on the circumstances, a choice of forum clause may be found contrary to public policy,[116] though the general rule is that such clauses are not unconscionable.[117] Such provisions will be honored "so long as they are procured freely and voluntarily, with the place chosen having some logical nexus to one of the parties or the dispute."[118] In a case involving the sale of computers from a website: "In the instant case, there is no discernable public policy obstacle to enforcing the choice-of-law provision, the parties agree that Texas law applies, Texas bears a reasonable relationship to the parties and the transaction because the defendant's principal place of business is in Texas, and the issues in this case involve basic contract law so there will be no substantial difference in the outcome of this case if Texas law is applied. Therefore, we apply Texas law to the substantive issues."[119] There must be some general connection between the jurisdiction selected in the license and one of the parties; typically, this is the licensor's primary place of business. "Consider the following: In *Caspi v. Microsoft Network, L.L.C.*,[120] the Court enforced a forum selection clause because the Microsoft Network did business nationwide. But what if it hadn't? This author knows of an ISP whose customer base is in northern Nevada and northeastern California. Yet at one time, its service agreement required that all arbitration and litigation occur in Florida. Would that had been enforceable? Probably not."[121] Some state institutions are restricted from entering contracts where the choice of law and forum is other than the jurisdiction in which the licensee-institution is located.[122] From the licensor perspective, including consent to jurisdiction is also desirable; that is, not only does the licensee agree to try any disputes in courts of the state jurisdiction and under the laws of the stated jurisdiction but consents to service of process by that jurisdiction as well. "To avoid any potential dispute, the parties should include a statement of the venue and affirmative consent of the stated jurisdiction. The parties should also include such words as 'sole' or 'exclusive' to further limit potential disputes over the enforceability of such clauses, and the contractual language should state that the forum selection clause applies to 'any dispute arising out of or related to the agreement,' which would include tort as well s contract claims."[123] A forum selection clause is a material term.[124] Inclusion of such on an invoice alone would be insufficient. It must be in the agreement or, in the case of the invoice scenario, negotiated.[125]

GRANT OF RIGHTS

Licenses state what rights are being granted to the licensee (the library) and its users—a license to make certain uses of certain content under certain terms and conditions. The license operates as a permission (to make such uses) and a promise (not to sue if the uses are confined to those articulated in the agreement and in fulfillment of any other conditions the agreement imposes). The license typically states the nature of the "grant," such as "CQ Press hereby grants to you a revocable, non-exclusive, nontransferable, non-sublicensable limited right and license to access and use those portions of the Site and Services accessible to the general public without a password or logon for your own personal research use, subject to this Agreement." This grant can be revoked ("revocable"); the licensee is not the only holder of such grant ("non-exclusive"); the library cannot in turn license the content to someone else ("non-sublicensable"); the rights granted are not all of the exclusive owner's rights under section 106 ("limited right and license"); use must be for personal and research use ("for your own personal research use"); and the "access and use" rights are subject to conditions ("subject to the Agreement"), that is, the terms of the agreement related in the various provisions of the agreement.

A sublicense would be different from an assignment. In an assignment, instead of the library remaining as licensee, the library-licensee transfers the license to another licensee, or in the more anticipated scenario (in terms of what a prohibition assignment tries to prevent), the licensee somehow merges or a successive entity is formed (e.g., a two-year community college is now made a baccalaureate-degree-granting university). A sublicense would be where the library in turn licenses (grants) access to the licensed content to others, whereby it would act as a content aggregator and allow access through some portal of its own.

HEADINGS

As with statute titles or headings, similar prefatory phrasings in license provisions have no legal effect. Rather, the meaning and effect of the license, as with any contract, are determined by the substances of its actual terms and not the title or headings given to such words.[126] "As such, the parties should ensure that each section heading clearly reflects the provision it contains and includes language that clearly indicates the section headings are for convenience of reference only and are not intended to have any substantive significance."[127] Street and Grant suggest including the following language: "Headings. The section headings in this Agreement are for convenient reference only and shall be given no substantive or interpretive effect."[128] Another alternative is to state in an "interpretation" provision that "the headings used in the license are for convenience only and are not intended to be part of any interpretations of the license."[129] However, mislabeling or the misalignment of heading and content, particularly where the content goes to the heart of the bargain or concerns important disclaimers or warranties, may lead to claims of unconscionability.[130]

IMPOSSIBLE TERMS

It is difficult to correctly label the sorts of clauses discussed in this section, as readers are unlikely to find this heading in any license agreement. The point is that a license may contain conditions with which it is impossible, or at least very difficult, to comply. These conditions typically relate to obligations imposed on users over whom the library does not have effective control. Consider the following language from the American Physical Society Online: "Authorized Users may: download search results...provided that such data is used solely for their personal use or research and are not made available to anyone who is not a subscriber... The Subscriber specifically agrees that use by the Subscriber or Authorized Users other than indicated above is a violation of the terms of this Agreement." First, how is the institution-library-subscriber to ensure that students or faculty use this for personal use or research and not for income-generating consulting, which faculty often do, or that a student does not pass an article along to a sibling taking a similar class at another institution? If this happens, the license, by its terms, makes such incidental use a breach ("specifically agrees...is a violation"). It might better to include an exception for incidental commercial or public use and to indicate that the licensee institution must undertake reasonable efforts to inform users of these conditions but does not promise to enforce such terms. The American Society of Civil Engineers requires only that "reasonable vigilance" be employed to ensure that only authorized users "access the Online Journals."

Reasonableness is also a common standard to ensure that all users follow the terms of the agreement. But what are reasonable steps? Is making the users aware of the terms sufficient, or must the licensee also enforce those terms? The American Statistical Association and Institute of Mathematical Statistics state: "Licensee agrees to take reasonable and necessary steps to prevent violations of the terms of the agreement by their users, including suspension of access privileges for known violators." Project MUSE uses similar wording: "Subscribers are expected to make their best feasible efforts to enable access to the Project MUSE Database only to faculty, students, staff, alumni, and walk-in library patrons using the campus physical library facilities." The International Federation of Library Associations and Institutions (IFLA) suggests that licensees have the responsibility to educate users regarding proper use of content, to take reasonable measures to prevent unlawful use and stop infringing use, but not to face secondary liability for the conduct of users.[131] However, the user should not be bound by these obligations.[132]

Anticipate how faculty, staff, students, patrons, and others may want to use the licensed content and then work to have such uses listed in the agreement, but be careful not to obligate the library or institution to ensure that uses not listed or prohibited are not in fact undertaken by your faculty, staff, students, patrons, and others. Mergent includes the concept of incidental public use this way: Mergent allows that the "Customer may use, access, copy, store display and create derivative works of (collectively 'Use') the Data for its internal business purposes and may use minor portions of the Data, as part of reports, or separately given to clients of Customer, whether electronic or other present or future media." Mergent also expects destruction of any of its products after termination, including a certificate.

What sort of certificate is unclear. Is a notarized statement indicating that the following list of efforts to purge was undertaken sufficient? Mergent will indicate what must be done, but it might be good to know up front what those expectations are. "Customer will, as Mergent shall direct, either return to Mergent or destroy all Data that cannot feasibly be returned and will furnish to Mergent a certificate, satisfactory in form and substance to Mergent, of such destruction." Such clauses signal another area of impossible conditions that relate to destruction or deletion of content after the agreement is terminated—an obligation to find and destroy any copies patrons, students, faculty, and others might have downloaded. Depending on the institution, this could be a monumental task. The better provision would be to agree to undertake reasonable efforts to destroy or, better, to send three notices to users that such content should, if stored electronically, be deleted.

Consider the wording from Associated Press Images: "Upon the termination or expirations of Your rights with respect to a Content element under an Invoice or a License Agreement, You agree to cease all use of such Content and shall promptly delete or destroy any digital copies." And from Alexander Street Press: "Upon any termination, the Customer will erase all electronic storage of copies of the Product(s)." Given how pernicious electronic copies are, this might be a difficult promise to fulfill. Consider CSA Illumina: "In the event the license granted under this agreement is terminated you shall disable all Products in your possession. This includes the destruction of any CD-ROMs, FTP databases or any software as well as any downloaded copies retrieved from the Products." Complete compliance is likely an impossible event, but the subscriber can certainly promise to inform users of the conditions but not promise to enforce them or guarantee 100 percent compliance.

Wharton Research Data Services (WRDS) wants similar purging ("promptly destroy any and all machine readable material containing any portion of the Service and/or an and all related documents" and "expunge any and all documentation produced by WRDS that was accessed by Subscriber pursuant to this Agreement") and requires the subscriber to "certify in writing to WRDS Subscriber's compliance with" those requirements. Another impossible post-termination destruction is found in the infoUSA license: "Upon termination of the Agreement for any reason Licensee shall cease any and all use of the Products and ensure that all copies of the Products and any related data and information is deleted from its computers and, if applicable, returned to infoUSA no later than five (5) days after termination of this Agreement." First, five days is an incredibly short amount of time in which to accomplish any obligation—even five business days is short. (Also, in an earlier provision, the licensor could terminate without notice and a right to cure in certain circumstances: "infoUSA may immediately terminate this Agreement if Licensee causes or facilitates any unauthorized use or distribution of the infoUSA data." It is assumed at least notice of the termination would be given or otherwise awareness of it known—i.e., the data cannot be accessed—which would trigger the five-day destruction/return proviso.) It is also odd, assuming the licensee has printed some data, that such data is not protected by copyright (names and addresses), which under the copyright law would be public domain content, and yet the licensor requires it all to be destroyed or returned.

A more reasonable response is for the licensee to agree to destroy, delete, and so on, any of the licensed content upon discovery of such content but only upon discovery in the normal course of business, rather than to agree to undertake specific steps to uncover the information. If a trove of files containing such licensed content is discovered, it will of course be destroyed or otherwise made inaccessible.

Perhaps falling more toward impractical than impossible is a prohibition found in both SilverPlatter WebSPIRS and WilsonSelect: "use any Database in any way unless you have agreed to be bound by this license" and "Use the Subject Database(s) in any way unless and until the Subscriber has agreed to this license." This raises some questions: If access to the database is not given until the agreement is signed, then what purpose does this clause have? If one could access the content before signing, then how would one know that such license or term exists? Again, be cautious of promising what is either impractical or impossible to accomplish.

INCORPORATION AND RESULTING OWNERSHIP OF CONTENT BY LICENSOR

Some agreements—and this is more typical in software agreements and rare in database or other content agreements—attempt to claim ownership in content that might be created with or incorporated with the licensed content. For example, the American Statistical Association and Institute of Mathematical Statistics: "All copies of the Database and any portion of the Database merged into or used in conjunction with another database or computer program will continue to be the property of Licensors and subject to the terms and conditions of this Agreement." Such provisions in content agreements are onerous and should be avoided.

INDEMNITY AND LIMITATION OF LIABILITY

Indemnification is one of the most important provisions a license can contain. Licenses without an indemnification provision should not be signed. With such a clause, the licensor is stating that if the licensee's use of the licensed content according to the terms of the agreement is found to be infringing (where the licensor did not possess the right to make such content available for such use), the licensor will defend in court and cover the licensee for any damages it incurs as a result of such a lawsuit. In a software license, it is typical to limit the indemnification to certain sorts of damages alone, such as those for bodily injury or tangible property loss, for example: "If our software fried your server when you installed it, we'll owe you a server. But if it just crashed or slowed down your server, which prevented you from getting your orders out on time, which in turn resulted in two of your clients dropping your service, we won't pay you the lost profits from those clients."

Some agreements require that the licensee indemnify the licensor. Ovid desires the licensee do this: "Subscriber agrees to indemnify OVID from and defend at its own expense...against any and all claims of third parties...arising out of or related to Authorized Users use of the Products or any materials provided hereunder." At least in return Ovid agrees to indemnify "Subscriber...from and against any and all liability, damages, loss or expense arising from any claim, action or proceeding based upon or arising out o any actual or alleged infringement upon, violation or misappropriation by Ovid of any third party proprietary rights...in consequence of the authorized use or possession of the Software or Documentation supplied by Ovid under this Agreement." Notice that the licensee must indemnify for harm arising from use related to the products, while Ovid need only indemnify for use relating to the software or documentation. Other vendors offer similar one-sided indemnification: "You hereby agree to indemnify, defend and hold Elsevier... harmless from and against any and all liability, losses, damages and costs, including, without limitation, reasonable attorneys' fees, arising from your use of the Site or Content." Gartner likewise desires the library to pony up: "User agrees to indemnify, defend and hold harmless Gartner...from and against all losses, expenses, damages and costs, including reasonable attorneys' fees, arising out of the use of the Products by User or User's account." These provisions should be avoided.

Indemnifications contain two aspects: first, an obligation to defend the claim and be responsible for all costs associated with that defense and, second, to pay for any damages that result from the lawsuit. "Whereas the warranty 'guarantees' the rights, the indemnity provides for financial compensation should the warranty be false. An indemnity clause states that the licensor must pay the cost of any legal expenses and other claims that arise from breaching the warranties in the agreement."[133] From the licensor's perspective, claims arising from intellectual property infringement and personal injury and possibly harm to personal tangible property should be indemnified and not others. From the licensee's perspective, this should be expanded to include claims arising from the licensor's negligence or willful misconduct in the performance of the agreement.[134] "[F]ailure to include an indemnification provision may limit an injured party's recovery under the laws of those states that have not adopted the doctrine of comparative negligence and still recognize the doctrine of contributory negligence."[135] In the context of database content licenses, it could be argued that the indemnification should include the cost of supplying an alternative product while the litigation is proceeding. If it came to this, a dispute by a third party over whether the licensor possessed the legal right to make the content available to the licensee might take months to resolve, all the while the licensed content might not be available. Therefore, the indemnification should include a backup plan, either a substitute of content or the financial means to allow the licensee, if it so chooses, to obtain a replacement product, that is, the same or similar database from another vendor. Indemnifications often include the right of the licensor to control aspects of the litigation for which it is footing the bill. This may raise a conflict of interest in "that the licensee may be motivated to settle the suit on terms favorable to the licensee, but which may have a disastrous impact on the licensor's business if the decision voids the intellectual property rights of the licensor or otherwise creates negative precedent of the licensor that impacts its business in the future."[136] The choice of options with respect to the litigation should rest with the licensee, as should any settlement, or, as an alternative, upon the mutual and reasonable agreement of both parties, and litigation and settlement decisions should be based on mutual agreement.

> Express contract terms dealing with a transferor's obligation (or right) to defend, bear the cost of litigation, and to indemnify the transferee for claims and loss caused by infringement litigation are common. Often, they stem from the realization that the licensor holds the most relevant information and the most significant stake in any infringement litigation. This latter feature is important in licensing since the infringement claim against the licensee directly threatens the viability of the licensor's own work product. In some cases, therefore, undertaking an obligation to defend infringement claims against the licensee does not simply allocate risk between the parties, but places control in the licensor who desires that it reside there for reasons other than risk of loss between the immediate parties.[137]

The indemnification can also address the library's attorneys' fees and the cost of implementing any nonmonetary awards as well, which still might bear a price tag.

Licensors typically condition the indemnification on prompt notice of any suit, assistance and cooperation in the defense, and exclusive control of the litigation—unless the licensor fails to promptly undertake defense, at which point the licensee should have the right to assume it won defense and have the licensor compensate it for the expense associated with its own defense. This is not an unreasonable request. Remedy is often to adjust the content so it is noninfringing, enter into a license to make the infringing content available, or offer a substitute. If none of these is possible, then a refund is the appropriate response.

Some licenses will indicate that should the original copyright owner sue, the aggregator licensor will indemnify the licensee. This is an important clause to have, as it may require some legal process to establish a claim of estoppel, or it may be that the copyright owner is claiming the use exceeds that allowed. The Accessible Archive contains a broad statement of indemnification: "The Licensor shall indemnify and hold Licensee and Authorized Users harmless for any losses, claims, damages, awards, penalties, or injuries incurred, including reasonable attorney's fees, which arise from any claim by any third party of an alleged infringement of copyright or any other property right arising out of the use of the Licensed Materials by the Licensee or any Authorized User in accordance with the terms of this Agreement. This indemnity shall survive the termination of this agreement." This last sentence is also important. The library may terminate the database subscription, and so the library will no longer make course packs from this content. But the statute of limitations for copyright infringement is three years. If making those course packs would be infringing and the copyright owner wanted to take a chance that estoppel would not apply, the copyright owner would in theory have three years after the library ceased use of the content in which to sue for infringement. In our scenario, upon termination of the license with the aggregator, the library could keep using the course packs semester after semester, in which case the statute of limitations would begin a new three-year tolling period with each new use (i.e., with each semester), so it is important that the indemnification survive the end of the agreement.[138] ARTstor offers its licensees indemnification as well, against claims of infringement brought by third parties "against Licensee and/or it Authorized Users, but only if such threatened claim(s) or claim(s) arise out of Permitted Uses or the ARTstor Digital Library." It is also common when offering such indemnification that the licensor desires to "control the defense of such claims and/or threatened claims, and Licensee shall: (i) immediately notify ARTstor upon learning of any such claim and/or threatened claim" and in general cooperate in its defense. "CQ Press reserves the right, at its own expense, to assume the exclusive defense and control of any matter subject to indemnification by you. This indemnity shall be in addition to and not limited by any other indemnity." In other words, the licensor could hire the most expense law firm in the world and the licensee would still be obliged to pay for it. A more reasonable provision allows for litigation defense reasonably agreed upon by the parties.

INTERLIBRARY LOAN

Section 108 rights of users can also be impacted by licensing. Under the copyright law, if the library obtained a print subscription to various titles, this would typically be via a sale, not a license. Once the print edition was in the possession of the library, the library could, consistent with section 109, lend the copy of the volume or, consistent with section 108, make a copy (reproduce) and offer this copy through interlibrary loan[139] (make a public distribution of) to a requesting patron at another library. As with other license provisions, many approaches are found in provisions relating to use of the licensed content to fill requests for this content, typically in the form of an article or other document, from a patron at another library—what librarians as well as the copyright law refer to as interlibrary loan.

Such restrictions again underscore the differences between copyright law and the law of license. Consider the following language and the restrictions it places on interlibrary loan privileges otherwise available under section 108. Euclid Prime suggests that requests for electronic ILL be negotiated additionally: "Provisions for sharing by the Licensee of the electronic version of Euclid Prim articles . . . may be negotiated between Duke University Press and the Licensee." On the other hand, the American Chemical Society license states that with some limitation the library "may use the ACS Products to fulfill requests for InterLibrary Loan (ILL) . . . to support non-commercial scholarly research by patrons of other libraries such as public, school, or college libraries." The provision goes on to offer a modification of the rule of five from the 1976 act guidelines on interlibrary loan, the CONTU Guidelines on Photocopying and Interlibrary Arrangements,[140] whereby a library is allowed to request up to five articles from one serial title within a given calendar that are no more than five years old but with significant modification. First, all requests are counted toward the five-article limit, not just those published within the past five years. Second, all requests are counted toward the single title condition; in other words, all items count toward the five copies from one source: "The borrower may make up to 5 (five) free article copies of individual articles, individual book chapters, proceedings, Reagent Chemicals monographs other individual items from the ACS Products per year for InterLibrary Loan purposes." This means that you can, in a given calendar, use the ACS content to fill five ILL requests and five requests alone. Even if each of the five requests is from a different publication within the licensed content, each request still counts toward the cap. After that, "Additional requests may be fulfilled only if the applicable single copy fees are paid with either to the Copyright Clearance Center or directly to the ACS through it sales procedures for single articles, individual book chapters, proceedings, Reagent Chemicals monographs other individual items from the ACS Products."

Format of the ILL can also be an issue. Section 108(d), the copyright law provision specifically authorizing ILL, does not place any limitation on the format the reproduced copy must take. Note also that ILL can be supported by fair use, which in some cases might be more advantageous than section 108. Consider a request for a clip from a VHS cassette from a patron at another library. The lending library could just send the entire tape for a designated loan period, but this act does not implicate either fair use or section 108; it is merely a public distribution allowed by section 109. The library could make a copy of the two-minute clip from the film, but this would not be allowed under 108(i), which prohibits the use of "a motion picture or other audiovisual work other than an audiovisual work dealing with news" for transactions under subsections (d) or (e).[141] However, if the clip was for use in preparing an article or presentation on film history, for example, it is very likely the use would be fair use and the interlibrary transfer of the clip could be made. The American Physical Society Online allows faxed, mailed, or hand-delivered ILL only, and only on condition that the request comes from a "noncommercial library located in the same country as the licensee." Springer allows for mailing or faxing "to fulfill requests from an academic, research, or other non-commercial library" and specifically forbids for-profit use: "Requests received from for-profit companies or directly from individuals may not be honored." The American Society of Civil Engineers (ASCE) allows for electronic delivery through "secure transmission using Ariel or its equivalent, whereby the electronic file is deleted immediately after printing, provided the institution is not-for-profit and within the same country as the Subscriber" and "supply of such copies must conform to CONTU guidelines or similar restrictions to 'fair use' provisions under copyright." This last proviso is significant for two reasons. First, the license promotes and requires the use of guidelines. The ILL guidelines are not the law, and, consequently, recent cases reveal advocacy on the part of many commentators for libraries to move away from use of the guidelines as a measure or standard of best practice. Second, the CONTU guidelines, at least those relating to ILL, fall under section 108, not section 107 (the fair-use provision), so it is odd to make this connection. Cambridge Journals Online contains a similar "electronic forward and delete" proviso ("secure electronic transmission, whereby the electronic files is deleted immediately after printing"). Unlike the ASCE, but like others, use must be for "research or private study but not for commercial use." Springer also allows electronic delivery via "secure" systems "as demonstrated by the ARIEL and Prospero."

The American Mathematical Society (AMS) allows either print or electronic copies for ILL (the licensee selects option A or B) and also references section 108 and the 1976 CONTU guidelines: "with the same limitations that apply to paper copies for that purpose made from the print edition of the journals. Specifically, copies must be made in compliance with Section 08 of the Copyright Act of the U.S. and be within the CONTU guidelines." However, if the option for electronic copies is chosen (apparently a licensee must choose one or the other option and cannot deliver copies in print to some patrons and deliver electronic copies to other patrons), additional reporting beyond the CONTU guidelines (which require the library of the requesting patron to keep records of filled ILL requests for three years) requires the fulfilling library also to keep and report requests it fills every six months and send the report to the AMS via e-mail: "The subscriber agrees to track such electronic interlibrary loans and report them to the AMS every 6 mths [*sic*] in the following manner: Name of requesting school/library, Journal title, # of articles requested." The CONTU guidelines attempted to offer a numerical standard interpreting the section 108(g)(2) restriction on ILL for qualifying libraries, in other words, that such ILL "arrangements...do not have, as their purpose or effect, that the library or archives receiving such copies or phonorecords for distribution does so in such aggregate quantities as to substitute for a subscription to or purchase of such work." The CSA Illumina provision attempts to offer a similar but also nebulous standard, whereby ILL "is allowed provided that the loan is not done in a manner or magnitude that would replace the recipient library's own subscription to either the Products or the purchase of the underlying Work." ProQuest uses identical language: "provided that the loan is not done in a manner or magnitude that would replace the recipient library's own subscription to either the Products or the purchase of the underlying Work." JSTOR expresses a similar intent but includes reference to the guidelines again: "provided that such use is not at a volume that would substitute for a subscription to the journal or participation in JSTOR by the receiving institution and is in accordance with United States or international copyright laws, guidelines or conventions. By way of example, Institutional Licensees shall comply with the CONTU Guidelines." MathSciNet allows "hard copies" alone, but the "copies must be made in compliance with Section 108 of the Copyright Act of the U.S. and be within the CONTU guidelines." Ovid allow for print copies and delivery "through Subscriber's traditional ILL policies and procedures," which of course could vary from subscriber to subscriber. The Springer ILL provision makes a similar request upon the library fulfilling the request: "Licensee agrees to fulfill ILL requests in Compliance with Section 108 . . . and [the CONTU] Guidelines for the Proviso of Subsection 108(g)(2)."

The American Fisheries Society allows interlibrary loan provided a copyright notice is used and the article is delivered to the requesting patron in print (though it could be delivered to the requesting library in electronic form). How the licensee-library—the fulfiller of the request—would ensure compliance with this request, other than to make such a request, receive some acknowledgment that indeed the requesting library will follow this command, and hope the requesting library honors its pledge, is difficult to conceive. WilsonSelect is the simplest: "Use the Subject Database to fulfill interlibrary loan requests." One advantage, depending on the contents of the database or resources licensed, is that ILL rights could be expanded in the license when compared to existing law. This is so because under the copyright law ILL (i.e., making a copy and then making a public distribution of this copy to a patron at another library—a section 108 transaction) is limited to certain categories of works: "The rights of reproduction and distribution under this section do not apply to a musical work, a pictorial, graphic or sculptural work, or a motion picture or other audiovisual work other than an audiovisual work dealing with news."[142] If the content includes "pictorial or graphic works published as illustrations, diagrams, or similar adjuncts to works of which copies are reproduced or distributed," then ILL is also allowed under section 108.[143] Of course, physically lending a book, periodical, DVD, CD, and so on, is not what the copyright law considers ILL under section 108 (ILL requires the item to be copied first and then the copy transferred to another library); rather, such a transaction is a mere public distribution and, if the item is lawfully made, is allowed under section 109, the same way that circulating the item to the library's own patrons is allowed under the same provision.

A growing issue involves using licensed content to fulfill requests from libraries outside of U.S. jurisdiction. While the clauses discussed here contain a variety of restrictions, none limit the use to in-country loans, though some do require the transaction to mirror that under section 108 and the CONTU guidelines. "Review of ILL clauses in research library licenses indicate that the majority of publishers allow ILL, the majority of publishers do not restrict ILL to the same country, and there is no uniformly adopted language or permission describing ILL services."[144]

Again, ensuring that the requesting foreign library complies with U.S. law may be asking too much, but at least the sourcing U.S. library can request assurances (acknowledgment through the request form, a click-to-agree button, etc.) that the requesting entity will comply with U.S. law. Unless prohibited by the terms of the license, a clause allowing ILL should also extend to international ILL as well. Some licenses, though, restrict further distribution of content unless the use falls under the enumerated permitted uses. As one report concluded: "We believe that US copyright law supports the ability of domestic libraries to participate in ILL arrangements and to send copies of some copyrighted works to foreign libraries, provided the libraries meet the requirements of the law. Although the law is not necessarily explicit about the conditions for sending copies of works through ILL, a few simple steps taken by libraries should provide greater assurance that the arrangements are serving the needs of libraries, researchers, and copyright owners."[145] One of the suggestions is to have the requesting library make an assertion (check a box or click to agree) that its use of the requested item or, to the best of its knowledge, the use of the item by the requesting library patron will conform to U.S. law under either fair use or section 108(g)(2) and "not have, as their purpose or effect, that the library or archives receiving such copies or phonorecords for distribution does so in such aggregate quantities as to substitute for a subscription to or purchase of such work." Again, the library should not promise that such compliance with U.S. law is achieved, as this would be another instance of an impossible clause. The best option would be to engage in notice or other reasonable and recommended efforts, as the *Report of the Task Force on International Interlibrary Loan and Document Delivery Practices* suggests.[146]

INTRANET POSTING AND OTHER INTERNAL USES

Does the library desire to share content through a closed and secure network, an internal library, or a campus intranet? Some licenses prohibit this outright, while others may have a general restriction of posting or further distribution. For example, while ProQuest "endorses the Interlibrary Loan and Scholarly Sharing provisions...Beyond these uses, you may not redistribute any material retrieved from the Products nor allow any use that will infringe the copyright or other proprietary right of ProQuest or its licensors." JSTOR clearly prohibits use of content in course packs and reserves: "Institutions and users may not...reproduce or distribute Content in bulk in any form, such as by including Content in course packs, electronic reserves, or organizational intranets." Kraus Curriculum Development Library (KCDL) indicates that the "Subscriber may not (i) redistribute that material over any network (including any local area network)." Review license provisions to determine if any anticipated uses of the licensed content would be curtailed. One compromise would be to offer that such systems be secure and restricted to authorized users and that all users receive general notice, through an AUP, for example, to ensure that uses conform to the copyright law.

LAW, CHOICE OF

As with choice of forum, many licenses also contain the choice of law.[147] Likewise, the choice of law should have some relation to one or both parties and to the forum chosen.[148] Article 2 of the UCC codifies this standard and indicates that the state chosen must have a "reasonable relationship" to the transaction.[149] "This allows the parties to choose their law in cases where no mandatory fundamental policy would otherwise govern, and also to choose their law even if the choice avoids a mandatory, fundamental policy rule unless there is no reasonable basis for the choice or if the choice violates the fundamental public policy of a state that would be the applicable state law and has a greater interest in resolving the dispute than does the chosen state."[150] A licensor chooses a jurisdiction based upon where it is located, a jurisdiction with which it is familiar. As a business strategy, some vendors may incorporate and have headquarters in jurisdictions where state contract or other law may be more favorable to their objectives. "In selecting the governing law, the parties should seek the existence of a well-developed body of law relating to licensing and evaluate the state's other laws, such as whether the state is a contributory or comparative negligence state."[151] Legal outcomes based on review of existing state law are predictable in a jurisdiction with which the vendor is familiar. Predictability in the market breeds confidence in the marketplace, and this leads to a more robust market, at least in theory. As a practical matter, predictability in terms of the law "reduces litigation costs while increases the likelihood of settlement."[152]

Many state libraries or the libraries of the educational entities within the state are prohibited from entering into any contracts where the governing law or forum is anything but the law of the home state. The infoUSA agreement recognizes this, and its governing law and forum provision ("All legal proceedings relating to the subject matter of this Agreement shall be maintained in the state or federal courts sitting in Douglas County, Nebraska and each party agrees that jurisdiction and venue for any such legal proceedings shall lie exclusively with such courts") adds the following sentences: "Notwithstanding the foregoing, infoUSA acknowledges that governmental entities are governed by the laws of the state in which they are organized. As such infoUSA waives enforcement of the portion of this Agreement which requires the use of Nebraska law and Nebraska courts, where Client is a governmental entity."

Choice of law clauses will be followed unless they violate a fundamental policy of the forum state. If no choice is stated, courts use standards that typically seek to assign the law of the most logical or significant contact with the transaction. "Cases of non-enforcement are significant only because they are so uncommon. The rule of enforcement holds unless the contract choice is over-ridden by a fundamental public policy of the forum state, by a specific mandatory rule that precludes a particular choice, or by the fact that the clause was obtained by fraud or duress exists. That being said, courts in some states have recently found fundamental public policy objections to some otherwise ordinary choices of law."[153] Beware of licenses that select the laws of Virginia or Maryland, the two states that have enacted UCITA (see Chapter 11 for discussion of UCITA).

LOOK AND FEEL PROTECTIONS

After some confusion in early software case law, courts now generally agree that duplicating the look and feel of a program without actually copying any of the code does not violate the copyright owner's exclusive rights,[154] and yet here it is in the NetLibrary-OCLC license: "Member will not, and will not attempt to, develop any products or services that contain the 'look and feel' of any of NetLibrary's products and services." Again, this provision is another example of a license protecting what copyright does not.

MERGER OR INTEGRATION CLAUSE

One of the initial provisions in any contract, including database or other content license agreements, is a merger or integration clause. Where prior agreements exist, an integration clause operates to negate such prior agreements. The provision does much more than this; it excludes other conduct, documents, and so forth, in the interpretation of the agreement. So if the librarian is relying on content gleaned from other sources to impact the license once signed, the gist of this extraneous content should be reduced to writing, expressed in a license term, and included in the agreement. Otherwise, by operation of this provision, such content will not be considered part of the agreement. Moreover, assenting to a contract with such a provision agreement means that the licensee has agreed to this result as well. Such provisions attempt in a sense to "codify" the parol evidence rule into the contract. The provision in essence says this document alone is to be used when interpreting the contract; everything the parties need to know is contained herein.

As explained by a recent decision: "The other provision is a merger clause that indirectly excludes reliance on extra-contractual statements not expressly set forth or referred to in the Contract by barring extraneous evidence to prove the Contract's terms...Both clauses, in effect, invoke the parol evidence rule, which precludes a court from considering extrinsic evidence of prior or contemporaneous agreements in order to change, alter, or contradict the terms of the integrated contract."[155] If the contract represents an integration, then the use of parol evidence is precluded to supplement the contract, in other words, to vary, add to, or contradict its written terms. An example of parol evidence would be a prior oral or written agreement or a contemporaneous oral agreement. This is different from evidence that might assist in the interpretation of the terms that are determined to be a part of the agreement, whether added by the application of parol evidence or not. This is so because evidence concerning interpretation is not evidence concerning parol agreements. Such evidence can take the form of course of performance, course of dealing, usage, or usage of trade. An integration clause is often prefaced by a phrase including the words "entire agreement." An example is the CSA Illumina license: "This agreement constitutes the entire agreement between the parties... supersedes any and all previous and contemporaneous understandings or agreements...The terms of your purchase Orders, in any, are for your convenience and do not supersede any term or condition of this agreement." The point here is to consider whether other elements surrounding the license need to be brought into the specific language of the agreement, such as descriptions of service functionality or compatibility stated in person by a sales representative or found in promotional material received in the mail or in a prior agreement between the parties. If so, get this language into the license, or the integration clause will prevent such elements from having legal effect, as the licensee has agreed through this clause specifically to exclude them.

MONITORING

Usage data but not user data should be permissible as long as such usage data is compiled anonymously. The licensee should not undertake terms and conditions that may impact user expectations of privacy.[156] As discussed in greater detail in the discussion of clauses under Impossible Terms and Enforcement in this chapter, the licensee should be cautious in agreeing to monitor for compliance and to what such clauses may also include, for example, a requirement to report the results of such monitoring to the licensor. The ARTstor license states that "Licensee shall have no obligation to monitor or ensure that Authorized Users are printing copies of ARTstor Content using the print functions(s) described herein" and, later, "it is understood that Licensee shall have no obligation to monitor or ensure that Authorized Users are only downloading ARTstor Content using the download function(s)." It may be acceptable to respond to abuse should it be discovered or the licensee become aware of it; it is another thing to be required to go looking for it. Provisions requiring monitoring and reporting should be tempered to protect patron expectations of privacy and the practical realities of monitoring and enforcement obligations. While reporting of noncompliance may appear benign; if the file-sharing era has taught us anything, it is that notice of potential infringing activity is often closely followed by a request for subscriber or user identity. Such monitoring and reporting should not be required or, at the most, be required only in egregious (defined by a percentage of the database or number of articles, perhaps) circumstances or those involving a repeat offender.

NOTICE, WHEN EFFECTIVE

Determining when and how notice is effective under the agreement is important. Does the agreement alter the traditional mailbox rule (the basic contract concepts of notice were discussed in Chapter 2)—that is, is notice effective when posted? The parties should also consider the acceptable form of the notice. Is e-mail sufficient? Such mechanisms along with fax can be wrought with problems, "as notice could be contractually satisfied and the cure period started without the intended recipient ever realizing it."[157] Remember, the licensee might desire to be notified when changes in content are made or, more important, when changes in the terms of the agreement are proposed. When and how is acceptance effective? "At a minimum, notice should be effective upon receipt, and the sending party should be obligated to send copies to at least two other individuals, at least one of which should be outside of the receiving part, that is, their lawyer. Further, if notice is sent electronically, a written confirmation copy should also be sent."[158] Harris points out that for the sender some form of receipt acceptance can be designated or, in the absence of this, a default acceptance set at a certain number of days after sending. "It is important that the specifics of delivery of the notice are set out in the license; for instance, that the notice should be in writing and delivered by hand, and actual delivery would constitute the time and date of delivery; or if by fax, that a fax back confirming delivery should be sent; or if sent by certified or registered mail, that the notice be deemed to be delivered five days after sending it."[159] For example, Google: "You acknowledge and agree that the form and nature of the services which Google provides may change from time to time without prior notice to you ... Google may stop (permanently or temporarily) providing the Services (or any features within the Services) to you or to users generally at Google's sole discretion, without prior notice to you." Oftentimes licenses contain language that allows the licensor to change the terms of the agreement at will. For example, the Ovid license states: "The terms and conditions of this Agreement may be changed from time to time, upon written or electronic notice to Subscriber; provided, however, that such changes or modifications do not materially diminish the use and value of the Products to Subscriber." Is this a disguised way of saying that changes to nonmaterial terms may be made unilaterally by the licensor "upon written or electronic notice"? If such terms are material, then a change in terms would require explicit assent, and, thus, some notice of this change should precede such alteration.

In general, notice effective upon receipt is the far better rule from the licensee perspective than the traditional mailbox rule, but do not forget to define what constitutes receipt. In other words, has the item actually been read by a librarian or the licensee, or is it merely in his or her e-mail inbox? The license should indicate when notice is required and how far in advance of an event notice is due, what forms of notice are acceptable, and when the notice is effective.

NOTICE OF CHANGES TO TERMS

See NOTICE, WHEN EFFECTIVE; TERMS, CHANGES TO

NOTICE OF COPYRIGHT OR OTHER WARNINGS AND ATTRIBUTIONS

Some licenses prohibit removal of the copyright notice that accompanies the licensed content when accessed by authorized users or otherwise dictate the use of copyright notices or other indications of product attribution. For example, users under the Johns Hopkins University Press license may not "remove, cover, overlay, obscure, block. Or change any copyright notices, legends, or terms of use; or modify or create a derivative work from the Online Reference content without the prior written permission of the copyright holder." JSTOR does not allow the licensee and its users to "modify, obscure, or remove any copyright notice or attribution included in the JSTOR archive." Springer also indicates: "No copyright notices, trademark or proprietary notices, author attribution or other notices or disclaimers included by Springer or any member of the Springer Group in the Springer Content may be removed." This would arguably violate section 1202, removal of copyright management information.[160]

Other licenses impose terms regarding attribution information. For example, the Associated Press Images license commands: "You shall include the credit line set forth in the metadata for any Content." The Taylor and Francis Group license goes further, requiring no changes whatsoever: "Any alteration, amendment, modification or deletion from the License Material, whether for the purposes of error correction or otherwise," is prohibited. The OCLC license provides: "Subscriber shall not omit, obscure or hide from any Authorized Users any notice of a limitation of warranty, disclaimer, copyright, patent, trademark, trade secret, usage limitation or any logo, splash screen or any other terms and/or conditions intended to be displayed to an Authorized User of the FirstSearch service by OCLC or any database supplier thereto." Marquis Who's Who states that it allows users to "print out or copy discrete insubstantial portions of information from the Database solely in conjunction with those uses [from the previous clause: 'business information, research and educational purposes'] and for professional writings provided that proper attribution is provided and all other copyright and other notices contained therein are maintained." MathSciNet concludes its use provision with the following sentence: "Authorized users who do download search results must maintain all copyright and other notices." Several observations may be made regarding such provisions. While such requests of notice or attribution appear reasonable at the outset, consider whether the system will automatically include such notice. How would the licensee prevent users from manually or digitally removing it? Depending on the circumstances, does such requirement fall into the impossible-provision realm? Is it more reasonable to inform authorized users of their obligation to retain such notices when present or to include same if absent? Finally, consider that removal of such information may constitute a violation of the prohibition against alteration of copyright management information under section 1202, if done intentionally.

PERFORMANCE TESTING

If the license is for a library service program or system (automated catalog, circulation, serials management, etc.), it is important to include a provision for acceptable level of performance—not just with your data but with your system. "When this exchange is occurring, it is common for one or both parties to the agreement to want to set forth a procedure and/or metric by which the parties can definitively and objectively determine that the providing party has satisfied its obligation to the receiving party by providing the proper and functional deliverable. First, the acceptance clause sets forth a time period for acceptance."[161] It is also common to establish the time period within which acceptable performance must be achieved, a so-called drop-dead date beyond which, if "no formal acceptance or rejection is completed by that date, the product is deemed accepted by the receiving party."[162] Careful consideration should be given to what constitutes an acceptable level of performance, operability, integration with existing computing and network systems, and so on.[163]

PROHIBITED USES

Prohibited use listings are the clauses that often take away fair-use or other rights which would otherwise exist under the copyright law, and they may in effect expand the licensor's control rights over the content and impact other rights of the licensee and its authorized users. "In many cases, it is just as important to identify the rights that the other party does not obtain through the license grant, and that section may be just as important as the license grant itself."[164] One option is to include an "except" clause: "X, Y, and Z…are prohibited, except as permitted in [reference appropriate section of the agreements where permitted uses are listed]." This indicates that the permitted uses operate as specific exceptions to prohibited uses. The task then is to ensure that each use you desire is reflected in the referenced section. One point is to ensure that the restrictions are consistent with the permissions. Harris lists a number of typical "usage restrictions."[165] Some specific and problematic provisions are also covered independently in this chapter.

Consider the Greenwood Press license that prohibits the licensed content from being "copied, modified, distributed, or made available in any media, including with limitation, electronic media, with or without charge, to any persons other than Authorized Users." Rights of public distribution under section 108 or 109 may be affected. Under section 108, a library can reproduce and make a public distribution of content in its collections through interlibrary loan systems, and under section 109, a library can circulate or lend the content in its collections (i.e., physical items on its shelves that were purchased) to patrons at other libraries. Both activities would be prohibited. Patrons at other libraries are not authorized users under the agreement. The next sentence takes away fair-use rights that might apply to software: "Licensee may not decompile, disassemble or otherwise reverse engineer the software." Software licenses often prohibit reverse engineering, and yet under some circumstances reverse engineering of software is fair use.[166] A similar result is accomplished by the American Chemical Society prohibition "not to forward, transfer, sell, rent, or otherwise knowingly distribute or provide access to the contents of ACS Products or any portions thereof, to any third party." At least the prohibitions are in effect only if the subscriber knows of the use.

Other restrictions can prohibit derivative works under any conditions, some that might otherwise be fair use. The Accessible Archive indicates that the "Licensee shall not modify or create a derivative work of the Licensed Materials without the prior written permission of Licensor." Likewise, under the American Chemical Society license, the user "agrees not to modify, alter, or cerate derivate works of the materials contained in the ACS Products." It seems the American Physical Society Online prohibits even the quotation of an excerpt in another work: "include any article files, or material obtained from any APS Online Journal in other works or otherwise create any derivative work based on any materials obtained from any APS Online Journal."

Some licenses state prohibitions in the negative and with a broad sweep. Consider this Associated Press Images admonition: "You acknowledge and agree that You have no right to use, copy, published, display, transmit, broadcast or otherwise exploit any Content except as expressly authorized in Sections 2.2, 2.3 or 2.4 of these License terms, or as expressly authorized in a separate written agreement (a 'License Agreement') between You and AP."

The BioMed Central license allows linking but prohibits framing. Further, any linking that is done must not imply endorsement and cannot be to a site containing distasteful or offensive material. It is understandable that the license would prohibit linking from an infringing site, but the terms *distasteful* and *offensive* are void of legal meaning and full of various subjective meanings: "provided you do not create a frame or any other bordered environment around the content and provided that any such linking does not imply any endorsement of an product or services and provided further that the website lining to the Web Site does not contain any intellectual property right, including but without limitation copyright, trademark, design right, or patent, infringing, distasteful or offensive material." BioOne: "Unless specifically authorized in writing by BioOne or the copyright holder, no alteration of the words or their order is permitted." So paraphrasing from BioOne's content is out unless you have written permission. Consider the nature of some serial publications, special issues, for example, where every article might be of value and relevant to a particular class. Yet the JSTOR license indicates that users may not "download or print, or attempt to download or print, and entire issue or issues of journal or substantial portions of the entire run of a journal." The point is to review the prohibited uses and determine whether the licensee and its users can abide by the listed restrictions. Some restrictions are unique to certain licensors and may appear surprising to the uninitiated.

PROPRIETARY RIGHTS

As a license is not a sale, licenses often reiterate this fact. Mere acquisition of an item for inclusion in a library collection does include a license to make a backup copy, for example.[167] Moreover, there may be other content involved, such as that protected by trademark or trade secret, or other information that the licensor considers proprietary. As articulated by one court: "Both the district court and defendants also read too much into the phrase 'proprietary rights.' They equate it with ownership, and it often may be used that way. But 'proprietary rights' is not a term of art or of immutable meaning. With respect to intellectual property and patentable inventions or innovations, at least, the term may include interests derived from ownership, though falling short of ownership. Proprietary rights, for example, may include a grant of exclusive use of a process or technological advance without transferring full ownership ... The court[168] uses the term 'proprietary rights' to describe an exclusive licensing agreement Koch obtained from a Swiss corporation for the manufacturing and marketing of a product in North America."[169] Licenses contain reminders and restrictions on the use of such content.

Proprietary rights clauses have been the subject of litigation, but not in library or related contexts. Most disputes relate to patent or other development agreements between two businesses where one party gives the other party access to proprietary content. Often the dispute relates to the use the licensee makes of the proprietary content to compete against the licensor. For example, in *Asset Marketing Systems, Inc. v. Gagnon*, the court considered the following extended proprietary rights provision: "In June 2003, Gagnon proposed that AMS execute an Outside Vendor Agreement (OVA). The OVA included a Proprietary rights clause providing: Client agrees that all designs, plans, specifications, drawings, inventions, processes, and other information or items produced by Contractor while performing services under this agreement will be the property of Contractor and will be licensed to Client on a non-exclusive basis as will any copyrights, patents, or trademarks obtained by Contractor while performing services under this agreement. On request and at Contractor's expense, Client agrees to help Contractor obtain patents and copyrights for any new developments. This includes providing data, plans, specifications, descriptions, documentation, and other information, as well as assisting Contractor in completing any required application or registration. Any source code or intellectual property will remain the property of Contractor. Trademarks, service marks, or any items identifying said Company shall remain the Company's said property. Contractor will allow Company non exclusive, unlimited licensing of software developed for Company."[170] In a library content and service license, the provision may not be as extensive but nonetheless present. The OverDrive Digital Library Reserve Content Service Plan contains such a provision in its simplest form: "Sole ownership of copyrights and other intellectual and proprietary rights to the Application Services shall remain solely with OverDrive or its suppliers." The BioOne license contains the following coupling—a statement of proprietary rights with the obligations imposed on the other party to protect those rights: "Each party shall use its best efforts to safeguard the intellectual property, confidential information and proprietary rights of the other party and third parties. This intellectual property, confidential information and proprietary rights shall include but not be limited to the source code of both BioOne and third parties." The Nature (Academic) license includes the provision as a prohibiting (on the uses undertaken by the licensee) condition: "otherwise use the Licensed Material supplied in accordance with this Agreement in a manner that would infringe the copyright or other proprietary rights contained within it." The Gale license includes a broad statement of the range of proprietary copyrighted and trademarked information: "The information available on Thomson Gale products is the property of Thomson Gale or its licensors and is protected by copyright and other intellectual property laws. This site contains copyrighted material, trademarks and other proprietary information, including without limitation, text, software, photographs, video, graphics, trademarks, service marks, logos, designs, and music and sound (the 'Content'), and such Content is protected under U.S. Copyright laws, U.S. Trademark laws as well as international copyright and trademark laws and treaties." Identifying what is a patent, trademark, or work of protected authorship (copyright) might be relatively easy—for example, a patent registration number or trademark symbol might accompany the property and its use—but different entities have different ideas about what should be confidential and proprietary (e.g., a trade secret). It is best to obtain some clarification or identification of the information to be held confidential or the terms under which such information may be disclosed. Is the pricing information, for example, confidential? It is unclear whether the search software (and its source code) is protected by patent or copyright (intellectual property) or is considered a trade secret to which an entity would in theory have a claim of proprietary right. Again, having some idea of the sort of information the licensor is claiming is proprietary would be useful, as would understanding the impact of that claim and what safeguard entails.

RECITALS, THE "WHEREAS" CLAUSES

It is typical for contracts to include a list of recitals, statements prefaced by the word "whereas."[171] A recital constitutes "[a] preliminary statement in a contract or deed explaining the reasons for entering into it or the background of the trans-action, or showing the existence of particular facts... Traditionally, each recital begins with the word whereas.—Also termed whereas clause."[172] While "recitals may be read in conjunction with the operative portions of a contract in order to ascertain the intention of the parties,"[173] recitals do not have legal import apart from a particular contract: "it is standard contract law that... [they] cannot create any right beyond those arising from the operative terms of the document."[174] While not a substantive part of the license terms, recitals do have an important purpose. "Recitals to a contract provide explanations of those circumstances surrounding the execution of the contract. Ordinarily, recitals are only preliminary in nature and will not, of themselves, be considered binding obligations on the parties or an effective part of their agreement unless referred to in the operative portion of their agreement."[175] This may in turn assist in the interpreting of the substantive provisions of the contract. "'Whereas' clauses, a background section, or several recitals... [are] used to set forth facts pertaining to the agreement which both parties agree up front as fact and agree not to dispute at a later date. Therefore, care should be taken to ensure that these recitals are accurate and based all on fact (i.e., not opinion). In essence, the recitals are admissions of fact by both parties that are difficult, if not impossible, to dispute at a later date. The preamble and recitals are important since it sets the stage for the agreement and may be the most-read portion of the agreement when executives want to decide what deal was made, with whom, and for what purpose."[176] An example would be a recital that included the following or similar language: "whereas the licensor, a standard-setting leader in the provision of online content" or "whereas the licensee has relied on the previous track-record of the licensor in selecting the licensor." A licensor would not want to be held to any suggestion of conduct, nor from the licensee's perspective should the following or similar language be included: "whereas the licensee, having conformed to and fulfilled the obligations in previous agreements."

If the recitals make some mention of the past expertise of a party, this may impact the reasonable efforts a party must undertake. This may be of greater concern in automation software or other service than in content or database agreements.[177] If the service results from a request for proposal (RFP), include notation of this in the recitation; consider also incorporating the standards listed in the call for proposals into the contract.[178] The point is that where the recitals become a substantive part of the agreement, the licensor should be willing and bound to stand behind such statements. If this is so, some licensees may desire a phrase be inserted that indicates recitals are indeed a "substantive" part of the agreement.[179]

A related point to consider is that the laws of some states give recitals (remember, both parties signing the agreement have agreed to the language in the recital, as well as in the other provisions of the agreement) legal significance, treating the recital as conclusive evidence of the facts stated, for example, when a recital contains a statement of fact. A similar result occurs in litigation, when the parties stipulate before the court that for purposes of a particular motion, for example, the facts are true and are not in dispute.

Whereas clauses may contain assertions that the vendor has the requisite experience and/or skill to provide the automated cataloging, circulation, or other data management service it promises to provide and in the manner indicated by the terms of the agreement: "From the developer's viewpoint, its statement of qualifications should be more factual and less like a sales pitch."[180] The recitals can set forth the respective intent of the parties, but recitals should not be used as another way to insert and enforce obligations or standards of conduct on either party.

REMEDIES OTHER THAN DAMAGES

Some license agreements limit recourse to nonmonetary forms. Though unlikely to be found in a database or content agreement, in software agreements, clauses to avoid are the so-called self-help provisions. For example, a licensor might try a remedy, if it believes the library is in material breach, by taking measures to disable the library network to prevent continued breach. On occasion, courts have held that certain intrusive forms of self-help, such as disabling systems, have constituted a violation of the federal computer crime statute.[181] "Electronic self-help is controversial because of the power it gives licensors over integral software enterprises."[182] The better alternative is to require notice of breach and reasonable efforts to cure before any termination or suspension right would be contemplated. Other licenses may limit remedy to termination, often without any measure of refund. Consider the following from the Access NewspaperARCHIVE: "If you do not agree with any of these terms and conditions, your sole remedy is to discontinue use [*sic*] the Service." It is more typical in such circumstances for the licensor to suspend service (as opposed to termination), if the license gives the licensor that right. This also can be problematic, as such scenarios typically do not allow for a refund and, in the author's opinion, instead allow the licensor to impose a form of unilateral penalty on the licensee (see Chapter 16 for an example and discussion of a suspension right and its interrelationship to other provisions). It is also common to limit remedies to restoration of service. In the other extreme is the Access NewspaperARCHIVE, which allows either party to terminate at any time ("Either you may cancel or NewspaperARCHIVE may terminate your membership at any time") but restricts the licensee's remedy to the right to terminate alone, no cure, no damages, and so on ("Cancellation of your Account is your sole right and remedy with respect to any dispute with NewspaperARCHIVE").

REMOTE ACCESS

Considering the preferences by library constituents today, some form of remote access is present in most licenses. The Accessible Archive verifies or regulates remote access by use of "controlled by the Licensor though the use of IP [Internet protocol] addresses (listed in Appendix C) and/or passwords." The American Chemical Society requires the licensee to submit a proposed list of IP addresses for review: "Only those IP addresses submitted by the Licensee and listed on Attachment B will have access to the material." Access to ACS products from within the authorized site is controlled by IP addresses: "Licensee is responsible for providing valid IP addresses for their organization on Attachment B. The form of these IP addresses must be acceptable to the ACS. Only those IP addresses submitted by the Licensee and listed on Attachment B will have access to the material. Licensee is responsible for providing reasonable security to ensure that only Authorized Users have access to its internal network." Alexander Street Press requires "remote [users] access [content] through an authentication (proxy) server that guarantees access only by Authorized Users." Project MUSE is more generous, allowing that "distance learners, alumni, and other off-campus affiliates may access Project MUSE if their internet access is through the campus network or via secure proxy server." UlrichsWeb states access is available "remotely (from locations other than the Licensed Locations) via protected referral URL and/or protected proxy server of Subscriber." Again, the concept is expressed in various ways. Review of provisions relating to remote use and who can qualify for remote access and how that access may be achieved should be made. Consider the conceivable ways in which library users might access information and ensure that, if off-site access is one of the ways, the license language is broad enough to accommodate such access.

RENEWAL

The library-licensee should consider how renewal is treated. So-called evergreen clauses are common. Such provisions indicate that renewal is automatic. "As a threshold matter, evergreen clauses are legally valid. When a contract is renewed via the operation of an evergreen clause, all of the attendant contractual obligations naturally continue for the period of renewal."[183] An option not to renew is provided, but often with an advance notice of at least a month or sometimes 45 or 60 days or more. The Digital Library Reserve Content Service Plan (OverDrive) includes a two-year evergreen provision, coupled with a 90-day period of notice to not renew: "The Agreement shall automatically renew for successive terms of twenty four (24) months unless either party provides written notice of intention not to renew ninety (90) days prior to the expiration of the then current term." It might be convenient to have renewal be automatic, such as with Access NewspaperARCHIVE: "your subscription will be automatically renewed and payment charged to your account as specified in your chosen billing method." However, if this is a chosen option or is the only option, it might be best to add that renewal is automatic unless the price changes, or changes beyond a certain percent, in which case notice of the change would be given and a time period within which the library-licensee could decide not to renew. Oddly, the Access NewspaperARCHIVE license states: "Subscription costs may be changed by the NewspaperARCHIVE at any time and each renewal of your subscription will be at the then standard renewal cost for the period which you originally selected when you subscribed." Again, change of price should be a trigger for notice vis-à-vis the renewal process. Alexander Street Press contains a similar provision: "the charges may change periodically." The author would submit that price is a material term. Therefore, such change should be subject to the general rule (and it is hoped there is a provision in your license agreement to this effect) that changes in price require notice and assent before acceptance; in other words, in the case of a change in price or fee structure, renewal cannot be automatic or conditioned on further use (Access NewspaperARCHIVE: "Everytime you use a NewspaperARCHIVE service, you reaffirm that (i) NewspaperARCHIVE is authorized to charge your designated payment method").

One option where automatic renewal is contemplated is to have this renewal be automatic (including the options not to renew with a reasonable notice period within which the renewal must be made) except when the price or subscription fee will change (in the case of flat-fee subscriptions) or the rate on which the fee is based is changed. The American Mathematical Society includes a provision for notice to be given if the price changes: "The annual fee for this subscription may be raised by written notice to the subscriber, given at least three months prior to the next succeeding renewal date." Should the price go up too high, the three-month notice provision gives the licensee enough time to decide not to renew, in other words, allows a cancellation right: "Either party may terminate this Agreement, effective on the next renewal date, by at least 30 days written notice to the other party." MathSciNet has a similar price change notice provision operating in conjunction with a nonrenewal or cancellation right (which, like others, it refers to as a right to terminate) of at least 30 days' written notice to the other party (as "either" party may "terminate" in this fashion): "The annual fee for this subscription may be raised by written notice to the subscriber, given at least three months prior to the next succeeding renewal date."

Where renewal or nonrenewal involves a time frame within which action must be taken, consider whether the time frame is reasonable. Mergent also uses an automatic renewal, but if either party desires not to renew, then "written notice of its intention not to renew" must be given to the other party "at least sixty (60) days before the end of the then applicable term in which case the Agreement will terminate with the expiration of the then applicable term." In contrast, Mergent may terminate "upon 10 days written notice" for nonpayment or without notice "in the event Customer commits any material breach hereof." In cases of breach, Mergent expects to nonetheless be paid: "Termination by Mergent for nonpayment or material breach will not relieve Customer of its obligation to pay the fees due for the breach of the Term." Ovid also uses automatic renewal unless 60 days' notice is given. Longer periods, measured in months, are assumed to be calendar days, but shorter limits, typical for termination, with clauses of 5, 7, or 10 days, might matter if in calendar days. A five-day notice of termination given on the Friday before a holiday weekend in the summer would be effective on the following Tuesday—leaving essentially one business day to respond. For example, Ovid license states: "If Subscriber or Authorized User is in breach of the terms and conditions of the Agreement, they will have ten (10) business days in which to cure the breach. If they have not cured the breach, Ovid may terminate"; infoUSA also contains an automatic renewal provision but has a shorter "out" period: one can decline to renew as late as 30 days before the end of the current subscription term: "This Agreement shall automatically extend for periods of one (1) year each (a 'Renewal Term') following the conclusion of the Initial Term and each Renewal Term, if any, thereafter, unless terminated prior to such extension. If either party does not want the Agreement to automatically extend at the conclusion of a term, then such party shall give the other party written notice to that effect not less than thirty days before the expiration of the existing term." If a credit of time or days of service was issued during the current subscription period under a downtime provision, for example, then consider whether the credit has altered the duration of the current subscription, as this may impact the requisite time frames as well.

RESERVATION CLAUSES

One concept stressed throughout this book is that a license trumps copyright. This is because if the licensee agrees not to exercise fair-use or other rights the copyright law provides for users (and possibly to undertake other obligations and follow other restrictions), then contract law (the license) does trump copyright law, as the library will be bound to those restrictions under the terms to which it agreed. "Only an affirmative promise by the library that it will not engage in activities other than those specifically discussed in the license would be sufficient to bar a library from engaging in ILL."[184] But what if those rights are specifically addressed in the agreement? Suppose the license merely states that the licensor "reserves all the rights not otherwise granted." What impact does the provision have on the rights not granted? Such clauses are called reservation (of rights) clauses. From the licensor's perspective, the use of a reservation clause is recommended: "Finally, the licensor should also seek to add a provision that any rights not expressly granted to the licensee are reserved by the licensor. This type of provision makes clear that any actions by the licensee beyond the scope of the license granted are a breach of the agreement."[185] However, many courts conclude that such provisions are without legal effect. "To the extent that HRCI relies on the boilerplate reservation of rights provision in the License Agreement, that reliance is misplaced. The reservation of rights provision states: 'All rights not specifically granted to licensee hereunder are expressly reserved by Licensor.' The law in this Circuit is clear, however, that such a clause adds nothing to the substantive prohibitions in the Agreement."[186] To be sure, such clauses indicate that unless the licensor has granted specific rights, those rights are retained by the licensor. "The reservation clause stands for no more than the truism that Stravinsky retained whatever he had not granted. It contributes nothing to the definition of the boundaries of the license."[187] By the same token, a reservation clause cannot take away rights from others by a failure to elucidate those rights. As one commentator explained: "The inclusion of a generic savings clause, such as 'All rights not specifically granted to Licensee are expressly reserved,' has no effect on a library's rights under fair use and Section 108, and hence does not bar lending under ILL arrangements. A publisher's rights are expressly limited by the exceptions in the law, including Sections 107 and 108, so they have no right to forbid activities that Sections 107 and 108 allow."[188] However, if restrictions on section 107, 108, or other rights provisions are stated in the agreement, as prohibited uses, for example, then the library will be bound to honor those restrictions. The library should also avoid agreeing to provisions that forbid all uses other than those specifically granted, as such clauses may indeed impact fair use, section 108 rights such as interlibrary loan, and other rights under the copyright law.

SCHEDULES

Some licenses use schedules to include additional information pertinent to the agreement. If schedules are made part of the agreement, then each requires dating and initialing.[189] Schedules should be referenced in the agreement. For example, the Nature Academic license leaves it to the schedule to define the "Chargeable Users: as set out in the Schedule... Customer Support: the Helpdesk (as set out in the Schedule... License Fee: as set out in the Schedule; Licensed Material: those agreed Nature, NPG Journals, Third-Party Journals, Palgrave Macmillan Journals and Palgrave Macmillan Third Party Journals and/or News elements indicated on the Schedule... Network: the Licensee's local area network system of connected computers at the Site, the IP address for which is set out in the Schedule... Schedule: the attached schedule preceding the Terms to this Agreement." Court have concluded that schedules become part of the agreement: "The Hunters allege that these breaches arise out of four of the contracts signed at the Loan's closing: the Letter, the Draw Schedule, the Construction Agreement, and the Note (collectively, the 'Agreements'). It is undisputed that the Agreements were *valid* and binding contracts."[190] Any schedules mentioned in the license should be reviewed. A court will not view a failure to review all relevant documents favorably. Such mistakes would be unilateral and the fault of the inattentive party.[191]

SELF-HELP

See REMEDIES OTHER THAN DAMAGES

SEVERABILITY

This may be more properly termed survivability of a provision in the agreement. As discussed in an early chapter, the right to and supremacy of contract is near sacrosanct in U.S. law. As a result, courts will do everything in their power to retain the agreement in a dispute over the validity of a contract or any of its terms. "The rule of severability provides that a contract may survive if an illegal clause can be severed from the remainder of the contract without defeating the primary purpose of the bargain."[192] One question courts ask is whether the offending language can be removed but the remaining terms and the contract as a whole remain intact and enforceable. Rather than voiding the entire agreement, "the severability clause allows terms of the agreement that are unenforceable to be severed such that the balance of the agreement can be fully enforced."[193] The offending portions are severed and the contract as a whole, sans the offending language, survives. Severability clauses are common in contracts of all sorts and are valid.

SIGNATURES AND SEAL

Be sure that the person signing the license has the legal authority to do so. To avoid any issues of content inclusion, never sign a blank page, that is, one that contains only the signature lines or spaces. Rather, the signature lines and spaces should follow immediately the last sentence of the agreement. "Doing so limits the potential of fraud through the addition of additional clauses without the knowledge of the other party."[194] Likewise, signatures should be in nonblack ink, assuming the contract is in black ink; creating the signatures in a different color ink than that used in the contract ensures that the original contract is clearly identifiable and distinct from copies.

Some agreements may be signed under seal. Thought to be perfunctory in effect, such designation can have practical impact. "The law regarding contracts under seal has been changed by statute in most of the states. Although in several States the effect of the statutes is unclear, contracts under seal are clearly recognized in the statutes of limitations of 20 American jurisdictions, and the seal seems to be recognized in five States where there is no special period of limitations. In many of the jurisdictions thus recognizing the seal there seems to be no statute or decision depriving the seal of its common-law effect as a substitute for consideration."[195] In addition, under some state laws, such designation may extend the statute of limitations, often doubling, tripling, quadrupling, or further extending the time period within which a claim for breach may be brought: "Finally, AITF argues that even if the D.C. statute of limitation applies, has begun to run, and has not been tolled, the applicable period of limitation is the 12 years provided to sue upon a contract under seal rather than the three-year limit upon all other contract actions. While the notes giving rise to this action were stamped with Petra Banks corporate seal, that does not automatically render them obligations made 'under seal.' A signature over the word 'seal' may operate to place a contract under seal, but the use of a corporate seal is only a mark of identification and genuineness absent any indication, in the document itself or elsewhere, that the parties intended to create an obligation under seal. AITF points to no such indication. We therefore conclude that the three-year limitation period for contracts not under seal applies in the present case."[196] Many companies no longer have or use an actual seal or stamp: "It is true that the presence of a corporate seal may not by itself make a document an instrument under seal...That is the case because corporate seals are routinely employed for identification and as a mark of genuineness, a use which does not necessarily evince an intention to create an instrument under seal. Thus, in order for a document to be an instrument under seal for statute of limitations purposes, something more than a corporate seal, such as, for example, a recitation that the document is 'signed and sealed,' is required...There is no requirement that proof of the parties' intent to create a sealed instrument be proved by extrinsic evidence...Thus, a proper determination of whether a document is under seal is limited in the first instance to an examination of the face of the document itself."[197] As a result, for contracts intended to be made under seal, the word *SEAL* should appear.

SUBLICENSE OR TRANSFER

It is typical for the license agreement to prohibit transfer of the license to another party, even a successor entity. Under the terms of most agreements, the preferred solution to a change in entity status, merger (several small colleges combine into a new corporate entity), dissolution (bankruptcy or some other termination of operations), and so on, is termination of the license agreement with a new agreement struck between the successor entity and the other party. For example, the Greenwood Press license indicates: "This Agreement is non-transferable and may not be sold, assigned, transferred or sublicensed to any other person or entity, including without limitation by operation of law, without the prior written consent of the Licensor." Likewise EBSCOhost prohibits assignment ("This Agreement and the license granted herein may not be assigned by the Licensee to any third party without written consent of EBSCO"), as does LexisNexis, without prior written notice ("The subscribing organization or individual may not assign its rights or delegate its duties under the subscription to access the Online Services without the prior written consent of the provider of the Online Services"), and Springer (no assignment without notice, but licensor can assign: "Licensee may not assign or transfer, directly or indirectly, all or part of the rights or obligations under this Agreement without prior written consent from Springer. Springer may assign this Agreement"). Licensor assignment might occur where the licensor distributes the content directly but later decides that an aggregator would better distribute its content; it might then assign the right to that entity. The license should at least contain the possibility of assignment, subject to the consent of the other party. The licensor should likewise not be able to assign without the permission of the licensee or at least notice of assignment with a chance to terminate.

Clauses like this drive home the point that licensed content is not bought and sold; there are no statutory so-called first-sale rights, as would exist with a book under section 109, to make subsequent public distribution of the content. The Gartner license forbids "sublicensing, leasing, selling, offering for sale or assigning the Product," a list which reads very much like the various public distribution rights granted users and libraries, archives, and educational entities in specific under section 109—for example, "Nothing in the preceding sentence shall apply to the rental, lease, or lending of a phonorecord for nonprofit purposes by a nonprofit library or nonprofit educational institution."[198] If the library purchased a set of photographic reproductions, it could treat the images as it would a collection of books or a print journal subscription. The Associated Press Images license ("You may not, directly or indirectly, sublicense any rights granted herein or redistribute any Content") makes it clear that this is not possible. Brepolis indicates that parent or affiliated organizations (it does not define this term, however) are excluded: "These rights are not extended to Licensee's subsidiaries, parent organizations or to any other affiliated organization or person. The Licensee may not transfer, sublet or confer the rights that are granted to him to any other organization or person." Again, such changes in legal status are unlikely in the future of a public institution, but a private entity such as a corporate licensee or most licensors might undergo such changes through merger, acquisition, consolidation, and so forth. So having continuation of the agreement in light of such an event should be articulated, at least with permission of the other party. The phrase "which shall not be unreasonably withheld" could be added to "without consent" to indicate the permission, to allow that such assignments should be withheld only for good reason and not denied when the change in legal status may not alter the substantive workings of the affected party. As a result, rights should be equal between licensor and licensee.

SURVIVABILITY OF CERTAIN CONTRACT PROVISIONS AFTER TERMINATION

Certain terms often survive the agreement, or there are obligations post termination imposed on the licensee, such as destruction of all copies of the licensed content in its possession. Classen identifies a cluster of typical surviving provisions: those relating to price and payment, proprietary rights, confidentiality and security, patent and other proprietary rights indemnification, general indemnity, limitations on liability, choice of law and choice of forum, arbitration (if applicable), bonds, and business continuity planning, in other words, disaster recovery, if applicable.[199] For example, the BioOne license indicates: "Upon termination the following rights and obligations continue: continuation rights under ¶ 2.1.2, permitted uses under paragraph 3, the prohibited uses under paragraph four, disclaimer of warranties under ¶ 5.1, notice to users of intellectual property under ¶ 5.5 and the safeguarding of intellectual property, confidential information and proprietary rights under ¶ 5.9. If the licensor continues to offer access even after termination, then the same terms (rights and obligations) continue to apply." From the licensee perspective, the warranty and indemnity provisions need to survive the duration of the agreement, as the licensee and its authorized users are likely to continue to use the licensed content obtained during the time the subscription was in place and thus the library needs the assurance (warranty) that the licensor had the legal right to make the content available to continue and protection (the indemnity) in case the licensor was wrong in that warrant as well.

TECHNICAL SUPPORT AND DOCUMENTATION

The scope and availability of technical support should be articulated in the license, including what forms it will take (e-mail, phone, live web chat, etc.) and the hours during which each form is available. If less than 24/7 help is to be provided, what time zones and whose calendar of days (calendar days, weekdays, business days excluding holidays—U.S. or Canadian holidays, etc.) will be used must be determined. Documentation and technical assistance during installation and upgrades are paramount in library automation or other service agreements. "The Agreement should contain a schedule specifying in considerable detail exactly what must be delivered as Documentation."[200] What is deliverable and when it is deliverable are important documentation questions in software agreements. "While some service vendors will provide client training on a casual basis during project development, a client that desires staff training should not rely on casual arrangements."[201] If training is included, the scope and duration should be stated. Does training survive the implementation period?

TERMINATION RIGHTS

Under what conditions is termination possible, and are the termination rights balanced between the parties? Does each party possess the right to terminate without cause with adequate notice, or is this right reserved for the vendor alone? If termination occurs, is a refund owed the licensee? The author would argue that even in cases where the termination results from the alleged fault of the licensee, a lack of refund acts as a penalty. Is a period of cure required before any termination can occur? Is there sufficient (form and mode) notice before termination can occur, in any case? Some courts see a distinction between termination and cancellation, though most licenses reviewed for this book do not appear to entertain the difference. In defining the two in § 2-106, the UCC underscores the critical distinction: "Termination occurs when either party pursuant to a power created by agreement or law puts an end to the contract otherwise than for its breach. Cancellation occurs when either party puts an end to the contract for breach by the other and its effect is the same as that of termination . . . Breach, or the absence thereof, is the essential difference."[202] Or perhaps in a more elaborate manner: "The result of a cancellation is something at odds with, or inconsistent with, the terms of the contract, obligation, or instrument canceled. To end a contract in a manner inconsistent with its terms is the difference that distinguishes a cancellation from other words of art describing the termination of a contract. Where payments under a contract are contingent, the cessation of payments upon the occurrence of the contingency is in no way inconsistent with the terms of the contract. Thus, the contingent obligation to make payments under a contract may well be described as having been satisfied when, upon the happening of the contingency, no further obligation exists; the happening of the contingency does not, however, in a legal sense, cancel the obligation, since, under the terms of the contract, no further obligation comes into existence."[203] For example, BioOne has automatic renewal but allows for expiration (termination, i.e., a right not to renew granted by the terms of the agreement) "upon tender of sixty (60) days notice by either party" or cancellation under various scenarios, including "a material or persistent breach of any term" by either party. Springer uses an identical provision. Most licenses, however, are not that careful with language. For ease of discussion, if the license refers to "a termination" or "may terminate," this phrasing is used herein. The American Mathematical Society includes mutual termination rights but is more true to a cancellation right, a decision not to renew, as termination rights cannot be exercised at any time: "Either party may terminate this Agreement, effective on the next renewal date, by at least 30 days written notice to the other party." The Kraus Curriculum Development Library (KCDL) license specifies how notice is to be given: "This Agreement may be terminated at any time for any reason by either party with 30 days written notice specifying the grounds for termination, delivered as described in Section 8 of this agreement." This is an odd provision. Why would one party need to specify the "grounds for termination" if such termination can be "at any time" and "for any reason"?

Termination rights are often woefully one-sided. Typically, the licensor can choose not to renew the license, but this is really not a termination right, just a logical right not to renew (though in evergreen agreements, notice of nonrenewal must be given first). A termination right allows a party to end the subscription before the term of the agreement is up. Consider Associated Press (AP) Images: "AP may terminate any license granted hereunder or in any Licensee Agreement at any time for any reason whatsoever immediately upon notice given to You. In such event, Your sole remedy in such event shall be to receive the amounts You actually paid to AP in respect of such Content." A so-called termination of convenience, such clauses "permit the owner to unilaterally cancel its contractual obligations [by terminating the contract] and still avoid committing a breach of contract which would expose it to damages. We agree that the act of terminating the contract is not itself a breach of contract by Gulf Liquids because it was merely exercising its right to terminate the contract with or without cause."[204] Likewise, SilverPlatter WebSPIRS can terminate in response to a breach of any term: "If the

Customer or an Authorized User breaches any term of this Agreement, SilverPlatter may, in addition to its other legal rights and remedies, terminate the license granted hereunder on 7 days' notice to the Customer, unless such breach has cured within such notice period." Here also is the stark impact of being responsible for the acts of your customers, clients, or patrons. (Note here that "customer" refers the licensee library or institution.)

Material breach should trigger a cancellation right, but not breach of just any term. Consider too cure rights and how the failure to cure is linked to termination. Often the cure right that is available after a notice of breach is received is of rather short duration—seven days: "ASP [Alexander Street Press] may, in addition to its other legal rights and remedies, terminate this license 7 days after written notice to Customer, if Customer has not remedied the breach within the 7 days." Once sufficient notice is received, the tolling of the cure right begins, and where this cure right must be exercised within a very limited number of days, it is important to determine whether the duration is expressed in calendar or business days. The infoUSA license contains a material breach trigger but with a more reasonable time to cure proviso: "Either party may terminate the Agreement if the other materially breaches any term or condition of the Agreement and fails to remedy such breach within thirty (30) days after written notice of such breach or becomes subject to any receivership, insolvency, bankruptcy, moratorium or similar proceeding for more than thirty (30) days." As in most content licenses, "material breach" is not defined. However, the next sentence appears to create an exception: "infoUSA may immediately terminate this Agreement if Licensee causes or facilitates any unauthorized use or distribution of the infoUSA data." Such act would surely be a material breach, for which apparently there is no notice requirement nor right to cure. Lexis effects its termination ten days after the library is in "receipt of an appropriate notice of termination, unless a later date is specified in the notice." The American Physical Society (APS) Online is shorter still: "the Agreement will terminate unless within five (5) business days after receiving written or e-mail notice of the violation, Institutional Subscriber implements procedures, reasonable satisfactorily to APS, to prevent future violation." Here, at least, the concept of cure is tied to procedures to prevent recurrence. Again, some thought to mutually agreeable reasonable cures is preferred from the licensee's perspective. Note that APS uses business days, but the other example licenses just state "days," which could be calendar days. Both ARTstor ("to the extent practicable, to notify Licensee in advance before disabling access to Licensee's Local Content") and MWW ("will provide the Licensee written notification of any intent to terminate") will provide notice if a termination event will occur and offer time to correct, "although ARTstor would make reasonable efforts to collaborate with an institution to resolve such infringements before terminating such access," and MWW would "allow the Licensee a reasonable time frame to correct the breach."

CSA Illumina appears to give either party, in response to the other's breach, the right to terminate: "If a party breaches any material term of this Agreement and does not cure after 30 days written notice, the Agreement may immediately be terminated in whole or as to the affected Product." Observe that a notice of breach would need to precede any termination by 30 days, during which time the party in breach would have a right to cure without further threat of termination. The American Mathematical Society includes mutual termination rights, but these are more true to cancellation rights, in other words, a decision not to renew, as the termination cannot be exercised at any time: "Either party may terminate this Agreement, effective on the next renewal date, by at least 30 days written notice to the other party." ARTstor: "in the event that either Party believes that the other Party has materially breached . . . such party shall so notify the breaching Party in writing. The breaching Party will have 60 days from the receipt of such notice to cure the alleged breach and to notify the non-breaching part in writing that such cure has been effected. If the breach is not cured within the 60-day period, the non-breaching party shall have the right to terminate the Agreement upon written notice." What breaches are material? Consider two approaches. FirstSearch indicates that "subscriber's obligations under the Section 6 are material to this agreement." EBSCOhost, for example, considers lack of payment or delay in payment a material breach: "Failure or delay in rendering payments due EBSCO under this Agreement will, at EBSCO's option, constitute material breach of this Agreement." Again, it is important to define what breaches are material and the consequences of those breaches. Finally, where termination occurs, there should be a refund right for payments made by the licensee. The licensor might agree to a refund only when the licensee was not at fault for breach, but it could be argued that if the licensee does not have a refund right even when the licensee was at fault, then the lack of a refund acts as a penalty or fine and represents payment for a service the licensee is no longer receiving.

TERMS, CHANGES TO

Can terms of the license be changed? If so, how is change accomplished, and does the licensee (usually it is the licensor that desires the right to change terms at any time) have the right to receive notice with a right to accept or decline the new term or, in the alternative, to terminate the agreement if the changes are not acceptable but the licensor refuses to modify the changes? Change of terms clauses operate in conjunction with other provisions. "Continued use equals assent" can be dangerous because, as such, it tacitly represents agreement to the changes.

Observe the following clause, found in the preamble of an agreement clause in a license reviewed by the author: "We may alter this agreement at our discretion and your continued use after any change indicates your acceptance of that change." According to decisions such as *Douglas v. Talk America, Inc.*, such a clause in a consumer or mass-market license would, without more notice, be unenforceable. "Talk America posted the revised contract on its website but, according to Douglas, it never notified him that the contract had changed. Unaware of the new terms, Douglas continued using Talk America's services for four years."[205] The court concluded that the new terms were not part of the agreement: "Even if Douglas had visited the website, he would have had no reason to look at the contract posted there. Parties to a contract have no obligation to check the terms on a periodic basis to learn whether they have been changed by the other side."[206] A proposed new term once the contract is formed represents an offer for additional terms that requires assent. "Further, the assent of both parties to a modification is necessary; the mental purpose of one of the parties to a contract cannot change its terms."[207] This is basic contract law, as expressed by one court: "It is axiomatic that parties to an existing contract may modify the agreement by mutual assent."[208] Similar to the *Douglas* facts (though this case involved a mass-market or consumer license), consider the example from Cengage Learning: "We may amend the Terms at any time by posting the amended terms to the site." Under the precedent discussed here and in previous chapters, this language is insufficient to bind licensees to new terms merely posted on its website. "In order to modify a contract, the parties must mutually assent to the new terms."[209] On the chance that some courts may uphold this provision (a possibility in a negotiated license agreement), do not agree to any such clause. Do not allow the license agreement to alter the basic premise of contract law: "As a general principle, a contract cannot be modified unilaterally; rather, the parties must mutually consent to the modification. Thus, a party to an existing contract may modify that contract only with the assent of the other party to the contract."[210] Notice of change and assent to that change must be forthcoming and assent explicit. The ARTstor license is consistent with the basic principles of contract formation, modification, and assent and indicates that the terms and conditions "may be amended from time to time" but that material terms ("materially conflict" with the existing terms) are provided with 30 days' notice of such changes, though the notice may be in electronic form such as e-mail. If the licensee objects, then the licensor will "use all reasonable efforts to agree upon mutually acceptable language." Changes would become effective upon mutual agreement, though the license is silent as to how assent would be made.

TRADEMARKS

License agreements in the library setting relate to content protected by copyright, but there may be times when trademark is involved. The Digital Content Reserve Content Service Plan (OverDrive) refers to content that can be the subject matter of trademark: "OverDrive reserves the right to display its branding, trademarks, logos, and/or other third party marketing or promotional material related to the

Application Services on the Library Website." As a result, some license agreements specifically claim ownership rights in their trademarks. For example, in the Engineering Village license: "All trademarks appearing on this Site are the property of their respective owners." Likewise, ScienceDirect: "All trademarks appearing on this Site are the property of their respective owners." Cengage Learning goes further: "All trademarks, service marks, trade names, logos and graphics ('Marks') indicated on this site are registered trademarks of Cengage Learning, its affiliates and/or licensors, in the United Sates and other countries. You may not make any use of Cengage Learning's Marks without the prior written consent of Cengage Learning." The sine qua non of trademark infringement is use of a similar mark such that it causes confusion as to the origin or source of the goods or services. This might occur, as unlikely a scenario as it might be, when a licensee-library places on its website a logo or other trademark as a hot-button link to activate and access the database of the licensor such that it appears that the library created and populated the database. It is more likely the library merely wants to indicate in an attractive way, through use of logos as hot-button links, that JSTOR and other vendors' products are available for use by faculty, staff, and students. Even if use by the library would infringe a trademark, there are fair-use concepts in trademark law, called nominative fair use, that would likely allow for use of the name to identify to library users that such products are available.[211] JSTOR anticipates such uses and that the door swings both ways: "Neither JSTOR nor Institutional Licensee may use the other's name or trademark's in a way likely to cause confusion as to the origin of goods or services, or to endorse or show affiliation with the other, except as specifically approved. Notwithstanding the foregoing, (i) JSTOR may use Institutional Licensees' names and/or the names of the libraries in brochures or other materials to identify Institutional Licensees as participants in JSTOR along with other participants, and (ii) Institutional Licensees are encouraged to use JSTOR's name and logo to announce participation to Authorized Users and to train Authorized Users on the use JSTOR." Likewise, Mergent allows that "Customer may only use such trademarks to identify the source of the Data in accordance with the terms hereof, and will not seek to register or use all of [*sic*] any part of such Trademarks as a corporate name or designation." Perhaps impractical is the Springer license, expressing concern that use of its mark meets its quality standards and so desires access to the library network under a section titled "Springer's Trademarks": "Springer shall have the right to review and approve all uses on Licensee's secure network of the publication titles, trademarks, logos, colophons, proprietary legends or legal notices provided by Springer in connection with the applicable publications or Springer Content, in order to ensure compliance with this Agreement and Springer's quality control standards." If use of a licensor trademark is contemplated as a visual cue to patrons when navigating a library webpage, catalog, and so forth, it is best to secure this right in the license. As with the copyright license continuum, a license agreement overrides any trademark fair-use rights as well.

WARRANTIES AND DISCLAIMERS

Licenses often disclaim all warranties associated with the condition of the licensed content but one. Licensors will make at least one sort of warranty: that the licensor has the right to make the content available, and that by doing so, in a database, it is not infringing copyright, another intellectual property right, or some other right of someone else. A licensor should also indemnify the licensee should its warrant prove to be incorrect. This warranty as well as the indemnification should survive the agreement, as the licensee might continue to make use of content obtained from the licensed content (database) after the agreement ends—unless of course the license contains one of those wacky provisions obligating the licensee to destroy all of the licensed content it its possession at the time of termination of the agreement.[212] If this content turns out then to be infringing, the strict nature of copyright liability will impose the liability upon the individual user (infringer) and potentially, vicariously (also strict), upon the institution-licensee as well. The window for infringement would exist for three years beyond cessation of the use of the content (not just three years from the license termination date), the length of the statute of limitations for civil copyright infringement.

From the licensee's perspective, the agreement should indicate that the licensor makes the following warranties: that it has valid title to the content or otherwise has the legal ability to offer the content under the terms of the agreement; if a license for a software service (library automation system), that the system will operate within certain service levels and performance standards; that service (development, support, or maintenance) should be rendered in a professional and workmanlike manner, as courts have generally held that there is no implied warranty for the provision of services.[213]

From a licensor's perspective, a warranty that is "to the best of its knowledge"[214] is preferable. From the licensee's perspective, this is unwise: "Make sure that the warranty is straightforward and unambiguous. Wording like 'to the best of the publisher's knowledge' is not acceptable."[215] Springer contains just such a weak expression of noninfringement: "Springer warrants that it will use commercial reasonable efforts in its production of media for delivery of the Springer Content to the Licensee and that, to the best of its knowledge, use by Licensee of the Springer Content pursuant to the terms and conditions of this Agreement will not infringe the rights of third parties." In the realm of liability, best liability or even best practices may not be good enough.

Warranties come in two flavors: express and implied. An express warranty is created "by making statements relating to software or other information in banner advertisements, sales literature, and advertisements. Website promotional materials, product descriptions, samples, or advertisements may create express warranties."[216] Implied warranties are not stated explicitly but exist based on language used in the license: "Unless the contract expressly disclaims or modifies it, a license contains an implied warranty that the transferor has a right to make the transfer. At least in cases involving transferors that are commercial parties regularly involved in such transactions, the transaction may also contain a warranty that the transferred subject matter will be received free of any claim that it infringes third-party rights. When or whether such obligation arise depends both on the terms of the contract and on the type of subject matter to which the transaction pertains."[217] Most licenses contain express warranties relating to the ability of the licensor to make the content so licensed available. For example: "Licensor [Greenwood Press] represents and warrants that it has the right and authority to make Licensed Materials available pursuant to these terms and conditions and that providing the Licensed Materials to Licensee does not infringe upon any copyrights, patent, trade secret, or other proprietary right of any third person." In another example: "ProQuest warrants that it has all rights necessary to enter into this Agreement and to provide the Products to you." The Accessible Archive license contains similar language: "Licensor warrants that it has the right to license the rights granted under this Agreement to use Licensed Materials . . . and that use of the Licensed Materials by Authorized Users in accordance with the terms of this Agreement shall not infringe the copyright of any third party." In a technical sense, this is not the case. A use under the terms of the agreement by an authorized user might indeed be a technical infringement of copyright, for example, the right to construct course packs in excess of fair use. This is the whole point of licenses from the library perspective— that the library might obtain some broader set of use rights than it might otherwise have under the copyright law. What the sequence of permissions assures the database aggregator, the library, and its patrons is that a promise has been made by the original copyright owner not to sue if the use conforms to the terms of the license. These terms are transferred down the chain of permission and may also at times be the reason some terms an aggregator presents are not open for discussion, as the aggregator is likewise subject to a license agreement. "If an express promise or representation becomes part of the bargain, that express promise is enforceable."[218] Consider the use in the American Fisheries Society license of a simple and effective sentence: "No warranties are required of the subscribing institution and AFS offers none." At least it's balanced.

HAPI Online offers several warranties unrelated to intellectual property rights, in other words, either that material is not infringing or it has permission to supply same; rather, it "warrants that HAPI does not and will not contain any libelous, slanderous, or obscene materials, and does not and shall not violate any persons right of privacy."

Related to this is a warranty that the licensor is not aware (to the best of licensor's knowledge) of or engaged in any pending litigation or threat of litigation, nor is it aware of "any basis for any such action"[219] that might interfere with the licensor's ability to enter into the agreement in general or to make warranties related to third-party intellectual property rights. The JSTOR license is more typical, offering assurances regarding the noninfringing (or "I won't sue you if...") nature of the content supplied: "JSTOR represents and warrants under the laws of the United States that use of the JSTOR Archive by Authorized Users in accordance with the terms of this Agreement shall not infringe the copyright of any third party. The fore-going shall not apply, however, to... usage of the JSTOR Archive by Institutional Licensees or Authorized Users in violation of these terms and Conditions of Use."

"Hidden" in Gale's disclaimer of the usual warranties is one a bit more troubling. See if you can spot it: "Gale and its affiliates, agents and licensors disclaim all warranties and cannot and do not warrant the accuracy, completeness, currentness, noninfringement, merchantability or fitness for a particular purpose of the information available through the service or the site itself." The disavowing of any responsibility that the information it supplies might be infringing is troubling. Gale is basically indicating that it makes no promises the content it is supplying to you is not already infringing some right. Not only is there no warranty that it can supply the content, but it is specifically disclaiming any implied license indicating that it does have right. Unfortunately, "[a] warranty clause in the license should reflect your comfort and not your suspicion."[220] Elsevier, in its ScienceDirect agreement, states: "This site and all content, products and services included in or accessible from this site are provided 'as is' and without warranties or represen-tations of any kind (express, implied, and statutory, including but not limited to the warranties of title and noninfringement and the implied warranties of merchantability and fitness for a particular purpose) all of which Elsevier disclaims to the fullest extent permitted by law. Your use of the site is at your sole risk." Likewise, WilsonSelect includes in its laundry list of disclaimers that "any Wilson Product or any of the content therein provided by Wilson" is made available "without warranty of any kind" and in specific is "provided 'as is,' without warranty of kind to subscriber, authorized users or any third party, including but not limited to, an express or implied warranties of merchantability; fitness for subscriber's purpose or system integration; accuracy of informational content; non-infringement; quiet enjoyment; and title." Such express disclaimer negates any implied warranty that the licensor has the authority to make available the licensed content.

ENDNOTES

1. Liblicense, Licensing Digital Information: A Resource for Librarians, http://www .library.yale.edu/~llicense/index.shtml (a web resource on licensing includes sample

license language and commentary). A listing is also found at Tuula Haavisto, Licensing and Public Libraries, http://www.ifla.org/IV/ifla66/papers/041-126e.htm. See also Duncan E. Alford, *Negotiating and Analyzing Electronic License Agreements*, 94 Law Library Journal 621 (2002).

2. See, for example, Principles for Licensing Electronic Resources promulgated jointly by the American Association of Law Libraries, the American Library Association, the Association of Academic Health Sciences Libraries, the Association of Research Libraries, the Medical Library Association, and the Special Libraries Association. That statement is available at http://www.arl.org/sc/marketplace/license/licprinciples.shtml. The University of California Libraries Collection Development Committee, Principles for Acquiring and Licensing Information in Digital Formats (May 1996), http://libraries.universityofcalifornia.edu/cdc/principlesforacquiring.html.

3. Licenses from following entities were included in this review: Access NewspaperARCHIVE, Accessible Archives, Alexander Street Press, American Chemical Society, American Fisheries Society, American Mathematical Society, American Physical Society Online, American Society of Civil Engineers, American Statistical Association and Institute of Mathematical Statistics, ARTstor, Associated Press Images, Bibliography of Asian Studies Online, BioMed Central, BioOne, Bowker's Books in Print, Brepolis, Cambridge Journals Online, Cengage Learning, Columbia International Affairs Online, CQ Press, CSA Illumina, EBSCO eBook Collection (formerly NetLibrary), EBSCOhost, Engineering Village, Euclid Prime, Evergreen ILS, FirstSearch, Gale, Gartner, Google, Greenwood Press, Gutenberg-e Columbia University Press, HAPI Online, ISI Web of Knowledge, Johns Hopkins University Press, JSTOR, Kraus Curriculum Development Library, Koha, LexisNexis, Marquis Who's Who, MathSciNet, Mergent, NewGenLib, Online Computer Library Center, Oxford English Dictionary, Ovid, Project MUSE, ProQuest, ScienceDirect, SPIE Digital Library, Springer, Taylor and Francis Group, *The Chronicle of Higher Education*, UlrichsWeb, SilverPlatter WebSPIRS, Westlaw Campus Research, WilsonSelect, and Wharton Research Data Services.

4. Raymond T. Nimmer, 2 Information Law § 11.53 (database updated in Westlaw, November 2011).

5. *Id.*

6. AT&T Mobility LLC v. Concepcion, 131 S.Ct. 1740 (2011).

7. Brower v. Gateway 2000, Inc., 697 N.Y.S. 2d 569 (Sup. Ct. 1998), ICC arbitration clause held unconscionable: procedural ("contract formation process") and substantive ("substance of the agreement in order to determine whether the terms unreasonably favor one party") unconscionability. But see Filias v. Gateway 2000, Inc., 1997 U.S. Dist. LEXIS 7115 (E.D. Mich. 1997), transfer of venue to Chicago, in accordance with ICC arbitration clause.

8. See, for example, 17 U.S.C. § 108(a): "Except as otherwise provided in this title and notwithstanding the provisions of section 106, it is not an infringement of copyright for a library or archives, or any of its employees acting within the scope of their employment,

to reproduce no more than one *copy or phonorecord* of a work..." See, for example, 17 U.S.C. § 109(a): "Notwithstanding the provisions of section 106(3), the owner of a particular *copy or phonorecord* lawfully made under this title, or any person authorized by such owner, is entitled, without the authority of the copyright owner, to sell or otherwise dispose of the possession of that *copy or phonorecord*." See, for example, 17 U.S.C. § 108(a): "Except as otherwise provided in this title and notwithstanding the provisions of section 106, it is not an infringement of copyright for a library or archives, or any of its employees acting within the scope of their employment, to reproduce no more than *one copy or phonorecord* of a work..."

9. Directive 96/9/EC of the European Parliament and of the Council of 11 March 1996 on the legal protection of databases, Official Journal L 077, March 27, 1996, pp. 20–28 (EU Database Directive).

10. U.S. v. Swartz, Criminal Complaint, at ¶ 10, No. 1:11-cr-10260-NMG (Dist. Mass., filed July 7, 2011).

11. See Druyan v. Jagger, 508 F. Supp. 2d 228, 237–238 (S.D.N.Y. 2007) and the cases discussed therein.

12. Nimmer, *supra* note 4, at § 11.80.

13. Guideone Insurance Co. v. U.S. Water Systems Inc., 950 N.E.2d 1236, 1241 (Ind. App. 2011).

14. Janowsky v. U.S., 23 Cl. Ct. 706, 715 (1991): "a contract is voidable at the option of the government when the official who made the agreement lacked actual authority to bind the government." See also Empresas Electronics Walser, Inc. v. U.S., 1980 WL 99733 (Ct. Cl.), cert. denied, 449 U.S. 953 (1980), an agency "can disavow" the unauthorized promises of its agents; and Century 21 v. Larry J. Hellhake and Associates, Inc., 636 P.2d 168 (Idaho 1981), an agreement between a partner and a partnership found voidable for lack of authority.

15. Lesley Ellen Harris, Licensing Digital Content: A Practical Guide for Librarians 90 (2d ed. 2009).

16. See U.S. v. Swartz, Criminal Complaint, at ¶ 10, No. 1:11-cr-10260-NMG (Dist. Mass., filed July 7, 2011).

17. Elsevier B.V. v. UnitedHealth Group, Inc., 2011 WL 1002659, *1 (S.D.N.Y. 2011).

18. Clinical Insight, Inc. v. Louisville Cardiology Medical Group, PSC, 2011 WL 1549478, *2 (W.D.N.Y. 2011) (slip copy): "Plaintiff also alleges that the defendant has exceeded the number of users authorized to use Pronto, but has failed to pay additional licensing fees for use of the software by those users."

19. See Licensing Principles, prepared by IFLA's Committee on Copyright and other Legal Matters (CLM), 2001, http://www.ifla.org/V/ebpb/copy.htm (Principles P10–P12).

20. Association of Research Libraries, Strategic and Practical Considerations for Signing Electronic Information Delivery Agreements (prepared by Patricia Brenan et al.), http://www.arl.org/sc/marketplace/license/licbooklet~print.shtml (faculty, staff, students, campus, branch campus, colleges and departments, noninstitutional patrons,

walk-ins, visitors including faculty, authorized account holders, distance learners, consultants, public libraries, consortia and state institutions, local academic libraries, network consortia libraries, users defined geographically).

21. Harris, *supra* note 15, at 72–73.

22. The sentence reads in full: "'Authorized Users' are (a) full and part time students and employees (including faculty, staff, affiliated researchers, and independent contractors) of Licensee and the institution of which it is a part, regardless of the physical location of such persons and (b) library cardholders or patrons not affiliated with Licensee who are physically present at Licensee's site(s) ('walk-ins')."

23. See Community for Creative Nonviolence v. Reid, 490 U.S. 730 (1989).

24. The complete provision reads: "Access to the ACS Products from within the Authorized Site is controlled by Internet Protocol (IP) addresses. Licensee is responsible for providing valid IP addresses for their organization on Attachment B. The form of these IP addresses must be acceptable to the ACS. Only those IP addresses submitted by the Licensee and listed on Attachment B will have access to the material. Licensee is responsible for providing reasonable security to ensure that only Authorized Users have access to its internal network."

25. The American Society of Civil Engineers indicates that an "'Authorized Site' is a localized site (one geographical locations) that is under a single administration."

26. The Accessible Archives provision begins with a two-word header functioning sentence "Authorized Users" then indicates the two categories of authorized users, introducing each with a header functioning sentence ("Persons Affiliated with Licensee" and "Walk-Ins").

27. For example, the American Physical Society Online provides for the concept of others besides employees, faculty, staff, and students who might also be properly in the library: "An Authorized User is any individual who is an employee, faculty, staff and/or student officially affiliated with the Subscriber, and persons with legal access to the library's collections and facilities on-site." The American Society of Civil Engineers states that "Authorized Users" includes "persons with legal access to the library's collections and facilities at the Authorized Site, using an IP address within the range identified in the Appendix" (p. 5).

28. Harris, *supra* note 15, at 52–54, lists a number of uses to consider adding: view, reproduce, store or save, search, browse, retrieve, display, download, print, forward electronically, email to oneself, fax, electronic link[ing], caching, closed network access such as intranet, extranet, LAN or WAN, post on a website, use for interlibrary loan, index, include in course packets (print or digital) or training manuals, include in electronic [or print] reserves, use in distance education as part of course content separate from an e-reserve or e-course pack, back-up (server) copies, and back-up (archival) copies for a specific period of time. See also under "usage or authorized uses" the following: "personal, noncommercial, scholarly, research, scientific, educational, review or comment, private use or research, electronic reserves, class packages,

training courses, internal research in the course of employment, business, or profession" (*id.* at 57). Likewise IFLA indicates consideration of various principles.

29. Licensing Principles, prepared by IFLA's Committee on Copyright and other Legal Matters (CLM), 2001, http://www.ifla.org/V/ebpb/copy.htm: "P15. At a minimum the license should permit users to read, download, and print materials for their own personal purposes, without restrictions."

30. See Tomas A. Lipinski, *A Functional Approach to Understanding and Applying Fair Use,* in 45 ANNUAL REVIEW OF INFORMATION SCIENCE AND TECHNOLOGY (ARIST) 525 (Blaise Cronin ed., 2010) (pp. 525–621).

31. Harris, *supra* note 15, at 54.

32. S.O.S., Inc. v. Payday, Inc., 886 F.2d 1081, 1087–1088 (9th Cir. 1989).

33. Jacobsen v. Katzer, 535 F.3d 1373, 1380 (Fed. Cir. 2008).

34. Netbula, LLC v. BindView Development Corp., 516 F. Supp. 2d 1137, 1150 (N.D. Cal. 2007).

35. Sun Microsystems, Inc. v. Microsoft Corp., 188 F.3d 1115, 1121–1122 (9th Cir. 1999).

36. The Johns Hopkins University Press license allows a variety of "personal" uses. For example, users may "download and print one copy of each chapter or entry for personal use" and "send one copy by email, hard copy, or fax to one person in the Subscriber's campus/institutional network at another location for that individual's personal use."

37. 17 U.S.C. § 101: "To perform or display a work 'publicly' means to perform or display it at a place open to the public or at any place where a substantial number of persons outside of a normal circle of a family and its social acquaintances is gathered; or to transmit or otherwise communicate a performance or display of the work to a place specified by clause (1) or to the public, by means of any device or process, whether the members of the public capable of receiving the performance or display receive it in the same place or in separate places and at the same time or at different times."

38. *Id.*

39. See Kupetz, *Beware When Dealing with Licensors of Intellectual Property: Avoiding Potential Pitfalls Facing Licensees and Lenders When Bankruptcy Intervenes,* 17 COMPUTER LAW 21 (2000); Kupetz, *Dealing with Issues in Chapter 11 Cases Filed by Licensors of Intellectual Property,* 16 E-COMMERCE AND STRATEGY 1 (2000); and Bartlett, *Effects of Bankruptcy on Licensing Under 11 U.S.C. § 365 (n),* 5 JOURNAL OF PROPRIETARY RIGHTS 20 (2000).

40. BLACK'S LAW DICTIONARY (9th ed.) (Bryan A. Garner ed., 2009) (no pagination in Westlaw), defines executory as something "[t]o be performed at a future time; yet to be completed" and an executory contract as a "contract that remains wholly unperformed or for which there remains something still to be done on both sides, often as a component of a larger transaction and sometimes memorialized by an informal letter agreement, by a memorandum, or by oral agreement."

41. See 11 U.S.C. § 365. See, for example, RCC Technology Corp. v. Sunterra Corp., 287 B.R. 864, 865 (M.D. Md. 2003): "However, there is a long line of authority holding that intellectual property licensing agreements such as the SLA [the Software Licensing

Agreement at issue in the case] are executory contracts"; reversed and remanded 361 F.3d 257, 264 (4th Cir. 2003), but agreeing that the contract was executory: "On this point, we agree with the district court that the Agreement was executory when Sunterra petitioned for bankruptcy"; and In re Chiwich, Inc., 54 B.R. 427, 430 (S.D.N.Y. 1985): "The court emphasized the fact that the licensee was required to do more than merely account for and pay royalties. The licensee was also required to deliver written quarterly sales reports and keep books of account subject to inspection. In the instant case, Farmland is similarly required to furnish the debtor with sales reports (on a monthly basis) and to keep books of account and records reflecting the licensed sales which must be open to the debtor's inspection at all reasonable times. Additionally, Farmland is required to protect the debtor's rights in the licensed trademarks. Manifestly, the licenses in the instant case are executory as to both the debtor and Farmland and, therefore, they are executory contracts within the meaning of 11 U.S.C. § 365(a)."

42. See 11 U.S.C. § 362.

43. The automatic stay rules are contained in section 362 of the bankruptcy laws and provides for example that the filing of a petition for bankruptcy "operates as stay... any act to collect, assess, or recover a claim against the debtor that arose before the commencement of the case under this title [and] the setoff of any debt owing to the debtor that arose before the commencement of the case under this title against any claim against the debtor." 11 U.S.C. § 362(6) and (7).

44. H. WARD CLASSEN, A PRACTICAL GUIDE TO SOFTWARE LICENSING FOR LICENSEES AND LICENSORS 109–110 (3d ed. 2008), citing 11 U.S.C. § 365(e)(1), § 365(b) and (c).

45. *Id.* at 110, citing In re Computer Communications, Inc., 824 F.2d 725 (9th Cir. 1987); "unilateral termination of agreement to buy hardware and software from bankrupt debtor violates bankruptcy code as ability to terminate stayed by bankruptcy filing. Debtor awarded $4 million in damages" (*id.*).

46. *Id.* at 871.

47. *Timberline Development LLC v. Kronman*, 263 A.D.2d 175, 178 (N.Y.A.D. 1 Dept. 2000), citations omitted.

48. Classen, *supra* note 44, at 128, quoting Allen v. Williamsburgh Savings Bank, 69 N.Y. 314, 322 (1877), and citing Kroboth v. Brent, 215 A.D.2d 813, 814 (3d Dept. 1995), and National Data Payment Systems v. Meridian Bank, 212 F.3d 849, 854 (3d Cir. 2000).

49. Nimmer, *supra* note 4, at § 11.76, footnote omitted.

50. HOWARD O. HUNTER, MODERN LAW OF CONTRACTS, § 8:10, database updated April 2011 (General rules of implication under contextual approach—Best-efforts clauses—Performance).

51. Classen, *supra* note 44, at 129.

52. *Id.*, citing Durham v. Warner Elevator Manufacturing Co., 139 N.E.2d 10 (Ohio 1956), Restatement (Second) of Torts § 324A (1965).

53. "'Reasonable Efforts' shall mean activity reasonable calculated to obtain the approval by action or expenditure not disproportionate in the circumstances. Although definitions

of this type are subjective, a subjective definition is often better than no definition at all" (Classen, *supra* note 44, at 860).

54. Adapted from Classen, *supra* note 44, at 851.

55. See Feist Publications, Inc. v. Rural Telephone Service Co., 449 U.S. 340 (1991).

56. Adelman v. Christy, 90 F. Supp. 2d 1034, 1043 (D. Ariz. 2000). "Adelman's Bibliography appears to be the printout of a computer research query or database, arranged in chronological order...Although Adelman may have invested time and money in compiling this list, the Bibliography is only subject to minimal protection under copyright law...Thus, even if Christy had reproduced and sold copies of a similar *bibliography*, Adelman's grounds for relief on the basis of copyright infringement would be weak. Christy is not alleged to have copied or distributed a bibliography, however. Rather, Adelman alleges that Christy used the *information* contained in the bibliography as a source for *Perfect Medicine*...To the extent that Adelman claims some form of copyright in the *underlying* source items in the Bibliography—namely the materials she allegedly turned over to Christy—Adelman's reasoning is flawed. It is undisputed that Adelman does not hold a copyright in any of the underlying research sources. She holds copyright only in what she has created: a compilation of source material on her specific topic. Her doubtless hard work of compiling the list of relevant sources does not vest in Adelman a copyright that would disallow others from using those original sources for research" (*id.* at 1044, emphasis in original).

57. Nimmer, *supra* note 4, at § 11.151.

58. In re Qintex Entertainment, Inc., 950 F.2d 1492, 1497 (9th Cir. 1991).

59. "Licensors will often include a definitive list of 'material' breaches in the contract. Licensees should resist this approach as it may limit their ability to terminate the agreement if the licensor's non-performance does not fall into one of the enumerated breaches" (Classen, *supra* note 44, at 65).

60. Nimmer, *supra* note 4, at § 11.151.

61. For a thorough discussion of circumvention in the library context see, TOMAS A. LIPINSKI, THE COMPLETE COPYRIGHT LIABILITY HANDBOOK FOR LIBRARIANS AND EDUCATORS 265–292 (2006).

62. See U.S. v. Swartz, Criminal Complaint, No. 1:11-cr-10260-NMG (Dist. Mass., filed July 7, 2011).

63. 18 U.S.C. § 1030. See, for example, Ticketmaster L.L.C. v. RMG Technologies, Inc., 507 F. Supp. 2d 1096, 1113 (C.D. Cal. 2007).

64. F. LAWRENCE STREET AND MARK P. GRANT, LAW OF THE INTERNET, Appendix 1-A, at 1-A-128 (2001, updated through release #19, Dec. 2011). "Overreaching raised doubt as to the validity of the claim of confidentiality" (*id.* 1-A-159). "Exceptions to confidential information vary among agreements due to different client policies, the perceived value of the information, and the relative bargaining position of the parties" (*id.* at 1-A-160).

65. Genelle I. Belmas and Brian N. Larson, *Clicking Away Your Speech Rights: The Enforceability of Gagwrap Licenses*, 12 COMMUNICATIONS LAW AND POLICY 37, 73 (2007): "First Amendment

jurisprudence provides considerable support to the concept of a right to hear. Using the First Amendment to attack gagwrap clauses directly would require that state action be found first. Even without state action, however, the First Amendment provides a significant public policy basis upon which gagwrap clauses might be found to be unenforceable. It remains to be seen how this public policy rationale will work with the *Restatement of Contracts* framework when evaluating gagwrap clauses"; and Anthony G. Read, *Notes: Dewitt Clauses: Can We Protect Purchasers Without Hurting Microsoft?*, 25 Review of Litigation 387, 420–421 (2006): "Software vendors use DeWitt Clauses to protect themselves against inaccurate benchmarks. Some consumers and writers contend software vendors also use the clauses to protect themselves against accurate benchmarks. There is an excellent possibility...that a court would apply the doctrine of copyright misuse and rule DeWitt Clauses unenforceable. If the clauses are unenforceable, vendors would be open to damage from inaccurate benchmark results. Consumers would also be more likely to receive inaccurate benchmark data. If DeWitt Clauses are unenforceable, what is the alternative? What can be done to create the proper balance...A statute based on the IBM Clause would provide adequate protection for the consumer. There would be no practical restriction on release of valid benchmark results. As long as minimum technical requirements are met, publishers would freely inform potential consumers of software and hardware performance. Vendors would also have a measure of protection against false test results while being prevented from suppressing accurate results. The IBM Clause would provide adequate protection for the consumer. The IBM Clause should be either adopted by all vendors or enacted by statute. It is the most effective and fair method to ensure that the valid interests of all parties are protected."

66. Raymond T. Nimmer and Jeff C. Dodd, Modern Licensing Law, § 12:29, database updated in Westlaw, October 2011, emphasis added.

67. People v. Network Associates, Inc., 758 N.Y.S.2d 466, 470 (N.Y. Sup. 2003). Motion granted "to the extent of permanently enjoining respondent Network Associates, Inc. d/b/a McAfee Software from distributing, advertising and selling its software which contains the" language in question (*id.* at 471).

68. Robert A. Hillman and Jeffrey J. Rachlinski, *Standard-Form Contracting in the Electronic Age*, 77 New York University Law Review 429, 470, footnotes omitted.

69. Raymond T. Nimmer, Law of Computer Technology, § 7:133, database updated in Westlaw, September 2011.

70. UCITA, Section 103, Official Comment 3 (Public Policy Invalidation).

71. UCITA, Section 111, Unconscionable Contract or Term, Official Comment 2 (Basic Policy and Effect). See also UCITA, Section 112, Manifesting Assent; Opportunity to Review, Official Comment, 8 (Opportunity to Review): "Common law does not clearly establish this requirement, but the requirement of an opportunity to review terms reasonably made available reflects simple fairness and establishes concepts that curtail procedural aspects of unconscionability."

72. Street and Grant *supra* note 64, Appendix 1-A, at 1-A-67.

73. See, for example, MICHAEL R. COHEN, 25B WEST'S LEGAL FORMS, INTELLECTUAL PROPERTY § 23:75, current through the 2010 update (Sound recording agreement—Includes options for record company to continue exclusive rights to artist; artist hires producer).

74. Harris, *supra* note 15, at 116.

75. Blackwell Publishing, Inc. v. Excel Research Group, Inc., 661 F. Supp. 2d 786, 791 (E.D. Mich. 2009). The court observed that "Excel is not an authorized user...license... permits students to 'print' and 'download' material. It does not allow students to copy and pay for material at an offsite copy shop...Excel's argument that its activities are protected by license agreement fails" (*id.* at 791).

76. Street and Grant, *supra* note 64, Appendix 1-A, at 1-A-169.

77. Classen, *supra* note 44, at 855–856.

78. *Id.* at 50.

79. New York ex rel. Cuomo v. Dell, Inc., 514 F. Supp. 2d 397, 400 (N.D.N.Y. 2007), claiming breach of contract by defendant for "repeatedly misrepresenting the nature, availability and terms of its customer service and technical support [and] repeatedly failing to provide consumers with adequate customer service and technical support; " and Toomey v. Nextel Communications, Inc., 2004 WL 5512967, *1 (N.D. Cal. 2004) (unpublished), alleging that the defendant "Nextel failed to market Toomey's system or to provide adequate customer support."

80. Adapted from Classen, *supra* note 44, at 851.

81. INTERNET LAW AND PRACTICE § 23:4 (2006), chapter author Keith Witek: "This latter approach is only advisable, if at all, for short agreements where the definitions are easy to find and are not that difficult to construct." See also Principle 6, Licensing Principles, prepared by IFLA's Committee on Copyright and other Legal Matters (CLM), 2001, http://www.ifla.org/V/ebpb/copy.htm.

82. Harris, *supra* note 15, at 49: "Placing all of the definitions in a single location in the license can make it easier to consult that section when coming across various terms in the agreement that are defined in it."

83. INTERNET LAW AND PRACTICE § 23:4 (2006), chapter author Keith Witek commenting on the more acrimonious or aggressive business-to-business setting: "The games that are played in the definitions section, especially when definitions are interwoven and embedded to ridiculous levels, are endless. Make sure the definitions, as applied in the context of the agreement, make sense and are reasonable in all circumstances."

84. Street and Grant, *supra* note 64, Appendix 1-A, at 1-A-46.

85. *Id.* at 1-A-116.

86. "A 'derivative work' is a work based upon one or more preexisting works, such as a translation, musical arrangement, dramatization, fictionalization, motion picture version, sound recording, art reproduction, abridgment, condensation, or any other form in which a work may be recast, transformed, or adapted. A work consisting of editorial revisions, annotations, elaborations, or other modifications which, as a whole, represent an original work of authorship, is a 'derivative work'" (17 U.S.C. § 101).

87. See Window Headquarters, Inc. v. MAI Basic Four, Inc., 1994 WL 673519 (S.D.N.Y. Dec. 1, 1994), but not when in bold and on the opposite page. Sierra Diesel Injury Service v. Burroughs Corp., 656 F. Supp. 2d 426 (D. Nev. 1987), aff'd 874 F.2d 653 (9th Cir. 1989).

88. Nimmer, *supra* note 4, at § 11.113.

89. Recursion Software, Inc. v. Interactive Intelligence, Inc., 425 F. Supp. 2d 756, 786 (N.D. Tex. 2006): "Regardless of whether Interactive has offered sufficient evidence to support its implied warranty claims (which it has not), those claims fail for the simple reason that implied warranties were effectively disclaimed by the license agreements."

90. "As is" means the item is "[i]n the existing condition without modification . . . [in] a sale of property 'as is' means that the property is sold in its existing condition, and use of the phrase as is relieves the seller from liability for defects in that condition.—Also termed *with all faults*." BLACK'S LAW DICTIONARY, *supra* note 40, emphasis in original.

91. "[T]he term [merchantability] means that a good sold carries with it an inherent soundness which makes that good suitable for the purpose for which it was designed." Agri-Business Supply Co. v. Hodge, 447 So. 2d 769, 773 (Ala. Civ. App. 1984).

92. "[T]he implied warranty of fitness for a particular purpose is a warranty implied by law when a seller has reason to know that a buyer wishes goods for a particular purpose and is relying on the seller's skill and judgment to furnish those goods." Martinez v. Metabolife Intern., Inc., 6 Cal. Rptr. 3d 494, 500 (2003).

93. Ambassador Steel Co. v. Ewald Steel Co., 190 N.W.2d 275, 279 (Mich. App. 1971).

94. Harris, *supra* note 15, at 81.

95. For a discussion of section 512 see Lipinski, *supra* note 61, at 141–185.

96. "*Droit moral*, or moral right, is generally summarized as including the right of an artist to have his work attributed to him in the form in which he created it to prevent mutilation or deformation of the work." Museum Boutique Intercontinental, Ltd. v. Picasso, 880 F. Supp. 153, 157 at n. 3 (S.D.N.Y., 1995). "The moral rights include the right of integrity, the right of attribution, the right of disclosure (i.e., the right to decide if and when the work should be presented to the public), and the right of withdrawal (i.e., the right to remove the work from public eye). Sometimes the rights are defined and distinguished differently." Nadav Shoked, *The Community Aspect of Private Ownership* 38 FLORIDA STATE UNIVERSITY LAW REVIEW 759, 821, at note 304 (2011). "American copyright law, as presently written, does not recognize moral rights or provide a cause of action for their violation, since the law seeks to vindicate the economic, rather than the personal, rights of authors." Gilliam v. American Broadcasting Companies, Inc., 538 F.2d 14, 24 (2d Cir. 1976).

97. See 17 U.S.C. § 106A.

98. U.S. v. Swartz, Criminal Complaint, at ¶ 32, No. 1:11-cr-10260-NMG (Dist. Mass., filed July 7, 2011). For another perspective on the circumstances see Timothy Lee, *Former Reddit Co-owner Arrested for Excessive JSTOR Downloads*, July 19, 2011, http://arstechnica.com/tech-policy/news/2011/07/reddit-founder-arrested-for-excessive-jstor-downloads.ars.

99. U.S. v. Swartz, Criminal Complaint, at ¶ 18a, No. 1:11-cr-10260-NMG (Dist. Mass., filed July 7, 2011).

100. U.S. v. Swartz, Criminal Complaint, at ¶ 18b, No. 1:11-cr-10260-NMG (Dist. Mass., filed July 7, 2011): "Accesses from this address continued until the middle of the day, when JSTOR spotted and blocked this IP Address as well."

101. U.S. v. Swartz, Criminal Complaint, at ¶ 18b, No. 1:11-cr-10260-NMG (Dist. Mass., filed July 7, 2011).

102. U.S. v. Swartz, Criminal Complaint, at ¶ 23–¶ 24, No. 1:11-cr-10260-NMG (Dist. Mass., filed July 7, 2011).

103. See U.S. v. Swartz, Criminal Complaint, at ¶ 34–¶ 37, No. 1:11-cr-10260-NMG (Dist. Mass., filed July 7, 2011), alleging one count of wire fraud and three counts of computer crime (18 U.S.C. § 1030). For additional discussion of the charges and circumstances wee, Nancy Sims, *Library Licensing and Criminal Law: The Aaron Swartz Case*, 72 COLLEGE AND RESEARCH LIBRARIES NEWS 534 (2011).

104. In the Matter of Quad/Graphics, Inc., 174 Misc. 2d 291, 664 N.Y.S. 2d 225 (N.Y. Super. Ct. 1997).

105. The ALA website contains a section titled "State Privacy Laws Regarding Library Records" that contains links to the state privacy laws regarding library records for all U.S. jurisdictions: http://www.ala.org/ala/aboutala/offices/oif/ifgroups/stateifcchairs/stateifcinaction/stateprivacy (accessed September 11, 2011).

106. Classen, *supra* note 44, at 859.

107. Street and Grant, *supra* note 64, Appendix 1-A, at 1-A-115.

108. Harris, *supra* note 15, at 87.

109. Pillsbury Co., Inc. v. Wells Dairy, Inc., 752 N.W.2d 430, 440 and 441 (Iowa 2008).

110. "Both parties should also insist on having the right of termination if the event of the force majeure continues for a set period of time" (Classen, *supra* note 44, at 134).

111. *Id.*

112. Nimmer, *supra* note 4, at § 11.88.

113. See Carnival Cruise Lines v. Shute, 449 U.S. 585 (1991).

114. Koch v. America Online, Inc., 139 F. Supp. 2d 690, 694 (D. Md. 2000).

115. The Bremen v. Zapata Off Shore Co., 407 U.S. 1 (1972). See also Hughes v. McMenamon, 204 F. Supp. 2d 178 (D.Mass. 2002), forum selection clause in AOL click-wrap agreement upheld.

116. Chong v. Friedman, 2005 WL 2083049, at *4 (Cal. App. 2005) (unpublished): "Because Nevada law does not have a comparable franchise disclosure law, it fails to further the public policy interest that California has recognized in enacting the CFIL—namely, the interest in protecting franchisees from fraud or the likelihood that a franchisor's promises would not be fulfilled. Accordingly, the choice of law provision of the license agreement is invalid as contrary to public policy."

117. See Carnival Cruise Lines v. Shute, 499 U.S. 585, 594 (1991): "It bears emphasis that forum-selection clauses contained in form passage contracts are subject to judicial

scrutiny for fundamental fairness. In this case, there is no indication that petitioner set Florida as the forum in which disputes were to be resolved as a means of discouraging cruise passengers from pursuing legitimate claims. Any suggestion of such a bad-faith motive is belied by two facts: Petitioner has its principal place of business in Florida, and many of its cruises depart from and return to Florida ports. Similarly, there is no evidence that petitioner obtained respondents' accession to the forum clause by fraud or over-reaching. Finally, respondents have conceded that they were given notice of the forum provision and, therefore, presumably retained the option of rejecting the contract with impunity. In the case before us, therefore, we conclude that the Court of Appeals erred in refusing to enforce the forum-selection clause." See also Koch v. America Online, Inc., 139 F. Supp. 2d 690, 694 (D. Md. 2000): "Use of a form contract... even by the party with superior bargaining power, does not necessarily make a forum selection clause enforceable"; and Fi-Med Management Inc. v. Clemco Medical Inc., 2011 WL 2133345, *2 (E.D. Wis. 2011) (slip copy): "The forum selection clause here is unambiguous and thus expresses the intent of the parties, and as such, it is valid and enforceable under federal and Wisconsin law... Absent unconsionability, fraud, or a violation of public policy, the forum selection clause will be enforced. None of the foregoing is argued here by defendants."

118. Merican Online, Inc. v. Superior Court, 108 Cal. Rptr. 2d 699, 707 (2001). See also Salco Distributors, LLC v. Icode, Inc., No. 8:05-CV-642-T-27TGW, 2006 U.S. Dist. LEXIS 9483 (M.D. Fla. Feb. 22, 2006), purchaser's signature acknowledging the express language of a purchase order that incorporates an end-user license agreement (EULA) expresses the parties' intent to be bound by the EULA and its exclusive forum-selection clause.

119. Hubbert v. Dell Corp., 835 N.E.2d 113, 120 (Ill. App. 2005).

120. Caspi v. The Micrsoft Network, L.L.C., 732 A.2d 528 (N.J. 1999).

121. L. J. KUTTEN, 2 COMPUTER SOFTWARE 9:64, database updated April 2012: EULAs and specific legal issues—Is the forum selection clause effective?

122. Harris, *supra* note 15, at 88: "In the United States, if your library is part of a state institution, you may be required to have the laws of that state govern your agreement (or to omit including a governing jurisdiction)."

123. Classen, *supra* note 44, at 138, citing Terra International Inc. v. Mississippi Chemical Corp., 922 F. Supp. 1334 (N.D. Iowa 1996).

124. Vanlab Corp. v. Blossum Valley Foods Corp., 2005 WL 43772, *3 (W.D.N.Y.) (unpublished).

125. Lively v. IJAM, Inc., 114 P.3d 487, 493 (Okla. Div. 4 2005).

126. See, for example, Ott v. All-Star Ins. Corp., 299 N.W.2d 839, 844 (Wis. 1981): "it is the substantive meaning and operation of Addendum 5, rather than the place of physical insertion in the original agreement or the heading of the Article, which must determine its legal nature and effect." See also First Securities Co. v. Storey, 49 P.2d 862, 863 (Cal. App. 2 Dist. 1935): "The legal effect of the terms of the signed document is not enlarged by the heading of the latter, nor by the allegations in the pleading setting forth appellant's interpretation of the meaning of the document."

127. Classen, *supra* note 44, at 5871.

128. Street and Grant, *supra* note 64, Appendix 1-A, at 1-A-84.

129. Harris, *supra* note 15, at 89.

130. See Blankenship v. Northtown Ford, Inc., 420 N.E.2d 167 (Ill. App. 1981), a provision containing a warranty disclaimer in the contract under a misleading or mislabeled section heading held void.

131. Licensing Principles, prepared by IFLA's Committee on Copyright and other Legal Matters (CLM), 2001, http://www.ifla.org/V/ebpb/copy.htm (Principle 18).

132. Licensing Principles, prepared by IFLA's Committee on Copyright and other Legal Matters (CLM), 2001, http://www.ifla.org/V/ebpb/copy.htm (Principle 19).

133. Harris, *supra* note 15, at 81.

134. Classen, *supra* note 44, at 55–56.

135. *Id.* at 55.

136. *Id.* at 58.

137. Nimmer, *supra* note 69, at § 11.110, footnote omitted.

138. See Lloyd Noland Foundation, Inc. v. Tenet Healthcare Corp., 277 Fed. Appx. 923, 928 (11th Cir. 2008): "a contractual indemnity agreement with no termination provision survives the performance of an underlying contract."

139. Licensing Principles, prepared by IFLA's Committee on Copyright and other Legal Matters (CLM), 2001, http://www.ifla.org/V/ebpb/copy.htm : "P29. Provisions for interlibrary loan or equivalent services should be included."

140. The CONTU Guidelines on Photocopying and Interlibrary Arrangements provides that "As used in the proviso of subsection 108 (g) (2), the words '. . . such aggregate quantities as to substitute for a subscription to or purchase of such work' shall mean: a with respect to any given periodical (as opposed to any given issue of a periodical), filled requests of a library or archives (a 'requesting entity') within any calendar year for a total of six or more copies of an article or articles published in such periodical within five years prior to the date of the request." Reprinted in U.S. COPYRIGHT OFFICE, CIRCULAR 21: REPRODUCTION OF COPYRIGHTED WORKS BY EDUCATORS AND LIBRARIANS, http://www.copyright.gov/circs/circ21.pdf.

141. 17 U.S.C.§ 108(i): "The rights of reproduction and distribution under this section do not apply to a musical work, a pictorial, graphic or sculptural work, or a motion picture or other audiovisual work other than an audiovisual work dealing with news, except that no such limitation shall apply with respect to rights granted by subsections (b) and (c), or with respect to pictorial or graphic works published as illustrations, diagrams, or similar adjuncts to works of which copies are reproduced or distributed in accordance with subsections (d) and (e)."

142. *Id.*

143. *Id.*

144. James G. Neal et al., *Report of the Task Force on International Interlibrary Loan and Document Delivery Practices*, RESEARCH LIBRARY ISSUES: A QUARTERLY REPORT FROM ARL, CNI, AND

SPARC 275, 3–5 (June 2011), available at http://publications.arl.org/rli275/. *Report of the Task Force on International Interlibrary Loan and Document Delivery Practices* (June 2011), http://publications.arl.org/1acgvq.pdf.

145. Brandon Butler et al., *White Paper: US Law and International Interlibrary Loan,* RESEARCH LIBRARY ISSUES: A QUARTERLY REPORT FROM ARL, CNI, AND SPARC 275, 15 (June 2011), http://publications.arl.org/rli275/. *Report of the Task Force on International Interlibrary Loan and Document Delivery Practices* (June 2011), http://publications.arl.org/1acgvq .pdf.

146. "[I]t may be helpful to explain to foreign ILL partners that US law bars domestic libraries from reproduction and lending that violates Section 108 or is not within fair use, with a clear statement that these two provisions may apply. It may also help to make the representations more explicit. For example, request forms could be changed to include verification similar to the following: This request is in compliance with US Copyright Law, including either Section 107 (fair use) or Section 108(g)(2), which provides that requests will not be made in such aggregate quantities as to substitute for a subscription to or purchase of such work.' The requesting library represents that it complies with US law and that receiving the copy will not violate the copyright, importation, or other laws of the requesting library's country." Brandon Butler et al., *White Paper: US Law and International Interlibrary Loan,* RESEARCH LIBRARY ISSUES: A QUARTERLY REPORT FROM ARL, CNI, AND SPARC 275, 15, http://publications.arl.org/rli275/. *Report of the Task Force on International Interlibrary Loan And Document Delivery Practices* (June 2011), http://publications.arl.org/1acgvq.pdf.

147. See Licensing Principles, prepared by IFLA's Committee on Copyright and other Legal Matters (CLM), 2001, http://www.ifla.org/V/ebpb/copy.htm: "P4. The choice of applicable law should be acceptable for both parties. Preferably it should the national or state law of the licensee."

148. See Vanier v. Ponsoldt, 833 P.2d 949, 959 (Kan. 1992), choice-of-forum provision valid if forum selected bears a reasonable relationship to transaction and if contract was not entered into under fraud or duress.

149. UCC § 1-105.

150. Nimmer, *supra* note 4, at § 11.86.

151. Classen, *supra* note 44, at 136.

152. *Id.*

153. Nimmer, *supra* note 4, at § 11.84.

154. See Lotus Development Corp. v. Paperback Software International, 740 F. Supp 37 (D. Mass. 1990), various aspects of the graphics interface for Lotus 1-2-3 "merge with the idea" and are therefore not copyrightable. See also Apple Computer, Inc. v. Microsoft Corp., 799 F. Supp. 1006, 1023 (N.D. Cal. 1992): "Purely functional items or an arrangement of them for functional purposes are wholly beyond the realm of copyright as are other common examples of user interfaces or arrangements of their individual elements—the dials, knobs and remote control devices of a television or VCR, or the

buttons and clocks of an oven or stove. Of course, the elements of these everyday user interfaces are seldom conflated into metaphoric images, but that does not mean that the user interface of a computer is less functional."

155. Sweetwater Investors, LLC v. Sweetwater Apartments Loan LLC, 2011 WL 3841343, *8 (M.D. Ala. 2011) (slip copy), quotations omitted.

156. See Licensing Principles, prepared by IFLA's Committee on Copyright and other Legal Matters (CLM), 2001, http://www.ifla.org/V/ebpb/copy.htm (Principles 20 and 21).

157. Classen, *supra* note 44, at 139.

158. *Id.*

159. Harris, *supra* note 15, at 89.

160. 17 U.S.C. § 1202(b)(1) describes liability separate from copyright infringement for those who "intentionally remove or alter any copyright management information [CMI]." CMI "means any of the following information . . . including in digital form. The title and other information identifying the work, including the information in the notice of copyright, or its author, owner. With the exception of public performances of works by radio and television broadcast stations, the name/identifying information about the performer whose performance is fixed other than an audiovisual work . . . in the case of an audiovisual work, the name/identifying information about, a writer, performer, or director who is credited in the audiovisual work. Terms and conditions for use of the work. Identifying numbers or symbols referring to such information or links to such information. Other information as the Register of Copyrights may prescribe by regulation." 17 U.S.C. § 1202(c)(1)–(8). See also Murphy v. Millennium Records, LLC, 2011 WL 2315128, *6 (3d Cir.), removal of photographer's "gutter" credit from magazine photograph posted on website not fair use: "we find that CMI, as defined in § 1202(c), is *not* restricted to the context of 'automated copyright protection or management systems.' In this case, the mere fact that Murphy's name appeared in a printed gutter credit near the Image rather than as data in an 'automated copyright protection or management system' does not prevent it from qualifying as CMI or remove it from the protection of § 1202." See also McClatchey v. Associated Press, 2007 U.S. Dist. LEXIS 17768, *5 (W.D. Pa. 2007): "Moreover, Section 1202(c) defines the term broadly to include 'any' of the information set forth in the eight categories, 'including in digital form.' To avoid rendering those terms superfluous, the statute must also protect non-digital information."

161. INTERNET LAW AND PRACTICE § 23:8 (2006), chapter author Keith Witek.

162. *Id.*

163. One example: "The acceptance criterion or requirements that are needed to definitively determine acceptance or rejection are often set forth by the parties in user manuals, the agreement itself, an exhibit to the agreement, a statement of work (SOW), a specification sheet, or other like technical documents that are often attached to the agreement, incorporated clearly into the agreement by a concise reference, or separately signed by the parties. The acceptance clause will generally state that the receiving

party will test the deliverable against the criteria/metrics set forth, and determine whether or not the product meets or does not meet those criteria within the allotted time period." INTERNET LAW AND PRACTICE § 23:8 (2006), chapter author Keith Witek. "One of the primary purposes of the acceptance clause is to obtain final closure to the delivery and performance obligations of the delivering party up front. Often, this closure on the deliverables and there conditions is of benefit to both the parties. This determination can also draw a distinct line between the 'development phase' of the relationship and the 'ongoing maintenance phase.' Each of these phases generally has different assumptions of risk and financial/resource obligations." *Id.*

164. INTERNET LAW AND PRACTICE § 23:5 (2006), chapter author Keith Witek.

165. Harris, *supra* note 15, at 58–59: "substantial or systematic copying," "transmitting content," "removing the publisher's copyright notice on any content," "modifying or altering the content," "merging, value-adding, or including content with any other product, service, or database, or creating a derivative work," "undertaking any activity that may harm the content owner's ability to sell his or her content," making a commercial use ("in any commercial manner"), and "sharing the content."

166. Evolution, Inc. v. SunTrust Bank, 342 F. Supp. 2d 943 (D. Kan. 2004), decompilation of software in order to extract unprotected elements fair use; Sony Computer Entertainment, Inc. v. Connectix Corp., 203 F.3d 596 (9th Cir. 2000), cert. denied 531 U.S. 871 (2000), copying computer code to extract unprotected elements fair use; Atari Games Corp. v. Nintendo of America, Inc., 975 F.2d 832 (Fed. Cir. 1992), reverse engineering (copying) of computer program as intermediate step to extracting unprotected elements can be a fair use; and Sega Enterprises Ltd. v. Accolade, Inc., 977 F.2d 1510 (9th Cir. 1992), decompilation of software program to extract unprotected elements fair use.

167. See Lowry's Reports, Inc. v. Legg Mason, Inc., 271 F. Supp. 2d 737, 750 (D. Md. 2003): "The mere transfer of a copyrighted newsletter does not imply a license to engage in copying that newsletter," citing 17 U.S.C. § 202.

168. Referring to Koch Engineering Co. v. Faulconer, 610 P.2d 1094 (Kan. 1980).

169. Jones v. Noblit, 2011 WL 4716337, *6 (Kan. App. 2011) (unpublished).

170. Asset Marketing Systems, Inc. v. Gagnon, 542 F.3d 748, 750–751 (9th Cir. 2008).

171. Succession of Ramp, 212 So.2d 419, 423 (La. 1968): "This contract of compromise is constructed of several introductory paragraphs each commencing with the word 'whereas,' and of a conclusion beginning with the word 'therefore.' 'Whereas' simply means 'when in fact,' 'considering that,' 'because,' 'by reason of.' The clauses of a contract which begin with the word 'whereas' simply state the reasons for the confection and the mental intent of the parties. That portion of a contract which follows the word 'therefore' is simply the response to the reasoning and the mental intention of the parties."

172. BLACK'S LAW DICTIONARY, *supra* note 40.

173. KMS Fusion, Inc. v. United States, 36 Fed. Cl. 68, 77 (1996).

174. Grynberg v. Federal Energy Regulatory Commission, 71 F.3d 413, 416 (D.C. Cir. 1995).

175. First Bank and Trust Co. of Illinois v. Village of Orland Hills, 787 N.E.2d 300, 308 (Ill. App. 1 Dist. 2003). See also All Metals Fabricating, Inc. v. Ramer Concrete, Inc., 338 S.W.3d 557, 561 (Tex. App. El Paso 2009), citations omitted: "A recital is a formal statement or setting forth of some matter of fact, in any deed or writing, in order to explain the reasons upon which the transaction is founded. Recitals are generally not part of a contract unless the parties intended them to be, and will not control a contract's operatives clauses unless those clauses are ambiguous. The recitals may be looked to in determining the proper construction of the contract and the parties' intent."

176. INTERNET LAW AND PRACTICE § 23:3 (2006), chapter author Keith Witek, citation omitted.

177. See, for example, Data Processing Services, Inc. v. L. H. Smith Oil Corp., 492 N.E.2d 314, 320 (Ind. App. 4 Dist. 1986), court held among other things that the computer programmer breached implied promise of having reasonable skill and ability to do job for which it contracted: "The trial court found: (a) DPS represented it had the necessary expertise and training to design and develop a system to meet the needs of Smith; (b) DPS lacked the requisite skills and expertise to do the work; (c) DPS knew it lacked the skill and expertise; (d) DPS should have known Smith was dependent upon DPS's knowledge and abilities; and, (e) DPS should have foreseen Smith would incur losses if DPS did not perform as agreed. These findings demonstrate DPS breached its implied promise of having the reasonable skill and ability to do the job for which it contracted."

178. Street and Grant, *supra* note 64, Appendix 1-A, at 1-A-45: "If the services have been engaged on the basis of an RFP and a responding proposal by the developer, it is generally advantageous, from the client's viewpoint, to recite such facts in the agreement and to incorporate the RFP and proposal into the four corners of the contract." However, the RFP itself is typically not incorporated wholesale into the agreement, for hopefully obvious reasons, as Street and Grant further explain: "While the RFP and response are often useful as negotiating tools, they are not usually attached to and included in the agreement. RFPs and responses tend to lean toward being sales documents, and as the agreement is considered the final understanding between the parties, such exhibits might create ambiguities. However, if the response is very specific about the tasks that will be performed for the price bid, a developer may want to attach the response, or a portion thereof, in order to clearly delineate the task promised to be performed" (*id.* at 1-A-108).

179. Classen, *supra* note 44, at 261–262: "NOW THEREFORE, in consideration of the foregoing Recitals, which shall be deemed to be a substantive part of this Agreement, and the mutual covenants, agreements, representations, and warranties hereinafter set forth, the parties hereto do hereby agree . . . "

180. Street and Grant, *supra* note 64, Appendix 1-A, at 1-A-106.

181. See, for example, North Texas Imaging, LLC v. Eisenberg, 1996 WL 1359212 (C.D. Cal. Aug. 19, 1996); and YourNet Dating, Inc. v. Mitchell, 88 F. Supp. 2d 870 (N.D. Ill. 2000).

182. MICHAEL RUSTAD, INTERNET LAW IN A NUTSHELL 135 (2009).

183. Trustees of B.A.C. Local 32 Ins. Fund v. Fantin Enterprises, Inc., 163 F.3d 965, 968–969 (6th Cir. 1998).

184. Brandon Butler, Appendix A: Legal Licensing Issues, *Report of the Task Force on International Interlibrary Loan and Document Delivery Practices* (June 2011), http://publications.arl .org/1acgvq.pdf.

185. MICHAEL A. EPSTEIN AND FRANK L. POLITANO, DRAFTING LICENSE AGREEMENTS, § 1.02 (2011).

186. Hard Rock Café, International. (USA) Inc. v. Morton, 1999 WL 717995, *23 (S.D.N.Y. 1999) (unpublished).

187. Boosey & Hawkes Music Publishers, Ltd. v. Walt Disney Co., 145 F.3d 481, 488 (2d Cir. 1998). See also Random House, Inc. v. Rosetta Books LLC, 150 F. Supp. 2d 613, 621 (S.D.N.Y. 2001): "Similarly, Rosetta's argument that the contractual clause in which the authors reserve motion picture and broadcasting rights for themselves in certain contracts also means that the authors reserved the ebook rights is without merit. Such reservation clauses, unless they expressly cover the new use in question, contribute nothing to the definition of the boundaries of the license."

188. Brandon Butler, Appendix A: Legal Licensing Issues, *Report of the Task Force on International Interlibrary Loan and Document Delivery Practices* (June 2011), http://publications.arl .org/1acgvq.pdf.

189. See Street and Grant, *supra* note 64, Appendix 1-A, at 1-A-108: If "the schedules and exhibits are not specified, their identification as part of the Agreement requires initialing and dating by both parties."

190. Hunter v. Sterling Bank, 750 F. Supp. 2d 530, 539 (E.D. Pa. 2010). See also America's Choice, Inc. v. Bienvenu, 700 F. Supp. 2d 1, *6 (D.D.C. 2010): "ACI also argues that because the April Contract left the method of rendering compensation to a future determination, *see* Pl.'s Ex. 17 at § 5 ('The method(s) of rendering compensation will be delivered in accordance with a schedule developed by the contractor and ADE.'), the contract was not valid. Along similar lines, ACI argues that the greater specificity in the July Agreement (i.e., which of the schools would receive the services and how payments would be scheduled) demonstrates that the April Contract was not enforceable. The Court finds that the refinements in the July Agreement did not change the overall objectives and scope of the April Contract and do not make the April Contract void. Parties may refine terms in a contract to supplement prior agreements, but that does not mean the prior agreement was never valid."

191. See, for example, Baldor Electric. Co. v. Sungard Recovery Services, LP, 2006 WL 3735980, *11 (W.D. Ark. 2006) (unpublished): "It is clear to the Court that if there were a unilateral mistake at all based on any perceived ambiguity by the Plaintiff as to the term of the Agreement, it arose from the Plaintiff's laxity in assessing and confirming the agreed term prior to entering into the Agreement and subsequent Schedules. The Court cannot rescind valid contracts because one party subsequently discovers that it failed to appraise itself of certain available facts which would have affected its decision

to enter into the Agreement. It is the Court's opinion that unilateral mistakes, which arise through no fault of the other party, but simply through the mistaken party's own negligence or want of due care, afford no basis of relief by rescission."

192. Dawson v. Goldammer, 722 N.W.2d 106, 111 (Wis. App. 2006).

193. In re Idearc Inc., 442 B.R. 513, 519 (N.D. Tex. 2010).

194. *Id.* at 142.

195. Restatement (Second) of Contracts § 26 (1981) (Statutory Note).

196. A.I. Trade Finance, Inc. v. Petra Intern. Banking Corp., 62 F.3d 1454, 1467 (D.C. Cir. 1995) (citations omitted). See also Ripps v. Powers, 356 Fed. Appx. 352, 355 (11th Cir. 2009): "Ripps claims that the notarized contract is 'under seal' and therefore subject to a ten year statute of limitations, Alabama law is clear that for a contract to be 'under seal' it must express that intention in the body of the contract. The written contract in this case states no such intention."

197. Burgess v. Square 3324 Hampshire Gardens Apartments, Inc., 691 A.2d 1153, 1156 (D.C. 1997), citations omitted.

198. 17 U.S.C. §109(b)(1)(A).

199. Classen, *supra* note 44, at 353–354.

200. Street and Grant, *supra* note 64, Appendix 1-A, at 1-A-117.

201. *Id.* at 1-A-53-54.

202. International Therapeutics, Inc. v. McGraw-Edison Co., 721 F.2d 488, 491–492 (5th Cir. 1983).

203. Estate of Frane v. C.I.R., 98 T.C. 341, 365–366 (1992).

204. Gulf Liquids New River Project, LLC v. Gulsby Engineering, Inc., 2011 WL 662672, *7 (Tex. App.–Houston [1 Dist.] 2011), citation and internal quotation omitted.

205. Douglas v. Talk America, Inc., 495 F.3d 1062, 1065 (9th Cir. 2007).

206. *Id.* "Nor would a party know when to check the website for possible changes to the contract terms without being notified that the contract has been changed and how. Douglas would have had to check the contract every day for possible changes. Without notice, an examination would be fairly cumbersome, as Douglas would have had to compare every word of the posted contract with his existing contract in order to detect whether it had changed" (*id.* at note 1).

207. Riceland Seed Co. v. Wingmead Inc., 2011 WL 3925366, *4 (Ark. App. 2011) (unpublished).

208. Perry v. Estate of Carpenter, 918 N.E.2d 156, 1163 (Ill. App. 1 Dist. 2009).

209. Holland v. Continental Telephone Co. of the South, 492 So.2d 998, 999 (Ala. 1986).

210. Star leasing Co. v. G&S Metal Consultants, Inc., 2009 WL 714146, *7 (Ohio App. 10 Dist.).

211. New Kids on the Block v. News America Publishing, 971 F.2d 302, 308 (9th Cir. 1991), use of the plaintiffs' trademark in another's own goods and services if (1) the product must not be readily identifiable without the use of the trademark, (2) no more of the trademark is used by the plaintiff than is reasonably necessary to identify the product,

and (3) the defendant must not act in such a way as to suggest sponsorship or endorsement by the plaintiff.

212. See Lloyd Noland Foundation, Inc. v. Tenet Healthcare Corp., 277 Fed. Appx. 923, 928 (11th Cir. 2008): "a contractual indemnity agreement with no termination provision survives the performance of an underlying contract."

213. Classen, *supra* note 44, at 39–61.

214. Street and Grant, *supra* note 64, Appendix 1-A, at 1-A-129, also adding that claims be made under laws of United States and only after "prompt notice" is also made.

215. Harris, *supra* note 15, at 80.

216. Rustad, *supra* note 182, at 126.

217. Nimmer, *supra* note 4, at § 11.109.

218. *Id.* at § 11.114.

219. Classen, *supra* note 44, at 346.

220. Harris, *supra* note 15, at 99.

▶ 15

FOUR COMMON LIBRARY LICENSES DECONSTRUCTED

This chapter includes a walk-through or review of several license agreements. The chapter includes actual licensing agreements, rather than constructing a mock, model, or sample license agreement, for several reasons. First, the chapter's content represents what the reader would actually find, demonstrating the similarities as well as the variations across agreements. Second, it allows for a realistic assessment of the license agreements, each in all its glory, with quirks, inconsistencies, internal connections, and intuitions. The discussion also includes references to broader concepts discussed in the body of the book but extrinsic to a particular license agreement to reaffirm several of the text's themes—the first of which is to contrast copyright and, on occasion, other laws or legal regimes (e.g., in the European Union) with contract law; the second, that the law of licensing is the law of contract, within which there may be variation in particular circumstances because the law of contract is state based. Basic contract law principles as well as advanced licensing concepts are often at play in these agreements. This chapter provides reinforcement of these principles and concepts. The paragraph numbering or notation is original to the particular license agreement reviewed.

THE Access NewspaperARCHIVE LICENSE DECONSTRUCTED

Terms of the Access NewspaperARCHIVE License	Comments on the Terms of the Access NewspaperARCHIVE License
Terms and Conditions.	
NewspaperARCHIVE is an Internet service (the Service) owned and operated by Heritage Microfilm Inc. (hereafter "we", "our" or "us").	This sentence identifies the licensor.

(continued)

Terms of the Access NewspaperARCHIVE License	Comments on the Terms of the Access NewspaperARCHIVE License
"You" or "your" means an adult user of the Service for itself and you as parent or guardian for any minor which you allow to access the Service, for whom you will be held strictly responsible.	This sentence identifies the licensee. The sentence also indicates, due to the fact that in many states contracts which a minor enters are voidable, it is actually the parent or guardian who makes the contract and then allows the minor to use the service. In such circumstances, the license makes clear that the parent is responsible for the minor's use. In theory, a parent would be liable for the infringing (copyright) acts of the minor child under the concept of vicarious liability. But see *Capitol Records, Inc. v. Foster*, 2007 WL 1028532, *3 (W.D. Okla., 2007) ("In *Santangelo* [*Elektra Entertainment Group, Inc. v. Santangelo*, 2005 WL 3199841, *3 (S.D.N.Y.)], the court denied the defendant's motion to dismiss the plaintiffs' direct infringement claim against her, but expressed skepticism that 'an Internet-illiterate parent, who does not know Kazaa from a kazoo' could be held liable for copyright infringement committed by a child who downloads music over the Web without the parent's knowledge or permission but using the parent's Internet account. While the Court is not prepared to pronounce the plaintiffs' secondary copyright infringement claims to be frivolous or objectively unreasonable, they would certainly appear to be untested and marginal.") Having said this, whether a parent is strictly liable for the harm (tort) caused by his or her minor child is often a question of state statutory or common law other than contract. See, e.g., B. C. Ricketts, *Validity and Construction of Statutes Making Parents Liable for Torts Committed by Their Minor Children*, 8 A.L.R.3d 612 (originally published in 1966; ALR databases are made current by the weekly addition of relevant new cases). Such statutes often limit liability to "willful, malicious, intentional, or unlawful acts of their minor children . . . Generally, unless the act of the child was performed willfully, wantonly, or through gross negligence, its parents will not be held vicariously liable, and some statutes are expressly limited to situations where the child acts willfully and maliciously." Laura Hunter Dietz, *Statutory Liability* 59 AM. JUR. 2d § 103 (database updated, November 2011).
Your use of the Service indicates that you are bound by this agreement with us.	Contract law requires assent before the terms of an agreement are binding. Assent can be indicated by an act. The license states that "use" equates to that assent. This can be a valid mechanism of assent in online settings, but it must be clear from the circumstances of access (e.g., through use of an on-screen click-to-agree prompt) that the user-licensee understood this to be the case before proceeding and that the terms were available for review. When applying this license, a question arises as to whether "use" always equates with assent or agreement. This is critical if there will be a change of terms whereby any continued use of the archive equates to acceptance of the new terms. This result may not be what the licensee expects or desires.

(continued)

Terms of the Access NewspaperARCHIVE License	Comments on the Terms of the Access NewspaperARCHIVE License
If you do not agree with any of these terms and conditions, your sole remedy is to discontinue use of the Service.	This sentence suggests that use again equates to assent and the cessation ("if you do not agree") equates to nonassent. This is a clumsy mechanism through which a licensee must indicate "I agree" and "I disagree," as use of the archive is precisely what the licensee hopes to achieve from the agreement. This may be problematic where the user-licensee has assented already (by use), for how is nonassent (through discontinued use) to be distinguished from the user-licensee who is merely taking a break from his or her assented use? Use-as-assent provisions are fraught with problems and should be avoided if possible. The sentence also indicates that nonuse is the sole form of remedy (see next Comment and that regarding ¶ 2.3. Cancellations). The provision also indicates that negotiation is not an option; either "use it or lose it," as the expression goes, and that remedy is limited under the agreement to cessation of service. Finally, and with respect to new terms, is there a requirement that notice be given of the new terms? If not, how would a licensee know to stop using the service in order to manifest nonagreement with the change (see next Comment)?
We may alter this agreement at our discretion and your continued use after any change indicates your acceptance of that change. If you do not want to be bound by a change, discontinue use of the Service and contact NewspaperARCHIVE Customer Support for cancellation of membership (see section 2.3 for cancellations).	This sentence indicates that changes in terms may be made by the licensor. So far, so good. But it is problematic to assume acceptance of changes in terms of service on continued use of the service for at least two reasons. First, there is no indication that in a given situation an existing user-licensee would know that there have been changes; that is, there is no notice of change proviso that indicates notice of changes will be given first, with the opportunity not to be bound by the change (in the case of this license, by stopping further use), whereby continued use would then equate to assent. Second, assent to those changes (from the licensor's perspective) is taken to be by an act that (from the licensee's perspective) one would expect an existing user-licensee to undertake (i.e., to make use of the service). Again, the sole response to disagreement (remedy) is cessation of the service, but it is not at all clear how an existing user-licensee knows when and if changes to the terms with which he or she might want to disagree (i.e., not be bound) and cease use. A party should not be bound by terms of which he or she is unaware. The provision should contain a notice of change proviso, whereby notice of term change is communicated to the licensee with further reiteration that continued use at that point equates also to assent to the new terms. Considering the use-as-acceptance default here, any notice should be effective upon receipt (defined as actual reading) and not upon sending. Otherwise, how would the licensee know that a new term has been proposed? Further, if the licensee disagrees with a change and stops use, is a refund owed for any payments made in advance of use (see, e.g., ¶ 2.1. Information about Charges and Fees.

(continued)

Terms of the Access NewspaperARCHIVE License	Comments on the Terms of the Access NewspaperARCHIVE License
NewspaperARCHIVE contains graphics, information, data, editorial and other content accessible by any Internet user and similar content which is accessible only to our subscribing members (the Content). Whether in the free section or in the subscription section of the Service, all Content is owned and/or copyrighted by Heritage Microfilm Inc. or third party providers and may be used only in accordance with this limited use license.	These sentences remind users that at least some of the content in the database service is protected by copyright and, regardless of whether copyright protection applies, the licensor still owns the content (so no first-sale rights, which, under section 109 of the copyright law, apply to owners of content, not those with mere access or in possession of the content). Some content may not be protected by copyright: "information" or "data" such as facts would not be protected by copyright, and courts have held that news stories are thin copyright for purposes of fair-use analysis. See, e.g., *Los Angeles Times v. Free Republic*, 2000 U.S. Dist. LEXIS 5669 (C.D. Calif. April 4, 2000). Certainly the newspaper article in which facts are presented is protected, but the underlying facts of the story are not. Furthermore, as the case law suggests, protection under the copyright law is "thin" at best. Yet contract vis-à-vis the terms of this agreement overrides copyright to the extent that the restrictions or prohibitions are articulated in the agreement. This is one purpose of a license from the licensor's perspective: to place additional restraints on the use of content through contract law that the copyright law does not. Finally, the archive is itself a licensee, obtaining some content from other "third party providers" through license, so some limitations on the use of content may be imposed by those providers and are passed along to licensees here.
NewspaperARCHIVE is protected by copyright as a collective work and/or compilation, pursuant to U.S. copyright laws, international conventions, and other copyright laws.	Serial publications are often protected as a collective work. Section 101 defines a collective work as "a work, such as a periodical issue, anthology, or encyclopedia, in which a number of contributions, constituting separate and independent works ... are assembled into a collective whole." Organizations of fact-based content (e.g., a statistical database) are often protected as a compilation. Also defined in section 101, a "compilation is a work formed by the collection and assembling of preexisting materials or of data that are selected, coordinated, or arranged in such a way that the resulting work as a whole constitutes an original work of authorship. The term 'compilation' includes collective works." Thus, a collective work is a type of compilation. All collective works are also compilations, but not all compilations are collective works. "A sound recording consisting of greatest hits from the 1980s would be a collective work. A collage of public domain film clips would be a compilation." WILLIAM F. PATRY, PATRY ON COPYRIGHT, § 3:61 at note 3 (database updated in Westlaw, February 2012). Collective works "are distinguished from the other types of compilations by the requirement that the individual elements forming the collective work must 'constitut[e] separate and independent works in themselves.' Periodicals and anthologies are examples of collective works. By contrast, noncollective work types of compilations consist of uncopyrightable individual elements, such as data." *Id*. at § 3:64, footnote to the statutory definition of

(continued)

Terms of the Access NewspaperARCHIVE License	Comments on the Terms of the Access NewspaperARCHIVE License
NewspaperARCHIVE is protected by copyright as a collective work and/or compilation, pursuant to U.S. copyright laws, international conventions, and other copyright laws. *(continued)*	collective works omitted. International copyright conventions also protect collective works and compilations but perhaps without the fine distinction or delineation of U.S. law. Article 2(5) of the Berne Convention appears to conflate the two concepts: "Collections of literary or artistic works such as encyclopedias [*sic*] and anthologies which, by reason of the selection and arrangement of their contents, constitute intellectual creations shall be protected as such, without prejudice to the copyright in each of the works forming part of such collections." Berne Convention for the Protection of Artistic and Literary Works, http://www.wipo.int/treaties/en/ip/berne/trtdocs_wo001.html#P85_10661.
Limited Use License. You are licensed to use the Content only for personal or professional research, and may download Content only as search results relevant to that research.	The licensor appears, by restricting use to "personal or professional research," to prohibit shared or public uses. A librarian could not use the library acquisitions credit card and purchase a subscription for all patrons as this would not be a personal use. Services such as iTunes and e-readers have similar restrictions. See also H. WARD CLASSEN, A PRACTICAL GUIDE TO SOFTWARE LICENSING FOR LICENSEES AND LICENSORS 267 (3d ed. 2008), indicating that "personal" requires that "[u]se of the software is 'personal' to the Customer only." Each patron would in theory need to become an individual licensee. If personal is the opposite of professional, then it is unclear what restriction on use and downloading the clause accomplishes other than to require that either be for research. If the only limitation intended is that a use be for "research," then that is the only restriction that should avail. But that is not what is written: research, but upon condition, with it being allowed in a personal or professional context alone. So to have meaning and purpose, there must be some sort of research that is not allowed. Otherwise, why qualify it? So circulating an article regarding the impact of nutrition on recovery time between workouts to your spotters at the local health club would be prohibited because while this is research it is neither professional nor personal; it is public. However, a download of an article to use to prepare for a presentation at the next corporate marketing meeting would be allowed; it is likely not personal but it surely is professional. Professional use in a corporate or academic setting (distributing an article at a company staff meeting or passing the article among your students) would be public but appears allowed, as this would be professional. Also allowed would be a use that is for your own preparation of an upcoming family reunion, and thus personal—but sharing the article with the attendees at a talk on genealogy or family reunions given at your local library would not be allowed: while it is research, it is also neither professional nor personal. Perhaps this is still not what the licensor intends, but it demonstrates the problem with applying simple words of English. In this case, perhaps use of the descriptor "private" or a restriction on "further distributions" might be a better choice, depending on what restricted uses are desired.

(continued)

Terms of the Access NewspaperARCHIVE License	Comments on the Terms of the Access NewspaperARCHIVE License
The download of the whole or significant portions of any work or database is prohibited.	This sentence reminds users that while the database may consist of unprotected elements (e.g., out-of-copyright newspaper articles or a factual recounting of a deceased person's accomplishments in an obituary), if you "take" too much, you are likely taking what is original in the way the elements are "selected, coordinated, or arranged," that is, the compilation copyright. Use of the word "significant" might suggest both qualitative and quantitative taking, recalling a similar assessment in the third fair-use factor ("amount and substantiality"). This would also indicate that some amount less than the entire database is still too much, but it is unclear when this threshold is reached. Perhaps the licensor is intending an amount, either quantitatively or qualitatively, that would constitute a commercially viable subpart (even if a commercial use is not made of it) such that the licensee would be tempted to terminate or not renew the agreement because he or she already possesses the needed elements. If this is so, the license should state it in a way a licensee could apply when downloading from the database.
Resale of a work or database or portion thereof, except as specific results relevant to specific research for an individual, is prohibited.	This sentence confirms (see earlier "Limited Use License") that "professional" uses may be commercial and these uses are allowed in some circumstances ("except as specific results relevant to specific research for an individual"), but in general, sales of the licensed content are not, such as access by a document delivery service that comes to your publicly accessible library to fulfill client requests by retrieving articles using this service.
On line or other republication of Content is prohibited.	This sentence attempts to clarify that all uses involving reposting are prohibited (e.g., to a corporate intranet board or to an online classroom through a course management system). It would also appear to prohibit inclusion of the licensed content in a course pack or otherwise in handouts to students, as this is surely a republication. This sentence would not appear to prohibit all public distributions (i.e., the passing around an article at a corporate marketing meeting example in a previous Comment).
Violation of this License may result in immediate termination of your membership and may result in legal action for injunction, damages, or both.	In addition to a cancellation right (see ¶ 2.3. Cancellations), which each party possesses (remember that if you do not like a change in terms, your one and only option is to cease use through cancellation!), if the licensor does not like what you are doing under this agreement, the licensor may terminate (without refund) or suspend the service (whereupon a refund is due) under ¶ 4. Termination. This sentence indicates that in addition to termination the licensor may seek other relief, including both nonmonetary (injunctive relief) and/or monetary remedy (damages).

(continued)

Terms of the Access NewspaperARCHIVE License	Comments on the Terms of the Access NewspaperARCHIVE License
You may use access software provided on the Service only while on line and may not download, copy, reuse, or distribute that software, except where it is clearly stated in connection with software that it is made available for offline use and a license for that use is provided in connection with that software.	This sentence reminds the user-licensee that the right to access and use the content and any intellectual property rights in the content are different from the underlying operating or navigation software (as well as any intellectual property rights in the software). Rights in such software are far more restricted.
User Provided Content. Portions of the Service will contain user provided content, to which you may contribute appropriate content. For this content, NewspaperARCHIVE is a distributor only.	The licensor is indicating that it is not responsible for content created by the licensee or by others that is then submitted to the service. As a distributor, tort liability, such as defamation, exists only if the distributor (and in this instance the licensor) had knowledge of the unacceptable nature of the content and failed to remove it. See *Cubby v. CompuServ*, 776 F. Supp. 135, 140 (S.D.N.Y. 1991). Federal law alters that standard, providing distributors or, in the words of the statute, a "provider of an interactive computer service" immunity from civil liability for harms arising from the speech of third parties, which here would be "user provided content." 47 U.S.C. § 230(c)(1): "No provider or user of an interactive computer service shall be treated as the publisher or speaker of any information provided by another information content provider." See, for example, *Zeran v. America Online, Inc.*, 129 F.3d 327 (4th Cir. 1997): Section 230 offers complete immunity from defamatory harms resulting from the acts of a service provider, either as publisher or distributor. See also *Blumenthal v. Drudge*, 992 F. Supp. 44, 52 (D.D.C. 1998): Section 230 immunity applies in circumstances where the "interactive service provider has an active, even aggressive role in making available content prepared by others."
By submitting content to NewspaperARCHIVE, you grant Heritage Microfilm Inc. a limited license to the content to use, host, distribute that Content and allow hosting and distribution on co-branded Services of that Content.	This sentence indicates that submission ("submitting") equals assent to allow the licensor to host and distribute the submitted content; that is, the licensee grants the licensor a license (albeit a limited one) to use the content he or she submits. One problem: What if the licensee in a particular submission does not have the legal right to grant such license (i.e., the content was not the licensee's to submit) and by submitting the content the licensee violates the copyright of another? The next Comment attempts to address this quandary.

(continued)

Terms of the Access NewspaperARCHIVE License	Comments on the Terms of the Access NewspaperARCHIVE License
You should submit only content which belongs to you and will not violate the property or other rights of other people or organizations. Heritage Microfilm Inc. is sensitive to the copyright and other intellectual property rights of others. We will not edit or monitor user provided content, with the exception that, to promote privacy.	This provision of course expresses what licensees should do ("should submit only. . ."), but it may not reflect what licensees in fact do. The provisions add a further reminder that the licensor is not responsible for submitted content which violates intellectual property laws; that is, do not rely on the licensor to remove it ("edit"). The licensor may edit or monitor for abuse only such content that might violate another's privacy rights ("with the exception that"). The licensor will not undertake such efforts with respect to possible violations of copyright law. In other words, the evidence of a licensee's infringement by submitting content that the licensee did not have a legal right to submit will be there as evidence for the entire world, or at least other users, to see. Under the rules of copyright liability, once the licensor is aware that some user-submitted content is infringing, it will likely remove said content to be free from liability. See *Gershwin Publishing Corp. v. Columbia Artists Management, Inc.*, 443 F.2d 11 59, 1162 (2d Cir. 1971): "one who, with knowledge of the infringing activity, induces or causes, or materially contributes to the infringement of another." Failure to delete content once made aware of its infringing nature is material contribution; see *A&M Records, Inc. v. Napster, Inc.*, 239 F.3d 1004, 1022 (9th Cir. 2001). The licensor should require that user-submitted content be posted on condition that the licensee-poster claims it has the right to make such submissions and indemnifies the licensor for any copyright or other liability it might incur because of the infringing nature or illegality of the content so submitted.
Heritage Microfilm Inc. also reserves the right to remove any user provided content that comes to its attention and that it believes, in its sole discretion, is illegal, obscene, indecent, defamatory, incites racial or ethnic hatred, or violates the rights of others.	The licensor does claim the specific right to remove content that is illegal if it chooses to do so, and this could include content that does violate intellectual property laws, such as copyright, and of course content from among the other categories listed. The right of the licensor to enforce the remaining triggering characterizations appears similar to many web service acceptable use policies or codes of behavior. Yet this provision does not grant the licensee the right to force the licensor to enforce these terms, in other words, to force the licensor to remove content that was submitted by some other licensee that the licensee finds objectionable. See *Noah v. America Online, Inc.*, 2003 U.S. Dist. LEXIS 8242 (E.D. Va. 2003): "Terms of agreement regarding online comportment standards ("Community Guidelines") created no contractual duty on the part of AOL; rather, the "plain language of the Member Agreement makes clear that AOL is not obligated to take any action"; affirmed *Noah v. AOL-Time Warner, Inc.*, 2004 WL 602711 (4th Cir. 2004) (unpublished).

(continued)

Terms of the Access NewspaperARCHIVE License	Comments on the Terms of the Access NewspaperARCHIVE License
Liability Disclaimer. The information, products, and services included on this Web Service may include inaccuracies or typographical errors. Changes are periodically added to the information herein. Heritage Microfilm Inc. and its third party suppliers provide all Content in this Service "AS IS," and without any warranty of any kind. Heritage Microfilm Inc. and its third party suppliers make no representations concerning the suitability, reliability, or accuracy of the content or the service provided on the Service for any purpose.	The first sentence indicates that the content may not be error free, so do not make any reliance (in a legal sense) upon it. Also (second sentence), the content may be altered or items may come and go, so do not rely on what content was in the service today or when the product was demonstrated at the annual American Library Association conference; it may not be there tomorrow. Here is the big one: the content is provided "AS IS" (notice this is capital script, so it is important), which in legal terms means "licensee, beware," and "no representations . . . for any purpose"—no promises whatsoever are made relating to content quality, veracity, and so on; the content is made available as is.
We and our third party suppliers disclaim all warranties, expressed or implied, in connection with the Content and the services provided on the Service, including conditions of merchantability, fitness for a particular purpose, title and non-infringement.	The licensor is reneging on any expectation the licensee might reasonably have. Legally, the licensor is disclaiming all warranties—warranties that courts over the years have determined are reasonable: for consumers or purchasers to expect certain characteristics of the product or service, that a product is not damaged or broken (merchantability) and that it works, or that the service functions (fitness for a particular purpose), and so forth. This is not the case with this sentence. In fact, the licensor does not even warrant that its provision of the content through the license is not infringing. This promise (and an indemnification) should be included. Moreover, this language should be in capital letters. In many license agreements or contracts, such warranty language is in capital script.
In no case will we or our third party providers be liable for any direct, indirect, punitive, special or other damages including, without limitation, lost or delay of use, lost profits, loss of data or any other damage in	This first sentence fits with the later sentence in capitals (see "IF YOU ARE DISSATISFIED . . ."), as both relate to damages. The licensee cannot obtain any monetary damages whatsoever (at least that is the suspected intent of the clause), either from the licensor or, where the licensor obtains content from another (is itself a licensee), from that third-party provider of content. Injunctive relief may be possible, such as a court order for specific performance, for example, turn the service back on and restore the licensee's access (see "IF YOU ARE

(continued)

Terms of the Access NewspaperARCHIVE License	Comments on the Terms of the Access NewspaperARCHIVE License
contract, tort, equity or any other legaltheory, even if advised of the possibility thereof.	DISSATISFIED....").
Heritage Microfilm Inc. may, from time to time, provide opportunities to users of the Web Service to link to or buy services from third parties. Sites of those third parties may be subject to terms and conditions different from those found here. Heritage Microfilm Inc. makes no warranty concerning third party provided goods or services and you agree that any recourse for dissatisfaction or problems with those goods or services will be sought from the third party provider and not from Heritage Microfilm, Inc.	It is unclear what purpose the second sentence serves. It appears out of place, other than to indicate that instead of incorporating third-party provider content into its service, the licensor will allow licensees to deal with and obtain content from those third-party providers directly. Again, should licensees deal directly with third-party providers of content, the licensor is reminding the licensees that the "goods or services" so provided may be subject to other terms and limitations. Any dispute arising out of such "goods or services" must be taken up with the third-party provider.
Because some states/jurisdictions do not allow the exclusion or limitation of liability for consequential or incidental damages, this limitation may not apply in part to you.	In other words, some state's lawmakers believe that customers, consumers, licensees, and so on, have the right to damages; it is too important to allow the right to be contracted away! As a result, in some states, such provision may be null and void, without legal effect or unconscionable. This agreement does not contain a severability clause, which is an affirmation that should one provision of the agreement prove illegal and a court strike or sever it from the agreement, the remaining provisions will stay in effect.
IF YOU ARE DISSATISFIED WITH ANY PORTION OF THIS WEB SERVICE, OR WITH ANY OF THESE TERMS OF USE, YOUR SOLE AND EXCLUSIVE REMEDY IS TO DISCONTINUE USING THIS SERVICE.	This is important, so it is also in capital script. Translating the legalese: "Our product: love it or leave it!" Again, the sole action available to the licensee in regard to a dispute over the quality of the content or the quality of the service is to stop using the content or the service. As stated earlier (see "In no case will we...."), there are no monetary damages available, and this provision would also appear to preclude injunctive relief as well.

(continued)

Terms of the Access NewspaperARCHIVE License	Comments on the Terms of the Access NewspaperARCHIVE License
1. Registration and Security. **1.1. Registration Information.** As part of the registration process, you will select a password and Subscriber name ("Username"). You must provide Heritage Microfilm Inc. with accurate, complete, and updated registration information. Failure to do so will breach this Agreement. You understand that you may not (1) select or use a name of another person with the intent to impersonate that person; (2) use the Rights of any person other than yourself without authorization; or (3) use a name that we, in our sole discretion, deem offensive.	It is unclear what sort of registration information must be submitted. If individual users (employees, students, patrons, customers of the licensee, etc.) must submit this information, and if query information is also collected, retained, and able to be associated with a particular user, then records that are generated—records that in public (in terms of funding) library content would constitute a protected record—potentially raise issues of patron privacy with each search. Under many state statutes, a registration or other record that links the identity of a library patron with his or her use of library materials, services, and so forth, is protected. See, for example, Wis. Stat. § 43.30: "Records of any library which is in whole or in part supported by public funds . . . indicating the identity of any individual who borrows or uses the library's documents or other materials, resources, or services may not be disclosed." However, in the vendor environment, if the vendor creates and retains such records, even where the search was conducted from terminals located in the library, those records would not be protected under state library confidentiality statutes. If this information is not forthcoming from the licensee, the licensor can consider this a breach of the agreement and may terminate the agreement without any requirement to offer a refund (see ¶ 4. Termination). If users are required to submit registration information, this might raise issues for the licensee in the case of a reluctant or unwilling user, not to mention that if such information is collected, depending on the nature and scope of the other information collected, it might result in an unprotected record of the user's reading habits (or in the least of the user's searching habits). Under clauses (1) and (2) of the second sentence, the license prohibits what would under traditional tort-privacy law be the right to prevent appropriations of one's name, likeness, image, and so on. State identity-theft statutes may also prohibit such use. The third clause allows the licensor to exert a bit of a comportment standard: if the licensee chooses a username such as "accessnewspaperarchivesucks," the licensor would have the right to prohibit it. See Donald E. Biederman, *Interactive On-Line Entertainment*, 367–368, in COUNSELING CLIENTS IN THE ENTERTAINMENT INDUSTRY (2001) (647 PLI/Pat 263): "A complaint has been filed against several domain names which purport to protest Guinness Beer: Guinness-Sucks.com, Guinness-Beer-Sucks.com, Guinness-Beer-Really-Sucks.com, Guinness-Beer-Really-Really-Sucks.com, and variations of the above addresses without the hyphens. 5. Verizon Communications attempted to preempt a 'sucks' parody site and itself registered 'verizonsucks.com' as well as fifty-six other self-critical names. Nevertheless, Web publisher 2600.com registered 'verizonreallysucks.com' and promptly received a cease and desist

(continued)

Terms of the Access NewspaperARCHIVE License	Comments on the Terms of the Access NewspaperARCHIVE License
	letter. Consequently, 2600.com responded by registering the name 'VerizonShouldSpendMoreTimeFixingItsNetworkAndLessMoneyOnLawyers.com'" (footnotes omitted). See also Jacqueline D. Lipton, *Commerce versus Commentary: Gripe Sites, Parody, and the First Amendment in Cyberspace*, 84 WASHINGTON UNIVERSITY LAW REVIEW 1327 (2006). So a username of the sort "HeritageMicrofilmblows" or NewspaperArchivecanbiteme" would likely not be allowed.
As you submit information, you understand that the network of Internet Sites are owned and operated by Heritage Microfilm Inc. in Iowa, USA. The Sites are operated in the United States of America and operated to be in compliance with the laws of the United States.	These sentences are getting close to traditional "choice of law" statements. In other words, the licensor will operate as if U.S. law and, in particular, the laws of the state of Iowa govern its conduct and decision making. It is typical to indicate also the particular state laws that govern as well, which for this licensor would be Iowa. The next provision indicates this is so.
Access is governed by these terms and conditions under the laws of the State of Iowa and the United States.	The so-called choice of law is Iowa. Federal laws may of course apply as well, such as the Magnuson-Moss Warranty-Federal Trade Commission Improvement Act (or Magnuson-Moss for short), codified at 15 U.S.C. §§ 2301–2312—although there is a question of whether this federal warranty protection applies to computer information, as the statute refers to a "consumer product" obtained as the result of a "sale." Even if such federal laws do apply, such warranties were disclaimed (see under "Liability Disclaimer": "We and our third party suppliers disclaim . . ."). Oddly, the choice of forum provision (i.e., that disputes must be adjudicated in the state or federal district courts of Iowa) is found later in ¶ 6. Miscellaneous.
Registration as a user of or subscriber to any of the Sites or services provided on them results in your customer information being stored and processed in the United States, and you, in registering or subscribing, specifically consent to that storage and processing. You may	The first sentence makes the licensor aware that licensee information can be stored and processed in the United States and that the licensee consents to such use. It is unclear whether the service is constructed to collect the customer information of the licensee's constituents (such as employees, patrons, etc.) who might also use the sites or services. If this is the case, users of the service might want to be aware that their search histories might be coupled with identifying information, stored, processed, and retained. While it appears this subscription is not institutional but individual, the privacy issues, though singular, remain. As mentioned earlier (see ¶ 1.1. Registration Information), if a qualifying library maintained such search records of a patron's search of its catalog, the content would be protected under many states'

(continued)

Terms of the Access NewspaperARCHIVE License	Comments on the Terms of the Access NewspaperARCHIVE License
access that information at any time to confirm its correctness and to keep it current in connection with your registration or subscription. If you are subscribing or registering for use of this site from outside of the United States of America, you consent to the storage and processing in the United States of the personal data you submit, within the scope of the Privacy Policy of Heritage Microfilm, Inc. You may and should review and correct this information regularly.	library confidentiality statutes. Also, it is not at all clear that the licensor is the only entity that may process the information so stored (i.e., that once processed the information will not be shared). There is no guarantee that the licensor would not release customer information to a third party that, for example, might be interested in marketing related products to the licensee or its constituents (assuming such information is so collected). In the world of personal information mining and marketing, "processing" is a concept for various uses of this sort. The right to access and collect stored personal data is one of the bulwark principles of privacy protection, one of the so-called Fair Information Principles, as articulated in several government reports. See U.S. SECRETARY'S ADVISORY COMMITTEE ON AUTOMATED PERSONAL DATA SYSTEMS, RECORDS, COMPUTERS AND THE RIGHTS OF CITIZENS (1973); U.S. SECRETARY'S ADVISORY COMMITTEE ON AUTOMATED PERSONAL DATA SYSTEMS, PERSONAL PRIVACY IN AN INFORMATION SOCIETY (1977); and Fair Information Practice Principles, http://www.ftc.gov/reports/privacy3/fairinfo.shtm. (The five principles are Notice/Awareness, Choice/Consent, Access/Participation, Integrity/ Security, and Enforcement/Redress.) The second sentence here indicates that if the licensee is outside the United States, the same rules apply. In Europe, for example, under its Privacy Directive (Directive 95/46/EC of the European Parliament and of the Council of 24 October 1995), strict rules apply for the collection and onward movement of personal information. Under the Privacy Directive, such rights may not be contracted away, and such a clause may not be enforceable in Europe. The license agreement allows subscribers to "access that information" and admonishes the subscriber to "review and correct this information" on a regular basis. However, there is no discussion of how the information might be used or shared by the licensor. It might also be worthwhile to review the Privacy Policy of Heritage Microfilm, Inc., for further clarification, the terms of which, however, are not part of this agreement.
1.2. Authorized Use. You must be 18 years or older to subscribe.	The licensor wants to ensure that all licensees have the capacity to contract. Many states make voidable contracts entered into by minors when a contract's provisions are detrimental to the minor's interest. As discussed earlier under "Terms and Conditions" (see "'You' or 'Your' means an adult user..."), the license anticipates that a licensee might allow minors to access and use the content, but the licensee would be "strictly liable," at least in the mind of the licensor.
You are responsible for all usage or activity on NewspaperARCHIVE via your password account. Distribution of your	The agreement indicates that the licensee is responsible for all account activity on his or her password, whether authorized or not. Even consensual uses (granted by the licensee) by others are not permitted. In the licensor's view, such uses remain unauthorized. Worse, such password sharing by the licensee is considered a breach and grounds

(continued)

Terms of the Access NewspaperARCHIVE License	Comments on the Terms of the Access NewspaperARCHIVE License
password for access to NewspaperARCHIVE to others is expressly prohibited and shall constitute a breach of this Agreement.	for termination, which, as other provisions indicate, translates to no more access and no refund as well (see ¶ 4. Termination). This provision underscores the nonpublic nature of the licensee, as discussed under "Limited Use License" earlier.
Any fraudulent, abusive, or otherwise illegal activity may be grounds for termination of your account, at our sole discretion, and you may be referred to appropriate law enforcement agencies. You shall notify us by regular mail or by e-mail at Customerservice@ newspaperarchive.com of any known or suspected unauthorized use(s) of your account, or any known or suspected breach of security, including loss, theft, or unauthorized disclosure of your password or credit card information. You will be responsible for maintaining the confidentiality of your password.	As a follow-up to the previous Comment, should the licensee's password fall into the hands of someone else, the licensee is nonetheless responsible for the havoc the third person might wreak on others. Unauthorized disclosure of your password obligates the licensee, if aware of or with suspicion of that disclosure, to inform the licensor of the occurrence. It is assumed that the sentence in the previous Comment regarding disclosure and breach is for intentional or consensual disclosures, not all distributions, or the licensee will be responsible for even unauthorized disclosures, that is, with "distribution" constituting breach, which is subject to termination and loss of subscription fee, as there is no refund where termination is due to breach. This assumption is questionable, as the next sentence admonishes: "You will be responsible for maintaining the confidentiality of your password." Does this "responsibility" include unauthorized distributions? Provisions such as this should be amended to clarify that the licensee is not responsible for unauthorized distribution or disclosure of a password and such occurrence does not constitute breach if the licensee promptly contacts the licensor of such release. The licensor expresses concern regarding appropriate use of a user's account, but then if unauthorized use is suspected, the licensee is admonished to use snail mail or e-mail, which is unlikely to be monitored 24/7.
You will never be required to reveal your password to any representative or agent of NewspaperARCHIVE.	This sentence reaffirms that the licensee's password is secret. It should never be revealed, even to Access NewspaperARCHIVE employees.
2. Fees and Payments. **2.1. Information about Charges and Fees.** NewspaperARCHIVE charges are billed in advance monthly, quarterly, or annually according to your plan for the NewspaperARCHIVE Online Service. This means that once you have become	Licensees pay up front the cost of future access to the service. The subscription, once commenced, is perpetual or evergreen, in that renewal is automatic. (See discussion in ¶ 4. Termination.) Apparently, different periods of renewal and payment plans are available ("monthly, quarterly, or annually"), and some methods of payment trigger a surcharge, "such as payment from your a subscribing member, your subscription will be automatically renewed and payment charged to your account as specified in your chosen billing method. These payments will be charged based on checking account." It is unclear if payment through PayPal or a similar online

(continued)

Terms of the Access NewspaperARCHIVE License	Comments on the Terms of the Access NewspaperARCHIVE License
a subscribing member, your subscription will be automatically renewed and payment charged to your account as specified in your chosen billing method. These payments will be charged based on the subscription program you have chosen. Surcharges may apply if you use certain payment methods (such as payment from your checking account). All charges are nonrefundable unless provided otherwise in your subscription plan. You can contact a NewspaperARCHIVE customer service representative at 1-888-845-2887 to get information about billing or to determine the status of your bill and the amount of any surcharge.	debit system (deductions direct from the licensee's checking account) would trigger the surcharge, the amount of which is not indicated here. It is also unclear whether all payments are "nonrefundable unless otherwise provided in your subscription plan," or whether the surcharge alone would be nonrefundable. In other words, does use of the phrase "all charges" in the second-to-last sentence refer to payments in general, including the membership fee (see next Comment), if there is one, the subscription fee, and any surcharges? In the alternative, does this apply to items that are specifically designated as charges, that is, in addition to the subscription fee? Use of the word "charges" in the first sentence suggests that the licensor refers to the monthly, quarterly, or annual subscription fees as "charges" in this context. As a result, the licensee should be aware that no payment, including the subscription fee, and made in advance, is ever refundable unless this provision is explicit in the license. As written and presented here, such clause is absent, though the second-to-last sentence indicates that it is possible ("unless provided otherwise") to include such a provision. A license should always provide for a refund or, at the option of the licensee, a credit. Avoid a credit in hours or length of service, as this can change renewal and term of subscription dates by adding hours or days which can then be more difficult to track. If a credit is taken, it is best to secure a credit in dollars that can be applied as the licensee chooses, to cover subscription fee or, as in this license, surcharges.
Any trial promotion (such as free trial time) must be used within the specified time of the trial. You must cancel your Account before the end of the trial period to avoid being charged a membership fee. Please note, however, that even during any free trial or other promotion, you will still be responsible for any purchases and surcharges incurred using your Account.	This is important, thus the use of bold print. In the previous Comment, the term "charges," which includes the "subscription" fee and "surcharges," is used. Here, a "membership fee" is now mentioned. It is unclear whether this membership fee refers to the normal subscription fee or if there is indeed a one-time-only initial charge to subscribe to become a member. Further use of the term "membership" (see ¶ 2.2. Payment Responsibilities) suggests that the licensor intends the term to mean the general subscription fee and not a separate initiation fee, which a licensor might want to charge, for example, as an offset against the maintenance cost of an archive for postsubscription access. The last sentence reiterates that "surcharges" are an additional cost, but since during a "free trial period" there would be no "certain payment methods" prior (see ¶ 2.1. Information about Charges and Fees), this reference to "surcharges" indicates that there are indeed assessments that might be charged even during the "free trial time" in addition to those which might be charged during subscription, such as for "payment from your checking account." It might be useful to obtain a complete list of these surcharges up

(continued)

Terms of the Access NewspaperARCHIVE License	Comments on the Terms of the Access NewspaperARCHIVE License
	front, even before agreeing to any free trial period. Moreover, even if the licensee is in a free trial time and decides not to become a subscriber, the licensee must take affirmative action to execute this intent beyond simply not choosing to subscribe; rather, the licensee must undertake effort to "cancel" the account "to avoid being charged a membership fee." It appears that nonuse alone does not equate to cessation of the agreement when one is in a trial period, as a user must "cancel your Account before the end of the trial period to avoid being charged a membership fee," which once triggered by noncancellation becomes automatic ("once you have become a subscribing member, your subscription will be automatically renewed")! (Compare to the admonishment under "Terms and Conditions": "If you do not agree with any of these terms and conditions, your sole remedy is to discontinue use of the Service.") So in the trial period, nonuse will get you nowhere, except into an evergreen membership! Again, it is unclear whether this fee is the same as the subscription fee or an additional fee due when activating a membership. Other costs may arise due to actual "purchases" and appear distinct from the membership or subscription fee.
2.2. Payment Responsibilities. You must select a payment method to pay newspaperARCHIVE for membership fees and all purchases made from NewspaperARCHIVE. You must give NewspaperARCHIVE accurate billing and payment information and keep this information up-to-date. You agree to pay NewspaperARCHIVE for all charges incurred under your Account, including all applicable taxes, fees and surcharges. You authorize NewspaperARCHIVE to charge your designated payment method for these charges. If newspaperARCHIVE does not receive payment from	Here again is reference to the term "membership fees" and "purchases" as two distinct sources of "charges." The third sentence obligates the licensee to pay for all taxes, fees and surcharges, and the next sentence authorizes the licensor to deduct ("to charge your designated payment method") those charges. Since a previous provision indicated that billing is done in advance of services, a licensee could be charged and billed, and the money deducted from his or her account, before being aware that such charges, say, those in addition to the subscription fee, had arisen, been encumbered, and paid out. If for some reason the automated payment cannot be made—perhaps the licensee anticipates a dispute over a fee and places a hold on the account—the licensor still has the right to demand payment from some other method.

(continued)

Terms of the Access NewspaperARCHIVE License	Comments on the Terms of the Access NewspaperARCHIVE License
your designated payment method, you agree to pay all amounts due upon demand by NewspaperARCHIVE.	
Every time you use a NewspaperARCHIVE Service, you reaffirm that (i) NewspaperARCHIVE is authorized to charge your designated payment method; (ii) NewspaperARCHIVE may submit charges incurred under your Account for payment; and (iii) you will be responsible for such charges, even if your membership is canceled or terminated.	This sentence reminds the licensee that use equals assent. Here, use also constitutes an affirmative act of consent to being charged for the use of the service as well as being responsible for additional charges that might accrue through use of the service, even if the membership is canceled. Is there a click-to-agree or other assent mechanism in place when a subscriber logs in so that he or she realizes that use equals assent to pay for any charges incurred through use (i.e., some prompt with words to this effect: "By submitting this query you agree to . . .")? There is reference to "charges incurred under your Account," but it is unclear if this is a reference to "surcharges" or all charges. (See Chapter 7 for a review of typical online assent mechanisms, such as click-wrap and browse-wrap.) The "even if" proviso suggests that charges could be surcharges or subscription fees and anticipates a scenario where the license is canceled but use continues nonetheless, allowing the licensor to charge for an additional subscription fee as well as for any surcharges associated with the continued use.
After 30 days from the date of any unpaid charges, your Account will be deemed delinquent and NewspaperARCHIVE may terminate or suspend your Account for nonpayment. NewspaperARCHIVE reserves the right to assess an additional 1.5 percent (or the highest amount allowed by law, whichever is lower) per month late charge if your payment is more than 30 days past due and to use alternate means to collect any unpaid charges. You are liable for any fees, including attorney and collection fees incurred by NewspaperARCHIVE in its efforts to collect any remaining balances from you.	If the licensee, for example, has put a hold on the account (see scenario in ¶ 2.2. Payment Responsibilities) because an anticipated dispute was brewing, and this period of nonpayment lasted more than 30 days, then the licensor may terminate membership (subscription) or suspend access to the service (likely continuing to charge the licensee for future periods of subscription with denial of access, i.e., suspension). In licensing, suspension is different from termination, with the former concept meaning that access is no longer forthcoming (but may be restored) but the agreement continues. In the 30 days without payment scenario, the licensor can also charge interest (another surcharge) and pursue legal remedy for the nonpayment and give the bill to the licensee for its efforts ("liable for any fees, including attorney and collection fees").

(continued)

Terms of the Access NewspaperARCHIVE License	Comments on the Terms of the Access NewspaperARCHIVE License
You are responsible for all charges incurred under your Account, including applicable taxes, fees, surcharges and purchases made by you or anyone you allow to use your Account (including your children, family or friends). You must notify NewspaperARCHIVE about any billing problems or discrepancies within 90 days after they first appear on your Account statement. If you do not bring them to the attention of NewspaperARCHIVE within 90 days, you agree that you waive your right to dispute such problems or discrepancies.	Again, this is important, thus the use of bold print. If for any reason someone obtains access to the licensee's account, the licensee is financially responsible. It is odd that one bold proviso anticipates that such "responsible" use includes use by others made with the consent of the subscriber ("or anyone you allow to use your Account") when an earlier provision under ¶ 1.2. Authorized Use warned: "Distribution of your password for access to NewspaperARCHIVE to others is expressly prohibited and shall constitute a breach of this Agreement." Perhaps illogical, this provision still suggests a sequence of events where the subscriber would log on for another person—consensual use without sharing of the password, thus the prohibition of ¶ 1.2. Authorized Use is honored—and the other user goes hog wild, racking up surcharge after surcharge (Ignoring the subscriber's admonition: "You can use my account but don't print anything; the archive charges an arm and leg to print"). The subscriber is responsible for those charges. By the same token, and in the absence of all-inclusive language, the subscriber would not be responsible for surcharges incurred by someone who is not authorized by the subscriber, as only those "surcharges and purchases made by you or anyone you allow to use your Account" are assignable to the subscriber's account.
	If the licensee desires to dispute any charges ("purchases," "surcharges," or "membership"/"subscription" fees), this must be done within 90 days of the item appearing on the "Account statement." This period runs from the date the licensor posts the charge on the licensee's account, which is likely not the same as the date the licensee receives the account statement in the mail or otherwise learns of it. While three months is a long time, there may still be occasion where having the full 90 days would be necessary; for example, the licensee would need to audit the statement and compare the charges against a record of actual uses. Some licensees may not keep such logs or records routinely, and billing departments may not have access to such records or logs, nor able to decipher or match charges against actual uses even if such are kept. It is also unclear what sort of contact with the licensor satisfies the 90-day notification requirement. This is important because the failure to do this within the time period is taken as assent or agreement to the charges ("you waive your right to dispute"). Is contact with any employee sufficient, or must contact be made to the billing department of the licensor or to the customer service department (as directed in the cancellation process)? Remember to keep payments for other charges current because if the licensee stops payments as part of the "billing problems or discrepancies," and this period is longer than 30 days from the date of the charge, the licensee will be deemed delinquent

(continued)

Terms of the Access NewspaperARCHIVE License	Comments on the Terms of the Access NewspaperARCHIVE License
	under the nonpayment provision in ¶ 2.2. Payment Responsibilities. Finally, there is no mention of what happens or what recourse is available when a billing dispute arises and it cannot be resolved. Is cancellation the sole remedy, as it is with other disputes under the agreement? ¶ 2.2. Payment Responsibilities suggests that it is: the sole remedy is cancellation in disputes over "the amount or type of fees, surcharges, applicable taxes, billing methods, or any change to the fees, applicable taxes, surcharges or billing methods."
2.3 Cancellations. Either you may cancel or NewspaperARCHIVE may terminate your membership at any time.	The first sentence indicates that there are two ways out of the license. The significant difference between the two is that cancellation is the right of the licensee and termination is the right of the licensor. Remember that during a suspension the licensee is likely still obligated to pay subscription fees! (See ¶ 2.2. Payment Responsibilities.) While either can be done at any time, the conditions and consequences of each differ, as noted in the following two Comments ("You can cancel your membership . . ."; Cancellation of your Account . . .").
You can cancel your membership by calling, by sending a fax, or by sending a letter to the NewspaperARCHIVE Customer Service Department. Cancellation will take effect within 72 hours of receipt of your request. NewspaperARCHIVE will send you confirmation of your cancellation. If you cancel near the end of your billing period and are inadvertently charged for the next month's fee, call NewspaperARCHIVE to have the charges reversed.	Unlike the dispute issues discussed previously, there is indication here of the department to which a cancellation should be directed and the acceptable mode (phone, fax, or mail, but no e-mail) to convey that cancellation. While cancellation is effective "within 72 hours of receipt of your request" and the licensor will send the licensee a confirmation, there is no indication when that confirmation will be sent or that it will indicate the date of receipt (i.e., 72 hours after which date the cancellation takes effect). Consider a situation where the licensee believes a proper cancellation process has been executed. The licensor thinks not (perhaps the licensee sent the cancellation notice by e-mail or to the wrong fax number), or perhaps the licensor is slow to read its mail or check its mailbox. The licensee waits patiently for a confirmation that never comes, all the while being billed for a subscription—rightly, as the licensor does not have proper notice of the cancellation yet. But the licensee thinks the process is over and so ceases using the service but is still paying for it. Worse, any refund is calculated from the official date of cancellation, not cessation of use. Having some definite period within which cancellation confirmation must be made and indicated would solve or at least minimize these sorts of issues. Once cancellation is effective, the licensee should refrain from using the service or additional subscription fee and surcharges may apply per ¶ 2.2. Payment Responsibilities. If for some reason the licensee is charged for the subsequent month in error ("inadvertently"), a reimbursement is possible, but this request would also be subject to the 90-day "billing problems or discrepancies" proviso. In large organizations, an audit match of billing statements

(continued)

Terms of the Access NewspaperARCHIVE License	Comments on the Terms of the Access NewspaperARCHIVE License
	with actual use might take some time to accomplish. The remaining and important unanswered question is whether any refund (proration) is made for cancellation before the end of a billing period where there is no inadvertent charge for the next month's fee, for which a complete refund would be due ("charges reversed"). Since a refund or proration is possible in some circumstances of termination (see discussion of suspension under ¶ 4. Termination), it should also be possible in cancellations too.
Cancellation of your Account is your sole right and remedy with respect to any dispute with NewspaperARCHIVE. This includes, but is not limited to, any dispute related to, or arising out of: (1) any term of this Member Agreement or the enforcement or application of this Member Agreement by NewspaperARCHIVE; (2) any policy or practice of NewspaperARCHIVE, including the NewspaperARCHIVE Copyright Policy and Privacy Policy, or the enforcement or application of these policies by NewspaperARCHIVE; (3) the Content available on NewspaperARCHIVE Services or the Internet or any change in Content provided by NewspaperARCHIVE; (4) your ability to access and/or use the NewspaperARCHIVE Services; or (5) the amount or type of fees, surcharges, applicable taxes, billing methods, or any change to the fees, applicable taxes, surcharges or billing methods.	This sentence perhaps should be in bold! It sure is important. Regardless of the nature of the dispute with the licensor, the sole remedy of the licensee is to cancel the subscription ("membership"). It would appear that an issue over a charge, for example, could still be raised per a previous provision (see "You are responsible for all charges incurred . . ."), that is, the "90-day billing problems or discrepancies" rule, but if the issue could not be resolved, the sole recourse would be to accept the licensor's position/response or cancel.

(continued)

Terms of the Access NewspaperARCHIVE License	Comments on the Terms of the Access NewspaperARCHIVE License
In the event that your Account is terminated or canceled, no online time or other credits will be credited to you or can be converted to cash or other form of reimbursement.	This sentence would appear to reference something other than an inadvertent charge for an entire billing period but more likely refers to credits issued for perhaps downtime exceeding the terms or a failed print or download that was charged but never received, was brought to the attention of the licensor within the 90-day period for billing challenges, and which the licensor agreed was in error. It might be understandable that a credit of "online time" would be lost in cases of termination or cancellation. Notice that even though such "online time or other credits" are not negotiable tender at cancellation or termination, mention of such credits here indicates that such are available in other circumstances, that is, can be credited against future surcharges or converted to cash or other form of reimbursement for continuation of the subscription. It is unclear (lack of reference elsewhere in the agreement) how these credits would be generated or why such credits could not be converted to a dollar figure through proration of the monthly fee. Where the credit represents a monetary response, for example, a billing dispute forwarded within the 90-day objection period and resolved in favor of the licensee, and since all charges are made automatically (charged against the licensee's "designated payment method"), it is unclear why a reverse charge (credit) could not be given to the licensee directly through the same automated account mechanism that delivered the payment to the licensor in the first instance. In other circumstances of cancellation or termination under the agreement, this is possible, that is, where the credit results from the inadvertent charge "for the next month's fee" and the accommodation by the licensor is to have the "charges reversed." As a result, it is not clear what other sorts of credits could be issued that could not translate into a clear and precise monetary amount for which the ameliorating response by the licensor should be to credit the licensee's account directly, that is, reverse the charges for those credits as well.
NewspaperARCHIVE must give you express permission before it will reactivate your Account if NewspaperARCHIVE previously terminated your membership for violating the NewspaperARCHIVE Terms and Conditions or due to an outstanding balance. Active NewspaperARHIVE members	In cases of termination by the licensor in response to violation of the terms or for nonpayment (of "an outstanding balance"), any reactivation of membership must be made by the licensor. Regardless of the reason for termination, a current licensee cannot allow the use of its account by a former, terminated licensee. The circumstances of termination are oddly articulated in a later section. The final sentence here, again, contemplates that one subscriber could let another person use his or her account without actually sharing the password by logging on personally and then letting the other individual use the service under the subscriber's account. However, this shared access (as opposed to a shared password, which is prohibited by ¶ 2.1.

(continued)

Terms of the Access NewspaperARCHIVE License	Comments on the Terms of the Access NewspaperARCHIVE License
may not allow former NewspaperARCHIVE members whose memberships have been terminated to use their Accounts.	Information about Charges and Fees and discussed earlier) is prohibited when the other nonsubscribing person is one whose account was previously terminated. So remember to ask! Unlike under ¶ 2.1. Information about Charges and Fees, there is no indication if such act would constitute a breach similar to the one caused by password sharing.
2.4. Subscription Costs. Subscription costs may be changed by NewspaperARCHIVE at any time and each renewal of your subscription will be at the then standard renewal cost for the period which you originally selected when you subscribed.	Reading this sentence in conjunction with a later sentence indicates that prices may change at any time, but notice of "pricing or material changes" must be given 30 days in advance (see ¶ 5. Modifications to This Agreement and the Service: "NewspaperARCHIVE will provide you with notice of any change in pricing or material changes to the Terms and Conditions at least thirty (30) days in advance"). However, accepted pricing changes would continue through the duration of the initial term of membership, that is, "for the period which you originally selected when you subscribed." New prices carry through into a renewal, with the renewal subscription cost being based upon (1) the new rates and (2) the length of the original subscription (e.g., quarterly, period).
3. Communications Between NewspaperARCHIVE and You. NewspaperARCHIVE will send electronic mail to you, for the purpose of informing you of changes or additions to NewspaperARCHIVE, or of any NewspaperARCHIVE related products and services. You may opt out of this notification service by sending an e-mail to customerservice@ newspaperarchive.com.	Notification of changes in content, related products, or services are made via e-mail, but there is no mention that changes in terms would be likewise so communicated. If the licensor is willing to send notice of "changes or additions," it does not seem too burdensome to also require notice regarding changes of terms as well.
For further information on our use of subscriber demographic information, see the Privacy Policy on the Service.	In the first sentence of ¶ 3. Communications Between NewspaperARCHIVE and You, the licensor will send e-mail to the licensee regarding "related products and services"—in other words, advertisements or junk mail. Entities often share customer information with other entities that might also desire to solicit this customer. This provision relating to communications between the licensor and "you," the licensee, points the licensee to the licensor's practices regarding how customer advertisements or junk mail. Entities often share customer information with other entities that

(continued)

Terms of the Access NewspaperARCHIVE License	Comments on the Terms of the Access NewspaperARCHIVE License
	might also desire to solicit this customer. This provision relating to communications between the licensor and "you," the licensee, points the licensee to the licensor's practices regarding how customer information is used, perhaps indicating the conditions under which such information is made available to third parties. Again, it might be worthwhile to review the Privacy Policy of Heritage Microfilm, Inc., for further clarification, the terms of which are not part of the agreement.
4. Termination. Should you breach this Agreement, NewspaperARCHIVE will revoke your license to use the Service and suspend your right of access. In such a case, no portion of your subscription payment will be refunded. Should NewspaperARCHIVE decide to suspend the subscription service for any reason other than breach, it will refund to you the unused portion of your subscription payment, which will be your sole and exclusive remedy upon such a suspension of service.	In previous provisions, the word "termination" was used; now there is reference to revocation and suspension. Revocation may be intended as a form of termination, as a consequence of certain conduct (a breach) that leads to termination. Suspension carries the same result, but its cause is something "other than breach," in which case a refund is due the licensee. Worse, in instances of breach-termination, no proration is given for the remainder of the billing cycle for which the licensee's account was already billed. In other instances of termination, a refund or proration is made for the "unused portion of your subscription payment," but this raises some questions. It might be nice to know in what other circumstances the licensor could suspend service! Is notice required before such suspension occurs? In cases of breach too? And in either case, is a right to cure available before suspension occurs? Suspension is used elsewhere in this agreement, but it is never explained under what circumstances it would apply.
5. Modifications to This Agreement and the Service. NewspaperARCHIVE in its sole discretion may change or discontinue any or all aspects of the NewspaperARCHIVE Services without notice, including access to support services, Content and other products or services ancillary to the NewspaperARCHIVE Services or a NewspaperARCHIVE membership.	The modifications provision confirms again that changes in "Content" as well as services may occur. Recall that content is the "graphics, information, data, editorial and other content accessible by any Internet user and similar content which is accessible only to our subscribing members (the Content)." If the licensee would consider these changes material or at least important, then perhaps notice should be required at some trigger point in advance—for example, change or loss of content constituting 5 percent or 10 percent of the licensed titles, or loss of the most significant make-or-break title(s) (i.e., the reason the licensee subscribed is to have access to this title). The licensee could submit that loss of content at some point might constitute a significant change and that notice-cancellation-refund is an option or at least an "online time or other credit . . . will be credited to you or can be converted to cash or other form of reimbursement."

(continued)

Terms of the Access NewspaperARCHIVE License	Comments on the Terms of the Access NewspaperARCHIVE License
NewspaperARCHIVE may modify the NewspaperARCHIVE Terms and Conditions, change its fees and change its billing methods at any time. NewspaperARCHIVE will provide you with notice of any change in pricing or material changes to the Terms and Conditions at least thirty (30) days in advance. If you disagree with any proposed change, your sole remedy is to cancel your membership before such change takes effect (See section 2.3 regarding cancellations). Otherwise, you will be bound by the revised terms if you keep your membership. NewspaperARCHIVE will not refund any charges if you choose to cancel your membership for this reason.	Changes in the terms or pricing may also occur. The licensee must receive notice of changes to "pricing or material changes" to the agreement at least 30 days before the changes go into effect. However, the other sorts of material terms are not defined. It is also not clear whether the 30-day notice period tolls from when the notice is made/sent by the licensor (the mailbox rule) or upon receipt by the licensee (and how receipt is defined, i.e., received in house or actually read). If the licensee views particular terms as so-called mission critical, these should be included as material, for which the notice mechanism would apply. However, there is no opportunity to negotiate over any change. Again, the sole response or remedy by the licensee is either to accept the changes or to cancel. Cancellation must occur before the changes are in effect, which may mean a fast turnaround or decision time if cancellation is contemplated: provision of notice of change by licensor, receipt and consideration of impact of change by licensee, sending of cancellation notice by licensee to licensor, notice effective "within 72 hours of receipt" by licensor. After provision of the notice of change by the licensor, if the licensee does nothing, the inaction will be deemed acceptance: "you will be bound by the revised terms if you keep your membership." The final sentence contains two important pieces of information. If the licensee cancels in response to a change in pricing or terms and misses the 30-day cancellation window, there will be no refund. This sentence also implies that in other circumstances of cancellation a refund would normally be forthcoming. Since in a previous provision the licensee "may cancel . . . membership at any time" (¶ 2.3. Cancellations)—though this provision is silent on the issue of refund there is mention of having "charges reversed" and credits converted or paid—it might be best to forward another logical, legitimate, and documented reason for cancellation and secure the right to a refund. Of course, the licensor may argue the other reason was mere pretense and refuse a refund.
6. Miscellaneous. **6.1.** If you have any questions about this privacy statement, the practices of this site, or your dealings with this Website, you may contact: Customer Service. This Subscriber Agreement is governed by the law of the State of Iowa, without regard to its principles	Again, there is reference to the privacy policy, along with reference to the practices and dealings of the site (how this differs from practices and dealings of the NewspaperARCHIVE is unclear). Questions should be directed to the customer service department. The second sentence reiterates the choice of law: the applicable law is that of the state of Iowa and, where applicable, the laws of the United States. The next sentence indicates the choice of forum: state or federal courts in Cedar Rapids. This designation of law and forum is made without application of the conflict of laws. "Conflict of Laws is that part of the law of each state which determines what effect is given to the fact that the case may have a significant relationship to more than one state," per RESTATEMENT 2d

(continued)

Terms of the Access NewspaperARCHIVE License	Comments on the Terms of the Access NewspaperARCHIVE License
on conflicts of laws, and the federal law of the United States of America. Any action to enforce this Agreement shall be brought in the federal or state courts located in Cedar Rapids.	CONFLICT OF LAWS § 2 (Subject matter of Conflict of Laws). "Conflict of Laws covers an extremely wide area, embracing all situations where the affairs of men cut across state lines. Important matters falling within the scope of a state's Conflict of Laws rules include: Judicial jurisdiction and competence ... Foreign judgments ... Choice of law" (*id.* at comment a, Matters falling within the field of Conflict of Laws). Though remedy in disputes over terms, policies, the licensed content, the availability, or the charges or processing of the charges as well as dispute over changes in pricing or terms is limited to cancellation and possible refund, there may be other issues over which litigation may occur, such as whether a particular clause is lawful or enforceable. If so, then the proper address for service of process is provided.
6.2. Official correspondence must be sent via postal mail to: NewspaperARCHIVE.com Attn: Customer Service 4069 21st Ave. S.W., Cedar Rapids, IA 52404.	

THE BioOne LICENSE DECONSTRUCTED

Terms of the BioOne License	Comments on the Terms of the BioOne License
THIS LICENSE IS AGREED as of this [ ] day of [ ], [ ], BY AND BETWEEN 1. BioOne, a non-profit corporation with offices at 21 Dupont Circle, Suite 800, Washington, DC 20036 (hereinafter referred to as 'BioOne') and 2. [ ] with offices at [ ] (hereinafter referred to as the 'Licensee').	The opening sentence identifies the parties, the licensor and licensee, including the legal address of each party, again indicating where process would be served if the need arose. A notice provision can indicate that this is the postal address to which correspondence should be sent and, of course, indicate the mode of correspondence—certified mail, return receipt requested, and so on.
IT IS AGREED AS FOLLOWS:	There is mutual agreement (expressed by the concluding signatures found immediately preceding Appendixes A and B to this license) as to the terms of the agreement; that is, both parties (listed in the previous sentence) express assent to be bound by the terms of the agreement, problematic in so-called browse-wrap agreements but an essential component of any valid contract.

(continued)

Terms of the BioOne License	Comments on the Terms of the BioOne License
1. Key Definitions In the License, the following terms shall have the following meanings:	The license defines a number of terms at the outset. The more significant terms are defined, the more precise and useful the agreement will become.
1.1. Authorized Users. Authorized Users are those individuals officially affiliated or registered with the Licensee, for example, those serving in the capacity of employees, consultants under contract with the Licensee, full- or part-time faculty and other teaching staff (including temporary or exchange faculty for the duration of their assignment), persons officially registered as full- or part-time students, registered patrons, and Walk-in Users. Authorized Users also include persons affiliated with remote sites of the Licensee as specified in Appendix D, provided such Authorized Users will work from, or otherwise maintain affiliation with, these access sites.	The list of authorized users is rather complete and includes arguably visiting faculty ("exchange faculty") but may not include visiting scholars engaged in researching or consulting, unless employed by the licensee ("consultants under contract with the Licensee") but are not teaching or otherwise said to be "faculty." It is conceivable that a visiting consultant could be "under contract" but not employed; that is, the contract could pertain to conditions of the exchange, but the juxtaposition of the phrase after "employees" suggests that the licensor may intend to be including what would under the copyright law, for example, be any person in the stead of independent contractor (i.e., anyone other than an employee but still doing work for the licensee). It is unclear whether alumni or members of the local community are included as well. However, since the definition includes those persons "officially affiliated or registered with the Licensee" and later "registered patrons," alumni, community guests, and so forth, would likely be included, assuming the institution vests such persons with this status, that is, allows alumni and the general public to be registered library patrons or possess some affiliated status. This assumes, as is the case with some colleges and universities, that all graduates are automatically members of the alumni association, thus making all alums "officially affiliated" with the institution. Likewise, if alums or members of the local community are registered patrons, such persons would also be authorized users. This category could also be used to include visiting nonteaching scholars or consultants as long as such persons are "registered patrons." The institution may have rules regarding who can or cannot be a library patron for whom a registration record exists, arguably satisfying the definition. Language such as this underscores the flexibility with which the institution may need to respond in order to take full advantage of the terms of a license. Observe also that Walk-In Users are included as Authorized Users (see also the discussion in ¶ 1.8. Walk-in Users). There is also provision for remote sites, as some institutions may have multiple or extension campus locations. It is not clear if there is a geographic limit as to how far away the remote site can be (e.g., another state, country, or continent). Since the list of remotes sites must be included as Appendix D, the licensor would have an opportunity to object to such inclusions if it so desired.

(continued)

Terms of the BioOne License	Comments on the Terms of the BioOne License
1.2. Commercial Use. Use for the purposes of monetary reward (whether by or for the Licensee or an Authorized User) by means of the sale, resale, loan, transfer, hire or other form of exploitation of the Licensed Materials. Recovery of direct and indirect cost by the Licensee from Authorized Users, or use by the Licensee or by an Authorized User of the Licensed Material in the court [*sic*, "course"?] of research funded by a commercial organization, is not deemed to constitute Commercial Use.	The licensee is allowed to charge Authorized Users if it so wishes on a cost-recovery basis for the actual cost of a document ("direct" cost), for example, or for the paper used to print out the document or to render librarian search assistance to the Authorized User ("indirect" cost). If the licensed content is used in conjunction with a grant awarded from a commercial entity, such as a pharmaceutical company, such use is not per se commercial use. What would be commercial use is the reproduction of the licensed content to satisfy third-party requests as part of a pay-per-document service the institution also administers, as this scenario would be beyond mere cost recovery. See *Ryan v. CARL Corp.*, 23 F. Supp. 2d 1146 (N.D. Cal. 1998). The UnCover service, a partnership between CARL Corporation and Dialog, Inc., is "a for-profit company that functions like a private interlibrary loan service. UnCover maintains an internet database that contains the titles, but not the text, of about eight million articles from about seventeen thousand periodicals. UnCover's customers, mostly libraries and some individuals, can search the database by title, author, periodical title, and subject. When a customer requests an article, an UnCover representative goes to a library that carries the periodical and copies the article. The article is then electronically stored by UnCover, so that later orders for the same article can be filled without a return trip to the source library. The article is then sent to the customer who placed the order. The fee charged depends on how quickly the customer needs the article" (*id.* at 1147). Even though "loan" is included in the list of prohibited activities, the prohibition would not appear to impact traditional interlibrary loan services even if a charge is associated with it, as such monies are not in the form of "reward" but again are based upon a general cost-recovery formula.
1.3. Electronic Reserve. Any electronic or other databased collection of articles, chapters, or other materials from different copyrighted sources compiled for a specific course or series of instruction by the Library.	The definition of electronic reserve is broad enough to include library as well as online course management systems and includes information literacy and other instruction by the library undertaken outside of formal course work. The intent of the provision is to allow the library to collect such articles, chapters, and so on, in support of teaching.
1.4. Fees. The fee(s) set out in Appendix B, or in new Appendices to this License that may be agreed to by the parties from time to time.	This sentence indicates that fees may change and that the new fee structure becomes part of the agreement ("agreed to by the parties from time to time"). Initial fees are listed in Appendix B, with changes listed in additional appendixes. It might be wise to include the process of that agreement, considering what constitutes adequate notice of change and assent to the change, and the timing of that notice.

(continued)

Terms of the BioOne License	Comments on the Terms of the BioOne License
1.5. Licensed Material. The electronic material listed in Appendix C, or in new Appendices to this License that may be agreed to by the parties from time to time.	This sentence likewise indicates that the content may change over time and that those changes become part of the agreement. The initial content ("licensed material") is found in Appendix C, with updated content lists in additional appendixes. Both ¶ 1.4. Fees and ¶ 1.5. Licensed Material indicate that a new fee structure as well as changes to content are also subject to the mutual assent of both parties (i.e., "agreed to by the parties"). Again, similar concerns over notice, timing, and assent should be indicated, typically elsewhere in the agreement.
1.6. Secure Network. A network (whether a standalone network or a virtual network within the Internet) which is only accessible to Authorized Users approved by the Licensee and whose conduct shall be subjected to regulation by the Licensee.	This sentence anticipates that the network for accessing the content should be secure, through, for example, the use of a password or other verification system that allows access only by authorized users. In addition, the licensee institution must have some sort of "acceptable use policy" (AUP) or similar set of guidelines or code of behavior that governs the conduct of users of the network and some level of authority to enforce those standards of conduct (i.e., "subject to regulation"), at least that appears to be the likely intent of the provision.
1.7. Subscription Period. That period nominally covered by the volumes and issues of the Licensed Material listed in Appendix C, regardless of the actual date of publication, or as otherwise pro-rated for less than one full calendar year in the Licensee's initial Subscription Period or in new **BioOne®** **Subscriber License**. Appendices to this License that may be added subsequently by mutual agreement of the parties hereto.	Rather than titles alone, the licensed content listed in Appendix C is identified by the volume and issue ranges (and not necessarily publication dates). Additional appendixes may be added again when agreed to by the parties, though expressed here by the concept of "mutual agreement" or assent of both parties (e.g., the signature or initial of each party on the appendix itself). Apparently the term of the license is a calendar year, with the licensed volume and issue ranges so correlating, though in the instance of a subscription beginning during the year the list of licensed material would be adjusted or prorated.
1.8 Walk-in Users. Persons who are not officially affiliated with the Licensee, but who are occasional users of the Licensee's library or information service and who are permitted to access the Secure Network from computer terminals within the Institution only. The payment of a fee in	The first sentence, when read in conjunction with ¶ 1.1. Authorized Users, indicates that there are two subsets of authorized users: those "individuals officially affiliated or registered," such as employees, consultants under contract, faculty and teaching staff, registered students, and registered patrons, and those individuals who are *not* officially affiliated with the licensee. The agreement refers to this, the second subset of authorized users, as walk-in users. Such a person would not be registered (i.e., the library does not have an informational record of the user), but he or she may nonetheless access the licensed content via the institution's secure network (see ¶ 1.6. Secure Network). However, the access

(continued)

Terms of the BioOne License	Comments on the Terms of the BioOne License
order to be considered a Walk-in User is deemed not to constitute Commercial Use under Para. 1.2 above.	is restricted to computer terminals at the actual physical location of the institution. The institution may charge such persons for terminal access, and this charge will not constitute commercial use under ¶ 1.2. Commercial Use.
2. Agreement. **2.1.** BioOne grants the Licensee the non-exclusive and non-transferable right to give Authorized Users access to the Licensed Material through BioOne's server(s) for the purposes of research, teaching and private study, subject to the terms and conditions of this License, and the Licensee agrees to pay the Fee.	The rights granted to the licensee are nonexclusive; there are other licensees out there with similar (or different, depending on what terms those other licensees secured!) rights. Second, the nonexclusive rights granted are not transferable (as with many a landlord-tenant agreement, there is no subletting!). If the licensee is the ABC College, the college cannot transfer the license to the XYZ School of Visual and Performing Arts. A rare but important circumstance is whether a successor entity can assume the license. Is this a prohibited transfer? This would be a situation where the ABC College licensee and XYZ School merge to form the LMNOP University. If such a situation is contemplated, it might be important to determine whether this is possible. Likewise, if both the college and school are current subscribers, then would consolidation of the dual licenses be possible, that is, does the termination provision allow for one to terminate? (See ¶ 6.2.3; termination is allowed in cases of insolvency or receivership, liquidation, or similar external administration, but these suggest a negative context; a merger might not be contemplated within such a list of terminating events.) Authorized users may use the services for purposes of "research, teaching and private study." While study must be "private" (as opposed to group study?), the listing is broad enough to include uses that are arguably quite public or nonprivate, such as teaching (at least under the copyright law classrooms are places of public performance and display) and research, which can be collaborative (arguably also then public) and which might include dissemination of the research (which is surely public). These uses need not be private. The "grant" is made subject to the terms of the agreement, indicating that the licensor can "terminate the license grant if the Customer breaches any other terms of the Agreement." H. WARD CLASSEN, A PRACTICAL GUIDE TO SOFTWARE LICENSING FOR LICENSEES AND LICENSORS 267 (3d ed. 2008). The concluding phrase indicates that there are terms and a fee to pay.
2.1.1. The Subscription Period for individual journals shall be as set out in Appendix C or in new Appendices to this License that may be added subsequently from time to time by mutual agreement of the parties hereto.	While the subscription period is identified in Appendix C or in additional appendixes, again subject to agreement of both the licensor and licensee, the duration of that period is one year (see ¶ 6. Term and Termination).

(continued)

Terms of the BioOne License	Comments on the Terms of the BioOne License
2.1.2. On termination of this License, BioOne shall and Licensee may provide continuing access for Authorized Users to that part of the Licensed Material which was published or added to the Licensed Material within the Subscription Period, either from BioOne's server(s), or from a third party's server, or by supplying electronic files to the Licensee. The terms governing access to this material shall be those in effect at the termination of the license.	This is an archive provision of sorts. After termination (and regardless of the cause or circumstances of the termination), the licensor is obligated to provide ("BioOne shall") continued access to the content that was created ("published or added") during the term this license was in effect. The decision whether to allow all authorized users access to the content rests with the licensee ("Licensee may"). The licensee may want to allow such access to certain classes of users (e.g., faculty) or to individual users on a case-by-case basis. The access might be from BioOne still or BioOne might itself contract with a third party to provide such access, or it may simply send the files of the relevant content to the licensee. The latter option might be desirable, as the licensee would then have complete control (subject to the terms of the agreement in force at the time of termination); in other words, if on a licensor or third-party server, issues of downtime due to maintenance or system failure persist, but with the latter option, such issues would be within the control of the licensee. Continued online access or in-house retention of content created and added to the database during the period of subscription is an important "archive" right and duplicates or mimics the purchases of a traditional subscription to a periodical, with the difference here that the subsequent "archived" use is subject to the license agreement, whereas with a traditional purchase of a periodical subscription use of the issues/volumes after the subscription ends would be governed by the copyright law.
3. Permitted Uses. **3.1.** The Licensee may, subject to Para. 4 below:	Paragraph 4 lists the prohibited uses, which take precedent over the uses permitted, unless listed in specific here.
3.1.1. Make temporary (less than 24 hours) local electronic copies by means of caching of all or part of the Licensed Material as is necessary to ensure efficient use by Authorized Users, provided that such use is subject to all the terms and conditions of this Agreement and does not result in the making available to Authorized Users of duplicate copies of the Licensed Material.	Transitory (compare 17 U.S.C. § 110(2): "transient or temporary storage") or cache (compare 17 U.S.C. § 117(a)(1): "essential step in the utilization of the computer program in conjunction with a machine") storage approaches are allowed if necessary for "efficient use." Such uses may result technically in more than one copy per user; see, for example, ¶ 3.1.4 (permitted uses: provide single print or electronic copies of an artucle) and ¶ 4.2 (prohibited uses: systematic "print or Telectronic copies of multiple extracts"). However, this is allowed if buffer, server (etc.), other copies are created in the provision of the single, allowed copy to an authorized user, provided such automatic processing does not result in the making of actual multiple copies to the authorized user.

(continued)

Terms of the BioOne License	Comments on the Terms of the BioOne License
3.1.2. Allow Authorized Users to have access to the Licensed Material, from BioOne's server or from another server designated or approved in writing by BioOne via the Secure Network.	Authorized users have access to the licensed content from the server of the licensee "or from another server" authorized in writing by the licensor. In either case, access by authorized users must be via the secure network of the licensee, that is, accessible to approved (by the licensee) users alone (e.g., via password) whose use of the network is also "subject . . . to regulation by the Licensee."
3.1.3. Allow Walk-in Users to have access to the licensed Material, from BioOne's server or from another server designated by BioOne at computer terminals within the Library Premises only.	Walk-in users are also allowed access, again from the licensor's server or an authorized alternative. While walk-in users are a category of authorized user, such users may access and use the licensed content only from terminals located physically in the library. This provision would prevent the licensee from allowing a "walk-in" with his or her own laptop to obtain licensed content through issuance of a temporary password or other mechanism, for example, that would allow remote access.
3.1.4. Provide single printed or electronic copies of single articles at the request of individual Authorized Users.	The default mode of reproduction is singular. See also ¶ 4.2 (prohibited uses: "systematically make print or electronic copies of multiple extracts"). In other words, authorized users get one copy and one copy only. What is the scope of the words "provide" and "at the request of"? If the licensee-library allows authorized users to print out or download an article, has the licensee provided it? And if the print or download is triggered by the authorized user hitting the "enter" key or by a point-and-click over a print icon on the terminal screen, has the licensee provided the article via a "request"? If so, then in situations where the licensee allows users to reproduce the licensed content, the licensee must somehow limit the reproduction to a single copy of the same item. It is hoped that the provision anticipates those scenarios where the licensee-library actually makes the copies for users, through some sort of document-on-demand patron service. The language in ¶ 3.1.4 parallels the rights given to qualifying libraries and archives in 17 U.S.C. § 108(d). Regardless, ¶ 3.2 indicates users may print only "single copies" of the licensed content. Under either a restrictive interpretation here or ¶ 3.2, the question is whether the licensee technologically can prevent a given user from repeatedly hitting the enter key or clicking the print icon multiple times. See discussion under ¶ 3.2.
3.1.5. Provide interlibrary loans.	This provision makes clear that the licensee may use the licensed content as a source for interlibrary loan. But see ¶ 4.3. Again, this grant parallels the right given to qualifying libraries and archives in 17 U.S.C. § 108(d).

(continued)

Terms of the BioOne License	Comments on the Terms of the BioOne License
3.1.6. Display, download or print the Licensed Material for the purpose of internal promotion or testing, or for training Authorized Users.	Even if use may not appear to be for "research, teaching and private study" or "compiled [by the library] for a specific course or series of instruction," the use is nonetheless allowed for promotion or testing within the licensee institution or for information literacy outreach to authorized users. At worst, the provision implies that the activity of librarians during instructional or literacy sessions is not "teaching" per ¶ 2.1 but is rather considered "training."
3.2. Authorized Users shall be informed that they may, subject to Para. 4 below: **3.2.1.** Search, view, retrieve and display the Licensed Material. **3.2.2.** Electronically save parts of the Licensed Material for personal use. **3.2.3.** Print off single copies of parts of the Licensed Material.	The licensee has an obligation ("shall") to inform all authorized users of the use rights each possesses, subject of course to ¶ 4 (prohibited uses, which take precedent over the uses permitted unless made specific here): the right to access and use the licensed content, the right to download ("[e]lectronically save") parts of the licensed content for their own ("personal") use, to print single copies of parts of the licensed content. Why downloads or "electronic copying" is not so similarly restricted is unclear. Most important, a requirement to inform users of their rights (and by defining the copying right as a single-copy rule, imposing a prohibition on multiple copying unless otherwise permitted herein) is not the same as an obligation to enforce such terms.
3.3. Authorized Users, except Walk-in Users, shall be informed that they may, subject to Para. 4 below: **3.3.1.** Create multiple copies of a discrete excerpt from the Licensed Material for classroom instruction use, consistent with existing "fair use" law and regulation. Each such copy shall carry appropriate acknowledgment of the source, listing title and author of, title and author of work, and publisher. **3.3.2.** Incorporate parts of the Licensed Material in Electronic Reserves for the use of Authorized Users in the course of instruction. Each such item shall carry appropriate acknowledgment of the source, listing title and	A second set of use rights applies to all but walk-in users, again subject to subsequent overriding prohibitions. The licensee has a similar obligation ("shall") to inform all authorized users of the use rights each possesses subject again to ¶ 4, which lists the prohibited uses, which take precedent over the uses permitted unless listed in specific here. First listed is a circumstance where multiple copies are allowed: making multiple copies for classroom use. This provision does not necessarily allow the creation of the typical course packs (which are copied, assembled, and reproduced in quantity for later distribution and, while in support of education, are not necessarily for "classroom instruction use"). The use of the word "discrete" reinforces the concept of specification, of a separate item or cluster of discontinuous items as opposed to widespread taking, such as an entire volume. Regardless, any such course-pack creation or other multiple-copy use, such as making a copy of a single article for each student, is limited to what would otherwise be fair use under the copyright law. It is uncertain what is meant by "and regulation," as there are few if any regulatory provisions in Title 37, CODE OF FEDERAL REGULATIONS (C.F.R.), governing fair use. Perhaps it is a less than accurate reference to the various fair-use guidelines, one of which addresses multiple copying for classroom use, but these are not found in the C.F.R. Even so, the licensor here has given the licensee nothing more in terms of copyright privileges than what the licensee would have had in the absence of the license, that is,

(continued)

Terms of the BioOne License	Comments on the Terms of the BioOne License
author of extract, title and author of work, and publisher. The electronic copy of such items shall be deleted by the Licensee when it is no longer required for such purpose. **3.4.** Nothing in this License shall in any way exclude, modify or affect anything the Licensee or any Authorized User is allowed to do in respect of any of the Licensed Materials consistent with existing "fair use" law, defined by the U.S. Copyright Code of 1976 (17 U.S.C. § 105–107).	under the copyright law, assuming it would have had similar access to or availability of the content. This also means that rather than clarifying that making multiple copies for classroom use is allowed, the licensee must undertake a similar "is my use fair" analysis for each such use of the licensed content ("consistent with existing 'fair use'"). The license has not necessarily increased any efficiency in the use of materials for multiple-copy classroom use. Regardless of scope, any such multiple copying must contain explicit source and citation information. These rights, which all but walk-in users possess and of which the authorized users must be informed by the licensee, include the right to use the licensed content in electronic reserves. Paragraph 3 does not affirmatively allow for use of the license content in print reserves, unless such use can be argued to fall under ¶ 3.1.4, as the modifier "electronic" is used twice, once in conjunction with the noun "reserves" and a second time with respect to "copies." Again, any e-reserve copy must contain proper source and citation information. More important, after the course ends, the e-copy on reserve must be "deleted . . . when no longer required for such purpose." If the same part of the licensed content is used again in conjunction with a course, it must be retrieved again and placed on e-reserve. What if the course is likely to be taught again? Can access merely be toggled off or the file removed to another part of the e-reserve server, or must the e-copy be deleted and then reacquired or copied from the database as the course is offered again? It could be argued that if the course is offered every semester, including summer term, the article is continuously used in "the course of instruction." It would seem that less seldom offerings would trigger the "when it is no longer required for such purpose" and require deletion and not mere restriction of access to that reserve copy. A strict reading of the provision would require at the end of every semester that the e-copy be deleted and reacquired at the start of the next. A final statement also reaffirms that the license agreement does not impact fair-use rights of the license. However, given the confusion and misconceptions (at least in the opinion of this author) among many users regarding fair use, this statement does little to bring any further degree of certainty to copyright transactions involving the licensed content. Even so, a more forceful phrasing might be to include among the list of permitted uses "any use permitted under the copyright law" and not under fair use alone but of the uses in 17 U.S.C. §§ 107–122.
4. Prohibited Uses. **4.1.** Neither the Licensee nor Authorized Users may remove or alter the authors' names,	This provision indicates that removing certain citation information is not permitted, including copyright notices, designations of trademark, other identifiers, and any disclaimers that might appear in the articles and other content. Removal of such information might

(continued)

Terms of the BioOne License	Comments on the Terms of the BioOne License
copyright notices, trademarks, or other means of identification or disclaimers as they appear in the Licensed Material.	also violate 17 U.S.C. § 1202(b)(1): "No person shall, without the authority of the copyright owner or the law intentionally remove or alter any copyright management information [CMI]." CMI "means any of the following information . . . including in digital form . . . The title and other information identifying the work, including the information set forth on a notice of copyright. The name of, and other identifying information about, the author of a work. The name of, and other identifying information about, the copyright owner of the work, including the information set forth in a notice of copyright." 17 U.S.C. § 1202(c)(1)–(3). Under a recent court decision, CMI need not be in digital form to be subject to the prohibition on removal. See *McClatchey v. Associated Press*, 2007 U.S. Dist. LEXIS 17768, *5 (W.D. Pa. 2007): "Moreover, Section 1202 (c) defines the term broadly to include 'any' of the information set forth in the eight [statutory] categories, 'including in digital form.' To avoid rendering those terms superfluous, the statute must also protect non-digital information." See also *Murphy v. Millennium Records, LLC*, 2011 WL 2315128, *6 (3d Cir.) ("we find that CMI, as defined in § 1202(c), is *not* restricted to the context of 'automated copyright protection or management systems' In this case, the mere fact that Murphy's name appeared in a printed gutter credit near the Image rather than as data in an 'automated copyright protection or management system' does not prevent it from qualifying as CMI or remove it from the protection of § 1202.")
4.2. Neither the Licensee nor Authorized Users may systematically make print or electronic copies of multiple extracts of the Licensed Material for any purpose other than temporary caching as permitted in Para. 3.1.1.	Except as discussed in ¶ 3.1.1 and referenced here relating to caching, the multiple copying of numerous items from the license content is prohibited. This provision refers to copies (plural) of multiple extracts and not a single copy of multiple extracts or the phrase would have read "make a print or electronic copy of multiple extracts," not "multiple copies of a discrete excerpt . . . for classroom instruction use" as in ¶ 3.3.1, for example. Otherwise, this prohibition would conflict with ¶ 3.3.1 and likely ¶ 3.3.2. This paragraph also supports the conclusion that while e-reserves are allowed (a single copy of multiple extracts, per ¶ 3.3.2), course packs are not (systematic multiple copies of multiple extracts). This is also why a cache right (copies of "all or part" of the licensed content within a 24-hour period) is specifically granted in ¶ 3.1.1, as an exception to the general prohibition here. Those other two paragraphs also reflect a more narrow use than that contemplated here. Paragraph 3.3.1 refers to "multiple copies" for "classroom instruction use," and ¶ 3.3.2 associates e-reserves created in the "course of instruction." A similar prohibition exists in 17 U.S.C. § 108(g): "systematic reproduction or distribution of single or multiple copies or phonorecords of material described in subsection (d)."

(continued)

Terms of the BioOne License	Comments on the Terms of the BioOne License
4.3. Neither the Licensee nor Authorized Users may mount or distribute any part of the Licensed Material on any electronic or other data network including, without limitation, the Internet and the World Wide Web, other than through a Secure Network.	Any posting or distribution of the licensed content on a course website or electronic interlibrary loan must be through a password-protected access or other secure mechanism. See ¶ 1.6, listing the requirements of a secure network. If, for example, electronic interlibrary loan cannot be conducted within a secure network ("only accessible to Authorized Users approved by the Licensee"), which it might not be if the requesting party is external to the licensee, then e-ILL is not allowed under this license. There is not necessarily a conflict between ¶ 4.3 and ¶ 3.1.5 (interlibrary loan). Rather, ¶ 3.1.5 still operates. Interlibrary loan is allowed, but it cannot in this instance be fulfilled electronically unless done via a secure network (which in the absence of the license, under 17 U.S.C. § 108(d) and (e), such third-party requests could, e.g., be filled and delivered electronically using standard webmail). The request of a patron from another library filled with an item sourced from the licensed content would need to be reproduced and distributed in print form. This result achieves consistency between the two provisions, with the permitted uses in ¶ 3 subject to the prohibitions listed in ¶ 4.
4.4. BioOne's explicit written permission must be obtained in order to: **4.4.1.** Reproduce the whole or any part of the Licensed Material for any Commercial Use. **4.4.2.** Systematically make available or distribute the whole or part of the Licensed Material to anyone other than Authorized Users. **4.4.3.** Publish, distribute or make available the Licensed Material, works based on the Licensed Material or works which combine it with any other material, other than as permitted in this License. **4.4.4.** Alter, abridge, adapt or modify the Licensed Material, except to the extent necessary to make it perceptible on a computer screen, or as otherwise	Commercial uses are prohibited here but defined in ¶ 1.2. The use of the word "systematically" appears again but is not inconsistent with use of this word in ¶ 4.2, as that provision refers to reproduction and this provision refers to access ("make available or distribute") and to persons who are not authorized users. The licensed content cannot be distributed, nor derivative use made of it, nor may it be combined with other content unless permitted by this agreement (see ¶ 4.4.3). One example would be in reserves under ¶ 3.3.2 ("Incorporate parts of the Licensed Material in Electronic Reserves for the use of Authorized Users in the course of instruction"), with electronic reserve defined as a combination of items (¶ 1.3. Electronic Reserve: "Any electronic or other databased collection of articles, chapters, or other materials from different copyrighted sources compiled for a specific course or series of instruction by the Library.") In ¶ 4.4.4, derivative use is again prohibited ("alter, abridge, adapt"). A derivative use is defined in part as "any other form in which a work may be recast, transformed, or adapted" (17 U.S.C. § 101). Changes "to the extent necessary to make it perceptible on a computer screen" for authorized users are allowed, though this would appear to be more a change in format, not content, as are others specific in the agreement. This would appear to allow adjustments for those with visual impairments. However, no changes in word order or deletions whatsoever are allowed. Such slight alterations, without a change in meaning, would arguably not be derivative under the copyright law in the absence of the license agreement. See *Clean Flicks of Colorado, LLC v. Soderbergh*, 443

(continued)

Terms of the BioOne License	Comments on the Terms of the BioOne License
permitted in this License, to Authorized Users. Unless specifically authorized in writing by BioOne or the copyright holder, no alteration of the words or their order is permitted.	F. Supp. 2d 1236 (D. Colo. 2006): "[D]efendants add nothing new to these movies. They delete scenes and dialogue from them" (*id.* at 1241). "[T]he infringing copies of these movies are not used in a transformative manner, they are *not derivative* works and do not violate § 106(2)" (*id.* at 1242).
5. Warranties. **5.1.** BioOne warrants to the Licensee that it is duly licensed to use, in accordance with the terms and conditions hereof, the Licensed Material and that the Licensed Material, if used as contemplated in this License, does not knowingly infringe any copyright or other proprietary or intellectual property rights of any natural or legal person. BioOne will not be responsible for any claim, loss or liability attributable to errors, inaccuracies or other defects in the Licensed Material or any part thereof whether arising from any intentional act or omission or (to the maximum extent permitted by relevant laws) any negligence or otherwise, and BOTH PARTIES EXPRESSLY EXCLUDE ANY LIABILITY FOR BREACH OF ANY IMPLIED OR EXPRESS WARRANTY AS TO TITLE, MERCHANTABILITY OR FITNESS FOR A PARTICULAR PURPOSE, BIOONE SHALL NOT BE LIABLE FOR ANY DIRECT OR INDIRECT, INCIDENTAL, SPECIAL, CONSEQUENTIAL OR PUNITIVE DAMAGES ARISING OUT OF USE OF ANY OF THE LICENSED MATERIAL. BioOne's maximum liability to Licensee	The licensor attempts to make several important promises or warranties here. The licensor is careful not to "represent" the following assurances, as that might give rise to a claim based in tort, not contract alone, which use of "warrant" signifies. That is, the licensor warrants that it has the authority to license the content to the licensee and that if licensee follows the terms of the license in its use of the licensed content the licensee should not be violating anyone's copyright or other intellectual property right, for that matter, at least not knowingly ("warrants ... Licensee ... is duly licensed to use in accordance with the terms ... if used as contemplated ... does not knowingly infringe ..."). The problem is that the law of direct (liability for infringing conduct undertaken by patrons or staff) and vicarious (in essence, liability as the employer of infringing employees) copyright infringement is a strict liability law. One does not need to know of the infringing nature of his or her conduct to be liable under copyright, nor does the institution need to know or be aware of the infringing conduct of its employees to be likewise liable vicariously for this conduct. So really all the licensor has warranted is that the licensor would not be a contributory infringer (for which knowledge or a reason to know of the infringement is one prerequisite for liability) for your direct infringement nor subject to criminal liability for copyright infringement (which requires intent), nor be a likely willful infringer (which requires a reckless disregard for the infringement; knowingly infringing a work would satisfy a claim for willful damages in a civil copyright suit). This warrant of noninfringement should extend to all uses made of the licensed content in accordance with the terms herein, not just those which the licensor asserts it knows does not infringe: BioOne should warrant that the "Licensed Material ... does not infringe any copyright ..." Most important, such warrant, whatever its scope, is rather empty without an indemnification that should the licensor be incorrect (imagine that) and the use turns out to be infringing, the licensor will cover any negative legal repercussion. The licensor should agree to indemnify the licensee should this scenario occur: "We made a mistake. We didn't have the right to make it available. It's infringing, and your use of it is likewise infringing, but to make up for it we will foot the litigation

(continued)

Terms of the BioOne License	Comments on the Terms of the BioOne License
hereunder is limited to the Fee paid by Licensee to BioOne for the then current Subscription Period.	bill and any damages awarded should you be sued and lose." Often licensors provide indemnification on condition that the licensor be able to make decisions related to the litigation defense. Implied or express warranties are disclaimed by both parties (though warranties of title, merchantability, and fitness would not be the licensee's to honor or disclaim). THAT'S WHY CAPITALIZATION IS USED—it is telling the licensee, "Hey, this is important, so pay attention!" The licensor is also prohibiting recovery of all sorts of damages. In any event, monetary liability is limited to the price of the annual subscription rate. Other than a lawsuit for specific performance where damages would not be an issue, it is unlikely this low-dollar ceiling would make litigation attractive to a licensee, but of course this might depend on the subscription fee and the will of the licensee.
5.2. BioOne shall: **5.2.1.** Make available the electronic copy of each journal covered by this License promptly after it is available.	The licensor promises to make the electronic version of its print publications available soon after publication in print. How soon? Promptly. If the time period between print release and online availability matters to the licensee, it would not be unreasonable to request a specific time period within which online availability must occur (e.g., with 7 days, 5 working days, 48 hours, etc.).
5.2.2. Provide the Licensee with information sufficient to enable access to the Licensed Material, within no more than 5 working days of the receipt by BioOne of a complete list of Authorized IP Addresses for the Licensee, or any revisions thereto.	Apparently, when it wants to, the licensor can turn a task around within one business week. Let us hope it can add content to its database as fast (see previous Comment). Of course, this provision indicates that information will be provided within five working days of receipt of the authorized IP addresses ("information sufficient to enable access to"), not necessarily that access will be provided—though it is logical to assume that providing instructions regarding how to access the licensed content without also providing the access itself would be worthless.
5.2.3. Use all reasonable efforts to ensure that the BioOne server(s) have adequate capacity to support the usage of the Licensee and its Authorized Users at a level commensurate with the standards of access to information services of similar scope operating via the World Wide Web, as such standards evolve from time to time over the term of this License.	The licensor promises to have the computing capacity to support the use of all its nonexclusive licensees and their users. The estimate of what would be sufficient capacity ("reasonable efforts") is based on industry standards, expectations, and experiences of similar information providers. This is not a promise that the licensor's servers will never go down or that its website will never crash. See ¶ 5.2.4.

(continued)

Terms of the BioOne License	Comments on the Terms of the BioOne License
5.2.4. Use all reasonable efforts to make the Licensed Materials available to the Licensee and to Authorized Users at all times and on a twenty-four hour basis, save for routine maintenance and down-time, and to restore access to the Licensed Material as soon as reasonably possible in the event of an interruption or suspension of the service. BioOne will make all reasonable efforts to notify Licensee of scheduled downtime at least 24 hours in advance. In the event of an interruption or suspension of service lasting more than 72 consecutive hours, the Licensee's contract will be extended by an equal number of hours.	There is no promise that the service will never experience interruption. The licensor will use "all reasonable efforts" to ensure this does not happen but makes no claims that such event will never occur. In fact, downtime is anticipated for "routine maintenance." If the server or website does crash, the licensor will restore access "as soon as reasonably possible." When downtime is planned, the licensor will make "all reasonable efforts to notify" the licensee at least a day in advance. "Reasonable efforts" is a phrase with legal meaning (see discussion in Chapter 14 under Best or Reasonable Efforts), but a reasonably possible effort does have separate legal meaning apart from its common meaning or usage of the phrase. It is hoped that if, say, a retail store were planning to close its doors for a period of remodeling, it would know this more than a day in advance. Likewise, the licensor should provide more than a day's notice of scheduled downtime—thus the concept that it is "scheduled," as the licensee would surely desire to inform its users that the service would not be available. It is not clear why, if the downtime is planned, notice cannot always occur or occur with more lead time and with an indication of the duration of the downtime. Though it is conceivable that in response to an emergency the licensor needs to schedule downtime the very next day, there could still be language inserted to the effect that, except in response to exigent circumstances, notice must be given seven (or some other reasonable and realistic number of) days in advance. If the downtime exceeds three days, then a credit (in days) is given to the licensee, with its contract extended by an equal number of hours. First, it is not clear if scheduled downtime ("routine maintenance") is included within the concept of "interruption or suspension of service" so that such loss of service qualifies also for the credit. Notice also that the credit is not applied against the next subscription period (assuming with this level of service the licensee desires to continue), but that it extends or pushes out the end of the contractual period and therefore the renewal date as well. Second, if the downtime is less than three days straight, does the licensee qualify for credit? It should; otherwise the licensee is paying for up to three days of service it will not receive. The author also prefers a licensee to have the option of refund or credit against the next subscription period, not an extension of current subscription period, which can cause all sorts of problems by pushing out the date of renewal invoice, notice of nonrenewal, and so forth. Further, there is no indication of how many times "scheduled downtime" can occur in a year. Note that there is no monetary compensation and that the credit (in hours of service, not in dollars against future charges) is offered only if the downtime is continuous. A situation of repeated

(continued)

Terms of the BioOne License	Comments on the Terms of the BioOne License
	downtimes, say, every other day for two weeks (seven days total), would result in no obligation, other than reasonable notice that it is going to happen again, and without a credit of hours to the licensee's account. It might be a good idea to ask for a record covering the past five years of the number of such planned and unplanned occurrences and the duration of each. All time during which the service is unavailable should be compensable, at least calculated to a reasonable portion of a day, such as to the nearest hour. Finally, suppose the service is suspended for 144 hours straight, so the contract is extended by an equal number of hours, or by six days. This would also mean that that the contract renewal date (and anniversary date, assuming no future credited interruptions of service) has also moved out by six days. It would be important to note this change of date, as other time periods in the license are marked from the anniversary date, which has just shifted.
5.3. BioOne reserves the right at any time to withdraw from the Licensed Material any item or part of an item for which it no longer retains the right to publish, or which it has reasonable grounds to believe infringes copyright or is unlawful. BioOne shall give notice to the Licensee of such withdrawal. In the event that the total amount of material removed constitutes more than ten percent (10%) of the total content of the Licensed Material, BioOne will refund ten percent (10%) of the then current Subscription Fee.	Recall how the licensor indicated in ¶ 5.1 that it would not knowingly supply the licensee and its users with content that is infringing, but it still might do so by accident, mistake, and so on, or perhaps its rights to supply the content ended (this happens often with aggregators); that is, the license it had to supply content from another source ended as the licensor was itself a licensee. Therefore, there are situations for various reasons where the licensor can no longer continue to offer some of the licensed content. The licensor might also determine that content is otherwise unlawful; it could be defamatory, for example. If this is the case or it has reasonable grounds to believe this is so, the licensor has the right to withdraw the content. If this occurs, the licensor will give notice of such event, which is a good thing, but again there is no indication of how much lead time will be given to the licensee. Considering the circumstances of how such a situation might arise (the licensor gets sued or receives a cease-and-desist letter), "you'll know when we know" might be the best one could expect. Unlike planned downtime for maintenance, this discovery might arise without notice to the licensor as well and, given the nature of copyright liability, might require immediate action, so a reasonable time frame regarding notice might be as soon as practical or as soon as possible. If the removal equates to 10.1 percent or more, assuming fractions of a percent are calculable ("more than ten percent," so 10 percent loss is still okay under this provision), then a monetary refund is due. While a more than 10 percent loss is the trigger, under the clause as it is written, 10 percent of the current subscription price is also the cap of the refund amount, regardless of amount. What if the content so removed equals 24 percent of

(continued)

Terms of the BioOne License	Comments on the Terms of the BioOne License
	the total content? Why can't the refund represent a like percentage of the subscription fee, 24 percent? Why this limit exists is not clear. Why not offer a comparable refund for loss of content: 24 percent less content equals 24 percent less subscription fee, or whatever the reduction represents. Also what happens if 2 percent is removed each month throughout the year? It is unclear from the clause whether the measure of removal is made in the aggregate—could the licensor withdraw 2 percent each month without any adjustment? The use of the phrase "the total amount of material removed" suggests that an aggregate tally is undertaken, but this could be made clear along the lines of something like: "In the event that the total amount of material removed during a Subscription Period constitutes more than 10 percent of the total content of the Licensed Material, BioOne will refund a portion of the current Subscription Fee equal to an amount above 10 percent that the loss represents." If calculating insubstantial loss is an issue, the threshold could be set lower, not at zero, where any reduction in content equates to a reduction in subscription fee, however small or insignificant, but, say, at 1 or 2 percent. For a licensee that does not desire to deal with refunds, deposits, and so on, a choice of refund or credit is also conceivable: "...will at the option of the licensee either issue an immediate refund or apply a credit toward the next Subscription Period a portion of the..." Finally, the juxtaposition of this provision implies that an adjustment is made only when the licensor loses the right to continue making the content available or concludes that it is infringing or otherwise unlawful. It might be useful to know if content has been removed for other reasons in the past, by choice, for example, because the licensor did not believe it was useful any longer. Asking for a record of all incidents of withdrawals in the past five years might be useful information to have during negotiation over or consideration of the license. A further revised provision might read: "In the event that the total amount of material removed for any reason during a Subscription Period constitutes more than 1 percent of the total content of the Licensed Material, BioOne will at the option of the licensee either issue an immediate refund or apply as credit toward the next Subscription Period a portion of the current Subscription Fee equal to an amount above 1 percent that the loss represents." Of course, turnabout is fair play, so if the amount of content increases by some percent, should the licensee be required to pay an additional amount? If a license contemplates an upward adjustment, it is typically tied to the number of users, not content, as it is expected that as new volumes or issues are produced the content is added to the database; that is, it is part of the subscription price to include both previous and future issues.

(continued)

Terms of the BioOne License	Comments on the Terms of the BioOne License
5.4. BioOne will ensure that an electronic archive of all Licensed Material is made available through BioOne. If BioOne is unable to ensure that this responsibility is met, the archive will be transferred to one or more depositories.	The licensor indicates that it or a third party will maintain an electronic archive of all material made available through its services. Either BioOne will do this or it will have a third party retain the content in deposit. It is assumed that content which over time BioOne did not have the right to provide will not be included in either its own electronic archive or the third-party repository. This might occur where there is material that BioOne no "longer retains the right to publish, or which it has reasonable grounds to believe infringes copyright or is unlawful," per ¶ 5.3. The provision does not indicate the archive will not include material removed under ¶ 5.3; arguably, such content would have been "published," at least at some point (and for which at that time the licensor had the legal right to publish), and thus could conceivably be retained in an archive, but perhaps the licensor would not desire this result for obvious legal (liability) reasons.
5.5. The Licensee shall: **5.5.1.** Use reasonable efforts to ensure that Authorized Users are appropriately notified of the importance of respecting the intellectual property rights in the Licensed Material and of the sanctions that the Licensee imposes for failing to do so.	These paragraphs are important! Following are the obligations the licensee must undertake. Regarding ¶ 5.5.1 and ¶ 5.5.2, it would be best for BioOne's wording to indicate what constitutes reasonable efforts, as the licensor and licensee might have divergent views here. Is a general intellectual property warning on the library website—on the page where the list of databases appears—sufficient, or is some other mode of notice expected? The sentence also anticipates that the licensee will have a code of conduct (or policy or other mechanism) for both students and employees, indicating that failure in "respecting" (what measure of respect is used remains unclear) intellectual property rights is subject to discipline or met with a response mechanism consistent with a violation of other rules, policies, and so on. Again, the mode of notice is not stated. Is inclusion in a student or employee handbook or on the dean of faculty and dean of students webpage sufficient? This provision is a general one of respect for the law; the next provision, in ¶ 5.5.2, is specific to licensed content. The concept of reasonable efforts represents a somewhat lesser though implicit requirement that a party act reasonably under the situation, while "best efforts" represents a higher standard of behavior: what is reasonable practice among similarly situated parties, what is typical and reasonable for vendors, what conduct, response, and so on, is typical or reasonable for a public library or college or university of similar character and resource to undertake (see discussion in Chapter 14 under Best or Reasonable Efforts).
5.5.2. Use reasonable efforts to ensure that Authorized Users are made aware of and undertake to abide by the terms and conditions of this License; and immediately	As in ¶ 5.5.1, it is not clear from this provision how notice of the terms of the license is transmitted to the authorized users. Does the licensee need to have every user, when accessing or logging into the licensed content, click-to-agree, with the entire license agreement (or a summary of pertinent terms prepared by the library) available for review by users? What additional "reasonable efforts" must be

(continued)

Terms of the BioOne License	Comments on the Terms of the BioOne License
on becoming aware of any unauthorized use or other breach, inform BioOne and take reasonable steps, including appropriate disciplinary action, both to ensure that such activity ceases and to prevent any recurrence.	undertaken, other than the threat of misconduct charges or similar penalty to encourage users to "abide by the terms and conditions" of the license? (Again, see the discussion in previous Comments and in Chapter 14 under Best or Reasonable Efforts). Assuming the licensee becomes aware of nonconforming use with the terms of the license and the licensee intervenes in some way to effect correction, why must the licensee inform the licensor? What does this accomplish other than to tip off the licensor to a potential target of litigation, if the licensor might desire to pursue independent legal action against the perpetrator of the malfeasance? As discussed in the previous license agreement review, care must be taken not to reveal any personally identifiable information regarding the subject of the unauthorized use. While raising patron privacy issues in a general sense, releasing a record of search query and use that reveals patron John Smith downloaded and made multiple copies of an entire volume of the licensed content on June 1 would violate some state patron library confidentiality statutes that protect the identity of patrons and their use of library resources, services, or materials. Other states' statutes that protect registration and circulation records and borrowing of materials alone would likely not be violated by such an act. Does the licensee have some discretion in its response, or must it impose "sanctions" or some form of "disciplinary action"? It might be conceivable, through some sort of "teaching moment" response, to correct the nonconforming conduct and ensure that it does not occur again. See also ¶5.8. The library can promise that as an institution it will not engage in such practices and will inform users of such restrictions, but how would the licensee ensure that users do not undertake such behavior? True, the licensee as employer can incorporate such restrictions into its work rules, but employees have been known on occasion to violate a work rule, policy, or procedure. The efficacy of 100 percent compliance should be considered before agreeing to any such obligation. A better alternative is an obligation to give notice to users, to intercede when deviation is discovered (without an obligation to monitor), and, if an employee is the source, to take appropriate response, treating the matter as the violation of a work rule.
5.5.3. Keep full and up-to-date records of all Licensee's authorized IP Addresses, and if appropriate, provide BioOne with periodic lists of additions, deletions or other alterations to such records as agreed between the parties from time to time.	Since the licensee must use a secure network and the access provided by the licensor is to authorized sites alone, keeping this list up-to-date ensures that all intended users from intended locations are able to access the licensed content. See Appendix D (Subscriber IP addresses should be submitted on the BioOne Order Form/Price List).

(continued)

Terms of the BioOne License	Comments on the Terms of the BioOne License
5.5.4. Use its best efforts to ensure that only Authorized Users are permitted access to the Licensed Material. Subject to the provisions of Section 5.6, allowing access to the Licensed Materials to persons not Authorized Users shall constitute a material breach of this License not capable of remedy for purposes of Section 6.2.2 if the Licensee knew or reasonably should have known that such person was not an authorized user.	"Best efforts" is a legal term of art indicating the level of effort to which a party to the contract is obligated. Some courts view it as a step above reasonable efforts. It signals not only a standard industry practice but places that knowledge in the context of the specific parties and circumstances. (See the discussion in Chapter 14 under Best or Reasonable Efforts). "[T]he question remains: 'How hard must one try if one has undertaken to use best efforts?'... As mentioned above, the answer depends on the terms (and nature) of the agreement, Defendants' ability, and Plaintiffs' justifiable expectations." *Samica Enterprises, LLC v. Mail Boxes Etc. USA, Inc.*, 637 F. Supp. 2d 712, 718 (C.D. Cal. 2008). "We conclude that the 'best efforts' standard is primarily a subjective one, relating in this case to the capabilities and circumstances of Carlson alone. In order to have relevance to the determination of Carlson's best efforts, the efforts of M&M (or any other distributor) would have to take place under similar circumstances where evidence of M&M's efforts would bear in some meaningful way on Carlson's capabilities to perform similarly." *Carlson Distributing Co. v. Salt Lake Brewing Co., L.C.*, 95 P.3d 1171, 1179 (Utah App. 2004). The concept does not entail extraordinary expense. "In light of these precedents, the Court is comfortable in concluding that a party's diligent, reasonable, good faith effort to fulfill the obligations imposed by the contract is good enough to qualify as 'best.'" *Reyelt v. Danzell*, 509 F. Supp. 2d 156, 165 (D.R.I. 2007). In this instance, what is the most common and effective way for the licensee to regulate off-site (outside of the library, not necessarily the campus) access to a library network? Username and password would appear typical. "'Best efforts' does not require a party to ignore its own interests." H. WARD CLASSEN, A PRACTICAL GUIDE TO SOFTWARE LICENSING FOR LICENSEES AND LICENSORS 129 (3d ed. 2008). The license must ensure that access to the licensed content is by authorized users alone, which can include walk-in users; see ¶ 1.8. Allowing unauthorized users to access the licensed content can constitute a material breach if the licensee "knew or reasonably should have known" that such person was not an authorized user. Since walk-in users are allowed, few conceivable scenarios would entail some sort of hacked remote access, which the licensee would somehow know or be aware of and do little to stop it. Such a course of action would be unlikely. The "knew or reasonably should have known" standard is arguably a more rigid standard than that used for contributory copyright (know or reason to know) infringement and may require some active inquiry or assessment on the part of the licensee. "Should know" implies, as it does in tort law, an affirmative duty to verify the existence or nonexistence of the occurrence. At least as far as tort law is concerned, it would require that the licensee is under a duty

(continued)

Terms of the BioOne License	Comments on the Terms of the BioOne License
	to use reasonable diligence to ascertain the existence or nonexistence of the fact in question (i.e., that the person is indeed an authorized user). RESTATEMENT OF TORTS 2d § 12, comment a. Moreover, a breach hereunder is not subject to the remedy rule of ¶ 6.2.2 (termination upon material or persistent breach and a failure to cure within 30 days of written notice). In other words, there is no cure right; that is, stopping the unauthorized user from further use of the licensed content will not cure ("remedy") the breach, and such unauthorized use remains a material breach. How would the licensor know of such occurrences? Recall under ¶ 5.5.2 that the licensee must "immediately on becoming aware of any unauthorized use or other breach, inform BioOne." Considering this discussion, "the parties should avoid adopting a 'best efforts' standard unless it is clearly defined . . . A potential definition might be: 'Reasonable diligence necessary to further the intentions of the parties hereunder.'" H. WARD CLASSEN, A PRACTICAL GUIDE TO SOFTWARE LICENSING FOR LICENSEES AND LICENSORS 129 (3d ed. 2008).
5.6. Nothing in this License shall make the Licensee liable for breach of the terms of the License by any Authorized User provided that the Licensee did not cause, knowingly assist, or condone the continuation of such breach after becoming aware of an actual breach having occurred.	The previous provision dealt with use of the licensed content by unauthorized users, licensee responsibility for this use, and its impact (i.e., material breach). This provision deals with authorized users who nonetheless violate the terms of use. This provision reflects a less rigid standard of responsibility for the licensee and is somewhat akin to a contributory infringement standard in copyright law. Contributory infringement occurs when "one who, with knowledge of the infringing activity, induces or causes, or materially contributes to the infringement of another." *Gershwin Publishing Corp. v. Columbia Artists Management, Inc.*, 443 F.2d 1159, 1162 (2d Cir. 1971). As long as the licensee does not cause, knowingly assist, or condone the continuation of such breach after becoming aware of it, the licensee will not be responsible for the breach of authorized users. The use of "cause" suggests an affirmative act (a faculty member ordered students to engage in one of the prohibited acts, e.g., ¶ 4.1, "remove or alter the authors' names, copyright notices, trademarks, or other means of identification or disclaimers as they appear in the Licensed Material"). For assistance to result in responsibility under this provision, it must be provided with the knowledge that it would result in breach (a librarian familiar with the terms helps a student "systematically make print or electronic copies of multiple extracts of the Licensed Material for a . . . purpose other than temporary caching," prohibited under ¶ 4.2, e.g.). Users might engage in breaching conduct routinely, however, unless the licensee becomes aware of a specific instance and does nothing to prevent its continued breach (e.g., if a student mounts or distributes a part of the licensed material on an electronic or other

(continued)

Terms of the BioOne License	Comments on the Terms of the BioOne License
	data network, such as the World Wide Web, perhaps on the student's individual page hosted on the campus website, which is prohibited under ¶ 4.3, and the licensee fails to remove the content, the licensee is not liable for breach by the student).
5.7. The Licensee shall, in consideration for the rights granted under this License, pay the Fee in accordance with Para. 2.1 within 60 days of signature and, if applicable, within 60 days of each subsequent renewal.	The subscription fee (the initial fee as well as a renewal) is due within 60 days. Once the contract is signed (the initial fee), the licensee has 60 days to pay the fee. So if the contract is signed on day one with subscription to begin in 30 days, the fee would be due within 30 days after of the commencement of the subscription period or 60 days from signature. Since nonrenewal (see ¶ 6.1) must be made at least 60 days before expiration of the current one-year term (i.e., on or before the 61st day before expiration of the current term), it is arguable that if no such notice is sent, then renewal occurs on the 60th day before expiration of the current term (i.e., by which time the licensee failed to indicate nonrenewal), with the new term of course beginning on the day after the end of the current subscription period. But when is payment for it due? In this example, the date for payment of the renewal fee is the date of the conclusion of the current subscription period (i.e., 60 days after renewal), which was evident here at midnight of the 61st day before expiration of the then-current term when the licensee failed to issue a notice of nonrenewal or cancellation per ¶ 6.1. This in turn makes the payment for renewal due, not 60 days after the renewed subscription period begins or 60 days after signature or 30 days after commencement, but, rather, payment of the renewal fee is due on the date of the new subscription period, the anniversary date. Perhaps this is not what is intended, but it appears to be what is written. If renewals are intended to be due within 60 days of the anniversary date, then the actual 60-day period for payment of the renewal fee should be clarified: "The Licensee shall, in consideration for the rights granted under this License, pay the Fee in accordance with Para. 2.1 within 60 days of signature and, if applicable, within 60 days of the commencement of each subsequent renewal period." With this language, the subscription period would still begin on day one, end on day 365, with nonrenewal due by day 305, but with no cancellation, the renewal fee would be due on day 425, or 60 days into the renewed subscription period. Of course, the actual date of nonrenewal, payment, and so on, could shift if the subscription period is moved out due to a credit, as discussed previously.
5.8. BioOne and the Licensee shall both permit and enable the collection and distribution	A record of searches that a particular library patron conducted through the library's network, whether of the catalog, Internet, or other resource, and tied to this individual, would be a protected

(continued)

Terms of the BioOne License	Comments on the Terms of the BioOne License
of usage data for BioOne's and the Licensee's use. BioOne use of such data will be approved by the Board of Directors. Such usage information shall be compiled in a manner consistent with the applicable privacy laws, and the anonymity of individual users and the confidentiality of their searches shall be fully protected. In the case that either party assigns its rights to another party under Para. 7.1 herein, the other party may at its discretion require the assignee to either keep such usage information confidential or destroy it.	record in some states (but not all, as many state statutes protect only the identifiable records of items borrowed; some extend this to items used, assuming such data would be collected). Such statutes, however, do not reach the records a licensor may create; therefore, it is wise to include such a provision (or at least make patrons aware that such a search record does not fall under same statute and is not protected). Observe that this provision indicates the "information shall be compiled in a manner consistent with the applicable privacy laws," but such statutes would have little impact on this provision, as the state library privacy statutes referenced do not prohibit collection or generation of the record but rather what is done with the patron information once collected or compiled; that is, they regulate its disclosure. This may be the more important concern. The opening sentence allows the licensor as well as the licensee to collect and retain such records. Control over the subsequent use of the record is the key. The next sentence indicates that the licensor's use of the record is subject to the desire of its board of directors. However, the provision does go on to state that "anonymity of individual users and the confidentiality of their searches shall be fully protected," and if this applies to the record of their searches, the protection appears adequate. A similar protection can extend ("keep . . . confidential or destroy") to a successor entity should assignment of the license occur, but this protection is at the option of the nonassigning party. If the licensor assigns the license, then the licensee-library may impose this restriction on the successor licensor, but if the licensee assigns the license because, as in the discussion of ¶ 2.1, it became a new legal entity, then it would be up to the licensor to impose this restriction or not. It might be better to have the trigger available where the assigning party has not already included it in the assignment agreement. One strategy to employ would be to hold the licensor to the same standard as the library-licensee, under whatever state library privacy statute is applicable to the library: "Licensor shall hold as confidential any information relating to Authorized Users and their use of the Licensed Content to the same extent that the Licensee is held under the applicable state statute [insert reference to state statute]," or words to that effect. See Chapter 17 for additional formulations.
5.9. Each party shall use its best efforts to safeguard the intellectual property, confidential information and proprietary rights of the other party and third parties. This intellectual property,	Identifying what is a patent, trademark of work of protected authorship (copyright), and so on, might be relatively easy (i.e., a patent registration number or trademark symbol might accompany the property and its use, but different entities have different ideas about what should be confidential and proprietary—e.g., a trade secret). It is best to obtain some clarification or identification of the information to be held confidential or the terms under which such

(continued)

Terms of the BioOne License	Comments on the Terms of the BioOne License
confidential information and proprietary rights shall include but not be limited to the source code of both BioOne and third parties.	information may be disclosed. Is the pricing information, for example, confidential? It is unclear whether the search software (and its source code) is protected by patent or copyright (intellectual property) or whether it is considered a trade secret to which an entity would in theory have a claim of proprietary right. Again, it would be useful to have some idea of the sort of information the licensor is claiming is proprietary and to understand the impact of that claim (i.e., what safeguards entail). To review the sort of undertakings ("best efforts") or how to assess the level of effort required, see discussion under ¶ 5.5.4 and the expanded discussion in Chapter 14.
6. Term and Termination. **6.1.** This Agreement shall commence on the date first set forth above and continue for one (1) year. Unless terminated sooner in accordance with its terms or allowed to expire (upon tender of sixty (60) days notice by either party), this Agreement will be automatically renewed for successive one (1) year terms, subject to applicable adjustment to the License Fees.	The term of the current subscription and of subsequent renewals is one year. Termination can occur as articulated in subsequent provisions. Expiration (i.e., nonrenewal) is also possible, but notice of the intention not to renew the license must be made by the licensee 60 days in advance. Renewal in this sense is evergreen. From the perspective of the licensee, 60 days is quite a large window. Assuming some annual assessment is made of the service, this review would need to occur at least a month before the 60-day notice period or it will be too late. It would be necessary, a good three to four months before the current subscription period ends, to conduct an adequate review of the service and the agreement, decide whether to renew, and, if not, get the notice of nonrenewal out before the 60-day window closes. Observe there is no right of cancellation under the agreement. Nonrenewal is possible with proper notice—a licensee cannot, as the provision states, allow the agreement to "expire" without an additional affirmative act: "upon tender of sixty (60) days notice"—and of course there are several ways to terminate, but short of termination, the parties are stuck with each other in yearly increments, unless a credit pushes out the subscription period.
6.2. This License is terminated if either party gives written notice to the other in the following circumstances: **6.2.1.** The Licensee defaults in making payment of the Fee in accordance with Para. 2.1 and fails to remedy such default within thirty (30) days of notification in writing by BioOne.	The prefatory sentence in ¶ 6.2 (either party can terminate under circumstances of ¶¶ 6.2.1–6.2.3 upon written notice to the other party) appears clear but in conjunction with the subprovisions becomes far less so. Does it mean that after any of the circumstances in ¶¶ 6.2.1–6.2.3 have occurred (two of which contain additional notice mechanisms) that "either party" may trigger termination of the license upon written notice to the other party? This might not be what was intended, that the licensee could terminate in a case of nonpayment, but it is what is written. In addition, under ¶ 6.2, it is not clear when the termination is effective. Is termination effective upon receipt of the written termination or upon its sending (i.e., the mailbox rule—notice

(continued)

Terms of the BioOne License	Comments on the Terms of the BioOne License
6.2.2. Either party commits a material or persistent breach of any term of this License and fails to remedy the breach (if capable of remedy) within thirty (30) days of notification in writing by the other party. **6.2.3.** Either party becomes insolvent or becomes subject to receivership, liquidation or similar external administration.	effective when sent). So the licensee could terminate also if it chose not to pay, received a reminder ("written notice") from the licensor and still refused to pay (failed "to remedy such default"), and then gave written notice that it was terminating. This might be a termination option for a licensee that missed the 60-day notification of nonrenewal deadline. There is a right to cure, that is, pay the outstanding fee, satisfaction of which would then prevent either party from terminating as the circumstance of the subprovision would not be met and no trigger of a termination right in ¶ 6.2 would arise. Under ¶ 6.2.2, if a party is in material breach or is in continuous ("or persistent") breach of a nonmaterial term and receives notice of the breach and fails to cure ("remedy") the breach, then either party may terminate after sending a written notice and the breach is not cured within the 30-day cure period. So if the licensee is in material breach, for example, it is allowing any visitor to its website to access the licensed content (violating the authorized user and secure network provisions), receives written notice of same from the licensor, fails to cure the situation within 30 days, and sends a written notice to the licensor, it may terminate. It is not clear what a persistent breach is or how it differs from a material one. A material breach could of course be persistent or not, but the provision does not say "a material and persistent" or "a material breach that is persistent." If by persistent the provision means a nonmaterial breach that is persistent, the provision should state so ("either a material breach or nonmaterial persistent breach"). Recall there is one scenario where cure of a material breach is not available: use of the licensed content by an unauthorized user under ¶ 5.5.4 where "the Licensee knew or reasonably should have known that such person was not an authorized user." It might be desirable to indicate which other provisions' violations would constitute a material breach, that is, what are the material terms of the agreement. Under ¶ 6.3.2, if either party ceases to financially exist (insolvent, receivership, liquidation, etc.), either party may terminate upon written notice. In this instance, there is no triggering notice that must be first sent, as in ¶ 6.2.1, by the licensor in situations of nonpayment, by the licensee, or by either party for material breach of the other in ¶ 6.2.2. As indicated, the wording of the prefatory provision suggests that in any of the three scenarios either party may terminate upon notice. So if the licensor goes into bankruptcy and the licensee does not desire to wait and see if the licensor will emerge from bankruptcy or if a government bailout might be forthcoming, the licensee can terminate upon written notice. Suppose this event occurs and the licensee gives proper notice of termination. Of course the licensee might desire to keep the agreement in force,

(continued)

Terms of the BioOne License	Comments on the Terms of the BioOne License
	enjoying the benefits of continued access to the licensed content and hoping the licensor emerges viable from bankruptcy. In the instance of termination, a refund may be due the licensee, but in the event of bankruptcy, the licensee may be standing in line with all the other unsecured creditors to see if the debt is dischargeable or will at least be reduced to some "percent on the dollar"—and in bankruptcy proceedings it is not uncommon to have that amount be 10 cents on the dollar, or 10 percent. Contracts for information, such as database subscriptions, would not be subject to a security interest under article 9 of the UCC (which would then make the licensee a secured party, thus possessing a higher priority in the order in which claims against the bankrupt estate are settled), nor under UCITA in the two jurisdictions that have enacted UCITA. "UCITA § 103(c) provides that to the extent of a conflict of interest between UCITA and Article 9 of the Uniform Commercial Code, Article 9 governs." In effect, this is saying that UCITA does not cover security interests, which are the province of article 9. LORIN BRENNAN ET AL., THE COMPLETE UCITA, vol. 1, § 103(D), at 103–151 (2004). This may not be the intent of the paragraph (that the licensor gets to terminate in ¶ 6.2.1 if the licensee does not pay, the party not in breach can terminate under ¶ 6.2.2, and the party that goes bankrupt can get out of the contract under ¶ 6.2.3), but this is what the contract says. At least in circumstances of bankruptcy, executory contracts are rather difficult to uphold (i.e., to force the other party to perform) if the other party is not in business anymore (i.e., ceases legally to exist). Another compounding factor in licensee bankruptcy is the so-called stay rules, which suspend the collection of debts and may include recent payments, whether the initial subscription or renewal fee by the licensee if bankrupt or a refund owed it if the licensor is the bankrupt party. See discussion under Bankruptcy in Chapter 14.
6.3. On termination all rights and obligations of the parties automatically terminate except for: **6.3.1.** Those specified in Paragraphs 2.1.2, 3, 4, 5.1, 5.5 and 5.9 above. **6.3.2.** All obligations in respect of Licensed Material to which access continues to be permitted.	Upon termination, the following rights and obligations continue: continuation rights under ¶ 2.1.2, permitted uses under ¶ 3, the prohibited uses under ¶ 4, disclaimer of warranties under ¶ 5.1, notice to users of intellectual property under ¶ 5.5, and the safeguarding of intellectual property, confidential information, and proprietary rights under ¶ 5.9. If the licensor continues to offer access even after termination, then the same terms (rights and obligations) continue to apply. The warrant that licensed content was made available infringement free (¶ 8.1) and the indemnification it made if that was not the case (¶ 8.2) should survive termination as well, or the licensee would need to consider ceasing use of any licensed content it might still possess or take the chance, albeit a very remote one, that some of the content could later be found to be infringing.

(continued)

Terms of the BioOne License	Comments on the Terms of the BioOne License
6.4. On termination of this License for cause, as specified in Paragraphs 6.2.1 to 6.2.2 above, the Licensee shall immediately cease to distribute or make available the Licensed Material.	Where the licensee does not pay the required subscription fee, receives notice of the arrearage, fails to cure within the 30-day period, or is in material or persistent breach of a term of the agreement and receives notice of termination from the licensor, the license terminates. Under ¶ 6.2.2, the licensor could also be in material or persistent breach (as could the licensee, in which case the notice of termination would come from the licensor) and be subject to a termination for cause notice from the licensee. Regardless of who gives notice (or, more important, who has the *right* to terminate in the ¶ 6.2.1 and ¶ 6.2.2 scenarios), the licensee has an obligation to cease making the licensed content available to any users, authorized or not, regardless of whether it technically could still access the licensed content and offer others access to it. The point is, if the licensor sent a termination notice that the licensee wanted to dispute, the termination notice (claiming, e.g., that it did in fact cure the breach of which it was accused), it would still have to cease providing access to the content, as termination would have occurred and the obligation here would be triggered. However, recall ¶ 2.1.2 for circumstances under which a portion of the licensed content may still be made available: "BioOne shall and Licensee may provide continuing access for Authorized Users to that part of the Licensed Material which was published or added to the Licensed Material within the Subscription Period" subject to the same terms "in effect at the termination of the license."
6.5. On termination of this License by the Licensee for cause, as specified in Para. 6.2.3, BioOne shall within thirty (30) days repay a prorated proportion of the Fee as represents the paid but unexpired part of the Subscription Period.	If the licensee terminates under ¶ 6.2.3 because it ("for cause") ceases to financially exist (insolvent, receivership, liquidation, etc.), then the licensor will in essence offer a refund, "a prorated proportion," representing the amount already paid but that will not be applied, that is, the remaining term of the subscription period. This refund might be useful in instances where the licensee terminated due to financial hardships (i.e., insolvency, receivership, liquidation, etc.). If the same fate befalls the licensor, where it is no longer providing access, the licensee might also desire a refund. There is no indication that, if termination is for nonpayment of a future amount or for breach (material or persistent) on its part, any refund would be forthcoming. While it might be expected, in instances of some fault it is still unfair in the opinion of the author because in either scenario the licensee is not getting what it paid for. For refund to be considered in the first instance, it must have been paid. So where nonpayment triggers a termination sequence, the dispute must have been over the nonpayment of renewal. This is unlikely, as renewal must occur 60 days before expiration of the contract; if it does not but the licensee does not pay the renewal fee, there are no monies upon which to draw in the first instance unless an enormous amount

(continued)

Terms of the BioOne License	Comments on the Terms of the BioOne License
	of credit (assuming such provision where included) for downtime had built up. If so, then a refund of these credits should be due. Likewise, in a situation where the licensee is in breach and termination results, to withhold refund for services paid but that will not be delivered in effect results in a penalty payment by the licensee to the licensor. Compensation for breach should be dealt with by the damages and remedy provisions, not by a back door through forfeit of the fees already paid (i.e., the refund). Moreover, in a situation where the licensor is in breach and terminates under ¶ 6.2.2, why can't the licensee expect a refund in those cases as well? It might be best to amend ¶ 6.5 to allow for a refund to the licensee at least in those circumstances where either party went belly-up and where the licensee terminated the agreement because the licensor was in breach.
7. General. **7.1.** This License may not be assigned by either party to any other person or organization without the prior written consent of the other party, which consent shall not unreasonably be withheld.	Paragraph 7 contains several clusters of provisions; the first two address assignment. The default "rule" here is that assignments are not permitted by either party unless the other party gives explicit consent. Consent, however, may not be withheld without good reason. The unreasonableness standard would allow two institutions, such as two colleges, one of which is a licensee, to merge into a university and license could be assigned from the college to the new legal entity, though it might be expected that the subscription fee would need to be adjusted to accommodate the increase in authorized users. It would be unreasonable for the licensor to not agree to assignment based on the circumstances of merger alone. Likewise, if the licensor merged with another licensor, the licensee could not on the basis of merger alone reject the assignment of its subscription to the new entity. A reasonable objection in this instance might be a previous disastrous experience that the licensor had with the other college which required termination for material breach by the licensor.
7.2. If rights in all or any part of the Licensed Material are assigned to another publisher, BioOne shall use its best efforts to ensure that the terms and conditions of this License are maintained.	If the licensor, upon written consent by the licensee per ¶ 7.1, assigns the license to another licensor, it will use its best efforts to ensure that the successor licensor accepts in the assignment the terms of the current agreement with the licensee. Again, "best efforts" is a legal concept; see discussion in ¶ 5.5.4 and in Chapter 14.
7.3. Alterations to this License and to the Appendices to this License (which may be altered separately from the body of	Any changes to the agreement must be with mutual ("both parties"), express ("recorded in writing") consent ("signed by"). Unilateral changes are not allowed, especially of material terms. Changes to the appendixes must also conform to the same standard, although as the parenthetical phrase suggests, such changes can be

(continued)

Terms of the BioOne License	Comments on the Terms of the BioOne License
this License without affecting the validity of the License as a whole) are only valid if they are recorded in writing and signed by both parties.	executed without necessarily affecting the actual terms; see end of table for a description, but not explanation, of the appendixes, A, B, C, and D, to which the provision from time to time refers.
7.4. Any notices to be served on either of the parties by the other shall be sent by prepaid recorded delivery or registered post to the address of the addressee as set out in this License or to such other address as notified by either party to the other as its address for the service of notices and all such notices shall be deemed to have been received within 3 business days of posting.	This is an important provision, as it indicates the circumstances of valid notice under the license, that is, when the other party is deemed to be aware of the contents of a correspondence. The provision adopts a delayed mailbox rule. Notices are effective when sent (i.e., posted or put in the mailbox), not when actually received or read, which can be two very different events, datewise. Here the notice is effective ("deemed to have been received") three days after posting. As the form of notice anticipates hard copy ("to the address of the addressee"), this is a true mailbox rule in concept and application, with the addition of a three-day proviso. However, since either "prepaid recorded delivery or registered post" is acceptable, it is possible that some private carrier through "prepaid recorded delivery" service (although it is not clear what "recorded" is intended to require) other than the U.S. Post Office may be used. The place of the direction of the notice is tied to postal address. This is why, in the very first sentence of the agreement, the address of the licensor is given and the license is required to supply the same ("with offices at"). If another address is to be used, it must be so indicated ("or to such other address as notified by either party to the other as its address for the service of notices"), although a party would have to follow the procedure and use the existing address in the opening sentence of the agreement to give proper notice to the other party that a different address other than the one set out in the agreement should be used for "notices" under the agreement.
7.5. Either party's failure to perform any term or condition of this Agreement, as a result of circumstances beyond its control (including, without limitation, war, strikes, floods, governmental restrictions, power, telecommunications or Internet failures or damage to or destruction of any network facilities, or other Acts of God) shall not be deemed to be, or to give rise to, a breach of this Agreement.	This is a force majeure provision. The licensor is not responsible for forces beyond its control. If an "act of God" prevents the licensor from performing its obligations under the agreement, the licensor cannot be deemed in breach under the license. While such circumstances cannot constitute a breach for which termination might then be possible, it is not unreasonable to request that where service is suspended by the licensor a refund or credit is due the licensee; otherwise the licensee is insuring or underwriting the disaster that befell the licensor—that is the role of its insurers, not its licensees! The licensee may literally have to wait out the storm, be without service for some period, and be unable to terminate for cause, but it should never be required to pay for services it does not receive, whether through fault of its own, the licensor, or the Almighty. Some licenses cap the duration of the force majeure,

(continued)

Terms of the BioOne License	Comments on the Terms of the BioOne License
	providing a time beyond which the force majeure can be deemed a default. Finally, it is one thing to indicate that a force majeure is not a breach, and quite another to say that the licensor should continue to receive compensation for the lack of service during this period. The licensee should never pay for service it does not receive. In occurrences of force majeure, a refund should be available. Under ¶ 5.2.4, a credit in hours, including those from force majeure, would be available, at least for those events which result in "an interruption or suspension of service lasting more than 72 consecutive hours, the Licensee's contract will be extended by an equal number of hours."
7.6. The invalidity or unenforceability of any provision of this Agreement shall not affect the continuation in force of the remainder of this Agreement.	This is a severability, or perhaps more accurately a survivability, clause. In the instance where a provision is deemed invalid (e.g., a new state law now prohibits waivers of warranties of merchantability) or becomes otherwise unenforceable (e.g., a court rules that in the circumstances of the parties a particular clause is unconscionable), the entire agreement is not somehow invalidated; rather, the offending provisions alone are affected and voided, and the remaining terms remain in effect.
7.7. The failure of either party to require performance by the other party of any provision of this Agreement will not affect its full right to require such performance at any subsequent time; nor will the waiver by either party of a breach of any provision of this Agreement be taken or held to be a waiver of the provision itself.	This is another very important provision impacting the ability of either party (but more likely the licensee) to claim the terms of agreement were somehow changed by conduct, through the grant of an implied license. Simply because one party was in a performance-related breach and the other party did not object, for example, under ¶ 6, it does not mean the other party is prohibited from enforcing the provision and claiming breach of performance the next time a similar triggering event occurs. Thus the adage "Do as I say (as in writing) not as I do" applies here. In circumstances of nonperformance-related breach (or where nonperformance was granted by specific permission), the waiver of the breach does not alter the obligation of the party to honor the terms of the same provision in the future. While the requirements of waiver are not indicated, it is assumed the waiver must be express, written, and signed by the waiving party.
As witness the hands of the parties the day and year below first written. **For BioOne Date [ ].** *By its agent Publishers Communication Group* Name [ ] Title [ ] Signature [ ] **For the Licensee** Date [ ] Name [ ] Title [ ] Signature [ ] **For the Licensee** Date [ ].	Each party must sign and date the agreement expressing consent to be bound by its terms. The title of each party is also required; this relates to authority. The licensee should verify who within its organization has the legal authority to bind the organization and take steps to ensure that only this individual or individuals sign this or other similar agreements.

(continued)

Terms of the BioOne License	Comments on the Terms of the BioOne License
Appendix A. BioOne. 2 Amendment **THIS AMENDMENT TO THE SUBSCRIBER LICENSE** executed in [ ], 200_ (*Month, Year*), by and between PCG as agent for BioOne and [ ] (Licensee) **IS AGREED TO** as stated herein. 1. **Licensed Material** is hereby defined as inclusive of the electronic publications in the new collection produced and updated by BioOne as "BioOne.2," in addition to the original collection produced and updated by BioOne and now named "BioOne.1". 2. **Fees** are as stated in the BioOne Order Form/Price List as applicable to the Licensee, and as such will be invoiced to Licensee for the **Subscription Period**. 3. All other terms and conditions of the **Subscriber License** will remain unchanged unless modified by mutual agreement of the parties hereto. As witness the hands of the parties the day and year below first written. **For BioOne Date** [ ]. *By its agent Publishers Communication Group* Name [ ] Title [ ] Signature [ ] **For the Licensee** Date [ ] Name [ ] Title [ ] Signature [ ].	Appendix A indicates that there are two sources in terms of content (a basic collection designated by "1" and a second new collection designated as "2"). Fees are listed elsewhere.
Appendix B. Fees. BioOne subscriber fees, credits and discounts are included as part of the BioOne Order Form/Price List. BioOne does not require pricing be included as part of this Subscriber License.	This fee schedule indicates that fees are not found as a separate appendix or attachment; rather, the fee schedule along with credits and discount rates are found on the "Order Form/Price List." The appendix indicates that the licensor "does not require pricing be included as part of this Subscriber License" but the licensee might desire access to current fee, credit, and discount information.

(continued)

Terms of the BioOne License	Comments on the Terms of the BioOne License
Appendix C. List of Licensed Material included in the BioOne Database. A list of titles available as part of the BioOne service may be found on the BioOne Web site, and is subject to change from time to time. BioOne does not require the list of title be included as part of this Subscriber License. For purposes of this Subscriber License, the Licensed Material shall include (*check one*): ___ the BioOne Databases identified as "BioOne.1" and "BioOne.2" ___ or the BioOne Database identified as "BioOne.1" only ___ or the BioOne Databases identified as "BioOne.2" only.	Appendix A indicates that there are two sources in terms of content: a basic collection designated by "1" and a second new collection designated as "2." Thus, three choices in terms of content licensing options are available: the licensee may choose to license "1" or "2" or both "1" and "2"; again, access to fees for each option might be useful information for the licensee. Specific titles are not listed here but "may be found on the... Web site" but are "subject to change from time to time." While the right to withdraw content is provided to the licensor in ¶ 5.3, the licensee is reminded that content is subject to change at any time, although the presence of the phrase here does operate as an enforceable waiver because it is not obvious or conspicuous in an appendix. Rather, the legal validity of this comes through its placement in ¶ 5 with other provisions of warranty and waiver. While the licensor "does not require the list of title be included as part of this Subscriber License," as with the fee schedule, the licensee might desire that this information be included here, if the list is not excessive.
Appendix D. Licensee's Authorized Access Sites. Subscriber IP addresses should be submitted on the BioOne Order Form/Price List. BioOne does not require IP addresses be included as part of this Subscriber License.	The list of IP addresses from which access to the licensed content may be made is not needed here because it is included, with other significant information, on the Order Form/Price List. The definition of *authorized* is critical to the agreement, and disputes may develop over access to these users (e.g., ¶ 5.5.4): "Use its best efforts to ensure that only Authorized Users are permitted access to the Licensed Material," and thus it is important that the licensee keep the list up-to-date.

THE Nature (Academic: Americas) LICENSE DECONSTRUCTED

Terms of the Nature (Academic: Americas) License	Comments on the Terms of the Nature (Academic: Americas) License
TERMS. **1. INTERPRETATION.** **1.1.** In this Agreement (as defined below), unless the context requires otherwise, the following expressions have the following meanings: "**Agreement**": means as defined in	This license agreement defines a number of terms. Definitions avoid guesswork. Should a word of phrase be assigned its meaning in everyday language, the dictionary definition? Is the word or phrase a term of legal significance or of legal art? Definitions can in a sense set the record straight, without having to rely on external sources of interpretation, or the surrounding context for that matter,

(continued)

Terms of the Nature (Academic: Americas) License	Comments on the Terms of the Nature (Academic: Americas) License
the Schedule; **"Authorized User"**: (a) every member of the teaching and research staff employed by or otherwise accredited to the Licensee whether full-time or part time; (b) every student enrolled or accredited to the Licensee for the purposes of full-time or part-time attendance; (c) individual members of the public registered as users of the Licensee's library or information service; and (d) individual members of the public permitted to use the Licensee's library or information services; in each case who are permitted general access to the Network by the Licensee; **"Chargeable Users"**: as set out in the Schedule; **"Customer Support"**: the Helpdesk (as set out in the Schedule) providing reasonable e-mail and telephone support; **"Commencement Date"**: as set out in the Schedule; **"Full Staff and Students"**: the full time students enrolled or accredited to the Licensee and the full time teaching and research staff employed by or otherwise accredited to the Licensee (relevant to **Nature** and **Scientific American** only); **"License Fee"**: as set out in the Schedule; **"Licensed Material"**: those agreed **Nature, NPG Journals, Third-Party Journals, Palgrave Macmillan Journals** and **Palgrave Macmillan Third Party Journals** and/or **News** elements indicated on the Schedule; **"Network"**: the Licensee's local area network system of connected computers at the Site, the IP address for which is set out in the Schedule; **"Non-Scientific Department Staff and Students"**: the full-time students enrolled or	which again may be subject to alternative interpretation. This section of the agreement attempts to take two steps forward in that regard but seemingly takes one step backward with the caveat "unless the context requires otherwise." The phrase is also presented as an override to the remaining defining text of the section ("unless"). In other words, these definitions operate unless the context "requires" the parties to do otherwise, but there is no indication of when that occurs, so the parties are back to figuring when the context of the word or phrase requires deviation from a definition presented in this section. It might be a better strategy for the licensor to locate where in the agreement the terms listed here appear and then determine whether in a particular context the licensor desires an alternate definition. This will save the licensee from proffering an alternative interpretation and avoid a possible dispute. If the parties are taking the time to define terms, effort should be made to include alternative meanings of the terms the parties are deciding in fact to define. Users include "teaching and research staff," whether full or part time, who are employed or otherwise "accredited" (yet it is not clear what "accredited" means in this instance and whether the term is broad enough to include visiting scholars). Left out of this category are other employees who are not teachers or researchers but might desire to use the database. A later definition of "full staff and students" does little to alter this supposition, as the qualification there is again on "teaching and research staff." Included again are students, whether part or full time, who are "enrolled or accredited" (again, use of the term "accredited" raises a query as to whether it would include exchange students who perhaps enroll at their home institution). Other members of the public, if registered library patrons, are also included, and in theory nonteaching and research staff could conceivably fall into this category. A final category includes other members of the public who for some reason (through library policy, perhaps) are not registered patrons but nonetheless are permitted to use the licensee's library or information services. Perhaps employees, students, and residents of the local community can be registered library patrons; this latter category would allow others to access the licensed content and would encompass what other agreements might label as walk-in users. Notice that customer support is "reasonable" e-mail and phone support, but no indication of the hours of service is mentioned here.

(continued)

Terms of the Nature (Academic: Americas) License	Comments on the Terms of the Nature (Academic: Americas) License
accredited to the Licensee and the full-time teaching and research staff employed by or otherwise accredited to the Licensee, excluding those in the scientific departments (relevant to **Palgrave Macmillan Journals** and **Palgrave Macmillan Third Party Journals**); "**Renewal Date**": means as defined in Clause 4.1; "**Schedule**": the attached schedule preceding the Terms to this Agreement; "**Scientific Department Staff and Students**": the full time students enrolled or accredited to the Scientific Department of the Licensee and the full time teaching and research staff employed by or otherwise accredited to the Scientific Department of the Licensee (relevant to **NPG Journals (excluding Scientific American) and Third-Party Journals** only); "**Site**": the premises located at the Site Address set out in the Schedule; and "**Supply Period**": as set out in the Schedule or as otherwise extended pursuant to Clause 4.1.	Some scope of the licensed content is given, not in specific titles but by publisher group, though "Third-Party Journals" is not terribly descriptive. A schedule of specific titles is available and precedes the actual terms of the agreement, defined as the "schedule." A number of items are delineated in attached schedules, such as the "chargeable users," fee structure for those chargeable users, the IP network addresses of the licensee, the site of the licensee, the commencement date, and supply period. There is distinction made between nonscientific department staff and students and scientific department staff and students, both of which are defined again with reference to "teaching and research staff," but such staff and students can also be accredited to qualify even if not employed or enrolled, respectively.
1.2. The Agreement contains the entire agreement and undertaking between the parties relating to the Licensed Material and supersedes any prior agreement.	This is an integration clause indicating that, as the expression goes, "what you see is what you get" (or as Peggy Lee sang in 1969, "Is that all there is, my friend?," to which the answer here is an emphatic yes). Integration clauses are used to remind both parties that neither should rely on any prior or external writings, as the current iteration of the relationship and understandings of the parties is expressed in present agreement and this agreement alone.
1.3. The termination of this Agreement shall not prejudice the rights and remedies of either party against the other in respect of any prior breach of covenant, terms, warranty or condition.	Termination of the agreement does not affect the ability of either party to claim ("rights and remedies") that a provision ("covenant, terms, warranty or condition") of the license was breached or otherwise failed to be performed by the other party prior to termination. After termination, one party is able to pursue legal remedy for harms that occurred during the pretermination period.

(continued)

Terms of the Nature (Academic: Americas) License	Comments on the Terms of the Nature (Academic: Americas) License
1.4. The failure of any party to enforce any provision of this Agreement on any one occasion shall not affect its right to enforce another provision or the same provision on another occasion.	An implied license or implied waiver shall not be construed by any course of conduct. To be more precise, by a course of inaction in response to some breach, the nonacting party has not impacted its ability to enforce the same provision if or when a violation occurs on a later occasion. Otherwise, such inaction or nonresponsiveness might lead the breaching party to have reasonable reliance on the meaning of the inaction or lack of response, in other words, that the nonacting party did not care that the provision was breached. Through legal concepts such as estoppel, the breaching party might then be able to prevent the nonacting party in a similar instance from exercising its rights under the contract the next time this party engages in the same conduct.
1.5. Nothing contained in this Agreement shall constitute or shall be construed as constituting a partnership, joint venture, or contract of employment between the parties.	This provision confirms that, other than a vendor-customer relationship through license of specified content, no additional legal relationship is formed between the parties as a result of entering into the license agreement.
2. DELIVERY AND GRANT OF RIGHTS. **2.1.** In consideration of the payments made by the Licensee, and subject to the Licensee observing its obligations under this Agreement, the Licensor grants to the Licensee the following non-exclusive rights ("the Rights") for the Supply Period: **(a)** access via the Network at any time (subject to Clause 7) the Licensor's server, or as the case may be any service provided by an agent on its behalf, for the purpose of accessing the Licensed Material for research, teaching, and private study purposes by means of workstations located at the Site connected to the Network;	The consideration the license provides in return for access to the licensed content comes in two forms: first, the payment of a fee, and, second, a promise to honor the obligations placed upon the licensee and as expressed in the agreement. Access is expressed through a series of rights granted to the licensee: the first is 24/7 ("at any time") for purposes of "research, teaching, and private study" from access terminals as identified in the schedule of authorized IP address locations. Notice that only study must be private as opposed to public? Certainly teaching is a public undertaking, at least as far the copyright law considers use of content in the classroom a public display or public performance. Research could be both: private when conducted from the person's office computer and public when the research results are disseminated in a journal. Does this mean the content cannot be used for public study? What would public study be as opposed to private study? If there is concern over some likely activities related to study, the provision should be clarified. Some anticipated uses are public, such as teaching and research, since at least collaborative research could be quite public. This type of use is allowed; only study uses must be private.

(continued)

Terms of the Nature (Academic: Americas) License	Comments on the Terms of the Nature (Academic: Americas) License
(b) make the Licensed Material accessible directly or remotely via the Network to the Authorized Users for their research, teaching, and private study purposes in accordance with the Licensee's customary policies and practices acceptable to the Licensor;	The licensee can offer on-site or remote access of the licensed content to authorized users, again for purposes of "research, teaching, and private study." Teaching is of course a public function, but research could be either private or public (i.e., the research could be conducted by a solitary scientist in a personal laboratory or it could be collaborative, involving dozens of researchers from multiple institutions, where the authorized user of the licensee is but one of many). However, the act of study is qualified on condition that it is "private," with again the same concern that the licensed content could not be used for group study or other collaborative learning.
(c) permit Authorized Users to print and/or download individual articles and other individual items from searches of the Licensed Material for research, teaching, and private study purposes by means of workstations located at the Site connected to the Network;	Printing and downloading individual items is allowed from workstations located on site (previously defined as "the premises located at the Site Address set out in the Schedule"), and while remote users can access the licensed content per ¶ 2.1(b), it is not clear from ¶ 2.1(b) that authorized users using remote access may also print or download, though it is difficult to fathom how one would stop such conduct. Remote users are likely accessing the content through library website servers, and this may constitute a sufficiently placed "site" for purposes of printing or downloading. When printing or downloading for purposes of study, the use must again be private as opposed to public study. Similar issues are raised when considering group or collaborative forms of study. There is no "private" condition on "research" or "teaching," as these would more naturally appear to be public; for example, research may be done collaboratively or disseminated and in the classroom under the copyright law would be deemed a public display or performance or at least would be a place of public display or performance (see, e.g., 17 U.S.C. § 110). Further, it is unclear what the concept of "individual" is meant to convey ("download individual articles and other individual items"), as the term is used to modify two examples in the plural ("articles" and "items"), so the clause cannot operate to limit each user to one article or item alone. It may intend that if more than one article or item are downloaded or printed, the items must be printed or downloaded one at a time (i.e., individually). However, it would appear that disabling or disallowing a "print all" or "download all" or similar mark or drag-and-print or download feature would be under the control of the licensor in designing the user interface to its content and not rest with the licensee. It might also, in the

(continued)

Terms of the Nature (Academic: Americas) License	Comments on the Terms of the Nature (Academic: Americas) License
	alternative or in addition, mean that a set of articles or items that are related cannot be downloaded or printed; the articles or items must be individual (or, as in the previous BioOne license agreement, "discrete"). For example, an entire special issue of a journal on a special topic could not be downloaded or printed. Perhaps the intent of this clause is to prohibit substantial (or some other amount of) printing or downloading, but, if so, it is awkwardly expressed here. It might be advisable to inquire what practical circumstance of downloading or printing the licensor desires to limit or prevent and go from there, crafting a revised provision that allows for all other downloads or prints than those of concern.
(d) permit teaching staff accredited to the Licensee to reproduce individual articles from the Licensed Material for distribution to students accredited to the Licensee for the purpose of including such individual articles in course study packs;	The licensed content can be used in the compilation of course packs ("course study packs"). Again, the use of "individual articles" is problematic. Is this "individual" qualification intended to prevent more than one article from the licensed content being included in any one course pack? Here the context perhaps does suggest that "discrete" or "singular" is intended; that is, no entire special journal issue or series of reports on the same topic is allowed to be included in course study packs. The provision uses the term "reproduce" and not "print," suggesting that a reproduction in a course study pack could be digital (e.g., on a CD-ROM).
(e) reproduce single copies of individual articles from the Licensed Material in hard copy print form for distribution without charge in hard copy form (but not electronically) to individual libraries of not for profit, non commercial organizations in accordance with fair usage guidelines. No right or license is hereby granted to any person provided with such a copy to copy or otherwise deal with that individual article; and	This provision contains a print or "hard copy" rule. The provision appears to allow interlibrary loan (ILL) in print form if the requesting library is nonprofit or noncommercial and the filling of the request is made without charge. What is odd is that, under the copyright law, the ILL privileges are found in section 108 and the so-called ILL "rule of five" guideline is derived from an interpretation of 108(d) and 108(g) and is not found in the fair-use provision of section 107, a section that also has a number of associated "guidelines" relating to classroom use of protected material. It is unclear, then, if filling such requests is to conform to the guidelines promulgated under 107 ("fair usage guidelines"), as this would appear rather limiting and inappropriate for ILL. For example, under the classroom guidelines, this would mean an article used for ILL would be limited to a length of 3,500 words or limited to nine instances per semester per the "classroom" guidelines. It may just be that the licensor is unaware of the source of the interlibrary right in the copyright law. The last sentence indicates that a person who receives an article from the licensed content under this provision is not granted any additional rights to reproduce

(continued)

Terms of the Nature (Academic: Americas) License	Comments on the Terms of the Nature (Academic: Americas) License
	the article or "deal with" it. The concept of "deal" might be included to prevent a particular sort of dissemination to another as part of that person's business. See the previous discussions of *Ryan v. CARL Corp.*, 23 F. Supp. 2d 1146 (N.D. Cal. 1998). However, such third-party persons would not be bound by this agreement and have public distribution rights under 17 U.S.C. § 109 regarding the lawfully made copy received through ILL.
(f) create a hypertext link to any part of the Licensed Material provided that no person other than an Authorized User may use such hypertext link.	Access to the licensed content can also be provided via a hyperlink, but the link must be accessible only to authorized users within, for example, a course management system that is password protected so that only teachers and students in a particular class can access the space associated with that class. Instead of posting an article from the licensed content on the course space, a hyperlink to the licensed content where the article can be found is posted.
2.2. The Rights are personal to the Licensee and do not extend to its subsidiary or parent organizations, or to any other related or affiliated organizations. The Licensee may not assign, sub-license, transfer, charge or otherwise dispose of its rights under this Agreement without the prior written consent of the Licensor.	The first sentence indicates that the rights granted in the license do not apply across the organization of which the licensee may be a part. In the case of the University of Wisconsin, Milwaukee (UWM), this would prevent the rights under the agreement from extending to the University of Wisconsin System, of which UWM is a part, or to the UWM Foundation, with which it is affiliated. This does not mean that authorized users might not be drawn from persons affiliated with those other entities if those individuals otherwise qualify (e.g., "individual members of the public permitted to use the Licensee's library or information services"). The second sentence prohibits assignments or a transfer of a similar vein of the license. Given the tenuous economic future that some institutions of higher education may face, if such merger, acquisition, or other subsuming act is contemplated, such language could be added. Although it is unlikely the licensor would want to risk loss of the successor licensee as a client, having such future continuation subject to the permission of the licensor (and in writing) may offer the licensor the opportunity to condition its consent on pricing terms more favorable to it ("Yes, you can transfer the license to the new University of XYZ from the old ABC College, but since you're part of a university now your rate is higher"). The provision could be amended to state that assignments to a successor organization or entity are allowed and that other assignments when reasonable are also allowed or that consent not be "unreasonably withheld," as in the BioOne license.

(continued)

Terms of the Nature (Academic: Americas) License	Comments on the Terms of the Nature (Academic: Americas) License
2.3. Title to, and ownership of, the Licensed Material (including any copies made by or on behalf of the Licensee including by the Authorized Users) is not transferred to the Licensee and remains vested in the Licensor, subject to the Rights granted in Clause 2.1 and Clause 4.6. The Licensee acknowledges that any rights not expressly granted in this License are reserved to the Licensor.	This is a license of the contents, not a sale of copies of the content. Section 109's so-called first-sale rights do not apply, nor do other use or user rights under copyright law apply for that matter—rights (found in sections 107–122 of the copyright law) that might apply if this were a purchase of copies of the licensed content. A licensee is not an owner. The use rights granted are those found in ¶ 2.1 and retention rights are found in ¶ 4.6. The last sentence reiterates the reality that a license is outside the application of the copyright law and rights granted to users under it—rights that often depend on ownership of a lawfully made copy of the work. To some extent, the last sentence states the obvious: rights not granted by the licensor remain with the licensor.
2.4. The Licensee is responsible for the provision of and payment for the computer equipment and telecommunication services necessary for access to and use of the Licensed Material. The Licensor shall not issue credits or refunds against charges incurred by the Licensee in relation to such telecommunication services or those incurred contacting Customer Support. The Licensee accepts that the Licensor has no control over such telecommunication services and that the Licensor shall have no liability to the Licensee for the acts or omissions of providers of telecommunication services or for faults in or failures of their apparatus or of the Licensee's computer equipment.	All related computing, networking, and related costs associated with access to and use of the licensed content are the responsibility of the licensee, even if this means that upgrades in specifications are needed. No credit or refund will be issued as an offset against such costs, nor against other related expenses, such as long-distance phone calls to contact the licensor's customer service center.
2.5. The Licensor may assign this Agreement without the consent of the Licensee.	In contrast to the licensee's situation (assignment upon consent of the licensor), the licensor may assign the agreement at any time and without the consent of the licensee. At least the licensee should have notice from the licensor if such assignment occurs (e.g., the licensor is acquired or bought by another publisher). In addition, the licensee could be given the right to terminate the license (and receive a refund) if the licensor assigns the license to another, though it is likely that the licensee desires that the agreement remain in force and access to the content continue.

(continued)

Terms of the Nature (Academic: Americas) License	Comments on the Terms of the Nature (Academic: Americas) License
3. USAGE RESTRICTIONS. Except as expressly permitted in Clause 2.1, the Licensee warrants that it will not, nor will it license or permit others to, directly or indirectly, without the Licensor's prior written consent:	In addition to requiring that any use or other rights granted to the licensee by the licensor must be explicit in order to exist under the agreement ("expressly permitted in Clause 2.1"), the license includes a number of prohibitions, carving out additional pieces of the "information space" of use, access, and so forth, regarding the licensed content. In addition, this provision requires the licensee promise that certain uses of the licensed content will not occur. Uses that under the copyright law and regarding content purchased or acquired under it by sale, gift, and so on, and that might otherwise be lawful are here nonetheless prohibited. This is a significant concession; the promise to forgo these rights is worth something, that is, surrender of those rights for some other rights of use, access, and so forth, that would not exist if use of the content were governed by the copyright law alone. In addition to the license fee paid by the licensee, surrender of these rights would constitute consideration (thus use of the word "warrants"). What is problematic is that not only will the licensee promise not to engage in such uses but that it will not "permit others" (e.g., students, patrons) to do so either. While employees might be considered part of the institution in a legal sense, through principles of agency law, students and other patrons drawn from the public are not and would be considered third parties to the contract. Yet the licensee promises here to impose such obligations upon such persons, to ensure that others comply with the terms of the agreement as well. How the licensee is to fulfill this promise is unclear. Oddly, the provision does not use the term "Authorized Users" but uses "others" to suggest a larger range of potential persons, therein widening the range of persons for whose conduct the licensee is responsible. A better approach than "warrants"—that is, the licensee promises that it (or its employees) will not engage in any prohibited use nor will it permit others to do so—would be to warrant that the licensee will use reasonable efforts to achieve such compliance by authorized users (students could be included here, as the licensee arguably has a greater ability to control their conduct, as with its employees, than, say, the general public) and to use reasonable efforts to notify others of these restrictions. This is a far more achievable result.
(a) sell, distribute, license, rent or otherwise exploit the Licensed Material, or any element of it, for any commercial purpose;	Forget fair commercial use (the vast majority of fair-use cases arise in commercial settings; see Tomas A. Lipinski, *A Functional Approach to Understanding and Applying Fair Use*, 45 ANNUAL REVIEW OF INFORMATION SCIENCE AND TECHNOLOGY 525, Blaise Cronin ed., 2010). Any commercial purpose whatsoever, even a

(continued)

Terms of the Nature (Academic: Americas) License	Comments on the Terms of the Nature (Academic: Americas) License
	commercial use of de minimus or incidental purpose, is prohibited. While the provision lists selling, licensing, or renting, activities which the licensee or its users might not by design engage in, "distribution" or "otherwise exploit" can cover a wide range of activities. See *Ryan v. CARL Corp.*, 23 F. Supp. 2d 1146 (N.D. Cal. 1998). The provision could be altered to allow for incidental or de minimus commercial uses.
(b) make the Licensed Material, or any element of it, available by any means to persons other than Authorized Users;	While the licensee may be able to limit access to the licensed content to authorized users only, the licensee would have little effective control over authorized users then making the licensed content available ("by any means") to others. It is hoped that the provision is not intended to reach such once-removed or downstream uses. Also, no system is perfect, and there may be occasion when the security measure employed by the licensee fails or ceases to be as effective as the licensee or licensor would like it to be. Yet under these circumstances, the limits of the provision are not met. Remember that the licensee agreed "that it will not, nor will it . . . permit others to, directly or indirectly, without the Licensor's prior written consent" do any of the following acts enumerated in (a) through (j). There should be allowed incidental infractions for those beyond the immediate and reasonable control of the licensee. Perhaps ¶ 2.1 should be amended to read: "The Licensee warrants that it will not intentionally permit and will undertake reasonable efforts to prevent others to, directly or indirectly, without the Licensor's prior written consent . . ."
(c) make the Licensed Material, or any element of it, available on, or by, electronic bulletin boards, news groups, Web sites, FTP or any other means of posting or transmitting material on the Internet, an on-line service or wide area network;	Posting any of the content ("or any element of it") to a bulletin board, blog, and so forth, is prohibited. Again, forget fair use; even quoting a line within such a post is prohibited. The licensee must also ensure (as it promised or warranted that it would) that "others," including authorized users, must not engage in such use either. The law of agent and principal might again suggest that "it" in "Licensee warrants that it will not" includes the licensee as a legal entity as well as its employees, who are the legal agents of the entity when acting in their capacity as employees. The "others" in the phrase "nor will it license or permit others to" applies to those outside the agent-principal relationship, such as students and "walk-ins" or members of the public. Again, the efficacy of such an impossible standard is nothing short of confounding. Informing authorized users of such restrictions or taking remedial measure upon discovery of deviating conduct is one thing, but promising that all comers will not engage in such uses sets a near-impossible bar.

(continued)

Terms of the Nature (Academic: Americas) License	Comments on the Terms of the Nature (Academic: Americas) License
(d) remove or obscure the Licensor's copyright notice from the Licensed Material including hard-copy print-outs;	This provision requires only that the licensee not remove, obscure, or otherwise make less visible the copyright notice that might accompany the licensed content. This is reasonable; the concern over the extension of the promise to "others" notwithstanding, as noted. See the discussion regarding Copyright Management Information in the BioOne agreement.
(e) use the Licensed Material to create any derivative work, product or service, or merge the Licensed Material with any other product, database, or service;	The right to make derivative works is a right of the copyright owner. 17 U.S.C. § 101 defines a derivative work as one that is "based upon one or more preexisting works, such as a translation, musical arrangement, dramatization, fictionalization, motion picture version, sound recording, art reproduction, abridgment, condensation, or any other form in which a work may be recast, transformed, or adapted." Inclusion of such a prohibition is common even in Creative Commons licensing, but such exclusive right, in the absence of a license, would under the copyright law be subject to fair use. If the licensor fears use of the licensed content in competing products—a reasonable concern—then language should be referenced to prevent this result; see ¶ 3.0(a), which prohibits commercial use altogether. Second, in an educational setting, the creation of derivatives can be a valuable part of the learning process—mash-ups in the arts, translations by language students, and so forth. It might be advisable to allow derivatives for classroom use with no further distribution allowed. This compromise would assuage licensor fears while allowing the maximum educational use of the licensed content. Another alternative is to include a general provision ensuring that all uses which would otherwise be fair use under the copyright law are permitted. Finally, "merge" appears to imply incorporation or integration into some similar function, into a product, database, or service, rather than simply combining content with other content. Otherwise, placing articles or items from the licensed content together with similar items from other vendors into a course pack or onto a distance-education course management webpage might be prohibited.
(f) alter, amend, modify, translate, or change the Licensed Material;	Again, a range of fair use or derivative use (such as a translation) rights is prohibited. Translating a sentence from an article sourced from the licensed content to use in a term paper or scholarly article would be prohibited but surely fits fair use. A more reasonable approach is to limit such uses to what would otherwise be fair use or to place some incidental or insubstantial cap on how much could be used (e.g., de minimus). Further, some uses are not derivative (i.e., do not step on the owner's exclusive right to make derivative uses) but would likely be

(continued)

Terms of the Nature (Academic: Americas) License	Comments on the Terms of the Nature (Academic: Americas) License
	prohibited under the broad rule of no alterations, amendments, or modifications allowed herein. For example, under *Clean Flicks of Colorado, LLC v. Soderbergh*, 433 F. Supp. 2d 1236 (D. Colo. 2006), editing out content from a feature-length film did not constitute the creation of a derivative work ("But because the infringing copies of these movies are not used in a transformative manner, they are not derivative works and do not violate § 106(2)" (*id*. at 1242). The study materials based upon the book *Big League Sales Closing Techniques* were found not to constitute a derivative work in *Peter Letterese and Associates, Inc. v. World Institute of Scientology Enterprises, Inc.*, 533 F.3d 1287, 1299 (11th Cir. 2008) ("*Big League Sales* is neither a derivative work nor a factual compilation," *id*. at 1213). Likewise, creation of dictionaries or similar guidebooks is not derivative. See *Warner Brothers Entertainment, Inc. v. RDR Books*, 575 F. Supp. 2d 513, 539 (S.D.N.Y. 2008): "Under these circumstances, and because the Lexicon does not fall under any example of derivative works listed in the statute, Plaintiffs have failed to show that the Lexicon is a derivative work." While not derivative, some uses might be viewed as alterations. Again, if the licensor fears use of the licensed content in competing products—a reasonable concern—then language should be substituted to prevent this, and such overbroad and sweeping language should be excised.
(g) undertake any activity that may have a damaging effect on the Licensor's ability to achieve revenue through selling and marketing the Licensed Material;	This is an onerous provision in the opinion of the author. It conceivably covers a wide range of activity. For example, the provision prevents the licensee from making any negative comment, either formally in a published review or informally on a board, blog, list, and so forth, about the licensor or its product or service. Again, under the opening proviso to clauses (a) to (i), "the Licensee warrants that it will not, nor will it license or permit others to, directly or indirectly, without the Licensor's prior written consent" do any of the following acts, and this language would include permitting employees to make the following comment: "The content isn't bad for the price but don't expect the new sales reps or customer service to ever be of any help. Think twice before subscribing to or renewing this one!" Suppose other librarians read this post and decide to cancel their subscription (see the discussion of termination rights in ¶ 4). This "activity" certainly impacts "on the Licensor's ability to achieve revenue through selling and marketing the Licensed Material." Such review or comment goes against concepts of open communication and furthermore does not violate any of the exclusive rights of the copyright owner, such as the derivative right. See *Ty, Inc. v.*

(continued)

Terms of the Nature (Academic: Americas) License	Comments on the Terms of the Nature (Academic: Americas) License
	Publication International Ltd., 292 F.3d 512, 520 (7th Cir. 2002): "Ty acknowledges as it must that a collectors' guide to a series of copyrighted works is no more derivative than a book review is." On the right to reproduce the work as long as the reviewer or guide author does not quote too much of the original, the right of reproduction would not be violated either. See *Warner Brothers Entertainment, Inc. v. RDR Books*, 575 F. Supp. 2d 513 (S.D.N.Y. 2008): "By condensing, synthesizing, and reorganizing the preexisting material in an A-to-Z reference guide, the Lexicon does not recast the material in another medium to retell the story of Harry Potter, but instead gives the copyrighted material another purpose . . . Under these circumstances, and because the Lexicon does not fall under any example of derivative works listed in the statute" (*id.* at 539); "While it is difficult to draw the line at each entry that takes more than is reasonably necessary from the Harry Potter series to serve its purposes . . . the Lexicon disturbs the balance and takes more than is reasonably necessary to create a reference guide" (*id.* at 549).
(h) otherwise use the Licensed Material supplied in accordance with this Agreement in a manner that would infringe the copyright or other proprietary rights contained within it;	This provision indicates the licensee cannot engage in conduct that would otherwise, in absence of the agreement, constitute copyright infringement. Sounds reasonable, and yet other provisions take away use rights that would otherwise, in the absence of the agreement, exist under the copyright law. In return for the surrender of those rights, the licensee ought to get a few it would not otherwise possess in return—uses that would be infringing under the copyright law but are allowed under the license. If this provision stood alone instead of in addition to (f) and (g) or a modified (e), as suggested previously, it might be more palatable. In other words, one would expect to be prohibited from engaging in copyright infringement with the licensed content if this were the only limitation. However, other provisions have already reduced the "information space" of lawful uses. Further, it might be reasonable to articulate some sense of which other "proprietary rights" the licensor believes are contained within the licensed content. Is the licensor asserting a trade secret claim? If so, what portion of the licensed content is trade secret? Does the licensed content contain images that might include a trademark? What is the nature of those rights, and what is the concern of the licensor?
(i) make the Licensed Material or any part of it available by remote access to any person other than Authorized Users; or	The provision indicates that the licensee warrants it will not make the licensed content available by remote access to anyone other than authorized users. Sounds reasonable, but absolutes are always dangerous. The provision promises perfection, no mistakes,

(continued)

Terms of the Nature (Academic: Americas) License	Comments on the Terms of the Nature (Academic: Americas) License
	no errors, no failure of whatever security measures the licensee employs to achieve these ends. No system is that good! And what about human error? A better, more achievable approach would be to promise to use best efforts to prevent unauthorized access, employing current industry or institutional standards, and best practices to prevent access from those users who are not so authorized under the agreement.
(j) make mass, automated or systematic extractions from or hard copy storage of the Licensed Material.	This clause prohibits robots, scrapers, or similar programs from extracting material from the licensed content. The provision also prohibits storing the content—though it is unclear if "hard copy" is meant to apply to print storage alone. Would the prohibition include storage on a CD-ROM as well as on a departmental server? It would appear the intent is to reach at least some digital file formats, such as those stored on a disc (which could be a kind of "hard copy"). Again, the underlying issue is appreciating the reasonable concern of the licensor and at the same time accommodating the educational or research uses of the licensee. A substantial, significant, or other portion standard could be inserted here if extraction is the concern, which would prohibit only those mass, automated, or systematic extractions that are substantial (quantitative) or significant (qualitative). Also, there might be times when such mass, automated, or systematic extraction or storage, even though insubstantial or insignificant, might be necessary as part of a larger project studying retrieval capabilities, search capacity, and so on, but would nonetheless involve a violation of this provision. (The author recalls using a legal database both as a source of documentation and as a tool to collect such documentation and running repeated searches in different files. It sure would have been great to use a program that would run those searches in various populations automatically, but use of such a tool would have been prohibited under this language.) Considering the scholarly nature of the user audience ("Nature: Academic"), an exception might be appropriate: "except for bona fide research purposes undertaken by an Authorized User, with access to hard copy storage limited to Authorized Users."
4. TERM AND TERMINATION. 4.1. This Agreement shall begin on the Commencement Date and continue for the initial period of the Supply Period as defined in the Schedule. The Licensor may agree to extend	The initial duration of the agreement is set out in the "Schedule" and is renewed at one-year increments. While the provision indicates that renewal can occur, there is no indication of the renewal process other than a general reference in ¶ 5 that any fee is due "within 30 days of the date of invoice" with failure to pay any fee, including the initial or annual renewal fee, constituting a material breach under ¶ 4.2. While credits are not

(continued)

Terms of the Nature (Academic: Americas) License	Comments on the Terms of the Nature (Academic: Americas) License
the Supply Period for additional one-year periods, from the end of the initial period or any subsequent additional one-year period (the "Renewal Date"), subject to payment of appropriate fees and acceptance thereof by the Licensor.	given under ¶ 2.4 for telecommunication, computing, or other access costs, it may be possible to secure a credit (or refund) for excessive downtime. The more significant question is whether this credit extends the duration of the agreement, which may have implications relating to due dates for nonrenewal notices, payment of subscription renewal fees, and so on, or simply operates as a credit against future payments (or refund in case of nonrenewal). Such options should be at the discretion of the licensee. Oddly, ¶ 4 does not indicate the process for nonrenewal or expiration of the agreement. It should. Otherwise, how is one to distinguish a nonrenewal from a failure to pay the next year's invoice on time? Triggering one of the following provisions (various sorts of termination scenarios) appears a clumsy way to end a subscription amicably, that is, in cases other than material breach (see ¶ 4.2). On the other hand, expecting a commercial relationship to continue forever is just as unreasonable.
4.2. Either party may terminate the Supply Period at any time upon written notice to the other if the other party commits a material breach of any term of this Agreement (for the avoidance of doubt non-payment of any fees as they fall due under this Agreement by the Licensee shall constitute a material breach). The termination will become effective thirty days after receipt of written notice unless, in the case of a remediable breach, during the relevant period of thirty days the defaulting party has remedied the breach.	If one party is in material breach of any term of the agreement, the other party (the nonbreaching party) has the right to terminate upon written notice to the breaching party. The termination is effective 30 days after receipt of written notice, with the particulars of proper notice further governed by ¶ 11. However, each party has the right to cure (i.e., to fix the problem): "in the case of a remediable breach, during the relevant period of thirty days the defaulting party has remedied the breach." While at least one form of material breach is defined (nonpayment of any fees), remedial breaches are not defined. There is no process for notice if the breaching party effects cure. If the party in breach remedies the breach, then written notice should be required to be given to the nonbreaching party (i.e., the one seeking termination) that this will now not occur because the problem is fixed. Of course, the parties might argue over whether certain conduct meets the requirements for material breach in the first instance ("You're in material breach"; "No, we're not in material breach") and then argue over whether certain conduct has in fact cured or remedied the breach ("We fixed the problem"; "No, you haven't"). As the initial notice of intended termination can begin the debate over breach and its materiality, a required notice from the curing party (the party in alleged breach) to the nonbreaching party can bring issues of insufficient cure into the open rather than the curing party believing things are now bright and rosy while the termination-seeking party who sent the initial notice is eagerly awaiting the day of termination. All the while the party in breach could have been attempting additional cure, assuming this party

(continued)

Terms of the Nature (Academic: Americas) License	Comments on the Terms of the Nature (Academic: Americas) License
	wanted to salvage the relationship and continue with the agreement in effect. The provision makes clear ("for the avoidance of doubt") that nonpayment of fees "as they fall due" (which under ¶ 5.1 is "within 30 days of the date of invoice," not the anniversary date, so it might be advisable to inquire how early renewal invoices go out) constitutes a material breach, giving the licensor the opportunity to terminate. It is logical that such term (i.e., nonpayment or untimely payment of the fee) would be material. It could be argued that changes in fee structure are also material, as are changes in content and terms relating to what can and cannot be done with the licensed content. While it is clear that nonpayment is a material breach, should it not also be subject to the right of cure, as nonpayment would surely be a case of a "remediable breach" (i.e., one that is able to be cured by payment)? So, a licensee that did not pay the renewal fee within 30 days of the date of invoice would receive a written notice of termination but still have 30 days within which to cure, that is, a total of 60 days from the date of the original invoice to pay the renewal fee, assuming default, notice, and cure. Since the fee is paid in advance of the "Supply Period" there would likely be an opportunity upon receipt of the invoice reflecting an increase to either negotiate a lower rate or decide not to renew. However, changes to the licensed content or use rights and restrictions should require written notice of the change as well and a right to terminate, as these might constitute a material term to the licensee. It is not unreasonable to define what other terms "shall constitute a material breach" here. "Thus, it has been said that a 'material breach' is a failure to do something that is so fundamental to a contract that the failure to perform that obligation defeats the essential purpose of the contract or makes it impossible for the other party to perform under the contract. In other words, for a breach of contract to be material, it must 'go to the root' or 'essence' of the agreement between the parties . . . A breach is 'material' if a party fails to perform a substantial part of the contract or one or more of its essential terms or conditions, the breach substantially defeats the contract's purpose, or the breach is such that upon a reasonable interpretation of the contract, the parties considered the breach as vital to the existence of the contract . . . In many cases, a material breach of contract is proved by the established amount of the monetary damages flowing from the breach; however, proof of a specific amount of monetary damages is not required when the evidence establishes that the breach was so central to the parties' agreement that it defeated the essential purpose of the contract."

(continued)

Terms of the Nature (Academic: Americas) License	Comments on the Terms of the Nature (Academic: Americas) License
	RICHARD A. LORD, 18 WILLISTON ON CONTRACTS § 63:3 (4th ed. 2008), footnotes omitted. Once material breaches are identified a point of debate might continue to be whether a particular conduct constitutes a breach. In the case of an aggregator, changes to the content might only trigger a notice and termination right if some threshold is met (e.g., 5 percent loss or change in content), or at least a right to refund, prorated to reflect what the loss of content represents to the overall database. See ¶ 4.4 discussing refund and ¶ 4.3 discussing "termination" by the licensor of "any part(s) of the Licensed Material." It can be argued that all terminations have a right of refund (credit would be illogical since the agreement is now ended). Without a refund, then retaining the subscription without return operates as a sort of penalty or forfeiture of sorts, to the advantage of the licensor, of course.
4.3. Licensor may terminate the Supply Period or the Supply Period for any part(s) of the Licensed Material only at any time upon thirty days' written notice to the Licensee.	While the licensor can terminate at any time and without cause upon 30 days' written notice (the process of notice is covered in ¶ 11), the licensee's options (other than nonrenewal) for termination are limited to those circumstances where the licensor is in material breach (¶ 4.2), the licensor goes out of business (¶ 4.5), or there is an act of God (inability to perform obligation for more than 30 days as a result of force majeure under ¶ 10). Unlike ¶ 4.2, which indicates a notice-upon-receipt rule, such a clause is absent here, so the general rule of "notice" under ¶ 11 operates herein: a party is deemed to have receipt within 48 hours of posting. Since this provision vests the licensor with broad power to terminate, the provision should at least be amended to make notice effective upon actual receipt, not by some event triggered by the licensor ("48 hours after posting") alone. It is not unreasonable for both parties to have equivalent termination rights, again with the right of refund owing to the licensee in all instances, even material breaches; otherwise, nonpayment of the refund operates as a fine or penalty (at least in the author's opinion). Apparently the licensor can terminate the entire agreement or terminate the agreement with respect to selected portions of the licensed content: "or the Supply Period for any part(s) of the Licensed Material only." Again, notice must be in writing, 30 days in advance of the termination date. It is unclear whether elimination of content from the licensed database is the same as termination of some "part(s) of the licensed content." If it is, then the licensor has the right to do it, but such elimination is at least subject to the refund right under ¶ 4.4. If it is not the same, and also if loss of significant content triggers a termination right under ¶ 4.2, then there is inconsistency between paragraphs 4.2 (material

(continued)

Terms of the Nature (Academic: Americas) License	Comments on the Terms of the Nature (Academic: Americas) License
	breaches subject to termination with right to cure) and 4.3 (licensor right to terminate "parts"). Furthermore, if loss of content is subject to ¶ 4.2, does substitution of similar content constitute a cure? If the licensee considers some titles irreplaceable or nonsubstitutable and if loss content is a material breach, then ¶ 4.2 should be amended to exclude the cure right in those instances. Based on the discussion so far, the agreement should make clear that such changes in content (again, consider a triggering threshold number or list of must-have titles) should either be subject to unilateral choice by the licensor under ¶ 4.3 but qualifying for refund under ¶ 4.4 or constitute a material breach under ¶ 4.2, which would also require a refund per ¶ 4.4 ("by the Licensee under Clause 4.2") with a right to cure. In either case and under either paragraph, written notice is required to be given by the terminating party, but with the 30-day period commencing under ¶ 4.2 on the date the notice is received by the nonbreaching, nonterminating party, and under ¶ 4.3 commencing upon "48 hours after posting," the time at which notice is deemed received.
4.4. If termination of the Supply Period occurs as a result of notice being given by the Licensee under Clause 4.2, 4.5 or 10.2 or by the Licensor under Clause 4.3 or 10.2 the Licensor shall repay the Licensee a pro-rateable proportion of the License Fee as represents the paid for but unexpired Supply Period at the date of termination. If the Supply Period is terminated for any part(s) of the Licensed Material only under Clause 4.3 then the Licensor shall repay the Licensee a pro-rateable proportion of that part of the License Fee that represents the Licensed Material so terminated only.	If the licensee decides to terminate under ¶ 4.2 (the licensor is in material breach), ¶ 4.5 (the licensor goes belly-up), or ¶ 10.2 (either party may terminate where an act of god like an earthquake, flood, or fire prevents either licensee or the licensor from fulfilling its obligations for more than 30 days), or if the licensor decides to terminate either because it can (under ¶ 4.3) or because either it or the licensee suffers an act of God that prevents it from fulfilling its obligations for more than 30 days, then the licensee is owed a refund: "Licensor shall repay the Licensee a pro-rateable proportion of the License Fee as represents the paid for but unexpired Supply Period at the date of termination." If the licensor terminates under ¶ 4.2 because the licensee is in material breach, then there is no refund due the licensee. The author would argue that a refund is still due the licensee in this case. The provision could be simplified to indicate that in any case of termination a refund is due. Even in a case of termination with fault (e.g., the licensor terminates under ¶ 4.2 because it believes the licensee to be in material breach), why should the licensee not receive a refund? Without a refund, the provision operates as a penalty, forfeit, or surcharge for services paid but no longer rendered. As discussed previously, where the licensor decides to terminate without cause under ¶ 4.3 but only with respect to a part of the licensed content, then a different prorated refund is made; that is, instead of a refund equal to the

(continued)

Terms of the Nature (Academic: Americas) License	Comments on the Terms of the Nature (Academic: Americas) License
	fee paid multiplied by the number of days left on the contract divided by the number of days in the entire contract period, the refund here is calculated by multiplying the fee paid by a percentage representing the licensed content that is removed or terminated as a part of the entire content licensed originally. It is not clear if this count ("terminated for any part(s) of the Licensed Material") is made based on the number of words, the number of items (articles or titles), file space, bits, and so or, or perhaps based on the cost of the content to the licensor that is reflected in the subscription fee ("proportion of that part of the License Fee that represents the Licensed Material so terminated"). This should be clarified. The provision also indicates that repayment is in the form of a refund, not a credit, and its calculation suggests, as suspected that under ¶ 4.3, the licensor can indeed unilaterally terminate (remove) content. The licensee should receive notice in such cases and have the right to terminate; in other words, a better placement for the provisions relating to removal should be under ¶ 4.2.
4.5. Either party may terminate the Supply Period forthwith on notice in writing to the other if the other party is unable to pay its debts or ceases or threatens to cease to carry on business, goes into administration, receivership or administrative receivership, or any event analogous to any of the foregoing occurs in any jurisdiction.	If one party has financial difficulties such that it can no longer "pay its debts" or is in some form of bankruptcy ("administration, receivership or administrative receivership") or the situation is so dire that it "ceases or threatens to cease" carrying on business, then the other party can terminate. The licensee can terminate if the licensor is so strapped or the licensor may terminate if the licensee is in the proverbial financial pickle. Notice that the termination right is due the financially stable party, not the party in trouble, though either party would have this right should the other become so positioned. The financially stable party must offer written notice of its intent to terminate. According to ¶ 4.4, discussed previously, a ¶ 4.5 termination is a termination that qualifies for a refund. In a situation where the licensee terminates upon written notice in response to the dire financial straits of the licensor while a refund is due the licensee under ¶ 4.4, it might not be realistic to expect one. If the licensor is in some form of bankruptcy, any licensee would likely be an unsecured creditor and would more or less get in line with all the other database customers as well as other unsecured creditors. An example of a security interest that would then position a party to a contract to become a secured creditor of the licensor might be the company that sold the computer hardware, servers, and so forth, to the licensor, assuming a security interest existed and was perfected under the applicable law. It is typical in those situations that percentage on the dollar owed is all that can be recovered. In

(continued)

Terms of the Nature (Academic: Americas) License	Comments on the Terms of the Nature (Academic: Americas) License
	some circumstances, the U.S. Bankruptcy Court might discharge the debt altogether. Licenses for information products like a database are not governed by the UCC, governed by UCITA where enacted, but would not constitute a secured transaction. A license agreement governing access to a database is within the scope of UCITA: "UCITA governs access by Fortune 500 businesses to sophisticated databases as well as distribution of software to the general public; it also covers custom software development and the acquisition of various rights in multimedia products" (UCITA, Prefatory Note). However, UCITA transactions are unsecured transactions. In a situation where the licensor terminates because the licensee is in bankruptcy, there would be no refund (though, as discussed, the author would argue there should nonetheless be a refund) due the licensor as ¶ 4.5 is not one of the two forms of termination triggered by notice from the licensor that qualifies for refund under ¶ 4.4: "termination . . . occurs as a result of notice being given . . . by the Licensor under Clause 4.3 or 10.2." In this scenario, the licensee is out the fee already paid. However, the U.S. Bankruptcy Court has the authority to stay transactions within 90 days of filing for bankruptcy. In other words, the court might order the return of the fee paid to the licensor into the bankruptcy estate if it was paid within 90 days of filing. The automatic stay rules are contained in § 362 of the bankruptcy laws and provide, for example, that the filing of a petition for bankruptcy "operates as stay . . . any act to collect, assess, or recover a claim against the debtor that arose before the commencement of the case under this title [and] the setoff of any debt owing to the debtor that arose before the commencement of the case under this title against any claim against the debtor," per 11 U.S.C. § 362(6) and (7). Such monies would be aggregated into the bankrupt estate and then shared prorated among the creditors according the statutory priority rules. The secured creditors, if there are any, as well as any other priority claims, such as for unpaid taxes and attorneys' fees, would be settled before any unsecured claims, the priority and ordering of such creditors established under the bankruptcy statute. The unsecured creditors would be paid last with the residuary estate. A license agreement of this sort is not a secured transaction, as there is no collateral to secure. Rather, such contracts are executory and subject to special discharge rules vested in the bankruptcy trustee, as a bankrupt entity might have difficulty fulfilling or continuing performance obligations. See 11 U.S.C. § 365. See, for example, *RCC Technology Corp. v. Sunterra Corp.*, 287 B.R. 864, 865 (M.D. Md. 2003): "However, there is a long line of authority holding that intellectual property

(continued)

Terms of the Nature (Academic: Americas) License	Comments on the Terms of the Nature (Academic: Americas) License
	licensing agreements such as the SLA are executory contracts," reversed and remanded, 361 F.3d 257, 264 (4th Cir. 2003), but agreeing that the contract was executory: "On this point, we agree with the district court that the Agreement was executory when Sunterra petitioned for bankruptcy"; see also *In re Chiwich, Inc.*, 54 B.R. 427, 430 (S.D.N.Y. 1985): "The court emphasized the fact that the licensee was required to do more than merely account for and pay royalties. The licensee was also required to deliver written quarterly sales reports and keep books of account subject to inspection. In the instant case, Farmland is similarly required to furnish the debtor with sales reports (on a monthly basis) and to keep books of account and records reflecting the licensed sales which must be open to the debtor's inspection at all reasonable times. Additionally, Farmland is required to protect the debtor's rights in the licensed trademarks. Manifestly, the licenses in the instant case are executory as to both the debtor and Farmland and, therefore, they are executory contracts within the meaning of 11 U.S.C. § 365(a)." A thorough discussion of the interplay between the operation of license terms and the bankruptcy laws is beyond the scope of this book, but such issues should be considered.
4.6. On expiry or termination of the Supply Period, Licensee shall have no rights of any kind to any Licensed Material published after the date of termination. On expiry or termination of the Supply Period, otherwise than as a result of notice being given by the Licensor under Clause 4.2, 4.3 or 4.5, the Licensee's non-exclusive license of the Rights shall, subject to (except as otherwise set forth in this Clause 4.6) all the terms and conditions in this Agreement (including without limitation this sub-clause 4.6, Clause 4.8 and the other provisions of this Clause 4), continue indefinitely in respect of the Licensed Material first published during the Supply Period as follows: (a) Those	The first sentence of this paragraph is reinforcing that, unlike a sale, where the purchaser of a copy or phonorecord of a work protected by copyright would have rights of public distributions in that item under 17 U.S.C. § 109, a licensee does not purchase a physical copy but merely purchases access, in this case to the contents of an online database, and thus there are no ownership rights in the licensed content. However, the license grants nonexclusive rights to maintain indefinite access to the licensed content added to the database during the duration of the agreement ("continue indefinitely in respect of the Licensed Material first published during the Supply Period") but not that content "published prior to the Supply Period to which access may have been granted during the Supply Period." Subject to additional conditions ("except as otherwise set forth in this Clause 4.6"), the agreement treats the license more like a sale or traditional library serial subscription in this respect, except that the continuation access and use rights are subject to the terms of the initial agreement ("On expiry or termination of the the Supply Period . . . the Licensee's non-exclusive license of the Rights shall, subject to . . . all the terms and conditions in this Agreement" and "SUBJECT ALWAYS to the Licensee's continued compliance with the terms of this Agreement"), including in

(continued)

Terms of the Nature (Academic: Americas) License	Comments on the Terms of the Nature (Academic: Americas) License
agreed Nature and NPG Journals elements indicated in Section A and B of the Schedule and those agreed Palgrave Macmillan Journals elements indicated in Section E of the Schedule SUBJECT ALWAYS to the Licensee's continued compliance with the terms of this Agreement and payment of such reasonable annual access fee as Licensor may from time to time charge (or such alternative supply arrangement terms and costs as the parties may agree); and (b) Those agreed Third Party Journals elements indicated in Section C of the Schedule (the "C Content") and those agreed Palgrave Macmillan Third Party Journals elements indicated in Section F of the Schedule (the "F" content) SUBJECT ALWAYS to the Licensee's continued compliance with the terms of this Agreement and payment of such reasonable annual access fee as Licensor may from time to time charge (or such alternative supply arrangement terms and costs as the parties may agree); PROVIDED THAT due to rights restrictions it may only be possible to allow access to the C Content and/or the F content via the Network for a limited period or not at all. The Licensor shall, after the end of such limited period or if it is not able to allow any access via the Network and provided that it has the rights to do so, deliver the C Content and/or F content in a physical storage media	theory termination rights: "including without limitation this sub-clause 4.6, Clause 4.8 and the other provisions of this Clause 4." One of the additional conditions of access to content listed in Schedules A, B, and E "first published during the Supply Period" is that the licensor can charge an annual maintenance fee, "and payment of such reasonable annual access fee as Licensor may from time to time charge (or such alternative supply arrangement terms and costs as the parties may agree)." Similar charges can apply to content listed in Schedules C and F. The parties may disagree as to what is reasonable. Is this an amount similar to the original fee or some percentage of the current subscription fee? And will it be calculated the same way, based on FTE or number of subscribers ("Chargeable Users")? This provision contains too many monetary uncertainties as written. Since this right is part of the agreement, the licensee might be led to believe that this continuation right is built into the original fee structure. Not so, as the licensor can decide when to charge it. There should be some identified triggers as to when this could be imposed (e.g., costs rise beyond a certain percentage of current charges) and how much it would be (e.g., "in no event shall the post expiry or termination annual access fee be greater than 20 percent of the highest annual fee paid during any previous Supply Period," or words to that effect). Another hidden result is that the licensor may be able to pull back content from continuation access arrangement. So in this respect the continuation arrangement is less like a purchase or acquisition. Again, the point is that if the licensee bargained for continuation rights, the licensee may not have those rights to the extent it believed originally it possessed (e.g., "due to rights restrictions it may only be possible to allow access to the C Content and/or the F Content via the Network for a limited period or not at all"). Should this occur, the licensee will receive a copy "in a physical storage media." The agreement does not define what this is. Does paper count? Use of the word "media" suggests it does not, but it could still be some sort of analog storage (e.g., on tape). Or is it desirable to have the content in a digital form? If so, this should be made explicit and subject to the request or option of the licensee or perhaps cued to the then-current (at the time of delivery) industry standard for storage. It also important to note that such media may be subject to additional terms (the "media license"), which if in conflict with the terms of the original agreement take precedence and supersede the original terms: "SUBJECT ALWAYS to the Licensee's compliance with the terms of any additional license terms notified to the Licensee on delivery of the Media ... the terms of the

(continued)

Terms of the Nature (Academic: Americas) License	Comments on the Terms of the Nature (Academic: Americas) License
(the "Media") to the Licensee SUBJECT ALWAYS to the Licensee's compliance with the terms of any additional license terms notified to the Licensee on delivery of the Media (the "Media License") that are appropriate for such physical media (for the avoidance of doubt, in respect of the use of the Media and the C Content and/or F content by the Licensee the terms of the Media License shall prevail over the terms of this Agreement if there is a conflict or other inconsistency) and payment of such reasonable supply fee as Licensor may from time to time charge to cover its handling costs (or such alternative supply arrangement terms and costs as the parties may agree) (the **Post Supply License**"). For the avoidance of doubt, the Post Supply License shall not include access to any Licensed Material published prior to the Supply Period to which access may have been granted during the Supply Period.	Media License shall prevail over the terms of this Agreement if there is a conflict or other inconsistency." There could be additional fees associated with the delivery of the physical storage media as well: "and payment of such reasonable supply fee as Licensor may from time to time charge to cover its handling costs (or such alternative supply arrangement terms and costs as the parties may agree)." Again, the same concerns regarding the payment of a continuation fee apply to the "reasonable supply fee" as well. Will the fee apply in the case of all content delivered in physical storage media? If not, what is a reasonable trigger, and how will the reasonableness of the fee be determined—tied to an industry standard, perhaps? The provision contemplates a subsequent agreement, the so-labeled Post Supply License, which of course would require review before assent. This continued-access right does not apply if the agreement is terminated as a result of the licensor giving notice to the licensee under ¶ 4.2 (where the licensee is in material breach), ¶ 4.3 (a "because the licensor felt like it" termination), or ¶ 4.5 (where the licensee is bankrupt or in similar financial straits): "otherwise than as a result of notice being given by the Licensor under Clause 4.2, 4.3 or 4.5." Because of this loophole, a wily licensor knowing that it could not continue to offer the content added during a Supply Period might choose to terminate under ¶ 4.3 and, under ¶ 4.6, avoid any continuation obligations, including delivery of the "physical storage media." Of course, it is unreasonable to expect the licensor to supply content that it no longer possesses the legal right to provide, but the point is that if those access rights were obtained in consideration of fees, surrender of rights, or assumption obligations (i.e., things of value), and this access right is no longer available, then the licensee has obtained nothing of value from the licensor for the considerations of value it did render. The content to which continued access exists is found in various schedules of the original agreement. Notice that this continuation right or Post Supply License does not apply to content already in the database at the time of initial agreement nor added after the agreement ended but only that content added during the subscription period (the "Supply Period"), even if during the agreement access was available to it: "shall not include access to any Licensed Material published prior to the Supply Period to which access may have been granted during the Supply Period." If the licensee is willing to pay additional access fees from time to time as the licensor sees fit to charge ("may from time to time charge") because the licensee considers the content valuable and necessary but cannot access future content (added after the expiry or

(continued)

Terms of the Nature (Academic: Americas) License	Comments on the Terms of the Nature (Academic: Americas) License
	termination), then the licensee might consider simply extending the agreement through renewal to ensure access to this content, depending on a comparison of the renewal fee versus the "reasonable supply fee . . . or such alternative supply arrangement." To make this assessment, one would need to obtain, and so should ask for, three pieces of information: first, a list of "reasonable annual access fee[s]" and "reasonable supply fee[s]" the licensor has charged "from time to time" to other licensees; second, any subsequent access agreements ("alternative supply arrangement terms and costs as the parties may agree"); finally, where delivery of "physical storage media" was made, any examples of the Post Supply License that governed such transfers. If it no longer believes this content to be of value and chooses not to renew the agreement, then it is unclear why the licensee should be expected to pay for continued access to content it no longer deems necessary.
4.7. Without prejudice to any other rights the Licensor may have, the Licensor may suspend the provision of the Licensed Material to the Licensee with immediate effect on written notice without liability if the Licensor believes the Licensed Material is being used in a manner that contravenes the provisions of this Agreement or the Media License or in the event of delay or failure to pay in accordance with clause 5.	So much for the language in the other termination provisions of ¶ 4 regarding written notice and 30 days to cure—under this provision there is no cure right as well as no refund right (see ¶ 4.4 articulating the provisions under which a refund operates). It is difficult to figure how use of the licensed content "used in a manner that contravenes the provisions" is different from use of content that is prohibited under the agreement or is outside the permitted uses and would constitute a breach under ¶ 4.8, or perhaps a material one as well under ¶ 4.2. However, the impact here is different, as ¶ 4.7 refers to a suspension (for which there would be no refund) and not a termination (which in some cases qualifies the licensee to a refund). This provision applies, however, to a subset of potential material breaches: conduct that involves use of the licensed content not in accordance with the terms of use. (While nonpayment is a material breach under ¶ 4.2, is it a breach unrelated to use of the licensed content?) However, this provision also indicates that suspension can occur "in the event of delay or failure to pay in accordance with clause 5," where payment is due "within 30 days of the date of invoice." Yet under ¶ 4.2 a material breach includes nonpayment ("for the avoidance of doubt non-payment of any fees as they fall due under this Agreement by the Licensee shall constitute a material breach"). Of course, this provision allows, short of termination, the licensor to suspend service. While "breach" is a concept discussed in numerous court cases, the concept of "contravention" is not. It would be useful to define how contravention differs from breach. On the other hand, if breach is subsumed under contravention

(continued)

Terms of the Nature (Academic: Americas) License	Comments on the Terms of the Nature (Academic: Americas) License
	then, for example, where a licensee is "mak[ing] the Licensed Material, or any element of it, available by any means to persons other than Authorized Users" in "contravention" of ¶ 3(b) or the licensee fails to pay in accordance with ¶ 5, the licensor could under ¶ 4.7 suspend service while at the same time file notice of termination under ¶ 4.2, for which no refund is allowed. Taken together, one could argue that the two provisions equate more or less to a right of automatic termination (while suspension takes effect immediately, notices are effective "within 48 hours after posting") on the part of the licensor. The same argument of overlap could be made regarding the general breach provision of ¶ 4.8. Again, the difference here is in result, that is, suspension, not termination. If the library is unsuccessful in striking this provision, suspension should at least be conditioned upon notice (effective upon receipt, not 48 hours after posting), with perhaps a shorter period of imposition, such as five business days, and with a right to cure still available within that shorter time frame. Otherwise this provision operates as a penalty: "While you're not in breach, we don't like the way you're using our product so we're suspending service." Further, there is no indication of when or how the service is to be restored (i.e., the suspension lifted). Otherwise, the impact on the licensee and its patrons, constituents, and so forth, could be disastrous (e.g., access to the licensed content suddenly suspended during finals week). Moreover, any right to suspend should be based on a good faith or objective standard and not the subjective ("Licensor believes") standard of the provision as written. In the copyright law, it is common to include a subjective as well as an objective standard and the same might be incorporated here, for example, 17 U.S.C. § 504(c)(2): "infringer believed and had reasonable grounds for believing." Finally, the concept of contravention might be interpreted to be broader than an actual violation of a term to reach conduct that is contrary to the spirit of a provision as opposed to deviation from the actual letter of a provision. And since there appears no limit on the duration of the suspension, it could be argued that this provision actually appears to contravene the essence of ¶ 4.2 and ¶ 4.8 (i.e., terminate only after the period of cure has passed).
4.8. The Licensor may terminate this Agreement (including the Post Supply License) at any time upon written notice to the Licensee if the Licensee commits	Under ¶ 4.2, either party could terminate with notice if either thought the other was in material breach; and if the licensor was at fault (i.e., the licensee sent a notice if its intent to terminate), the licensee could request a refund. Under this provision, the licensor alone can terminate for any breach, even a Agreement or

(continued)

Terms of the Nature (Academic: Americas) License	Comments on the Terms of the Nature (Academic: Americas) License thirty days after receipt of written notice unless, in the a
breach of any term of this case of a remediable default, during the relevant period of thirty days the Licensee has remedied the default.	the Media License. The termination will become effective nonmaterial breach. While the notice of termination is subject to a 30-day cure period, during which time the licensee has the opportunity to cure, there is no right to refund per ¶ 4.4 (in contrast to the refund provision of ¶ 4.4 and like the termination by the licensor for material breach of the licensee under ¶ 4.2). As indicated under the cure proviso of ¶ 4.2, there is no direction as to how a fix or cure is to be communicated and the standards under which satisfaction of cure is made. Language could be inserted that notice of cure is effective upon sending, must be acknowledged, and must be to the mutual and reasonable satisfaction of both parties. First, the licensee should also have the right to terminate for breach by the licensor. If the contract ends due to the exercise of termination rights, then in any case, and especially where under a revised ¶ 4.8 the licensor is in breach, the licensee should receive a refund.
4.9. On termination of the Supply Period as a result of notice being given by the Licensor under Clause 4.2, 4.3 or 4.5 or on termination of the Post Supply License as a result of notice being given by the Licensor under Clause 4.8, the Licensee shall have no further rights of any kind in the Licensed Material and the Licensee agrees to destroy and use its best endeavours [sic] to procure that all Authorized Users destroy, all Licensed Material stored on its Network or in CD-ROM or other hard copy form both on paper and in any digital information storage media or other physical media storage, including, but not limited to, system servers, hard disks, diskettes, and backup tapes.	If the licensor terminates because it believes the licensee is in material breach (¶ 4.2), the licensor feels like terminating (¶ 4.3), or the licensee is going bankrupt (¶ 4.5) or is in a continuation arrangement (a Post Supply License) and the licensor believes the licensee is in breach (¶ 4.8), then all bets are off; in other words, there are no further continuation rights. Worse, the licensee agrees to use its best efforts to destroy and have its authorized users destroy "all Licensed Material stored on its Network or in CD-ROM or other hard copy form both on paper and in any digital information storage media or other physical media storage, including, but not limited to, system servers, hard disks, diskettes, and backup tapes." This is quite a task! It might be more reasonable to indicate what conduct satisfies the "best endeavours" obligation. It is also unclear if "best endeavours" is meant to express the concept of "best efforts" as opposed to a lesser standard of "reasonable efforts." Does the licensor expect the licensee to treat noncompliance by an authorized user the same as a deviation from a work rule or student code of conduct? Or is a more reasonable response one where destruction will occur when it knows or has reason to know the content exists, or that the licensee will send out several notices of such requests once a week for a period of six weeks after termination? On the other hand, why is the licensee asked to do this at all? The right of users to obtain a copy for various uses is granted in ¶ 2. Why must this right in essence be given back, even in situations where the licensee is in material breach or bankrupt?

(continued)

Terms of the Nature (Academic: Americas) License	Comments on the Terms of the Nature (Academic: Americas) License
4.10. When calculating the reasonable annual access fee payable by the Licensee pursuant to clause 4.6 the Licensor shall be entitled to increase such fee on an annual basis including but not limited to reflect any increase in the number of Chargeable Users, any change in the business of the Licensee or any increase in supply or other costs incurred by the Licensor.	**4.10.** When calculating the reasonable annual access fee This provision logically indicates that because the annual fee is based upon FTE or "Chargeable Users," should the number of users increase, the annual fee will also increase. What is oddly missing is what happens if the number of FTE or "Chargeable Users" decreases? It would be expected that the annual fee would then decrease, but this is not explicit. Though the licensee might expect this to occur (and the licensor might agree to make this adjustment as well), the right to a decrease would not be enforceable under the terms of the agreement as written. It would be better to have a clause that indicates the annual fee for the upcoming academic year will be adjusted to reflect the actual FTE or "Chargeable Users" reported in the previous academic year or to reflect current FTE or "Chargeable Users" at the time of initiation and each subsequent renewal. Also, in the provision, it is the right of the licensor to increase the annual fee for other reasons as well ("the Licensor shall be entitled to increase such fee on an annual basis *including but not limited to*"). The additional reasons for increase should be articulated or at least subject to the mutual agreement of both parties. While it can be expected that prices would rise from year to year, the point is that this provision allows the licensor to do this unilaterally. The licensee has either to accept the increase or consider nonrenewal. It is argued that price is one of three most important or material terms of a content agreement (along with knowing what content is licensed and what can or cannot be done with the content so licensed). A contemplated increase in price should be conditioned upon adequate notice, the opportunity to negotiate with the option not to renew should an acceptable price not be mutually agreed upon. Further, the provision says nothing of decreases in chargeable users of supply or other costs. Finally, why are the changes in business circumstances subject to a right of adjustment, and what are such changes? Suppose the annual revenue and thus profits of the licensor decrease because licensees are finding the provisions of its license too onerous. Does this trigger a right of the licensor to increase your fee to offset these losses? Going from the black into the red would certainly be a change in the business of the licensor. Such changes should be described and a triggering threshold articulated, or the proviso should be removed. Taking into account these considerations, a revised provision might read: "When calculating the reasonable annual access fee payable by the Licensee pursuant to clause 4.6 the Licensor shall adjust such fee based on the following: any change in the number of Chargeable Users, any change in supply or other costs incurred by the Licensor or when agreed upon both parties, upon a change in other circumstance."

(continued)

Terms of the Nature (Academic: Americas) License	Comments on the Terms of the Nature (Academic: Americas) License
5. LICENSE FEE. **5.1.** The Licensee agrees to pay to the Licensor the License Fee and any other payments under this Agreement within 30 days of the date of invoice.	The initial license fee and subsequent renewals, or perhaps a continuation fee or transfer cost of the "physical storage media" under ¶ 4.6 ("payment of such reasonable annual access fee as Licensor may from time to time charge"), are due 30 days after invoice. Since ¶ 4.2 indicates that nonpayment within the allotted time is a material breach, triggering termination and suspension rights, it may be wise in terms of renewal to indicate either a date earlier than which the renewal invoice cannot be sent or for renewals to indicate a different due date (30 days before the end of the current fee period), regardless of when the licensor sends the notice. Otherwise, the licensor could in theory send the renewal notice three months in advance of the renewal date, but the licensee would be obligated to pay the fee two months in advance of the renewal date (or 30 days after invoice). Moreover, it is unclear whether the date of the invoice is on the date sent (a mailbox rule), perhaps falling under the notice rules of ¶ 11, or is effective upon receipt. It is also assumed the counting days are calendar days and not weekdays or business days. If the invoice is considered a "notice" under the agreement, then ¶ 11 clarifies that indeed a mailbox rule or at least a modified mailbox rule is in effect; any notice sent is deemed received 48 hours after posting regardless of when actually received or read by the licensee. Since nonpayment can trigger material breach and suspension, it might be best to adopt a "notice effective upon acknowledged receipt" rule.
5.2. All amounts payable by the Licensee under this Agreement shall be exclusive of any sales, use, value added or similar taxes.	Fees due under the agreement are exclusive of any tax.
6. NATURE, NPG JOURNALS, AND/OR THIRD-PARTY JOURNALS, PALGRAVE MACMILLAN JOURNALS AND/OR PALGRAVE MACMILLAN THIRD PARTY JOURNALS LICENSE FEE (NOT APPLICABLE TO NEWS). **6.1** Where the Licensed Material includes **Nature, NPG Journals,** and/or **Third-Party Journals, Palgrave Macmillan Journals** and/or **Palgrave Macmillan Third Party Journals** elements	Paragraph 4.10 also made reference to "Chargeable Users" and the annual fee calculation, that is, a possible fee increase due to an increase in Chargeable Users. This provision reiterates this calculation but adds that the licensee "warrants" that the number of chargeable users is what the licensee said it was, or at least that the number has not exceeded what it said it was: "warrants that its Chargeable Users during the 12 months prior to the Commencement Date did not exceed the number of Chargeable Users as stated in the Schedule." The significance of a warranty is that it is a promise, not a condition (for which nonperformance would be an available response).

(continued)

Terms of the Nature (Academic: Americas) License	Comments on the Terms of the Nature (Academic: Americas) License
the License Fee is calculated on the basis of Chargeable Users. The Licensee warrants that its Chargeable Users during the 12 months prior to the Commencement Date did not exceed the number of Chargeable Users as stated in the Schedule in respect of **Nature, NPG Journals** and/or **Third-Party Journals, Palgrave Macmillan Journals** and/or **Palgrave Macmillan Third Party Journals**.	
6.2. The License Fee is assessed on the number of the Licensee's Chargeable Users during the 12 month period prior to the Commencement Date for the initial 12 month period of the Supply Period and for each 12 month period prior to any subsequent 12 month extensions agreed to by the Licensor. The Licensee must immediately notify the Licensor if at any time the actual number of Chargeable Users exceeds the number of Chargeable Users stated in the Schedule. The Licensee acknowledges that in the event that such number of Chargeable Users increases during the initial 12 month period of the Supply Period or in any subsequent 12 month extension period agreed to by the Licensor the License Fee will be increased in accordance with the Licensee's then applicable charges for any subsequent 12 month extension period agreed to by the Licensor.	The fee is calculated by multiplying a base rate or figure by the number of chargeable users. The counting period is the year prior to initiation or renewal. It is understandable that the licensor desires the fee to accurately reflect the actual number of users, but this desire cuts both ways. The licensee would not want to overpay. If there is an increase, the "Licensee must immediately notify the Licensor if at any time the actual number of Chargeable Users exceeds the number of Chargeable Users stated in the Schedule." Why? Oddly, there is no provision directing the current fee to then be adjusted upward; rather, the future fee would be so adjusted: "the License Fee will be increased in accordance with the Licensee's then applicable charges for any subsequent 12 month extension period agreed to by the Licensor." The licensor may require such reporting so that when it sends a renewal invoice it can reflect the then-current number that is used to calculate the renewal fee. Likewise, in ¶ 4.10, the licensor can increase the fee if the number increases, but neither there nor here is an accommodation should there be basis for decrease in the fee. As in ¶ 4.10, there should be provision for the downward adjustment of the fee due to a decrease in the chargeable users as well. Also, a better mechanism for reporting increases (and decreases if the provision is added) should be considered, as enrollments (admissions, withdrawals, etc.) may come and go and changes in employment occur. One option would be to indicate the upcoming fee should reflect the current number of chargeable users at the time of receipt (or payment) of the invoice, the number to be reflected by the licensee on the return (payment) of the invoice. If the licensor desires to be informed of changes in the number of chargeable users throughout the year, a different trigger than "any time the actual number of Chargeable Users exceeds the number

(continued)

Terms of the Nature (Academic: Americas) License	Comments on the Terms of the Nature (Academic: Americas) License
	of Chargeable Users." A better trigger would be to offer quarterly or term (spring, summer, and fall semester enrollments) reports or indicate that a report of change is due if it represents a change of 5 percent or more from the figure reported in the invoice payment.
7. LICENSEE'S UNDERTAKINGS. **7.1.** The Licensee will take all reasonable steps to ensure that the Licensed Material is used only in accordance with the terms and conditions of this Agreement and shall inform Authorized Users of the permitted use restrictions and other provisions set out in this Agreement.	The licensee agreeing to the terms as presented commits to a number of obligations or "undertakings," some of which may be challenging to fulfill or which the licensee may not wish to fulfill. Under this provision the licensee must inform all authorized users of the "use restrictions and other provisions" of the agreement and take "all reasonable" steps to ensure compliance with the terms of the agreement by authorized users. "Reasonable steps" does not have legal meaning, as would the phrase "reasonable efforts"—though perhaps this is intentional here. Further, any such notice delivered or disseminated to authorized users as well as other efforts at compliance should also stress the permitted uses. It might be desirable to articulate what the respective parties understand by the phrase "all reasonable steps." Other than providing notice ("shall inform") and other information outreach, it is unclear what else the licensee should be doing to accomplish this. What are the scope, the form, and the frequency of the required informing? Must the entire agreement be made available? Is a binder behind the reference desk or a webpage of all license agreements sufficient? What other steps are contemplated by the licensor? Considering the number of agreements with similar requirements that might be in effect, short of creating some sort of spreadsheet of permitted and prohibited uses and alerting users to this information, it is difficult to fathom what more proactive measures could be undertaken other than general awareness. Perhaps a comment in the employee and student code of conduct handbook or network acceptable use policy (AUP) that a violation of said terms (with link to the full agreement or spreadsheet summary of the restrictions and permitted uses) would suffice, or perhaps a similar prompt on the login screen to the database portal or access screen to where detailed information is available. A click-to-agree prompt could be included to the effect that "Yes, I have read the terms and conditions, and I agree to abide by the restrictions as well as permitted uses governing my access to this database." It could be made clear that deviation is subject to the same processes and discipline as other policy violations. However, short of actual monitoring or use of some technological means to achieve compliance, it is unclear what might constitute such reasonable steps.

(continued)

Terms of the Nature (Academic: Americas) License	Comments on the Terms of the Nature (Academic: Americas) License
7.2. The Licensee shall put into place reasonable procedures to monitor the compliance with the terms and conditions of this Agreement by the Authorized Users.	Here it is! This provision requires monitoring in some form. Although the provision does not indicate that the monitoring must be real-person, real-time (i.e., looking over the shoulders of users oversight). Monitoring technology similar to that which might be used, for example, to detect and curb copyright infringement over peer-to-peer networks would appear a reasonable procedure. Again, beyond such automatic processes of awareness or short of actual notice of noncompliance discovered in the course of routine business, it would be unwieldy to promise more. Such monitoring can easily lead to compounding problems regarding patron privacy, not to mention the efficacy of fulfilling such promises, as discussed in greater detail in other licenses in this chapter and in Chapter 14.
7.3. The Licensee will notify the Licensor immediately of infringements that come to the Licensee's notice and the Licensee agrees to co-operate with the Licensor as appropriate to stop further abuse should it occur.	The standard for contributory liability under the copyright law is knowing or having reason to know, and not a "should know" standard. As a result, the licensee should not be required to do more. This provision reflects no more than this and arguably less, as its trigger is actual knowledge. Once "infringements" are known ("come to the Licensee's notice"), the licensee must notify the licensor of the event and cooperate with the licensor "as appropriate" to stop it. However, since the licensee agreed to monitor in ¶ 7.2, it is far more likely that increased knowledge of abuse will occur, triggering the reporting obligation here. It is only natural that the licensor now desires to know if the licensee has discovered any noncompliance—first, because the licensor might want to assess the level of licensee effort put forth under ¶ 7.1 and ¶ 7.2 and, second, because the licensor might find the abuse so egregious that the licensor now wants the licensee to identify the offending person in order to commence legal proceedings against him or her. (The privacy issues related to such a sequence of events have been discussed in reviews of other license agreements.) The use of the word "infringements" is an odd choice, as the license terms prohibit more than just copyright or trademark infringement. Therefore, it could be interpreted that only noncompliance with terms of the agreement which also constitutes copyright infringement need be reported. This may not be what the licensor intends, but this is what the words suggest. The reporting burden is not present in current copyright law, either by the courts or under the codification of secondary liability processes under § 512. True, an obligation to respond is required (i.e., to undertake measures to end the known or discovered infringement), but there is no obligation to then report such incidents to the copyright owner. This obligation should not be entered into lightly, not only for the subsequent issues that such reporting can raise but also

(continued)

Terms of the Nature (Academic: Americas) License	Comments on the Terms of the Nature (Academic: Americas) License
	for the increased administrative burden. Reporting should be at the option of the licensee if, for example, the licensor could help in curbing an egregious or pervasive problem of abuse.
7.4. Subject to Clause 4.9, nothing in this Agreement shall make the Licensee liable for breach of the restrictions set out in the terms and conditions of this Agreement by any Authorized User as long as the Licensee complied with the terms of Clauses 6, 7.1, 7.2 and 7.3 and did not cause, intentionally assist in or encourage such breach nor allowed it to continue after having received notice of such breach whether from the Licensor or otherwise. However, in the event of continuing abuse the Licensor shall be entitled to terminate this Agreement.	Assuming the licensee reported the proper number of chargeable users under ¶ 6, notified users of the license terms, and undertook reasonable steps to ensure compliance by users under ¶ 7.1, including monitoring under ¶ 7.2 or where termination occurred (subject to ¶ 4.9)—that is, as a result of termination by the licensor under ¶ 4.2 (material breach by licensee), ¶ 4.3 (at the whim of the licensor), ¶ 4.5 (bankruptcy or similar strait of the licensee), or ¶ 4.8 (breach by the licensor)—but the licensee undertook efforts to ensure destruction of the licensed content remaining in its possession or in the possession of users, then the licensee is not liable for a breach of the terms by users. However, the licensee must not have caused, intentionally assisted, or encouraged the breach, or, once aware of such breach, failed to intercede to stop such continued breach. This provision, subject to the additional conditions of those provisions noted previously, adopts, as did ¶ 7.3, an actual knowledge standard into the agreement. Observe that the knowledge of the breach could come from the licensor, another user, or a licensee-employee. The provision does not, however, adopt the "reason to know" standard of contributory liability but instead appears to rely on actual knowledge or awareness. The last sentence appears to suggest that where the licensee is not contributing to the breach (i.e., the licensee did not "cause, intentionally assist in, or encourage such breach nor allowed it to continue after having received notice") but repeat episodes of abuse continue to arise, the licensor may terminate. This would require increased vigilance on the part of the licensee and would allow termination where the licensor, after a number of abuses, is convinced that the licensee is simply not a good risk and desires the right to terminate. However, use of the word "continuing" ("in the event of continuing abuse") might suggest reference to a specific event and its continuation as opposed to a general climate of repeated but discrete breaches. Because of the impact of such breaches, clarifying when the termination right exists is prudent.
7.5. The Licensor shall be entitled to monitor the use of the Licensed Material through the Licensor's servers, or as the case may be any service provided by an agent on its	The licensor is allowed to monitor activity of authorized users through its servers. or if the licensor uses a third party to host its content, the third party may monitor on its behalf. If the licensor or its agent will be collecting information that would tie a specific user to the subject matter of an inquiry, then the licensor should be obligated to keep such information confidential and held to at

(continued)

Terms of the Nature (Academic: Americas) License	Comments on the Terms of the Nature (Academic: Americas) License
behalf, so as to monitor compliance with this Agreement.	least the same restrictions relating to use of this information as is the library through its state law and any other policy the library adopted regarding patron privacy. Such information, if done by a patron in a state-supported or -funded library, from, say, a search of the library's online catalog, would likely be a protected record under most state library patron confidentiality statutes. (Again, see the detailed discussion of these issues in the reviews of previous license agreements.)
8. WARRANTIES, UNDERTAKINGS AND INDEMNITIES. 8.1. The Licensor warrants to the Licensee that it has full right and authority to grant the Rights to the Licensee and that the use by the Licensee of the Licensed Material in accordance with this Agreement will not infringe the rights of any third party.	This is a significant and necessary clause. The licensor promises that the licensed content it is making available to the licensee is that content to which it has the legal right to make available to the licensee, and under the terms of this license it is making that content available.
8.2. The Licensor shall indemnify the Licensee for the amount of any award of damages against the Licensee by a court of competent jurisdiction as a result of any claim arising from a breach of the warranty in Clause 8.1 provided that the Licensee must inform the Licensor immediately upon becoming aware of any claim, not attempt to compromise or settle the claim and give reasonable assistance to the Licensor who shall be entitled to assume sole conduct of any defence [*sic*] and shall have the right at its option: (a) to procure the right for the Licensee to continue using the Licensed Material; (b) to make such alterations, modifications or adjustments to the Licensed Material that it	Coupled with the previous provision, these are the two must-have provisions in any content license. A promise that the licensor possesses the right to make the licensed content available and under the terms so presented means little if there is no indemnification behind this promise. Here the licensor is indicating that if it turns out in the end that it did not have the right to make the licensed content available or to grant, for example, the right to use the content in "course study packs" under ¶ 2.1(d) and now the licensee is sued for copyright infringement by the copyright owner, the licensor is responsible for damages that might result from such a lawsuit. A provision for attorneys' fees should also be included. For the indemnification to operate, the licensee must notify the licensor "immediately upon becoming aware of any claim." The licensee and licensor are in essence in it together, sink or swim. Provision to make reasonable efforts to inform would be better. In addition, the licensee must in essence let the licensor take charge of the litigation and not try to settle, for example, in return for cooperating in litigation with the licensor. A better approach is to have settlement or other decision be made at least subject to mutual agreement. It is argued that the licensee should have this option, not the licensor, "as the Licensee cannot allow its business interest to be determined by the Licensor." See H. WARD CLASSEN, A PRACTICAL GUIDE TO SOFTWARE LICENSING FOR LICENSEES AND LICENSORS 335 (3d ed. 2008), suggesting use of the following sentence: "No settlement of claim will be binding on Licensee

(continued)

Terms of the Nature (Academic: Americas) License	Comments on the Terms of the Nature (Academic: Americas) License
becomes non-infringing without incurring a material reduction in performance or function; or (c) to replace the Licensed Material with non-infringing substitutes provided that such substitutes do not entail a material reduction in performance or function.	without Licensee's prior written consent" (*id*. at 334). If such circumstances arise, the licensor has several options: negotiate for the use of the content to continue and, short of that, to replace the lost titles, items (articles), and so on, with substitutes or to delete the offending content ("alterations, modifications or adjustments to the Licensed Material that it becomes non-infringing"). First, any substitution right should be subject to the mutual but reasonable agreement of both the licensor and licensee (as there may be dispute whether the *Journal of Lunacy* really is an adequate substitute for *Idiots Quarterly*). Second, the concepts of deletions and substitutions "without incurring a material reduction in performance or function" should be further defined, as it appears to combine mismatched concepts. If the reality is that some titles, items (articles), and so on, will no longer be available, it is difficult to see how this would impact performance or function in a technical sense in which these concepts are most commonly considered other than to say, "The database doesn't perform as well because I can't find any articles from *ABC Journal* anymore" or similar characterization. Rather, "material reduction" should be defined by numbers, percentages, specific "must-have" titles, or some discrete trigger or discernible event, or a dispute may again arise in interpretation. Such reduction (see discussion under ¶ 8.7) should be dependent upon adequate notice to the licensee and should come with a termination right or a refund right, if there is material reduction either qualitatively and quantitatively in the licensed content available, or should the parties be unable to agree on a substitute. It is also odd that the right to make alterations, modifications, adjustments, or replacement is conditioned on no "material reduction in performance or function," as this phrase would more properly belong in a license for software, for a product that is supposed to do something, not in a license for an information database. True, the software that underlies the user interface might fall into this category; but there should be some measure included where the alterations, modifications, adjustments, or replacements are of the content itself. In other words, the provision should indicate which "alterations, modifications, adjustments, or replacements" to content are permissible or capable of "fix" and which are not. Further, a final option, again at the discretion of the licensee, should be to terminate and obtain a full refund. Actually, the licensor should welcome this option or it might otherwise be obligated to provide a "fix" regardless of cost. See H. WARD CLASSEN, A PRACTICAL GUIDE TO SOFTWARE LICENSING FOR LICENSEES AND LICENSORS 334 (3d ed. 2008). The paragraph fails to indicate what will

(continued)

Terms of the Nature (Academic: Americas) License	Comments on the Terms of the Nature (Academic: Americas) License
	result if the licensee fails to notify or provide reasonable assistance or does attempt to compromise or settle. The intent may be to then release the licensor from its obligation to indemnify, but the provision does not state this result. If this is the intent, then any revised indemnification paragraph should condition release of that obligation only where such failure or other conduct materially prejudices the licensor's ability to defend such claim.
8.3. The Licensor shall not be liable to the Licensee for any loss or damage whatsoever resulting from omissions or inaccuracies in the Licensed Material regardless of how caused. The Licensor does not warrant that access to the Licensed Material will be free from errors or faults. In the event of a fault, the Licensee shall notify Customer Support of the same by telephone, electronic mail or in writing.	This is a common and, from the licensor's perspective, necessary provision, as it would indeed be unreasonable to expect a promise that the information contained in the licensed content is free from all error. However, if errors are discovered, the licensee must ("shall") report the error to the licensor by phone, e-mail, or traditional post letter. While this might be a professional courtesy, and will only make the licensed content more useable in the future, this is not the licensee's responsibility and it is unclear why it should be required here.
8.4. Without prejudice to the generality of the foregoing, the Licensor shall not be liable for any claim arising from: (a) any failure or malfunction resulting wholly or to any material extent from the Licensee's negligence, operator error, use other than in accordance with the User Documentation or any other misuse or abuse of the Licensed Materials; (b) the failure by the Licensee to implement recommendations previously advised by the Licensor in respect of, or solutions for, faults in the Licensed Material; or (c) the decompilation or modification of the	Damages resulting from liability are limited in a paragraph titled "liability" (¶ 12), but the liability itself is limited here ("the Licensor shall not be liable") under a general paragraph titled "warranties, undertakings, and indemnities." Clause (a) states that the licensor will not be responsible for problems with use of the licensed content that are due to the fault of the licensee, such as "negligence, operator error," or use in contradiction of the directions ("User Documentation") or terms of the agreement ("any other misuse or abuse of the Licensed Materials"). If the licensee uses the help desk to obtain customer support (see ¶ 1.1: "'Customer Support': the Helpdesk (as set out in the Schedule) providing reasonable e-mail and telephone support") and the licensee fails to implement the recommendations, then the licensor is not responsible either. Decompilation, modification, merger, repair, adjustment, alteration, or enhancement—all are arguably prohibited under clause (f) ("alter, amend, modify, translate, or change the Licensed Material") and (j) ("make mass, automated or systematic extractions from or hard copy storage of the Licensed Material") of ¶ 3.0 already. Here, clause (c) states that the licensor is again not responsible for any problems that might result from such tinkering with the licensed content. Under clause (d), unless the downtime exceeds

(continued)

Terms of the Nature (Academic: Americas) License	Comments on the Terms of the Nature (Academic: Americas) License
Licensed Material or its merger with any other program or any maintenance repair adjustment alteration or enhancement of the Licensed Material by any person other than the Licensor or its authorized agent; or (d) the Licensee or any Authorized User being unable to exercise the Rights due to the Licensed Material being unavailable as a result of any act or omission of the Licensor provided that the period for which the Licensed Material is not available shall not exceed a period of 50 hours (in aggregate) in any continuous period of 1000 hours.	50 hours in a continuous 1,000-hour period or 5 percent, the licensor is not liable if the licensed content is "unavailable as a result of any act or omission of the Licensor." However, why a continuous period of a little over four days (4.16) days is used is unclear. What if the licensed content is unavailable every other month for two days? This would not trigger the proviso but would still represent a significant amount of time over the period of a year. Again, any aggregated downtime should be compensable, as a credit or refund at the option of the licensee, with the latter preferred.
8.5. The Licensee shall use its best efforts to safeguard the intellectual property, confidential information including without limitation the terms of this Agreement, and proprietary rights of the Licensor.	It is not uncommon for business-to-business agreements to contain language that requires a party to protect from disclosure, for example, the trade secrets to which in the course of the relationship the other party is exposed or is given access. However, the problem here is that the provision is very vague. While intellectual property might be known to include copyright, trademark, patent, and trade secret, it is unclear what sort of information would constitute confidential and proprietary information. There should be a requirement that the licensor at least describe the sorts of information which the licensor desires to be so treated by the licensee and some indication of what best efforts entail, as the licensee may not be prepared or experienced with the standards that the business community employs to protect such information ("best efforts") and the expectation is what is reasonable for a similarly situated library-licensee.
8.6. THE LICENSED MATERIAL IS PROVIDED "AS IS." NEITHER THE LICENSOR NOR ANYONE ELSE MAKES ANY WARRANTIES OF ANY KIND, EITHER EXPRESS OR IMPLIED, INCLUDING, BUT NOT LIMITED TO, WARRANTIES OF SATISFACTORY QUALITY,	These are warranties that many states require conspicuous language to waive, thus the all capital letters. Under UCC § 2-316(3)(a), an "as is" warranty generally means that the item is sold in its present condition and that it may contain faults. See also BLACK'S LAW DICTIONARY (9th ed.) (Bryan A. Garner ed., St. Paul, MN: West Publishing, 2009) (no pagination in Westlaw), where an "as is" warranty is "[a] warranty that goods are sold with all existing faults." The next sentence reiterates that no warranties, express or

(continued)

Terms of the Nature (Academic: Americas) License	Comments on the Terms of the Nature (Academic: Americas) License
ACCURACY OR FITNESS FOR A PARTICULAR PURPOSE. EXCEPT AS OTHERWISE EXPRESSLY PROVIDED IN THIS CLAUSE 8 AND CLAUSE 12, ALL CONDITIONS, WARRANTIES, TERMS, REPRESENTATIONS, AND UNDERTAKINGS EXPRESS OR IMPLIED, STATUTORY OR OTHERWISE IN RESPECT OF THE LICENSED MATERIAL ARE TO THE FULLEST EXTENT PERMITTED BY LAW EXPRESSLY EXCLUDED. NO ORAL OR WRITTEN INFORMATION OR ADVICE GIVEN BY ANY REPRESENTATIVE OF THE LICENSOR OR BY ANYONE ELSE SHALL CREATE ANY WARRANTIES.	implied, are given by the licensor, except those offered elsewhere in ¶ 8 or in ¶ 12 relating to the liability and damages for which the licensor is still held. The inclusion of warranties includes warranties of satisfactory quality and accuracy or fitness for a particular purpose. An "implied warranty of fitness for a particular purpose" is a warranty [that is] implied by law if the seller has reason to know of the buyer's special purposes for the property—that the property is suitable for those purposes" (*id.*). A more general warranty that the product is fit to be sold is an implied warranty of merchantability, that is, a "warranty that the property is fit for the ordinary purposes for which it is used" (*id.*). A warranty of satisfactory quality is an "implied condition in every contract of sale (unless expressly excluded) that goods being sold would meet reasonable requirements or standards in terms of appearance, durability, fitness for use, freedom from material defects, safety in use, etc." (from BusinessDictionary.com, http://www.businessdictionary.com/definition/satisfactory-quality.html). Some licenses contain disclaimers of all three. Compare the disclaimer at issue in *Long v. Hewlett Packard Co.*, 2007 WL 2994812, *6 (N.D. Cal.) (unpublished): "TO THE EXTENT ALLOWED BY LOCAL LAW, THE ABOVE WARRANTIES ARE EXCLUSIVE AND NO OTHER WARRANTY OR CONDITION, WHETHER WRITTEN OR ORAL, IS EXPRESSED OR IMPLIED AND HP SPECIFICALLY DISCLAIMS ANY IMPLIED WARRANTIES OR CONDITIONS OF MERCHANTABILITY, SATISFACTORY QUALITY, AND FITNESS FOR A PARTICULAR PURPOSE." The final sentence indicates that no information whatsoever, whether in written form or oral, will give rise to any warranty. This would prevent the assertions made by the sales representative at the annual American Library Association conference that the licensed content would indeed "do Windows" or that "Yes, it does contain a full run of all titles ever published under the XYZ moniker" or that the schedule of updates listed in the documentation or brochures is written in stone or any other assertions made by the rep to get you to subscribe to the service.
8.7. The content of the Licensed Material is subject to change without notice.	This is an unreasonable clause. While it might be impractical for an aggregator licensor to anticipate changes in its legal relationship with its own vendors that might affect its ability to license content to licensees, it could nonetheless be argued that the makeup of the licensed content (i.e., the subject matter of the agreement) is a material term, a change to which would require notice and assent. The licensor would surely know of these changes itself, and it is not unreasonable to ask that the licensee be informed of such changes at least on a quarterly basis and,

(continued)

Terms of the Nature (Academic: Americas) License	Comments on the Terms of the Nature (Academic: Americas) License
	if substantial, going to the heart of the agreement, to have such changes trigger a termination right or at least a right to renegotiate a price if a reasonable substitute is not added. Such terms might be considered material. Perhaps the only or main reason for entering into the agreement was to have access to *ABC Journal* or the *XYZ* family of journals. If these titles are now no longer part of the licensed content available, the impact on the licensee is significant and it does go to the heart of the bargain, so to speak; it is material. The licensee should receive notice and have the opportunity to either terminate the agreement or continue but on condition that it receive a prorated refund in the percentage (in titles, items, i.e., individual articles) that the deletion represents to the initial total of titles, items, and so on, or some other price adjustment or credit. Of course, the licensor may then insist that as titles, items, and so on, are added a prorated increase should also occur. This is not the same. The loss of the key *ABC Journal* likely represents a greater value to the licensee than the addition of the *Journal of Useless Facts* to the licensor or licensee, for that matter. Second, the addition of new volumes as time moves forward is expected; it is the nature of serial subscriptions, unless of course the content agreement is for retrospective access alone. If the loss of some titles does not matter to the licensee, then no adjustment need be contemplated through the license terms, unless some percentage net-loss threshold is met. Otherwise, inclusion of a list of those "must-have" journals could be considered, triggering a termination or refund right or at least a substitution subject to the reasonable and mutual agreement of both parties. Nonetheless, notice of any changes would still be desirable from a courtesy (of the licensor) and customer service (to the licensee's users) perspective. It would not appear that requesting routine and quarterly updates, for example, of the licensed content would be unreasonable.
9. USAGE STATISTICS (RELEVANT TO NATURE, NPG JOURNALS, THIRD-PARTY JOURNALS, PALGRAVE MACMILLAN JOURNALS AND/OR PALGRAVE MACMILLAN THIRD PARTY JOURNALS AND NEWS). The Licensor confirms to the Licensee that usage statistics covering the online usage of Nature, NPG Journals, Third-Party	This provision indicates that usage statistics will be provided (the licensor "confirms"; it does not promise) by the licensor to the licensee for its "private internal use" alone. The second sentence makes reference to the COUNTER (Counting Online Usage of Networked Electronic Resources, http://www.projectcounter.org/code_practice.html) Code of Practice, making "all reasonable endeavours [*sic*] to" conform to such standards. Further, the "Licensor shall not be required to disclose any information to the Licensee which it is prohibited from disclosing to the Licensee due to any legal or regulatory constraint imposed upon it including without limitation any applicable privacy or data protection

(continued)

Terms of the Nature (Academic: Americas) License	Comments on the Terms of the Nature (Academic: Americas) License
Journals, Palgrave Macmillan Journals and/or Palgrave Macmillan Third Party Journals and News covered by this Agreement will be provided. The Licensor further confirms that it shall use all reasonable endeavours [*sic*] to ensure that such usage statistics will adhere to the specifications of the COUNTER Code of Practice, including data elements collected and their definitions; data processing guidelines, usage report content, frequency and delivery method PROVIDED THAT these statistics are strictly for the Licensee's private internal use and the Licensor shall not be required to disclose any information to the Licensee which it is prohibited from disclosing to the Licensee due to any legal or regulatory constraint imposed upon it including without limitation any applicable privacy or data protection legislation or regulations or contractual obligations.	legislation or regulations or contractual obligations." This is good, as there might be some statistics the licensor believes are proprietary and which would be subject to trade secret protection. This would in theory be interpreted as a legal constraint imposed upon it, albeit by its own legal counsel, or the legal constraint might come in the form of a contractual obligation with the owners of the "Third-Party Journals" it provides. If there were a clause in those contracts similar to ¶ 3(g) herein, and if for some reason the usage statistics indicate problems with the third-party journals, then revealing the statistics might impact the ability of the third party to generate revenue from the content it is licensing to the licensor (so it can license it to the licensee). This would be a qualifying legal constraint, one based in contract law. If the statement is intended to express the licensor's concern for the privacy of the licensee's users and personal data that such statistics might include, then the COUNTER Code of Practice may be insufficient, unless the licensor or any party with which it might also share such usage statistics is under similar constraints. Considering the nature of the licensed content, the reference is likely to the Code of Practice for Journals and Databases (Release 3, August 2008). One provision this code reflects is a concern for user privacy: "7.4.1. Privacy and user confidentiality. Statistical reports or data that reveal information about individual users will not be released or sold by vendors without the permission of that individual user, the consortium, and its member institutions (ICOLC Guidelines, October 2006)." Thus, personal information will not be sold or released without permission, but this suggests that the licensor might indeed possess such information or is able to generate it or collect it in the first place. The point is that the licensor might not be subject to other legal restraints regarding release of such information to the same extent a library funded in whole or in part with public funds might be, for example, subject to the relevant state library confidentiality statute. It might be desirable to request that the licensor comply with similar privacy guidelines that exist in the licensee's library patron confidentiality statute or to adhere to so-called Fair Information Practice Principles (available at the same extent a http://www.ftc.gov/reports/privacy3/fairinfo.shtm) that also include protocols for processing and retention as well as for collection, access, and dissemination. On the other hand, the licensor might be subject to other constraints that would restrict the statistics it could share with the licensee. The licensor may be subject to "data protection legislation," such as the Privacy Directive (Directive 95/46/EC of the European Parliament and of the Council of 24 October 1995),

(continued)

Terms of the Nature (Academic: Americas) License	Comments on the Terms of the Nature (Academic: Americas) License
	which provides a comprehensive scheme of protection regarding the collection and onward movement of personal information. It might be wise to review the COUNTER Code and related documentation to determine under which protocols the licensor would acquire, process, share, and so on, search and use data and if these protocols are sufficient; to consider what data the licensee would desire to receive; and to inquire if any other restraint or obligation (regulatory, contractual, etc.) would prevent the release of such information to the licensee.
10. FORCE MAJEURE. **10.1.** Either party's failure to perform any term or condition of this Agreement as a result of conditions beyond its control such as, but not limited to, war, strikes, floods, governmental restrictions, power failures, or damage or destruction of any network facilities or services, shall not be deemed a breach of this Agreement.	It is not uncommon to include language that excuses the non-performance of one party when the cause of the nonperformance is the result of a natural disaster or other significant event beyond the control of the party. Such provision is not made here. In fact, just opposite is the case, as the clause makes clear that such events do not constitute a breach of any sort, material or otherwise. The mere occurrence of such catastrophe does not trigger a termination right, as such is not considered a breach: "Either party's failure to perform any term or condition . . . shall not be deemed a breach of this Agreement." However, termination rights arise if the failure to perform an obligation persists as a result of force majeure for more than 30 days. Even if such force majeure does not trigger a termination right under ¶ 10.2, the licensee should not pay for service it does not receive, especially when the cause is not its fault. There should be a refund or credit at the option of the licensee. Likewise, if the disaster befell the licensee, then it would be obligated to pay for service which it could not use but which it did however receive. The purpose of a force majeure provision is to ensure that such suspension of service does not trigger a breach/termination right, but it should not also operate as a payment provision.
10.2. If any event set out in Clause 10.1 shall continue for a period in excess of 30 days either party shall be entitled to terminate this Agreement forthwith by written notice to the other.	Regardless to which party the unfortunate event befalls, either party may terminate "forthwith" upon "written notice to the other" if the ¶ 10.1 event persists for more than 30 days. Of course, the force majeure is different from the impact from this event, so it is unclear if the force majeure must exist for more than 30 days (e.g., the fire must burn, the storm must rage, etc., for more than 30 days). While the hurricane that befell New Orleans and its libraries did not last for more than 30 days, the flooding as well as the consequences of the storm persisted for a much longer period. But in other cases the power outage from, say, a tornado might last less than 48 hours, but the lightning strike and outage might have fried the servers, which are taking longer to restore. Such effects are assumed to be included. Observe that the list

(continued)

Terms of the Nature (Academic: Americas) License	Comments on the Terms of the Nature (Academic: Americas) License
	includes some human-made events, such as a labor strike. Some force majeure clauses restrict the list of events to those of nature ("acts of God") alone. It might make the provision more useful to indicate the "due to the occurrence of events beyond its control [i.e., the force majeure] or the impact of such events..." or words to that effect. Consider: "The parties' performance under this Agreement is subject to acts of God, war, government regulation, terrorism, disaster, strikes (except those involving the Hotel's employees or agents), civil disorder, curtailment of transportation facilities, or any other emergency beyond the parties' control, making it inadvisable, illegal, or impossible to perform their obligations under this Agreement. Either party may cancel this Agreement for any one or more of such reasons upon written notice to the other," from *OWBR LLC v. Clear Channel Communications, Inc.*, 266 F. Supp. 2d 1214, 1216 (D. Hawaii 2003). Recall from ¶ 4.4 that such termination is subject to a refund, however, if the event befell the licensor such that the licensed content was not available for 30 days and the licensee decided to terminate; it has been without the service for more than a "period of 50 hours (in aggregate) in any continuous period of 1000 hours" and thus would be able to make a claim under ¶ 8.4. It might be easier to indicate that loss of service under these circumstances is also subject to a refund or, in the alternative, through a revised downtime provision that all downtimes are, at the option of the licensee, subject to credit or refund (which in this case the licensee would choose).
11. NOTICE. Any notice to be served on either party by the other made under this Agreement shall be in writing sent by prepaid recorded delivery or registered post to the address of the addressee as set out in the Schedule or to such other address as notified by ether party to the other as its address for service of notices and all such notices shall be deemed to have been received within 48 hours after posting.	The provision is titled and uses the word "notice," as does the termination provisions of ¶ 4.2 (for material breach of either party), ¶ 4.3 (anytime by the licensor), ¶ 4.5 (bankruptcy or similar financial strait of either party), ¶ 4.7 (licensor believes the licensee is engaging in contravening conduct), or ¶ 4.8 (licensor believes the licensee is in breach). However, only in ¶ 4.2 and ¶ 4.8 does each respective provision indicate that receipt of the notice is effective upon receipt. In all other cases, the general rules of "notice" elucidated under this provision operate. It is unclear whether this provision applies to all correspondence between the parties or only those provisions which use the term "notice." For example, do the formalities apply to correspondence regarding fee payment, such as invoices? Since fees are due within 30 days of invoice, it might be desirable to define the date of invoice, that is, either under a somewhat modified mailbox rule as here ("48 hours after posting") or effective upon receipt. While it might not be desirable to have simple communication be subject to such

(continued)

Terms of the Nature (Academic: Americas) License	Comments on the Terms of the Nature (Academic: Americas) License
	formalities, the sending of the invoice (i.e., its effective date) is one area where specificity is in order. Depending on what other provisions the licensee is able or not able to secure, changes in content or changes in billing/invoice processing (like a change in where to send payment) might also be important to delineate and likewise make effective upon receipt. As in ¶ 4.2 and ¶ 4.8, notice should be effective upon receipt or upon acknowledgment of receipt, which this clause suggests is easy to determine (i.e., occurred at some point at least by requiring use of "prepaid recorded delivery or registered post"). In either case, the licensee will need to ensure coverage or monitoring of mail during vacation, illness, or other absences. In any case (notice effective upon posting, 48 hours after posting, receipt, or acknowledgment of receipt), the provision should indicate the party (by title) or department to whom the "notice" should be addressed or labeled, as well as some general reference to the subject matter of the notice or correspondence; this signals staff of its legal significance, such as "c/o Office of Copyright Management... important account information enclosed," with return address/sender information or other relevant designation, as opposed to correspondence about a new product or additional service.
12. LIABILITY. **12.1.** Neither party excludes or limits liability to the other party for death or personal injury caused by its own negligence or any other liability the exclusion or limitation of which is prohibited by law.	Losses come in two forms: business or economic loss and personal (injury). This provision preserves the latter category, as the law views harms to a person somewhat of a higher priority than mere harm to business interests, and thus makes such harm compensable. Harms of a personal nature ("death or personal injury") remain recoverable. Also, if the law otherwise prohibits the limitation of any other liability, those losses will remain recoverable as well.
12.2. Except as provided for in Clause 12.1 above, the liability of the Licensor in respect of any and all claims (whether in contract or in tort) arising out of or in connection with this Agreement is limited in respect of each event or series of connected events to the greater of US$10,000 or an amount equal to the fees paid under this Agreement.	The harms that are recoverable are nonetheless limited under this provision to either the annual fee or $10,000, whichever amount is greater. This is a common provision inserted to discourage dispute and encourage the disgruntled and harmed licensee to merely ride out the remainder of the current subscription and then not renew. As observed earlier, the process, and arguably therefore the option to not renew short of nonpayment, which triggers a termination right without any refund one would be due under ¶4.2, is not contemplated in any provision in this agreement.

(continued)

Terms of the Nature (Academic: Americas) License	Comments on the Terms of the Nature (Academic: Americas) License
12.3. Except as provided for in Clause 12.1, notwithstanding anything else contained in this Agreement, in no event shall the Licensor be liable to the Licensee for: (a) loss of profits, business, revenue, goodwill, anticipated savings; and/or (b) indirect, special, incidental or consequential loss or damage; and (c) any inaccuracy in the Licensed Material.	This provision again reiterates that business losses are not recoverable, nor are contractual damages, that is, the litany of damages in (b), available other than actual damages which are limited to the greater of either the annual fee or $10,000 under ¶ 12.2. Finally, there can be no recovery for loss to due to inaccuracy of the licensed content.
13. GOVERNING LAW. This Agreement, and the rights and liabilities of the parties with respect to this Agreement and its subject matter, shall be governed by the laws of the State of New York, without reference to the principles of conflicts of laws thereof. Any dispute arising out of or relating to this Agreement or its subject matter not settled by the parties may be resolved only by the courts of the State of New York or, if subject matter jurisdiction exists, by the United States federal courts, with venue in the County of New York (in the case of state court) or in the Southern District of New York (in the case of federal court). Each of the parties hereby consents to the jurisdiction of such courts over it in any action involving any such dispute. Each of the parties agrees not to commence or maintain a legal proceeding involving any such dispute in any forum except a court of the State of New York located in New York County or the United	This is a choice of law ("shall be governed by the laws of the State of New York") as well as a choice of forum ("may be resolved only by the courts of the State of New York or, if subject matter jurisdiction exists, by the United States federal courts" within the state of New York) and specific venue ("County of New York" in the case of state court or in the Southern District of New York") provision. This designation is made without application of the relevant rules regarding the conflict of laws (this concept was discussed in the explanation of a previous license agreement). The parties may not raise a question as to the proper forum. It is typical in contract disputes involving parties from different states that each party desires the litigation to be resolved in the courts physically located in its own state, whether state or federal court. Jurisdictional disputes such as this are determined by the initial court of petition and involve elaborate rules of due process law and general equity. For the non–New York resident licensee, this would be done by filing a motion in the relevant court located in the licensee's state, but this act is prohibited: "Each of the parties agrees not to commence or maintain a legal proceeding involving any such dispute in any forum-venue except a court of the State of New York located in New York County or the United States District Court for the Southern District of New York." The previous sentence eliminates such disputes, as both parties consent to the jurisdiction of either the state of New York located in the County of New York or the federal district court for the Southern District of New York located in the city of New York. Moreover, the licensee is prohibited from challenging the jurisdiction (venue) of the specific, applicable New York court in New York court as well, "and agrees not to contest the venue of any action involving any such dispute in the County of New York or the Southern District of New York." BLACK'S LAW DICTIONARY

(continued)

Terms of the Nature (Academic: Americas) License	Comments on the Terms of the Nature (Academic: Americas) License
States District Court for the Southern District of New York (other than to enforce a judgment [sic] obtained in such courts) and agrees not to contest the venue of any action involving any such dispute in the County of New York or the Southern District of New York, as the case may be, nor to assert in any such court the doctrine of forum non conveniens or the like.	(9th ed.) (Bryan A. Garner ed., St. Paul, MN: West Publishing, 2009) (no pagination in Westlaw) defines "forum non conveniens" as "The doctrine that an appropriate forum—even though competent under the law—may divest itself of jurisdiction if, for the convenience of the litigants and the witnesses, it appears that the action should proceed in another forum in which the action might also have been properly brought in the first place." While these restrictions apply equally to both licensee and licensor, the licensor based in New York is happy to litigate disputes on its own turf, so to speak, as it might be easier to litigate in the jurisdiction where its offices are located and its lawyers are likely more familiar with this state's contract law, which may have been a contributing reason for incorporation or location of the business in New York as well. However, should litigation occur in the proper New York court and the licensee prevailed in the dispute and desired to enter or enforce the judgment against the licensor in a court in its home state, this is possible ("other than to enforce a judgement [sic] obtained in such courts").
14. SEVERABILITY. In the event any provision of this Agreement is held by a court or other tribunal of competent jurisdiction to be contrary to law, the remaining provisions of this Agreement will remain in full force and effect.	This provision indicates, if a particular section or paragraph of the license is invalidated by a court, that such action does not void the entire agreement. Rather, only this section or paragraph is no longer in effect; the remaining provisions are unaffected, and the agreement stays in force, with both parties bound to honor the remaining terms.
15. WAIVERS. No provision of this Agreement or breach thereof may be waived except in a writing signed by the party against whom the waiver is sought to be enforced.	Any waiver granted in response to breach of a provision or release of an obligation under the agreement must be in writing and signed by the party "against whom the waiver is sought," that is, the party to whose detriment the waiver will operate. For example, if the licensor waives its right to terminate at any time and for any reason under ¶ 4.3, it would forgo an important right. Thus, the licensor must put in writing and sign its desire to waive the exercise of its termination right. This provision can be viewed in tandem with ¶ 1.4 ("The failure of any party to enforce any provision of this Agreement on any one occasion shall not affect its right to enforce another provision or the same provision on another occasion"), where failure to enforce a provision does not signal any sort of waiver, implied license, or so on. Here, if one party so intends to waive an obligation, such intent must be express.

(continued)

Terms of the Nature (Academic: Americas) License	Comments on the Terms of the Nature (Academic: Americas) License
16. THIRD PARTY RIGHTS. Nothing in this Agreement is intended to confer rights on any third party, whether pursuant to the Contracts (Rights of Third Parties) Act 1999 or otherwise.	Historically, a person not a party to a contract does not have any rights under that contract; in other words, a third party may not maintain any legal action for breach or enforcement. Likewise, the terms of the agreement are not binding, nor do they have any legal force against those third parties. The reference to the Contract (Rights of Third Parties) Act 1999 is a reference to an English law that modified the traditional rule of contract privity that only those parties to the contract, those in privity with the contract, had rights to enforce it. See BLACK'S LAW DICTIONARY (9th ed.) (Bryan A. Garner ed., St. Paul, MN: West Publishing, 2009) (no pagination in Westlaw): "The relationship between the parties to a contract, allowing them to sue each other but preventing a third party from doing so." "At common law, the concept of 'privity,' which appears to have originated in an early English case, prevented persons who were not actual parties to the contract, with the exception of certain third-party beneficiaries, from suing for breach of warranty," per RICHARD A. LORD, 18 WILLISTON ON CONTRACTS § 52:38 (4th ed. 2008), footnotes omitted. In 1999, Parliament passed the Contracts (Rights of Third Parties) Act, which provided that "a person who is not a party to a contract may in his own right enforce a term of the contract if (a), the contract expressly provided that he may, or, (b), subject to subsection (2), the term purports to confer a benefit on him" (§ 1 [1990 c. 31] § 1, http://www.legislation .gov.uk/ukpga/1999/31/contents). "The English Contracts (Rights of Third Parties) Act of 1999 was Parliament's attempt to allow third parties, under some limited circumstances, to be beneficiaries of a contract between two others." HOWARD O. HUNTER, MODERN LAW OF CONTRACTS § 20:4, rejection of doctrine in England (database updated March 2011). The implication of the application of privity in commonwealth jurisdictions to licenses was discussed by one commentator: "Finally, there is considerable uncertainty about the validity and thus enforceability of shrinkwrap licenses, yet the market is said to crave certainty. Indeed, certainty is one of the reasons touted as justifying licensing agreements. Why, then, have copyright owners in New Zealand, the United Kingdom and Australia failed to see whether their licensing agreements will be upheld by taking a test case . . . There are two reasons for this. The first is that in the United Kingdom, prior to the passing of the Contracts (Rights of Third Parties) Act 1999 (UK), the doctrine of privity of contract meant that even if licensing agreements were valid, in the vast majority of cases, the agreement was between the purchaser and the supplier. The copyright owner

(continued)

Terms of the Nature (Academic: Americas) License	Comments on the Terms of the Nature (Academic: Americas) License
	would therefore have been unable to enforce that agreement because it was a third party," per Alexandra Sims, *Copyright and Contract*, 22 NEW ZEALAND UNIVERSITIES LAW REVIEW 469, 486 (2007), footnote omitted. In the United States, an assessment must still be made to determine whether extension of a right under the contract is proper. "Determining whether an enforceable third party beneficiary contract exists requires two additional steps: First, the technical prerequisites of a third party beneficiary contract must be examined, applied, and, of course, met. Second, the several varying classes of cases in which third persons have, or may have, an interest in an agreement made between two or more other contracting parties must be analyzed and differentiated," per RICHARD A. LORD, 18 WILLISTON ON CONTRACTS § 37:1 (4th ed. 2008), footnotes omitted. This modernization of contract, whether in the United Kingdom or United States, is more or less moot here, as the provision makes clear that any expanded rights of privity granted by law, such as the 1999 Act of the British Parliament, are reneged in a sense under this agreement. Third parties have no rights under the contract to enforce a provision of the agreement.

THE AMAZON.COM KINDLE LICENSE DECONSTRUCTED

In fall 2011, Kindle products became available via public library distribution (see Matt Hamblen, *Kindle Books Now Ready for Borrowing from Public Libraries*, September 21, 2011, http://www.computerworld.com/s/article/9220163/.) This agreement (last updated February 16, 2011, and available at http://www.amazon.com/gp/help/customer/display.html/ref=hp_left_sib?ie=UTF8&nodeId=200506200) is included here for two reasons. First, it represents the sort of license that accompanies end user content such as readers, music downloads, and so on, which generally otherwise prohibits the public distribution of such content. Second, even with an OverDrive agreement in place, an individual library patron would still need to have a Kindle, accompanied by some iteration of this agreement in place. So be wary of similar agreements with such prohibitions if your goal is to circulate such content directly to patrons or students instead of via a distributor. Further, if library users are accessing such content with their own Kindle devices, this agreement, or one with similar language, would likely govern the use of their devices.

Amazon.com Kindle License Agreement and Terms of Use	Comments on the Amazon.com Kindle License Agreement and Terms of Use
This is an agreement between you and Amazon Digital Services, Inc. (with its affiliates, "**Amazon**" or "**we**"). Please read this Amazon.com Kindle License Agreement and Terms of Use, the Amazon.com privacy notice located at www.amazon.com/privacy and the other applicable rules, policies, and terms posted on the Amazon.com website or the Kindle Store (collectively, this "**Agreement**") before using the Kindle or any Reading Application or Digital Content. By using the Kindle, any Reading Application, or any Digital Content, you agree to be bound by the terms of this Agreement. If you do not accept the terms of this Agreement, then you may not use the Kindle, any Reading Application, any Digital Content, or the Service; and you may return the Kindle for a refund in accordance with the applicable return policy. [Reference to terms for UK residents omitted.]	This phrase identifies the parties with precise detail. Subsequent definition offers more in regard to the licensor. While the license agreement and terms of use are referenced here and found in the agreement, additional policies are referenced in the agreement but located elsewhere. Terms appear elsewhere as well. While there is an integration clause (see under ¶ 4: Complete Agreement and Severability; integration and severability are discussed in Chapter 14), a later issue may nonetheless arise as to whether such additional content is part of the agreement and terms or at least might be used as parol evidence (discussed in Chapter 2) and/or to interpret the agreement. A sentence in a later paragraph attempts to give priority to these terms: "Those terms [referring to] "The Content Provider may include additional terms for use within its Digital Content."] will also apply, but this Agreement will govern in the event of a conflict." The next sentence is very important. Under this agreement, use equates to assent: "By using the Kindle, any Reading Application, or any Digital Content, you agree to be bound by the terms of this Agreement." While it does not say your sole remedy is to cease use of Kindle or its related products, the licensee is to not use those products if the terms are not accepted, accomplishing more or less the same result as the NewspaperARCHIVE license already discussed. The last phrase is somewhat odd, relating to return. Such allowance is typical in "pay now, terms later" agreements like shrink-wrap licenses, but here the terms are accessed before payment, download, or so forth, is necessary. Assuming a licensee would change his or her mind and later decide the terms were not acceptable, the sentence implies that one could cease use and return the Kindle for a refund, according to the return policy. (Note: The return policy was not examined.)
For the purposes of this Agreement: "Content Provider" means the party offering Digital Content in the Kindle Store, which may be us or a third party; however, for Digital Content designated as active content in the Kindle Store, "Content Provider" means the publisher of the Digital Content.	A number of terms are defined here. The provider of content for the device could come from Amazon ("we") or a third party. The content on the device is separate from the device itself ("our portable electronic reading device"). As a result, there may be a legal issue as to whether those who purchase the device own this device (Kindle or an "other device") and its attendant operating software ("software" or "reading application"), similar to recent questions raised regarding cell phones and their users. An argument can be made that such purchasers are not licensees but owners of the device and its operating software with first-sale, fair-use, and other rights

(continued)

Amazon.com Kindle License Agreement and Terms of Use	Comments on the Amazon.com Kindle License Agreement and Terms of Use
"Digital Content" means digitized electronic content, such as books, newspapers, magazines, journals, blogs, RSS feeds, games, and other static and interactive electronic content.	under the copyright law applying (see discussion under ¶ 1: Use of Digital Content and under ¶ 2: Use of Wireless Connectivity).
"Kindle" means our portable electronic reading device.	
"Kindle Store" means our storefront through which you can shop for Digital Content or other items offered by us or third parties and manage your Digital Content and account settings.	
"Other Device" means a computer or device other than a Kindle on which you are authorized to operate a Reading Application.	
"Periodicals" means Digital Content made available to you on a subscription basis, such as electronic newspapers, magazines, journals, blogs, and other subscription-based content.	
"Reading Application" means software (including any updates/upgrades to that software) we make available that permits users to shop for, download, browse, and/or use Digital Content on an Other Device.	
"Service" means the wireless connectivity that we provide Kindle users, the provision of Digital Content, Software, and support and other services that we provide Kindle and Reading Application users, and the terms and conditions under which we provide each of the foregoing.	
"Software" means the Reading Applications and all software on the Kindle (including any updates/upgrades to that software), and any related documentation that we make available to you.	

(continued)

Amazon.com Kindle License Agreement and Terms of Use	Comments on the Amazon.com Kindle License Agreement and Terms of Use
1. Digital Content **Use of Digital Content.** Upon your download of Digital Content and payment of any applicable fees (including applicable taxes), the Content Provider grants you a non-exclusive right to view, use, and display such Digital Content an unlimited number of times, solely on the Kindle or a Reading Application or as otherwise permitted as part of the Service, solely on the number of Kindles or Other Devices specified in the Kindle Store, and solely for your personal, non-commercial use. Unless otherwise specified, Digital Content is licensed, not sold, to you by the Content Provider. The Content Provider may include additional terms for use within its Digital Content. Those terms will also apply, but this Agreement will govern in the event of a conflict. Some Digital Content, such as Periodicals, may not be available to you through Reading Applications.	This section has the language that prevents libraries, or anyone for that matter, from circulating or making any other public distribution of such content: "and solely for your personal, non-commercial use." Public distribution (sharing with your friend and family or circulating from a library) of an e-version of a latest best seller is not personal use. True, the "Digital Content is licensed, not sold," but does that apply to the pieces of the Kindle service? What about the device itself or its operating software? If it is a sale, then the user is the owner of the device, along with its operating software. There is a legal argument that can be made for ownership of the device and its attendant software. However, the content remains subject to license and the restrictions previously explained. Recent comment was made suggesting that the device and its operating software might indeed be owned by purchasers and not licensed: "Moreover, the Register cannot clearly determine whether the various versions of the iPhone contracts with consumers constituted a sale or license of a copy of the computer programs contained on the iPhone. The contractual language is unclear with respect to particular copies of the computer programs. Although Apple retains ownership of the computer programs, the contracts also expressly grant users ownership of the device. Since the 'copy' of the computer program is fixed in hardware of the device, it is unclear what ownership status is to be given to the particular copy of the computer program contained in the device. Apple unquestionably has retained ownership of the intangible works, but the ownership of the particular copies of those works is unclear. Moreover, the state of the law with respect to the determination of ownership is in a state of flux in the courts. Both proponents and opponents cited case law in support of their respective positions, but the Register finds it impossible to determine how a court would resolve the issue of ownership on the facts presented here." *Exemption to Prohibition on Circumvention of Copyright Protection Systems for Access Control Technologies*, 75 FEDERAL REGISTER 43825, 43829 (July 27, 2010). In recommending another category of exempted works (firmware on wireless telephone handsets), the register of copyrights made a similar statement: "The wireless networks asserted that by using a cellphone on another network, an act that is not authorized under their contracts . . . Proponents of the class asserted that the owners of mobile phones are also the owners of the copies of the computer programs on those phones and that as owners they are entitled to exercise their

(continued)

Amazon.com Kindle License Agreement and Terms of Use	Comments on the Amazon.com Kindle License Agreement and Terms of Use
	privileges under Section 117 of the Copyright Act, which gives the owner of a copy of a computer program the privilege to make or authorize the making of another copy or adaptation of that computer program under certain circumstances. The wireless networks responded that their contracts with their customers restrict the uses of the customers' mobile phones and retain ownership of the copies of the computer programs that are loaded onto the mobile phones and enable the phones to operate . . . The Register has reviewed the appropriate case law with respect to who is the 'owner' of a copy of a computer program for purposes of Section 117 when a license or agreement imposes restrictions on the use of the computer program and has concluded that the state of the law is unclear. The Register cannot determine whether most mobile phone owners are also the owners of the copies of the computer programs on their mobile phones. However, based on the record in this proceeding, the Register finds that the proponents of the class have made a prima facie case that mobile phone owners are the owners of those copies. While the wireless networks have made a case that many mobile phone owners may not own the computer program copies because the wireless network's contract with the consumer retains ownership of the copies, they have not presented evidence that this is always the case even if their interpretation of the law governing ownership is correct. The record therefore leads to the conclusion that a substantial portion of mobile phone owners also own the copies of the software on their phones." *Exemption to Prohibition on Circumvention of Copyright Protection Systems for Access Control Technologies*, 75 FEDERAL REGISTER 43825, 43830–43831 (July 27, 2010), concluding that an owner of mobile phone is allowed to make a copy of the phone operating software or modifications to it under section 117. The point is that if a purchaser owns his or her copy of a Kindle and its operating software in the same way iPhone and mobile phone purchasers do, then first-sale rights to make public distributions such as lending and make fair-use modifications under the copyright law apply. The case law is too underdeveloped at this time to say with certainty, but a legal argument can nonetheless be made for this result.
Limitations. Unless specifically indicated otherwise, you may not sell, rent, lease, distribute, broadcast, sublicense, or otherwise	Here is additional language that would prevent a public library, or anyone for that matter, from circulating or making any other public distribution of such content: "[Y]ou may not sell, rent, lease, distribute, broadcast, sublicense, or otherwise

(continued)

Amazon.com Kindle License Agreement and Terms of Use	Comments on the Amazon.com Kindle License Agreement and Terms of Use
assign any rights to the Digital Content or any portion of it to any third party, and you may not remove or modify any proprietary notices or labels on the Digital Content. In addition, you may not bypass, modify, defeat, or circumvent security features that protect the Digital Content.	assign any rights to the Digital Content or any portion of it to any third party." There is also a CMI (Copyright Management Information) provision of sorts, prohibiting removal or alteration of copyright or other proprietary notices (e.g., trademark). The companion to section 1202 (the CMI provision of the copyright law) is section 1201, prohibiting circumvention of technological protection measures, and it is also paralleled here ("may not bypass, modify, defeat, or circumvent security features").
Periodicals. You may cancel your subscription as permitted in our cancellation policy in the Kindle Store. We may terminate a subscription at our discretion, for example, if a Periodical is no longer available. If we terminate a subscription before the end of its term, we will give you a prorated refund. We reserve the right to change subscription terms and fees from time to time, effective as of the beginning of the next subscription term.	Here is reference to another policy (cancellation), so, along with at least the "applicable return policy," additional information would be needed before assessing the overall value and pluses and minuses of the Kindle and related products and services. The licensee may cancel, according to the other policy, but Amazon may cancel at its "discretion," though a "prorated refund" is due. If the licensee terminates, then a refund is subject to the terms of the "applicable return policy" (again, not located herein). Having such important rights as refund and termination available elsewhere is problematic; worse, as a later provision (under ¶ 4: Amendment—"We may amend any of the terms") allows for change of terms via posting on the Amazon website (along with acceptance of new terms made by continued use of the product or service), this is very problematic because a user would need to check at least several policies before obtaining a complete picture of this transaction. One would also need to check the website from time to time or perhaps daily to determine the current sets of applicable terms.
2. Wireless Connectivity **Use of Wireless Connectivity.** Your Kindle uses wireless connectivity to allow you to shop for and download Digital Content from the Kindle Store. In general, we do not charge you for this use of wireless connectivity. Your Kindle may use wireless connectivity to make other services available to you for which we may charge you a fee, such as personal file download and subscriptions when you are located in another country. The fees and	This clause indicates the wireless capabilities of Kindle but also refers to a possible fee the licensee may incur when using the product/service overseas. Of course, like a good part of the important stuff, the actual terms and fee schedule are located elsewhere, which of course Amazon "may change from time to time." Good luck keeping track of the numerous polices and their potential changes. Changes to material terms, like price and refund, should require assent before the change becomes part of the agreement. Further, notice of all changes should derive from the licensor and not rely on the efforts of each individual licensee to ascertain. (See Chapter 14, Terms, Changes to.)

(continued)

Amazon.com Kindle License Agreement and Terms of Use	Comments on the Amazon.com Kindle License Agreement and Terms of Use
terms for such services are located in the Kindle Store and may change from time to time. If your Kindle functions with third party services, such as WI-FI access points, a third party may charge you fees for the use of those services.	
Your Conduct. You may use the wireless connectivity provided by us only in connection with the Service. You may not use the wireless connectivity for any other purpose.	While you cannot use the connectivity provided for any other purpose, the following provision indicates that Amazon may not be able always to have that connectivity available. As a prior provision forbade the user to "bypass, modify, defeat, or circumvent security features," any patch or other modification in the connectivity mechanism to achieve "other purpose" (interoperability) would be prohibited. Again, recent discussion in the regulatory process regarding circumventing and cell phone owners indicates that if the user is determined to be the owner of the phone and its attendant software, so-called jailbreaking in order to allow interoperability may not be a circumvention of the operating software: "The Register does not find that the contract between Apple and purchasers of the iPhone authorize modification of the iPhone. Moreover, the Register cannot clearly determine whether the various versions of the iPhone contracts with consumers constituted a sale or license of a copy of the computer programs contained on the iPhone. The contractual language is unclear with respect to particular copies of the computer programs . . . Since the 'copy' of the computer program is fixed in hardware of the device, it is unclear what ownership status is to be given to the particular copy of the computer program contained in the device." *Exemption to Prohibition on Circumvention of Copyright Protection Systems for Access Control Technologies*, 75 FEDERAL REGISTER 43825, 43829 (July 27, 2010). While there are factual differences between the prohibition of this provision and the jailbreaking of cell phone firmware to make further use of the cell phone as it was intended (i.e., to make phone calls or other network communications), the register concluded that such jailbreaking was fair use and that a regulatory exemption from the prohibition of section 1201 was warranted: "On balance, the Register concludes that when one jailbreaks a smartphone in order to make the operating system on that phone interoperable with an independently created application that has not been approved by the maker of the smartphone or the maker of its operating system, the

(continued)

Amazon.com Kindle License Agreement and Terms of Use	Comments on the Amazon.com Kindle License Agreement and Terms of Use
	modifications that are made purely for the purpose of such interoperability are fair uses. Case law and Congressional enactments reflect a judgment that interoperability is favored. The Register also finds that designating a class of works that would permit jailbreaking for purposes of interoperability will not adversely affect the market for or value of the copyrighted works to the copyright owner. Accordingly, the Register recommends that the Librarian designate the following class of works: Computer programs that enable wireless communication handsets to execute software applications, where circumvention is accomplished for the sole purpose of enabling interoperability of such applications, when they have been lawfully obtained, with computer programs on the telephone handset" (*id.* at 43830). Applying a similar rationale to the Kindle, it could be argued that making modifications relating to interoperability with other devices, content, or systems is possible, at least until Congress or the courts make a definitive response on the matter.
Availability. If your Kindle is located in an area in which it cannot maintain wireless connectivity, you may not be able to use some or all of the Service. We are not responsible for the unavailability of wireless connectivity for your Kindle or any corresponding loss of Service. Events beyond our reasonable control (such as changes in service or terms by wireless carriers) may impact the terms or circumstances under which we provide you wireless connectivity and may result in a change to these terms or a temporary or permanent modification or loss of wireless connectivity for your Kindle.	Since Amazon is itself a licensee of wireless connectivity, changes in its own licensee agreements may also impact the available connectivity it does have. Amazon would certainly be aware of such changes and should make that information available to Kindle licensees. Further, if the scope or range of connectivity is determinable by geographic region, again, a schedule of any blackout or noncoverage areas should be available, and if changes are made, the licensee should be made aware of such changes. If so, then, depending on the location where the licensee intends to make use of his or her Kindle, this might be a material term as well, that is, if a licensee intends to use the device where there has been a "permanent modification or loss of wireless connectivity."
3. Device and Software **Use of the Software.** You may use the Software only on a Kindle or through a Reading Application on an Other Device. You may not separate any individual component of the	The ownership of a particular copy of the software that "sits" on a Kindle is an unfolding legal question. (See discussion in Chapters 1 and 4 regarding the first-sale doctrine and its applicability to component pieces of software systems. Unfortunately, the U.S. Supreme Court will not resolve the issue in the near term, per *Vernor v. Autodesk, Inc.*, 621 F.3d

(continued)

Amazon.com Kindle License Agreement and Terms of Use	Comments on the Amazon.com Kindle License Agreement and Terms of Use
Software for use on another device or computer, may not transfer it for use on another device or computer or use it, or any portion of it, over a network, and may not sell, rent, lease, lend, distribute, or sublicense or otherwise assign any rights to the Software in whole or in part. Additional terms apply to some of the third party software or materials on the Kindle, and will govern in the event of a conflict with this Agreement. For more information, see the Legal section in the Kindle Settings menu.	1102 (9th Cir. 2010), cert. denied 132 S.Ct. 105 (Oct. 3, 2011).) If the software is truly obtained through license, then such "transfer" of "any individual component of the Software" is prohibited. Otherwise, first-sale rights might allow the buyer-owner (licensee) to "sell, rent, lease, lend, [or] distribute" components of the software. Even an owner of a particular copy of the software (embodied in a particular Kindle) would not have the ability to "assign any rights to the Software in whole or in part" as the rights in the underlying intellectual property remain with the copyright owner. Finally, additional terms might apply to some software supplied by third parties, but unlike other policies relating to services or products under its control where the terms of this agreement prevail in cases of conflict, here Amazon does not own the software, so the "additional terms . . . will govern in the event of conflict with this Agreement."
Automatic Updates. In order to keep your Software up-to-date, Amazon may automatically provide your Kindle or Other Device with updates/upgrades to the Software.	This provision gives Amazon the right to make updates, that is, to make changes to your Kindle's operating software. Be wary if similar language ever applies to a Kindle service that is accessible from your own computer or other device because the change made might impact other software on such devices
No Reverse Engineering, Decompilation, Disassembly, or Circumvention. You may not modify, reverse engineer, decompile, or disassemble the Kindle or the Software, whether in whole or in part, create any derivative works from or of the Software, or bypass, modify, defeat, or tamper with or circumvent any of the functions or protections of the Kindle or Software or any mechanisms operatively linked to the Software, for example, by augmenting or substituting any digital rights management functionality of the Kindle or Software.	The reverse engineering, decompilation, and disassembly of software to achieve interoperability can be fair use. *Sony Computer Entertainment, Inc. v. Connectix Corp.*, 203 F.3d 596, 609 (9th Cir. 2000) stated: "Connectix's reverse engineering of the Sony BIOS extracted from a Sony PlayStation console purchased by Connectix engineers is protected as a fair use"; *Sega Enterprises Ltd. v. Accolade, Inc.*, 977 F.2d 1510, 1514 (9th Cir. 1992) offered: "In light of the public policies underlying the Act, we conclude that, when the person seeking the understanding has a legitimate reason for doing so and when no other means of access to the unprotected elements exists, such disassembly is as a matter of law a fair use of the copyrighted work"); and *Atari Games Corp. v. Nintendo of America, Inc.*, 975 F.2d 832 (Fed. Cir. 1992) commented: "Reverse engineering, untainted by the purloined copy of the 10NES program and necessary to understand 10NES, is a fair use" (*id*. at 843). "This 'reverse engineering' process, to the extent untainted by the 10NES copy purloined from the Copyright Office, qualified as a fair use" (*id*. at 844). This right is precluded here. Further, circumvention for reverse similar purposes is also possible

(continued)

Amazon.com Kindle License Agreement and Terms of Use	Comments on the Amazon.com Kindle License Agreement and Terms of Use
	under section 1201(f)(1): "a person who has lawfully obtained the right to use a copy of a computer program may circumvent a technological measure that effectively controls access to a particular portion of that program for the sole purpose of identifying and analyzing those elements of the program that are necessary to achieve interoperability of an independently created computer program with other programs, and that have not previously been readily available to the person engaging in the circumvention, to the extent any such acts of identification and analysis do not constitute infringement under this title." Not that a Kindle user would want to engage in such practices, but there may be efforts to make such readers or the content usable with other content or viewable on other devices. Such efforts at interoperability are significant statutory rights. Licensees here have surrendered those rights.
4. General Compliance with Law and Reservation of Rights. You will use the Kindle, the Software, the Service, and the Digital Content in compliance with all applicable laws. Neither the sale or transfer of the Kindle to you, nor the license of the Software or Digital Content to you, transfers to you title to or ownership of any intellectual property rights of Amazon or its suppliers or the other Content Providers. All licenses are non-exclusive and all rights not expressly granted in this Agreement are reserved to Amazon or the other Content Providers.	Regardless of whether a Kindle user obtains ownership over any particular copy of a device or attendant software, with the result that the copyright law would govern use of the device or software, the underlying intellectual property rights in either remain with "Amazon or its suppliers or the other Content Providers." This would occur whether the transactions herein are true sales or licenses.
Export Regulations. You will comply with all applicable export and re-export restrictions and regulations, and you will not transfer, or encourage, assist, or authorize the transfer of, the Kindle, Digital Content, or Software to a prohibited country or otherwise in violation of any such restrictions or regulations.	For an overview of possible applicable regulations, see, generally, Benjamin H. Flowe, *Coping with U.S. Export Controls*, in EXPORTING TECHNOLOGY AND SOFTWARE, PARTICULARLY ENCRYPTION 87 (2011) (Practising Law Institute Commercial Law and Practice Course Handbook Series, 943 PLI/Comm 87, PLI Order No. 29564).

(continued)

Amazon.com Kindle License Agreement and Terms of Use	Comments on the Amazon.com Kindle License Agreement and Terms of Use
Information Received. The Software will provide Amazon with data about your Kindle and its interaction with the Service (such as available memory, up-time, log files, and signal strength). The Software will also provide Amazon with information related to the Digital Content on your Kindle and Other Devices and your use of it (such as last page read and content archiving). Annotations, bookmarks, notes, highlights, or similar markings you make using your Kindle or Reading Application and other information you provide may be stored on servers that are located outside the country in which you live. Any information we receive is subject to the Amazon.com privacy notice located at www.amazon.com/privacy.	Amazon is collecting quite a bit of information about how a licensee uses his or her Kindle, such as what pages you flip through, those you reread, likely how long you spend on a page, and any annotations, bookmarks, notes, highlights, or similar markings you make. Use of such information is subject to the Amazon privacy policy, again located elsewhere and not necessarily a part of this agreement (and likely it can be changed at any time without notice as well). Such information can also be tracked when public library patrons use Kindle products and services obtained through their public library's subscription service. If the public library collected this information itself, the record of patron reading habits would be protected under most states' library patron confidentiality statutes. If the "Informaton Received" provision is in the Kindle agreement to which either the library or its patrons subscribe, patron reading history will be collected without any assurance of privacy other than Amazon's own policy. STATE LIBRARY PATRON CONFIDENTIALITY PROTECTIONS WOULD NOT APPLY (this language appears in capital script here because it is very important). This could lead to a serious compromise of public library patron reading habits, preferences, and other information. (A thorough review of the Amazon.com privacy policy is beyond the scope of this book, but if past recountings are any indication of future practice, there is cause for concern. See *Add Amazon.com to the List—Class-Action Lawsuit Alleges Data Privacy Violations*, posted by Nicole Friess (March 11, 2011), http://www.infolawgroup.com/2011/03/articles/privacy-and-security-litigatio/add-amazoncom-to-the-list-classaction-lawsuit-alleges-data-privacy-violations/ (2:11-CV-00366 RSL, W.D. Wash., filed March 2, 2011), http://www.scribd.com/doc/50083197/Del-Vecchio-v-Amazon-Complaint. See also *Who Cares about Amazon.com's Privacy Policy?*, recounting similar concerns in September 2000, http://www.pcworld.com/article/18705/who_cares_about_amazoncoms_privacy_policy.html. This license is a nonnegotiated, consumer license. If it were negotiable, one alternative would be to insert language into the license that obligates Amazon to offer a level of privacy protection equal to that of the public library making the Kindle content available—privacy protection that the public library is required by state law to offer. For further discussion see Chapter 17, under Compliance Obligations...and the Impact on Patron Privacy.

(continued)

Amazon.com Kindle License Agreement and Terms of Use	Comments on the Amazon.com Kindle License Agreement and Terms of Use
Information Provided to Others. You are responsible for any information you provide to others using a Kindle or a Reading Application. Any information you provide to a third party will be subject to the privacy notice or any similar terms that the third party provides to you, and will not be subject to the Amazon.com Privacy Notice.	If you want to share information with folks similar to that which Amazon.com is collecting, then all bets are off. Moreover, Amazon is not responsible for the use of the personal information that you supply to others.
Patents. The Kindle, Software, and Service, and/or methods used in association with any of the foregoing, may be covered by one or more patents or pending patent applications.	In addition to copyright, some of the Kindle products and services may be covered by patent as well—although recent events have challenged the validity of the Kindle Fire patent: *SmartPhone Technologies, LLC v. Amazon.com, Inc.*, Dkt. No. 6:2011cv00530 (E.D. Texas, filed October 7, 2011).
Changes to Service. We may modify, suspend, or discontinue the Service, in whole or in part, at any time.	Is suspension or discontinuation of service the same as a previously noted termination, whereby the licensor owes the licensee a refund? If not, there should be a credit in instances of suspension (if restoration of service is contemplated) and a refund in circumstances that mimic or for practical purposes equate to a termination.
Termination. Your rights under this Agreement will automatically terminate if you fail to comply with any term of this Agreement. In case of such termination, you must cease all use of the Software, and Amazon may immediately revoke your access to the Service or to Digital Content without refund of any fees. Amazon's failure to insist upon or enforce your strict compliance with this Agreement will not constitute a waiver of any of its rights.	If termination occurs under this provision (but who makes that determination, Amazon?), then not only does your access cease ("Amazon may immediately revoke your access"), but there is no refund! All breaches are deemed material, and thus termination is the result. There is no advance notice with a right to cure. Without a refund, the provision operates as a fine or penalty, as discussed previously. This provision also includes a statement of nonwaiver—that Amazon's lax conduct in failing to enforce a term in the past (or its failure to "automatically terminate" for a past infraction) does not mean it waives its right to enforce and terminate without refund a user's access in the future.
Disclaimer of Warranties. USE OF THE SERVICE, KINDLE, KINDLE STORE, DIGITAL CONTENT, AND SOFTWARE IS AT YOUR SOLE RISK. EXCEPT FOR THE ONE-YEAR LIMITED KINDLE WARRANTY, NO ORAL OR WRITTEN INFORMATION OR ADVICE	For a thorough discussion of waivers, see the previous licenses in this chapter and the discussion in Chapter 14 under Warranties and Disclaimers. Here there is a one-year warranty. Further, any communication made by a representative of Amazon or otherwise communicated by it does not mean anything; it does not constitute a promise or warranty. The Kindle products and content are made

(continued)

Amazon.com Kindle License Agreement and Terms of Use	Comments on the Amazon.com Kindle License Agreement and Terms of Use
GIVEN BY AMAZON OR AN AUTHORIZED REPRESENTATIVE OF AMAZON CREATES A WARRANTY, AND THE SERVICE, KINDLE, KINDLE STORE, DIGITAL CONTENT, AND SOFTWARE ARE PROVIDED "AS IS" WITH ALL FAULTS AND WITHOUT WARRANTY OF ANY KIND, AND AMAZON, ITS SUPPLIERS, ITS LICENSORS, AND THE OTHER CONTENT PROVIDERS DISCLAIM ALL WARRANTIES, EXPRESS OR IMPLIED, SUCH AS THE IMPLIED WARRANTIES OF MERCHANTABILITY, FITNESS FOR A PARTICULAR PURPOSE, ACCURACY, QUIET ENJOYMENT, AND NON-INFRINGEMENT OF THIRD-PARTY RIGHTS. THE LAWS OF CERTAIN JURISDICTIONS DO NOT ALLOW THE DISCLAIMER OF IMPLIED WARRANTIES. IF THESE LAWS APPLY TO YOU, SOME OR ALL OF THE ABOVE DISCLAIMERS, EXCLUSIONS OR LIMITATIONS MAY NOT APPLY TO YOU, AND YOU MAY HAVE ADDITIONAL RIGHTS.	available "as is" and without other implied warranties. Of course, some states do not think it is fair to waive implied warranties, so by statute such disclaimers are invalid. Amazon of course knows this, so it adds: "The laws of certain jurisdictions do not allow the disclaimer of implied warranties. If these laws apply to you, some or all of the above disclaimers, exclusions or limitations may not apply to you, and you may have additional rights."
Limitation of Liability. TO THE EXTENT NOT PROHIBITED BY LAW, AMAZON, ITS SUPPLIERS, ITS LICENSORS, AND THE OTHER CONTENT PROVIDERS WILL NOT BE LIABLE TO YOU FOR ANY INCIDENTAL OR CONSEQUENTIAL DAMAGES FOR BREACH OF ANY EXPRESS OR IMPLIED WARRANTY, BREACH OF CONTRACT, NEGLIGENCE, STRICT LIABILITY, OR ANY OTHER LEGAL THEORY RELATED TO THE SERVICE, KINDLE, OTHER DEVICES, KINDLE STORE, DIGITAL CONTENT, OR SOFTWARE, SUCH AS ANY DAMAGES ARISING OUT OF LOSS OF PROFITS, REVENUE, DATA, OR USE OF THE SERVICE, KINDLE, OTHER DEVICES, KINDLE STORE, DIGITAL CONTENT, OR SOFTWARE OR ANY ASSOCIATED PRODUCT, EVEN IF AMAZON HAS BEEN	For a thorough discussion of limitation on liability (damage) provisions, see the licenses discussed in this chapter and Chapter 14, under Damages and under Disclaimers. Various damage claims are prohibited. As is typical, the total amount recoverable is limited to the price paid for the content or product ("In any case, Amazon's and the other content providers' aggregate liability under this agreement with respect to any claim relating to purchase of digital content is limited to the amount you actually paid for that digital content, and, with respect to any other claim, is limited to the amount you actually paid for the Kindle"). In other words would you sue Amazon.com over its Kindle if the most you could obtain in damages would be the price of the Kindle? Not likely. Therefore, from Amazon's perspective, mission accomplished. It is unlikely that anyone would sue for this amount. Again, some states do not think this is fair and so prohibit such limitations: "The laws of certain jurisdictions do not allow the exclusion or limitation of incidental or consequential

(continued)

Amazon.com Kindle License Agreement and Terms of Use	Comments on the Amazon.com Kindle License Agreement and Terms of Use
ADVISED OF THE POSSIBILITY OF SUCH DAMAGES. IN ANY CASE, AMAZON'S AND THE OTHER CONTENT PROVIDERS' AGGREGATE LIABILITY UNDER THIS AGREEMENT WITH RESPECT TO ANY CLAIM RELATING TO PURCHASE OF DIGITAL CONTENT IS LIMITED TO THE AMOUNT YOU ACTUALLY PAID FOR THAT DIGITAL CONTENT, AND, WITH RESPECT TO ANY OTHER CLAIM, IS LIMITED TO THE AMOUNT YOU ACTUALLY PAID FOR THE KINDLE. THE LAWS OF CERTAIN JURISDICTIONS DO NOT ALLOW THE EXCLUSION OR LIMITATION OF INCIDENTAL OR CONSEQUENTIAL DAMAGES. IF THESE LAWS APPLY TO YOU, SOME OR ALL OF THE ABOVE EXCLUSIONS OR LIMITATIONS MAY NOT APPLY TO YOU, AND YOU MAY HAVE ADDITIONAL RIGHTS.	damages. If these laws apply to you, some or all of the above exclusions or limitations may not apply to you, and you may have additional rights." Oddly, the agreement does not forbid class actions, so this may be the only viable form of litigation. See *Add Amazon.com to the List— Class-Action Lawsuit Alleges Data Privacy Violations*, posted by Nicole Friess (March 11, 2011), http://www .infolawgroup.com/2011/03/articles/privacy-and- security-litigatio/add-amazoncom-to-the-list-classaction- lawsuit-alleges-data-privacy-violations/ (2:11-CV-00366 RSL, W.D. Wash., filed March 2, 2011), http://www.scribd .com/doc/50083197/Del-Vecchio-v-Amazon-Complaint.
Governing Law. The laws of the state of Washington, U.S.A., without regard to principles of conflict of laws, will govern this Agreement and any dispute of any sort that might arise between you and Amazon.	Here is the choice of law. Oddly, the state and federal courts in Washington state are not indicated as the choice of forum as well, but see the next provision.
Disputes. Any dispute arising out of or relating in any way to this Agreement in which the aggregate total claim for relief sought on behalf of one or more of the parties exceeds U.S. $7,500 will be adjudicated in any state or federal court in King County, Washington, U.S.A., and you consent to exclusive jurisdiction and venue in such courts.	The agreement does not prohibit users from suing Amazon, though a previous provision (Limitation of Liability: "In any case, Amazon's and the other content providers' aggregate liability under this agreement with respect to any claim relating to purchase of digital content is limited to the amount you actually paid for that digital content, and, with respect to any other claim, is limited to the amount you actually paid for the Kindle.") limits damages to the cost of the device or content in dispute. This provision merely adds that if you do decide to sue and potential damages in question are more than $7,500, then choice of forum is limited to the state or federal courts in King County, Washington. Considering that the current price of a Kindle with WiFi is $79, or $149 for a Kindle Touch with 3G network capabilities (price checked on May 5, 2012, at http://www.amazon.com/dp/B0051QVESA/?tag= googhydr-20&hvadid=7895212208&hvpos=1t1&hvexid=

(continued)

Amazon.com Kindle License Agreement and Terms of Use	Comments on the Amazon.com Kindle License Agreement and Terms of Use
	&hvnetw=g&hvrand=315448961959020100&hvpone=&hvptwo=&hvqmt=b&ref=pd_sl_1h7nrm5wtl_b), it would take a rather intense period of inflation for the price of a device to ever meet this threshold.
U.S. Government Rights. The Software, Service, and Digital Content are provided to the U.S. Government as "commercial items," "commercial computer software," "commercial computer software documentation," and "technical data," as defined in the U.S. Federal Acquisition Regulation and the U.S. Defense Federal Acquisition Regulation Supplement, with the same rights and restrictions customarily provided to end users	For more information on the Federal Acquisition Regulation, see 48 C.F.R. Part 201, and on the Defense Federal Acquisition Regulation Supplement, see 48 C.F.R. Part 204 and Part 254.
Complete Agreement and Severability. This is the entire agreement between us and you regarding the Kindle, Digital Content, Software, and Service and supersedes all prior understandings regarding such subject matter. If any term or condition of this Agreement is deemed invalid, void, or for any reason unenforceable, that part will be deemed severable and will not affect the validity and enforceability of any remaining term or condition.	This provision is the integration clause, in spite of the numerous other terms and policies that are needed to obtain a complete picture of the Kindle and related service terms, which of course can change at any time. While "[t]his [may be] the entire agreement between" Amazon and a licensee, this agreement is clearly not the sole source of the terms regarding the use and relationship that results from this agreement. This provision is also the severability (or more properly survivability) provision. Should any provision be deemed invalid, void, or unenforceable by, say, a court (and there are several potential provisions!), this will not void or cancel the entire agreement, and the remaining terms (and assume the additional terms, policies, etc., located elsewhere) remain in effect, again subject to change at any time.
Amendment. We may amend any of the terms of this Agreement in our sole discretion by posting the revised terms on the Kindle Store or the Amazon.com website. Your continued use of the Kindle, Digital Content, Service, or Software after the effective date of any such amendment constitutes your agreement to be bound by such amendment.	Because this is a mass-market, consumer agreement, at least in the 9th Circuit, such changes might not be valid. According to decisions such as *Douglas v. Talk America, Inc.*, 495 F.3d 1062 (9th Cir. 2007): "Talk America posted the revised contract on its website but, according to Douglas, it never notified him that the contract had changed. Unaware of the new terms, Douglas continued using Talk America's services for four years" (*id*. at 1065). The court concluded that the new terms were not part of the agreement: "Even if Douglas had visited the website, he would have had no reason to look at the contract

(continued)

Amazon.com Kindle License Agreement and Terms of Use	Comments on the Amazon.com Kindle License Agreement and Terms of Use
	posted there. Parties to a contract have no obligation to check the terms on a periodic basis to learn whether they have been changed by the other side" (*id*). A proposed new term once the contract is formed represents an offer for additional terms that, in theory, requires assent. This is a nonnegotiated agreement with such suspect in terms of enforceability: "Nor would a party know *when* to check the website for possible changes to the contract terms without being notified that the contract has been changed and how. Douglas would have had to check the contract every day for possible changes. Without notice, an examination would be fairly cumbersome, as Douglas would have had to compare every word of the posted contract with his existing contract in order to detect whether it had changed" (*id*. at note 1). "Further, the assent of both parties to a modification is necessary; the mental purpose of one of the parties to a contract cannot change its terms," per *Riceland Seed Co. v. Wingmead Inc.*, 2011 WL 3925366, *4 (Ark. App. 2011) (unpublished). This is basic contract law, as expressed by one court: "It is axiomatic that parties to an existing contract may modify the agreement by mutual assent." *Perry v. Estate of Carpenter*, 918 N.E.2d 156, 1163 (Ill. App. 1 Dist. 2009). Under the precedent discussed here and in previous chapters, this language is insufficient to bind licensees to new terms merely posted on a website. "In order to modify a contract, the parties must mutually assent to the new terms." *Holland v. Continental Telephone Co. of the South*, 492 So.2d 998, 999 (Ala. 1986). On the chance that some courts may uphold this provision (a possibility in a negotiated license agreement), do not agree to any such clause. Do not allow the license agreement to alter the basic contract premise: "As a general principle, a contract cannot be modified unilaterally; rather, the parties must mutually consent to the modification. Thus, a party to an existing contract may modify that contract only with the assent of the other party to the contract." *Star Leasing Co. v. G&S Metal Consultants, Inc.*, 2009 WL 714146, *7 (Ohio App. 10 Dist.). Unless the subscriber desires to be checking the Amazon website for changes to the terms or other policies, such clause should be avoided. Amazon is also viewing continued use after a a change is posted as acceptance of this change even though there is no mechanism to alert a subscriber that there is a new change to review!

(continued)

Amazon.com Kindle License Agreement and Terms of Use	Comments on the Amazon.com Kindle License Agreement and Terms of Use
Contact Information. For help with your Kindle, a Reading Application, the Service or resolving other issues, please contact Customer Service by e-mail: kindle-cs-support@amazon.com/ or by phone at 1-866-321-8851 (toll free) when dialing in the US or at 1-206-266-0927 (charges will apply) when dialing outside the US. For communications concerning this Agreement, please contact Amazon by e-mail: kindleterms@amazon.com/.	Contact information is provided. Service is provided via e-mail and phone, but there is no indication if the communication is staffed 24/7 or some other subset of hours (and, if so, for what time zones). Do not attempt to call Amazon to review any of the issues discussed here, as such contact ("communications concerning this agreement") is limited to e-mail alone.

16

TWENTY SAMPLE KEY CLAUSES TO LOOK FOR IN CONTENT LICENSES

The clauses presented in this chapter are not exclusive. In other words, these clauses are not the only provisions of concern in licensing but do address significant issues. In some examples, the sample clauses do not represent the entire treatment of the topic in an agreement but target important licensee rights that are often excluded or are problematic. Also, the language is not set in stone. Particular situations and institutional preferences may dictate necessary changes. These clauses are merely starting points for consideration. Moreover, the author refrains from use of the word *model* in describing any particular language offered as a "model provision" for various reasons. First, licenses, like contracts, especially negotiated ones, are quite personal in the sense that the agreement is an expression of the meeting of the minds, of the agreement's two parties, and may reflect the combined parties' unique circumstances. One provision does not fit all. Second, the law of licensing—at least here in the United States—reflects often variable state law, which is one theme of this book. Third, a second theme of this work is to encourage the reader-licensee to become proactive or at least an active participant in licensing adoption and application. Often, even lawyers "model" provisions, whether a part of something larger or representative of the entire contract, document, or so forth, can lull one into a false sense of security or even laziness, not with any thought of maliciousness but just because it seems to be human nature. Again, such provisions are points of departure, examples, and so on, and are not to be taken as the beginning and the end. Rather, the point is to get the licensee thinking about what is in the agreement, what should not be in the agreement, and what could be in the agreement—in other words, to discover what is in the realm of possibility. After all, some licensors have been urging onerous provisions on licensees for years; we can afford to push back a little. Relationships between licensor and licensee can include give-and-take without animosity, but in contract law foresight is better than hindsight.

1. ARCHIVING (INCIDENTAL)

"Licensed content reproduced in print or electronic form during the duration of the agreement may be retained and used by the licensee or authorized users after termination of this agreement or after their status as authorized users has ceased. Aggregated groupings of content in electronic form may be retained after termination of this agreement by the licensee as long as no commercial use is made of the grouping. In the case of any particular grouping in electronic form where its contents are under copyright protection, the grouping made and retained by the licensee shall not constitute more than 1 percent [insert an alternative percentage], nor the aggregate of groupings made and retained by the licensee constitute more than 10 percent [insert an alternative percentage], of the licensed content, measured in terms of the numbers of items [insert an alternative measure] in the database at the time of the aggregation." This provision obviates the need to seek out and destroy the licensed content after the termination of the agreement. While the licensor may not agree, it also allows for somewhat more systematic retention of the licensed content—for continued use in electronic reserves, for example.

2. ASSENT

"Assent to this agreement shall be indicated by signature, whether actual or electronic, by the representative of each party vested with the requisite institutional authority to enter into such agreement. Under no circumstances shall use of the licensed content by the licensee constitute any of the following: assent to the initial agreement, intent to renew either the initial or a renewed term of subscription or the acceptance of a change to any term of the agreement." This provision indicates that assent to the agreement is explicit and by an authorized representative. Use alone cannot constitute assent.

"The continued use of the licensed content by the licensee or an authorized user or the continued supply of access to the licensed content by the licensor shall not constitute acceptance by either party of a change in terms to the agreement. The continued use of the licensed content by the licensee or an authorized user or the continued supply of access to the licensed content by the licensor after expiration of the current term of subscription shall not constitute renewal of the subscription period." In addition, a license agreement may provide that use of the licensed content by authorized users beyond a particular date or beyond some other event represents assent either to renewal of the agreement or to acceptance of a change in terms to the agreement.

"Assent to renew the agreement shall be demonstrated by payment of an undisputed renewal invoice within 45 days of receipt, where receipt occurs no earlier than 60 days and no later than 30 days before the anniversary date of the agreement." Assent should be made by explicit act, such as by payment of the renewal fee. This language also attempts to place receipt of the invoice and the due date for its payment in a reasonable time frame.

3. ASSIGNMENT

"Neither party may assign this agreement, except where one party changes legal form through merger, acquisition, or similar reconstitution, and the other party consents to the change, with consent not to be unreasonably withheld. If the assignment by the licensee results in a change in the value of the indicator used in determining the subscription fee [e.g., number of FTE students and employees], the subscription fee shall be adjusted proportionally by that corresponding indicator change, whether increased or decreased, and further adjusted for the remaining duration of the current subscription period." This provision allows for assignment of the agreement where it is logical that such assignment should occur. It also allows for adjustments to be made if the number of users under the assigned agreement changes (assuming the subscription fee is based on that number), whether up or down, but only assessed for the remaining term of the current subscription.

4. AUTHORIZED USERS

"Authorized users means those individuals who are registered users of the library, possess a campus network ID and password, or similar discrete designation of affiliation with the licensee." This provision does not include so-called walk-in or on-site users, which are typically listed under another subcategory of user. This concept of authorized user reflects the reality that this category of user possesses the highest level of access. The licensee must ensure that institutional policies and procedures accommodate such affiliation in order to maximize the benefit of the provision.

5. AUTHORIZED USES

"Allowed uses . . . any use that is lawful under the U.S. copyright law, its statutes (title 17, U.S. Code), its regulations (title 37, Code of Federal Regulations), or a court decision in effect at the time when use of the licensed content is made by an authorized user." This provision is a push-back against many license provisions that take away rights the licensee and its users would possess if the transaction and use of the licensed content were governed by the copyright law.

6. BONA FIDE RESEARCH

"Extraction of items from the licensed content, whether extracted individually or in clusters that is then aggregated into a discrete electronic grouping, is allowed for bona fide research purposes. Other aggregated electronic groupings are allowed of items if personal, noncommercial use is made of the grouping." This provision allows for systematic extraction for research.

"Use of automated, systematic, or similar search mechanisms of the licensed content is allowed for purposes of bona fide research as long as no commercial use is made of the search results." This alternate provision allows for systematic searching for research purposes.

7. CHANGE OF CONTENT

"Reporting period: Licensee shall be given notice to all changes to the schedule of licensed content titles/databases [choose one or insert another] on a monthly/quarterly [choose one or insert another] basis." This provision requires the licensor to provide periodic information on changes to the licensed content.

"A net decrease in content in excess of 10 percent [or alternate percentage] during any one subscription period, measured in the number of titles/items [choose one or insert another measure] available at the start of the subscription period, shall constitute a material breach for which the licensee may terminate this agreement upon notice to the licensor." Significant loss of content should trigger a termination right.

8. CHANGE OF TERMS, NOTICE AND TERMINATION

"Change of other terms requires notice be sent in accordance with the provision regarding adequate notice. Changes to material terms require notice in accordance with the provision regarding adequate notice and assent. Where required, assent shall be by separate acknowledgment either in writing, including by e-mail, or by an express online click mechanism. Continued use of or access to the licensed content after receipt of notice shall not constitute assent." In theory, this provision could apply to either party; that is, the licensee might desire to change a material term, would need to notify the licensor of the proposed change, and require assent to it by the licensor, with the continued supply of the service by the licensor to the licensee after receipt of notice not constituting this assent.

"If the licensee does not agree to a change in terms, the licensee may terminate this agreement and receive a refund of any prepayment. The amount of refund will be a figure representing a portion of the subscription period fee equal to the fraction of remaining days of the terminated subscription period over the total number of days in the subscription period." Changes in material terms by the licensor during a current contract should require assent and, if the licensee does not agree, should trigger a termination and refund right.

9. CREDIT AND REFUND

"When changes to the licensed content result in a net decrease in total content during any one subscription period in excessive of 1 percent measured in titles/items [choose one or insert another measure], on the start of the next subscription period the licensee shall be due a credit against

future payment of renewal and other fees or a refund, at the option of the licensee. The amount of credit or refund will be a percentage of the subscription period fee equal to the percentage of the net decrease in total content. "This provision secures a credit or refund for net loss of content. The "net" concept allows the licensor to attempt substitution, to not trigger a credit or refund right, as well as to add and subtract titles during a subscription period. Note that other provisions may reference or provide a credit or refund right.

10. DEFINITIONS

"Under this agreement... commercial use shall mean sale, rental, lease, lending of material from the licensed content, or a transaction of a similar nature, in return for monetary payment or use of the licensed content in direct competition with the licensor, except that nothing in this agreement shall prevent the licensee from participating in interlibrary loan or other library exchange arrangements sourced with material from the licensed content. "If acquisition of the licensed content were through sale, nothing would prevent such subsequent commercial transfer. However, as access is continual, there are limits on using the licensed content as a source of revenue. The provision does, however, preserve traditional library "exchange value" activities, such as interlibrary loan.

11. DISSEMINATION OF COMMENT

"Licensee shall not undertake any activity that may have a damaging effect on the licensor's ability to achieve revenue through selling and marketing the licensed content, except that nothing in this agreement shall prevent the licensee or its authorized users from making fair, reasonable, and lawful comment regarding the licensor, the licensed content, or the licensed service upon notice to the licensor received at least [insert number] hours/days [choose one] before/after [choose one] such comment is made public. "This provision preserves the right to comment on aspects of the licensor, the content, or the service, but it also preserves other clauses that may require confidentiality, such as pricing information. This provision also does not succumb to the 30-day period (or other period) required under a notice provision when offering public comment, as in cases of a wiki, blog, and so on, as such restriction would be contrary to the nature and context of the dissemination. Published review or comment in a serial may dictate advanced notice, *"or in instances of a review in a serial publication [insert a reasonable period of warning, depending on likely source of dissemination] days in advance of the expected publication date."*

12. DOWNTIME AND MAINTENANCE

"Licensor shall use all reasonable efforts [or use 'best efforts'] to make the licensed content available to the licensee and to authorized users on a daily, 24-hour basis, and to restore access to the licensed material as soon as reasonably possible in the event of an unscheduled

interruption in service. Licensor will make reasonable efforts [or use 'best efforts'] to notify licensee five business days in advance of scheduled interruption or suspension of service due to maintenance. Except where the force majeure provision applies, unscheduled or scheduled interruption or suspension of service lasting more than [insert amount, aggregate amount over a period of time, etc.] shall constitute a material breach of the agreement by the licensor. A refund or a credit against future fees at the option of the licensee, or a prorated credit or refund where interruption or suspension of service is partial, and where partial further adjusted in proportion to the loss of service measured in titles/items [choose one or insert another measure], shall be due the licensee where the aggregate time of interruption or suspension of service or partial service exceeds 60 minutes [or choose another number and/or measure] in any subscription period." This provision indicates that notice should be given for scheduled downtime or maintenance and that excessive loss of service other than by force majeure (where a breach or termination trigger might be a longer period of time) can constitute material breach. Finally, all loss of service beyond a very low threshold is subject to compensation, the form at the option of the licensee. Short of material breach, some agreed-upon level of loss of service is anticipated but nonetheless subject to credit or refund rights.

13. EXTRACTION LIMITS

"Reproduction of items from the database by any one user or by the institution shall be limited to an amount less than that which would render the continued access to the licensed content as a whole through renewal of the term of the agreement unnecessary. However, nonrenewal of this agreement shall not in and of itself serve as evidence that such reproduction has occurred." This provision gets to the heart of what most licensors fear and want to prohibit: that you take and retain so much from the licensed content over a subscription period or series of periods that you decide you do not need the service anymore. Many agreements do not entertain such rare possibilities, but should you find a nervous licensor, this language may address its fears without handcuffing the licensee or its users. Avoid inserting a number, even as a qualitative representation. Unless the parties are willing to partake in a somewhat futile exercise to identify a set amount—say, 20,000 downloads or copies a year, or some other number or a percentage of the total items (which would likely be a moving target for most databases, as the number of items may change throughout a given subscription period)—this is just as impractical as using a "significant" or "substantial" amount and also defeats the flexibility of a license in the first place.

14. FEES

"The annual subscription fee shall be based and adjusted on the following: any change in the number of authorized users, or any change in supply or other costs incurred by the licensor, or

when agreed upon by both parties upon a change in other circumstance. " Fee structures based on the number of users might increase or decrease based upon changes in this population. This provision accommodates either possibility. Of course, the licensor might adjust the rate as well. This is possible but would be subject either to negotiation or nonrenewal per other provisions. Other factors may impact the fee as well, but these would be subject to the consent of both parties. Of course, the content might change too. If the available amount goes down, the licensee might want the fee to be adjusted downward—but unless the licensee wants to pay more when content is added, it might be best to avoid such phrases. A possible added formulation might be something along the following: *"or any decrease [or change, if you are on a two-way street] in the licensed content measured in titles/items [choose one or insert another measure]. "*

15. FORCE MAJEURE

"Neither party shall be liable in damages or have the right to terminate this agreement for any delay or failure to perform any term or condition under the agreement if such delay or failure is caused by or is the result of conditions beyond its control including, but without limitation, acts of God, war, strikes, floods, governmental restrictions, power failures, telecommunications or Internet damage, destruction of any network facilities or services, or any other cause beyond the reasonable control of the party whose performance is so affected by such event. If any event or combination of events in the preceding sentence as well as the aftermath of such events shall continue for a period in excess of 30 days continuously or in the aggregate, either party shall be entitled to terminate this agreement upon receipt of notice by the other. In addition to a refund due under this provision the licensee shall be entitled to a credit or refund, at its option for any duration in loss of service exceeding [insert threshold, e.g., one hour, one day] under this provision or a prorated credit or refund where loss of service is partial, and where partial adjusted in proportion to the loss of service measured in titles/items [choose one or insert another measure]. " This provision places a limit on the toleration of the parties with respect to a force majeure. In all instances, credit or refund is due the licensee for all interruption in service.

16. INDEMNIFICATION

"The licensor shall indemnify the licensee for the amount of any award of damages against the licensee by a court of competent jurisdiction as a result of any claim arising from a breach of the warranty under [reference the warranty provision indicating that the licensor has the right to make the licensed content available] provided that the licensee informs the licensor as soon as practical upon becoming aware of any claim, not attempt to compromise or settle the claim, and gives reasonable assistance throughout the litigation to the licensor who shall be entitled to assume sole conduct of any defense, with decisions regarding litigation or settlement

made in conjunction with the licensee and upon consent of the licensee, with that consent not to be unreasonably withheld." This indemnification provision allows the licensor to control the course of the defense with reasonable input from the licensee.

17. NOTICE

"*Unless stated elsewhere, notice given under this agreement shall be in writing, sent by commercial delivery service or registered U.S. Postal Service with delivery signature confirmation to the person or address indicated in the communication schedule or to such other address as notified by either party to the other as its address for service of notices, and shall be effective when received. Receipt shall be deemed to occur upon acknowledgment through signature of delivery by the party in receipt of the notice.*" This provision establishes the default rule regarding the form and effect of notice under the agreement, adopting a notice upon receipt rule. The licensor may desire a modified mailbox rule, such as "*notice is deemed effective five business days after sending.*"

18. OBLIGATIONS OF THE LICENSEE

"*Licensee will make reasonable efforts to inform authorized users of the prohibited and permitted uses under the agreement through measures such as screen warnings or prompts hyperlinked to the relevant provisions of the agreement associated with use of the licensed content.*" This provision promotes compliance with the terms of the agreement without mandating it or imposing some impractical obligation upon the licensee.

"*Licensee shall not be required to monitor the use of the licensed content by authorized users in order to ensure compliance with the prohibited and permitted uses.*" This provision avoids heavy-handed compliance measures and preserves the status of the licensee in relation to library patrons, campus students, and so on, as intermediary and facilitator of access to information and not watchdog.

"*Upon knowledge of noncompliant use of the licensed content by an authorized user, the licensee shall undertake an appropriate and proportionate corrective response consistent with other institutional rules and policies regarding employee, student, patron, etc., conduct and behavior. Licensee shall not be required to notify the licensor of specific instances of noncompliance under this provision provided the licensee has responded as indicated here.*" This provision obligates intervention but is less heavy-handed than a reporting or "snitching" requirement.

"*Upon termination of this agreement the licensee shall send three notices to then-current authorized users of the licensed content regarding the retention and use of the licensed content after termination. The first notice is to be sent one week in advance of termination, the second notice one week after termination, and the third notice two weeks thereafter.*" Avoiding a promise of impractical obligations, if a "destroy after use" provision is insisted upon by the licensor, this approach is again less heavy-handed and a represents a reasonable obligation to assume.

In the alternative: *"Upon termination of this agreement the licensee shall send [choose an amount] notices to then-current authorized users of the licensed content regarding the possession and use of the licensed content after termination. The notices are to be sent once a week [or once every two weeks] beginning with a period two weeks in advance of termination."* This provision gives a slight variation on the previous one.

19. RENEWAL

"Unless renewed, this agreement will expire on the anniversary date of the initial date listed in the subscription schedule and shall renew every year thereafter on that date. Notice of nonrenewal must be given to the licensor by the licensee no later than 30 days before expiration of the current subscription period. Payment of an undisputed renewal fee must be made within 30 days of the anniversary date for renewal or, when in dispute, within 15 days of the resolution of such dispute." This provision allows for expiration or nonrenewal, avoiding the evergreen nature of many licenses (those having automatic renewal), and requires a reasonable period of notice for nonrenewal as well as for payment of a renewal fee, unless there is an issue regarding the amount of the fee.

20. TERMINATION

"Either party shall have the right to terminate without cause 60 calendar days after notice of the intent to terminate is received by the nonterminating party and with cause for material breach 30 days after notice of intent to terminate is received by the nonterminating party, provided the party in breach does not execute a cure of the material breach within 30 days after receipt of the termination notice. Where the remaining portion of the subscription period is less than 30 days the notice and cure period shall be the remaining number of days in the subscription period. Where notice of termination is tendered under circumstances described in the preceding sentence and the renewal fee paid, then any renewal shall be voidable (with full refund) at the option of the licensee and if so exercised a refund for the entire renewal fee shall also be due the licensee. In any case of termination before the expiration of the current subscription period the licensee shall be due a refund of any prepayment made and applied to the current subscription period. The amount of credit or refund being a figure representing a portion of the subscription period fee paid equal to the fraction of the remaining number of days in the terminated subscription, including the number of days the service was unavailable prior to termination over the total number of days in the subscription period." This provision offers equal termination rights with a reasonable period of notice and cure right, except where there are few days remaining in the current

subscription period. This mechanism also attempts to address the problems that could arise where material breach occurs in close proximity to the renewal (anniversary) date.

► 17

LOOK BEFORE YOU LICENSE: 126 QUESTIONS AND ANSWERS FOR EVALUATING LICENSES

Various resources exist for developing a checklist or similar tool with which one can evaluate a license agreement. For example, the *Principles for Licensing Electronic Resources*, developed by the major law library associations, can be readily adapted into a checklist for reviewing a license agreement.[1] A useful series of questions is found in Patricia Brennan, Karen Hersey, and Georgia Harper's *Licensing Electronic Resources: Strategic and Practical Considerations*.[2] A general set of principles that can also serve as a template for an audit, by the Association of Research Libraries, covers fifteen points.[3] Access to these and other compilations and collections is found on the Liblicense website of Yale University Library.[4] Short of constructing a list from scratch or adapting those mentioned, the following alphabetized list may be useful. In a given situation, one question or set of questions may be less relevant than another, or may even be irrelevant, and readers may think of additional questions and areas that could be included. However, this list is a good starting point for help in recognizing the potential issues and, hopefully, an inspiration for further exploration of problems and possibilities.

ARBITRATION

While it is not typical to include a provision that requires arbitration of disputes in information content or database licenses, the provision appears in many mass-market licenses and other software agreements. If the legal remedy is limited to arbitration, then disputes between the parties over application, interpretation, enforcement, and other areas of license provisions are not judiciable or subject to review by a court. Some licensees may prefer not to enter agreements with such requirements, and some states have legislation limiting the use of arbitration provisions in consumer contracts. However, recent U.S. Supreme Court precedent suggests such provisions, including class-action waivers that may be included in arbitration provisions, are valid, and state statutes to the contrary are preempted by federal law.[5] If arbitration is present in the license, the question is whether the arbitration mechanism presented is reasonable and meaningful, in terms of the ability for realistic redress of disputes that it offers.

1. If resolution of disputes under the agreement is limited to arbitration, is the process of arbitration reasonable, offering meaningful review of each party's position in a dispute? Or is the mechanism described one-sided, making it unlikely that a licensee would ever pursue action under it? In other words, is arbitration worth the time and trouble?

2. Does the arbitration process outlined in the license require an unreasonable escrow deposit or other payment before the process can commence, unreasonable costs—for example, travel— during the process, or does it otherwise limit the amount of recovery to the license fee, for example?

ARCHIVING (DURING AND POSTLICENSE)

The term *archiving* when applied to licensed content may refer to many activities, including conduct taken during the duration of the agreement, or it may refer to a bundle of access rights after the agreement ends. The concept can be applied with respect to individual or discrete items or to some subset or systematic amalgamation of items. While the licensee or an authorized user should be allowed to retain individual or discrete items (printed, downloaded, etc.) after termination, the right to make continued use of an extracted subset of the licensed content in a discrete grouping (such as that content to the database during the period of subscription) where each item in the grouping is still under copyright protection may need to be negotiated or otherwise discontinued. For those items no longer protected by copyright, the initial as well as continued noncommercial use of such grouping should be allowed, as the individual items in the grouping or subset are in the public domain and the extracted subset is likely not protected by the licensor's overall compilation copyright. Some licenses may allow for postlicense ("perpetual") access to material added to the licensed content during the duration of the agreement, though access may remain administered by the licensor or by a third party or, in some cases, directly by the licensee. Authorized users in possession of items from the licensed content should be allowed to retain such items for their personal, noncommercial use. Further, the licensee should not agree to the impossible task of destruction of such items.

Of course, many licensees desire to have extensive archiving rights. A licensor might be reluctant to provide such rights because nothing would prevent the licensee from failing to renew once retainable archive rights are obtained. The licensee would then have obtained and retained access to the licensed content while paying for only one year's subscription. This would be unlikely even in the world of print, as back issues would require some additional compensation. Of course, the licensee would incur the cost of maintaining the content in usable form, but this is a cost many would gladly bear. An alternative that might be more amenable to a licensor is to secure archive rights to the content added to the databases during the year or years of subscription. Previous years' archives might be subject to negotiation for an additional fee.

3. Does the licensee or its authorized users desire to have permanent or perpetual access to the licensed content or some subset of the licensed content? For example, would the licensee want access to material that was added to the licensed content during the duration of the agreement or to all licensed content that was added to the database prior to and through termination of the agreement?

4. Perhaps access to an archive or in e-reserves of material reproduced into some functional subset—for example, organized or searchable—is sought, fashioning the license transaction in terms of access and retention to be more akin to an acquisition-sale than a license? If so, is provision made for ensuring that such content remains available, accessible, etc., after the agreement ends, if the content may reside with a third party?

5. During the duration of the agreement, are authorized users able to create functional subsets of the licensed content for their own private use or for purposes of bona fide research and, in either case, making noncommercial use of the subset and to retain and continue use of such subset after the agreement ends?

ASSENT

The mechanism of expressing the parties' assent to the initial terms of the agreement or to amendment of those terms should be identified. Moreover, the mechanism of assent should be an explicit act. In the initial subscription, this is accomplished typically by a signature, which could be electronic under ESIGN or parallel state legislation (i.e., some form of UETA; see discussion in Chapter 5). More important is to consider how assent to changes in the terms is accomplished. A change in subscription price for the upcoming renewal indicated in a renewal invoice could be deemed accepted upon payment of the adjusted fee. This might be rather obvious, but how are changes to terms handled? Avoid provisions such as "subject to change without notice" or "as posted from time to time on our website." Whatever mechanism, the process should be clear. Avoid provisions that indicate "continued use constitutes acceptance to any changes to this agreement" or similar use-equals-assent clauses. There should be a separate notice provision indicating the form or mode of notice and when a notice is deemed effective. A change in a term should be subject to the notice provision and, if the term is material, require explicit consent to the change. While a printed addendum and signature might not be necessary in every case, the mechanism of assent must be clear and indicate the provision (change) that is being contemplated, that is, the subject of the assent. Under no circumstances should use or access (after notice of changes in terms was given) constitute assent. Likewise, use or access of the licensed content or continued use or access of the licensed content after expiration of the current term of the license should not be considered assent to renew the license. Assent should be demonstrated by signature, click-to-agree, or similar explicit act and not by conduct that a licensee would be expected to engage in, such as accessing a website (e.g., running a search). Avoid scenarios whereby such "assenting" use could be signaled by authorized users' continued access or use of the content as well.

6. *Does the agreement indicate that the method of assent is by signature, or other explicit act, and by the person authorized by the institution to enter into such agreements?*

7. *How does the licensee assent to renew the license?*

8. *How is acceptance to changes in the terms, including subscription fee, of the agreement accomplished (at least for material terms)? Is notice of changes required? If so, when is notice effective?*

9. *Does the agreement equate assent under any circumstances with mere access to or use of the licensed content?*

10. *Does any other act other than signature constitute assent, such as payment of an invoice to renew the subscription for another term?*

11. *Where notification of changes are by e-mail or other electronic form, is a "click-to-agree" mechanism through the licensor's website, for example, used? And is it clear to the average person what terms are the subject of change, and that clicking the "I agree" equates to assenting to the new terms?*

ASSIGNMENT

Licenses typically cannot be assigned. Often this prohibition applies to both parties. In situations of successor entities, for example, if the licensee merges with another institution, assignment might be desirable and not unreasonable to include. The licensee should assess the likelihood of this occurrence and determine the importance of this right and whether inclusion in the agreement is necessary. The same fate might befall the licensor as well. In these circumstances, assignment might be allowed only upon notice to the other party and require the consent of the other party as well, with consent not withheld unless there is good reason ("which shall not unreasonably be withheld"). Termination with refund to the licensee should be an option if a party to the license does not agree to the assignment. From the licensee's perspective, an example of a reasonable refusal to allow assignment would be a documented negative experience with another vendor—and this vendor is now the entity to whom the licensor desires to assign the license, as a result of, say, being bought out by this other vendor.

12. Does the agreement prohibit assignment of the license by either party?

13. If assignment is generally prohibited, is there exception for situations of merger, successor entity, or other logical scenarios?

14. If there is such exception, is assignment conditioned upon at least adequate notice to and, if possible, consent of the other party, with that consent unable to be withheld unless there is good reason, for example, a prior negative experience?

AUTHORITY

The license should indicate who has the authority to bind a respective party to the agreement. This identification is often made on the signature page. The agreement should also indicate (if applicable) that this person is the designated recipient of notice under the agreement, assuming there is a notice indicating the mechanics of proper notice. If the signatory is not the designated recipient of notice under the agreement, then another person, department, unit, or so forth, should be designated as the recipient of such notices. In all instances, the address of the target should be indicated with sufficient specificity. Some signatures are made "under seal" with one practical result being that the statute of limitations for settling disputes under the agreement may be extended.

15. Does the agreement identify the representative from each party who has the legal right to enter into contracts on behalf of that party and is the signature made "under seal"?

16. Is this person the legal representative to whom notice under the agreement is to be directed? If not, is that person, unit, department, etc., identified and articulated elsewhere in the agreement?

AUTHORIZED USERS

Ensuring that all users are in fact authorized users under the agreement is important. One way to solve the challenge of anticipating all the possible categories or groups of users to which full access rights are desired under the license is to link the concept of "user" in the agreement to those either registered by the library or the broader campus network system, in other words, to grant users some level of recognized affiliation. Then as unanticipated users or groups of users emerge, ensuring access through authorized user status is a rather simple process. (Walk-ins are typically given on-site access only and are typically dealt with under a separate designation.) The catch is then to make sure the institutional (campus or broader network) policies allow for the qualification and easy addition of such users to whatever designated status or level of access is necessary to achieve the intended result (e.g., issuing a library card, campus network ID and password, etc., which allows the user access to the licensed content from any location, whether on campus or through remote proxy server, etc.). Another approach is to attack the problem from the other side. Ensure that library-licensee policy is broad enough to accommodate the range of potential and desired users and then align the appropriate license terms to accommodate those authorized (from the perspective of the library-licensee) users. Where the "affiliated" or blanket approach is used, the following inventory can serve to ensure that the library or campus computing policies would accommodate the users so listed. Even with such an approach, the licensee will be back to square one in spite of a generous licensing provision where this provision is nonetheless limited by institutional reticence or lack of forethought and flexibility in its own policy. The other approach is to actually list all the anticipated user categories. Here is an example of the importance of "looking before you leap" and the value of making your list ahead of time before looking at the agreement to verify inclusion.

17. Does the license agreement accommodate or allow for access by the range of conceivable users in your present and future (at least for the duration of the current subscription period) circumstances?

18. Are the following users allowed access to the licensed content?
  ▶ *Are all categories of employees included, such as full-time employees but also those employed less than full time?*
  ▶ *Are independent contractors, consultants, and others who are doing work that directly supports the campus mission included? For example, would it allow access to a retired faculty member from another institution who is developing an online course module for use by the institution?*
  ▶ *Are volunteers, docents, or similar persons allowed access?*
  ▶ *Are visiting faculty, researchers, scholars, or more ephemeral guest lecturers that might be on campus for only part of the day or might join a distance-education chat room as an expert guest allowed access?*
  ▶ *Are alumni included? (Prospective students would be grouped under the "visitor" or other category.)*
  ▶ *Are part-time and full-time, degree and nondegree students included?*
  ▶ *Are exchange students, who may not be taking classes for credit but rather participating in an internship or other placement, included?*
  ▶ *Are continuing education, adult learners, "college for kids," and recreation as well as certificate or professional training students also included?*

▶ *Are visitors and other members of the general geographic community (as opposed to the institutional community)—in other words, walk-ins or similar individuals not affiliated with the institution past or present—included?*

19. If the library is a member of a consortia, system, or library network, are staff, patrons, and users of these other entities allowed remote access and on-site access (under the "walk-in" category), or are the limits of such access otherwise delineated?

20. Which categories of people previously mentioned will need remote access? If there is remote access via a proxy server, will all of these persons possess the required credentials that might be required (library card number or campus network username and password) in order to achieve the desired level of access?

21. Are any categories of users defined by geographical or jurisdictional limits—for example, legal residents of Milwaukee County? If so, does the license allow for such categorizations and for potentially shifting populations?

AUTHORIZED USES

What sorts of uses would you and your users like to make of the licensed content? Again, making a list before reviewing the actual agreement can be useful; it is a proactive rather than reactive strategy. As the license, not the copyright law, will govern the use of the content, you must include those uses which you might otherwise expect to be allowed under the copyright law. An alternative strategy is to again adopt a so-called blanket approach. Consider the following blanket-use clause linking authorized uses to the existing or future copyright law: "Allowed uses . . . any use that is lawful under the U.S. copyright law, its statutes (title 17, U.S. Code), its regulations (title 37, Code of Federal Regulations), or a court decision in effect at the time when use of the licensed content is made by an authorized user." Of course, such uses are not the only ones the licensee might desire.

The licensee and its users should be able to undertake a variety of uses, some of which may be beyond the limits of fair use or other provisions of the copyright law, or at least raise an unsettled issue (in terms of owner-versus-user positions on the matter). This is an opportunity to have the license agreement in a sense settle such concerns by expanding the scope of use rights beyond those of the copyright law and clarify some muddy areas of the law. This flexibility is an important asset of license agreements, and failure to take advantage of the opportunity greatly minimizes the license agreements' potential usefulness. A starting point for defining potential uses is suggested by the following list of questions.

22. Can a copy of an item from the licensed content be included as part of the reserve, course pack, anthology, or other reading, reference, or instructional support list for a particular course, in print or electronic form, either through the library or distributed through the campus course management system (i.e., in the web space of a particular class) or otherwise? Is it also possible for the same item to be used in multiple courses at one time and in multiple semesters, either individually or in combination with other items, whether such items are derived from the licensed content or elsewhere?

23. Can the licensed content be used to fulfill requests from other libraries or entities—for example, interlibrary loan and similar sharing or exchange relationships—and in either print or electronic form?

24. May authorized users make further noncommercial public distribution, public performance, or public display of the licensed content in print or electronic form to fulfill their own research, recreational, professional development, or similar interests, so long as the user parts with possession of his or her single copy of the item? (For example, a user could print an article, read it, and then pass the copy to a classmate, but could not post the article to a discussion board in an online classroom while retaining a copy on his or her laptop.) Is incidental commercial use or indirect commercial use allowed, such as background preparation for a seminar or workshop for which the authorized user will be paid?

25. Can the licensed content be combined, merged, compiled, and so forth, with other content?

26. Can derivative use be made of the licensed content (e.g., translating an article into a foreign language) as long as the use is limited to an institutional setting such as a classroom or an employee staff meeting with ownership of such derivative work retained by the creator or author (in the case of an employee in a work-made-for-hire scenario) or personal use of the derivative work? (Note that granting permission to make uses farther afield, e.g., for publishing the translation in a journal, may not be the licensor's to give.)

27. Can a single copy of an item or items from the licensed content be reproduced (printed, downloaded) by authorized users as well as "walk-in" users as long as the reproduction is for their personal and noncommercial use?

28. Does the license allow for the repeat reproduction of the same item or items as long as each subsequent reproduction occurs at a different time, that is, not as part of a concerted or related purpose? (For example, a user could print out a copy on a certain day, then misplace this copy and three weeks later print a second copy of the same article or download an item to his or her desktop computer, then months later, while traveling, access the same item remotely and download it to his or her laptop. In contrast, a walk-in user could not print out ten copies of the same item from the licensed content to distribute at a community meeting later that day, but nothing could prevent the walk-in user from printing one copy then making nine more at the local self-serve copy station or copy shop in the reference area of the library.)

29. Can authorized users make multiple copies of an item or items for other authorized users within a limited institutional setting, such as a classroom or in an employee staff meeting? (For example, a faculty member, teacher, or staff member would not be able to hand out multiple copies of an item at a seminar or other conference where he or she presented a paper, session, etc., but could do so for students enrolled in his or her Wednesday afternoon class.)

30. Does the licensee anticipate the need to make further public distribution and display of an item or items from the licensed content to other authorized users other than in the instructional settings previously noted? (For example, a user might want to include the item as an attachment in an e-mail to a standing committee of the institution or post it on a secure wiki to the committee membership or for a patron at another institution-library, including a patron and institution-library in a foreign jurisdiction.)

31. Is there a limit on the number of items the licensee or its users in the aggregate can obtain (print, download, etc.) over time from the licensed content? If so, how is this limit expressed— in terms of amount and time period, in number of items, titles, etc., as a percentage of the database or by some functional designation, for example, as an interrelated and searchable subset of the database?

In general, vague terms such as prohibiting reproduction of a "significant" or "substantial" amount might be difficult to articulate, much less administer. One approach is to understand the objective of the licensor through use of such a provision. One possibility is that the licensor does not want the licensee to download or otherwise reproduce sufficient amounts of the licensed content such that the copies compete or interfere with the need of the licensee to access the content in the future—to, in essence, obtain a copy of the database or a functional, competing subset of it such that the licensee no longer needs to continue to license the content but can instead draw upon its own store of the items. The following might offer a compromise without including clauses open to varied interpretations of meaning: "Reproduction of items from the database by any one user or by the institution shall be limited to an amount less than that which would render the continued access to the licensed content as a whole through renewal of the term of the agreement unnecessary. However, nonrenewal of this agreement shall not in and of itself serve as evidence that such reproduction has occurred." Again, the issue of how the institution will impose these restrictions on authorized users other than its own employees or perhaps students through codes of conduct is questionable. At the very least, employers are supposed to be able to control the actions of their employees, with the law generally holding that the employer is legally responsible for such conduct when undertaken in the furtherance of its employ. It might be better to agree to give users notice of this and any other restriction through reasonable methods but stop short of an impossible obligation to render the conduct of all users compliant to the license restrictions, even as to employees.

The licensee or user might desire to make a small database of related items upon which he or she might want to run searches, rather than need to access the entire database every time an item is needed. Some researchers might desire to study the search capabilities of the entire database or some subset of it.

32. Is such extraction and subset creation desired, as long as the use is noncommercial or for bona fide research or scholarship?

33. Related to this use, does an authorized user desire to run repeat, automated, or similar searches of the licensed content as a whole or as a subset for purposes of research, scholarship, or teaching?

BREACH, REMEDY, AND RIGHT TO CURE

Many agreements do not define what acts constitute a breach of the terms of the agreement other than to indicate that use of the licensed content or other conduct beyond the parameters articulated in the agreement violates the terms of the agreement and results in breach. Few agreements indicate what terms are material terms such that a breach of those enumerated terms constitutes a material breach. Breach may trigger additional rights or obligations—for example, a termination right, a right to cure the breach, an obligation to report the misuse—depending on whether the breach is material. While it is typical for a material breach to trigger a termination right on behalf of the nonbreaching party, a nonmaterial breach does not trigger this right. In addition, because remedy even in circumstances of material breach may be limited to termination of the agreement with damages for pecuniary loss foreclosed or limited to the subscription fee, the sequence of response to material breach is important. One approach is to require that, where the breach is material, notice be sent to the party in breach offering a right to cure the breach within a fixed amount of time with a right of termination at the option of the party not in breach should the cure not be made within the stated time period.

34. Does the agreement identify those terms that are material where conduct not in conformity with such terms constitutes a material breach? Is the remedy for material breach as well as nonmaterial breach, if any, articulated?

35. Is suspension of service or other so-called self-help measures a remedy of the licensor where the licensee is in breach? If so, is adequate notice of the impending suspension and a right to cure available to the licensee?

36. In cases of material breach does each party possess equal rights, for example, a right to terminate the agreement? If so, must the exercise of such right be predicated upon the receipt of notice by the party in breach from the nonbreaching party identifying the breach with termination effective within a fixed amount of time should the party in breach fail to cure the breach?

37. In case of suspension or termination (cancellation of the remainder of the license period), is a prorated refund available to the licensee so that the licensee does not pay for service it does not receive regardless of fault?

CHANGE OF TERMS

It is fathomable to conceive of the need for changes in the terms of license to be made on occasion—for example, the terms of agreements to which the licensor is party may have changed and those changes affect its abilities under the agreement to make the licensed content available in the future, or short of force majeure, there may be external events, marketplace or industry changes, for example, that necessitate change. Changes to material terms—terms that go to the heart of the bargain—price, content, use, etc.—should be conditioned upon clear notice of those changes and explicit assent to those changes. It could be argued that all changes, even nonmaterial or incidental ones, require notice; for example, a change in the dates of the licensor's billing cycle, while not a deal breaker, would be nice to know. Notice and assent should be required of all terms the parties have identified as material. As discussed, assent to changes should not be connected in any way to continued use of or access to the licensed content. Changes proposed in conjunction with a renewal period—such that the new terms go into effect at the same time as the new period begins—should be provided to the licensee at least 30 days in advance of the date by which renewal must be made, which may not be the same as the anniversary date of the current agreement. In this case, and where a change of terms is proposed in a negotiated contractual setting (as opposed to a mass-market agreement), the notice should be accompanied by sufficient opportunity to negotiate the change and opt for nonrenewal, all within the contractual time frame. There should be sufficient time to consider the terms and effect of termination where the proposed changes are unilaterally imposed. Depending on renewal and anniversary dates and the proximity of notice of change to those dates, there should be reasonable time to review the proposed changes; decide whether to negotiate and either accept or reject/terminate; and, depending on the how the dates fall and the terms of the agreement, issue notice of nonrenewal before either the changes are in effect or the option of nonrenewal has lapsed, or both. In cases of termination or nonrenewal, refund or credit rights should be available.

38. Is notice of any change of terms to the agreement required?

39. Is assent to a change in terms to the agreement required as well—at least for terms designated as material? In other words, what changes to the licensed content trigger a right to receive notice, and what changes to the licensed content require that the licensee assent to those changes?

40. What conduct qualifies as assent under the agreement? (See ASSENT)

41. If changes are to take effect in the new contract period, is there sufficient time to review the changes and take appropriate action (renew, reject and nonrenew, accept, etc.) before the date for renewal or nonrenewal passes? In other words, will changes in terms for the renewal period come in sufficient advance of the renewal date to allow for review and contemplation of the new terms?

42. Is there meaningful opportunity to negotiate proposed changes after receiving proper notice as articulated in the license?

43. Assuming notice of change in terms is given with an assent proviso (i.e., the licensee must consent to the change before the changes become effective), what options are available if the licensee does not agree to the terms? If the new terms will be effective in the new subscription period and the licensee does not agree to the terms, is the process for nonrenewal clear and straightforward, avoiding inadvertent acceptance/renewal?

44. If there is no opportunity to negotiate a proposed change in terms to take effect before the next subscription period, can the licensee terminate the agreement without penalty of any sort and with a right to refund?

CHOICE OF LAW, CHOICE OF FORUM

Is the law under which any dispute is to be resolved based on the state where the licensor is located or, more important, is it a state other than where the licensee is located? Likewise, what is the forum (federal or state) or court where the dispute is to be settled? In the case of a state institution, there may be prohibitions on entering into such contracts. Further, it is not unreasonable to obtain the right for the licensee to sue in courts of its own forum—in other words, federal and state courts with jurisdiction over it based on its permanent residence or official place of business and applying the law of the forum as well. At least in situations where the licensee is suing the licensor, or vice versa, the party instigating the lawsuit should have the right to bring this suit on its legal home turf, so to speak. Is this asking too much? This is a right European consumers have; in fact, European consumers can even require that suits against the consumer be brought in their home jurisdiction.[6] However, a library is likely a merchant, not a consumer, in such agreements, and its involvement could be construed in an agreement as a business-to-business or between-merchants transaction. The point is that the licensee should be aware of the implications of such provisions, especially where the licensor is based in a foreign country.

45. Does the agreement indicate the applicable law to be applied to disputes arising under the agreement?

46. Does the license agreement indicate which courts (and name the specific state and federal district courts) have jurisdiction over disputes arising under the agreement?

47. Does the agreement require the licensee to submit to the jurisdiction of the courts so indicated and prohibit the licensee from raising the issue of jurisdiction, a claim of forum non conveniens *before the court so indicated? See example and discussion in Chapter 15's deconstruction of the Nature (Academic: Americas) license.*

COMPLIANCE OBLIGATIONS...AND THE IMPACT ON PATRON PRIVACY

It is typical for the agreement to impose a number of obligations upon the licensee relating to what might be called compliance, with the goal of promoting and ensuring that the licensed content is used in conformity with the terms of agreement. Issues may arise related to these obligations, including efficacy and patron confidentiality. Turning a blind eye to misuse of the licensed content (or other material protected by copyright) is one thing; promising that all authorized users will comply with the license (or the law) is quite another. It is recommended that in situations where knowledge or awareness of misuse is not present, the most the licensee should be required to do is provide notice of those prohibited uses (as well as permitted uses, especially those in deviation from the copyright law—i.e., uses permitted by the license that are beyond those which copyright law would allow if it applied and of which the user would otherwise be unaware). While it is important to inform authorized users likewise of their use rights under the agreement (*see* AUTHORIZED USES), it could be argued that any such notices, except in their most rudimentary form, are cumbersome at best. Perhaps issuing a general warning notice at key points of access (in the acceptable use policy of the licensee, on the log-in page, etc.) that some content in the library is under license; that such licensed content is subject to the terms of the respective agreements; that these terms may provide rights lesser or greater than those governing content subject to the copyright law; and that for further information the user should follow the specific directions provided (e.g., "Click on the link below to see relevant terms" or "Click here to see the license agreement"). Yet this process could still be quite cumbersome. Different terms might apply to different content due to variation across vendors, so there would need to be some way to align the different agreements and respective terms with differing resources. This compromise might be acceptable from the perspective of the licensor and represents a far less ludicrous promise by the licensee than 100 percent compliance by all authorized users. While the licensee might accept an obligation to intercede if it knows or is aware of misuse of the licensed content and treat such deviation consistent with a violation of its other network policies, such as a prohibition against using campus e-mail to send harassing messages, additional obligations should be met with caution. The licensee should not be obligated to report such infractions to the licensor, nor should it accept any obligation to monitor use of the licensed content to ensure compliance. One problem with reporting such infractions, as opposed to an obligation to nonetheless intervene by arresting the misuse and promoting corrective, compliant action by the authorized user, is that alerting the licensor to a locus of misuse somewhere on the premises or network of the licensee—misuse which also might rise to a level of copyright infringement—is inviting further inquiry by the curious and now suspicious licensor. The next logical move is for the licensor to inquire after the name and particulars of the misuse as it contemplates legal action against the user. This leads to obvious issues of patron privacy in a legal as well as perhaps an ethical sense and at the least places the licensee in an awkward limbo between the licensor and end user, who may be a patron or student of the licensee. As previously stressed, one problem with the legal landscape of this setting is that such persons are third parties to the contract, not bound by the terms of an agreement between the licensor and the library-institution licensee. As a result, a promise by the licensee that authorized users will adhere to the terms of the license is problematic. The third-party status of authorized users can also be problematic from another perspective: while such persons are not bound by the terms of the contract, neither are they protected by it. It might be tempting for a licensor, once made aware of an incident of misuse, to enforce its copyright and other rights against the users who are misusing the licensed content. As a result, the licensee should not be obligated to report and document the misuse it observes but should be allowed to undertake corrective measures consistent with enforcement of other institutional facilities use and copyright compliance measures.

48. Does the license agreement obligate that the licensee promise all uses of the licensed content by all authorized users conform to or comply with the provisions of the agreement—in specific, the prohibited uses—and is the licensee required to use reasonable means to notify authorized users of prohibited as well as permitted uses of the licensed content?

49. Does the license require the licensee to monitor use of the licensed content by authorized users?

50. Upon discovering misuse by an authorized user, whether through monitoring or by other means, is the licensee required to notify the licensor of such misuse?

51. While not required to seek out misuse, if the licensee becomes aware of misuse by an authorized user, is it required to intercede in a manner consistent with infractions of its other policies related to employee, student, patron, etc., misconduct of computing, network, facilities, etc., such as its acceptable use policies?

52. Can the licensor monitor individual patron use in any way? If so, does the licensor have an obligation to adopt and enforce privacy protections regarding personally identifiable information or subject or use patterns of licensee-library patrons equal to or greater than those imposed on the library by a state privacy statute, other laws, or library policy?

In addition to language that would bind the licensor contractually to the same level of privacy (or greater) regarding patron information under which the library-licensee is bound by law or policy to follow, notice should be given to the patron in circumstances where control over use of the information is governed by or resides with a third party. Notice could be accomplished by placing signage near the terminals or on the screens from which the patron would access a vendor database ("Warning: You are about to leave...") or download content ("Warning: Your use of this e-content may be subject to observation by..."). These signs are especially important in situations where content is under the control of the licensor, such as when a database is accessed from the website of the vendor or content is tied to a device such as an e-reader or tablet that is under the control of the vendor or to which it has access. Language could be inserted into the license to ensure patron-user privacy along the lines of the following: "Licensor shall undertake reasonable measures ("reasonable efforts" would be better; "best efforts" would be best) to minimize the collection and retention of information that indentifies a patron or information regarding a patron (or use and define a concept of "personally identifiable information") or associates a patron with the use of the facilities or content, including but not limited to patterns of use, presence in the library, subject, search, or other use patterns." In addition, one of the two following statements should also be present: (1) "Patron information collected or retained by the licensor is confidential and shall not be released without the prior written and explicit consent of the patron and the licensee" or (2) "Any such patron information shall be protected to an extent equal to or greater than that imposed on the library by a state privacy statute, other laws, or library policy under which the licensee-library operates." (See also the discussion about fair information principles in Chapter 15's deconstruction of the Access NewspaperARCHIVE and Nature (Academic: Americas) licenses.)

CONSIDERATION

Consideration is essential to contract formation. Consideration can be thought of as the tie or glue that binds a party to the agreement. It is something of value. Obviously, the licensee offers payment of the license fee as partial consideration. Considering the other obligations the licensee may also assume or other rights surrendered (rights that would exist under the copyright law if it applied to use of the licensed content), the agreement should indicate that such promises are also part of the consideration offered in return for access and perhaps additional use rights (rights that would not exist under the copyright law if it applied to use of the licensed content).

53. Does the agreement indicate that the licensee enters into the agreement on the consideration of payment of the subscription fee as well as by assumption of the listed obligations and surrender of rights or other mutual promises?

CONTENT

In reasonable cases of singular, discrete, or limited number of titles, imprints, and so on, the subject of the licensed content should be articulated in at least a general sense—for example, which journal titles and for which years or volumes or which monographs by series, imprint, date range, and so forth, apply. Identification can be made through reference to accompanying schedules. Even, in the case of an aggregator, some initial list of scope or titles should be made available, upon the understanding that such list might reflect a snapshot alone, at some prior but recent point in time and not the date of assent to the initial agreement or renewal. A licensee may choose a vendor for a particular reason; for example, rather than looking for a general database of current news items or recent industry developments without much regard to specifics, the licensee seeks instead a particular family of newspapers or cluster of newsletters, with other titles being of little or lesser importance. Such titles or series would represent must-haves, so to speak, and go to the heart of the bargain. In this case titles, series, imprints, and so forth, should be listed in specific. Identification of a starting point is critical if a later refund, credit (in legal tender, not in hours of time, which may then extend the duration of the current subscription period), notice or notice/assent, or termination right is to be triggered by a change in the available content; in some cases, such change might constitute a material breach. An additional trigger might be set at a more general percentage change (more appropriately, a net decrease) in number of titles, individual items, and so on—in other words, loss of those considered less critical coupled with a right of cure, including a right of reasonable substitution if appropriate. A net loss of content, measured in some way, should trigger a credit or refund. Loss of those "mission critical" items goes to the heart of the bargain, the reason the license was obtained in the first place, and should again, within reason, trigger a material breach with termination rights. Termination for material breach often requires that notice be sent by the party not in breach with a right to cure. In a license for information, such as with a database, cure can be met by substitution of alternative content, subject to the agreement of both parties, which should not be unreasonably withheld.

54. Does the license agreement describe the content to be licensed with sufficient specificity such that any right of refund, credit, material breach, cure, termination, etc., is determinable?

55. Does a change in content, even if not accompanied by a right of refund, credit, material breach, cure, termination, etc., nonetheless require that notice of such change be given to the licensee in a timely manner?

56. Where the requisite change in content constitutes a material breach, does the licensor have the right to cure the breach and, if so, is substitution of content allowed? Is adequate substitution or cure determined through reasonable agreement of both parties?

57. If some definable net decrease in content does not constitute a material breach, does the change nonetheless trigger, at the option of the licensee, a credit that can be applied to a future subscription period or a refund?

CREDIT AND REFUND

Assuming that a fee is paid in advance—under some licenses such fees may be debited from the automated account of the licensee—a credit or refund, at the option of the licensee, should be available in identified circumstances, such as loss of service (downtime), force majeure, suspension, cancellation, and termination. Such a situation might arise where the charge is disputed and the supposed error is resolved in favor of the licensee. A termination might also trigger a refund. In noncancellation or nontermination scenarios, a credit is charged against future fees and can be in the form of a monetary adjustment or an extension of the length of service, with the former preferred over the latter. Adjustments to the length of current subscription period may complicate communications and trans-actions under the agreement if they impact the anniversary date, invoice, payment, and other deadlines. Many agreements do not offer refunds when termination is due to a material breach by the licensee. This author argues that nonrefunds of this nature are improper. Termination by the licensor in this instance represents a loss of something which is owed, that is, for which a fee has already been paid. The loss of refund in combination with loss of service through termination then operates as a fine, penalty, or unilateral imposition of damages. Likewise, in cases of loss of service for suspension (when deemed a fault of the licensee), downtime, including maintenance (unless calculated in the original fee), and force majeure, refund should be owed, as the licensee is otherwise paying for service it does not receive. Further, retention of prepayments by the licensor in such instances constitutes a penalty or forfeiture, which in many scenarios can be imposed at the discretion of the licensor. (For more information, see the previous discussion of Breach, Remedy, and the Right to Cure and, in situations of suspension, the licenses reviewed in Chapter 15.)

58. Where circumstances of suspension, other loss of service such as maintenance (with notice given in advance), and other downtime or qualifying change in content, for whatever reason, occur, does the agreement provide for the credit (against future payments or in hours, i.e., in extension of current service period) or refund, at the option of the licensee, of any fees paid by the licensee?

59. Does the agreement provide for a refund to the licensee of any fees paid where the agreement is terminated, regardless of the fault or reason for the termination?

CURRENCY

For the sake of clarity, the agreement should indicate upon which country's currency the dollar amounts described (e.g., subscription prices and any other charges) are based (e.g., Canadian, U.S., Australian).

60. Does the agreement indicate the national currency under which fees, refunds, etc., are calculated?

CUSTOMER SUPPORT

Many licenses indicate the form and availability of customer support. The licensee should consider whether this is sufficient.

61. Does the agreement identify the form of customer support the licensor will make available to the licensee (e.g., phone, e-mail) and provide adequate contact information?

62. Is the availability of support limited by day and time?

63. Does customer support include service (searching) as well as technical assistance?

DAMAGES

In addition to limiting the liability under the agreement (*see* DISCLAIMERS) for errors, omissions, and so forth, of the licensed content, contracts often limit damages recoverable as a result of any remaining liability from claims arising under the agreement to the greater of some low threshold or the amount of the current subscription fee. The resulting cap on damages is so low that the amount would fail to cover even the aggrieved party's attorney's fees, much less approach the compensation for the actual harm suffered. Some agreements limit the recoverable damages to the subscription fee only. This limit is put in place, of course, to discourage such claims in the first place. A laundry list of potential damages arising in tort or contract are often recounted for which recovery is not allowed, including loss of profits, business, revenue, goodwill, and anticipated savings, as well as indirect, special, incidental, or consequential loss or damage. This practice began in the early days of licensing and at that time was used extensively in the software industry to account for unforeseen but inevitable bugs or glitches in program code. The liability is often further limited to tort claims for personal injury alone, with the exclusion of pecuniary or business loss based in either tort or contract. Such limitations are the reality of licensing practice, and it is difficult if not impossible to change such practice. However, any such provision, if present, should apply equally to licensor and licensee. While it is understandable that the licensor does not want to be liable in contract or tort for harms arising from the licensed content—which might be deemed information-based harms—in instances of material breach in the form of, for example, nonperformance, there is no reason why compensable harm for loss of service to the entire campus during finals week should not be recoverable, at least in the opinion of this author. Of course, this provision would cut both ways: misuse of the licensed content would be subject to recovery for the actual harm caused by such misuse.

64. Does the agreement limit recovery for all claims based in contract or tort relating to the licensed content, or is recovery allowed for limited fault-based injuries, such as negligence, or limited to willful or intentional torts, such as fraud?

65. Does the agreement allow recovery for personal injury?

66. For the recovery that is allowed, does the agreement limit the damages to some monetary threshold or to the amount of the annual subscription fee? Does the license prohibit the withholding of a refund by the licensor in lieu of or as a partial fulfillment of damages assessed against the licensee?

67. Do the limitations on damages that are present apply equally to the licensor and licensee?

68. Are claims for material breach also subject to the limitations on damages?

DEFINITIONS

Licenses contain a section that includes a number of definitions, for example, defining "authorized users" or designating other categories of users, often assigned with a lesser level of access or use rights. Other concepts such as "notice" or "remote access" may be articulated in a specific section dedicated to providing definitions. Specific provisions may elsewhere by default define important rights, such as termination. If other provisions are applicable, consider including here a definition of which terms, if breached or changed, are material and trigger additional rights, such as credit or refund, termination, notice and cure, or notice and assent, as the case may be. If a phrase such as "reasonable efforts" is used (or "best efforts"), such concepts are legal terms often used in contracts, with courts defining such concepts; so if not otherwise defined in the contract, existing legal standards will apply. Either define the concept in the agreement or articulate examples where the term is used (e.g., "Reasonable efforts including but not limited to..."). One strategy is to read the agreement, making note of words or phrases used throughout that might be in need of defining, and then compare the list with the "definitions" provisions or other specific provision, such as those regarding "notice" or "force majeure," to determine whether the treatment is adequate. Another cluster of words or phrases may relate to permitted or authorized uses, such as commercial, noncommercial, personal, or private. Often licenses prohibit commercial use of the licensed content and restrict uses to private or personal sorts of uses (e.g., private study). Are *commercial* and *noncommercial* opposite terms? Is exchange of material from the licensed content for something of value also considered commercial, or is commercial intended to mean conduct that is in competition with the licensor or undertaken with the goal of monetary gain? In defining *private* or *personal*, is either concept intended to mean the opposite of *public*? If so, this may greatly limit the range of uses in networked or other shared environments. Another strategy is to consider inserting an exception for incidental commercial or incidental public use or to list with greater specificity the sort of uses prohibited or allowed.

69. Are the important terms or phrases in the agreement defined or are the meanings of those words or phrases clear from the context in which they are used? If not, consider including a definition in the paragraph or section of the license dedicated to defining terms and phrases. As a starting point, determine whether the following words or phrases are defined or articulated somewhere in the contract: permitted uses, prohibited uses, authorized users, *and related issues such as* remote access, licensed content, material breach, termination and cure rights, notice.

70. If some uses are limited to personal or private, do other provisions allow for uses in a library or educational setting that are "public," such as classroom use; internal use, such as group study; collaborative research use; use in staff meetings; or use in networked (by posting) settings?

71. If commercial use of the licensed content is prohibited, is the concept defined in such a way that it is not too limiting—for example, reaching use of the licensed content that is for direct profit or financial gain, or is in direct competition with the market for the licensed content alone—and excluding incidental commercial use and specific exchange value, such as participation in interlibrary loan or other resource-sharing arrangements?

DESTRUCTION OF CONTENT, POSTSUBSCRIPTION PERIOD

A license may contain a provision requiring that the licensee upon cessation of the agreement, whether by termination, nonrenewal, or other circumstances, destroy all copies of items from the licensed content that it or its authorized users possess. It is assumed that so-called walk-ins are a subcategory of authorized user. This is a ridiculous expectation and near impossible to meet. The better route is for the licensee to agree, at most, to use reasonable efforts to purge known copies under its control (e.g., on its servers) and to notify current authorized users with a request or series of requests within a given time frame after expiration of the agreement to do the same. It could be argued that this obligation is also unwarranted, but it is consistent with a view from the perspective of the licensor that a license is not a sale, and that once the term of the agreement ends all rights to that content should likewise cease. However, it is impossible to turn back the clock, so to speak, and expunge the existence of all copies of the licensed material, as if the agreement and the access it allowed never existed—especially for those persons who are no longer authorized users and no longer under the reach of the licensee, such as former students, or less subject to its current control, such as public library patrons.

72. Does the agreement require the licensee to destroy all copies of material sourced from the licensed content in its possession or in the possession of authorized users?

73. As an alternative, does the agreement require the licensee to use reasonable efforts (avoid the phrase "best efforts") to expunge copies of the licensed content of which it is aware and to expunge the same upon obtaining awareness of such content under its direct control?

74. Further, does the agreement obligate the licensee to make current authorized users aware, upon termination of the license, of the agreement of the cessation of access to the licensed content and to request any copies made by those users of material sourced from the licensed content be destroyed, making a reasonable number of such notifications within a reasonable time period after the end of the agreement (e.g., one notice every other week for a period of six weeks; one notice provided at one week, two weeks, and four weeks after termination of the agreement)?

DISCLAIMERS

It is common for licenses of all sorts, such as software or information products and services such as databases, where it is inevitable that errors, glitches, and so on, are present due to the nature of the content, to disclaim warranties related to the condition of the "product"—in this case, the licensed content and the information in it. The series of disclaimers ensures there is no guarantee, no expectation that things will always be perfect and free from error. This caveat makes licenses unlike the purchase of an automobile or a toaster, where the customer expects the product to function, the car to start and run without problems, and the toaster to darken the bread. But when the product is information, how is it expected to function? No one wants to buy a book full of typos, but what about the content itself? Is the information supposed to be accurate, up-to-date, free of all errors, and so forth? This may be the desire of the licensee—as well as the licensor, for that matter— but like some obligations imposed on the licensee regarding the compliance of authorized users or postlicense obligations relating to destruction of content, this too may be an impossible goal to achieve. As a result, such disclaimers nullify contractual guarantees, either imposed by legislatures or common law, that typically accompany transactions involving tangible products, often disclaimed with regard to information-based products and services. Perhaps this is a good thing. Otherwise, similar guarantees would be expected and might operate in other information product and service transactions, such as reference and other library services. The laundry list of possible warranty disclaimers includes expressed or implied warranties, conditions of merchantability, satisfactory quality, accuracy or fitness for a particular purpose, title, and noninfringement. Some states may legislate that some warranties are not able to be disclaimed, so a license might qualify its disclaimers with the phrase "to the fullest extent permitted by law," or words to that effect. Finally, the agreement may indicate that any oral or written information provided by any representative of the licensor does not create any warranty. This is included to ensure that, for example, any conversations with or any literature, brochures, and so on, distributed by the sales representative of the licensor at the annual library convention do not create any binding promise or warranty regarding what the product will or will not do or the nature of its content.

75. Does the license disclaim a series of warranties related to the information in the licensed content or the system or service that facilitates access to it? If so, are these disclaimers in bold or capital letters, as is often required by state contract law? Does your state law or the law of jurisdiction under which the agreement is to be interpreted foreclose disclaimers of certain warranties?

DOWNTIME OR MAINTENANCE

Time is money, as the saying goes, and so downtime for more than a day (24 hours) over the course of a subscription period—in some agreements measured in the aggregate (preferred), in other agreements measured in a smaller continuous time frame—should trigger a credit or refund right. It could be argued that even an hour of downtime should be compensable if it represents loss of access or service for which the licensee has already paid. If both credit and refund are anticipated under the agreement, the choice of which to take should rest with the licensee; after all, it is the licensee's money and is intended for the licensee's benefit. To be sure, such downtime might not trigger a termination right for material breach or additional damages, depending on how other provisions are constructed, but it should nonetheless trigger the right to be compensated for something the licensee paid for but did not receive, as most if not all subscriptions are based upon prepayment of the subscription fee. The license might state that downtime is compensated by an extension of an equivalent length of service or as an offset against future payments—a credit, more or less. If so, this should be at the option of the licensee, that is, to choose to take additional days of service, credit against future fees, or a refund. Also, if additional days are taken, the agreement should clarify whether this operates to extend the term of the current subscription period. It might be easier to treat it as a monetary credit, offset against future fees, to avoid changing the anniversary date or complicating renewal processes. In any case, in the event of nonrenewal, the licensee should be able to convert the days of subscription period extension or credit into a cash refund. Credit or refund might also arise where a dispute in fees is settled and adjusted in favor of the licensee. This assumes, of course, that prepayment occurred.

Most license agreements indicate some amount of downtime is anticipated during the term of the agreement. This may be due to upgrades, maintenance, and so on. Many agreements indicate that unless the downtime exceeds a certain amount—often stated in terms of a threshold of hours of service loss over a threshold time period, often stated in terms of days—no compensation is necessary. While the author agrees that such should not be considered material breach for which the termination right would apply (though in circumstances of significant loss of service, access to the licensed content would go to the heart of the agreement and surely be a material breach), this is nonetheless service for which the licensee is paying but does not receive, unless of course the fee is based on a daily rate that is then automatically adjusted to include at the outset such downtime, but this is unlikely. Furthermore, making the licensor financially responsible, short of material breach for lapses in service, is one of the best ways the author knows to ensure that such lapses are kept to a minimum. The financial responsibility should be expressed in the form of a credit, refund, or similar offset, and at the option of the licensee.

Offsets for consequential damages are not contemplated within this provision. For example, the service was down for two weeks so the licensee chooses a two-week credit to be applied to the next renewal fee. But because the service was down, a doctoral student could not finish cite-checking her dissertation, had to postpone her defense and subsequent graduation, and lost the job that was dependent upon timely completion of her PhD.

The author cautions against agreements that provide an offset in the form of a credit automatically applied that pushes out or extends the end of the current agreement period, as such adjustments can wreak havoc with notice, renewal, and payment dates and obligations. The better course of action is to take the credit and apply it against the next renewal agreement period, thus retaining the current anniversary date. Or, if the licensee is fed up with the shoddy service, the licensee can claim a refund and allow the current agreement to expire without renewal (watch for nonrenewal notice requirements; see RENEWAL, NONRENEWAL). In addition, the agreement should anticipate partial loss of service or downtime if this is conceivable or possible and adjust calculations proportionately. Finally, the licensor should be obligated to give adequate notice (of a reasonable amount measured in weeks, not days) of such lapses in service, at least for those reasonably under the control of the licensor, such as routine or scheduled maintenance or upgrades to service. To avoid hairsplitting, the agreement could indicate the calculation of credit or refund is made by rounding up to the nearest whole day beyond the first day (an aggregate 24-hour period).

76. Does the agreement state an acceptable period of downtime, nonservice, maintenance, etc., within which limits such lapse will not be considered a material breach?

77. If partial loss of service is possible, are such lapses accounted for proportionally and is the measure of proportion identified—in other words, number of titles, number of items, number of databases unavailable as a percentage of total titles, items, databases?

78. In cases of scheduled maintenance and other reasonably foreseeable losses of service does the agreement require the licensor to give the licensee at least five business days' notice of the event and a reasonably accurate estimate of the duration of the suspension of service or partial service?

79. In any case, is the licensee compensated and at its option by refund, credit, etc., for all the time the service is unavailable in excess of 24 hours (a shorter time frame, calculated to the nearest hour, would be better) in the aggregate in any subscription period, regardless of whether such unavailability triggers the material breach threshold (the acceptable period of downtime, nonservice, maintenance, etc.)?

80. If a credit option is available and selected, is the credit applied to the next subscription period as a monetary credit rather than as an extension of an equivalent number of days of the end of the current subscription period, the result of which would affect the expiration date of the current subscription period and push out the anniversary date?

81. Further, is any compromise in service by the licensor to the licensee likewise subject to compensation at the option of the licensee in proportion to the amount the loss or degradation of service represents to the service as a whole? In other words, a downtime of 25 percent equates to a refund, credit, etc., of 25 percent of the subscription fee, represented by the days affected. Finally, is the measure of proportion identified (e.g., number of titles, number of items, number of databases)?

FEES

Fees include the actual subscription cost as well as other charges. All fees should be identified in the license or its schedules. The period subscription price is a material term, and changes to it should be subject to notice and assent. Likewise, nonpayment is often considered a material breach. If so, there should an adequate invoice period offering a realistic opportunity to challenge the fee before the breach provision(s) would be triggered. One way to avoid this issue is to qualify the nonpayment as breach provision applicable to nonpayment of "undisputed" fees alone. Consider also whether the nonpayment would be subject to a "right to cure" under the agreement, which would typically also require that notice of breach be given with a subsequent period to cure the breach, satisfied by paying the fee (and therefore curing the breach). Fees should also be subject to credit/refund provisions. If the agreement makes reference to other fees or costs, these should be described or listed in the agreement or accompanying schedule to avoid surprises later.

82. Does the license agreement or its schedules indicate the period (monthly, quarterly, annually, etc.) of subscription fee or the rate on which it will be calculated?

83. Where other charges or fees are assessed, does the agreement or its schedules indicate the form, manner, and amount of such assessments?

84. Does the agreement provide that, before any fees are owed, an invoice must be received by the licensee indicating the amount, nature, and due date of the fee and, in advance of that due date, sufficient time is allowed for the licensee to seek clarification or dispute the proposed fee?

85. Are period renewal invoices received a reasonable time in advance of the anniversary date, with the due date for payment of the renewal fee also reasonable? For example, a renewal invoice would be received at least 30 days before expiration of the current subscription (the anniversary date), with payment due within 30 days of the expiration of the current subscription period (i.e., within 30 days of the anniversary date or 60 days after receipt of the invoice).

FORCE MAJEURE

Another common element in contracts is some variation of a force majeure, or acts of God provision, releasing the party from an obligation to perform under the contract where such performance is made impossible or very difficult due to circumstances beyond its control, for example, forces of nature related to weather or tectonic plate movement or human catastrophes such as war, terrorist attack, or other limitations (e.g., think of the failure of the U.S. power grid in the Northeast that forced much commerce and activities of daily life to a halt in August 2003). While the party affected by the force majeure should not be obligated to perform under the agreement, nor is this party liable for damages resulting from the occurrence of nonperformance (it could be the licensor's inability to make the service available as a result of a flood or the licensee's inability to make timely response to an invoice because its accounting system was toasted by a lightning strike and subsequent power outage), as performance is excused. Under the license, such an occurrence does not constitute material breach for which termination is a likely remedy. Some agreements are written broadly enough to include not only the event itself but the impact or fallout from it as well. For example, Hurricane Katrina lasted only a few days and the flooding persisted for days afterward, but even after structures were dry, it often took weeks or longer to make them usable or habitable again. However, some agreements may indicate that if the force majeure or its impact persists for more than a stated amount of time, the other party may terminate upon written notice. In any case, any downtime or suspension of service by the licensor should be subject to a credit or refund due the licensee, as such downtime is not part of scheduled maintenance and, it could be argued, the licensee, in cases of prepayment, paid for but did not receive regular and expected service. Allowing one party to suspend performance is one matter, but a licensee should not also be expected to pay for the nonperformance; thus, it is argued that the period of loss of service, while not terminating the agreement (unless some threshold is met), should still count toward the downtime/maintenance credit/refund provision.

86. Does the agreement contain a force majeure clause, describing the range of events both natural and human that are subject to it?

87. Is it clear from the provision that also included within the force majeure is the subsequent impact of the event and fallout from it, as well as the occurrence of event itself?

88. Does the force majeure provision release the affected party from performance under the contract for the duration of the event and a foreseeable period of impact, as well as from liability damages that befall the other party as a result?

89. Does the provision prohibit a party from terminating the agreement as a result of a force majeure befalling other party or, in the alternative, does the provision allow one party (typically the party not in crisis) or both parties to terminate the agreement if the event or its foreseeable impact persists for more than a stated time period?

90. In any case, is the licensee compensated and at its option by credit, refund, etc., for all the time the service is unavailable when the licensor is the party befallen by the force majeure? (While a force majeure excuses performance by one party, it should not obligate the other party to keep paying for the lack of performance.)

91. Further, is any compromise in service by the licensor to the licensee likewise subject to compensation at the option of the licensee in proportion to the amount the loss or degradation of service represents to the service as a whole? (For example, a 25 percent service loss equates to a refund, credit, etc., of 25 percent of the subscription fee represented by the days affected.) Finally, is the measure of proportion identified, for example, the number of titles, number of items, number of files or databases, size of record?

HEADINGS

The headings used throughout the agreement, like the title of statutory provisions, do not have legal meaning under the agreement.

92. Is it clear from the agreement that the headings, which may preface or accompany particular provisions, paragraphs, etc., are for the convenience of the reader and have no legal significance or impact on interpretation or application of the agreement?

INDEMNIFICATION

Any warranty made by the licensor that it has the legal right to make the licensed content available through the agreement is rather useless if the licensor does not back this promise with a further promise to, in essence, make the licensee whole from the legal repercussions of any error on this front. Likewise and often overlooked, an indemnification provision alone is also insufficient but for a different reason. With a warranty provision in place alongside the indemnification, the licensee, upon becoming aware that the licensor is in fact supplying the licensed content in an infringing manner, does not need to wait to be sued (and claim indemnification rights from the licensor under the agreement) but can claim breach of a material term with all the rights attendant to such claim under the agreement (termination, refund, etc.). This is the one warranty upon which the licensee should insist. Indemnification indicates that the licensor will provide or pay for any legal representation necessary—all costs, damages, and so on—that result from such an error, as it did not have the right to make the material available. Claims can arise because, without the legal right to make the licensed content available to the licensee and under the terms in the agreement, use of the content by the licensee under some provisions might constitute copyright infringement. The provision should include coverage of any costs incurred by the licensee to rectify any infringing representations of the licensed content, in other words, costs associated with withdrawing or expunging the infringing content. Often such indemnification is contingent upon the cooperation of the licensee in reporting any knowledge of infringement or claim of infringement, in desisting from continued infringement where possible, and in allowing the licensor to control the defense of any claim brought against the licensee regarding the licensed content under the agreement. It might be advisable to condition that any litigation decisions be made in consultation with the licensee and subject to the consent of the licensee as well; for example, the licensee should have some input into a decision to settle the case and the settlement amount, with such consent not to be unreasonably withheld.

93. Does the agreement indicate that the licensor will indemnify the licensee against any liability and the costs, damages, etc., resulting from its supply of the licensed content in error (not that the content has errors but that the licensor did not have the legal right to make available the licensed content), including costs associated with removing any infringing content or rectifying the problem?

94. Does the indemnification require prompt notice of any such claim by the licensee and continued cooperation by the licensee with the licensor in defense of such claim?

95. If the agreement indicates that indemnification is contingent upon any legal defense of infringement being under the control of the licensor, are decisions related to the litigation subject to the consent of the licensee, which is not to be unreasonably withheld?

INTEGRATION

The agreement should indicate that the agreement stands on its own and represents the complete expression of the parties' wishes, desires, and so on, superseding all previous agreements between the parties. While there may be attached schedules, previous or other agreements are not used to interpret the current relationship. There is no further incorporation of other documents, and any other information intended to be included in the agreement is merged or integrated into its current iteration and present in the document. If there are schedules describing the content, Internet protocol (IP) addresses, or other identification of users, and so forth, the schedules are identified in the agreement. If future schedules or changes to existing schedules (change in fee structure, change in number of authorized users or equivalents, etc.) are anticipated, this information is also stated and delineated.

96. Does the agreement indicate that it represents the complete expression of the parties' intent to enter into the agreement, superseding any previous agreements between the parties, and that no other documents should be used to interpret the agreement?

97. If there are attached schedules, are the schedules identified in the agreement? If amendment to the schedules is anticipated, is the amendment process and impact of that amendment described?

NOTICE: MECHANISM, WHEN EFFECTIVE

The notice provision should indicate the particulars of acceptable notice (form, direction, etc.) and when that notice is deemed effective.

98. Is the form of acceptable notice specified as print, electronic, or either?

99. Is the method of delivery of notice specified? If limited to print, is delivery by commercial delivery agency or U.S. Postal Service, in either case with a delivery-confirmation and/or a signature-confirmation mechanism?

100. Does the agreement indicate the person or department to whom or to where notices under the agreement are to be directed, including the particular address?

101. Is notice effective when sent (the mailbox rule), or some variation of it, for example, within 48 hours of posting or sending, as the case may be?

102. Alternatively, is notice effective when received (and by whom; see question 98) with a mechanism for acknowledgment of receipt required—for example, a delivery-confirmation or receipt—requested signature?

PROHIBITED USES, RESTRICTION ON OTHER RIGHTS

In return for granting authorized users authorized uses, the licensor will desire something of value in return and in addition to the subscription and other fees. It is typical that the agreement requires the licensee to make promises not to make certain uses of the licensed content and to fulfill other obligations. Expect a prohibition on commercial use of any of the licensed content. The licensor is not figuring in use of the licensed content by the licensee to fill requests from third parties who are then charged for the licensee's service. Other prohibitions on certain types of reproduction (downloads, extractions, etc.) and public distribution are often also included. Of course, there is no way for the licensee to prohibit its users, without its knowledge, from engaging in such practices other than to take reasonable steps to inform users of such prohibitions and to prevent such further prohibited uses when it does possess knowledge of such prohibited uses. However, a licensee should assume no obligation to actively police the conduct of all authorized users or ensure that users engage in no misuse whatsoever. Also, there may be prohibitions on revealing certain licensing terms related to pricing or other conduct that might interfere with ability of the licensor to obtain a profit or other benefit from its product (and prohibitions of this sort can be worded broadly and vaguely, as the previous sentence suggests). Service agreements may contain a gag or nondisclosure provision indicating that the entire contents of the agreement are to be treated as confidential and not to be shared under any circumstances. However, there are some prohibitions a licensee might not want to be obligated to honor: restrictions on uses that under the copyright law would be lawful should not be prohibited; obligations which are impossible or nearly impossible to perform or which require monitoring or enforcing restrictions upon users should not be required.

Some license agreements may require the licensee to abstain from engaging in other conduct unrelated to the use of the licensed content but related to it in other ways. This restriction may be stated in very general terms, such as a prohibition on engaging in any conduct that would interfere with the ability of the licensor to achieve or maximize revenue from the licensed product or service.

In the alternative, the agreement may in specific prohibit conducting benchmark testing on the service or dissemination of those results, or from disseminating reviews of or similar comments on the product. While performance testing might not be an option where the subject of the license is information, such as a database, and tests could be made of the search features that accompany the database, a more likely scenario involving such activity concerns the system software a library might license. For example, as a new cataloging upgrade or circulation module is introduced, the licensee might desire to put the system through its paces, so to speak, and then, as a service to the profession, disseminate the results by posting a summary on a library blog, wiki, old-fashioned electronic bulletin board, e-newsletter, and so forth. The licensor might have an interest in preventing such release or at least might desire "rebuttal" space. While such provision does not in a constitutional sense violate the free speech rights of the licensee, it nonetheless offends general concepts of free speech and expression. If the licensor is concerned about negative press, then such dissemination could be conditioned upon notice to the licensor. If the licensor desires to rebut such expression, it can then pursue identified avenues and attempt that rebuttal. In other situations, the licensor might desire to keep some information confidential, such as pricing.

103. Does the license agreement prohibit the licensee or its users from making fair, reasonable, and otherwise lawful comment on the quality of the service or content provided? Or is there a general prohibition on undertaking any activity that would have a negative impact on the ability of the licensor to generate revenue from the licensed product? If so, is there an exception if the licensee first provides notice to the licensor of the upcoming public comment or dissemination and an opportunity to respond?

104. Does the agreement prohibit the licensee from disseminating information regarding the terms of the agreement, such as pricing or discounts?

105. If the licensed content includes items that are not protected or are no longer protected by copyright, are there limitations on the extraction or use that can be made of these works? This would be in contrast to the copyright protection that would exist for a work consisting of the aggregate of items in the database, which might be protected as a compilation or collective work.

106. Is the licensee prohibited or otherwise limited from extracting a subset of unprotected (in terms of the copyright law) licensed content and manipulating the subset for its own needs? Where no such limitation exists, is extraction nonetheless prohibited if some threshold conduct or amount is reached (e.g., commercial use is made of the subset, any grouping of extracted content protected by copyright constitutes more than 1 percent of the licensed content at the time the extraction is made, or the aggregate of groupings constitutes more than 10 percent of the licensed content, etc.)?

RENEWAL, NONRENEWAL (EXPIRATION)

Renewal is common in licensing relationships. However, a change in terms, to become effective in the renewed subscription period, should be given with sufficient notice so that the other party may consider such terms, perhaps negotiate alternate changes, and ultimately decide whether to renew. The agreement, communications, or invoice of new terms may indicate that in these circumstances assent is demonstrated by payment of the proposed renewal fee. Any such notices of changes in terms should be given with sufficient notice to avoid invoice and fee payment issues. The date of invoice for renewal should be reasonable in relation to the anniversary or renewal date. In any instance, the licensee should have 30 days after the anniversary or renewal date in which to pay the renewal fee. Some agreements require the party seeking nonrenewal (typically the licensee) to notify the other party A period of 60 days is typical; from the licensee perspective, a shorter period is preferred. Some agreements require 90 days' notice of nonrenewal. Again, the street goes both ways: for the unusual situation in which the licensor desires not to renew, is the notice period (30, 45, 60 days, etc.) sufficient time for a licensee to find a replacement vendor? Without such notice required in the agreement, situations of automatic renewal are known as evergreen agreements.

107. Is the duration of the agreement and its anniversary date articulated?

108. Is the anniversary date firm, without the ability to extend such date through application of credit, for example? (See Downtime or Maintenance*) In situations of outstanding credit and nonrenewal (expiration), is the licensee due a refund, assuming the annual subscription or other fees are prepaid?*

109. Do both parties have the ability to allow the agreement to expire—in other words, to decide not to renew the agreement? Or is the agreement subject to automatic renewal (evergreen)?

110. Is notice required by one party to the other party in the situation of nonrenewal (expiration)? If so, is the required notice period reasonable, not being more than 60 days (fewer is better, especially in subscriptions less than a year) prior to the anniversary date for a subscription period of one year?

SEVERABILITY (OF "OFFENDING" PROVISIONS) AND SURVIVABILITY (OF THE AGREEMENT)

It is typical for license agreements to include a survivability or severability clause indicating that, should any provision of the agreement be deemed unlawful, inapplicable, void, and so on, by a court or legislature, the remaining provisions remain in effect. The agreement will not end because a provision or even several provisions are, in effect, redacted from the agreement. Courts in general take this stance, viewing the contract as near sacrosanct. As a result, a court will endeavor to leave undisturbed the overall agreement unless, sans the offending provisions, absurd results occur or the provisions go to the heart of the bargain such that the removal renders the agreement pointless. In other words, not so fast! It is not that easy to get out of the agreement even when it includes an invalidated provision.

111. Does the agreement indicate that, should one or more of the provisions be struck from the agreement by a court or made legally inapplicable by a legislature or otherwise invalid by law, the remaining provisions as well as the agreement as a whole will remain in effect?

SUSPENSION

The agreement should indicate the circumstances under which a unilateral suspension of service by the licensor is possible, other than by force majeure. Suspension should be very limited, if allowed at all; and if allowed, it should indicate how the duration of the suspension is calculated and under what circumstances the suspension ceases. Is suspension subject to a notice and cure right? Suspension should not occur unless there is adequate notice and a right to cure. In the opinion of the author, a suspension operates as a punishment. It is unfair to impose suspension, loss of service, without notice and a right to cure the breach, especially if no credit or refund is due for the period of suspension—though it could be argued suspension is punishment enough, that the licensee should not have to pay for it as well. If the suspension occurs in error, then a credit and refund should be due. Moreover, this improper loss of service might then constitute a material breach.

112. Under what circumstances, if any, can the licensor suspend access, short of termination?

113. Is adequate notice provided before suspension with a reasonable right to cure and prevent the suspension?

114. If the suspension is later found to be in error, can the licensee receive a credit or refund or view the improper suspension as a material breach? Is a credit or refund at the option and in the form of the licensee's choosing available?

TERMINATION (AND CANCELLATION) RIGHTS AND OBLIGATIONS

In addition to the right not to renew the agreement (nonrenewal or expiration), both parties should have equal termination rights, that is, the ability to end the relationship before the stated date of expiration of the current agreement. Some agreements refer to this voluntary ending of the agreement as *cancellation* and reserve the word *termination* for situations of cause (bankruptcy, material breach, etc.) alone. The triggers for exercise of this right should be articulated in the license. The agreement may allow the licensor to terminate at a whim, for any reason, as long as sufficient notice is provided. It is, however, typical to grant termination rights to both parties where the other party is bankrupt (or in some similar legal state such as receivership and is unable to pay its debt) or has committed a material breach of the agreement. All terminations should be subject to a period of adequate notice (30 days) and where applicable a right to effect a cure of the problem (within that 30-day period) and refund.

Termination rights should be equally available to both parties, but with reasonable notice. Notice is especially important to the licensee and arguably less so for the licensor. If a library decides to cancel its subscription, the impact on the licensor may be negligible; it would still continue to operate business as usual the very next day, with one less customer. However, the loss of access to content by the licensee and its patrons, clients, and so forth, would send staff scrabbling to ensure that coverage or access to the licensed content would somehow still be available or find a reasonable substitute, in other words, line up another vendor with the same or similar content. This may take some time.

Finally, what provisions survive the termination of the agreement or what obligations are imposed, such as destruction of the licensed content? H. Ward Classen identifies a cluster of typical surviving provisions: those relating to price and payment, proprietary rights, confidentiality and security, patent and other proprietary rights indemnification, general indemnity, limitations on liability, choice of law and choice of forum, arbitration (if applicable), bonds, and business continuity planning, that is, disaster recovery (if applicable).[7]

115. Is there parity in the termination (cancellation) provisions—that is, does the agreement give equal termination (cancellation) rights to the licensee as well as the licensor? If the licensor has the ability to terminate the agreement for any reason, does the licensee possess a similar right under the agreement to so the same?

116. Upon termination by either party does the licensee receive a refund for the payments already made? Does this termination refund include payment for any downtime experienced but not previously offset? If the offset is in the form of days of service (an extension of the contract by the days of downtime), then these days should be cashed in at the time of termination or nonrenewal.

117. Do both parties have the right to terminate due to bankruptcy or other legal designation of financial straits? If the licensor goes belly-up, is the licensee due a refund, application of the federal bankruptcy statutes notwithstanding?

118. If the licensor merges with another vendor or otherwise changes its business status, does the licensee have termination rights? Or is the licensee at least subject to notice and assent which cannot be unreasonably withheld?

119. Is notice of termination required in reasonable advance of the date of termination and, regardless of the reason or instigation of termination, is a refund available to the licensee?

120. If termination results because of breach, is a right to cure the breach available to the party in breach? If so, how is assessment and acknowledgment of cure to be accomplished?

121. Do any of the obligations survive the agreement and remain in effect after the term of the agreement or subscription period ends? What other obligations are imposed following termination?

WAIVERS

It is common in license agreements to include a provision relating to waivers—not the disclaimer of warranties (*see* WARRANTIES), but a waiver or release of an obligation or other responsibility of one party under the license, waived by the impacted party (or the party against whom the waiver operates). In essence, one party gets a pass. Any waiver should be explicit, limited, and written and signed by the appropriate authority. The waiver should be for a specific provision and a specific incident or occurrence (otherwise it might constitute a unilateral change in terms, even if to the benefit of the other party). Waivers should not be implied. Often in conjunction with this provision is one stating that, even in cases where a proper waiver is not made, inaction in response to or ignoring any infraction is not to be taken as a waiver, that such infraction of the other party's obligation or other responsibility is acceptable. Further, such inaction does not prevent the aggrieved party from enforcing its rights under the contract in the future. Inaction does not constitute an implied license in the future and does nothing to prevent the party from enforcing the provision in the future.

122. Are waivers prohibited by the agreement?

123. When waivers are allowed, are the waivers required to be in writing, with the appropriate signatures of the party granting the waiver, articulation of the specific conduct or circumstances of the waiver, and the period of the waiver (if applicable) indicated?

124. Does the agreement also indicate that inaction or nonenforcement of a right under the contract by one party in one instance of infraction does not prevent that party from acting and enforcing its right under the contract in the next instance of infraction?

WARRANTIES

While it is typical for the licensor to waive most, if not all, warranties on the veracity, quality, and so on, of the product or service offered (i.e., the licensed content) and for the licensee to agree to these waivers, there is one warranty the licensor should make. The licensor should warrant that it in fact has the legal right to license and make available the licensed content under the terms it offers. The licensor typically offers a nonexclusive (indicating in essence that the licensee is not its only client or customer) license to make certain uses of the licensed content. In tandem with this warranty, the licensor should provide an indemnification to the licensee that, if by chance it is wrong and it really does not have the right to offer the licensed content to the licensee with the result that use by the licensee of the content is infringing, the licensor takes full responsibility and agrees to provide legal representation, compensate for any damages assessed against the licensee, and so on. (*See* INDEMNIFICATION)

125. Does the agreement contain a provision indicating that the licensor has the legal right to make the licensed content available as part of the agreement?

126. If the licensor retains the right to withdraw content because it no longer possesses this right or has a reasonable belief that it no longer possesses this right, is the licensee compensated for the loss of such content if the licensor cannot supply a reasonably agreed-upon substitute? (*See* CREDIT AND REFUND)

ENDNOTES

1. American Association of Law Libraries, *Principles for Licensing Electronic Resources* (November 2004), http://www.aallnet.org/main-menu/Advocacy/recommendedguidelines/licensing-electronic-resources.html?css=print. This document covers numerous issues, including access, copyright and intellectual property, archiving, statistics/privacy, termination/renewal, dispute resolution, and warranties/quality of service, as well as a list of terms but, according to the website, the "terms are not defined . . . as definitions may vary from instance to instance."

2. See Patricia Brennan, Karen Hersey, and Georgia Harper, *Licensing Electronic Resources: Strategic and Practical Considerations* (January 1997), http://www.arl.org/sc/marketplace/license/licbooklet.shtml.

3. Association of Research Libraries, *Reshaping Scholarly Communication: Principles for Licensing Electronic Resources* (July 15, 1997), http://www.arl.org/sc/marketplace/license/licprinciples.shtml (definite or indefinite period, abrogation of rights under copyright, intellectual property rights, secondary liability, reasonable enforcement, preservation of user privacy rights, policy formation for improper uses, notice and reasonable time to cure improper use, user authentication access issues, archival or retention rights, fixed terms and notice of change with right of termination, indemnification by the licensor, user privacy rights, terms now rather than pay now terms later, and termination rights).

4. Licensing Digital Information, *Licensing Resources* (2008), http://www.library.yale.edu/~llicense/liclinks.shtml.

5. See AT&T Mobility LLC v. Concepcion et ux., 131 S.Ct. 1740, 1744 (2011) ("The revised agreement provides that customers may initiate dispute proceedings by completing a one-page Notice of Dispute form available on AT&T's Web site. AT&T may then offer to settle the claim; if it does not, or if the dispute is not resolved within 30 days, the customer may

invoke arbitration by filing a separate Demand for Arbitration, also available on AT&T's Web site. In the event the parties proceed to arbitration, the agreement specifies that AT&T must pay all costs for nonfrivolous claims; that arbitration must take place in the county in which the customer is billed; that, for claims of $10,000 or less, the customer may choose whether the arbitration proceeds in person, by telephone, or based only on submissions; that either party may bring a claim in small claims court in lieu of arbitration; and that the arbitrator may award any form of individual relief, including injunctions and presumably punitive damages. The agreement, moreover, denies AT&T any ability to seek reimbursement of its attorney's fees, and, in the event that a customer receives an arbitration award greater than AT&T's last written settlement offer, requires AT&T to pay a $7,500 minimum recovery and twice the amount of the claimant's attorney's fees") and discussion in previous chapters.

6. See, for example, Brussels Regulation on Jurisdiction and Enforcement of Judgments in Civil and Commercial Matters, article 2.1 (C. Reg. EC No. 44/2001, December 22, 2000) ("Subject to this Regulation, persons domiciled in a Member State shall, whatever their nationality, be sued in the courts of that Member State"). See also 80/934/EEC: Convention on the Law Applicable to Contractual Obligations Opened for Signature in Rome on June 19,1980, article 5.2: "a choice of law made by the parties shall not have the result of depriving the consumer of the protection afforded to him by the mandatory rules of the law of the country in which he has his habitual residence."

7. H. WARD CLASSEN, A PRACTICAL GUIDE TO SOFTWARE LICENSING FOR LICENSEES AND LICENSORS 353–354 (3d ed.) (Chicago: American Bar Association, 2008).

Case Index

A

A. A. Metcalf Moving & Storage Co., Inc. v. North St. Paul–Maplewood Oakdale Schools, 133n20

A&E Television Networks, House of Bryant Publications, LLC v., 361n34

A&M Records, Inc. v. Napster, Inc., 526

ABKCO Music Inc. v. Stellar Records, Inc., 350

Academy Chicago Publishers v. Cheever, 99

Academy Life Insurance Co., Kipperman v., 38, 83n47

Accolade, Inc., Sega Enterprises Ltd. v., 513n166, 626

Acuff-Rose Music, Campbell v., 339

Adelman v. Christy, 504n56

Adler v. Fred Lind Manor, 199n30

Adobe Systems, Inc., SoftMan Products Company, Inc. v., 23n36, 23n37, 180–184

Adobe Systems, Inc. v. One Stop Micro, Inc., 183

Adobe Systems, Inc. v. Stargate Software, Inc., 22n36

Adsit Co., Inc. v. Gustin, 255, 256, 272n23

Agarita Music, Inc., Bridgeport Music, Inc. v., 360n20

Agee v. Paramount Communications, 352, 353, 360n27

Agri-Business Supply Co. v. Hodge, 507n91

Alcatel USA, Inc. v. DGI Technologies, Inc., 207n85, 210nn110–111

All Metals Fabricating, Inc. v. Ramer Concrete, Inc., 514n175

Alliance Laundry Systems, LLC v. Thyssenkrupp Materials, 236–237

All-Star Ins. Corp., Ott v., 509n126

Amazon.com, Inc., SmartPhone Technologies, LLC v., 629

America Online, Inc., Koch v., 197n15, 509n117

America Online, Inc., Noah v., 526

America Online, Inc., Williams v., 257, 274n28

America Online, Inc., Zeran v., 525

America Online, Inc. v. Superior Court, 200n34

American Broadcasting Companies, Inc., Gilliam v., 507n96

American General Financial Services, Inc., Rivera v., 202n49, 206n77

American Medical Association, Practice Management Information Corp. v., 167–168, 211nn118–122

American Paper Recycling Corp., Little, Brown and Company, Inc. v., 43

America's Choice, Inc. v. Bienvenu, 515n190

ANC Sports, Inc., Angel Music, Inc. v., 361n33

Angel Music, Inc. v. ANC Sports, Inc., 361n33

Apple Computer, Inc. v. Franklin Computer Corp., 18n11

Apple Computer, Inc. v. Microsoft Corp., 511n154

Apple Inc. v. Paystar Corp., 49

Appleton v. Norwalk Library Corp., 95n146

Arizona Cartridge Remanufacturers Association v. Lexmark International, Inc., 269n2

Arizona Retail Systems, Inc. v. Software Link, Inc., 55

Arlington Independent School District, James T. Taylor & Son, Inc. v., 133n19

Ashcroft, Eldred v., 393n4

Assessment Technologies of WI, LLC v. Wiredata, Inc., 162–163

Asset Marketing Systems, Inc. v. Gagnon, 479

Associated Press, McClatchey v., 512n160, 552

AT&T, Ting v., 203n54

AT&T Mobility LLC v. Concepcion, 155–156, 159–160, 188, 205nn72–75, 296n47, 398, 679n5

Atari Games Corp. v. Nintendo of America, Inc., 513n166, 626–627

Attorney General v. Board of Ed. of City of Detroit, 94n145

Augusto, UMG Recordings, Inc. v., 35–36, 40, 46, 47, 74n28, 74nn30–31

Autodesk, Inc., Vernor v., 23n37, 41–42, 49, 84n56, 184–187, 188, 190–191, 221nn223–229, 222n231, 222n233, 223nn237–238, 224n242, 224n248, 625–626

A.V. v. iParadigms, Ltd., 104–105, 256–257, 296n44

Avins v. Moll, 93n142

T

▶ Subject Index

A

Abandonment
  of copyright protection, 304
  limited copyright abandonment with CC
    license, 324n37
ABC Sports, 341
Abrams, Howard B., 349–350, 362n52
Acceptance
  additional terms for contract and, 53–57
  clause in license, 512n163
  conditional acceptance, 86n75
  conditional acceptance/end of power to
    accept, 52–53
  counteroffers/end of power to accept,
    50–52
  end of power to accept, 49–50
  as essential element of contract, 27
  with EULAs, 279–283
  Hill v. Gateway 2000, Inc., 89n109
  lapse of time for, 85nn69–71
  by offeree, 59–63
  performance testing provision, 476
  repudiation by offeree, 63
  revocation and, 59, 90n115
  summary points about, 69
  of unsolicited merchandise for library,
    33
  website EULAs, 284–290
  See also Assent
Acceptance test specification, 443
Access
  archiving rights, license evaluation,
    646–647
  circumvention provision, 423–424
  EULAs for access to websites, 279–283
  remote access provisions, 482–483
Access NewspaperARCHIVE
  damages provisions, 441
  disclaimers, 445
  license, 519–543
  remedies provisions, 482
  renewal provisions, 483
Accessible Archives license
  archive provision, 399–400, 402
  authorized users provision, 410, 501n26

  authorized uses provision, 415
  cure, right to, 437–438
  customer support provision, 439
  disclaimers, 445
  enforcement provisions, 449, 450
  indemnity/limitation of liability
    provisions, 465–466
  prohibited uses provision, 477
  remote access provision, 482
  warranty, 497
Acts of God
  force majeure clause, 458, 641
  impossibility makes contract voidable, 108
  performance of contractual obligations
    impossible, 129
  provisions in Nature (Academic:
    Americas) license, 612–613
"Add Amazon.com to the List—Class-Action
    Lawsuit Alleges Data Privacy Violations"
    (Friess), 628
Additional terms
  of contract, 53–57
  Restatement (Second) of Contracts on,
    92n127, 92n129
  UCC § 2-207 on, 86n73, 86n77
Adhesion contracts
  bargaining power and, 201n37
  browse-wrap contracts as, 256
  click-wrap agreements as, 201n36
  definition of, 196n2
  enforceability of, 198n22
  limitation on remedies/class-action
    waivers, 158
  nonnegotiated licenses as, 248
  overview of, 148–149
  procedural unconscionability, 153–154
  summary points about, 192
  unconscionability in, 153–154
Admission charge, 363n54
Adobe Systems, Inc.
  EULA of, 220nn203–207
  recharacterization of license as sale case,
    180–184
ADR (alternative dispute resolution),
    398–399
  See also Arbitration

► About the Author

Tomas A. Lipinski, a native of Milwaukee, Wisconsin, completed his Juris Doctor (JD) at Marquette University Law School, Milwaukee, Wisconsin. He received his Master of Laws (LLM) from The John Marshall Law School, Chicago, Illinois, and his PhD from the University of Illinois at Urbana–Champaign.

Lipinski has worked in a variety of legal settings, including the private, public, and nonprofit sectors. He taught at the American Institute for Paralegal Studies and at Syracuse University College of Law. In summers he is a visiting professor at the Graduate School of Library and Information Science, University of Illinois at Urbana–Champaign. From 1999 to 2003, during summers, he taught at the Department of Information Science, School of Information Technology, at the University of Pretoria, Pretoria, South Africa. Professor Lipinski was the first named member of the Global Law Faculty, Faculty of Law, University of Leuven (Katholieke Universiteit Leuven), Belgium, in fall 2006, where he continues to lecture annually at its Centre for Intellectual Property Rights and Interdisciplinary Centre for Law and ICT.

Prior to becoming Executive Associate Dean at Indiana University School of Library and Information Science, in 2011, he was Director of the MLIS program at the School of Information Studies at the University of Wisconsin–Milwaukee. Beginning in January 2013, he will be Director of the School of Library and Information Science, Kent State University in Ohio.

Lipinski currently teaches and speaks frequently on various topics within the areas of information law and policy, especially copyright, licensing, privacy, and free speech issues in schools and libraries, and he continues to counsel libraries and schools in these areas. He is a national leader in copyright education, developing and teaching online continuing education courses for both ACRL and the University of Maryland College Park, Center for Intellectual Property. He chairs the Copyright Discussion Group for ACRL and is the chair elect of ALA's OIPT Copyright Education Subcommittee.

Monographs include *The Library's Legal Answer Book* (ALA, 2003), co-authored with Mary Minow; *Copyright Law in the Distance Education Classroom* (Scarecrow Press, 2004); and *The Complete Copyright Liability Handbook for Librarians and Educators* (Neal-Schuman Publishers, 2006).

Among his many articles are "The Myth of Technological Neutrality in Copyright and the Rights of Institutional Users," in the *Journal of the American Society for Information Science and Technology* (2003); as third co-author with Lee S. Strickland and Mary Minow, "Patriot in the Library: Management Approaches When Demands for Information Are Received from Law Enforcement and Intelligence

Agents," in 30 *Notre Dame Journal of College and University Law* 363 (2004); with Thomas Gould and Elizabeth Buchanan, "Copyright Policies and the Deciphering of Fair Use in the Creation of Reserves at Major University Libraries," in the *Journal of Academic Librarianship* (2005); with Elizabeth Buchanan, "The Impact of Copyright Law and Other Ownership Mechanisms on the Freedom of Inquiry: Infringements upon the Public Domain," *Journal of Information Ethics* (Spring 2006); as third co-author with Kathrine A. Henderson and Richard A. Spinello, "Prudent Policy? Reassessing the Digital Millennium Copyright Act," in *Computers and Society* (November 2007); as co-author with Hannelore Dekeyser, "Digital Archiving and Copyright Law: A Comparative Analysis," in 12 *International Journal of Communications Law & Policy* 180 (2008); and "A Functional Approach to Understanding and Applying Fair Use," in 45 *Annual Review of Information Science and Technology* (*ARIST*) (Blaize Cronin, ed., 2010).